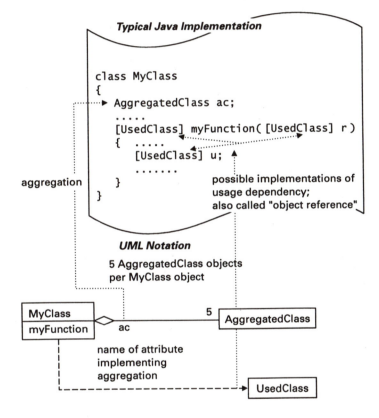

Typical Java Implementation

```
class MyClass
{
    AggregatedClass ac;
    .....
    [UsedClass] myFunction( [UsedClass] r )
    {  .....
        [UsedClass] u;
        .......
    }
}
```

aggregation

possible implementations of
usage dependency;
also called "object reference"

UML Notation

5 AggregatedClass objects
per MyClass object

MyClass
myFunction

◇── ac ──── 5 ── AggregatedClass

name of attribute
implementing
aggregation

UsedClass

SOFTWARE ENGINEERING
An Object-Oriented Perspective

SOFTWARE ENGINEERING
An Object-Oriented Perspective

ERIC J. BRAUDE
Boston University

JOHN WILEY & SONS, INC.
New York / Chichester / Weinheim / Brisbane / Singapore / Toronto

Acquisitions Editor   *Paul Crockett*
Editorial Assistant   *Jennifer Welter*
Marketing Manager   *Katherine Hepburn*
Production Services Manager   *Jeanine Furino*
Production Editor   *Sandra Russell*
Production Management Services   *Publication Services, Inc.*
Cover Image   *Trina S. Hyman*

This book was set in *10/12 Times Roman* by *Publication Services, Inc.* and printed and bound by *Hamilton Printing Company.* The cover was printed by *Phoenix Color Corporation*

This book was printed on acid-free paper. ∞

Library of Congress Cataloging-in-Publication Data:
Braude, Eric J.
  Software engineering : an object-oriented perspective / Eric J. Braude
    p. cm.
  ISBN 0-471-32208-3 (cloth : alk. paper)
    1. Software engineering. 2. Object-oriented programming (Computer science) I. Title.

QA76.758 .B74 2000
005.1'17--dc21

                                                                00-063345

Printed in the United States of America

10 9 8 7 6 5 4 3 2 1

To Judy, Michael, Miriam, and Rachel

"I have spread my dreams under your feet" — W. B. Yeats

CREDITS

PREFACE

This book is not just *about* software engineering: it also concerns how to do software engineering. Such a book has not been fully attempted in the past because no technical approach has enjoyed sufficiently broad acceptance. The object-oriented approach in particular has merely been included as a section in existing software engineering textbooks, despite the fact that a very large proportion of contemporary projects utilize object-oriented languages.

During the 1990s, the Object-Oriented Analysis and Design community fashioned an approach to application design, together with a corresponding notation: the Unified Modeling Language. The broad acceptance of this approach and language makes the new millennium's beginning an appropriate time to teach the doing of software engineering, not merely to talk about software engineering. Thus, although this book necessarily includes aspects of software engineering that are not object-oriented, it is designed to support instruction in the application of frameworks, use cases, and design patterns: It also relates object-orientation to requirements analysis and testing. As a result, instructors can spend less time trying to cover numerous approaches, and more time promoting depth and practice.

Any book showing how to do software engineering must include a case study. In addition, since software engineering deals largely with complexity, a software engineering textbook needs a substantial case study rather than a token one. Finally, the case study should be interesting enough to students so that they can envision building upon it just for fun. For these reasons, this book shows throughout how software engineering principles are applied to the construction of a particular role-playing video game. Video games afford a rich opportunity to demonstrate frameworks, design patterns, state behavior, concurrency, and nontrivial graphical user interfaces. Scientific and business examples complement the case study.

The typical software product is built by a team of software engineers, rather than by an individual working alone. To satisfy the corresponding educational need, this book provides extensive support for student teams. Watts Humphrey's pioneering work on the Personal Software Process [Hu] and the Team Software Process [Hu7] inspired much of this support.

AUDIENCE

This book is intended for senior-level undergraduates and first-year graduate students. Since the goal of the book is to produce good practice in developing software, the book will also be useful for practicing professionals who wish to improve their knowledge and performance. The text assumes familiarity with programming using classes and objects, preferably in Java.

ORGANIZATION

Each of Chapters 1, 2, 4, 5, and 6 is divided into two parts. This division is intended to help those readers and instructors who wish to progress rapidly through the fundamentals of requirements analysis and design. They can do this by first covering Part I of these chapters, returning later for the Part II's.

- The introduction provides a brief overview of software engineering, together with suggestions for student teams. This section also provides a summary of the case study so that students can be reassured that technical challenges do indeed await them beyond the "process" and project management concepts that they must understand.

- Chapter 1 provides an extensive account of the software engineering process. Section 6 is the heart of this chapter.

- Chapter 2 is concerned with how software projects are organized. Technical people sometimes try to avoid this subject, but they will be much happier in their team work if they understand organizational and management issues. In particular, Section 1, an introduction, and Section 4 on risk, discuss knowledge which is indispensable for software engineers.

Chapters 3 through 10 follow the logical order in which software is produced during each iteration.

- Chapters 3 and 4 concern requirements analysis: the process of understanding what is to be produced.

- Chapters 5 and 6 describe how products are designed and how designs are expressed.

- Chapter 7 discusses programming in the context of software engineering.

- Chapters 8 and 9 focus on the testing process.

- Chapter 10 discusses the activities required after the product has been released.

- References are found at the end of the book. Acronyms are summarized on page 511.

WAYS TO USE THIS BOOK

Although the sequence of the book's chapters is logical, it does not entirely parallel the way in which applications are actually produced. The *requirements analysis / design / program / test* sequence is usually repeated at least once. Chapters 1 and 2 discuss the ways in which this repetition can be organized.

There are several basic ways in which this book can be used, each motivated by different priorities, and these are discussed next.

THE LINEAR WAY TO USE THIS BOOK: Read the chapters in this order: Introduction / 1 / 2 / 3 / 4 / 5 / 6 / 7 / 8 / 9 / 10   The author has taught from this material by reviewing the preface and Introduction, followed by Chapters 1 through 10 in sequence. He has relied on chapters 1 and 2 for an overview, and encouraged class teams to first go through elements of the *requirements analysis/design/program/test* sequence with a *trivial* set of requirements. This accustoms the group to the idea of "process", exercises group interaction, and exposes the members to the problems to be faced. It requires little exposure to the substance of the material beyond chapter 2.

THE "TWO-PASS" WAY TO USE THIS BOOK: Read the chapters in this order: Introduction / 1 Part I / 2 Part I / 3 / 4 Part I / 5 Part I / 6 part I / 1 Part II / 2 Part II / 4 Part II / 5 Part II / 6 Part II / 7 / 8 / 9 / 10 The first pass covers the introductory sections of each chapter, and the second pass extends to the entire chapters. This sequence has the advantage of enabling teams to build a small prototype while reviewing the Part I sections, then embarking on the full development process afterwards. The author recommends that this prototype be extremely modest. Its main purpose should be to get the team working together, and to exercise aspects of the software engineering process. These activities take a long time for new teams. Useful features should not be expected.

The "career ladder" way to use this book:Read the chapters in this order: Introduction / 1/ 7 / 8 / 6 / 5 / 2 / 3 / 4 / 9 / 10 After introducing software engineering using Chapter 1, other instructors may prefer to order the topics according to the typical career of a software engineer within a company. Careers start with the role of *programmer* (this starts with Chapters 7 and 8, using the case study design of Chapter 6 as the basis for an example). Programmers are eventually given the responsibility of a *designer* (Chapter 6, using the case study architecture in Chapter 4). Designers typically transition into the role of *architect* (Chapter 5 using the requirements in the case study of Chapter 6). The final career level for which this book is relevant is *project leader* (Chapters 2, 3, 4, 9 and 10).

THE WEBSITE FOR THIS BOOK

Among the features of the book's web site at http://www.wiley.com/college/braude, are the following.

- Slides of all the figures and bullet sets in the book, in color, and in original PowerPoint form. This allows instructors to modify and customize the slides, and to selectively integrate them with other slides.
- Answers to the "general" exercises for faculty (in a password-protected mode)
- Java source code for the book's case study
- The case study documentation, for use as templates

There are many ongoing plans for the website, and the reader is referred there for its list of current features.

EXERCISES

There are three kinds of exercises in each chapter. "Review" exercises have short answers, and a solution or a hint to each is provided in the same chapter as the question. "Team" exercises provide specific goals and evaluation criteria for teams performing term projects. Solutions to the third exercise type, "general" exercises, are not provided in the book, but are available to instructors at the book's web site.

ACKNOWLEDGMENT

In my career as a software engineer and manager in industry, and in my present practice as a professor and consultant, I have been struck by how widespread a hunger there is for learning how to do software engineering "right", within the relentless pressures of business. I am grateful to my colleagues and industry students for taking the time with me to articulate this need.

For assisting me at every step in writing this book, my gratitude to Dick Bostwick is boundless. I am indebted to Tom van Court for his extensive and painstaking assistance. To my students at the Metropolitan College of Boston University: thank you all for your feedback. To the reviewers: your comments and reviews have made a significant, positive difference to this book. The reviewers included the following: Henry A. Etlinger, Rochester Institute of Technology; Michael Godfrey, University of Waterloo; David A. Gustafson, Kansas State University; Peter Hitchcock, DalTech, Dalhousie University; Floyd Lecureux, California State University—Sacramento; Steven P. Reiss, Brown University; and Laurie Werth, The University of Texas at Austin. I want to thank my colleagues and administrators at Boston University's Metropolitan College for their interest and encouragement. I am most grateful to Paul Crockett, Jenny Welter, and Bill Zobrist at John Wiley & Sons, and Jan Fisher at Publication Services, for working so diligently with me on this project.

Finally, this brief space allows me, however inadequately, to record my deep appreciation to my wife, Judy, and my son, Michael, for supporting my passion for writing this book.

Eric J. Braude
Boston University
Metropolitan College
Boston, Massachusetts; April 2000

BRIEF CONTENTS

CONTENTS

CHAPTER 2   *PROJECT MANAGEMENT*   **73**

CHAPTER 8   *UNIT TESTING*   **393**

CHAPTER 9   *SYSTEM INTEGRATION, VERIFICATION, AND VALIDATION*   **432**

CHAPTER 10   *MAINTENANCE*   479

INTRODUCTION

"... enterprises of great pith and moment ..."
— Hamlet

This **introduction** describes what Software Engineering is, and how this book is organized.

The creation of large software applications is one of the most important engineering challenges of modern times.

- SECTIONS 1 THROUGH 9   PAGE 1
- EXERCISES   PAGE 61

1. THE CONTEXT OF SOFTWARE ENGINEERING

Software engineering is by definition a kind of engineering, and it therefore has the same set of social responsibilities as all of the other kinds of engineering.

During the history of computing, much of the work of software people has been regarded as "development," that uses programming language skills but little *engineering* discipline. The Accreditation Board for Engineering and Technology defines engineering as shown in Figure 1. Much thought had been given to engineering as a human endeavor long before the birth of software. As of the early 2000s, software engineering is beginning to command the same degree of discipline from its practitioners as other branches of engineering such as electrical, mechanical, and civil. The nature of that discipline is the theme of this book.

How is software engineering different from, and how is it the same as, other kinds of engineering? One property that software engineering shares with the others is the necessity for a thorough description of what is to be produced, a process called "requirements analysis." On the other hand, software projects are subject to particularly frequent changes, including those imposed while the product is under development.

1

The *profession* in which

a knowledge of the *mathematical* and
natural sciences gained by study, experience,
and practice

is *applied with judgment*

to develop ways to *utilize,* economically, the
*materials and forces of nature for the benefit of
mankind*

—Accreditation Board for Engineering and Technology, 1996

Figure 1 A Definition of "Engineering"

2. THE ACTIVITIES OF SOFTWARE ENGINEERING

Two trends dominated software engineering in the 1980s and 1990s. One was the explosive growth of applications, including those associated with the Web. The other trend was a flowering of new tools and paradigms (ways of thinking, such as object-orientation).

Despite the advent of new trends, however, the basic activities required for the construction of software have remained stable. These activities include those listed in Figure 2 and Figure 3.

Development teams vary both the sequence and the frequency of these activities, as explained in Chapter 2. Software development in the real world is usually driven by a demanding list of features, as well as tight, market-driven deadlines. As a result, only well-organized groups of engineers, educated in the methods of software engineering, are capable of carrying out these activities appropriately. The alternative is often chaos, and sometimes disaster.

Software engineering involves *people, process, project,* and *product,* as suggested by Figure 4. The symbols used are from the Unified Software Development Process (USDP) of Jacobson, Booch, and Rumbaugh [Ja1], one of the processes for software development explained in this book. The icon shown in the "process" part of Figure 4 is explained in Chapter 1. The "project" diagram shows engineers doing various kinds of work, according to their role, and then passing the results to other engineers who then perform their roles.

- *defining* the software development *process* to be used
  - Chapter 1

- *managing* the development *project*
  - introduced in Chapter 2; also referenced in the remaining chapters

- *describing* the intended software *product*
  - Chapters 3 and 4

- *designing* the *product*
  - Chapters 5 and 6

- *implementing* the *product*
  i.e. programming it
  - Chapter 7

- *testing* the *parts* of the product
  - Chapter 8

- *integrating* the parts and testing them as a whole
  - Chapter 9

- *maintaining* the *product*
  - Chapter 10

Figure 2 Basic Activities of Software Engineering, 1 of 2

Figure 3 Basic Activities of Software Engineering, 2 of 2

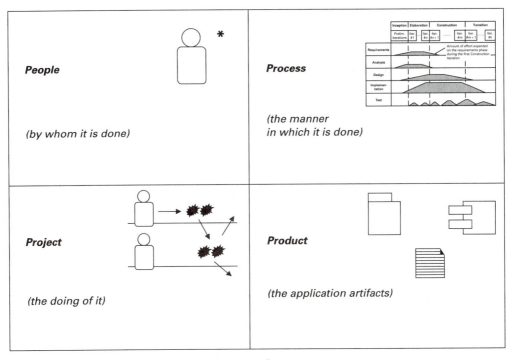

People *(by whom it is done)*	*Process* *(the manner in which it is done)*
Project *(the doing of it)*	*Product* *(the application artifacts)*

* Symbology from [Ja1]; explained in Chapter 1

Figure 4   The Four "P"'s of Software Engineering

The "products" of a software development effort consist of much more than the object code and the source code. For example, they also include documentation, test results, and productivity measurements. In conformance with the USDP, we will call these products *artifacts*. This book describes what a complete set of artifacts contains.

3. PROCESS

This section is summarized in Figure 5. The "waterfall" process begins with the specification of the requirements for the application, then proceeds to the design phase, then the implementation phase and, finally, the testing phase. The maintenance phase, described in Chapter 10, is sometimes included in the waterfall process. In this book, we have divided "design" into "architecture" (Chapter 5) and "detailed design" (Chapter 6), and "testing" into "unit testing" (the parts: Chapter 8), and system testing (the whole: Chapter 9). Software development rarely occurs in the strict "waterfall" sequence. Web development, for example, tends to skip back and forth among specification, design, integration, and testing. In practice, then, we often use *iterative* processes for software development, in which the waterfall is repeated several times in whole or in part. This is explained in Chapter 1. When performed in a disciplined manner, iterative styles can be highly beneficial.

Decisions about software process often take place at an organizational level (company, department, group, etc.) and so it becomes important to measure the software development capabilities of organizations. Several chapters discuss such a measure, the *Capability Maturity Model*[SM] (CMM). The CMM was developed by Watts Humphrey and the Software Engineering Institute (SEI). The SEI is described in Chapter 1.

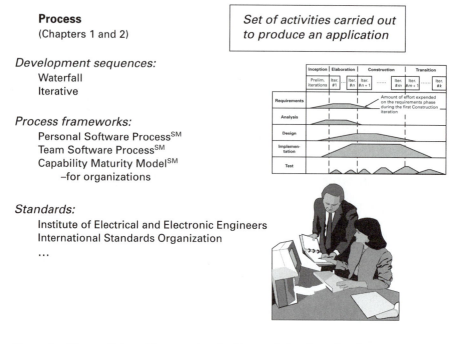

Process
(Chapters 1 and 2)

Set of activities carried out to produce an application

Development sequences:
Waterfall
Iterative

Process frameworks:
Personal Software Process[SM]
Team Software Process[SM]
Capability Maturity Model[SM]
   –for organizations

Standards:
Institute of Electrical and Electronic Engineers
International Standards Organization
…

Figure 5   "Process" (graphics reproduced with permission from Corel)

The software engineering capability of individual engineers can be developed and measured by the *Personal Software Process*[SM] (PSP) created by Humphrey [Hu]. The highlights of CMM and PSP are woven through several chapters of this book. A third level of software organization is Humphrey's *Team Software Process*[SM] (TSP) [Hu7] which describes the process by which teams of software engineers get their work done. The author believes that disciplined frameworks such as the CMM, PSP, and TSP will form a basis for the professional software engineer in the twenty-first century.

Well thought out documentation standards make it much easier to produce useful, reliable artifacts. Several standards are available. For the most part, this book applies the IEEE (Institute of Electrical, and Electronics Engineers) software engineering standards, many of which are also sanctioned by ANSI (American National Standards Institute). Many companies provide in-house standards. Although standards have to be modified over time to reflect new issues, the core of good standards has remained stable for a number of years. Unless they work from standards and, if possible, case studies applying them, teams typically waste a great deal of time dreaming up the structure (as opposed to the substance) of documents. Standards focus the process by providing a baseline for engineer, instructor, and students. In practice, they are modified and tailored to specific projects.

4. PROJECT

A *project* is the set of activities needed to produce the required artifacts. It includes contact with the customer, writing the documentation, developing the design, writing the code, and testing the product. Selected aspects of projects are summarized in Figure 6.

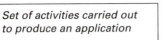

- *Object Orientation:* very useful paradigm

- *Unified Modeling Language:* design notation

- *Legacy systems:* common starting point

  · enhancement or usage of existing system

Figure 6   "Project"

The object-oriented paradigm (way of thinking) can be very useful for project development. It is particularly helpful in facilitating continual change because it can be used to organize designs and code in parts (classes and packages) that match the real-world problem.

The Unified Modeling Language (UML: see [Ra]) is an industry standard for describing designs, and is used throughout this book. Note that the UML is not a methodology in itself, but a notation. The UML is summarized on the book's inside covers.

Chapter 5 explores the ways in which the architecture of an application can be developed. The approach borrows from the exciting field of Design Patterns, and from research classifying software architecture. Chapter 6 completes the discussion of designs, demonstrating how complete details can be specified. Chapters 7 through 9 cover the integration and test of the application. Chapter 10 discusses maintenance, the last— and ongoing—process phase.

The overwhelming proportion of real world development work is not the building of brand new systems at all, but the enhancement or usage of existing ("legacy") systems. Even applications which are apparently new, usually have to coexist with legacy systems. One cannot understand how to deal with legacy systems, however, until one understands how systems should be put together in the first place, and so this book emphasizes nonlegacy applications. Readers desiring experience using legacy systems can use the completed *Encounter* case study for that purpose, and build a video game based upon it.

5. PEOPLE

The interactions among the *people* involved in a software project have profound effects on its success. This book does not attempt to do justice to people management except by raising selected personnel issues that vitally affect the software engineering enterprise. Teams work best when they know what they are supposed to do, and when the members have specific roles. To support this need, there are numerous "One way to . . . ." figures in this book (see, for example, Figure 9 on page 8), containing specific suggestions. The *Team Software Process*[SM] [Hu7] also has some useful words of wisdom on the management of teams, and some of these are provided in Chapter 2.

Another element of the "people" factor has to do with the project's stakeholders: the people who have a stake in its outcome. These include the customer, the end users, and the financial backers. Although these people can have a profound effect on the project, the management of stakeholders is beyond the scope of this book.

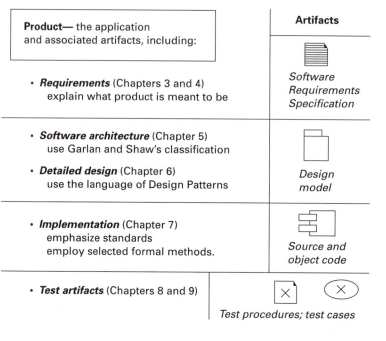

Figure 7   "Product"

6. PRODUCT

Finally, what about the *product* itself—not only the software application, but also its associated artifacts? Artifacts that constitute the product are summarized in Figure 7.

Chapters 3 and 4 on requirements analysis explain how to produce the requirements that specify what the product is meant to be. Although this specification task appears straightforward, it is difficult to carry out well in practice. Some requirements are best expressed using formal, mathematical methods. Chapter 5 explains how to specify the software architecture, following Garlan and Shaw's classification. Chapter 6 describes how to specify the detailed designs and includes the language of Design Patterns, a wonderful gift to the development community that helps us to communicate intelligently with each other about design. Chapter 7 discusses implementation (programming), emphasizing standards and formal methods. The latter help developers to write programs that are much easier to verify for correctness. Chapters 8 and 9 describe how to test the parts of an application, as well as the whole. Testing artifacts are described. These include the test procedures which specify how the tests are conducted, and the test cases which specify the input data for tests.

7. QUALITY

This section is summarized in Figure 8.

Even when developed by outstanding organizations, large applications contain defects. To accept this fact may sound defeatist, but it is not. To take a civil engineering analogy, there is undoubtedly peeling paint or equally minor defects somewhere on the Golden Gate Bridge at all times, so the bridge is not "perfect" but this does not matter. The important point is that the bridge satisfies specific quality standards such as the ability to carry trucks safely from one

Application must satisfy predetermined quality level.

Methods to attain quality level:
- *Inspection* (introduced in Chapter 1)
  - team-oriented process for ensuring quality
  - applied to all stages of the process

- *Formal methods* (introduced in Chapter 1)
  - mathematical techniques to convince ourselves and peers that our programs do what they are meant to do
  - applied selectively

- *Testing*
  - at the unit (component) level (Chapter 8)
  - at the whole application level (Chapter 9)

- *Project control techniques* (Chapter 2)
  - predict costs and schedule
  - control artifacts (versions, scope, etc.)

Figure 8   Quality

end to the other. So it is with software. But the question is, what is the equivalent of "peeling paint" for a software application? Software does not "wear out" in the manner of physical applications, and we require specific definitions of software quality.

Rather than insisting on perfection, we insist on standards of quality. This places upon us the obligation to define these standards exactly (i.e., numerically). Such numerical measures are known as "metrics." An example of a metric is "defects found per month of operation"—at a predefined level of severity. Once metrics are defined, and their acceptable limits specified, we need to ensure that the process used and the project executed measure up within acceptable ranges of these metrics. This text integrates quality considerations into every phase of development. It emphasizes three activities for ensuring quality: inspection, proof of correctness, and testing.

Inspection is a team-oriented process for ensuring quality, and is applied to all stages of the process. A *proof of correctness* is a mathematical or logical technique used to convince ourselves and our peers that a program does what it is meant to. Such proofs are *formal* (as opposed to vague) methods. We do not execute programs during this proof process: We inspect only their source. On the other hand, we do execute programs when *testing*. Testing at the unit (component) level is covered in Chapter 8. In Chapter 9, testing at the whole application level is covered in conjunction with the process of assembling the parts ("integration").

Novice software engineers are often surprised at how expensive and time-consuming testing is. The author has encountered many practicing software engineers who are exhausted by testing, and wish ardently for "a better way." The "better way" lies in process improvement, complete with inspections and appropriate formal methods.

To ensure quality standards, the materials ("artifacts") produced by the process are carefully managed. Many of them come in several versions, in which later versions improve upon or extend earlier versions. The management of these artifacts is called *configuration management,* and is discussed in Chapter 1.

Ensuring quality also requires that we are able to maintain control over the project, an achievement that turns out to be very difficult. In particular, we have to be able to maintain a good measure at all times of the resources used, the current capabilities, and where the application is relative to its schedule. Better, we should be able to predict these, using standard methods transferable among projects.

8. STUDENT TEAM PROJECT

The reader of this book should be simultaneously executing a software project, and will will gain most if that project is a team effort. For many, this is the first technical course they take in which teamwork is used. Many students look back on their team process as an adventure to be remembered. If the team avoids a few common pitfalls, the adventure can be one of the most enlightening and useful experiences of an academic program. The "One way to . . . ." figures distributed throughout the text are designed to help groups maximize the benefit of group work. In addition, the case study, described in Section 11, provides an example of a team project. Near the end of each chapter, a section entitled "Student Project Guide and Case Study Explanation" provides guidance to teams by showing how a hypothetical team went about developing the case study.

The earlier the team begins its work, the better. At this stage, the activities listed in Figure 9 should be completed.

Figure 10 contains some of the issues to be aired at a first meeting. Doing so can help to avoid future problems. One of the biggest sources of frustration is a lack of commitment of one or two team members (point 1 in Figure 10). It is far better to discuss commitments at the beginning than to try to fix the problem after the project is underway. To reduce the resentment that follows when some team members feel they are contributing much more than others, set in advance an expected number of hours of commitment per week. This also helps to make people work more efficiently.

A second issue (point 2 in Figure 10) concerns the trade-off between the desire to produce an impressive product and the desire to learn new skills. These are often contradictory. To produce the most impressive product, team members should specialize along the lines of their greatest strengths. This is a typical industrial mode. To learn the most, however, team members need to try activities with which they are inexperienced (e.g., team leadership). Teams have to decide how and when to trade off between these two goals by specifying when they will specialize and when they will try new roles. Instructors reward learning behavior by establishing evaluation criteria additional to the capability of the product produced. This

---

One Way To. . . Decide Initial Team Issues

1. Set the meeting agenda and time limits.
   (Chapters 1 and 2 cover this in more detail)

2. Choose the team leader.

3. Decide how the team will communicate.
   See Figure 11

4. Identify the customer.
   The party or parties who want this application.

5. Get an understanding of the project in general terms.
   Don't be embarrassed if project seems too vague to you. Probe until you are comfortable.

Figure 9 One Way to Decide Initial Team Issues

One Way To. . . Set Team Expectations

1. Get everyone's commitment to taking the required time
   - Define an expected average number of hours per week.
   - If not forthcoming:
     Industrial: alert management
     Academic: inform instructor; implement written mutual evaluations
   - Gather dates of planned absences.
2. Choose team emphasis: accomplishment/learning.
   - Accomplishment (capable product): get a good mix of leadership, technical, writing, customer relations.
   - Learning: sacrifice accomplishment by allowing members to experience new activities.
   - Understand manager's/instructor's emphasis.

Figure 10 One Way to Set Team Expectations

discussion will translate into specifics when we discuss scheduling and roles in Chapters 1 and 2. At this early stage, the team can only come to a general understanding, an example of which is the following.

> *We will schedule at least four members to participate in each activity of the process. One of these members should be the group's most knowledgeable for this activity.*

8.1 Group Communication

The beginning of a project is the time to pick communication practices to be used and then to practice using them. It is beneficial to write down how the team will communicate. An example is shown in Figure 11. Many problems arise from a failure to communicate fully.

One Way To. . . Specify How the Team Will Communicate

1. *General policy:* If in doubt, communicate. Redundancy is OK!
2. *Meeting:* The team will meet each Wednesday from 8 to 10:00 a.m. in room 671 unless notified of a change.
3. *Meeting alternative:* Team members should keep Mondays 4 to 6:00 p.m. open in case an additional meeting is required.
4. *Standards:* The word processing used will be *Ajax release 9.* E-mail should be via *BestMail release 4*—if this is not possible, the e-mail should be verified as being compatible, especially for attachments.
5. *Preferred mode of electronic communication:* Unless a communication is of very limited interest to the group, it should be posted to the group site, www.xxx.yyy with automatic notification to every member. The "subject" format should be *Attn. <name(s)>: subject matter.*
6. *Alternative mode of electronic communication:* For 1–1 communication of very limited group interest, members will use e-mail or telephone.
7. *Acknowledgement:* Team members should acknowledge all electronic communication specifically targeted to them, whether asked to acknowledge or not. Senders should follow up on all significant communication that is not acknowledged.

Figure 11 One Way to Specify How the Team Will Communicate

To avoid communication gaps, practice redundancy (e.g., send e-mail to members peripherally interested in the subject, not just to the principal recipient). Make sure that you are understood. Check your understanding by asking questions.

If the group consists of students housed in close proximity, or engineers occupying the same building, communication is potentially smooth. Even under these circumstances, however, communication gaps are common and one cannot assume that adequate communication will take place without a procedure like that outlined in the figure. Many teams—including some student teams—are widely distributed geographically, and the specific means of communication becomes especially important. Large projects are often developed by more than one team in more than one part of the country. Mergers, acquisitions, and joint ventures often result in multiple groups working together on single projects.

An increasing number of products are available to facilitate group work including groupware, video conferencing, and instant messaging. Despite these communication wonders, engineers are frequently surprised at how useful well run face-to-face meetings can be.

Group projects are adventures. Enjoy the ride.

9. CASE STUDY OVERVIEW

To unify and reinforce the many concepts presented in this book, a project case study, the *Encounter* video game, is developed throughout.

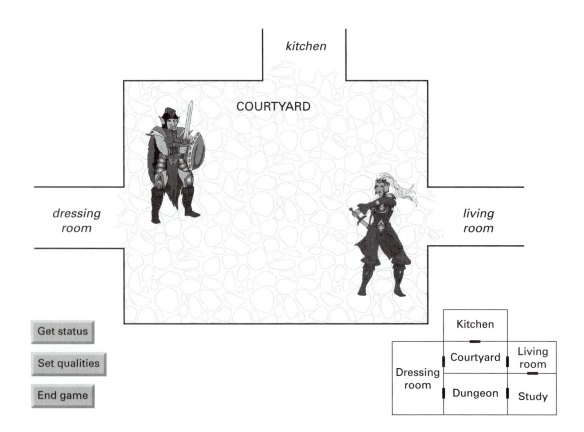

Figure 12   Sample Encounter *Screen (graphics reproduced with permission from Corel)*

Video games, in addition to their entertainment value, are among the biggest selling off-the-shelf software products (as reported in the *Economist,* 1998), and are serious business. Some foresee 32 million online video game players by 2002 (*The Boston Globe,* 1/21/00, page D12). We will suppose that a decision has been made to build a new role-playing game, which will be of interest to adults of both genders. Alas, *Encounter* is not worth playing yet (we don't have a big enough development war chest for this), but it does support the text's explanation of how products are developed from conception through maintenance.

This section provides a brief overview of the case study. Since the case study is an example for student projects to follow, this section provides student teams with an idea of what lies ahead.

9.1 Introduction to the *Encounter* Video Game

Encounter simulates all or part of the lifetime of the player's main character. Success in playing this game is measured by the "life points" maximum attained by the player, or by the ability of the player to live as long a life as possible. Figure 12 shows a typical screen shot: the courtyard area containing a player-controlled character on the right and a foreign character on the left.

Game characters have a fixed number of points allocated among qualities such as *strength, endurance, patience,* etc. Characters engage each other when they are in the same area at the same time. The result of the engagement depends on the values of the characters' qualities and on the environment in which the engagement takes place. Engagements are not necessarily violent or adversarial. Once an engagement is complete, the player's character is moved to a random area in the environment.

The interface for setting the qualities of a player character in *Encounter* is shown in Figure 13. Players can set the values of their qualities, except when in the midst of en-

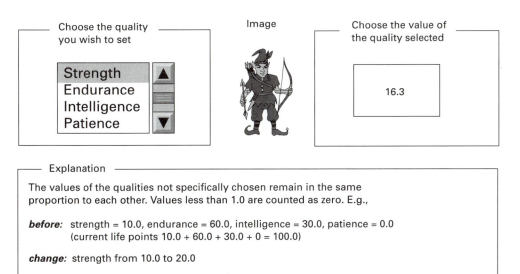

*Figure 13   User Interface for Setting Quality Values (graphics reproduced with
permission from Corel)*

gaging a foreign character. One challenge of the game is that the new quality values take effect only after a delay, leaving the player vulnerable for a period of time.

9.2 Requirements for *Encounter*

Many requirements for *Encounter* can be expressed by means of interactions between the application and an agency external to it, typically the user. Such interactions are called "use cases" (Jacobson [Ja]) and are explained in Chapter 3. For example, the *Engage Foreign Character* use case for the player is shown in Figure 14. The *Engage Foreign Character* use case is a sequence of actions that ensue whenever the player's main character and foreign character are in the same area at the same time.

Detailed requirements for *Encounter* can be expressed in several ways, including the use of "sequence diagrams," which are explained in Chapter 4. These are graphical representations of control flow which are particularly useful for visualizing use cases.

9.3 Design of *Encounter*

The architecture for *Encounter,* explained in Chapter 5, is decomposed into the parts illustrated in Figure 15. There are two sections to this architecture, namely, the *Role-playing game* layer and the *Encounter video game* layer. The *Role-playing game* layer consists of the *Characters, RolePlayingGame,* and *GameEnvironment* packages. The Encounter video game layer consists of the *EncounterCharacters, EncounterGame,* and *EncounterEnvironment* packages. As will be explained in Chapter 5, the *Role-playing game* layer is a *framework* because it can be applied to many different games.

The *Role-Playing Game* framework package deals with the movement of entities in role playing games. The *Characters* framework package involves both the characters con-

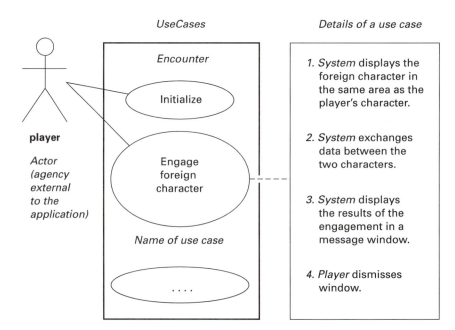

Figure 14   Engage Foreign Character *Use Case*

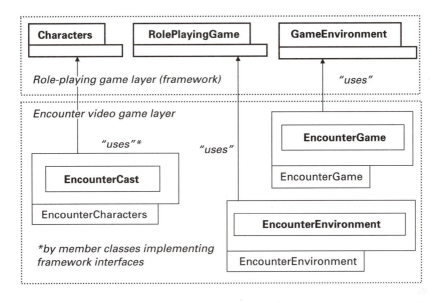

Figure 15   Framework/Application Dependency

trolled by the player, as well as those controlled by the application. The *GameEnvironment* framework package describes the layout of the video game.

The *EncounterGame* package consists of the classes controlling the progress of the game as a whole. The *EncounterCharacters* package encompasses the characters involved in the game. These include character(s) under the control of the player, as well as the foreign character(s). The *EncounterEnvironment* package describes the physical layout of *Encounter,* including the areas and the connections between them.

9.4 Testing of *Encounter*

The testing of *Encounter* consists of unit, integration, and systems tests. *Unit tests* involve testing the functions of a class, then testing the functions of the class in combination. The next level beyond unit tests is *integration testing.* This activity tests the overall functionality of each stage of the partial application. Finally, the application's *system tests* consist of testing the final product in its deliverable configuration. Chapters 7 and 8 discuss these and several other forms of testing.

9.5 Project Documentation for *Encounter*

The documents supporting a project correspond roughly to the waterfall process. The case study uses key documents described by the IEEE standards as follows. The *Software Quality Assurance Plan* for *Encounter* given at the end of Chapters 1 and 2 identifies project documentation, standards, reviews, audits, and risk management. *Encounter's Software Configuration Management Plan* given at the end of Chapter 1 explains how the documents and code are stored. The *Software Project Management Plan* stated at the end of Chapter 2 explains the manner in which the project is to be conducted. The *Software Requirements Specification* given at the end of Chapters 3 and 4 describes the requirements for the application. The *Software Design Document* given at the end of Chapters 5 and 6 describes the architecture and detailed design for the application. The *Software Test*

Document given at the end of Chapters 8 and 9 describes the way in which the application is tested.

EXERCISES

Solutions or hints are given at the end of this section to all exercises marked with "s" or "h" respectively.

1ˢ (a) What is "engineering"? Give a one sentence definition.

(b) How does "engineering" differ from "science"? Provide a key characteristic of each that is not true of the other.

2ˢ What are the four basic "P" components of a software engineering enterprise?

TEAM EXERCISES (TITLE: "COMMUNICATION")

For the following exercises, consider as a group how you will perform them, check the hints below, then carry out the assignment.

T1ʰ Decide who your team leader(s) will be. Note that being team leader provides you with practice that may be hard to otherwise get.

T2ʰ Decide how your team will communicate, specify your communication tools and methods, and test your communication methods. Be specific: you may change the specifics later.

T3ʰ Search the Web for the latest information on a topic determined by the instructor (e.g., the TSP). Note at least four of its basic goals and at least five of the techniques it uses. Post the references to the course forum or web site if there is one, and annotate your posting with the name of your group. State individual or group opinions of the topic or issue.

Your team response should be 4–7 pages long.

Evaluation criteria: (suggestions for the instructor)
α . *Clarity (A = very clearly written, with all salient points explained, and negligible redundancy)*
β . *Specificity (A = specific procedures as to how the team will communicate under most conceivable circumstances)*
γ . *Soundness of your topic summary (A = very clear that the writer understands the goals of the topic investigated; posting clearly organized)*

SOLUTIONS TO REVIEW QUESTIONS

1 (a) See the first sentence of this preface for a definition of "Engineering." "Science" is the enterprise that extends our knowledge and understanding using verifiable methods.

(b) Science and engineering intersect when the extension of knowledge leads to the solution of one of mankind's problems.

2 Process, project, people, and product.

HINTS TO REVIEW QUESTIONS

T1 hints: To distribute the benefit of team leadership practice, it can be beneficial to swap team leadership about halfway through the semester. Both team leaders can be chosen up front, and they can back each other up in case of emergency. Such backing up is a good practice in any case because the probability of a team leader having to quit a project or a class can be high. Note that the second half of a project typically requires the team leader to make decisions more quickly than the first half.

T2 hints: Examples are telephone, meetings, e-mail, forums, chat facilities, and websites.

1. Schedule regular face-to-face meetings at least once a week if possible. It is hard to convene an unscheduled meeting but easy to cancel a scheduled meeting.
2. E-mail is an essential tool, but can be problematic due to unpredictable delays. Messages can become unsynchronized, damaging the threads (subjects) of dialogs. This is especially serious near the end of a project when communication is frequent and of immediate importance.
3. Use a shared website or chat-type facility. Free services are available at [Ch], for example.
4. Do not merely state "we will use *Superword* for word processing." Specify a version number, and exchange a few messages to be sure. Don't change versions during the project without ensuring compatibility first.
5. Try out all the standards and methods that you have chosen.

   (Throughout this program of study, validate your plans and intentions with practical tests whenever possible. Try to use at least two independent tests. In general, assume that your project will be much more demanding in the future than it is at the beginning.)

T3 hints: Use this activity to stress your communication system. For example, you may want to set up a website to which team members are to add new TSP information. How will you organize this random activity? How can you obtain a useful result instead of a conglomeration of unconnected text?

CHAPTER 1

PROCESS

"How many ages hence
Shall this our lofty scene be acted over
In states unborn and accents yet unknown!"
— Cassius, from *Julius Caesar*

Good software engineers avoid repeating past project mistakes by documenting and improving upon their software development process.

Using the waterfall software development model as an overall project roadmap, this chapter covers the parts highlighted in Figure 1.1. The goals for this chapter are shown in Figure 1.2. Each of Chapters 1, 2, 4, 5, and 6 is divided into an "essentials" part, and an "at length" part. It is possible to cover only the "essentials" parts first, returning to the "at length" parts later. This ordering of the material provides teams with enough background to develop a small prototype of their term project—an implementation of minimal, selected aspects of the application, as explained in Section 5 of Chapter 3. This prototype can then be used to assist in the full requirements analysis process described in Chapters 3 and 4, and the design process in Chapters 5 and 6. Such a prototype should be *extremely modest,* its main purpose being to give the team practice in working together on the process.

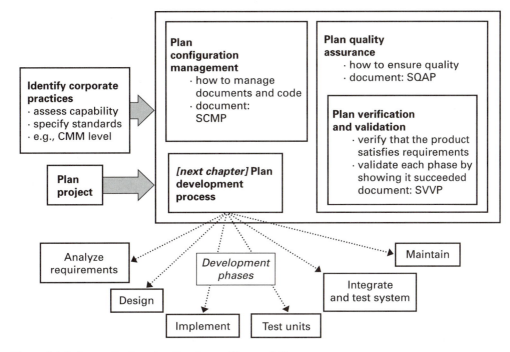

Figure 1.1 Software Engineering Roadmap: Chapter 1 Focus

- Distinguish among development processes
  - Indicate benefits and disadvantages
- Define software "quality" quantitatively
  - Institute collection
- Understand documentation needed
  - Approximately one document for each waterfall phase
  - Plan for configuration management

Figure 1.2 Learning Goals for This Chapter

▶ PART I: ESSENTIALS

1. INTRODUCTION TO THE SOFTWARE ENGINEERING PROCESS

Software engineering is the process of building applications of practical size or scope, in which the software effort predominates, and which also satisfy requirements for functionality and performance. For example, a word processor, spreadsheet, and operating system certainly qualify,

- *Stand-alone*
  - residing on a single computer
  - not connected to other software or hardware
  - *e.g., word processor*

- *Embedded*
  - part of unique application involving hardware
  - *e.g., automobile controller*

- *Real time*
  - must execute functions within small time limit
    - typically microseconds
  - *e.g., radar software*

- *Network*
  - consist of parts interacting across a network
  - *e.g., Web-based video game*

Figure 1.3 Some Application Types

and so does a program controlling an X-ray machine or troubleshooting a space station. *Programming* is one of the software engineering activities.

The difference between programming alone and software engineering is like the difference between bringing a patio table into existence and bringing a bridge into existence. These differ greatly in order of magnitude and required professional knowledge. Unlike the building of a patio table, bringing a bridge into existence entails professional and societal responsibilities. This book does not attempt to address societal issues, but it does provide the tools to do so in the form of rigorous requirements analysis, and quantified standards of quality.

The reach of software applications has expanded without precedent since the invention of the computer, and includes the categories listed in Figure 1.3. Software engineering must account for the building of all of these types of applications. The principles explained in this book cover all of these categories. Embedded and real-time applications require additional principles that are not covered.

1.1 A Typical Software Engineering Roadmap

How does one bring into existence applications of significant use and potentially great complexity? The following is a typical sequence of software engineering project activities (also see Figure 1.4).

1. First, we need to understand the nature of the project. This sounds obvious, but it usually takes quite a while to understand what customers want, especially when they do not know completely what they themselves want. The general magnitude of the available time, funding, and personnel should be understood. This helps to clarify the project's scope. For example, if we are given $10,000, one engineer, and one month to build a video game, its purpose would have to be a prototype only (as with the case study used in this book). On the other hand, a $5M budget, 20 engineers, and an 18-month time frame suggest a competitive product and an entirely different scale of operation.

1. Understand nature and scope of proposed product
    2. Select the development process and create a plan
        • *Section 4 and Chapter 2*
        3. Gather requirements
            • *Chapters 3 and 4*
            4. Design and build the product
                • *Chapters 5, 6, and 7*
                5. Test the product
                    • *Chapters 8 and 9*
                    6. Deliver and maintain the product
                        • *Chapter 10*

Figure 1.4 Typical Project Roadmap

2. Projects require documentation from the start—documentation that will very likely undergo many changes. For this reason, a means should be identified from the very beginning for keeping track of changes to both documents and code. This process, known as *configuration management,* is discussed in Section 7.3 of this chapter. Configuration management is not necessarily hard to carry out, but its absence creates nightmares of confusion and lost productivity. Next, the team has to identify the process that will be followed. Process options are discussed in Section 4. Sometimes, existing company guidelines mandate the process.

A typical next step is the development of the overall plan for the project, including the schedule. This plan is refined throughout the life of the project, as more becomes known about the requirements and the design. For example, all of the details of the schedule cannot be provided until the architecture has been identified.

3. The next step is the gathering of the requirements for the application. This consists largely of conversing with the stakeholders—those who have an interest in its outcome. This process is covered in detail in Chapters 3 and 4.

4. The next step is the designing and implementing of the product. Chapters 5, 6, and 7 describe this process.

Depending on the development process used, steps 3 and 4 may be repeated several times.

5. The emerging product and the final product have to be tested thoroughly, in several ways. This phase is covered in detail in Chapters 8 and 9.

6. Once the product has been delivered, it enters "maintenance" mode, which involves repairs and enhancements. Maintenance, which consumes as much as 80% of software engineering resources, is covered in Chapter 10 of this book.

2. HISTORICAL AND CONTEMPORARY PERSPECTIVES ON SOFTWARE ENGINEERING

This section provides some historical perspectives on software engineering. It then contrasts these perspectives with contemporary trends and influences.

2.1 Software Engineering Comes of Age

Software engineering is a very young branch of engineering. For this reason, it is in a state of rapid change. The British Computer Society, for example, started to award to software engineers Chartered Engineer status in the early 1990s. In 1998 it became possible for the first time to register somewhere in the United States as a professional software engineer: in the state of Texas. Nevertheless, at the close of the twentieth century, it is widely accepted that the prevailing way in which organizations develop software applications lacks sufficient discipline. One estimate places 75% of development organizations at a primitive level. Addressing this shortfall is a major goal of this book. Because of the richness of ideas about what good software engineering is, the student will find this a stimulating journey.

2.2 The Influence of Structured Programming and Object Orientation

Since the inception of software development, there have been several waves of improvement in the discipline. A remarkable one was occasioned by Edsger Dijkstra's letter to the Communications of the Association for Computing Machinery (ACM) called "GOTO's considered harmful" [Di1]. Dijkstra pointed out the disadvantages of goto's, which were prevalent in code at that time, and suggested *structured programming* to avoid their use. Behind Dijkstra's point is the observation by Bohm and Jacopini [Bo2] that essentially all programs can be expressed as a combination of statement sequences, branching, and iterations. Goto's—jumps from one part of a program to another without return — are not necessary. Eliminating goto's leads to structured programming.

   Structured programming, which most programmers now take for granted, uses sequence, branching, and iteration. To keep the parts of such a program to an acceptable size, we introduce functions. These invoke additional functions at lower levels, and so on down the hierarchy. This approach is suggested in Figure 1.5. The principles of structured top-down programming are as useful as ever, and software development could not have progressed without it. New, useful perspectives and paradigms, however, which build on structured programming, have subsequently been found. One of the biggest problems with

```
Function definition handleAccount(...)
    getDetailsFromUser(...)
    getAccount(...)                              TOP
    doTransaction(...)
    ......

Function definition getDetailsFromUser(...)    DOWN
    getName(...)
    ......

Function definition getAccount(...)
    getFirstName(......)
    ......

    ......
```

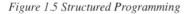

Figure 1.5 Structured Programming

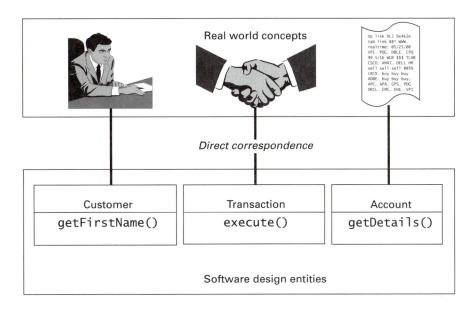

Figure 1.6 Object Orientation (Graphics used with permission from Corel.)

structured programming is that it is not designed to map onto entities in the real world, and this makes it hard to manage and adapt when requirements change.

In more recent times, *object orientation* (OO), the use of objects with data and functionality, has shown itself to be an extremely effective mode of thinking. OO is a medium of expression and implementation, rather than an architecture or a design. OO is effective because objects can represent the real-world parts of applications, narrowing the conceptual gap between the components of the real world and the components of the software. An example of how an application involving accounts and customers might be expressed in an OO context is suggested by Figure 1.6. By placing each element of functionality in an appropriate class, we can organize, design, and maintain applications much more easily. This book assumes a knowledge of object-oriented programming.

The development of *design patterns* (introduced in Chapters 4 and 5) further exploits the OO perspective by providing a stock of reusable design elements. Contemporary languages and systems such as Java and CORBA are based on the OO paradigm. CORBA allows an application to execute functions written in different languages, residing on different platforms. Other approaches to the creation of software are object-like—for example, Visual Basic and Microsoft's COM (described in the next section).

2.3 Reuse and Components

It is said that the production of automobiles was revolutionized by Henry Ford's observation that parts could be standardized, so that cars of a given model could use any instance of each required part. The reduction in costs resulting from this standardization made automobiles far more affordable.

To an increasing extent, we now expect to reuse ideas, architectures, designs, or code from one application to build others. If projects are planned in such a way that parts (often, collections of classes) can be reused, then costs can be reduced in the long run. Only *modular* applications have potentially reusable parts, however. An application is modular when

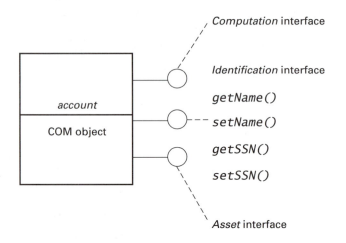

Figure 1.7 The COM Idea

its parts can easily be identified and replaced. For this reason, good software engineering stresses modularity, especially at the architecture stage (Chapter 5). Modular approaches are also important in the detailed design and in the implementation phases.

Reusability of developer knowledge has always been a major component of the experience of software engineers, and explains why experience with current technology is sought by employers. At the detailed design and implementation level, code reuse is increasing with the advent of standards such as COM and JavaBeans. COM objects are examples of modular tools. Figure 1.7 illustrates the idea of a COM object. The *account* COM object is effectively a Windows™ executable, which can be dynamically linked to any Windows™ application. It supports three interfaces. In particular, *account* supports the *Identification* interface, which means that it has a function *setName(...)* etc. The idea is that *account* can be reused any number of times since we know what it is capable of doing. COM objects can be composed of other COM objects, and can be as substantial as an entire spreadsheet.

At a general level, Meyer [Me] has defined a component as "a program element satisfying the following two properties.

- The element may be used by other program elements (*clients*).
- The clients and their authors do not need to be known to the element's authors."

A good reference for component viewpoints in general is [Sz].

2.4 Formal Methods

Software engineering methods that rely on mathematics as their basis are called *formal methods*. Dijkstra (e.g., [Di]), Hoare (e.g., [Ho]) and others pointed out some time ago that many programs can be considered mathematical entities, because they behave in precise ways. In addition, we are reminded that most other branches of engineering began as seat-of-the-pants enterprises, but eventually developed supporting mathematical bases. Electrical engineering, for example, has deep roots in mathematics, and mathematics is embedded broadly in the education of electrical engineers. Many argue that this will occur with software engineering as well.

Formal methods help to ensure reliability within programs by applying the existing, well-understood language of mathematics. They can be used during requirements analysis to define requirements precisely, and during implementation to ensure that code implements requirements. Formal methods are discussed in Chapters 4 and 7.

Formal methods typically use the *logical* aspects of mathematics. The *computational* aspects of mathematics are leveraged by the use of metrics, discussed below.

2.5 Usability

Users undergo a close, continual interaction with their software applications. In particular, the widespread use of graphical user interfaces suggests that many aspects of application development are rooted in areas other than mathematics or even algorithms (see, e.g., [We]). To an increasing extent, software designers must account seriously for the psychological basis of human-machine interaction. In this book, usability appears as part of requirements analysis (Chapters 3 and 4), design (Chapters 5 and 6), and usability testing (Chapter 9).

3. EXPECTATIONS FOR PROCESS, PROJECT, PRODUCT, AND PEOPLE

The four P's of software engineering were explained in the preface. Here is a recap. The goal of every software *project* is to produce a software *product* (e.g., a word processor). We are also concerned with the *process* by which projects produce products effectively. The fourth "P" is *people*. The interpersonal dynamics of a project team are critical to its success.

This book is designed to cover process, project, and product, but does not attempt to fully cover people issues. The text identifies key human factors for project success, especially in Chapter 2. References to the people aspect of software engineering can be found in Brooks ([Br1]) and Humphrey ([Hu6]).

There are five key expectations of contemporary software engineering, attributed mainly to Humphrey [Hu2] (see Figure 1.8). The first one is to decide in advance what the specific quality measures are to be for the project and the product. For example, "500 lines of fully tested code per person-month" and "no more than three defects per thousand lines of code." Point 2 advises gathering data on all projects to form a basis for estimating future projects. Point 3 states that all requirements, designs, code, and test materials should be freely and easily available to all members of the team. Point 4 effectively states that a process should be followed by all team members. The figure shows the role of the four P's in attaining the five key expectations, and it highlights the fact that none can be attained without the participation of the people on the project team. For example, writing programs only against designs (point 4B in Figure 1.8) is an expectation that can be enforced in *projects* and that requires the efforts of the project team's *people*.

Predetermining and attaining specific, measurable goals is an expectation of the project and of the actual *product*. All five expectations relate to the specific *project*, and all five are influenced by the activities of *people*.

3.1 Artifacts and Roles

The product of software engineering consists of far more than code. It includes *artifacts* such as plans, reports, and graphics. In addition, the software engineers fulfill a variety of *roles*. These

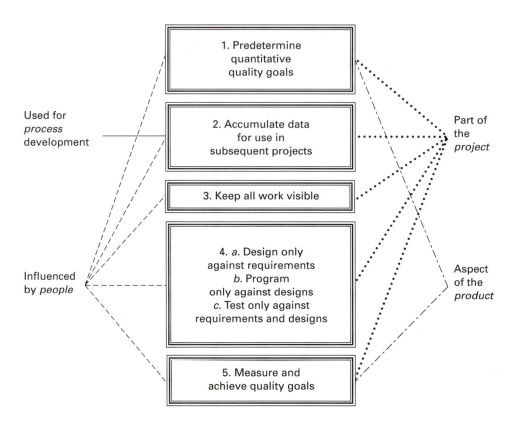

Figure 1.8 Five Key Expectations

roles are called "workers" in the Unified Software Development Process (USDP; described later in this chapter) [Ja1]. Figure 1.9 shows USDP symbols for artifacts and workers. As will be seen in Chapters 5 and 6, on design, specifying a design requires viewing it in several ways, called *models*. This is analogous to viewing the design of a building from various angles.

4. PROCESS ALTERNATIVES

Applications of realistic size are difficult to construct because of their complexity. The process under which they are constructed is a crucial factor in managing this complexity. There are several process alternatives, the most fundamental being the waterfall.

4.1 The Waterfall Process Model

The classical software development process model is the *waterfall model*. This is a sequence of activities (or phases) consisting of *requirements analysis, design, implementation, integration*, and *test*, as illustrated in Figure 1.10,

- *Requirements analysis* consists of gathering the requirements for the product, and its output is typically text. This is covered in Chapters 3 and 4.
- *Design* describes how the product will be structured internally, and is typically described by diagrams and text. This is covered in Chapters 5 (architecture) and 6 (detailed design).

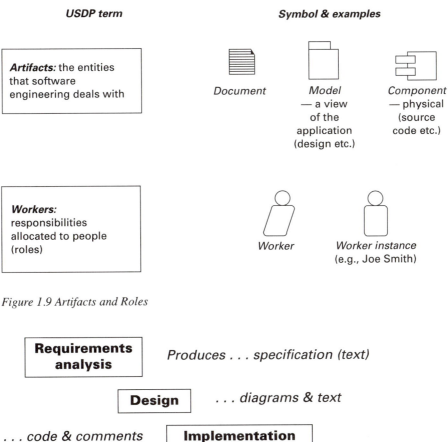

Figure 1.9 Artifacts and Roles

Figure 1.10 The Waterfall Model

- *Implementation* means programming. The product of this phase is code at any level, including that generated by high-level drop-and-drag systems, fourth generation languages, and so on. This is covered in Chapter 7.
- *Integration* is the process of assembling the parts to complete the product. Testing and integration are covered in Chapters 8 and 9.

These phases are not actually performed in a strict sequence, since there is some overlap between the parts of the process. The reason for this overlap is that it is usually impractical to fully complete any one of these phases before beginning the next one.

The phases shown in Figure 1.10 are sometimes augmented with additional phases such as the following:

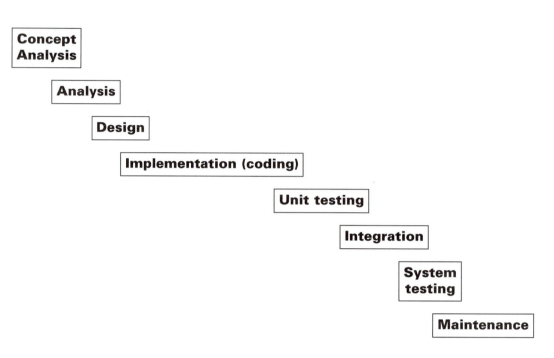

Figure 1.11 More Detailed Waterfall Model

- *Concept analysis,* at the beginning of the process, in which the application's overall philosophy is defined (described in Chapter 3)
- *Object-oriented analysis* between requirements analysis and design, in which the key classes are identified (described in Section 2.2 on page 20, and in Chapter 6)
- *Unit vs. system test,* which distinguishes between testing the parts of the application and testing the whole
- *Maintenance* at the end of the process, in which the application is repaired and modified so that it continues to be useful (described in Chapter 10)

A full version of the resulting waterfall is shown in Figure 1.11. The pure waterfall process is seldom carried out exactly as shown, except possibly on small projects, and for products that are very similar to those built previously by the same group. One of the reasons for this is the complexity of most applications. For example, this book employs a role-playing video game as a case study. There are so many variations in what "a role-playing video game" could mean that it is simply not practical to capture every last requirement before proceeding with a design and its implementation. Nevertheless, the waterfall process is the basis, or point of reference, for most other processes, and should always be considered as a viable process alternative.

Processes that apply the waterfall diagram repeatedly are called *iterative.* Not all of the waterfall steps, however, need be applied on each iteration. We will explain the spiral and incremental iterative processes next.

4.2 The Spiral Process Model

The *spiral* process recognizes the need to visit the *requirements analysis / design / implementation / test* sequence more than once. There are several reasons for this. A major one is the need to retire (take care of) risks. This is explained in Chapter 2. Another reason is to build an early partial version of the product that can be shown to the customer to obtain feedback; yet another is to avoid integrating a large code base all at once, as is called for by the waterfall process model. The idea is to build each version on the result of the previous one. This repetitive process forms a kind of spiral path, as illustrated by Figure 1.12.

To take our video game case study (introduced in the Preface) as an example, the first iteration could implement the preparation of the player's game character and his movement into an area. The second could allow movement from area to area, and the third could introduce foreign or alien encounters, and so on.

An additional advantage of iterative modes of software development is the possibility of collecting metric values about the process from each iteration. For example, by recording the time taken by the team to design and implement the first iteration, the predictions for subsequent design and implementation can be improved. This is particularly useful for organizations with little historical development data.

The spiral process matches the progress of typical projects; however, it requires much more careful management than the simple waterfall. One reason for this additional care is the fact that the documentation must be consistent whenever the project completes a full iteration. In particular, the code should implement the documented design and should satisfy the documented requirements. In addition, in order to optimize the team's productivity, it is often necessary to begin a new iteration before the previous iteration is complete. This places a special burden on the coordination of documentation.

For most projects, the benefits of spiral development outweigh its drawbacks. The U.S. Department of Defense recognized this in the 1980s, scrapping its prior assumption that all software projects are developed using the single waterfall process.

How many iterations of the spiral are necessary? This depends on the situation. A typical three person-month project with a four-month duration requires perhaps two or three iterations. In particular, the management overhead required to track five iterations for such a project usually cancels out the benefit of additional iterations. As shown in Section 4, the Unified Software Development Process assumes many iterations, and divides them into four groups.

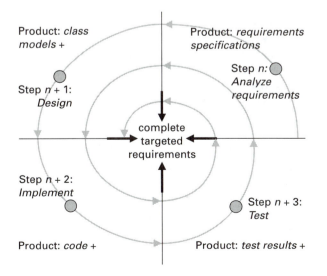

Figure 1.12 Spiral Development

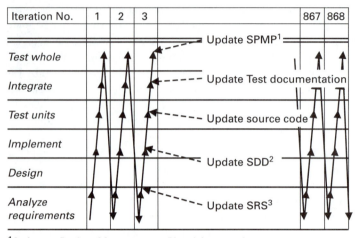

Iteration No.	1	2	3			867	868

[1]Software Project Management Plan (chapter 2)
[2]Software Design Document (chapter 5)
[3]Software Requirements Specification (chapter 3)

Figure 1.13 Incremental Development

When the rate of iteration increases so much that each iteration adds only a small amount of capability to the previous one, we call this *incremental* development.

4.3 The Incremental Process Model

Sometimes it is possible to inch a project forward in an almost continual process. This process model is particularly viable at the later stages of a project, when a product is in maintenance, or when the proposed product is very similar to a previously developed product. For example Cucumano and Selby [Cu] report on the process used within parts of the Microsoft Corporation, where code and documentation updates are submitted by a fixed time each *day* for integration and overnight testing. Other organizations report weekly schedules. In order to handle this degree of incremental development, the architecture must already have been clearly established and the documentation system must be extremely well synchronized (see Figure 1.13). To perform incremental development, a time interval is typically chosen, such as a week. The entire project (documentation, test, code, etc.) is then updated at the chosen interval. In theory, the increments can be worked on in parallel, but this is very difficult to coordinate. Incremental development works best if increment $n+1$ is started more or less after increment n is base-lined, and works worst if the parts require significantly longer to prepare than the chosen time interval. To understand why the latter is true, imagine needing to work on module 789, which depends on seven parts: 890, 23, 489, 991, 7653, 2134, and 2314. If the work requires nine weeks, then module 789 has to be built against the predicted state of the seven parts at the end of the nine weeks. This is very difficult to coordinate, because each of the seven parts may have been changed as many as nine times (once each week), and each change may depend on examining the effectiveness of previous changes.

Cucumano and Selby report that Microsoft typically decomposes projects into parts, applies the incremental synchronization process, and periodically "stabilizes" the application by combining the parts. They name this process "synch-and-stabilize."

4.4 The Unified Software Development Process

The Unified Software Development Process (USDP), due to Jacobson, Booch, and Rumbaugh, described in [Ja1], was published in 1999. This process is an outgrowth of earlier methodologies developed by these three authors, namely Jacobson's "Objectory methodology," the "Booch methodology" [Bo3], and Rumbaugh et al's "Object Modeling Technique" [Ru2].

Since iterative approaches repeat all or part of the waterfall process, they are sometimes complicated to describe, as evidenced by Figure 1.13. The USDP is an iterative process, which attempts to solve this problem by classifying iterations into the four groups, as listed in Figure 1.14. "Stakeholders" are people who have a stake in the outcome of the product. They include customers, of course, but also users (who may not be the customer), venture capitalists, user groups, and the developers themselves. The *Elaboration* iterations establish the key technical goal of selecting and confirming an architecture. The *Construction* iterations establish the basic product, but work is still required to make it releasable. The goal of the *Transition* iterations is to prepare the application for release to the customer.

By classifying iterations in this way, the USDP can be described using a matrix, as shown in Figures 1.15 and 1.16. As with most OO Analysis and Design processes, the waterfall phases shown by Jacobson *et al* also include an *Analysis* phase. The figure shows where this phase fits within the classical waterfall phases. "Analysis" consists of that part of the requirements process in which the basic classes of the application are selected and related. In addition, the USPD does not show the specific "Integration" phase normally shown by the classical waterfall process. This is due to the belief expressed by Booch [Booch-UML] that OO applications can and should employ continual integration. In other words, as new parts are added, the entire application is integrated, eliminating the need for a designated integration phase.

The approximate type and level of work for each USDP core workflow across the USDP iterations is shown in Figure 1.17. Most of the iterations involve most waterfall phases (USDP core workflows), but to differing extents. The *Inception* iterations involve mostly requirements analysis, some analysis, and may involve enough design and implementation to produce a preliminary prototype that can be used to discuss the project with stakeholders. The *Elaboration* iterations involve mainly requirements analy-

- *Inception iterations:* preliminary interaction with stakeholders
  - primarily customer
  - users
  - financial backers
  - etc.

- *Elaboration iterations:* finalization of what's wanted and needed; set architecture baseline

- *Construction iterations:* result in initial operational capability

- *Transition iterations:* complete product release

Figure 1.14 The Unified Software Development Process:
Classification of Iterations

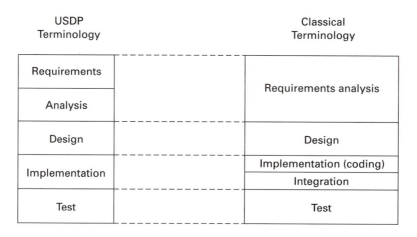

Figure 1.15 USDP versus Standard Terminology, Part I

USDP
Terminology

Classical
Terminology

USDP Terminology		Classical Terminology
Requirements		Requirements analysis
Analysis		
Design		Design
Implementation		Implementation (coding)
		Integration
Test		Test

Figure 1.16 USDP versus Standard Terminology, Part II

sis, but include some design and implementation. The *Construction* iterations involve mainly design and implementation, and the *Transition* iterations involve implementation and test.

The Unified Process produces six models (views of the application), as shown in Figure 1.18. These models will be discussed throughout this book, although not always by using USDP terminology. Briefly, the *Use-case model* describes the ways in which the application is to be used. The *Analysis model* describes the basic classes for the application. The *Design model* describes the relationship of the classes and selected objects. The *Deployment model* describes the allocation of the software to computers. The *Implementation model* describes how the code itself is to be organized. The *Test model* consists of test components, test procedures, and test cases.

	Inception	Elaboration			Construction		Transition		
	Prelim. iterations	Iter. 1	...	Iter. n	Iter. n+1	......	Iter. m	Iter. m+1	...... Iter. k

Requirements	Amount of effort expended on the requirements phase during the first Construction iteration
Analysis	
Design	
Implemen-tation	
Test	

Figure 1.17 Unified Process Matrix

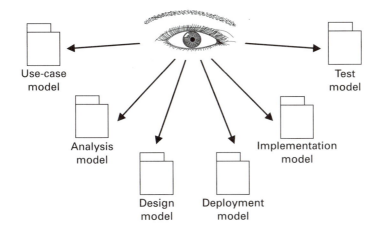

Figure 1.18 The Six USDP Models (Views of the Application) (Graphics reproduced with permission from Corel.)

4.5 Process Trade-offs

Table 1.1 summarizes the author's assessment of the trade-offs among pure waterfall, spiral, and incremental processes. Factors specific to individual projects could change this assessment. For example, the author rates *"Leverage of project metric data collection within project"* as "harder" for the pure waterfall process because metric data collected about each phase cannot be used much during the project (although it can be used for future projects). In spiral applications, however, metrics gathered from earlier iterations (e.g., lines of code per hour) can be used for later iterations.

The following are explanatory notes keyed to the table entries in Table 1.1.

TABLE 1.1   Process Trade-offs

| | | Iterative | |
Factor	Pure Waterfall	Spiral	Incremental
Ease of documentation control	Easier	Harder	Harder/ Medium (Note 1)
Enabling of customer interaction	Harder	Easier	Easier
Promotion of good design	Medium/ Easier	Easier (Note 2)	Harder
Leverage of metric data collected within project	Harder	Medium/ Easier	Medium/ Easier

1. The incremental process is feasible if the documentation set is complete and consistent to begin with. If this completeness and consistency is present, relatively small increments are fairly easy to document, and the development team obtains a great deal of practice updating all of the documents because the process is repeated many times.

2. Spiral development increments are few enough to permit design at a high level, but numerous enough to provide designers with a maturing understanding of the design problems. This accounts for their widespread use.

Figure 1.19 indicates how a team can decide which process it will use. To make the decision, one takes into account the time available, and the deliverables required by the instructor. Teams usually find two iterations comfortable. Three iterations have several benefits, especially the ability to practice collecting metric data during one iteration (e.g., lines of code), and then use this data on the next iteration. Fitting three iterations into a semester can be done only if the team is ambitious, efficient, and very well organized.

In any case, the large amount of time required to coordinate the artifacts for the first iteration is usually a surprise. For this reason, the capabilities of the first iteration should be kept extremely modest. A simple graphical user interface is often a good goal for this iteration, because it is typically straightforward, and can be shown to the customer (see chapter 2 for more on this). The first iteration accustoms the group to the mechanics of artifact coordination. This allows the team to concentrate on functionality and design for the second iteration, which coincides with the material covered in Chapters 3 through 9. If the group does plan a third iteration, its purpose should probably be to add functionality and to "polish" the product.

Incremental development can be planned for the tail end of the project, although this is somewhat ambitious for a term project. By that time, team members should be quite advanced, adeptly communicating, and confident that their process is smooth.

One Way To. . . Identify the Process You Will Use

1. Decide which of *waterfall, spiral,* and *incremental* processes is appropriate.
   Usually a spiral for a semester project.
   Combining parts is OK, e.g. start with spiral, end with *incremental.*

2. Decided how many iterations.
   Usually two for a semester project (there are many artifacts to coordinate at the end of each iteration).
   Three provides lots of practice—but this is a challenge; make the first increment as minor as possible.
   Three promotes the collection and use of metric data—use metric data collected from each iteration on next.

3. Rough out a weekly schedule.
   Coordinate with course assignments.
   (The next chapter discusses scheduling.)

Figure 1.19 One Way to Identify the Process You Will Use

5. DOCUMENTATION

5.1 Introduction to Documentation

Documentation is the lifeblood of software engineering. This includes documentation separate from code, as well as documentation closely associated with code. To understand the importance of comprehensive documentation, imagine being asked to contribute to a software project that is already well underway. Given the potential complexity involved, it would be as if you were asked to learn about an aspect of blood pathology, for example. To do this, you would want an overview of the subject, the motivation for knowing about it, an orderly flow from the overview to the details, diagrams showing interrelationships, copious notes on particular implementations, and so on. Omissions or contradictions would make it difficult or impossible to understand what is going on.

To illustrate the importance of software documentation at several levels, examine the code fragment shown in Figure 1.20. Without complete documentation, this code is impossible to interpret, and thus has little or no value. When we insert comments, and make the names more expressive, as in Figure 1.21, the result, while improved, is only marginally more useful. We may even be misled into believing we know its meaning and context, and the consequences may be more disastrous than if we acknowledge ignorance of the code's meaning.

When we look at the thoroughly documented code (Figure 1.22), however, its meaning becomes much clearer. The important new fact communicated by the documentation is that this tax rate applies only for a limited time period. The reference to a specific requirement in the SRS is another important piece of documentation. The symbols beginning with "@" are *Javadoc* reserved words, and will be explained in greater detail in Chapter 8.

But the story of this piece of code is not yet over. Surveying the configuration management document (the SCMP) tells us that we are currently developing version 2.7.3 of *tax()*, and that the version used is 2.3.4. In other words, the code fragment we have been looking at is pretty much irrelevant. The current version, 2.7.3, may look completely different.

We are still missing the whole picture. For example, do we know whether version 2.3.4 works as required? What class is this function a part of? What package? Even if we

```
int a(int i, char c)
{
        if(c== "m")
                if(i< 1000)
                        return 0;
                else
                        if(i< 10000)
                                return 500;
                        else
                                return 1200;
        else
                return 1300;
}
```

Figure 1.20 Undocumented Code

```
int tax(int anEarning, char aStatus)
{
        if(aStatus == 'm')
            if(anEarning < 1000)
                  return 0;  //  no tax for married, < $1000
            else
                  if(anEarning < 10000)
                        return 500;  //  married, $1000–$10000
                  else
                        return 1200;  //  married, >=$10000
            //  If not "married," apply single tax rate of $1300 regardless
        else
            return 1300;
}
```

Figure 1.21 Somewhat Documented Code

know the name of its package, what is the package's purpose? How does it relate to other packages? In other words, documentation gets its meaning not only from its text, but also from its context. A litmus test for good documentation is that a new engineer should be able to understand the project within a reasonable amount of time. To sum up: a project is the whole set of coordinated, well-engineered artifacts, including the documentation suite, the test results, and the code.

5.2 Documentation Standards

In the past, the establishment of standards has vastly magnified the benefits received from new engineering fields. Standards make interoperability possible: in other words, an idea or artifact produced for one application can be carried over to another. Standards improve communication among engineers. As a case in point, the establishment of electrical standards led to great leaps forward in our ability to produce useful products and services. Most large companies have developed standards for software development. Some customers, such as the U.S. Department of Defense, insist that their specified standards be used by contractors.

```
/**
 * This method implements requirement 4.3:
 * "State tax effective 9/1/98 - 12/31/99"
 * @ author Eric J. Braude
 * @ version 2.3.4 (8/6/98)
 * @ param anEarning: earnings 9/1/98 thru 12/31/99
 * @ param aStatus: 'm' signifies "married" (anything
 * else designates unmarried)
 */
int tax (int anEarning, char aStatus)
{ . . .
```

Figure 1.22 Documented Code

Most companies have discovered that simply publishing and disseminating standards does not lead to their acceptance. It is common to find thick volumes of company standards manuals gathering dust on engineers' bookshelves. The author has even observed brief reference cards on company standards being virtually unused, proving that size alone is not the deterrent factor. Nor does forcing engineers to attend standards training sessions necessarily make them comply with standards. To be effective, standards must be perceived by engineers as being helpful to them, rather than a set of hurdles. In addition, quantified goals, which require disciplined and documented approaches, tend to motivate teams.

Humphrey [Hu3] suggests that development teams decide collectively which documentation standards they will apply. In my opinion, this way of deciding is preferable, because the team will be motivated to follow its own decision. Another advantage is that the company effectively tries out several approaches, a process which is likely to produce superior choices in the long run. The disadvantage of allowing teams to pick their own standards is that groups within the same company often select different standards. This diminishes the possibility for comparisons between projects, and requires engineers who switch projects to learn a new document framework.

At a minimum, organizations have to make standards simple and clear. Organizations allow some flexibility and autonomy, but they also expect process improvement feedback in a standard manner. For example, an organization should expect data concerning the time spent on an application, and the lines of code, measured in a specified manner. Such measurement makes it possible to use the data across the organization. Process improvement involves an evolutionary metaprocess (a process concerning processes) within the organization. One example is the *Capability Maturity Model* (CMM), which classifies the software development organizations into five categories of increasing capability. The CMM is described in Section 8.3 on page 57.

The following organizations publish important standards. In all cases, the standards have to be modified somewhat to bring them up to date, because the deliberations required to create standards are much slower than the generation of new techniques and technology in the marketplace.

- The International Institute of Electronic and Electrical Engineers (IEEE, www.ieee.org) has been very active in setting software documentation standards for many years. Most of the standards are developed by distinguished committees of experienced, dedicated engineers from industry. Several of the IEEE standards have also become ANSI standards (the American National Standards Institute). This chapter, for example, refers to three IEEE standards (see Sections 6.5, 7.2, and 7.3).

- The International Standards Organization (ISO) has had significant worldwide impact, especially in manufacturing, and particularly among organizations doing business with the European Common Market (EC). The EC has mandated ISO standards for any company doing business with its member countries, and this has provided a powerful incentive for companies throughout the world to comply.

- The Software Engineering Institute (SEI) was established by the U.S. Department of Defense at Carnegie-Mellon University to help upgrade the level of software engineering by military contractors. The SEI's work has also been embraced by numerous commercial companies, which have identified software process improvement as a strategic corporate goal. We describe an important SEI capability standard, the Capability Maturity Model, in this chapter.

- The Object Management Group (OMG, www.omg.org) is a non-profit organization with about 700 member companies. OMG sets standards for distributed object-oriented computing. In particular, the OMG has endorsed the Unified Modeling Language (see inside covers) as its standard for describing designs. For example, the interface notation used in the COM of Figure 1.7 on page 22 is a UML notation.

The documents supporting a project vary among organizations, but they correspond roughly to the waterfall phases. ISO 12207 is one example of such a document set.

This book applies a consistent set of documentation standards, namely those due to the IEEE. Although the IEEE standards require occasional modernization, they help the engineer to recall most of the issues that need to be addressed, and they allow the engineer to concentrate on the application. When documentation standards are not used, engineers have to spend a significant amount of time organizing documents themselves, which is like reinventing the wheel. Figure 1.23 shows a typical documentation set using IEEE terminology. The case study uses most of the documents in the set. The fact that this documentation set parallels the waterfall process does not imply that the waterfall model must be used, but if it is not used, these documents must be revised and augmented each time that the waterfall phases are applied. This means that the documents must be very well organized. This is rather like the organization of a library in the sense that it is easy to add and remove books from a well-organized library.

Below is a description of each document in the IEEE set, with references to full descriptions in this book. Other standards bodies organize theirs in a similar way.

- SVVP: The software verification and validation plan. This plan explains the manner in which the project steps are to be checked, and the product is to be checked against its requirements. *Verification* is the process of checking that an application is built in a correct manner; *validation* checks that the right product has been built. These are explained in full in Section 6.6 on page 46. Frequently, it is an external organization that performs some or all of these functions (in which case it is specifically referred to as Independent V&V,—IV&V).

- SQAP: The software quality assurance plan. This plan specifies the manner in which the project is to achieve its quality goals. It is explained further in Section 6.5 on page 46, in the case study at the end of this chapter, and in Chapter 2.

- SCMP: The software configuration management plan. The SCMP explains how and where the documents and code, and their various versions, are stored, and how they

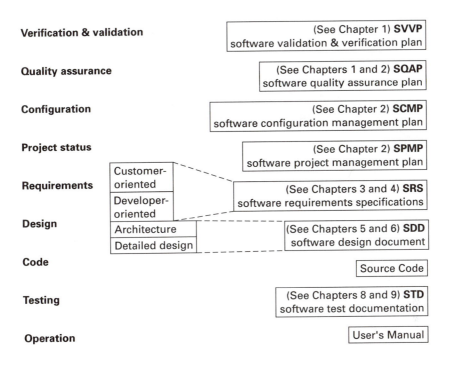

Figure 1.23 Project Documentation

fit together. It is not advisable to get started without such a plan because the very first document generated is bound to change, and we must understand how this change will be managed before we begin writing the document. The IEEE's SCMP standard is described in this chapter. For the case study, we will be content with the modest plan described at the end of this chapter. Medium to large companies generally try to work out configuration management details on behalf of all their projects, and engineers need only learn to follow the designated procedures in the official SCMP and use the designated tools. The SCMP is described further in Section 7 on page 49, and in the case study at the end of the chapter.

- SPMP: The software project management plan. This plan explains the manner in which the project is to be conducted. Typically, it cites a known development process, e.g., the company's standard process. The SPMP is discussed in Chapter 2, which covers project management.

- SRS: The Software Requirements Specification. This document states the requirements for the application and is a kind of contract and guide for the customer and the developers. The SRS is explained in Chapters 3 and 4.

- SDD: The Software Design Document. The SDD describes the architecture and design details of the application. Typically, diagrams such as object models and data flow diagrams are used. The SDD is explained in Chapters 5 and 6.

- STD: The Software Test Documentation. This document describes the way in which the application and its parts are to be tested. The STD is described in Chapters 8 and 9.

Projects sometimes employ documents additional to those described above (see, e.g., [IE]). The documentation for iterative development can be organized in at least two ways.

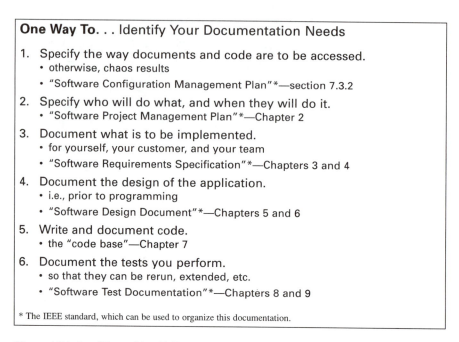

One Way To. . . Identify Your Documentation Needs

1. Specify the way documents and code are to be accessed.
   - otherwise, chaos results
   - "Software Configuration Management Plan"*—section 7.3.2
2. Specify who will do what, and when they will do it.
   - "Software Project Management Plan"*—Chapter 2
3. Document what is to be implemented.
   - for yourself, your customer, and your team
   - "Software Requirements Specification"*—Chapters 3 and 4
4. Document the design of the application.
   - i.e., prior to programming
   - "Software Design Document"*—Chapters 5 and 6
5. Write and document code.
   - the "code base"—Chapter 7
6. Document the tests you perform.
   - so that they can be rerun, extended, etc.
   - "Software Test Documentation"*—Chapters 8 and 9

* The IEEE standard, which can be used to organize this documentation.

Figure 1.24 One Way to Identify Your Documentation Needs

Some documents (e.g., the SDD) can contain a version for each iteration. Another way is to add appendices which account for progress on the application.

The Unified Modeling Language (UML) was developed as a way to standardize the description of software designs, particularly object-oriented designs. The UML has been accepted as a standard by the Object Management Group (see above). This book uses the UML as its notation for several artifacts, including the design and the physical configuration of source files. Selected UML is described inside the book's covers. Additional UML is described in the body of the text. Figure 1.24 summarizes the key documentation needs that every project has, regardless of whether or not it uses recognized documentation standards, such as the IEEE's.

▶PART II: AT LENGTH

This **part** of the chapter *can* be covered after covering subsequent chapters. Understanding the material in this part, however, is required to produce a quality software product.

6. QUALITY

There is a vast difference between simply producing a function and producing a *quality* function. The former consists of code that compiles and appears to "work," but about which nothing more can be said with certainty. A quality function, on the other hand, consists of code that

- Satisfies clearly stated requirements
- Checks its inputs; reacts in predictable ways to illegal inputs
- Has been inspected thoroughly by engineers other than the author
- Has been tested exhaustively in several independent ways
- Is thoroughly documented
- Has a confidently known defect rate, if any

The difference is like that between a shelf built by a homeowner, which is good enough to hold garden pots, and a beam in a bridge secure enough to ensure the safety of travelers.

Similarly, a high-quality quality design is typically

- Extensible (readily capable of being enhanced to provide additional functionality)
- Evolvable (readily capable of being adapted to altered requirements)
- Portable (applicable to several environments)
- General (applicable to several different situations)

Our goal is to specify standards for acceptability, and to create products that satisfy these specifications. In order to do this, we must know how to quantify quality, how to specify goals in terms of these quantities, and how to control progress towards these goals.

6.1 Metrics

Quantification is an essential part of engineering. For example, traffic engineers speak of *number of cars per hour,* and mechanical engineers of *load limits.* Software engineers also use measures, such as *lines of code, number of classes, number of defects fixed per month,* and *number of functions per class.*

Metrics cannot be separated from their context. For example, when two programmers produce different amounts of code to attain the same degree of reliability, functionality, readability, and efficiency, the version with the smaller number of lines of code is probably superior. In other contexts, however, more lines of code could indicate improved productivity. Taken over large numbers of sample points, and used together with other metrics, however, *lines of code* can be quite meaningful. For example, assuming that reliability metrics are at their required level, and that increasing lines of code reflect increasing capability in the application, the more lines of code produced per hour the better. Because of the variety of coverage among metrics, we usually collect several different kinds.

Metrics and their use are discussed throughout this book, and the habit of collecting metrics is stressed. The metrics we shall almost always include are

- Amount of work done, measured physically (e.g., lines of code)
- Time taken to do the work
- Defect rate (defects per 1000 lines of code, defects per page of documentation, etc.)

In addition, we shall often include a subjective rating of the quality of the work on a scale of 0 to 10.

The anticipated or desired values for metrics are forecast before the corresponding effort takes place, and then the results are compared with the forecast values. For example, our organization might inject (cause) 0.2 defects per page of requirements documents (one in five pages, as averaged over past projects). Our goal for the current project might be 0.15 per page. Our actual rate might turn out to be 0.17, which would indicate that our methods are superior to methods used in the past, but not good enough to support our goal of 0.15.

6.2 The Quality Assurance Process

The primary responsibility for the quality of an artifact rests with the person creating it. Nevertheless, "no man is an island." We all need to have our work reviewed by others (the author of this book included!). This is essential for preventing short-sightedness, unrealistic self-evaluation, and stagnation. It is also a social responsibility. Each piece of work of each engineer should be reviewed in detail by at least one other person, preferably by someone independent of the creator.

In addition to the responsibility of individual development engineers, and the review that their peers provide, many organizations identify a separate systematic and thorough review process, referred to as *quality assurance* (QA). The QA function includes reviews, inspections (a formal type of review described below), and testing. As illustrated in Figure 1.25, QA input should be sought from the beginning of each project. As suggested by Figure 1.25, it is ideal for QA to be involved with ensuring that a sound process is being used, and that the documentation is kept up-to-date. A QA representative can often participate in inspections. Ideally, QA should be performed by a separate organization. Many companies are too small for such specialization, in which case engineers perform QA functions on each other's work.

6.3 Black Box and White Box Techniques

Black box QA techniques deal with applications, or parts thereof, that have already been built. These techniques check whether or not the software conforms to its requirements. *White box* (or *glass box*) QA techniques deal with the components that make up the unit being tested. Turning on your TV, switching channels, and then observing their quality is a black box technique. Testing your television so that each circuit is exercised is a white box technique, because it involves the components that make up the TV. QA processes that

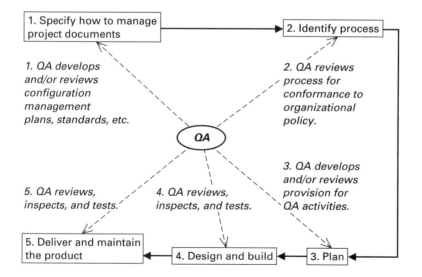

Figure 1.25 QA Involvement

are at neither of these two extremes are sometimes known as *gray box* techniques. Checking out each major component of your TV is a gray box technique. Strictly speaking, the difference between white box and gray box techniques is not always well defined.

Although black box and white box are most often thought of in the context of testing, these concepts apply to several quality assurance activities. White box techniques require the engineer to think about the structure, form, and purpose of the artifact being examined. This includes the use of formal methods, and, as will be discussed below, inspections. Black box thinking asks "does the entity we have built behave appropriately?" Black box and white box testing are explored in Chapters 8 and 9.

6.4 Introduction to Inspections

An *inspection* is a white box technique for ensuring quality. It consists of examining the parts of the project (requirements, designs, code etc.) to find defects. Inspections are performed by a group of the author's peers. This book introduces inspections very early because they should be used as soon as the first documentation of the project is produced. Since inspections were originally introduced to improve code, they are often referred to as "code inspections," even though their value has been shown to be greatest when used very early in the process, long before code is produced.

The inspection concept was established by Fagin [Fa], who observed the fact that the author of a work is usually able to repair a defect once he or she knows it to be present. Thus, a process should be used whereby the defects in the work are called to the author's attention before the author delivers the work to his management. This implies that inspections should be a peer process. This is summarized by Figure 1.26.

The principle of inspection can be expanded into four rules:

1. *Defects detection only*. Inspections specifically exclude the *repair* of defects. The repair process is left to the author, and no time should be spent during inspections even suggesting repairs. All suggestions should be made offline.

2. *Peer process*. Inspections are conducted by a group of software engineers. Inspection is not a supervisor-subordinate process. The *work in progress* is under inspection, not the performance of the author. The author is responsible only for the end product, and should be considered as having not yet delivered his work. The work brought to the inspection should be the author's best effort, not a draft of any kind. It is a waste of resources for a group to look for, find, and describe defects that the author would have found with reasonable effort.

AUTHORS CAN USUALLY REPAIR DEFECTS THAT THEY RECOGNIZE

COROLLARY:
Help authors to recognize defects
before they deliver their work.

COROLLARY:
Have their peers seek defects.

Figure 1.26 Principles of Inspection

3. *Specified roles.* Each participant adopts one of the following roles. To contain costs, one person can exercise two roles. Typically, the moderator can also be the reader. However, to avoid bias, the author should not adopt any other role.

- The *moderator* is responsible for seeing to it that the inspection takes place in a proper fashion. The moderator is also an inspector.
- The *author* is the responsible for the work itself, and repairs all defects found (offline). The author is also an inspector, and spends the time looking once again for defects.
- The *reader* is responsible for leading the team through the work in an appropriate thorough manner. The reader inspects at the same time.
- The *recorder* is responsible for writing down descriptions and classifications of the defects as decided by the team. The recorder is also an inspector.

The following are optional inspection roles. The necessity for their participation depends on the artifact being inspected.

- A *focused inspector* inspects for a specific criterion (e.g., reliability).
- A *specialized inspector* is a specialist in the area covered by the artifact under inspection (e.g., a radar expert for a radar control application).
- A plain *inspector* has no additional role besides inspecting the material for defects.

4. *Complete preparation.* Participants in inspections are required to prepare for the inspection at the same level of detail as the author. Inspections are not reviews, management overviews, or education sessions. Inspectors have to work at the same level of detail as the author. (This is what makes inspections expensive.)

Inspections should be applied as early as possible in the development process. For example, requirements should be inspected. Project management and configuration plans can also be inspected.

The following steps are required to execute an inspection (illustrated in Figure 1.27):

1. The inspection process begins with *planning.* "Planning" includes deciding which inspection metrics to collect, and identifying tools to be used in recording and analyzing these data.

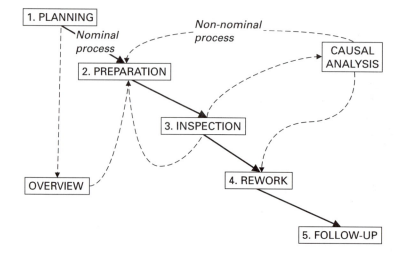

Figure 1.27 Inspection Process

2. As the project progresses, responsible people need to determine just which group of peers (fellow engineers) are to inspect which fragments of work. The fragments should have logical consistency, and should result in a 1–4-hour inspection meeting (discussed in step 5 below).

3. If necessary, an *overview meeting* can be organized to explain the unit under inspection. Meetings are expensive, and this type of overview should be avoided unless obviously necessary.

4. The next phase consists of *preparation*. This is when the inspectors review the work in complete detail at their own desks (e.g., checking that the code under inspection correctly implements the detailed design). What makes the inspection process valuable, but also expensive, is the fact that this detailed process is performed by several people. The process is *not* a "review," because inspectors work at the same level of detail as the author. Inspectors frequently enter the defects found into a database (e.g., web-accessible) together with descriptions and classifications. This helps to prevent duplication, and minimizes unnecessary meeting time. Some prefer to use paper to record their defects, and some consider the number of inspectors who recognize a given defect to be a useful metric.

5. Once every participant is prepared, the *inspection meeting* takes place. During this meeting, the participants honor their designated roles.

6. Normally, the author is able to repair all defects. This is the *rework* phase. If the inspection meeting decides, however, that the defects are so pervasive that a reinspection is required, then the item is *recycled* through the process.

7. If the defects are due to a misunderstanding or widespread misconception, it may be necessary to call a separate *causal analysis* meeting at which these causes are discussed. Again, since meetings are expensive, causal analysis meetings should not be scheduled casually.

8. The final *follow-up meeting* is a brief one, at which the moderator and the author confirm that the defects have been repaired. This is not intended to be a detailed review by the moderator. The onus for repair is on the author, who is responsible for the work.

9. As with all processes, the group meets to review the inspection process itself, and decides how it can be improved. This includes the improvement of inspection checklists.

Figure 1.28 shows the average relative times for each inspection process step, used as reference data by one of the author's clients. The inspection meeting time is shown as 1 hour for the sake of reference. Individual companies or development groups record inspection

Planning	1 hr x (1 person)
[*Overview: optional*	*1 hr x (3–5)]*
Preparation	1 hr x (2–4 people)
Inspection meeting	1 hr x (3–5 people)
Rework	1 hr x (1 person)
[*Analysis: optional*	*1 hr x (3–5)]*
Total: approx.	*7–21 person-hours*

Figure 1.28   Time/Costs per 100 LoC (Lines of Noncommented Code)— One Company's Estimates

	Defect found at inspection time	Defect found at integration time
Hours to detect	0.7 to 2	0.2 to 10
Hours to repair	0.3 to 1.2	9+
Total	1.0 to 3.2	9.2 to 19+

Figure 1.29 Hours per Defect: One Estimate

times and quantities inspected, and they estimate future inspections based on this historical data. The times shown in the figure may disturb the uninitiated, who may wonder whether it really does take that long to check code. Producing professional quality products does indeed take a substantial amount of time, and any failure to recognize the true costs ends up consuming far more time in the end. Inspections are estimated by Gehani and Lally [Ge] to consume 10–15% of the development budget.

Various studies (for example, [Fa]) have shown clearly that inspections, despite their expense in using a great deal of expert time, pay off handsomely. If one examines the cost of inspections, this may be hard to believe at first; however, this expense should be compared with the cost of not detecting defects during the phase in question. Eventually, defects have to be detected and then repaired. If this is not done close to the time of defect creation, the cost escalates dramatically. Figure 1.29 compares the cost to detect and repair defects at inspection time versus integration time. These estimates, drawn from a client of the author's, are conservative.

The figure indicates, for example, that it takes between 7/10 of an hour and two hours to detect (find) each defect if the search is performed as part of an inspection. On the other hand, it takes between 2/10 of an hour and as much as ten hours to find each one if the search for defects is performed when the application is integrated (i.e., at the end of the development process). Gathering these numbers for a particular development group and project is not difficult provided that testing and other times are recorded. For example, to determine the average time spent detecting a defect, one divides the number of hours spent testing by the number of defects found.

Quantified benefits of inspections from sources such as IBM, ICL, and Standard Bank are summarized in [Gi]. The benefits accrue from identifying defects earlier in the development cycle than they would otherwise have been identified. In these studies, the magnitude of the savings easily justifies the costs. Companies report that the earlier the inspections are conducted, the greater the cost benefit. In particular, a disproportionate number of product defects result from defective requirements. For example, imagine the cost to detect and repair the following defect in requirements:

Requirement implemented: *If the temperature is within 5.02% of the maximum allowable limit, as defined by standard 67892, then the motor is to be shut down.*
Real requirement: *If the temperature is within 5.02% of the maximum allowable limit, as defined by standard 67892, then the motor is to be powered down.*

The writer of the requirements considered "powered down" equivalent to "shut down." "Powered down," however, could refer to a process of switching off elements of the application in a specific order, perhaps waiting for one part to end before beginning the next part. "Shut down" could mean switching them all off at the same time. Additional specifics are required to define what this means.

Unfortunately, it is quite conceivable that a test involving the "maximal allowable temperature" can be performed only near the end of the development process, at which time the application would mysteriously shut down. The defect is trivial to inspectors of the *requirements*, but to *system testers* it could well be dramatically nontrivial.

As pointed out in the SQAP case study at the end of this chapter, "reviews" are generally not inspections. Reviews are meetings where work is discussed that is either in progress, or that has been completed. An example is a review at which alternative architectures are discussed. Although reviews are essential, they do not require the same detailed preparation as inspections, nor are the participants required to assume roles in the manner of inspections.

Figure 1.30 shows how your team can prepare for and conduct inspections. A significant amount of organizational work is required to carry out the steps in the figure. In the author's experience, companies generally find it a major challenge to organize and use the metric data collected because of a lack of simple planning. This is changing for the better as companies understand the strategic value of their data, and as students emerge from educational institutions expecting to record metrics. Student team work is an excellent place to practice metric collection and application. A simple solution to the challenge of metric data collection and use is to designate one person responsible for it. The data is generally used to measure quality and to estimate future time requirements.

Every phase of every part of a project is inspected. Due to the limited resources available to class teams, however, it may be necessary to inspect only selected parts of the project and product. Chapter 2 describes a "buddy" system in which each team member is shadowed by another individual on the team. This buddy should participate in the inspections of the team member's work: Time constraints may force inspections by the buddy alone. This is not ideal, but it is far superior to no inspection at all.

One Way To. . . Prepare for and Conduct Inspections

1. Build inspections into the project schedule.
   - Plan to inspect all phases, starting with requirements
   - Allow for preparation (time-consuming!) and meeting time

2. Prepare for collection of inspection data.
   - Include number of defects per work unit (e.g., KLOC), time spent
   - Develop forms: include *description, severity,* and *type*
   - Decide who, where, how to store and use the metric data
     - default: appoint a single person to be responsible
     - failure to decide usually results in discarding the data

3. Assign roles to participants.
   - Three adequate (*author; moderator/recorder; reader*)
   - Two far better than none (*author; inspector*)

4. Ensure every participant prepares.
   - Bring defects pre-entered on forms to inspection meeting.

Figure 1.30 One Way to Prepare for and Conduct Inspections

6.5 IEEE Standard for Software Quality Assurance Plans

Checklists of things to do and look for are particularly useful in making sure that all quality bases are covered: hence the use of existing standards. For example, Figure 1.31 shows the first six sections of the table of contents of IEEE standard 730-1989: *Standard for Software Quality Assurance Plans*. The remaining sections will be discussed in Chapter 2. Much of this standard is geared to large projects, but it is good for small projects too, and the standard helps us to remember all the factors that must be covered. It is a simple matter to discard a section that does not apply to a particular project.

The document specifies

- Who will be responsible for quality (Section 3)—a person, a manager, a group, an organization, etc.
- What documentation is required (Section 4)—(see Chapter 2, on project management)
- What techniques will be used to ensure quality (Section 5)—inspections, proofs of correctness, tests, etc.
- What procedures will be followed to manage the process (Section 6)—meetings, audits, reviews, etc.

6.6 Verification and Validation

Verification and *validation* (V&V) are part of the quality assurance plan. Verification asks "Are we building it right?" Mainly, this responds to the question "Are we building precisely those things in the present phase that were specified in the previous phase?" Validation responds to the question "Are we building the right thing?" In other words, "Are

---

1. **Purpose**
2. **Referenced documents**
3. **Management**
   3.1 Organization
   3.2 Tasks
   3.3 Responsibilities
4. **Documentation**
   4.1 Purpose
   4.2 Minimum documentation requirements
   4.3 Other
5. **Standards, practices, conventions, and metrics**
   5.1 Purpose
   5.2 Content

6. **Reviews and audits**
   6.1 Purpose
   6.2 Minimum requirements
   - 6.2.1 *Software requirements review*
   - 6.2.2 *Preliminary design review*
   - 6.2.3 *Critical design review*
   - 6.2.4 *SVVP review*
   - 6.2.5 *Functional audit*
   - 6.2.6 *Physical audit*
   - 6.2.7 *In-process audits*
   - 6.2.8 *Managerial review*
   - 6.2.9 *SCMP review*
   - 6.2.10 *Post mortem review*
   6.3 Other
   7–15. [*see next chapter*]

Figure 1.31 IEEE 730-1989 Software Quality Assurance Plans Table of Contents
Copyright © 1989 IEEE

we fulfilling what the customer wants and needs?" Figure 1.32 summarizes these oft-quoted terms, which are attributed to Boehm. Unfortunately, the terms *verification* and *validation* are not used consistently in the literature, but this book will abide throughout by the definitions just given.

To reinforce the verification/validation distinction, let us perform V&V on a simple example. The customer wants an application that "solves linear equations of the form $ax + b = c$." We translate this into a detailed requirement such as

1. The user shall be able to input numbers a, b, and c up to 10 digits long, with up to four places after the decimal point.

2. The application shall produce a solution to the equation $ax + b = c$ within 1/1000 of the exact answer.

Then we write a program to implement this requirement.

Validation of this product consists of running a set of tests on it. For example, we enter $a = 1$, $b = 1$, and $c = 1$, and validate that the program produces $x = 0$. (Chapters 8 and 9 discuss testing in detail.) Testing can only determine the presence of some of the defects; it cannot determine that all defects are absent. Thus, validation does not fulfill our responsibility to deliver a defect-free product.

Part of our remaining responsibility is to be sure that we have *built the application right* by checking that we proceeded correctly from the beginning of the process to the end. This is the *verification* process. In this particular problem, we need to verify the following steps.

1. Get the customer's requirements.
2. Write down the requirements in detail.
3. Code the application.
4. Test the application.

Thus, *verification* checks each of the following:

1→2: Do the requirements express what the customer really wanted? Some verification issues are as follows: Is $ax + b = c$ the correct form? (check with the customer on the

Verification:
   are we building *the thing right?*

Validation:
   are we building *the right thing?*

Figure 1.32 Meaning of V&V (Graphics reproduced with permission from Corel.)

precision interpretation); What if 0 is entered for *a*?, etc. Inspections of the requirements are also part of this verification process.

2→3: Does the code implement the written requirements? This requires an inspection of the code, in which the requirements are taken one at a time, and the matching code is identified. It could include a mathematical proof.

3→4: Does the test adequately cover the application? This also requires an inspection of the testing (see Chapters 8 and 9).

6.6.1 IEEE V&V Standard 1012-1986

The IEEE standard 1012-1986 for verification and validation, whose headings are reproduced in Figure 1.33, provides a framework with which to express the manner in which V&V is to be carried out. Standard 1012-1986 was reaffirmed in 1992. Ideally, V&V procedures can be specified across the board for *all* company projects. An ideal procedure is for an outside group to perform V&V; hence the term IV&V (independent verification and validation).

Figure 1.34 summarizes steps a team can take to produce a quality product. The first step in the figure, setting quantified quality goals, will appear impossible to groups with no historical metric data to use. In this case, it is best to take an educated guess. What is your maximum allowed number of defects per thousand lines of code? Would a good standard be as "*one* defect per KLOC of no higher than medium severity"? Choose a number that you feel represents your standard of quality. You will find it instructive when the actual number is computed, and you compare it with your estimate. (On the other hand, people tend to forget these results when they have not estimated them in advance.) When you do determine the actual number in your project, you will be in a better position to set realistic goals and schedules the next time.

The second point made in Figure 1.34 is to build continual inspection into the team's process. In the author's experience, engineers and students are usually surprised by the extent to which their work is improved by inspections. Although inspections pay off hand-

---

1. **Purpose**
2. **Referenced documents**
3. **Definitions**
4. **V&V overview**
   4.1 Organization
   4.2 Master schedule
   4.3 Resource summary
   4.4 Responsibilities
   4.5 Tools, techniques, and methodologies
5. **Lifecycle V&V**
   5.1 Management of V&V
   5.2 Concept phase V&V
   5.3 Requirements phase V&V
   5.4 Design phase V&V
   5.5 Implementation phase V&V
   5.6 Test phase V&V
   5.7 Installation and checkout phase V&V
   5.8 Operation and maintenance phase V&V
6. **Software V&V reporting**
   6.1 Required reports
   6.2 Optional reports
7. **V&V administrative procedures**
   7.1 Anomaly reporting and resolution
   7.2 Task iteration policy
   7.3 Deviation policy
   7.4 Standards, practices, and conventions

Figure 1.33 IEEE 1012–1986 Software Verification & Validation Plans Table of Contents (reaffirmed 1992)   Copyright © 1986 IEEE

One Way To. . . Produce a Quality Software Product

1. Quantify your quality goals.

   minimum: *number of defects per KLOC*

   team: *# defective requirements; # classes missing* from design; *# defects* in testing; *# defects found* in operation

   personal: apply *# of defects* to code, compile, unit test separately

2. Build inspections and reviews into the schedule.

   (see scheduling, next chapter)

   follow the inspection procedure (see Figure 1.27 on page 00)

3. Document your quality goals and procedures.

   use a documentation standard to avoid missing issues

   SQAP (see case study for example); if time allows: SVVP

Figure 1.34 One Way to Produce a Quality Software Product

somely, they consume a significant amount of time up front, and this should be taken into account when developing the schedule. Scheduling is discussed in Chapter 2.

The third point concerns the specification of quality goals and procedures. Using a standard such as the IEEE Software Quality Assurance Plan specifies the issues that must be covered. Writing and implementing a V&V plan is usually too demanding for inclusion in a one-semester term project.

7. DOCUMENTATION MANAGEMENT

7.1 Introduction to Documentation Management

Managing software project documentation requires a significant degree of organizational skill, because the document set is a large, living entity that undergoes continuous, concurrent modification by multiple people. Writing good, flexible documentation is similar in many ways to writing good, flexible code.

The management of documentation requires *completeness, consistency,* and *configuration.* We addressed *completeness* in Section 5.2 on page 37, in which a typical suite of documents is described that covers the development and maintenance process. *Consistency* means the document set does not contradict itself. For large document sets, it is hard to avoid occasional near-contradictory statements. *Configuration* is the coordination of the various versions and parts of the documents and code. Consistency and configuration management are addressed in the next sections.

7.2 Consistency and Single Source Documentation

One key to consistency is to specify each entity in only one place. We will call this *single source documentation.* For example, a requirement for a scientific application may be: "bacterial count, an integer between 1 and 100,000,000, shall be accessible at all times."

Such a requirement would be documented in the Software Requirement Specification (SRS). It is tempting to restate this requirement in several other places—e.g., in the source code, either in the function header or in-line comments. Another place where we might want to restate a requirement is in the user's manual. The value of restatements should be carefully traded off against the inherent difficulties that they cause. The reason for avoiding restatement is the inevitable change which takes place through the lifetime of a project. When the same fact is stated in several places, every one of those restatements must be changed simultaneously whenever the fact changes. This is a practical impossibility during the stress of project execution. Restatement leads to inconsistency, and inconsistency leads to failure. There *is* a need for references to the same idea from several places within documentation. One way to implement this without violating "single source documentation" is to try to hyperlink to the single source.

Figure 1.35 postulates a hyperlinked version of the documentation set, in which document parts reference relevant parts of other documents. For example, since each requirement leads to specific source code, the source code can hyperlink to the corresponding requirements in the SRS. Hyperlink technology permits each requirement to be traced to its test and implementation without being repeated. As of 2000, such hyperlinking is beginning to be exploited by several vendors of software tools.

The dynamic components shown in Figure 1.35 are those parts of the documents that must be updated and/or supplied while the project progresses. In other words, most of the documents are living entities which require continual "care and feeding." An example of this is the SCMP, which specifies current document versions. The SRS is frequently revisited to make additions and modifications during iterative development.

Sometimes we simply *must* restate a requirement in a different manner. User manuals, for example, generally have to be written in a manner different from that used in developer documentation, and so it is necessary to restate requirements in a new form. In

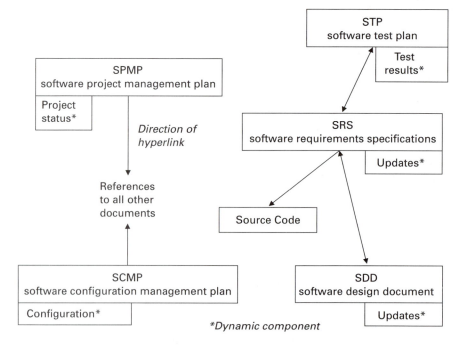

Figure 1.35 Example of Hyperlinked Documentation Set

addition, documentation must sometimes be expressed at more than one level of detail; for example, at one stage we may need to provide an overview, at another stage the details. These can easily become inconsistent. Hyperlinking holds promise for mitigating the resulting consistency problems by maintaining cross references. For example, a summary section could hyperlink to corresponding detail sections, or a requirement in the SRS could be hyperlinked to a corresponding section in the user manual. This does not prevent covering the same material twice, but it can facilitate consistency by having the two versions "virtually" side by side. Single source documentation is applied in the case study in Chapter 7, where function headers in the source code reference the corresponding SRS requirement.

Organizations, especially smaller ones, generally find it difficult to keep documentation synchronized. For example, after the initial draft of the requirements has been completed, engineers often add capabilities to the design and to the implementation without, unfortunately, updating the requirements correspondingly. Documents that are not consistent lose their credibility: Engineers become even less likely to update them, and the investment in their creation can easily evaporate. It helps to make updating as easy as possible for engineers, using techniques like those mentioned above, but doing so does not guarantee success. Only a cultural and educational process that convinces software engineers that consistent documentation is their professional obligation, can accomplish this.

7.3 Configuration Management

Projects change in two ways as they progress toward completion. The first is through the accumulation of new parts. The second kind of change consists of successive versions of these parts. "Configuration management" refers to the management of these parts.

An unfinished road project is an example of an engineering project. It can be readily observed, and certainly can't be lost! We have to be much more careful, however, in tracking the status of a software product under construction, because such a product *can* be lost, in part or in whole. Being "lost" in this context is actually not so much the result of misplacing files, but of not knowing which versions of files belong with which. Our first obligation in tracking software is to know exactly where the parts of the project are located and which ones fit together. The "parts" consist of far more than just the source code. They include all of the documentation, which even includes the project plan itself. For this reason we introduce configuration management early in this book. A plan must be in place to deal with changes to documents even before the Software Project Management Plan (SPMP) is developed (the subject of Chapter 2).

In addition, projects usually produce variants of the product as it emerges. For example, there are several ways of rendering video game scenes, and we might want to try out more than one of these renderings. At least one of these versions will not be part of the eventual product. Similarly, functions are frequently discarded because they become superceded by changes in requirements, or are replaced by more complete versions. In addition, a significant amount of support software is developed that enables the building of the product, but is not deliverable. All of these units must be tracked so that the project team understands exactly what it is dealing with at all times. Finally, when a project is complete, some of its software may be reusable. Untracked software is typically not reusable.

7.3.1 Configuration Items
To track the parts of a project, we must first identify them. *Configuration items* (CIs) are the project parts tracked by the configuration management system. For example, as shown in Figure 1.36, version 6 of the social security computation method of the payroll unit of an accounting system could be labeled configuration item "S6."

Units tracked officially
· down to the smallest unit worth tracking
· includes most official documents

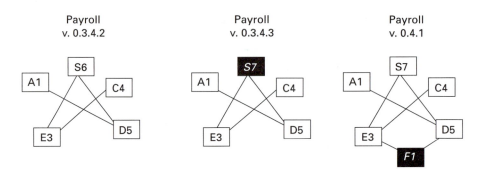

Figure 1.36 Configuration Items (CIs)

CIs can consist of other CIs. Thus, in Figure 1.36, the CI "Payroll version 0.3.4.2," the payroll unit of an accounting system, consists of version 6 of part S, version 1 of A, version 3 of E, and so forth. The configuration system has to be able to distinguish between variants in versions—for example, version 3.4 of the Payroll application containing CI S6, and one containing S7 (different versions of the social security computation method). The figure shows a change in Payroll version numbers that accommodate this, and a further change to accommodate the new method F1. Classes are typically CIs. Individual functions could be CIs, but this is not typical. We would not use CIs of finer granularity than functions, since tracking parts of functions is generally unmanageable. Significant data such as global tables, however, could be CIs.

Next, the use of CIs by multiple project personnel has to be managed. There is a huge potential for chaos when this is not performed carefully. Here are examples of this chaos:

- A software engineer retrieves a copy of class *Customer* to modify it and to make it more versatile. He completes his work, certifies it, and replaces the original. Later it is discovered that the new version causes problems, and it is decided to reinstate the old version while the new *Customer* class is reengineered. However, several other parts of the project are now built around the new version of *Customer*.

  The old version should be available, and it should be clear as to which parts of the application coordinate with the new version of *Customer* and which coordinate with the old one. Such clarity allows for the option of rolling back to previous versions when necessary. The requirements to which the old version conforms would be reinstated at the same time.

- Software engineers Abel and Beryl retrieve copies of class *Customer* in order to modify it. Abel completes his work and replaces the old *Customer* class with the new one. Beryl completes her work and replaces the old *Customer* class with the new one, losing Abel's modifications.

  Configuration management (CM) systems allow the "locking" of CIs so that CIs are effectively checked out to only one engineer, while all other engineers can work with a read-only copy.

- Procedure to identify CIs
- Locking
  - to prevent more than one person working on a CI at one time
- Authorization to check out
  - optional

- Check-in procedure
  - authorization process
  - involves testing etc.
- Historical record of prior groupings of consistent CIs

Figure 1.37 Configuration Management Requirements (Graphics reproduced with permission from Corel.)

Typically, CM systems satisfy the minimum requirements shown in Figure 1.37. For example, there are clear procedures under which CIs are checked out, new CIs added, and modified CIs checked in. This includes documentation and testing. In particular, a clear authorization process for checking in documents is essential. A single individual, such as the project leader, may be the authority; otherwise the authority may be a group, often referred to as the Change Control Board.

7.3.2 IEEE Standard 828-1990 for Software Configuration Management Plans
The IEEE has developed a standard for software configuration management plans, IEEE 828-1990. This can be very useful in making sure that all bases have been covered in the process of CM. Figure 1.38 shows the relevant contents of this standard. Section 3.3 of the SCMP documents the means by which the status of CM is to be communicated (e.g., in writing, once a week). Section 3.6 applies if a CM tool is used or if configuration management is handled by a subcontractor. The IEEE standard describes the purpose of each section of the above outline in detail. IEEE 828-1990 is used in the case study at the end of this chapter.

1. **Introduction**
2. **SCM management**
   2.1 Organization
   2.2 SCM responsibilities
   2.3 Applicable policies, directives, & procedures
3. **SCM activities**
   3.1 Configuration identification
      3.1.1 Identifying configuration items
      3.1.2 Naming configuration items
      3.1.3 Acquiring configuration items

   3.2 Configuration control
      3.2.1 Requesting changes
      3.2.2 Evaluating changes
      3.2.3 Approving or disapproving changes
      3.2.4 Implementing changes
   3.3 Configuration status accounting
   3.4 Configuration audits and reviews
   3.5 Interface control
   3.6 Subcontractor/vendor control
4. **SCM schedules**
5. **SCM resources**
6. **SCM plan maintenance**

Figure 1.38 IEEE 828-1990 Software Configuration Management Plan Table of Contents   Copyright © 1990 IEEE

One Way To. . . Plan Configuration Management

1. Roughly sketch out your SCMP.

   Determine procedures for making changes.

   Omit tool references unless already identified.

   See the case study for an example.

2. Specify what you need from a CM tool.

   For class use, maybe only *locking* and *backup*.

3. Evaluate tools against your needs and budget.

   Commercial tools are in wide use.

   For class use, try free document storage web sites; try simple method of checking out, e.g., renaming.

4. Finalize your SCMP.

Figure 1.39 One Way to Plan Configuration Management

Figure 1.39 shows how teams can go about deciding their CM methods. Several commercial configuration management tools, such as Microsoft's SourceSafe™ are in common use.

Class teams have succeeded fairly well with simple websites, such as www.egroups.com, that allow document storage. A simple checkout system is needed, one of which is to change the document type. For example, when the SQAP is checked out to Joe, the file is changed from *sqap.txt* to *sqap.joe*. Although configuration management applies to both documents and source code, the file-naming convention usually has to be planned separately. For example, we cannot change *myClass.java* to *myClass.joe* without disrupting compilation. Some groups maintain two vaults of files. One vault contains the current baseline, which cannot be changed without a formal process. The other contains versions that are currently being worked on.

Various free CM tools such as FtpVC are also available. Be sure that your process does not rely on excessive manual intervention, and that it does not result in a bottleneck where one person is overloaded. If you are considering using a tool, be sure that the length of the learning curve justifies its use. There are many other software engineering aspects to learn besides using a particular CM tool. Whatever system you select, try it out first on an imagined implementation. Make sure that the process is smooth. You do *not* want to worry about your CM process during the implementation phase, when time is limited.

Students teams generate numerous workable ideas based on free tools. In the work world, however, professional CM tools are a necessity.

8. INTRODUCTION TO CAPABILITY ASSESSMENT

Software development has become recognized as an extremely valuable organizational asset. But this raises the issue of how to assess this asset, and it leads to the question "how good are we?" Very few organizations are able to answer the question with "excellent."

This section describes ways to assess the software engineering capabilities of individuals, teams, and organizations. Watts Humphrey and the Software Engineering Institute have developed the *Personal Software Process*[SM], the *Team Software Process*[SM], and the *Capability Maturity Model*[SM] to assess these respective levels of capability. This section describes each of these, and relates them.

Software engineering can be viewed from the perspective of the individual engineer (described in Section 8.1), the team (Section 8.2), or the entire organization (Section 8.3).

8.1 Introduction to the Personal Software Process (PSP)

Humphrey has deftly defined just what skills a competent software engineer should possess. The result is the *Personal Software Process*[SM] (PSP), which "provides detailed estimating and planning methods, shows engineers how to track their performance against these plans, and explains how defined processes can guide their work" ([Hu4] p3). The PSP is intended to develop specific programming habits, especially in measurement (How much time have I spent on this code? To write how many lines? Generating how many known defects? etc.). The PSP assumes that the engineer already possesses programming language skills.

As shown in Figure 1.40, the PSP is divided into graduated stages of growth, named *PSP0, PSP1, PSP2,* and *PSP3.*

PSP0: The Baseline Process   PSP0 accepts the student's current development practices, but requires the student to

- Track time spent working on the project
- Record defects found
- Record the types of defects

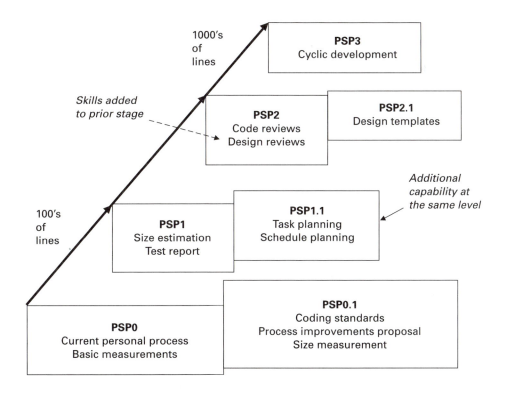

Figure 1.40 The PSP Evolution (Adapted from [Hu1])

PSP0 is augmented by PSP0.1, which requires the student to establish a

- Standard way to define a *"line of code"*
- Framework within which the individual can note ways to improve his or her development process

PSP1: The Personal Planning Process   PSP1 is designed to help the engineer understand the relationship between the size of programs and the time he or she takes to develop them. It is intended to provide an "orderly framework" within which the individual can perform estimates, make commitments, assess status, and record results. Software engineers are repeatedly asked by their managers "how long will it take you to do this." The PSP helps engineers to answer this question realistically.

PSP1 adds the following abilities to PSP0:

- Ability to estimate size
- Framework for reporting test results

PSP1 is augmented by PSP1.1, which adds the ability to

- Plan programming tasks
- Schedule programming tasks

PSP2: The Personal Quality Management Process   The PSP2 is designed to help engineers "deal realistically and objectively" with programming defects. The idea is to eliminate as many defects as possible before submitting the program for formal inspection. (Inspection was described in Section 6.4 on page 41.)

PSP2 adds

- Personal design reviewing
- Personal code reviewing

PSP2 is augmented by PSP2.1, which adds a

- Framework and checklist to ensure that designs are complete

PSP3: Cyclic Personal Process   PSP3 is designed to scale the PSP to deal with larger code units (in thousands of lines) by breaking up a large program into small increments.

PSP3 adds

- Applying the PSP to each increment, producing a high quality basis for the successive increments
- Using "regression" testing to ensure that tests designed for prior increments continue to succeed on new increments

8.2 Introduction to the Team Software Process (TSP)

As of 1999, Watts Humphrey reported encouraging results in establishing maturity goals and procedures for software teamwork. He has named this process the *Team Software Process*[SM] (TSP—see [Hu2]). The objectives of the TSP are shown in Figure 1.41 and Figure 1.42. The

- Build self-directed teams
  - 3–20 engineers
  - establish *own* goals
  - establish *own* process and plans
  - track work
- Show managers how to manage teams
  - coach
  - motivate
  - sustain peak performance

- Accelerate CMM improvement
  - make CMM 5 "normal"
- Provide improvement guidelines to high-maturity organizations
- Facilitate university teaching of industrial-grade teams

Figure 1.41 TSP Objectives 1 (Graphics reproduced with permission from Corel.)

Figure 1.42 TSP Objectives 2 (Graphics reproduced with permission from Corel.)

TSP's emphasis on team initiative and bottom-up interaction encourages an increased degree of professionalism among software engineers. For example, Humphrey states that it is unprofessional for engineers to provide management with schedules that cannot be accomplished, even when requested to do so. He counsels negotiation in such a situation. Professionalism, he reminds us, involves an obligation to serve society responsibly, in addition to serving employers. Also noteworthy is the TSP's emphasis on "coaching" by management external to the team. Management is expected not simply to give orders and specify deadlines, but to provide guidance, tools, and other required resources. We will return to the TSP when discussing project management in the next chapter.

8.3 Introduction to the Capability Maturity Model (CMM)

The ability of organizations to deliver quality software products depends upon many factors, both technical and human. The human issues range from the competence of individuals (addressed by the PSP) to issues of management and process. Improving the process within an organization is best performed in stages.

In the 1980s the Software Engineering Institute (SEI) established a simple classification of capabilities for contractors on behalf of the U.S. Department of Defense (DoD). DoD's plan was to restrict bidding on government contracts to contractors with specified capability levels. The SEI's system, known as the *Capability Maturity Model* (CMM), has been very successful in providing specific goals for organizational software engineering competence. Many organizations, defense and commercial alike, have used the CMM to measure their process improvement efforts. For example, instead of describing an organization as "pretty good" at developing software, one can be more specific, and state that the organization is "at CMM level three." The author's clients seeking to improve their CMM standings include a major defense contractor, but also a company developing spell checkers.

The CMM classifies organizations in five levels as follows.

Level 1: Initial Level 1, the "Initial" CMM level, expresses the most primitive status for software organizations. It recognizes only that the organization is capable of producing software products. The organization has no recognized process for software production, and the quality of products and projects depends entirely on the individuals performing the design and implementation. Typically, teams depend on the methods provided by a member

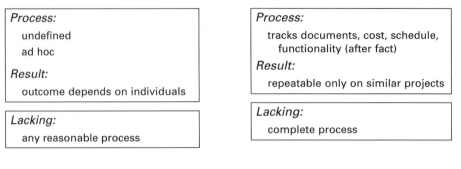

Process:
  undefined
  ad hoc
Result:
  outcome depends on individuals
	Process:
	  tracks documents, cost, schedule,
	    functionality (after fact)
	Result:
	  repeatable only on similar projects

Lacking:
  any reasonable process
	Lacking:
	  complete process

Figure 1.43 "Initial" CMM Level (1)   *Figure 1.44 "Repeatable" CMM Level (2)*

of the group who takes the initiative on the process to be followed. The success of one project has little relation to the success of another unless they employ common engineers, and are similar. When a project is completed, nothing is recorded about its cost, schedule, or quality. The result is that new projects are commonly performed no more competently than prior projects. This level is summarized in Figure 1.43.

Level 2: Repeatable   Level 2, the "Repeatable" CMM level, applies to organizations that are capable of tracking projects to some extent. They maintain records of project costs and schedules. They also describe the functionality of each product in writing. It is therefore possible to predict the cost and schedule of very similar projects performed by the same team. This is an improvement on level 1. What's needed for further improvement is the capability to make predictions independent of the particular people on the project teams. This is summarized in Figure 1.44. As of mid-1999, only a reported 20% of development organizations had attained level 2 or higher.

Level 3: Defined   Level 3, the "Defined" CMM level, applies to organizations that reduce excessive dependence on particular individuals by documenting and enforcing a standard process. Such a process is typically one of those described in this chapter (waterfall, spiral, etc., as described in Section 4 on page 00). Some organizations adopt existing standards such as IEEE's, while others define their own. Roughly speaking, as long as management enforces coordinated, professional standards, and engineers implement them uniformly, the organization is at level 3. This typically requires special training. Teams are allowed flexibility to tailor the organization's standards for special circumstances. This is summarized in Figure 1.45. Although level 3 organizations are capable of producing applications with consistent quality, and even though there are relatively few such organiza-

Process:
  documented
  standardized
  tailorable
Result:
  consistency

Lacking: predictable outcomes

Figure 1.45 "Defined" CMM Level (3)

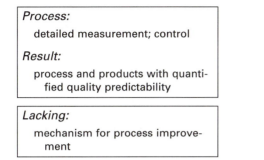

Process:
  detailed measurement; control

Result:
  process and products with quanti-
    fied quality predictability

Lacking:
  mechanism for process improve-
    ment

Figure 1.46 "Managed" CMM Level (4)

tions, they still lack predictive capability. They are able to make predictions only for projects very similar to projects performed in the past.

Level 4: Managed   Level 4, the "Managed" CMM level, applies to organizations that can predict the cost and schedule of jobs. One way they do this is to classify jobs and their components, and to measure and record the cost and time to design and implement those parts. Such measurements constitute historical metric data that are used to predict the cost and schedule of subsequent jobs. As Humphrey has pointed out, this is not "rocket science," but it does require a significant amount of organizational ability.

Level 4 almost appears to be the highest capability, but it is not. We know that software engineering changes rapidly. For example, the object-oriented paradigm has made rapid inroads into methodology: Reuse and new component concepts are having a growing impact. Future improvements and paradigms are unpredictable. Thus, the capabilities of a level 4 organization that does not change appropriately may well decline. This is summarized in Figure 1.46.

Level 5: Optimized   Instead of trying to predict future changes, it is preferable to institute permanent procedures for seeking out and exploiting new and improved methods and tools. Thus, level 5 organizations, at the "Optimized" CMM level, build in process improvement: In other words, their process (strictly speaking, a *meta-process*) includes a systematic way of evaluating the organization's process itself, investigating new methods and technologies, and then improving the organization's process. This is an impressive capability which, as of the beginning of 2000, few organizations possessed. With the passage of time since the CMM was promulgated, however, level 5 has become less of a dream, and more of a goal. Level 5 is summarized in Figure 1.47.

Process:
  continual process improvement
    through quantitative feedback
  extensible scope
  innovative ideas and technologies

*Figure 1.47 "Optimized" CMM Level (5)
    (Graphics reproduced with
    permission from Corel.)*

CMM Level	Focus	Key Process Area	PSP	TSP
5. Optimizing	Continuous process improvement	Defect prevention Technology change management Process change management	X X X	X X X
4. Managed	Product and process quality	Quantitative process management Software quality management	X X	X X
3. Defined	Engineering process	Organization process focus Organization process definition Tranining programs Integrated software management Software product engineering Inter-group coordination Peer reviews	X X X X X	X X X X X X
2. Repeatable	Project management	Requirements management Software project planning Software project tracking Software quality assurance Software configuration management Software subcontract management	 X X	X X X X X

Figure 1.48 Relating PSP, TSP, and CMM

8.4 Relating the PSP, TSP, and CMM

In [Hu3], Humphrey relates the three capability models discussed above. This comparison is shown in Figure 1.48. As an example of the relationship among the CMM, TSP, and PSP, note that "training programs" relates to the CMM only, since they are organization-wide and therefore not part of the PSP or TSP. Another example is that software configuration is required for teamwork, but it is not mandated for individual software development.

9. SUMMARY

Building software products is enormously challenging. The waterfall is the simplest process, and also the basis for processes such as spiral (or iterative) development. Incremental development is a third major process. Success depends upon a professional quality-oriented perspective, extensive support for individuals and teams (e.g., via the PSP/TSP processes), and the execution of a thorough, standardized development process (e.g., as assessed by the CMM). The ideal process includes both measurement and self-improvement. Figure 1.49 summarizes these points and also lists a typical set of project documentation.

- Software engineering an extensive challenge
- Major process models:
  - *waterfall, spiral, incremental*
- Capability frameworks: *CMM, TSP, PSP*
- Quality is the professional difference
  - metrics to define
  - inspection throughout
  - rigorous testing
  - include continuous self-improvement process
- Documentation: *SCMP, SVVP, SQAP, SPMP, SRS, SDD, STP, Code, User's manual*

Figure 1.49 Summary of the Ideal Software Engineering Process

EXERCISES

Solutions and hints are given at the end of this chapter to all exercises marked with "s" or "h" respectively.

REVIEW QUESTIONS

R1.1[h] a. Categorize the four ingredients of the software enterprise.

b. Are any of these ingredients generally more important than the others?

R1.2[s] (see text for answers) a. Name four major stages in the development of a software product.

b. What is the "waterfall" process?

c. How is the waterfall process applied in contemporary development?

R1.3[s] Name two software development processes besides the waterfall process.

R1.4[s] a. What is the difference between "verification" and "validation"? (see Section 6.6 on page 00 for answers)

b. What are advantages and disadvantages of specifying a V&V plan before a plan for conducting your specific project?

R1.5[s] Give two advantages and two disadvantages of using standards for documentation.

R1.6[s] a. What are metrics?

b. Name a reason why metrics are useful.

R1.7[s] a. Name the development process methodologies and/or assessments for personal, team, and organizations created by the Software Engineering Institute and Watts Humphrey.

b. Describe these methodologies in a paragraph each. State their purposes and a general description of what they consist of. (Solution: see Section 8 in this chapter.)

c. Check that you described all of the levels of the CMM in question (b) above.

TEAM EXERCISES

For each team exercise, consider as a group how you will perform it, check the hints below, then carry out the assignment.

T1.1[h] (Title: "CM Plan") Produce a software configuration management plan for your term project using IEEE standard 828-1990. The case study should guide your team, but your document will be more specific, reflecting the particular resources available to you. Do not include material unless it contributes to the document's goals. Avoid bottlenecks and unnecessary procedures. Include procedures for what to do if people cannot be reached and deadlines loom. Try out your plan by using it to produce the documents required by exercise T1.2 below.

Before you begin, estimate the number of defects per page the team thinks it will discover during its final review. Keep track of, and report the time spent on this effort by individual members and by total team effort. State the actual defect density (average number of defects per page). Assess your team's effectiveness in each stage on a scale of 0 to 10. Summarize the results using the numerical results, and state how the team's process could have been improved.

Criteria:

α. Practicality: How well does the plan ensure that documents and their versions will be secure, coordinated, and available? (A = plan very likely to ensure coordination and availability)

β. Specifics: How specific is the plan in terms of suitably naming places and participants? (A = no doubt as to what engineers must do)

γ. Process assessment and improvement: To what degree did the team understand the strengths and weaknesses of its process, and how specific are its plans for improvement? (A = full, quantitative understanding; plans for improvement very specific and realistic)

T1.2[h] ("V&V plan") Produce the relevant parts of a V&V plan, using IEEE standard 1012-1986. Measure and report the metrics described in problem T1.1.

Criteria:

α. Practicality: How well does the plan ensure that the work will be adequately verified and validated? (A = completely practicable in the environment of the project)

β. Specifics: How specific is the plan in terms of suitably naming places and participants? (A = spells out exactly how V&V will be performed in the environment of the development)

γ. Team participant perception: To what degree are participants likely to perceive your plan as a help to them? (A = written in a way that respects the time and efforts of engineers)

HINTS TO REVIEW QUESTIONS

R1.1 (a) *hint:* The four "ingredients" begin with the letter "p." (The answer appears below.)

T1.1 and **T1.2** *hint:* Do not fill in sections that are as yet unknown: Add only parts that you are confident of being able to implement within the semester. Make your plan realistic. For example, don't state that "all other team members will review each contributor's work" unless you are reasonably sure that this can be done within the probable constraints of your project. It is too early to make any assumptions about the architecture and design of the application.

SOLUTIONS TO REVIEW QUESTIONS

R1.2 (a) Requirements analysis, design, implementation, integration, and test

R1.3 Spiral and incremental processes

R1.4 (b) Among the advantages are that quality procedures can be specified across the organization, promoting uniformity in the organization's products. This saves time by avoiding the continual re-creation of the procedures from project to project. The disadvantages include the fact that we can't provide all of the details of the plan until the plan for the project has been settled. (For example, we can't specify the V&V schedule until then.)

R1.5 Standards save us the time of having to devise document headings. They tend to remind us of important issues we may not have thought about. Being standard, they provide some uniformity across projects. Disadvantages include the fact that users of standards sometimes feel obliged to provide material for every heading, even when the heading is not relevant or useful for the job at hand. This can lead to cynicism, and contempt for "boilerplate" and "paperwork." Standards can also blind us to the inclusion of additional sections that we need to address because of unique characteristics of our job. (e.g., the IEEE standards do not address certain issues peculiar to Web development).

R1.6 Metrics are numerical measures for software development. They are important because they bring discipline to the software development process, turning it from a mere activity into true engineering.

R1.7 Capability Maturity Model (CMM) for organizations, Team Software Process (TSP) for teams, and Personal Software Process (TSP) for individuals.

R1.1 (a) and (b) *answer:* "People, Process, Project, and Product." These are all important. In the author's opinion, none can be called more important than the other in general.

CASE STUDY 1:

SOFTWARE CONFIGURATION MANAGEMENT PLAN

[Note to the student: It is a good idea to have each team member sign off on the physical document. This process focuses their attention on the fact that they are accountable for its contents, and they will tend to ensure it is the document that they assumed it was.]

Approvals:

P. Jones _____ date: _____

L. Wilenz _____ date: _____

The table of contents of this SCMP follows that of IEEE standard 828-1990.

5/1/98 E. Braude: Created first draft

1/10/99 R. Bostwick: Reviewed

1/18/99 E. Braude: Expanded 3.2

5/18/99 E. Braude: Reviewed for release

4/30/99 E. Braude: Final editing

5/2/99 Released

1. INTRODUCTION

This Software Configuration Management Plan (SCMP) describes how the artifacts for the *Encounter* video game project are to be managed.

1.1 Acronyms

CI: configuration item—an item tracked by the configuration system

CM: configuration management—the process of maintaining the relevant versions of the project

SCMP: the Software Configuration Management Plan (this document)

1.2 Terms

Approved CIs: CIs signed off by project management

Artifact: A final or interim product of the project (e.g., a document, source code, object code, test result)

Master file: A particular designated file for this project, defined in Section 3.1.2.

2. SCM MANAGEMENT

2.1 Organization

[Note to the student: State how this is to be managed. Supply role(s), but no names or responsibilities. Names are supplied in a later section.]

A specific engineer, provided by the QA organization, will be designated as the "configuration leader" for the duration of the project.

2.2 SCM Responsibilities

[Note to the student: State the tasks that each role must carry out. If this is not stated, essential activities will not be done, and some activities will be done by more than one team member. Include backup responsibilities in case the main individual is incapacitated.]

2.2.1 Configuration Leader

[Note to the student: "Responsible" does not necessarily imply that the individual does all of the work—merely that he or she organizes the work, and sees to it that the work is done.]

The configuration leader shall be responsible for organizing and managing configuration management (CM). Whenever possible, the configuration leader shall discuss CM plans with the development team prior to implementation. He or she will maintain this document (the SCMP). The configuration

leader is responsible for the installation and maintenance of the configuration management tool(s) specified in Section 2.3. Archiving is to be performed in accordance with department policies 12345.

The SCM leader shall be responsible for acquiring, maintaining, and backing up the configuration tools used. He or she shall also develop a plan of action if tools become unsupported (e.g., by discontinuance of the vendor).

Additional responsibilities of the configuration leader are stated in Sections 3.3, 3.4, 3.5, and 3.6.

2.2.2 Project Leader
The project leader and his/her manager will take over the configuration leader's function only under exceptional circumstances. They are responsible for knowing all the relevant means of access to documents throughout the life of the project. The project leader shall ensure that archiving is performed in accordance with the policies in Section 2.3 below.

Additional responsibilities of the managers are stated in Sections 3.3 and 3.4.

2.2.3 Engineers
It is the responsibility of each engineer to abide by the CM rules that the configuration leader publishes. Engineers are also referred to "Standard Engineering Responsibilities," document 56789.

Additional responsibilities of the engineers are stated in Section 3 below.

2.3 Applicable Policies, Directives, and Procedures

[Note to the student: Activities such as CM are generally conducted in accordance with group or corporate guidelines. Student teams should identify and list their policies in this section. Policy 3 should be included.]

1. Configuration management for this project shall be carried out in accordance with the corporate guidelines for configuration management, corporate document 7890 version 6 (8/15/98).

2. In accordance with division software improvement policies, midstream and post-project review sessions are required, where improvements to these guidelines are to be documented for the benefit of the organization. These sessions are required to help prepare the division for level 5 CMM certification. The self-assessment results are to be sent to the manager of Software Self-assessment within three weeks of the assessment session. All "room for improvement" sections are to contain substantive material, with specific examples.

3. All current and previously released versions of CIs will be retained.

4. The master file (defined in Section 3.1.2) can be accessed only by the configuration leader and, in his or her absence, the department manager.

5. CM passwords should be changed in accordance with corporate security practices, with the following addition: No password shall be changed until the project leader, his manager, and the manager of QA have all been notified and have acknowledged the notification.

6. The project leader and department manager are to have complete access to all documents under configuration at all times. Access verification form www.ultracorp.division3.accessVerification is to be submitted every two weeks by the project leader to his or her manager.

7. The *Encounter* project will use *SuperCMTool* release 3.4, a configuration management product by SuperCMTool. [*Note to the student: These are fictitious names.*]

8. Archiving is to be performed in accordance with department policies 123456.

3. SCM ACTIVITIES

3.1 Configuration Identification

[*Note to the student: This section states how configuration items (CIs) come into*

being, and how they get their names. Without such procedures being stated and followed, chaos results.]

3.1.1 Identifying Configuration Items
The project leader shall be responsible for identifying all CIs. Engineers wishing to propose CIs shall secure his or her agreement, via e-mail or otherwise. If the project leader is unavailable for one business day following the engineer's e-mailed proposal for inclusion, the configuration leader shall have the authority to accept the proposed item.

3.1.2 Naming Configuration Items
The configuration leader shall have the responsibility for labeling all CIs. The file conventions shall be as follows

Root directory: *Encounter*

Subdirectory: *SRS* or *SDD* or ...

File *N-N-N.xxx* corresponding to version *N.N.N*

For example, version 2.4.8 of the SRS will be on file *Encounter/SRS/2_4_8.txt*.

The text file *Master* in the root directory states the versions of the CIs that comprise the current and prior states of the project. For example, *Master* could include information such as

The current version of *Encounter* is 3.7.1. It comprises version 2.4.8 of the SRS, version 1.4 of the SDD.

The previous version of *Encounter* was 3.6.11. It comprised version 2.4.8 of the SRS, version 1.3 of the SDD.

This information shall be maintained in a table of the following form.

Encounter Release	SRS version	SDD version	. . . .

3.1.3 Acquiring Configuration Items

[Note to the student: In specifying this section, imagine the most stressful part of the project, which is the implementation phase, involving several people in parallel. The process has to be very orderly, but it also has to allow engineers reasonable access to the parts of the project so that they can start work quickly.]

Engineers requiring CIs for modification shall check them out using *SuperCMTool's* checkout procedure. Note that *SuperCMTool* prompts the user with a form requesting an estimate of how long the checkout is anticipated, and stores this information for all requesters of the CI. Anyone requiring a CI that is currently checked out, should negotiate with the current owner of the CI to transfer control through *SuperCMTool*. A read-only version of the CI is available to all engineers. *Under no circumstances may an engineer transfer a CI directly to anyone.*

3.2 Configuration Control

[Note to the student: This section spells out the process whereby configuration items are changed. This process should be flexible enough to allow quick changes, but controlled enough to keep changes very orderly so that they improve the application, not damage it.]

3.2.1 Requesting Changes
As specified in the Software Project Management Plan [see Chapter 2], the team will designate an "inspector" engineer who is allocated to each team member. Before requesting a change, engineers must obtain an inspection of the proposed change from an inspection team or, if this is not possible, from their inspector engineer. To request the incorporation of a changed CI into the baseline, form www. ultracorp.division3.Encounter.submitCI must be submitted to the configuration leader and the project leader, along with the changed CI and the original CI.

3.2.2 Evaluating Changes

[Note to the student: For larger projects, a group of people, often called the Change Control Board, evaluates and approves changes. Student teams must make this process reasonably simple.]

The project leader or his designee will evaluate all proposed changes. The project leader must also specify the required quality standards for incorporation.

3.2.3 Approving or Disapproving Changes
The project leader must approve proposed changes. If the project leader is unavailable for three business days following the submission of a proposed change, the configuration leader shall have the authority to approve changes.

3.2.4 Implementing Changes

[Note to the student: To avoid chaos, it is natural to give to the CM leader the responsibility for incorporating changes; this can create a bottleneck at implementation time, however. Before this "crunch" occurs, the CM leader should find ways to remove this bottleneck by distributing as much work as feasible to the engineers making the changes.]

Once a CI is approved for incorporation into the baseline, the configuration leader shall be responsible for coordinating the testing and integration of the changed CI. This should be performed in accordance with the regression test documentation described in the Software Test Documentation. In particular, the configuration leader shall coordinate the building of a version for testing.

Version releases must be cleared with the project leader, or with the manager if the project leader is absent.

3.3 Configuration Status Accounting

The configuration leader shall update the configuration summary at least once a week on the project configuration website www. ultracorp.division3/Encounter/Configuration.

SuperCMTool's status report will be a sufficient format for the summary.

3.4 Configuration Audits and Reviews

[Note to the student: In industry, random audits are often employed. They are not commonly conducted by student teams due to a lack of resources, although some teams have carried them out successfully. Periodic reviews, as part of the regular team meetings, do not take much time, and they are recommended.]

The project manager shall schedule a review by the CM leader of the configuration at least once every two weeks, preferably as an agenda item for a regularly scheduled weekly project meeting. The CM leader shall review CM status, and report on the proposed detailed procedures to be followed at code and integration time.

Configuration efforts will be subject to random audits throughout the project's life cycle by the IV&V team.

3.5 Interface Control

The CM system interfaces with the project website. This interface shall be managed by the configuration leader.

3.6 Subcontractor/ Vendor Control

The configuration leader shall track upgrades and bug reports of *SuperCMTool*. He or she should be prepared with a backup plan in case the maintenance of *SuperCMTool* is discontinued. This plan is to be sent to the project leader within a month of the project's inception.

4. SCM SCHEDULES

[Note to the student: The SCM schedule can be provided here, or combined with the project schedule in the SPMP. In the latter case, this section would not repeat the schedule, but would merely point to the SPMP.]

The schedule for configuration management reporting, archiving, and upgrading is shown in Figure 1.50.

	Month 1				Month 2				Month 3				Month 4				Month 5			
	1	2	3	4	1	2	3	4	1	2	3	4	1	2	3	4	1	2	3	4
Stable CM	▲																			
						▲ Vendor backup plan due														
CM reviews	▲	▲	▲	▲	▲	▲	▲	▲	▲	▲	▲	▲	▲	▲	▲	▲	▲	▲	▲	
CM process improvement session													▲							▲
				◄					Random IV & V audits								►			

Figure 1.50   Configuration Management Schedule

5. SCM RESOURCES

Configuration leader will require an estimated average of six hours a week to maintain the system configuration for the first half of the project, and twelve hours a week for the second half. We have chosen not to call out separately the time spent by the other team members on configuration management.

6. SCM PLAN MAINTENANCE

[Note to the student: All project documents undergo change throughout the duration of the project. The SCMP is especially sensitive to change, however, because it controls change itself.]

Due to the importance of a stable SCM plan, all changes to this document must be approved by the entire CM team.

In view of the software development organization's goal to attain CMM level 5, the configuration leader will do the following for the CM process improvement sessions.

- Review the effectiveness of this plan
- Quantify losses due to defects in this plan
- Review the effectiveness of *Super CMTool*
- Investigate the literature for new CM methods; quantify the costs and benefits of improvements
- Investigate new CM tools
- Suggest specific improvements to this CM process
- List the benefits of improvements
- Provide cost estimates on effecting the improvements
- Prioritize the cost/benefit ratios of all the suggested changes

---

CASE STUDY 2:

SOFTWARE QUALITY ASSURANCE PLAN PART 1 OF 2 (SEE END OF CHAPTER 2 FOR PART 2)

Approvals:

P. Jones _____ date: _____

L. Wilenz _____ date: _____

The table of contents of this SQAP follow that of IEEE standard 730-1989.

E. Braude: created 1/17/99

R. Bostwick: reviewed 5/30/99 added substance to sections 7 through end

E. Braude: integrated and revised contents 5/31/99

1. PURPOSE

This document describes the plan by which the *Encounter* project will produce a quality product. This includes the maintainability of *Encounter*.

2. REFERENCED DOCUMENTS

See Section 4.2.

3. MANAGEMENT

3.1 Organization

[Note to the student: State what roles are involved in ensuring quality. Actual names are provided in Section 3.3.]

Each team member is responsible for the quality of his or her work. In addition, for the first three iterations of *Encounter*, an individual "quality assurance leader" is designated. Within the priorities set by the team, the QA leader will take the lead for projectwide quality issues. After iteration three, the SQA organization will provide a team of engineers to perform this function. The team will include the existing quality assurance leader.

3.2 Tasks

[Note to the student: State what needs to be done.]

QA tasks shall include

- Documentation
- Review meetings
- Verification (including inspections)
- Validation (mostly testing)
- Activities designed to improve the quality assurance process itself

These tasks are detailed in this document.

3.3 Responsibilities

[Note to the student: State who will do what, and who will fulfill the job functions.]

It is the quality assurance leader's responsibility to see to it that the tasks in Section 3.2 are done, and to ensure that the prescriptions in this document are followed, including scheduling the reviews specified.

The project leader will be responsible for ensuring that quality management is being performed.

[Note to the student: No name is mentioned here, because names are stated in the Software Project Management Plan, which is their proper place. Duplicating a name here would require us to update more than one document when there are changes.]

The requirements leader and the design leader have responsibilities described in Section 6 of this document.

4. DOCUMENTATION

4.1 Purpose

The purpose of this section is to define the documentation that will be used to ensure quality.

4.2 Minimum Documentation Requirements

[Note to the student: This section lists all of the project documentation, since it is the documentation that ensures the quality of the product.]

The following documents will be produced.

- SQAP: software quality assurance plan (this document)
- SCMP: software configuration management plan
- SPMP: software project management plan
- SRS: software requirements specifications
- SDD: software design document
- STD: software test documentation
- User's manual
- Maintenance plan

In addition to these documents, the Java source code will utilize Javadoc, and will therefore be capable of generating package-, class-, and function-level documentation.

4.3 Other

The SVVP (software validation and verification plan) will be generated and maintained by an organization independent of the SQA organization.

5. STANDARDS, PRACTICES, CONVENTIONS, AND METRICS

5.1 Purpose

This section describes the standards, practices, conventions, and metrics to be used for the *Encounter* project. These are intended not only to ensure quality for *Encounter*, but also to obtain quantitative metric data on the SQA process itself. This data is to be used to help elevate the CMM level of Gaming

Consolidated Industries (GCI), the developers of *Encounter,* from level 3 to level 4.

5.2 Content

[Note to the student: Describe the standards, practices, conventions, and metrics to be used. Organization-wide quality goals can be supplied here, or in a separate appendix. The contents of this section should be specific. For example, statements such as "quality should be as high as possible" should be avoided.]

Standards: The IEEE standards, with appropriate modifications, are to be used for documentation.

Practices:

1. Because delaying quality is expensive, GCI Inc. strongly encourages engineers to apply quality precepts while working, rather than as an afterthought.
2. GCI Inc. feels that no separate QA function that is external to the individual engineer, can by itself obtain higher quality than the developer. QA at GCI is considered primarily a coaching organization rather than a watchdog or punitive one. Engineers whose experience is not consistent with this practice are encouraged to contact the quality ombudsman at extension 7832.
3. All project artifacts are inspected, and all are made easily available to the team once released by the developer. This is done by placing artifacts under configuration management, where the contents can be seen at any time.
4. All processes are to be reviewed at least once for improvement, and the written results forwarded by the project leader to the software engineering laboratory. (See Section 6.2.10.)

Conventions: Where feasible, writing conventions should conform to the suggestions in *Writing for Computer Science: The Art of Effective Communication* by Justin Zobel (Springer Verlag; ISBN: 9813083220). The QA organization conducts monthly three-hour courses on writing styles and conventions. Attendance is funded by corporate overhead, not by project accounts.

Metrics: At least three metrics will be maintained for every process, and every document.

1. Time spent by individuals on subtasks
2. Quality self-assessment on a scale of one through ten, approximately in a bell-shaped distribution; self-assessment scores will not be used for the evaluation of personnel by management; failure to produce them may negatively impact the evaluation of an engineer by management, however
3. Number of defects per unit (e.g., lines of code)

GCI quality goals for delivered products are as follows.

[Note to the student: The numbers used here should be based on historical data obtained from the group that is developing Encounter.]

Detected within two months of delivery:

Requirements: No more than one minor defective detailed requirement per 100 requirements

Design: No more than one minor defect per five diagrams

Pseudocode: No more than two minor defects per 1000 lines [Note: pseudocode is described in Chapter 6]

Code: No more than two minor defects per KLOC (1000 lines of non-commented code)

The actual metric data from this project are to be reported as Appendix 1 to this document.

6.   REVIEWS AND AUDITS

6.1 Purpose

The purpose of reviews and audits is to provide a means of focusing the attention of engineers on quality of the application as it develops. Reviews carry this out in a scheduled and thorough manner. Audits do so on the basis of random sampling with short notice.

6.2 Minimum Requirements

[Note to the student: Large projects require the full set of reviews and audit listed here. At a minimum, student teams should conduct reviews and inspections of requirements and design, as well as post-mortem reviews. "Reviews" are discussions of proposed artifacts. "Inspections" are conducted on completed artifacts presented to the team.]

Refer to the SPMP for the schedule of reviews described below.

6.2.1 Software Requirements Review
This is a walk-through of the requirements document in the presence of the entire team. The review will be led by the project leader. It is expected that the requirements will not have been inspected prior to this review. This review is not intended to replace inspections of the requirements. The requirements leader (see SPMP) will be responsible for seeing to it that these inspections are carried out.

6.2.1A Software Requirements Inspection
All requirements will be inspected in accordance with GCI Inc's inspection process manual, document GCI 345678.

6.2.2 Preliminary Design Review
This is a review of alternative architectures with the entire team. The review will be led by the project leader or his or her designee. It is expected that the team will provide feedback, which will be reflected in the final design. The alternative architectures will not have been inspected prior to this review. The design leader (see SPMP) will be responsible for seeing to it that this review is carried out.

6.2.3 Critical Design Review
This is an inspection of the proposed architecture,

in the presence of the entire team. The design leader will be responsible for seeing to it that these inspections are carried out. The architecture will have been inspected prior to this review. If possible, the architecture will be decomposed into detailed designs of its parts, and these will undergo separate critical design reviews.

6.2.4 SVVP Review
Since V&V is to be conducted by an independent team, there will be no review of the SVVP Plan by QA.

6.2.5 Functional Audit
Prior to delivery, the project leader shall be responsible for checking that the product being delivered satisfies the requirements in the SRS. Where exceptions are necessary, the project leader shall obtain the prior consent of his or her management to allow the delivery. He or she shall communicate these exceptions to the customer by appropriate means, including a README file, and a cover letter citing this file.

6.2.6 Physical Audit
Prior to each delivery, the QA leader shall be responsible for checking that the physical software and its documentation designated for delivery are indeed delivered.

6.2.7 In-process Audits
Project personnel should expect random audits of their work. This will consist of visits to the work site by teams designated by division management. A day's notice shall be given for all visits. The subject of these audits will be the current work of teams and individuals that has been allocated to the project.

As the organization migrates to CMM level 5, all work will be made freely available to all team members and auditors at all times. The work will be organized in a clear, standard fashion, so that audits will be possible without any notice.

6.2.8 Managerial Review
The *Encounter* project shall be reviewed by the VP for Engineering during the first week of every month. It is the project leader's responsibility to schedule this review.

6.2.9 *SCMP Review* The QA leader shall review the status of CM on a monthly basis in a manner independent of the procedures specified in the SCMP.

6.2.10 *Post Mortem Review* As with all GCI projects, the *Encounter* team shall conduct post-mortems of all phases, in order to provide a log for future projects. These will include reviews of the project phase just completed, and reviews of the QA process itself. The QA team or QA leader shall file a process improvement report for every phase, and for the QA process itself, with the manager of the software engineering laboratory.

6.3 Inspections

All artifacts of the *Encounter* project will be inspected.

[Sections 7 through 15: See Chapter 2]

PROJECT MANAGEMENT

We few, we happy few, we band of brothers.
—Henry V

A **genuine** team spirit is essential for the successful development of applications. Relative to the waterfall software development process, this chapter covers the parts highlighted in Figure 2.1. The goals for this chapter are shown in Figure 2.2.

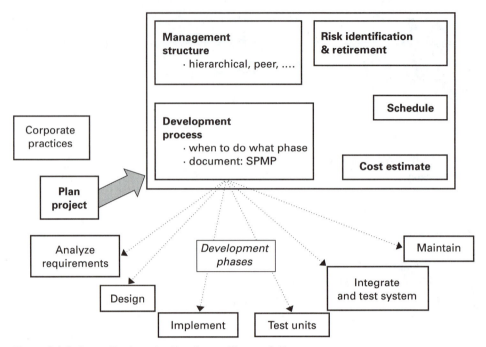

Figure 2.1 Software Engineering Roadmap: Chapter 2 Focus

- Understand the term "project management"
- Organize teams
- Specify project management plans
- Define and retire risks
- Estimate costs very early in the life cycle
- Create high level projects schedules
- Write a Software Project Management Plan

Figure 2.2 Learning Goals for This Chapter

▶ PART I: ESSENTIALS

1. INTRODUCTION TO PROJECT MANAGEMENT

1.1 The Meaning of "Project Management"

Project management consists of managing the production of a product within given time and funding limits. Since this requires human resources, project management involves not only technical and organizational skills, but also the art of managing people. Project management is no mundane activity: It can be as gripping as landing a jumbo jet on a short airstrip.

The project manager can control the following factors somewhat:

1. The total cost of the project
    *   *e.g., increase expenditures*
2. The capabilities of the product
    *   *e.g., subtract from a list of features*
3. The quality of the product
    *   *e.g., increase the mean time between failure*
4. The duration of the project
    *   *e.g., reduce the schedule by 20%*
    *   *e.g., postpone project's completion date one month*

Figure 2.3 The Variables of Project Management

1.2 The Constituents of Project Management

Project management comprises

*   Structure (organizational elements involved)
*   Managerial process (responsibilities and supervision of the participants)
*   Development process (methods, tools, languages, documentation, and support)
*   Schedule (times at which the work portions are to be performed)

1.3 The Principal Variables: *Cost, Capability, Quality,* and *Schedule*

Project planners can vary cost, capability, quality, and delivery date, as shown in Figure 2.3. The *degree* to which these four factors can be controlled depends on the project. Although *costs* may often appear fixed in advance, there is frequently some flexibility. For example, suppose that our customer is a chemist who needs molecular visualization in 2D. After viewing a prototype of 3D molecular modeling, our chemist customer might well look for additional funds, since the 3D prototype looks so much better than 2D. *Capabilities* are also not the fixed entities they may appear to be. For example, the customer may agree to drop a requirement if doing so shaves 15% off the project's duration (a capability / schedule tradeoff). Although it may sound heretical, even *quality* goals can be varied. When quality targets are set too low, they are offset by the resulting short- and long-term costs of rework and customer dissatisfaction. When quality targets are set too high, the cost of finding the very last minor defect may be prohibitive. Most of us would be unwilling to pay three times the price for a word processor in order to have a version without an acknowledged trivial defect. Completion *dates* can sometimes be negotiated. For example, a manager may be willing to change a completion date if the resulting end product is so capable that it is likely to capture the market.

One way to visualize these four variables is by means of a "bulls-eye" diagram. In this kind of diagram, each of the variables is plotted by means of an axis originating at the center. The axes are drawn symmetrically relative to each other. In the particular bulls-eye diagram shown, Figure 2.4, there are four variables, so that they form 90-degree angles. On each of these axes, the origin is the most unfavorable value, and the target value is marked on each axis the same distance from the origin, forming a quadrilateral. (If there

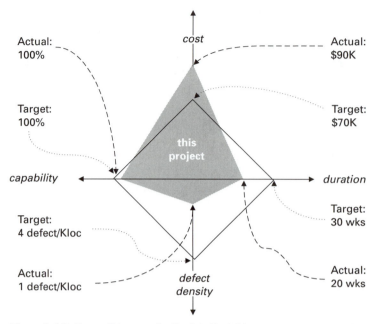

Figure 2.4 Bulls-eye Diagram for Project Variables

were five variables, they would form a regular pentagon, etc.) For example, on the "capability" axis, the origin denotes "no requirements satisfied," while the unit mark represents "100% of the requirements satisfied." The actual values are usually somewhere in between, though values could lie outside the polygon if they exceed goals, as shown in Figure 2.4. The status of a project can be visualized as a solid polygon, by joining the values on the axes and filling in the resulting polygon. The more the original regular polygon is filled in, the more we will accomplish our project goals. The example project shown falls short on most of the variables, but performs under its cost goals. This visualization helps a project manager to alter priorities so as to achieve goals in an even manner. For example, the leader of the project represented in the figure should permit higher spending so as to obtain the required defect density.

To summarize, project management deals constantly with trade-offs among cost, capability, quality, and completion date. Professional project managers quantify these trade-offs as much as possible.

1.4 A Typical Road Map of the Project Management Process

Figure 2.5 shows a typical sequence of activities required for setting up a project. Understanding the project (1) refers only to an overall comprehension of goals, rather than to gathering all the requirements. The latter is an extensive process, and is performed after the preliminary project plan has been drafted (see Chapters 3 and 4). We also need to understand the overall scope (extent) of the application. A banking application could have a very large scope as in "automate all bank transactions," a small one, such as "modify the bank statement program to sort by check number," or somewhere in between. The overall time frame (e.g., two months, two years) and the labor allocation must be appreciated in general terms. Next (2) comes the decision about which development process to use (e.g., waterfall, spiral, incremental, combination, etc., as described in Section 4 of Chapter 1).

1. Understand project content, scope, and time frame
    2. Identify development process
        (methods, tools, languages, documentation, and support)—Section 4 of Chapter 1
        3. Determine organizational structure
            (organizational elements involved)—see Section 3
            4. Identify managerial process
                (responsibilities of the participants)—see Section 3 of case study 1 at end of chapter
                5. Develop schedule
                    (times at which the work portions are to be performed)—see Section 6
                    6. Develop staffing plan—*see Section 3.5 of case study 1*
                        7. Begin risk management—*see Section 4*
                            8. Identify documents to be produced—*see SQAP 4.2*
                                9. Begin process itself—*described in Chapters 3–10*

Figure 2.5 Road Map for Project Management

This can be followed (3) by an overall organization of personnel (e.g., identification of the company units involved, number of team leaders, QA involvement). Once the players and their organization have been identified, we can concentrate on the way in which they are to interact to get the job done—the managerial process (4). This includes determining who will report to whom, or identifying a level TSP-type organization (introduced in Chapter 1 and elaborated on later in this chapter). Next (5), the overall schedule is established (i.e., what gets done when). After this (6), the staffing plan can be completed—an allocation of personnel and approximate person-days to the tasks (e.g., requirements analysis). It is not possible to be very specific (e.g., who will design what function) because the design has not yet been identified. Projects are almost always affected by "bad things" happening to them, and so the identification and management of risks in the project (7) should begin at once. The appropriate document set should be identified (e.g., IEEE documents SVVP, SRS) (8), and then the project itself can begin (9).

2. MANAGING PROJECT PEOPLE

2.1 Professionalism

One of this book's themes is the growing professionalization of Software Engineering: But what, exactly, does this mean? To illustrate the answer, consider the professionalism of surgeons. We expect that if a surgeon is in the midst of performing a four-hour brain operation, her professionalism will prevent her from obeying an order from a hospital administrator to reduce the operation's duration to three hours. In other words, "professionals" have societal responsibilities that supercede their requirement to satisfy the needs of their employers and supervisors. With so much of our modern world software-driven, software engineers have to assume increasing responsibility. This is obvious in the case of computer-controlled aircraft and the space shuttle, but it is also present to a degree in generating output such as insurance bills. Just as the public should not have to stop at every bridge and test it before crossing, they should not have to check every computation for correctness.

The practices of software engineers in planning, scheduling, designing, implementing, inspecting, and testing artifacts are coming under increasing scrutiny from inside and outside the profession. The legal profession's interest in year 2000 bugs is significant evidence for outside scrutiny. The application of metrics is a part of the solution. Authors such as Humphrey [Hu7] advise software engineers not to promise product delivery dates without a sound way of verifying the reasonableness of such dates. They counsel negotiation instead. The problem in the past has been that engineers have too often lacked the tools with which to justify their time and effort estimates. In the authors' opinion, this will change. Humphrey's Team Software Process (TSP) is an example of a very specific procedure for development using a consistent set of metrics.

Between 1994 and 2000, a joint committee of the IEEE and the Association for Computing Machinery worked to define the specific meaning of "professional" software engineers.

2.2 The Importance of People Management

The principal ingredient required to produce software is *people*. The engineers' technical skills count, of course, but these skills have to be brought to bear on the right problems at the right time. This requires a combination of teamwork and leadership. Our goal in this section is to become acquainted with typical personnel issues. We will regard people management issues from several viewpoints: that of the enterprise wanting the application, that of the managers responsible for seeing that it is created, and from that of the engineers involved.

Brooks [Br1] is famous for *The Mythical Man-Month*, which includes "Brooks's Law." According to this law, putting more people on a failing software project may not help, and may even make it worse. In other words, the additional man-month that the project appears to be gaining can be mythical indeed. Under good management, however, additional man-months can be quite useful.

DeMarco's and Lister's *Peopleware* [De2] is another influential work on project management in which the authors acknowledge the recurrent sentiment that if they could manage software projects over again (which is never possible), they would have done so differently. *Peopleware* consists of short essays, each "about a particular garden path that managers are led down, usually to their regret. What typically lures them into error is some aspect of management folklore, a folklore that is pervasive, and loudly articulated, but often wrong." Examples are "Take the worker's estimate and double it. Keep the pressure on. Don't let people work at home, they'll goof off." The author has observed that software engineers invariably want to be treated as professionals, and are eager to deliver professional results.

2.3 Enterprise Perspectives

From the perspective of the enterprise commissioning a project, its development is seen as contributing to the enterprise's goals, producing a product that more than justifies its cost. This perspective is primarily businesslike. The very name of the corporate organization responsible for project personnel illustrates the corporate perspective: "human resources"—a type of resource of the human variety that furthers the organization's goals.

2.4 Management Perspectives

It has been said that "there are no technical failures; only management failures." Although this is not literally true, it does remind us of the importance of management in the success-

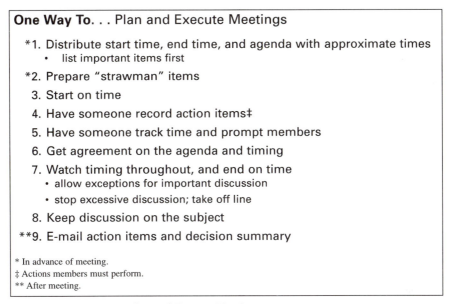

Figure 2.6 *One Way to Plan and Execute Meetings*

ful completion of engineering enterprises. The manager's perspective on his subordinates is typically a mixture of business concerns on one hand and, on the other hand, an interest in the people involved. Despite the frequent misgivings of those managed, the average manager tries to get the job done, and also tries to foster a contented workforce at the same time. This is in the manager's interest: Discontented workers are not productive. One of the manager's challenges is reconciling her goal of getting the job done as specified by management, with the job satisfaction of her staff. For example, upper management may stipulate that the work is to be done in an older language for compatibility, whereas the software engineers may want experience with a new language or system.

Managers ensure that the technical efforts of the engineers are directed appropriately. New managers in particular find it difficult to steer a course between dictating orders and allowing engineers to do whatever they think fit. A dictatorial attitude causes resentment and a decline in motivation, but a laissez-faire attitude results in wasted work, which breeds cynicism. The solution is leadership, the ability to draw out people's natural desire to cooperate and participate actively in a successful endeavor. Project leaders have varying degrees of management responsibility, depending on the magnitude of the project. On large projects, their duties consist mainly of management. On small ones they have to provide both management and technical leadership.

2.4.1 Conducting Meetings

One specific activity required of project managers is to hold meetings. Figure 2.6 lists some good meeting practices from which all team members can benefit. The items marked with a single asterisk should be performed before the meeting. Since groups are not particularly good at creating artifacts from scratch (especially designs), it is far better for someone to bring to the meeting a tentative ("strawman") version of the artifact to form the basis for discussion. For example, the design leader brings a tentative design, or the team leader brings a tentative work breakdown. The version should not be overly specific, because there must be plenty of room for input by the members.

One Way To. . . Specify Agendas

1. Get agreement on agenda and time allocation
2. Get volunteers to
   - record decisions taken and action items
   - watch time and prompt members
3. Report progress on project schedule—10 minutes
4. Discuss strawman artifact(s)—*x* minutes
5. Discuss risk retirement—10 minutes
   <more items>

   metrics and process improvement?

n. Review action items—5 minutes

Figure 2.7 One Way to Specify Agendas

Many meeting participants, but especially students, complain that meetings last too long without accomplishing enough. When the approximate time for discussions is agreed to in advance, however, members tend to focus on the issues to be resolved, and meetings can be quite effective. Deciding when to allow further discussion and when to break it off is a duty of the team leader. The keys to doing this are whether the discussion is productive, and whether the discussion of the present topic is preventing the discussion of more important ones, given the time remaining. It is also the leader's task to ensure that the discussion remains focused, and that a conclusion is reached. At times, the leader must step in and make a decision, because consensus is not always possible. The member recording action items also records decisions taken. This should generally be done in a summary form only, and is meant to remind everyone of the issues, not to specify details. Details are reflected in the project's documentation.

One good management practice is to create and follow agendas for meetings. An example of a generic agenda is shown in Figure 2.7. The figure mentions metrics and process improvement: These are discussed after a phase has been completed, not necessarily at every meeting. Risk retirement (covered in Section 4) should be an agenda item at every meeting during the first third of the project. Risk identification and retirement require discussion after that, but not as frequently.

2.5 Engineers' Perspectives

Finally, consider the "people" issues affecting the typical software engineer. Engineers want interesting work, they want opportunities to show that they are competent, they want to be recognized and rewarded, and they want cordial relationships with their teammates. A healthy self-respect is a prerequisite for these wants. One important source of self-respect in the workplace is a sense of quality. There is nothing new about this observation. If you hire a carpenter to build a kitchen, and you appreciate good workmanship, that carpenter is likely to be motivated. If you have little idea of what good workmanship is, your carpenter is less likely to enjoy the task. Thus, software engineers have to learn exactly what "quality" entails. For example, engineers have to learn how to estimate the effort required to produce a good product, how to prove to themselves and others that what they write works correctly, and how to measure the quality of their work.

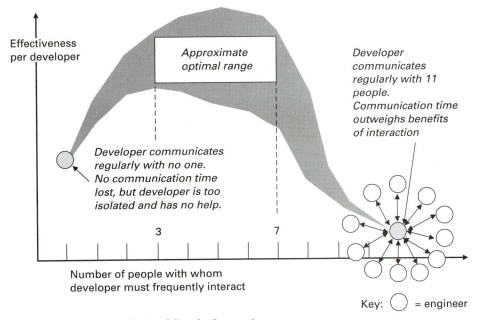

Figure 2.8 Approximate Optimal Size for Interaction

3. OPTIONS FOR ORGANIZING PERSONNEL

We will discuss the organizational aspects of project teams from two perspectives. First, what is the project responsibility structure? Second, where do the people come from and to whom do they report? In any event, little can be accomplished unless the participants are communicating properly.

3.1 Managing Communication

Experience of the author and others shows that the number of developers with whom each developer needs to interact on a regular basis should be between three and seven. (Humphrey [Hu7] suggests four to eight.) Formal studies on the effect of team size on performance are rare, but Figure 2.8 illustrates the extremes leading to the recommendations about team size. At one extreme, the developer works without interacting regularly with anyone on an individual basis. Although no time is spent on communication, such isolation typically results in misunderstandings of what is required of that developer, leading to a relatively low level of effectiveness. At the other extreme, the developer has to interact regularly with so many individuals that there is not enough time left over to perform development itself, again resulting in relative ineffectiveness. In particular, "regular communication" entails speaking with someone for something like two hours a week. If an engineer were in regular communication with ten others, then fully one half of his time would be spent communicating, leaving only half of the week for his individual contribution. Project organizers, whether planning twenty-person or hundred-person projects, have to take this into account.

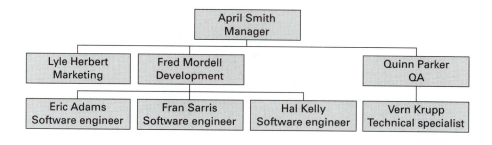

Smaller Projects:

No separate marketing?
No separate QA organization?

Larger Projects:

Subdivide QA into testing,...?
Subdivide Engineering into
       system engineering,...?

Figure 2.9 Hierarchical Project Management Organization

3.2 Options for the Structure of Responsibilities

The hierarchical management structure, typified by Figure 2.9, is one organizational extreme. In this organization, there is an overall manager, April Smith, with three people reporting to her. Lyle Herbert is responsible for the marketing aspects of the project. Presumably, the marketing group will interface with customers to ensure that the product is what the customer wants. Quinn Parker and his subordinate Vern Krupp are responsible for quality assurance. The advantages of this organizational scheme are that everyone understands the lines of authority and decision, and the number of people with whom each person must regularly interact is acceptable. The disadvantage is that team members tend to participate less in decisions because tasks are likely to be handed from above. All other things being equal, this is a fairly safe way to organize a project. Larger projects organized in this hierarchical style require broader and deeper organization charts.

At the other organizational extreme is a team consisting of a community of peers with equal authority. The advantage of this organization is the potential for motivation that comes with equal partnership in the project. This works particularly well if the group is small, highly competent, and accustomed to working together. The disadvantages include the difficulty of resolving differences, and the fact that "no one is in charge." Merely stating that all decisions are participatory and consensual (unanimous) does not automatically make this process work, in the personal experience of the author. Humphrey's Team Software Process™ (see [Hu3]) is a specific set of guidelines for such teams. Ultimately, a mix of peer participation and leadership responsibility must be established that is appropriate to the size of the project, its nature, its maturity, and the people involved.

One middle ground is a horizontal organization structure, shown in Figure 2.10. The idea is that team members are equals, except that Gil Warner is the designated leader. Ideally, he should encourage team members to participate, but he should be decisive when required. Figure 2.11 shows a more detailed way in which teams can be organized. If there are five team members, then one member may want to be the requirements leader as well as the implementation leader, since only one of these activities is very active at any given time. The requirements leader role could be dispensed with, although someone should be responsible for maintaining the SRS. Roles can be switched once during a three-month period to provide team members with broader experience. Since each role is critical, it is wise

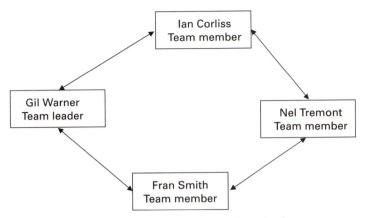

Figure 2.10 Horizontal Project Management Organization

One Way To. . . Organize a Team

1. Select team leader: responsibilities:
   - ensure all project aspects active
   - fill all gaps
3. Designate leader roles and document responsibilities
   - ⇑ team leader: *proposes and maintains* ...SPMP
   - ⇑ configuration management leader: ...SCMP
   - ⇑ quality assurance leader: ...SQAP, STP
   - ⇑ requirements management leader: ...SRS
   - ⇑ design leader: ...SDD
   - ⇑ implementation leader: ...code base
2. Leaders' responsibilities:
   - propose a strawman artifact (e.g., SRS, design)
   - seek team enhancement and acceptance
   - ensure designated artifact maintained and observed
   - maintain corresponding metrics if applicable
4. Designate a backup for each leader as indicated by the arrows above

---

Figure 2.11 One Way to Organize a Team

to designate a kind of "buddy system" for each leader. The buddy engineer can take over if the leader is incapacitated. He or she should inspect all of the other engineer's work. The backup scheme shown in Figure 2.11 promotes a smooth hand–over of artifacts from one phase to the next, since each engineer becomes familiar with the product of the phase prior to the one for which he or she is responsible.

As the number of participants in a project grows, the pure peer organization becomes impossible to use because the number of communication links (between all of the pairs) grows with the square of the number of participants. Three people entail three lines of communication, four people entail six, five people 10, six people 15, n people require $(n-1) + (n-2) + \cdots + 1 = n(n-1)/2$. 100 people would have to participate in 4950 lines of communication! One alternative for large projects is the organization shown in Figure 2.12, in which

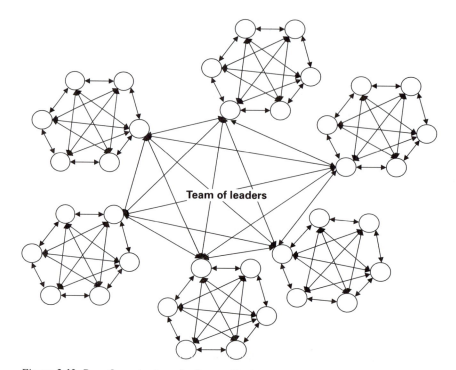

Team of leaders

Figure 2.12 Peer Organizations for Larger Projects

peer groups are small, and one member of each group is designated the communicator with the other peer groups. This type of organization tries to preserve the benefits of small teams but it harnesses the large number of people to build a large application.

It is conventional wisdom that the engineer who is good at both engineering and management is rare. The author has observed many engineers, however, who have done well leading groups, even when few expected them to be capable of it.

3.3 Sources of Project Personnel

In *project-oriented* organizations, project personnel report to the project manager organizationally. He or she is their boss. A software engineer is attached in all ways to a particular project, and has no organizational affiliation with the other software engineers on other projects within the company. This has the advantage of simplifying lines of authority, but the disadvantage of isolating engineers professionally. Very small companies, for example, are almost always organized on a project-oriented basis, but even large ones organize this way at times, especially when they try to emphasize customer focus.

Generally speaking, reporting structures in practice are more complex than purely project-oriented organizations, due to the use of *matrixing*. In matrixed organizations, employees belong to functional units (e.g., Engineering, Sales, etc.) and are loaned to projects (see Table 2.1). Thus, a software engineer's supervisor—the person responsible for evaluating him—would be a member of the software engineering functional unit. Within each project on which he is working, however, he would be supervised by a project leader. Engineers are usually involved on a regular basis with one project, sometimes two, but seldom more. For example, if the organization involved in the hierarchical project organization illustrated in Figure 2.9 above were matrixed, Lyle Herbert would be a member of the

TABLE 2.1   Matrixed Organization

Functional Unit	Project			
	Airline Reservation Project	Bank Accounting Project	Molecular Analysis Project	Fluid Mechanics Project
Project management department	Al Pruitt Full time	Quinn Parker Half time	Ruth Pella Full time	Fred Parsons Full time
Marketing department	Oscar Mart Full time	Pete Merrill Full time	Sue More Half time	Elton Marston Full time
Engineering department	Hal Egberts	Ben Ehrlich	Mary Ericson	Len Engels .....

marketing department. His boss would not be April Smith, but a manager in the marketing department. That marketing manager would consult with April when doing performance appraisals. Matrixed organizations have the advantage of improving skills and professionalism and the disadvantage of weakening lines of authority. Companies often try to find compromises between matrixed and project-driven organizations.

4. IDENTIFYING AND RETIRING RISKS

In this section we are going to be a little paranoid. We will think of our project as being under threat by nasty gremlins that pose risks to its success. We will then mount a vigorous defense.

4.1 Defining "Risks"

A *risk* is something which may occur in the course of a project, and which, under the worst outcome, would affect it negatively and significantly. Industry figures show an appalling number of failed software development projects. For example, Rational Corporation claims that "more than 70% of all software projects are challenged or severely impaired." The factors that eventually cause projects to fail appear as risks when recognized early enough, and the failure can possibly be averted by means of appropriate action. There are two types of risks.

1. Risks that can be avoided or worked around ("retired")
2. Risks that cannot be avoided

An example of the first type is "what if the project leader in this 15-person team leaves the company?" (Retire this by preparing a backup person.) An example of the second type of risk is "2100 flight data points must be gathered from airport personnel before we can deliver the product."

If the risks of the first type are recognized early enough, their retirement turns a failed project into a successful one. It is also highly beneficial to recognize the second type. Either the project can be stopped before wasting resources (so you can apply them productively elsewhere), or else the project can be rescoped or restaffed in order to minimize the risk.

Effective teams adopt a risk "mind-set" in which potential risks are continually sought.

(1) Identification
     Mind-set: *try to continually identify risks*

(2) Retirement planning

(3) Prioritization

(4) Retirement or mitigation

Figure 2.13 Four Risk Management Activities

1. Lack of top management commitment
2. Failure to gain user commitment
3. Misunderstanding of requirements
4. Inadequate user involvement
5. Failure to manage end-user expectations
6. Changing scope and/or objectives
7. Personnel lack required knowledge or skills

Figure 2.14 Risk Sources Ordered by Importance [Ke]

4.2 Risk Management Overview

Applications that are very similar to jobs carried out in the past by the same engineers may be free of risk: However, the universe of software applications is vast and growing rapidly. Many jobs consist of new ways of performing tasks, or are realizations of new ideas. For these reasons, software application development typically involves many risks.

Each identified risk should be welcomed by the project team because they can then start to do something about it. *The real problems are risks which have not been identified:* These are like land mines waiting to explode. Since a large percentage of projects are never completed (sometimes estimated at over 80%), constant attention to risks makes it more likely that a project either is in the successful 20%, or is cancelled before it wastes an embarrassing amount of money and damages careers.

Risk management consists of the activities shown in Figure 2.13. These activities should be carried on from the very beginning of the project, and continued in a disciplined fashion during its first quarter at least. Some teams appoint a member to the role of risk coordinator, responsible for encouraging the team members to detect risks, and to monitor their retirement.

4.3 Risk Identification

Risk identification consists of writing down all the worries and concerns of those connected with the project, then continually pressing all team members to think of even more concerns. Risk identification requires a skeptical mind-set similar to that required for inspection: a global search for defects in the development plan. Risk categories include underestimation of the job's size, too-rapid changes in requirements, inability to find an efficient enough implementation, deficiencies in staff skills, time lag in learning to use tools (e.g. CASE tools), and languages deficiencies (e.g., execution too slow). Figure 2.14 lists the most common project risk factors. These were found by Keil et al. ([Ke]) in studies in the United States, Hong Kong, and Finland.

It may appear strange that the top two risks have to do with lack of stakeholder commitment: Presumably, these are the very people who should be wanting the application. (A "stakeholder" is anyone having a stake in the project's outcome.) The stakeholder community

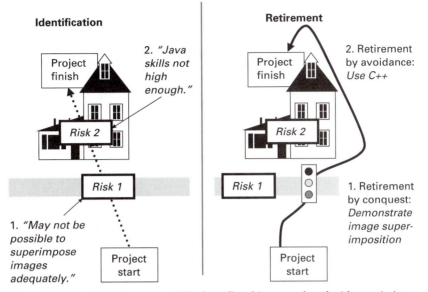

Identification

Retirement

Figure 2.15 The Risk Management Mindset (Graphics reproduced with permission from Corel)

is large, however. Like most groups, its members have differing motivations, which can be hard to reconcile. A failure to reconcile these motivations results in unstable requirements, which can devastate a project. Note that most of the categories in this list are of the same nature as Risk Source #1 and #2, except for item #7. It is noteworthy that technical issues constitute only 20% of the top ten factors, and are considered less important than most of the others. The remaining factors are political and organizational. One can summarize these findings by saying that the project leader has the lion's share of the work in staving off threats to the success of a project.

4.4 Risk Retirement

Risk retirement is the process whereby risks are reduced or even eliminated. There are then two ways to retire a risk. One is to make changes in the project requirements so that the issue causing the risk is no longer present ("avoidance"). A second way is to develop techniques and designs that solve the problem ("conquest," in a manner of speaking). One can compare risk retirement to the process of building a pedestrian walk from start to finish, as suggested in Figure 2.15, in which the obstacles are a street and a house.

When the team identifies an obstacle to constructing the walkway, the team can either avoid it by modifying direction, or else immediately begin development work to surmount the obstacle. In other words, risks can be either *avoided* (finding a way around instead of through the house in the example) or *conquered* (instituting a traffic light for the pedestrian walk to cross the street). The two *Encounter* project risks mentioned in the figure, as well as their retirement strategies, are explained below.

In a healthy project, risks are continually identified, and it is typical to have a backlog of risks waiting to be retired. This backlog should be prioritized, because there is often not enough time to retire them all. In a well-managed project, those risks not retired in advance will be the smallest, and will not be significant problems when encountered in the normal sequence of events. Table 2.2 explains one prioritization scheme. Each risk is provided with (1)

TABLE 2.2 A Way to Compute Risk Priorities

	Likelihood 1–10	Impact 1–10	Retirement cost 1–10	Priority computation	Resulting priority
	(1 = least likely)	(1 = least impact)	(1 = lowest retirement cost)		(lowest number handled first)
The highest priority risk	10 (most likely)	10 (most impact)	1 (lowest retirement cost)	(11–10) ×(11–10) ×1	1
The lowest priority risk	1 (least likely)	1 (least impact)	10 (highest retirement cost)	(11-1) ×(11-1) ×10	1000

an impact level, (2) the likelihood that it is a real risk, and (3) an assessment of the cost of retiring the risk. Each of these measures is on the same scale—say 1–10. These three numbers—or 11 minus the number as the case may be—are multiplied to give the risk's priority.

Table 2.3 identifies two risks for the *Encounter* video game. Risk #1, "Superimposing images," concerns image manipulation in Java. Let's suppose that no one on the team has experience with superimposing images. This is a required capability, because characters have to move about superimposed on backgrounds. Table 2.2 indicates the priority and retirement plan. We judge that this issue might turn out to be a real issue, but more likely it will not, so we set its "likelihood" (that our fear will be realized) to 3. If our fear is realized, on the other hand, we will have a very big problem, so we set impact to a full 10. We think that this risk will cost very little (i.e., will not take long) to retire, so we set "retirement cost" to 1. The retirement plan is simple: An engineer is set the task of reading the manuals and making sure that a figure can be easily and properly superimposed on a background image (i.e., without carrying a visible rectangle).

Risk #2 "Deficient Java skills" indicates the fact that 40% of the team is insufficiently skilled in Java. This is a judgment call, but the author of the risk is almost certain of this, so its likelihood is set to 9. Given that this is true, the project would be fairly seriously set back, but since not everyone in the team is required to program, the author of the chart believes that the effect on the project would be 6 out of 10. The cost of retiring this will be high, both in terms of time away from the job and also training time, so the retirement cost is set to 8. The author invented "Java level 2 certification" to illustrate the point that retirement plans should be entirely specific.

The use of metrics like these to prioritize risks can be useful, but should always be augmented with a healthy dose of common sense. For example, it is worth looking separately at risks that are "show stoppers" with high probability: Even though risk #1 is formally higher in priority than risk #2, retiring #2 requires more lead time, and so training work should be initiated at once. Teams try to obtain more than one perspective on risks. If there are many serious risks, it might be best to delay committing to the project until the risks have been retired.

Figure 2.16 lists specific steps that teams can take to carry out a regular risk retirement program. The process outlined in the figure attempts to maximize the benefit of meeting time by performing offline those aspects of risk that do not require the presence of the entire group.

TABLE 2.3 Sample Risk Analysis for *Encounter* Case Study

Risk Number	Risk Title (details given above)	Likelihood 1–10 (1=least likely)	Impact 1–10 (1=least impact)	Retirement Cost 1–10 (1=lowest retirement cost)	Priority lowest number handled first	Retirement/ Mitigation Plan	Responsible Engineer	Target Completion Date
1	Superimposing images	3	10	1	8	Experiment with Java images.	P. R.	2/1/99
2	Deficient Java skills	9	6	8	80	H.T., K.M., V.I., and L.D. to attend training course beginning 1/5/99 at Ultra Training Corp, obtain Java level 2 certification by 3/1/99 and level 3 certification by 4/15/99	H. L.	4/15/99
3	Alan Gray may be pulled off this project	3	7	9	288	Susan Ferris to inspect all of Alan's work	S.F.	Continual

One Way To. . . Identify and Retire Risks

*1. Each team member spends 10 minutes exploring his or her greatest fears for the project's success.

*2. Each member specifies these risks in concrete language, weights them, writes retirement plans (see format above), and e-mails to the team leader.

*3. Team leader integrates and prioritizes results.

‡4. Group spends 10 minutes seeking additional risks.

‡5. Team spends 10 minutes finalizing the risk table.

  ● Designates responsible risk retirement engineers

**6. Responsible engineers do risk retirement work.

‡7. Team reviews risks for 10 minutes at weekly meetings.

  ● responsible engineers report progress

  ● team discusses newly perceived risks and adds them

* in advance of first meeting
‡ at meeting
** between meetings

Figure 2.16 One Way to Identify and Retire Risks

5. CHOOSING DEVELOPMENT TOOLS AND SUPPORT

5.1 Process Methods

A decision has to be made as to what development methodology—or combination of methodologies—will be used. The choices are waterfall, spiral, USDP, and incremental methodologies, as described in Chapter 1.

5.2 Tools

Software engineering is a substantial market. A number of vendors sell tools and environments for helping engineers to develop software applications. These are often referred to as *Computer-aided Software Engineering* (CASE) tools. The issue of what should be included as a CASE tool has been discussed for years. At times, CASE tool supporters have promised much but delivered far less. Figure 2.17 lists the possible components of a CASE tool. Large projects simply cannot be managed without at least some of these CASE components. For example, in a large project, configuration management tools are indispensable.

5.3 Build or Buy Decisions

There are an increasing number of tools and applications on the market which promise to help, or form the basis for, new applications. For example, in planning for a Web-based auction application, we could compare the purchase of a ready-made auction framework with developing our own application. Typically, we can delay these decisions until the requirements are known, but they are discussed here since they are a part of project management.

A rational manner for approaching this kind of decision is to make a list of expenses, and to estimate the magnitude of each alternative. This is shown in Figure 2.18, which il-

- To support project management
  - schedule
  - work breakdown
- To support configuration management
- For managing requirements

- For drawing designs
  - functional
  - object-oriented
  - use-case-based
- Tracing tools
  - requirements to designs
  - designs to code
- To support testing
- To support maintenance

Figure 2.17 Potential CASE Tool Components (Graphics reproduced with permission from Corel.)

	Build Cost (in thousands)	Buy Cost	Comments
Tool	$0	$40	Purchase Ajax software
Feature 1	$5	$0	No customization
Feature 2	$10	$1	Customize tool
Feature 3	$15	$15	Tool no help
	$75	$98	

Do not buy tool (or application)

Figure 2.18 Build vs. Buy Decision-making

lustrates the decision-making about the purchase of the Ajax graphics software that would help us enhance the graphics of our video game.

Figure 2.18 computes the bottom line with and without purchasing Ajax's software. It breaks out the relevant desired graphics features, and estimates the cost of each. Ajax implements Feature 1, first-person perspective, completely (i.e., continually displays the view of the scene from the player's perspective). On the other hand, Ajax does not do a complete job of handling 3-D (Feature 2), so we will have to program to compensate for this. Finally, we need light reflection (Feature 3), where the scene gives the impression of a light source shining onto it from a single direction. Ajax helps here, but we will have to perform considerable programming to make it work. The table in Figure 2.18 could be an appendix to the project plan or the Software Design Document. A more realistic version of the table would compare the costs on a multi-year basis, and would include maintenance expenses. The more features we are required to implement ourselves, the less attractive the purchase.

Many decisions that are apparently intangible can be framed in a cost comparison form. Maintaining a written record of decisions such as quantitative build-or-buy trade-offs helps in communicating these decisions to the team and others. It also aids postmortems and process improvement.

5.4 Language Selection

The implementation language or languages have to be identified near the beginning of the project. Sometimes this decision is straightforward, as when the organization mandates a

TABLE 2.4 Example of Method for Deciding Language Choice.

Factor	Weight (1-10)	Benefit of Language 1 (1 to 10=best)	Benefit of Language 2 (1 to 10=best)
Internet-friendly	3	8	2
Familiarity to development team	8	3	9
Compilation speed	5	2	8
Runtime speed on processor p	1	7	3
Score		3*8 + 8*3 + 5*2 + 1*7 = 65	3*2 + 8*9 + 5*8 + 1*3 = 121

language, or when a language is the only one capable of implementing the requirements. Sometimes, however, the implementation must be chosen from several alternatives.

Table 2.4 shows examples of factors and weights that could enter into such a determination. The weights are factors in arriving at the bottom line. For example, the score for language 1 is 3*8 + 8*3 + 5*2 + 1*7 (weights underlined).

Decision-making tables such as this are not magic: They merely decompose large decisions (e.g., what language to choose) into smaller ones (e.g., Java is more Web-friendly than C++). Such decompositions provide more stability, but the conclusions that they provide are sensitive to the weighting chosen, the factors selected, and the judgments made. Their results should be augmented with some independent common sense.

5.5 Documentation

During the planning stage, teams decide what particular documentation set will be produced for the project. Alternatives were discussed in Chapter 1.

5.6 Support Services

Projects require support from system administrators, network administrators, database administrators, secretaries, and the like. The project manager has to ensure that these people are available. Humphrey's TSP actually designates one team member as the "support manager."

6. CREATING SCHEDULES: HIGH LEVEL PLANNING

With the information and work performed up to this point, the first version of a schedule can be developed. The form of schedule shown below, with horizontal time lines, is known as a Gantt chart. At this stage, the Gantt chart shows about as much as is known about the project (see Figure 2.19). Note that an alternative is shown in Figure 2.41 on page 108, which employs three iterations. Figure 2.20 shows one way to develop a schedule, the numbering being keyed to the example in Figure 2.19. Even though iterative methods allow for the gradual inclusion of requirements, it is still wise to indicate a date past which no one may introduce new requirements (step 3). The first iteration should be kept very modest (step 4). Even a trivial iteration has the advantage of exercising the team's process, which can take surprisingly long to get going. Bear in mind that it is usually easier to add

	Month 1				Month 2				Month 3				Month 4				Month 5			
	1	2	3	4	1	2	3	4	1	2	3	4	1	2	3	4	1	2	3	4

SCMP complete △   Begin system testing △ (2)

Milestones   △ SQAP complete

                                                                  (1*) Delivery △

                 △ SPMP rel. 1 complete

              (3) Freeze requirements △

Iteration 1   (4)

                          (6)

Iteration 2

Risk
identification and
retirement   (5)   Prep. for maintenance

Indicates the order in which the parts of this table were built

Figure 2.19 High-Level Task Chart with Fixed Delivery Date: Order of Completion

---

One Way To. . . Create an Initial Schedule

1. Indicate the milestones you *must* observe.
   - usually includes delivery date
2. Back these up to introduce the milestones you *need.*
   - e.g., begin system testing well before delivery

   > The remaining steps depend on the process used.
   > We will assume an iterative process.

4. Show first iteration: establishes minimal capability.
   - usually: keep it *very modest, even trivial, in capability*
   - benefit: exercises the development process itself
5. Show task of identifying and retiring risks.
   - starting from project inception
6. Show unassigned time (e.g., week) near middle?
7. Complete the schedule.

Figure 2.20 One Way to Create an Initial Schedule

capability to a modest set of requirements than to subtract capability from an overly ambitious set. An additional advantage of using a very small initial iteration for academic teams is the fact that the team has yet to learn about documenting projects, and should not yet be developing substantial requirements and design documents.

It is advisable to include comfort margins (step 6) in a schedule. This is because we can account for the factors we know about, but we can't honestly account for those that we don't know about. We must try to provide for the latter, however. In addition, people almost

	Month 1				Month 2				Month 3				Month 4				Month 5			
	1	2	3	4	1	2	3	4	1	2	3	4	1	2	3	4	1	2	3	4
Milestones					Freeze requirements △								Complete testing △				Release to production △			
						Karen vacation														
Iteration 1	2	2	2	3	2	2	3				Hal vacation									
Iteration 2									4	4	4	3	3	4	4	4	4	4	4	4
Risk Identification and retirement	2	2	2	1	1	1		4	To be assigned											
Given team size:	4	4	4	4	3	3	3	4	4	4	4	3	3	4	4	4	4	4	4	4

Figure 2.21 Level Labor Allocation for Fixed Labor Total

always expand tasks to fit allotted times: If no buffer time is built into the schedule, then all time lines butt up against one another, and typically begin to overlap in a frightening cascade. One way to provide for the unknown is to "tax" the tasks we know about by a reasonable amount of overestimation or "comfort." Another way, shown in Figure 2.19, is to build into the schedule a period (a week, for example) during which no specific tasks are scheduled. It is easier to modify a schedule by filling this "buffer" week than by rearranging tasks.

The schedule becomes increasingly detailed as the project progresses and the schedule is revisited. In particular, we define the individual tasks once the design is settled. At that point we also compute detailed labor allocations (i.e., who will work on what, and when). Subsequent chapters will revisit the effects on the schedule of each step in the development process. In some cases, it is possible to make gross labor distributions at a very high level. For example, if we know that four people are employed full time on the project from the beginning, then we should employ them all if we can. In this case, a labor allocation results such as that shown in Figure 2.21.

The schedule leaves a gap for unforeseen issues at the end of Iteration 1 in Month 2 Week 4, and Iteration 2 in Month 5, Weeks 3 and 4. No explicit obligations are assigned during these weeks. We can account for vacations, etc. at this point, which is why the labor allocations are not constant.

▶ PART II: AT LENGTH

This "at length" part *can* be covered after covering subsequent chapters.

7. INTEGRATING LEGACY APPLICATIONS

Most of the work performed by software engineers actually consists not of developing brand new products, but of extending existing systems or harnessing them to new applications. Such existing programs are termed "legacy" applications. Sometimes, the origin of

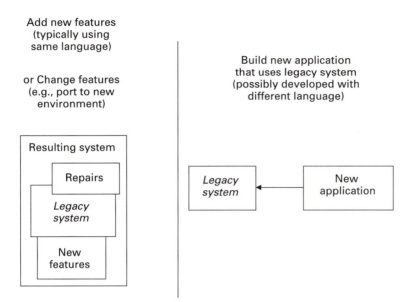

Figure 2.22 Legacy System Integration

an application is an exploratory project, rather than a planned development responding to a professional marketing study. The origin could be a rapid prototype that evolved in an unplanned manner into a profitable product, or an application written some time ago without the benefit of modern methods and documentation standards. In cases like these, the language, the documentation, the architecture, and/or the code may be technically lacking. Nevertheless, such applications can be in demand, and have typically been debugged through extensive usage. Often, discontinuing such an application would be folly, and replacing it would be prohibitively expensive.

To add to the capability of a legacy system, we can either integrate new features into it, or build the desired application separately and have it simply use the legacy system. These alternatives are illustrated in Figure 2.22. A common problem in using a legacy system is a difficulty in merely understanding what it does and how it does it—especially when it is poorly documented. Using a legacy system is easiest when the system was designed using good software engineering practices.

Rugaber and White [Ru] describe a case study in which the legacy "RT-1000" telephony system for automated call distribution was causing problems, even though it was making a great deal of money for its owner. It had originally been built by a team of 70 developers over a five-year period at a cost of millions of dollars, and it was deemed far too expensive to replace. The company decided to restore and enhance it. Among RT-1000's problems were

- No formal process used in building it
- No version control in place
- General lack of documentation
- No complete record of tests and test results, and no test automation
- Not year-2000 compliant

- Written in several languages, some out of date
- Its third-party components (e.g. a database management system) no longer supported by their vendors
- Customers relied on the exact form of RT-1000's output in order to provide input to other programs (e.g. displays) without the knowledge of RT-1000's owner

The restoration development team did their work over a period of three years. They

- Reduced the number of open defects from 300 to under 15
- Placed the source code under configuration control
- Automated over 80% of the existing test cases
- Replaced or upgraded third-party components or negotiated maintenance agreements with the remaining ones
- Obtained ISO-9001 certification for their process
- Encouraged regular customer visits to the development organization, thereby improving customer relations
- Added significant new functionality
- Rewrote parts in C

Rugaber and White report that their attempts to use a tool which automatically translated Fortran to C was technically successful, but produced code that could not be maintained.

Today's applications are tomorrow's legacy systems, so let's examine how this perspective affects the building of a new application such as the video game case study used in this book. This game is called *Encounter*. We will make *Encounter* easy to change and extend, since video game concepts tend to change a great deal. Using an object-oriented approach throughout helps in this respect by clarifying the parts, and minimizing assumptions about where and how *Encounter* will grow.

Suppose that an ardent group of psychologists hears about *Encounter,* and wants to use it to study of the effects of extended game play on the brain. Our legacy integration approach would be like that on the right side of Figure 2.22 above, since we would be building an application that uses *Encounter*. We would want the *Encounter* legacy system to exhibit an appropriate application programming interface (API). Such as API might consist of

```
void runForDuration(int numMinutes) // execute for an amount of time
void runScenario(Scenario aScenario) // execute a particular sequence
float getScore() // score the player
void setKeystrokeCounter(boolean aToggle) // time between key strokes
```

Part of our task would thus be to write software (called a wrapper, or adapter) that would allow the application to use these legacy system services. The *adapter* design pattern is discussed in Chapter 6.

Legacy applications are also discussed in Chapter 10 of this book, in the context of maintenance.

8. ESTIMATING COSTS: EARLY CALCULATIONS

8.1 Introduction

The cost of a project is of intense, continual interest to the stakeholders. At the wrong production price, even the most fantastic product can be disastrous. The simplest cost estimation is one in which the fixed cost is provided at the inception, no deviation being allowed under any circumstances. Although highly competent organizations are skilled enough to vary the remaining variables (capability, schedule, and quality) to meet a predetermined cost, absolute cost rigidity is not always practiced. Suppose, for example, that a project producing a very salable product runs out of funds when 90% complete. Rather than drop the entire project, an organization would typically do its utmost to find the funds for that last 10%. Even when the project's cost is rigid, it becomes necessary to estimate the cost of a given set of requirements and/or design to ensure that it conforms to the mandated cost, and if it does not, change it and then reestimate.

    The process of estimating costs (i.e., for fixed capabilities, quality level, and schedule) often starts at the inception of a project, and continues even after coding has begun. When a project is initiated, the team can have only the vaguest of ideas about its cost. If the cost estimation can be postponed until the project has been fleshed out, then it certainly should be, but there is always a need to estimate a "ballpark range" from a summary requirements statement. The more we learn about the requirements for the product and the more design we perform, the more precise we can be about its cost. This is illustrated in Figure 2.23.

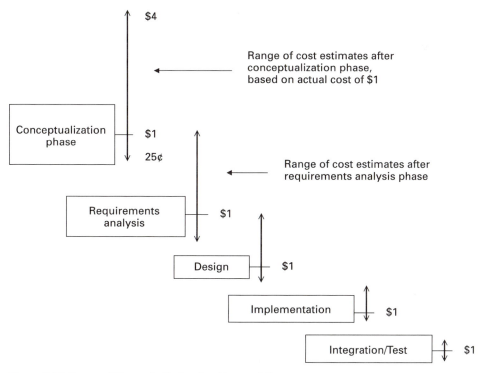

Figure 2.23 Range of Errors in Estimating Eventual Cost

1A.	Use comparisons with past jobs to estimate cost and duration directly or to estimate lines of code.

and/or

1B.	Use function point method to estimate lines of code.
	1B.1 Compute un-adjusted function points.
	1B.2 Apply adjustment process.

2.	Use lines of code estimates to compute labor and duration using COCOMO formulas.

Figure 2.24 Typical Cost Estimation Road Map

The fourfold estimation error shown in Figure 2.23 is due to a study reported by Boehm [Bo]. For an application which will eventually cost $100,000, for example, estimates made after the application's concept has been developed, can be as low as $25,000 and as high as $400,000. We use various techniques to sharpen our estimate of a project's cost, as early as possible, which amounts to reducing the height of the vertical lines in Figure 2.23. Only at the latter end of implementation can we have complete confidence in our estimates. (The estimates are far less useful at that time, however, since most of the money will already have been spent!) Since precision is practically impossible, a *range* is a good way to express projected costs, and this is applied in the above example.

It puzzles some people that we can even begin to think about costs without a design, and without detailed requirements, but this is a common practice in other fields. One can gain a rough estimate of the cost of building a house, for example, without any design or detailed requirements. For example, one can use rules of thumb such as "houses in this area cost about $100 per square foot to build," and so a 1000-square-foot house will cost about $100,000.

A good way to approach project cost estimation at the very early stages of a project is to develop estimates in several independent ways, then combine the results. One can even weight the estimates obtained according to one's level of confidence in each of them.

A sewing machine or lathe is a sophisticated tool which is useless without a practiced user. Similarly, the first time one uses early cost approximation measures, the results are unlikely to be reliable. With time, feedback, and calibration, however, one learns to use them with increasing precision.

Figure 2.24 shows a typical road map for the early estimation of project cost and duration. The next section shows an example of the use of past projects. The function point methodology and COCOMO (Constructive Cost Model) are explained below.

8.2 Estimating Lines of Code without the Function Point Process

This section discusses ways to estimate lines of code at a very early stage, well before any design work has been performed. Once design work is performed, the methods are based on the parts of the design, and become far more precise, as indicated above in Figure 2.23.

Several estimation methods, notably the COCOMO model, depend on the number of lines of code (LoC). "COCOMO" stands for Boehm's "Constructive Cost Model" ([Bo]). At the very early stages of a project, COCOMO may not sound very useful because coding is a long way off. When the product can be compared with other products, however, estimating lines of code is feasible. For example, we could estimate that our current satellite control job is comparable to our last satellite job, which required 3 million lines of FOR-TRAN: However, our current job has the additional requirement of being able to monitor hurricanes. It may be possible to roughly estimate the size of this additional piece based on other hurricane trackers (100,000 lines of FORTRAN, for example). When implementation languages change, industry-standard language conversion factors are used.

Organizations working above Capability Maturity Models level 1 must be able to record the person-hours and duration of the parts of jobs. In the absence of such data, we would have to compare our *Encounter* video game, for example, with other games. Obtaining data directly from other companies ranges from difficult to impossible. Trade publications and general industry announcements sometimes provide partial data. For example, we may know from industry announcements that "BugEye Inc." has worked on its new game for two years: The announcement may even mention a number of programmers. Such data is highly suspect, however, since companies regard their development knowledge as a corporate asset, and commonly exaggerate or underreport numbers as the case may be.

In the absence of historical data, it may be necessary to compare the project with related projects, (simulations, for example, in the case of our video game). Let's say that we have very little experience programming games, and some experience programming simulations and Java. Our lines-of-code estimation may have to be something like the following:

> *I once wrote a non-graphical simulation of a simple queue in C++, which required about 4–8 pages of code. At about 30–50 non-comment lines per page, this totals 120–400 lines. We will assume that Java requires the same number of lines. The first commercial release of Encounter has 4–15 such queues and 30–90 additional components of comparable size to make it interesting, so that yields between [(120 lines) × (34 components)] minimum and [(400 lines) × (105 components)] maximum as our range, or approximately 5000 to 42,000 lines of code. The use of graphics multiplies the effort by 1.5 to 4, depending on the degree of sophistication, so this gives us a range of 1.5 × 5000 to 4 × 42,000 = 7.5–170 K-lines (thousands of lines) of code. (Note: The case study in this book encompasses a prototype, which is far less ambitious than the version upon which this estimate is based.)*

By documenting this data on a spreadsheet we establish a baseline, and we can then sharpen our estimates as the project goes forward. Note that the range 7.5–170 K-lines is consistent with Figure 2.23 on page 97, in which a 16-fold range in estimates is expected at the conceptualization stage. The preceding calculation is a bottom-up approximation, since it estimates the cost of the whole from that of the parts.

An example of a top-down approximation follows, using industry data (or, preferably, historical data from the organization doing the work). Suppose we know that a very good video game required the services of 5–20 expert programmers for 1–2 years. Since we can invest only $\frac{1}{10}$ of the amount which was invested in that game, we will assume that ours will have about $\frac{1}{10}$ of its capability. Assuming 5–25 lines of (fully tested!) Java code per day, this yields

(1/10 capability of the famous game) × (5–25 lines per day) ×

(5–20 programmers) × (1–2 years) × (48–50 weeks per year) ×

(35–60 hours per week) ≈ 4.2-300 K-lines of code.

This range is different from the bottom-up estimate obtained previously, but it helps to ground our ideas about the job's magnitude, since the method used this time is quite different.

Free estimation tools, such as those at www.construx.com, are also available on the Web.

Recall from Chapter 1 that the Personal Software Process[SM] involves the intensive gathering of personal metrics. This essential practice equips the individual and the organization with historical data for use in subsequent lines-of-code estimation.

8.3 Function Points and Lines of Code

Starting in 1979 with Albrecht [Al], the more fundamental notion of *function points* was developed to assess the size of a project without having to know its design. The function point technique is a means of calibrating the capabilities of an application in a uniform manner, as a single number. This number can then be used to estimate lines of code, cost, and duration. Function points is an attractive concept, since it tries to get to the heart of a future product's capability: However, it takes a great deal of practice to apply it in an accurate and consistent manner.

Function point calculation comprises the following steps.

Function Point Step 1 Identify the functions (e.g. "retrieve," "display") that the application must have. The International Function Point Users Group (IFPUG; see [IF]) has published criteria as to what constitutes a "function" of an application in this sense. They consider user-level functionality, rather than programming-level functions as in C. Typically, a function is the equivalent of processing a screen or form on the monitor.

For our role-playing video game prototype, for example, we can identify the following functions:

(1) Set up the character representing the player
(2) Encounter a foreign character

Function Point Step 2 For each such function, compute its function point contribution from the sources shown in Figure 2.25. The following summarizes the sense of each contributing factor. The guidelines have to be carefully followed, otherwise it is hard to obtain consistent estimates.

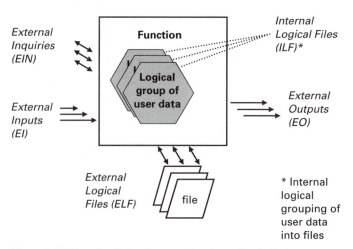

Figure 2.25 Function Point Computation for a Single Function

Parameter		simple				complex		
External inputs, *EI*	×	3	or	4	or	6	=	☐
External outputs, *EO*	×	4	or	5	or	7	=	☐
External inquiries, *EIN*	×	3	or	4	or	6	=	☐
Internal logical files, *ILF*	×	7	or	10	or	15	=	☐
External logical files, *ELF*	×	5	or	7	or	10	=	☐
						count Total		☐

Figure 2.26 Function Point Computations—Before Adjustment

		Simple		Medium		Complex		Sub-	Total
		count	*factor*	count	*factor*	count	*factor*	totals	
Ext. inputs		1	3	1	4	1	6	13	
comments:		Name		Ready/move		Qualities			
Ext. outputs		0	4	0	5	0	7	0	
Ext. inquiries		0	3	0	4	0	6	0	25
Int. logical files		1	7	0	10	0	15	7	
comments:		Data about the user's character							
Ext. interface files		1	5	0	7	0	10	5	
comments:		Data about the user's character							

Figure 2.27 Unadjusted Function Point Computation for Encounter *Function "Set Up Player Character"*

- *External inputs:* Only inputs that *affect the function in a different way* from each other are counted as separate. Thus, a function of an application that subtracts two numbers would have $EI = 1$, not $EI = 2$. On the other hand, if the character A can be input to request an addition and S for subtraction, these would contribute 2 to *EI*.

- *External outputs:* Only outputs which account for true separate algorithmic or nontrivial functionalities should be counted. For example, a process that outputs a character in several fonts would be counted as 1; error messages are not counted. Chart representations of data are counted as 2 (1 for the data and 1 for the formatting), and data sent to separate nontrivial destinations (e.g., printer and monitor) are counted separately.

- *External inquiry:* Each independent inquiry is counted as 1.

- *Internal logical files:* This counts each unique logical group of user data created by or maintained by the application. *Combinations* of such logical groupings are not counted; each functional area of the application dealing with a unique logical grouping increases the count by one.

- *External logical files:* This counts each unique grouping of data on files external to the application.

Function Point Step 3 As shown in the Figure 2.26, each of these parameter values is then factored by a number, depending on the degree of complexity of the parameter in the application. IFPUG ([IF]) has published detailed descriptions of the meaning of "simple" and "complex" in this context.

Applying this process to the two selected functions of the *Encounter* video game mentioned above, we obtain the spreadsheet tables shown in Figure 2.27 and Figure 2.28.

		Simple		Medium		Complex		Sub-	Total
		count	factor	count	factor	count	factor	totals	
Ext. inputs		0	3	0	4	0	6	0	
Ext. outputs		1	4	0	5	0	7	4	
comments:		Report on results							
Ext. inquiries		0	3	0	4	0	6	0	16
Int. logical files		1	7	0	10	0	15	7	
comments:		Data about the user's character							
Ext. interface files		1	5	0	7	0	10	5	
comments:		Data about the user's character							

Figure 2.28 Unadjusted Function Point Computation for Encounter *Function "Encounter Foreign Character"*

These Figures are highly preliminary, but they do begin to provide estimate parameters for the job. The total unadjusted function point estimate for these two *Encounter* functions is 25+16=41.

Function Point Step 4   Next, one computes weights for the 14 *general characteristics* of the project, each between 0 and 5. This is shown for the two selected *Encounter* functions in Figure 2.29 and Figure 2.30. We have actually used a range for each of these to reflect our current uncertainty about the application. Once again, it takes consistent experience to assess the appropriate values for these variables. For example, factor 6 asks for the degree of certainty that online data entry is required. We are certain that the user will need to input characteristics for the game characters, and so the value chosen is the highest: 5.

The total *General Characteristics* value (1 through 14) is between 24 and 41.

Function Point Step 5   Finally, the (adjusted) function point total is calculated by the formula shown in the Figure 2.31. This equation states that if there are no special demands at all on the application (total general characteristics = 0), then the function point measure should be scaled down from the unadjusted (raw) score by 35% (which explains the "0.65"). Otherwise the measure should be scaled up from the unadjusted amount by one percentage point for each general characteristic unit.

For the case study, a reasonable allocation of general characteristics is shown in Figure 2.29 and Figure 2.30. The total value of these is between 24 and 43, so the final (i.e., adjusted) function point computation is

$$41 \times [0.65 + 0.01 \times (24 \text{ to } 41)] = 41 \times [0.89 \text{ to } 1.06] \approx 36 \text{ to } 43.$$

8.4 Converting Function Points to Lines of Code

Once accurately obtained, function points are very useful. For example, they can be exploited as comparative metrics, allowing organizations to estimate jobs based on function point metrics of previous jobs. They can be converted to lines of code using standard tables. Lines of code can then be used to estimate total effort in person-months as well as duration (see next section). For example, [SPR] estimates 53 lines of Java source per function point. Using this factor for the *Encounter* example, we anticipate (36 to 44) × 53 ≈

```
        incidental       average      essential
    0———————1———————2———————3———————4——————5
  none              moderate      significant
```

                                          Case
                                          study

1. Requires backup/recovery?   *0–2*
2. Data communications required?   *0–1*
3. Distributed processing functions?   *0*
4. Performance critical?   *3–4*
5. Run on existing heavily utilized
   environment?   *0–1*
6. Requires on-line data entry?   *5*
7. Multiple screens for input?   *4–5*

Figure 2.29 General Characteristics for
Function Point: Adjustment Factors 1–7
Copyright © 1983 IEEE

```
        incidental       average      essential
    0———————1———————2———————3———————4——————5
  none              moderate      significant
```

                                                     Case
                                                     study

8. Master fields updated on-line?   *3–4*
9. Inputs, outputs, inquiries of files complex?   *1–2*
10. Internal processing complex?   *1–3*
11. Code designed for re-use?   *2–4*
12. Conversion and installation included?   *0–2*
13. Multiple installation in different orgs.?   *1–3*
14. Must facilitate change and ease-of-use
    by user?   *4–5*

Figure 2.30 Adjustment Factors 8–14   Copyright ©
1983 IEEE

(Adjusted) Function points =
[Unadjusted function points] ×
[0.65 + 0.01 × (total general characteristics)]

Figure 2.31 Computation of Adjusted Function Points

1.9–2.3 K-lines of Java source. As expected, this is much lower than the previous estimates of 4.2-300 and 7.5–170 K-lines of Java source. This is true because it applies to only two "functions" for *Encounter,* whereas the larger estimates were for a full game. Free function point calculation spreadsheets are available on the Web through [IF1].

8.5 A Further Function Point Example

Let's consider a simple system that tracks video rentals. We will confine the application to a customer-oriented application, in which customers rent videos and need information about availability.

		Simple		Medium		Complex		*Sub-*	**Total**
		count	**factor**	*count*	**factor**	*count*	**factor**	*totals*	
Ext. inputs		2	3	1	4	0	6	10	
explanation:		Name, ph. #		Video data					
Ext. outputs		0	4	1	5	0	7	5	
explanation:				Amount due					
Ext. inquiries		0	3	1	4	0	6	4	33
explanation:				Availability					
Int. logical files		2	7	0	10	0	15	14	
explanation:		Customers; Videos							
Ext. interface files		0	5	0	7	0	10	0	

Figure 2.32 Unadjusted Function Point Scores for Video Store Example

```
        incidental       average        essential
  0————1————2————3————4———— 5
none            moderate      significant
```

1. Requires backup/recovery?   4
2. Data communications required?   0
3. Distributed processing functions?   0
4. Performance critical?   3
5. Run on existing heavily utilized
   environment?   1
6. Requires on-line data entry?   5
7. Multiple screens for input?   3
8. Master fields updated on-line?   5
9. Inputs, outputs, inquiries of files
   complex?   2
10. Internal processing complex?   1
11. Code designed for re-use?   3
12. Conversion and installation included?   3
13. Multiple installation in different orgs.? 3
14. Must facilitate change & ease-of-use   *Total*
    by user?   2   *35*

Figure 2.33 Function Point Adjustment Factors for Video Store Example

We assume that the application requires two files only: one for customers and a second for videos. The unadjusted function point computation is as shown in Figure 2.32. Now we estimate the adjustment factors, as shown in Figure 2.33, yielding a "General Characteristics" total of 35. The Function Point formula gives

Function points =

[unadjusted function points] $\times$ [0.65 + 0.01 $\times$ (total general characteristics)]
= 33 $\times$ [0.65 + 0.01 $\times$ 35] = 33

This yields 33 $\times$ 53 = 1749 lines of non-commented source lines of Java code.

8.6 Function Point References

The function point method is summed up by Capers Jones [Jo], a practiced advocate of function point application. See also [Dr].

9. ESTIMATING EFFORT AND DURATION FROM LINES OF CODE

Once lines of code have been estimated (whether via function points or via a method like those in Section 8.2), they can be used to estimate labor requirements and project duration. Barry Boehm [Bo] observed that, roughly speaking, the labor required to develop applications increases faster than the application's size. The exponential function, with exponent close to 1.12, is used to express this relationship. Boehm's model also says that the duration increases exponentially with the effort, but with an exponent less than 1 (the exponent used in this case is close to 0.35). This reflects the observation that after a certain size (the "knee" in curve (2)), additional required effort has only a gradual lengthening effect on the time it takes to complete the project. These are illustrated in Figure 2.34, where LOC is short for "lines of code."

Using data from numerous projects, Boehm estimated the parameters for these relationships, assuming an exponential relationship. His formulas are illustrated in Figure 2.35. *Organic* applications are stand-alone applications such as classical (i.e., non-Web-enabled) word processors—or our *Encounter* case study. *Embedded* applications are integral to hardware-software systems (e.g., an antilock braking system). *Semidetached* applications are in between. A Web-enabled *Encounter,* for example, is semi-detached: It is not organic, but it is not as heavily embedded as the code in an antilock braking system, for example. *Encounter* would communicate with the Internet via signals that are only occasional when compared with the frequency of CPU instruction execution.

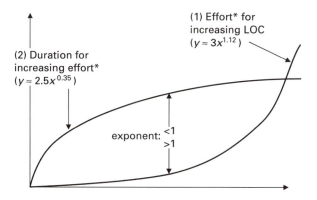

Applies to *design* through *integration* and *test.*
*"Effort"= total person-months required.

Figure 2.34 Meaning of the COCOMO Formulas   SOFTWARE ENGINEERING ECONOMICS by Boehm, B. W., © 1982 Reprinted by permission of Prentice-Hall, Inc., Upper Saddle River, NJ.

Effort in person-months = $a \times$ KLOC^b
Duration = $c \times$ Effort^d

Software Project	a	b	c	d
Organic	2.4	1.05	2.5	0.38
Semidetached	3.0	1.12	2.5	0.35
Embedded	3.6	1.20	2.5	0.32

Figure 2.35 Basic COCOMO Formulas (Due to Boehm [Bo])
SOFTWARE ENGINEERING ECONOMICS by Boehm, B. W., © 1982
Reprinted by permission of Prentice-Hall, Inc., Upper Saddle River, NJ.

Boehm's model says first that the required effort and duration have separate models (formulas) for each type of the application (differing in factors *a* and *b*). For example, a stand-alone job with 20,000 lines of code would take $2.4 \times 20^{1.05} \approx 51$ person months duration if organic (stand-alone) but about $3.6 \times 20^{1.2} \approx 76$ person months if embedded.

The duration formula can be expressed directly in terms of line-of-code (KLOC) as follows

$$Duration = c \times \text{Effort}^d = c \times (a \times \text{KLOC}^b)^d = c \times a^d \times \text{KLOC}^{bd}$$

At first glance, Boehm's duration formula may appear strange because the relationship between effort and duration would seem to be much simpler than his formula. For example, if we know that a job requires 120 person-months, and we put 10 people onto it, won't it get done in 12 months? This would indeed be the case if we could usefully and consistently employ all 10 people on the project from day one through day 365, but this is not usually possible. Think, for example, about day one: You do not know anything about the project, so what useful activities could all 10 engineers do that day? Thus, we know that if we allocate 10 engineers from the first day, then the 120 person-month job will actually take longer than 12 months.

Boehm's duration formula has the strange property of being independent of the number of people put on the job! It depends only on the size of the job. Actually, the formula assumes that the project will have roughly an appropriate number of people available to it at any given time (for example, one on day one, 30 on day 100—assuming that is what's needed).

Boehm's model, which has been tested extensively and is widely recognized, has been refined over time. However, a great deal of practice is required to use it effectively, and it is best used along with an independent method and a healthy dose of common sense (sometimes called a "sanity check").

Using Boehm's basic formula on the prototype version of *Encounter* (consisting of two basic functions), with 4–300 K-lines of code, we obtain 10 to 1000 person-months of effort, and 6 to 35 months in duration, as shown in Figure 2.36. Figure 2.37 sums up a way to obtain early estimates of the labor required for a project, and its duration.

	a	*K*	*b*	Approximation
Effort				aK^b
LO	2.4	4.2	1.05	10
HI	2.4	300	1.05	1000

	c	*P*	*d*	Approximation
Duration				cP^d
LO	2.5	10	0.38	6
HI	2.5	1000	0.38	35

Figure 2.36 Computing COCOMO Case Study Models SOFTWARE ENGINEERING ECONOMICS by Boehm, B. W., © 1982 Reprinted by permission of Prentice-Hall, Inc., Upper Saddle River, NJ.

One Way To. . . Estimate Cost and Duration Very Early in a Project

1. Use the function point method to estimate lines of code
2. Use Boehm's formulas to estimate labor required
3. Use the labor estimate and Boehm's formulas to estimate duration

Figure 2.37 One Way to Estimate Cost and Duration Very Early in a Project

10. THE TEAM SOFTWARE PROCESS

You don't want to worry continually about issues that are common to all software development projects, which could have been worked out in advance. The Team Software Process (TSP) settles a large number of software project management issues and practices for all team activities. The TSP provides guidance to groups on each of the project development phases after requirements analysis. TSP participants are required to be PSP-trained. The method is organized around iterations of the waterfall sequence, and requires that the team "launch" each iteration at a meeting where a number of predefined issues are addressed. Humphrey provides numerous detailed scripts. The phases can be iterated several times, requiring several launches. Launch issues to be settled are shown in Figure 2.38. Humphrey recommends that the items listed in Figure 2.39 be produced by each phase launch. Much of this is covered by the "*One way to .....*" scripts and the IEEE documents discussed in this book.

The *TSPi* is a version of the TSP which is scaled to fit an academic semester. The TSPi roles are *team leader, development manager, planning manager, quality/process manager, and support manager.* In this chapter, we have used the term "leader" instead of "manager" for a similar allocation of roles. The "support manager" is responsible for obtaining and supplying all the tools and environments, such as compilers, for example.

- Process to be used
- Quality goals
- Manner of tracking quality goals
- How team will make decisions
- What to do if quality goals not attained
  - fallback positions
- What to do if plan not approved
  - fallback positions

- Define team roles
- Assign team roles

Figure 2.38 TSP Launch: Issues to Settle (Graphics reproduced with permission from Corel.)

1. Written team goals
2. Defined team roles
3. Process development plan
4. Quality plan
5. Project's support plan
   computers, software, personnel etc.
6. Overall development plan and schedule
7. Detailed plans for each engineer
8. Project risk assessment
9. Project status report

Figure 2.39 To Be Produced by Each Phase Launch

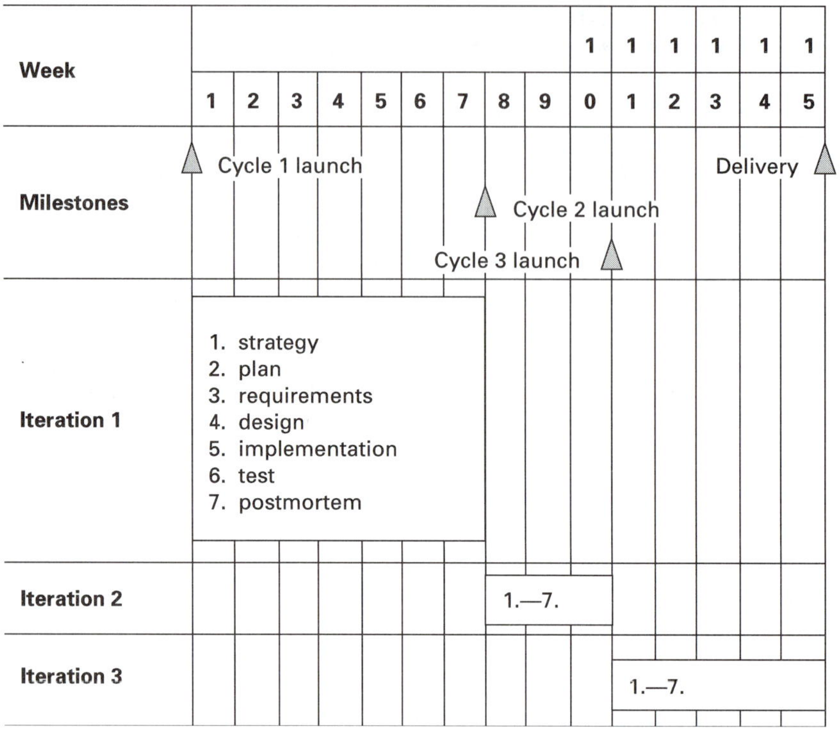

Week										1	1	1	1	1	1
	1	2	3	4	5	6	7	8	9	0	1	2	3	4	5
Milestones	Cycle 1 launch						Cycle 3 launch	Cycle 2 launch						Delivery	
Iteration 1	1. strategy 2. plan 3. requirements 4. design 5. implementation 6. test 7. postmortem														
Iteration 2								1.—7.							
Iteration 3										1.—7.					

Figure 2.40 TSPi Cycle Structure

Humphrey specifies a specific semester-long schedule for the TSPi, consisting of three iterations (he calls them "cycles") as shown in Figure 2.40.

The idea is that data obtained from each cycle can be used to estimate the metrics for the next cycle. Cycle 1 is comparatively long because it includes the team's first progression through the stages shown. It is intended to be a "minimal function working subset of the final product." Cycle 3 is long enough to wrap up the job completely. This leaves a relatively short middle cycle. "Strategy" (labeled "1" in Figure 2.40) refers to the overall way in which the team will go about building the cycle in question. This requires a high-level discussion of the requirements, a conceptual design, and an overall assembly plan for the components. These are then made into the concrete plan (2), the written requirements (3), and so on. Humphrey [Hu7] provides numerous, detailed scripts to accompany the TSPi.

11. THE SOFTWARE PROJECT MANAGEMENT PLAN

The project plan is documented so that everyone knows what to do, and when to do it. There are many formats for such a plan: We will use IEEE standard 1058.1-1987 (reaffirmed in 1993). The table of contents for 1058.1-1987, the Software Project Management Plan (SPMP), is shown in Figure 2.41, and is also used in the case study at the end of this chapter.

Section 1.1 in Figure 2.41, the overview, should identify the project, but should not attempt to cover its requirements (i.e., descriptions of its behavior). These are covered in the Software Requirements Specification, described below in Chapters 3 and 4. Repeating that

THE SOFTWARE PROJECT MANAGEMENT PLAN

1. **Introduction**
   1.1 Project overview
   1.2 Project deliverables
   1.3 Evolution of the SPMP
   1.4 Reference materials
   1.5 Definitions and acronyms
2. **Project organization**
   2.1 Process model
   2.2 Organizational structure
   2.3 Organizational boundaries and interfaces
   2.4 Project responsibilities
3. **Managerial process**
   3.1 Managerial objectives and priorities
   3.2 Assumptions, dependencies, and constraints
   3.3 Risk management
   3.4 Monitoring and controlling mechanisms
   3.5 Staffing plan
4. **Technical process**
   4.1 Methods, tools, and techniques
   4.2 Software documentation
   4.3 Project support functions
5. **Work packages, schedule, and budget**
   5.1 Work packages
   5.2 Dependencies
   5.3 Resource requirements
   5.4 Budget and resource allocation
   5.5 Schedule

Figure 2.41 IEEE 1058.1-1987 SPMP Table of Contents   Copyright © 1988 IEEE

material in the SPMP is not necessary, and would violate the goal of single-source documentation. The "deliverables" section (1.2) lists all of the documents, source and object code, to be produced. Section 1.3 describes the ways in which the SPMP is expected to grow and change. The Software Configuration Management Plan should have been developed by this time (see Chapter 1), so that versions of the SPMP will be properly controlled.

Section 2.1 refers to the process to be used (e.g., waterfall, spiral, incremental). Possible "organizational structures" were discussed in section 3.2 on page 82. Section 2.3 ("organizational boundaries and interfaces") describes the ways in which organizations will communicate with each other. This depends on the project's stakeholders (the people who have an interest in it). For example, how will engineering interface with marketing? regular meetings? e-mail?, etc. Section 2.4 states who is responsible for what. For example, in the horizontal organization in Figure 2.10 on page 83, just what is the "team facilitator" responsible for (the exclusive success of the project? personnel recommendations? leadership only?, etc.).

"Management objectives and priorities" (Section 3.1) is where the operational philosophy of the project can be stated. Not all projects have the same priority. For our video game, the first priority would probably be "the creation of a truly engrossing player environment." After all, if no one buys our game, all the other issues are moot. For critical medical applications, on the other hand, "safety" is the paramount priority. With other applications, reusability of parts may be a managerial priority.

Risk management (item 3.3 in Figure 2.41) was described in Section 4 on page 85. "Monitoring and controlling mechanisms" (3.4) specifies who will manage, control, and/or review the project, together with how and when this is to be done. For example, senior management needs to know how projects are progressing, so we would describe the process for keeping them informed here. The "staffing plan" states exactly who will fill each position. Thus, for example, Section 2 could state that the project will have a "Manager" with particular responsibilities, whereas Section 3.5 would state that Albert Smith will occupy that position.

The "technical process" in Section 4 is where constraints on the languages and tools used are provided (e.g., "this project shall use Java from Sun, version 1.2.1, and Rational Rose version 1"). Section 4 can include information on reuse requirements and on the use of techniques such as design patterns (see Chapters 5 and 6). The "Project support functions" section (4.3) is where we would reference or describe activities that support the development process, such as configuration management and quality assurance. If the support function is described in separate documents (e.g., the configuration management plan or the quality plan), we reference those documents. Otherwise we describe the support function in full.

Section 5.1 ("Work packages") describes how work is to be apportioned and delivered. Since the application's architecture has not yet been determined, the first release of this section is necessarily sketchy. For example, at this stage in the project, we can state that the technical supervisor is responsible for creating the Software Design Document, but we can't go into much more detail, because no design has yet been identified. The work package is made increasingly detailed on subsequent versions of the SPMP.

Section 5.3 ("Resource requirements") estimates the labor, hardware, and software required to build and maintain the application. The results of the cost estimation techniques above can be stated here. This section is revisited after the project progresses and more accurate and detailed estimates can be made.

Section 5.4 (Budget and resource allocation) describes how the resources (money, mostly) are to be allocated to the parts of the project throughout its lifetime. This consists mainly of person-day expenses, but also includes software and hardware.

Finally, Section 5.5 concludes the SPMP with a schedule, stating how and when the parts of the process are to be performed. This was described in Section 6 on page 92.

12. QUALITY IN PROJECT MANAGEMENT

Everyone wants to be in on the "good" projects, but we can't be unless we know just what "good" means. For this we need to define metrics, measure our projects against them, and then improve them until they become "good."

12.1 Process Metrics

12.1.1 Introduction to Process Metrics
Recall that CMM level 5 (Section 8.3 of Chapter 1, on page 57) requires continual improvement in the process itself. Although few organizations work at this level, its goals should always be kept in mind. In order to improve a project management process, we must be prepared to measure its effectiveness using process metrics. These are metrics that can measure the effectiveness of our process organization, including the way in which the steps are sequenced. We also separately measure the effectiveness of requirements analysis, design, code, and test.

12.1.2 Examples of Process Metrics
A common metric is the *defect detection rate* for a given detection phase and a given injection phase. For example, a "defect detection rate of 0.2 per 100 requirements defects at the implementation phase" would result if one defect in the requirements were detected at implementation time, as part of implementing 500 requirements.

When defect detection rates are compared with the norms for the organization, they measure the *process*, rather than just the project. Table 2.5 shows a project in which these defect data have been collected. For the sake of simplicity, we have omitted the test and post-delivery phases, which would complete the picture.

Let's focus on the detailed requirements part of Table 2.5. We noted from inspections that two defects per 100 were detected during the requirements phase. This compares fa-

TABLE 2.5 Defects by Phase

Phase Containing Defects	Phase in which defects detected (This project / *norm*)		
	Detailed requirements	**Design**	**Implementation**
Detailed requirements	2 / *5*		
Design	0.5 / *1.5*	3 / *1*	
Implementation	0.1 / *0.3*	1 / *3*	2 / *2*

Compare each of the following with company norms averaged over similar processes.

1. Number of defects per KLOC detected within 12 weeks of delivery
2. Variance in schedule on each phase

$$\frac{\text{actual duration} - \text{projected duration}}{\text{projected duration}}$$

3. Variance in cost

$$\frac{\text{actual cost} - \text{projected cost}}{\text{projected cost}}$$

4. Total design time/total programming time
   • should be at least 50% (Humphrey)
5. Defect injection and detection rates per phase
   • e.g., "One defect per class in detailed design phase"

Figure 2.42 Five Examples of Process Metrics

vorably with the organization's norm of five per 100. Looking across the "detailed requirements" row, we note that our process detected fewer than the normal rate of requirements defects during subsequent phases. This tells us that our project, and possibly the process we are using, is comparatively effective when it comes to producing quality requirements.

The results for design defects are as follows. We detected more than the usual number of design defects during inspections at the time they were produced, but recognized fewer design defects at a later stage. Since it is more expensive to detect and repair a defect later in the process, this indicates that our project, and possibly our process, are superior to the organization norms.

To complete the table, we would include similar defect data collected during testing, and during a specific time (e.g., three months) after product delivery.

The metrics shown in Figure 2.42 summarize appropriate process metrics, and include the defect metrics described above. Note that only the numbers *compared with company or industry norms* constitute the process metrics: The numbers alone are not sufficient to evaluate the process used. For example, if our project has one defect per KLOC after delivery, detected within the first six months, and the company norm (i.e., for the same period, per KLOC) is 1.3 defects, then our process may well be an improvement. To establish this, we would need to run several projects with a given process, and compare average data.

For more process metrics, see [IEEE 982]. The next section discusses ways to use metric data in order to improve the process.

7. Test
    - *can reference Software Test Documentation*

8. Problem reporting and corrective action

9. Tools, techniques, and methodologies
    - *can reference SPMP*

10. Code control
    - *reference SCMP*

11. Media control

12. Supplier control

13. Records collection, maintenance, and retention

14. Training

15. Risk Management
    - *can reference SPMP*

Figure 2.43 IEEE 739-1989 Software Quality Assurance Table of Contents, Part 2 of 2   Copyright © 1989 IEEE

One Way To. . . Gather Process Metrics

1. Identify and define metrics team will use by phase; include
    - time spent on 1. research 2. execution 3. review
    - size (e.g., lines of code)
    - # defects detected per unit (e.g., lines of code)(include source)
    - quality self-assessment of each other on scale of 1 to 10 (maintain bell-shaped distribution)

2. Document these in the SQAP.

3. Accumulate historical data by phase.

4. Decide where the metric data will be placed.
    - as the project progresses
    - SQAP? SPMP? Appendix?

5. Designate engineers to manage collection by phase.
    - QA leader or phase leaders (e.g., design leader)

6. Schedule reviews of data for lessons learned.
    - specify when and how to feed back improvement

Figure 2.44 One Way to Gather Process Metrics

12.2 IEEE 739-1989 SQAP: Part 2

As introduced in Chapter 1, quality considerations in a project can be spelled out in a quality document such as the SQAP. The latter half of the SQAP has the appearance of Figure 2.43. It is sometimes preferable if parts of the SQAP simply refer to other documents, as shown in Figure 2.43. Trying to duplicate them or parts of them violates our "single source" documentation rule. The case study illustrates how the remaining topics can be addressed.

Figure 2.44 contains a sequence of actions which can be taken throughout the life of a project in order to continually improve the process.

Table 2.6 is an example of the kind of data that can be collected about the process. It is applied to the process of collecting detailed requirements, which is covered in Chapter 4,

TABLE 2.6 Project Metric Collection for Phases

Requirements Document: 200 detailed requirements	Meeting	Research	Execution	Personal Review	Inspection
Hours spent	0.5×4	4	5	3	6
% of total time	10%	20%	25%	15%	30%
% of total time: norm for the organization	15%	15%	30%	15%	25%
Self-assessed quality 1–10	2	8	5	4	6
Defects per 100	N/A	N/A	N/A	5	6
Defects per 100: organization norm	N/A	N/A	N/A	3	4
Hours spent per detailed requirement	0.01	0.02	0.025	0.015	0.03
Hours spent per detailed requirement: organization norm	0.02	0.02	0.04	0.01	0.03
Process improvement	Improve "straw man" brought to meeting		Spend 10% more time executing		

Summary: Productivity: 200/22 = 9.9 detailed requirements per hour
Probable remaining defect rate: 6/4 × [organizational norm of 0.8 per hundred]
= 1.2 per hundred

but the table is applicable to most phases. The numbers are illustrative only, and should not be regarded as industry standards. A comparison with the organization's normative data reveals deficiencies in the team's meeting process, and in their individual execution (i.e., the actual writing process). This exposes problems in meetings, for example, which was subjectively evaluated "2" out of 10 by the team. It was determined (not visible in the data) that the meeting process would improve if the straw man proposal brought to the meeting was more finished.

The other problem observed is during the execution step, where the actual work of writing the requirements is performed. The defect rate is higher than normal (5 versus 3) and the self-assessed quality is a little below average (4). Compared with company norms, there appears to be room to spend more time executing the work (i.e., as individuals), thereby reducing the defect count, and improving the subjective self-assessment. The reader can observe from this process that a standard for counting the parts of the phase is fundamental to our ability to measure it. In this case, we are counting "detailed requirements," a concept that will be explained in Chapter 4.

The "remaining defect rate" refers to the number of defective detailed requirements per 100 remaining in the requirements document after this phase has been completed. This measures how effective we have been at this activity. The remaining defect rate is determined by computing a proportion of the organization's historical remaining defect rate. We know the latter by counting the defects per 100 detailed requirements found in past projects after the requirements document has been completed. These were found during design, implementation, and testing. The proportion used, 6/4, is "requirements defect rate found in this project" divided by the "average requirements defect rate." The principle is that the defect rates for a step are likely to be comparable to those for the previous step. A more reliable predictor would also take into account the defect rates for prior steps as well (during personal inspection, in this case). This would require linear regression.

Even in the absence of historical data, the team predicts in advance what the values of the metrics should and will be. With these advance predictions, teams tend to work better, and they tend to remember results. The data collected becomes the basis for future historical data. Managing all of this is not technically difficult, but it has to be done at the same time as many other urgent activities. For this reason, the assignment of clear responsibilities, and the regular review of the metric data is worked out at this early stage in the process. As will be seen in the next section, it is the process of feeding back process improvement that separates great development organizations from merely good ones.

13. PROCESS IMPROVEMENT AND THE CAPABILITY MATURITY MODEL

As described in the preceding chapter, the highest CMM level is attained by continually improving the process itself using a meta-process. But how can this be done on a regular basis? There are two levels of process improvement. The first improves the way the organization develops applications. The second improves the process being used in a current project.

13.1 Improving the Processes Used in an Organization

The overall improvement of process first requires a classification by job type and by process type. The job type classification depends on the organization. An example for a specialized shop is "motor control," "display," and "data collection," meaning that the applications dealt with in this organization have to be one of these types. Historical data can then be kept within this framework. Table 2.7 shows an example.

There would be similar tables for "display" and "data collection" applications. The question is "how can we use these to improve the process?" One way is to try to leverage the best parts of different processes. For example, according to Table 2.7, fewer defects are introduced at implementation time when the waterfall process is used for motor control applications, compared with the other processes, although a spiral with three iterations gave the best overall result. This suggests modifying our spiral process from Requirements(R)-Architecture(A)-Detailed design(D)-Implementation(I)-R-A-D-I-R-A-D-I to R-A-D-I-R-A-D-R-A-D-I, which retains a spiral with three iterations but which reduces the number of implementation iterations.

13.2 Improving the Process for a Project That Is Underway

The team can evaluate its performance on every process in a project, and then feed back the results for the next process, even while the project is underway. One way to do this is shown in Figure 2.45. An example of this procedure is shown in Table 2.8.

TABLE 2.7 Example of Process Comparison

Motor control applications	Process		
	Waterfall	Spiral, 2–4 iterations	Spiral, 5–10 iterations
Company average—Defects per thousand source lines of code at delivery time injected at . . .			
requirements time	4.2	3.2	2.4
architecture time	3.1	2.5	3.7
detailed design time	1.1	1.1	2.2
implementation time	1.0	2.1	3.5
Total	9.4	8.9	11.8

One Way To. . . Feed Back Process/Project Improvement

1. Decompose the process or subprocess being measured into *Preparation, Execution,* and *Review*
   • include *Research* if learning about the procedure
2. Note time taken, assess degree of quality for each part on a 1–10 scale, count defects
   • try to enforce a curve
3. Compute *quality/(percent time taken)*
4. Compare team's performance against existing data, if available
5. Use data to improve next subprocess
   • note poorest values first, e.g., low *quality/(percent time)*

Figure 2.45 One Way to Feed Back Process/Project Improvement

TABLE 2.8 Measuring Team Phase Performance

	For each part ...		
	Preparation	Execution	Review
% time	45	30	25
Quality (0 to 10)*	6	2	6
If low, investigate	—	*investigate*	—
Quality/(% time)	0.13	0.07	0.24
If low, investigate	*investigate*	*investigate*	—
Typical?	*No* [Joe lost specs]	*Yes*	*Yes*
Action	—	*Schedule 20% more time for execution, taken equally from other phases*	—

The lowest value for *quality* and also for *quality / (% time)* is for the *Execution* phase. The decision is made to take more time for this phase in the future, subtracting time from the other phases. The team will assess the impact of this, and decide whether or not there are other issues to resolve.

Organizations cannot reach pinnacle performance levels overnight, and so phased approaches have to be used to achieve high levels. Instead of trying to attain perfection in all ways at once, they can follow the PSP, TSP, and CMM, and lead teams through agreed-upon intermediate improvements in procedure and technique. The CMM levels provide a staged framework for process improvement. Organizations need to attain level 2 before embarking on level 3, and so on.

14. MISCELLANEOUS TOOLS AND TECHNIQUES FOR PROJECT MANAGEMENT

This section briefly discusses distance as a factor in software team formation. This is followed by a discussion of "extreme programming," an example of an approach to managing the process of developing applications. The final section discusses the use of triage as a general decision-making technique that can be useful for making reasonably fast decisions within complex situations.

14.1 Remote and International Teams

Managers naturally try to make use of worldwide programming talent to lower costs and improve quality. The per-hour costs of remote programmers are traded off, however, against the communication problems incurred by physical remoteness. The Internet has made remoteness less problematic. On the other hand, the requirement for more continual interaction with the customer is increasing for many applications, making face-to-face interaction essential. Options for remote teams are illustrated in Figure 2.46.

14.2 Extreme Programming

Extreme programming is a project management and development methodology created by Kent Beck [Be]. It is introduced here to provide the reader with some exposure to the wide variety of methods and techniques that are continually being tried, and to provide additional ideas for use in special circumstances. Interesting features of extreme programming include the emphasis on continual communication within the development organization and with the customer, radical simplicity (using the simplest solution possible), and pair programming. In pair programming, developers work in pairs at computers—never in isolation. The methodology is summarized in Figure 2.47.

We have already mentioned some of these techniques in other contexts. Having customer representatives on site with the developer has long been practiced by the Department of Defense for large projects: Extreme programming goes further, however, by having the customer representative participate directly in development (the author was once such a participant). This is a good idea in principle, although it introduces legal responsibility issues that not all organizations can handle. Perhaps the most radical feature of Beck's method is "pair programming," in which developers work only together in pairs at computers. This is, in effect, a form of continual inspection. Anderson et al. ([An]) report excellent results in their case study of extreme programming at Chrysler Corporation.

- Same office area
  - + ideal for group communication
  - − labor rates sub-optimal

- Same city, different offices
  - communication fair

- Same country, different cities
  - − communication difficult
  - + common culture

- Multi-country
  - − communication most difficult
  - − culture issues problematic
  - + labor rates optimal

Figure 2.46 Remote Team Configurations (Graphics reproduced with permission from Corel.)

Non-extreme	Extreme
• Customer separated	• Customer on team
• Up-front design	• Evolving design
• Build for future, too	• Just in time
• Complexity allowed	• Radical simplicity
• Tasks assigned	• Tasks self-chosen
• Developers isolated	• Pair programming
• Infrequent integration	• Continuous integration
• Limited communication	• Continual communication

Figure 2.47 Non-extreme vs. Extreme Programming (Adapted from [An])

Continual integration and evolutionary programming are particularly beneficial in some circumstances, such as the latter part of a project, and are reminiscent of the synch-and-stabilize methodology reportedly observed at Microsoft.

Every software engineer and project manager encounters a conflict between "radical simplicity" on one hand and an emphasis on generality and reuse on the other. The case study in this book emphases reuse: In many situations, however, a strong case can be made for radical simplicity. For example, you would probably feel less than comfortable if a contractor were to spend significant time refining his tools, designs, and methods for the benefit of his future jobs while he was building your house, unless you felt that his activities significantly improved your house.

14.3 Decision-Making with Triage

Executing projects is frequently an overwhelming experience. For example, a "to do" list of wants and needs accumulates quickly, and seems to grow during the project without bound. The natural way to deal with this is to prioritize. This ideal is frequently overwhelmed by events, however. For example, if we have a list of 100 things to do, and

if among top items in importance
    place it in <u>do at once</u> category
otherwise
    if item can be ignored without substantially
    affecting project
        place in <u>last to do</u> category
    otherwise
        place in <u>middle</u> category

Figure 2.48 Triage in Project Management

time for probably only 20 of them, then it is a waste of time to order all 100. *Triage* can be useful for situations like this.

Triage consists of making no more than two decisions about each item, as shown in Figure 2.48. Now, items from the "do at once" category are carried out until they are exhausted (if ever), and then we move on to the middle list etc. If necessary, items can be prioritized within their category. Little time is wasted in splitting hairs or wondering about the exact order of actions that will never be performed. As reported in Business Week [Bu], triage teams were used by Microsoft in combing through bug reports during the debugging of Windows™ 2000.

15. SUMMARY OF THE PROJECT MANAGEMENT PROCESS

The message of this chapter is that the way in which projects are managed is just as important as their technological aspects. Yourdon [Yo] goes so far as to claim that project management is the "silver bullet" that software professionals have been seeking to remedy the problems of late, overbudget, and inferior software products. The Software Project Management Plan is the principal vehicle for guiding the management of projects. A key aspect is the estimation of the project's costs, a process that requires continual revisiting throughout the life of the project. Major points of this chapter are summarized in Figure 2.49.

- Project management: "silver bullet"?
- "People" aspects co-equal technical
- Specify SPMP
- Define and retire risks
- Estimate costs using several methods
  - expect to revisit and refine
  - use ranges at this stage

- Schedule project with appropriate detail
- Maintain a balance among cost, schedule, quality, and functionality

Figure 2.49 Major Points of Chapter 2 (Graphics reproduced with permission from Corel.)

PROJECT MANAGEMENT PLAN FOR THE *ENCOUNTER* CASE STUDY

This section explains how the principles explained in this chapter are translated into practice, by using the case study as the example.

Before beginning the Software Project Management Plan (SPMP), the team met at least once to discuss the project in general terms, and Ed Braun was selected as team leader. The configuration management plan (SCMP) and quality plan (SQAP) were written.

SPG1. PREPARING FOR THE PROJECT PLANNING MEETING

Well before the meeting, Ed looked through the IEEE SPMP headings (refer to Figure 2.41) for the major issues, and drafted material for each of them. In the case of the *Encounter* video game, he considered these to be *objectives and priorities* (Item 3.1 in Figure 2.41), *project organization* (primary and backup roles, and their responsibilities) (2.4), *risk management* (3.3), and the *schedule* (5.5). Ed also drafted a brief paragraph for Section 1.1 (*project overview*). He left the staffing plan blank (i.e., who fills what role) because he felt it best to have members volunteer for roles at the meeting. He planned for the remaining issues to be filled in after the meeting. Via e-mail, Ed asked for a volunteer to perform cost estimation, since this is a technical task that requires significant lead time, and is best done by one, or at most two people.

Ed wrote up options for *objectives and priorities* rather than selecting the top priority, since he did not want the group to feel railroaded into a decision. He included "attaining quality goals," "developing something that the members can use" (a favorite of his), and "complete project on schedule" as options for the top priority. He was pretty sure that the group would agree to a flat

role-based organization as described in Section 2.10 on page 107, so he wrote this into the straw man document.

Via e-mail, Ed asked team members to think about the risks that they consider threatening to the project, and to send write-ups to him 48 hours before the meeting, in the form of Table 2.2 on page 88. Karen was concerned about the group's Java capabilities. She communicated with the rest of the team about their knowledge of Java, and described this risk as specifically as she could. She also researched companies that provide on site training at short notice. Her step-by-step risk retirement plan was included in the material she sent to Ed. Hal Furnass had a concern about superimposing images in Java, and he sent his risk identification and retirement write-up to Ed. The latter collected these in the straw man SPMP, and listed them in priority.

Ed then drafted the following agenda for the meeting:

Meeting to be held in Engineering 397 at 10:00 A.M. to 11:30 A.M. Saturday, September 11

1. Appoint record keeper and time keeper (5 minutes—10:05)

2. Approve agenda and times for this meeting (5 minutes—10:10)

3. Review SPMP sections supplied by Ed (25 minutes—10:35)

4. Allocate remaining SPMP section to writers (20 minutes—10:55)

5. Arrange review process (5 minutes—11:00)

—e-mail and/or meet

6. Brainstorm for additional risks (10 minutes—11:10)

7. Review action items (5 minutes—11:15)

8. Miscellaneous business (10 minutes—11:25)

Ed e-mailed the agenda and his strawman SPMP to the team members two days before the meeting, and asked them to read it over before the meeting. His version of the SPMP contained all of the IEEE headings.

SPG2. THE INITIAL PROJECT PLANNING MEETING

At the meeting, Ed asked Fern to record action items and major decisions, and asked Al to watch the time and remind the team if it exceeded planned limits. It was understood that these two roles would rotate among the members in future meetings. Most of Ed's ideas were accepted. Several changes to Ed's proposed schedule were suggested. Hal pushed very hard for a buffer week in which no tasks are assigned. Karen pointed out that no work should be assigned during the week before the midterm. There was also a discussion of using a simple waterfall to avoid the complications of revisiting document, but this was dismissed as not reflecting the real world. Fern pushed for incremental development because she wanted to begin coding as soon as possible, but there was little support for this because the team did not even have architecture yet. Members felt that "quality" was an area they needed the most practice with. After considerable debate about building an exciting computer game, the team decided that "the attainment of the specified quality parameters" would be its top priority. It was recognized that a quality game worth playing was out of the question in the time available, and that the actual capabilities would be have to be minimal. When the team arrived at role allocation, Karen volunteered immediately for the "design leader" role. There were three volunteers for "implementation leader" and none for QA leader. Ed compromised by suggesting that two of the three people split roles as QA and implementation leaders, switching halfway through the semester. The other roles were filled, and Ed reminded them of their responsibilities, and of their additional backup roles, as stated in the SPMP.

The discussion of how to allocate the writing of the SPMP went over its planned limit, but the discussion was productive and to the point, so Ed did not try to curtail it. It was decided that only two team members besides Ed would write the SPMP, and the rest would review their writing, since it would be too difficult in a short time to manage more people writing. After 10 minutes, the team found itself discussing very small sections, and Ed cut off discussion, promising to resolve the small differences offline, and e-mail the two members concerned a detailed allocation of the sections. The team decided that the writers would complete their sections by Friday at 6:00 P.M., and Ed would create the document from these and circulate the results to the team by Saturday at 3:00 P.M. Everyone would provide comments to Ed by Sunday at 3:00 P.M., and Ed would take all of these comments into account to finalize the document. A tentative meeting was set for Monday at 11:00 A.M. in Arts 283 in case it was necessary, and Ed was tasked with informing the team by Sunday night at 8:00 P.M. whether the meeting would be required or not.

Fern reviewed the decisions made—mainly who was to write what sections, and when the due dates were. The meeting adjourned.

SPG3. COMPLETING THE PROJECT MANAGEMENT PLAN

In writing the document details, the team realized that various issues had not been discussed at the meeting, including the details of "monitoring and controlling" (item 3.4 on Figure 2.41). Hal's initial write-up of this section spoke of many meetings at which the project was to be reviewed, but most of the other members felt that many of the meetings were unnecessary. After reading several proposals, Ed tried to resolve the e-mail discussion by proposing that project monitoring be accomplished at weekly meetings, supplemented by meeting at the inception of each phase (which he would try to fold into weekly meetings as well). The team agreed. To allow for the possibility that more project meetings would be needed, a second weekly time was selected which members would keep available, but would be used only if required.

[Note to the student: The case study contains material concerning liaison activities.

These are shown for illustration purposes, and would not normally be the responsibility of student teams. Some teams might want to designate a member as liaison to the instructor. This is usually best performed by the team leader. If the project has a true customer (i.e., the project is not just an invention of the team itself), then a liaison to the customer would be required: The requirements leader would normally have this task.]

EXERCISES

Solutions and hints are given at the end of this chapter to all exercises marked with "s" or "h" respectively.

REVIEW QUESTIONS

For hints and solutions, see below.

R2.1[h] Give five stages in the process of planning a software project.

R2.2[s] How would you organize responsibilities among three very experienced engineers on a three-person-month job? Describe in about three sentences how decisions would be made.

R2.3[s] What effective form of organization could one use for 100 engineers on a 4000-person-month job? Describe this is in about four sentences.

R2.4[s] List at least two consequences of failing to develop a written project plan.

R2.5[s] List a part of the SPMP that you are probably unable to supply at this stage. This refers to a part you will have to return to after more work has been performed on the project.

R2.6[s] Why plan for risk identification and retirement when developing the project plan?

R2.7[s] Describe a kind of project under which risk identification and retirement will probably not pay off.

R2.8[s] Cost estimation is important, but can you cite a circumstance under which it is probably not worthwhile to perform a cost estimation?

R2.9[s] Give one major advantage and one major disadvantage to the use of function points in estimation.

R2.10[s] Give one major advantage and one major disadvantage to the use of Boehm's methods in estimation.

R2.11[s] What are process metrics? Give three examples. What are they good for?

TEAM EXERCISES

T2.1 (SPMP) Develop a Software Project Management Plan for your project. Use (or tailor, or improve upon) the IEEE standard, as shown in the case study below. Include at least two iterations in the schedule. Obtain a rough estimate of the size of the product.

Before you begin, estimate the number of defects per page the team thinks it will discover during its final review. Keep track of, and report the time spent by individual members and by total team effort in the following stages: research, document preparation, review (including inspections). Show the actual defect density (average number of defects per page). Assess your team's effectiveness in each stage on a scale of 0 to 10. Summarize in a narrative, using the numerical results, and state how the team's process could have been improved. The team is encouraged to use additional metrics if they contribute to effectiveness in this and future efforts.

> *Evaluation criteria:*
>
> α. *degree of clarity of the plan and addendum—A = very clear writing; all specifics included, especially of risk retirement*
>
> β. *degree of realism of the plan and addendum—A = sets realistic goals and procedures (neither too ambitious nor too modest)*
>
> γ. *extent to which the plan and addendum include all relevant specifics—A = > 95% of knowable, relevant specifics included*
>
> δ. *extent to which the plan and addendum exclude irrelevant material—A = < 5% of details supplied irrelevant*
>
> ε. *usefulness of your self-assessment*

T2.2   (SQAP) Produce a realistic software quality assurance plan for your project. Measure the time spent on this effort by individual members and by the complete team.

Provide the corresponding metric data and self-assessment for this assignment, as described in T2.1 above.

> *Criteria: as for T1.2*

HINTS FOR REVIEW QUESTIONS

R2.1   Refer to the "roadmap for project management" in Figure 2.5.

SOLUTIONS TO REVIEW QUESTIONS

R2.2   Assuming that team members are interested, a good way to organize a small project is to establish it as a community of equals, designating someone as the project leader. He or she would provide leadership, break ties, and monitor the schedule. Individuals on the team can each take on a responsibility for a particular part of the process.

R2.3   A job this size requires considerable regimentation in overall structure. A management hierarchy has to be selected (at least a project manager/section heads/software engineers). A relatively small team of senior engineers would have to be assigned to build initial requirements analysis and architecture. Once the job is decomposed into parts, section heads can be assigned responsibility for each part, and each part can be provided with a staff of engineers. Section heads may decide to apply peer teams within their organizations.

R2.4   Without a written plan, even the most competent of developers will waste time and effort. Whether or not we express a plan in writing, some sort of plan exists, if only in the minds of several engineers. When not written, the plan has to be conveyed by word of mouth. Although this sounds quaint, it is unprofessional in the extreme, and highly unlikely to result in a professional product. In passing information by word of mouth, issues become distorted, including:

- What development process is being used.
- Who is to do what, and when they are to do it.
- What risks loom in the future. Without a risk identification and retirement plan, the development effort is at the mercy of unknown future obstacles.

R2.5   One can provide a schedule in outline, but it is not possible to provide many details yet. This is because details require us to know how the job breaks down, and we do not know this yet, because we have not done any architectural design work.

R2.6   Every project has risks to cost, schedule, and quality. Trying hard to identify them at the very beginning provides the maximum amount of time to retire them: This minimizes the damage that such risks can inflict.

R2.7 It is possible that the process of identifying and retiring risks yields few of them, and of those few, the circumstances for their retirement would have been encountered anyway. In such cases, one would have wasted the time spent on this activity, and the only tangible result would be peace of mind.

R2.8 One is tempted to answer this question by citing very small projects that *have* to be performed, regardless. One would argue that the time taken to make the estimate would cut too much into the time taken to perform the job. But even this situation does not justify skipping cost estimation. You can think of cost estimation as absorbing a fraction of the time it takes to execute the job. The size of the job is not highly relevant. If the practitioner is completely unpracticed and unschooled in the art of estimation, it may indeed be unjustified. After all, taken to its logical conclusion, it can't be a good thing for three engineers to learn about estimation for two weeks, then apply what they have learned, when the job is a 2-person-month effort! For large jobs, on the other hand, such time spent learning is much less of a problem.

R2.9 Advantage: the ability to make estimates very early in the development process. Disadvantage: the potentially wide variation in function point calculation, especially by inexperienced practitioners or for unique programming applications

R2.10 Advantages: the ability to estimate both labor and duration; the precision of the formulas. Disadvantage: the method's reliance on lines of code, since this is often unknown.

R2.11 Process metrics measure the effectiveness of a process. For example, we can ask whether within our particular organization at a particular time, a simple waterfall method is superior to a spiral method. Measures which accomplish this include

- (Total time spent on design)/(Total time spent on development)
  - Should be 0.5 or slightly greater, typically
- (Defects per 1000 NCSLOC in delivered code) / (Company average)
- (Fraction of undocumented requirements) / (Company average)
- [(Actual duration of project) / (Estimated duration of project)] / (Company average)

The last three metrics suggest measures of the process, although each individual project may be different enough to distort the measure. The test mentions metrics that focus on the effectiveness of parts of the process.

CASE STUDY 1:
SPMP FOR THE *ENCOUNTER* VIDEO GAME

Approvals:

F. Lowrey   _____

A. Arneson   _____

M. Moray   _____

H. Little   _____

5/1/98 E. Braun: initial version

2/2/99 H. Furnass: reviewed and made miscellaneous suggestions for improvement

5/16/99 E. Braun: made schedule more detailed, included references to IV&V

5/29/99 E. Braun: final review for release

1. INTRODUCTION

1.1 Project Overview

[Note to the student: Every project has a unique history and vision. This is the place to state these. The size of this section depends on whom the SPMP is written for. If it is mostly for the team's benefit, then this section should be small, confining itself to a high level, but including specific items that reflect the team's consensus on overall scope. If the readership of the document goes well beyond the team, this paragraph will

have to explain more about the context of the project.]

This project is organized to produce a role-playing video game called "Encounter." This game will be developed in several stages since the customer intends to specify the requirements in stages, following the demonstration of each version. The early versions are for educational purposes, as examples of software engineering practice, and as legacy systems on which students may build their own video games. The later versions are expected to be either freeware games, or commercial products marketed by a game marketing organization.

1.2 Project Deliverables

The following are to be delivered at the times shown:

Version 1 (prototype) and supporting documents listed below: week two of month two

Version 2 and supporting documents listed below: week three of month five

The supporting documents are this SCMP,* SQAP,* SVVP,* SCMP,* SRS,* SDD,* STD,* Source code, Compiled Java byte code, Software Maintenance Plan,* and User Manual.

Acronyms are defined in Section 1.5 below.

1.3 Evolution of the SPMP

[Note to the student: explains how and by whom this document will be maintained. It will have to be modified in several ways (e.g., with a more detailed schedule as more is known about the requirements). If a specific person is not tasked to maintain this document, it will be worked on sporadically or not at all.]

This document shall be maintained on a weekly basis by the project leader. It is subject to configuration management by means of the SCMP. It is the project leader's responsibility to submit this document as a CI, and to keep it up to date. This SPMP mainly follows the format of IEEE 1058.1-1987.

1.4 Reference Materials

[IEEE] The applicable IEEE standards are published in "IEEE Standards Collection," 1997 edition.

[MPACL5] This document is to conform to the company's "Master Plan for the Attainment of CMM Level 5"

[Braude] The principal source of textbook reference material is "Software Engineering: an Object-Oriented Perspective" by E. Braude (Wiley, 2000)

1.5 Acronyms

CI = Configuration Item

CMM = Capability Maturity Model—the SEI's model for organizational improvement

IEEE = Institute of Electrical and Electronics Engineers

QA = Quality Assurance

SEI = Software Engineering Institute, Pittsburgh, PA

SCMP = Software Configuration Management Plan

SPMP = Software Project Management Plan (this document)

SRS = Software Requirements Specification

SDD = Software Design Document

STP = Software Test Plan

tbd = to be decided

2. PROJECT ORGANIZATION

2.1 Process Model

The first two versions of this project will be executed using a Spiral Development process with an iteration corresponding to each version. The iterations are to be grouped according to the classification used in the USDP. (*The Unified Software Development Process*, by Jacobson, Rumbaugh, Booch; Addison-Wesley; 1999). The USDP groups iterations into Inception, Elaboration, Construction, and

---

*IEEE standards will be used for each document with an asterisk.

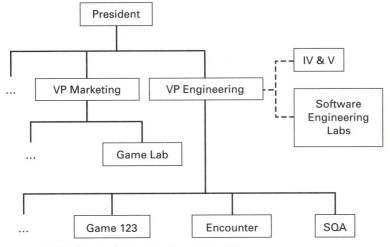

Figure 2.50 "Gaming Industries Consolidated"

Transition iterations. The first iteration will be considered the only Inception iteration. The second iteration is the first of the Elaboration iterations. This will be version 1 of *Encounter*. The number of subsequent iterations, and the nature of version 2 is to be decided after the customer has witnessed a demonstration.

2.2 Organizational structure

Figure 2.50 shows the organization of the *Encounter* project within Gaming Industries Consolidated. The project shall be organized as a team of peers with designated roles. The roles are *team leader*, the configuration management leader, the quality assurance leader, the requirements management leader, the design leader, and the implementation leader. In addition, there are *liaison* roles to marketing and to the software engineering laboratory. These roles are shown in Figure 2.51. The *Encounter* project will employ inspections, as described in the SQAP. Each team member will be included in the inspection of all of the work of the other team members, as indicated in Figure 2.51. This will occur either as part of a regular group inspection

or, if time does not allow this, an inspection performed by the author and his backup.

2.3 Organizational Boundaries and Interfaces

[Note to the student: Name the people and organizations with which the team will communicate.]

The project team shall interface with the following individuals and organizations: VP Engineering, Marketing, Game Laboratory, the Independent V&V Team, and the Software Engineering Laboratory.

2.4 Project Responsibilities

The responsibilities of the participants in the project are shown in Table 2.9. Being responsible for a document includes the following:

• Making sure that the document is created on time

• Having the team leader identify the writers of the document

• Keeping the document up-to-date throughout the project life cycle

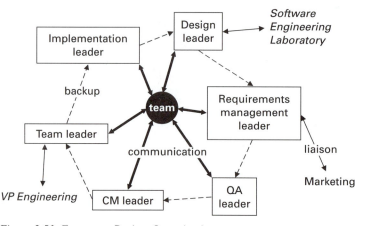

Figure 2.51 Encounter Project Organization

TABLE 2.9 ENCOUNTER PROJECT RESPONSIBILITIES

Member	Team Leader	CM Leader	QA Leader	Requirements Management Leader	Design Leader	Implementation Leader
Liaison Respon- sibility	VP Engineering			Marketing	Software Engineering Lab	
Document Respon- sibility	SPMP	SCMP	SQAP STP	SRS	SDD	Code Base

3. MANAGERIAL PROCESS

3.1 Management Objectives and Priorities

[Note to the student: These express the relative priority of schedule, budget, and capability. Capability is divided into extent to which requirements are satisfied, degree of quality, and reusability. Strictly speaking, reusability is an aspect of the requirements.]

The highest management priority shall be the attainment of the specified quality parameters. The second priority is that the product be on schedule. The third priority shall be satisfying as many requirements as possible. The fourth priority of this project is to produce reusable classes for use by other video game projects. A desirable video game is expected only for version 3 and higher.

3.2 Assumptions, Dependencies, and Constraints

[Note to the student: State any assumptions being made about issues and events external to the project; constraints on the project caused by external issues and events]

None

3.3 Risk management

[Note to the student: Elaborate on the risks as specific "bad happenings": Do not leave as generic titles. For example, "deficient Java skills" by itself does not specify the issue. Perhaps the project can be performed adequately by a team whose Java skills have deficiencies.]

Table 2.10 shows a format for risk reporting and retirement. Each project meeting is to have an agenda item for risk identifica-

TABLE 2.10 Risk Table for *Encounter*

Risk #	Risk title (detailed description follow)	Likelihood to occur (L, 1–10)	Impact (I, 1–10)	Retire-ment cost (R, 1–10)	Priority do in order (11-L)× (11-I)×R	Retire-ment or mitigation plan	Respon-sible engineer	Target completion date
1	Super-imposing images	3	10	1	(11-3)× (11-10) ×1=8	Experiment with Java images	PR	2/1/99
2	Deficient Java skills	9	10	7	(11-9)× (11-10) ×7=14	All on referenced list to attend training course beginning 1/5/99 at Ultra Training Corp, obtain ABC certification by 3/1/99 and XYZ certification by 4/15/99	HL	4/15/99
3	. . .	. . .	. . .	. . .		. . .	. . .	. . .

The method for computing relative priority is from Braude, Chapter 2, Section 4.4

tion brainstorming, and reporting on risks that have been identified. Risk #1 "Superimposing images" concerns image manipulation in Java. This is a required capability, because characters have to move about, superimposed on background images. No one in the team has experience with placing the image of a character against a background without carrying a rectangle along with the character. We do not know if this is easy, difficult, or impossible to do.

Risk #2 "Deficient Java skills" indicates the fact that 40% of the team is not sufficiently skilled in Java to implement the movement of and interaction of character images. We anticipate that it will also be necessary to scale the game environment, which no one on the team has any experience with. We do not know whether the capabilities that our customer has in mind are do-able with Java, and even if they are, we do not know how long it will

take to come up to speed. This could damage the project irreparably.

3.4 Monitoring and Controlling Mechanism

[Note to the student: It is usually advisable to schedule regular meetings (typically weekly). When there is no business, such meetings can easily be cancelled. On the other hand, scheduling a meeting on short notice is difficult because team members accumulate other commitments. Even teams which work together every day need to schedule regular review meetings to avoid drifting.]

The entire team will meet at the beginning of each phase (requirements, design, and implementation) of each iteration. There will be weekly project meetings on Tuesdays from 10:00 A.M. to noon. Every effort will be made to accomplish all team business during that

Responsibility	Leader	Facilitator	Marketing liaison	QA liaison	Game lab liaison	Risk retirement
Report at weekly meeting	X		X	X		X
Circulate weekly report				3*		
Circulate biweekly report					4*	
Circulate monthly report	1*		2*			

*Report formats	
1	see CI 34: "monthly project status form"
2	see CI 87: "monthly marketing status form"
3	see CI 344: "weekly QA status form"
4	see CI 48: "biweekly game lab result form"

Figure 2.52 Program Monitoring and Control

time. Team members are requested to keep Friday mornings from 9:00 A.M. to 11:00 A.M. open for an additional meeting, in case such a meeting becomes necessary. The team leader will inform the team by Thursday at 4:30 P.M. if the latter meeting is to take place.

[Note to the student: In a realistic project, various people would be responsible for periodic reports, typified by Figure 2.52.]

3.5 Staffing Plan

The roles will be filled as in Table 2.11. Each team member has an additional role as a backup and inspector, as shown in Figure 2.52.

4.   TECHNICAL PROCESS

[Note to the student: This section describes the technology that will be used, but we restrict it to aspects that are not specifically requirements.]

The SRS describes several aspects of the required technical process. This section describes those aspects of the process which are not explicitly stated in the SRS.

4.1 Methods, Tools, and Techniques

The *Encounter* project will use Rational Rose™ for design, and will be imple-

mented in Java. Object orientation is to be used throughout. Javadoc will be used for documentation as much as possible (see the SRS for this requirement). Refer to Section 2.1 (process model) for a description of the process.

4.2 Software Documentation

See the SQAP Section 4.2.

4.3 Project Support Functions

A technical support specialist will be assigned halftime throughout the life of the project.

5.   WORK PACKAGES, SCHEDULE, AND BUDGET

5.1 Work Packages

The work breakdown structure is shown in Figure 2.53. The bottom line shows the person-months available for each month.

[Note to the student: We have not yet performed any design, so it is too early to actually name the engineers who will work on specific parts. These names will be added here after the designs for the various configurations have been determined.]

TABLE 2.11 *Encounter* Staffing Plan

Name	Team Leader	CM Leader	QA Leader	Requ. Management Leader	Design Leader	Implementation Leader
Ed Braun	X					X
Al Pruitt		X				
Fern Tryfill			X			
Hal Furnass				X		
Karen Peters					X	
Liaison with	VP Eng.			Marketing	Soft. Eng. Lab	

	Month 1				Month 2				Month 3				Month 4				Month 5			
	1	2	3	4	1	2	3	4	1	2	3	4	1	2	3	4	1	2	3	4
Milestones		SCMP				SQAP								Freeze requirements				Complete testing	Delivery	
			SPMP release 1																	
Tasks		Iteration 1																		
		Risk I & R									Iteration 2									
E. Braude	1	1	1	1	1	1	1	1	1	1	1	1	1	1	1	1	1	1	1	1
A. Pruitt	1	1	1	1	1	1	1	1	1	1	1	1	1	1	1	1	1			
F. Tryfill	1	1	1	1	1	1	1	1	1	1	1	1								
H. Furnass	1	1	1	1	1	1	1	1	1	1	1	1	1	1	1	1	1	1	1	1
K. Peters	1	1	1	1	1	1	1	1					1	1	1	1	1	1	1	
F. Smith (tech support)	.5	.5	.5	.5	.5	.5	.5	.5	.5	.5	.5	.5	.5	.5	.5	.5	.5	.5	.5	.5
TOTAL	5.5	5.5	5.5	5.5	5.5	5.5	5.5	5.5	4.5	4.5	4.5	4.5	4.5	4.5	4.5	4.5	4.5	4.5	3.5	3.5

Figure 2.53 Work Breakdown Structure for Encounter Project

5.2 Dependencies

[Note to the student: relationship among the work packages. This section will be revisited after the design has been determined. At this point, we are only able to provide very high-level dependencies.]

Iteration two is dependent on the completion of iteration one.

Engineers Sellars and Furnass are working on the Game 123 project, and there is a 50% chance that they will be unavailable for the first month of this project.

5.3 Resource Requirements

[Note to the student: The cost to build the first three iterations of Encounter is estimated in Section 8 of this chapter. The computations and results would be placed here, or in an appendix.]

The project will require seven engineers, one half-time secretary, one half-time tech support.

The hardware resources are eight 500mHz Pentium computers running Windows 95 and Symantec Visual Café

TABLE 2.12 Very Rough Estimate of Application Size Prior to Requirements Analysis

Method	Minimum	Maximum	Comment
(1)	7.5*	170	
(2)	4.2	300	
(3)	11.4	46	1.9–2.3 for two identical functions × 6–20 times as many in complete application
Most conservative	11.4	300	Maximum of minimums and maximum of maximums
Least conservative	4.2	46	Minimum of minimums and minimum of maximums
Widest range	4.2	300	Minimum of minimums and maximum of maximums
Narrowest	11.4	46	Maximum of minimums and minimums of maximums

*All figures in K-lines of Java source code.

version 3.0. Each of these computers should have at least 128 MB RAM and 6GB of disk space.

5.4 Budget and Resource Allocations

[Note to the student: This section explains how funds are to be spent. This begins with the cost estimates which were carried out in Section 8 of this chapter. Cost estimates are refined as the project progresses.]

Estimate before beginning requirements analysis:

We have estimated the size of this effort in three different ways.

1. Using an informal top-down estimate based on the experience of team members with somewhat similar projects.

2. Using a top-down approximation with industry game development data.

3. Using function points on two known functions, extrapolating to the entire application.

The results are shown in Table 2.12.

[Note to the student: There are many ways of presenting this data, depending on the needs of management and the development staff. Some of these are shown in Table 2.12. Without performing requirements analysis, estimates are still very rough.]

The reason for the very wide range is that the figures have been obtained with negligible interaction with the customer.

Estimate using customer requirements, before beginning detailed requirements:

to be supplied

Estimate using detailed requirements, before beginning architecture:

to be supplied

Estimate using architecture, before beginning detailed design:

to be supplied

Estimate using detailed design, before beginning implementation:

to be supplied

Estimate at the end of iteration 1, before beginning iteration 2:

to be supplied

Estimate at the end of iteration 2, before beginning iteration 3:

to be supplied

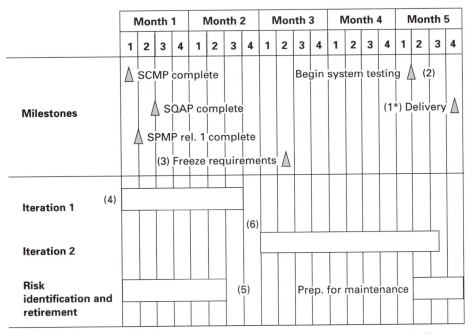

*Indicates the order in which the parts of this table were built

Figure 2.54 High-level Task Chart for Encounter With Fixed Delivery Date

5.5 Schedule

[Note to the student: If we are given a fixed completion date, and have identified the general process that we will use, we may have enough information to provide a high-level schedule. We increase the amount of detail in the schedule as more becomes known about the design.]

The schedule is shown in Figure 2.54. Refer to the SQAP for the schedule of quality activities.

6. ADDITIONAL COMPONENTS

6.1 Index

to be supplied

6.2 Appendices

to be supplied

CASE STUDY 2:

SOFTWARE QUALITY ASSURANCE PLAN PART 2 OF 2

See Chapter 1 for Part 1 of this SQAP (Sections 1 through 6).

7. TEST

[Note to the student: This section describes how testing is to be managed. The text here should refer to, but not duplicate the software test documentation.]

For the first three iterations, the QA leader will perform all of the Quality Control (QC) functions. For subsequent iterations, the QC team, appointed by the QA department manager, will take over this function. A description of the QC team will be supplied. The

Encounter development team is responsible for testing individual methods and combinations of methods in a class ("unit testing"). The quality leader and the QC team are responsible for all other testing. (See *Braude* Chapters 8 and 9 for the background information on these types of tests). Refer to the Software Test Documentation for details on testing *Encounter*.

8. PROBLEM REPORTING AND CORRECTIVE ACTION

[Note to the student: This section explains how defects come to be recognized, described, and repaired. They do not follow the details of IEEE standards. The reader is referred to the IEEE standards, as well as to Humphrey [Hu] for additional defect severity and type classifications.]

The Problem Reporting Form to be used by the *Encounter* development team in response to a software problem report generated by QA is shown in Figure 2.55. To use this form, engineers should execute the *describeDefect* application on directory *QA*. The defect number will appear automatically, and the application will ensure that the appropriate fields are filled in.

The values for severity are as follows:

Major: results in requirements not satisfied

Trivial: will not affect the execution of the application or its maintenance

Minor: neither major nor trivial

Engineers are not encouraged to create defect reports for trivial defects, but to send e-mail to the engineer most likely to be in a position to repair the defect.

The documentation defect type are missing material, unclear, ambiguous, incomplete, redundant (within or between documents), and contradictory.

The code defects type are syntax, logic, data (i.e., allows a wrong variable value), and insecure (allows unacceptable security breach).

The QA leader and, later, the QA team will create and maintain a database of problem reports that describe the deficiencies, discrepancies, and anomalies for *Encounter*. They ensure that defects are consistently recorded on this form, and that they are routed and repaired in a consistent manner. Problem reports shall be routed in accordance with the SCMP.

After iteration three, when a problem is encountered, the QA manager will distribute the problem report to the members of the Change Control Board (CCB). For the first three releases, the configuration specialist will carry out the functions of the QA team, and the project leader will perform all of the CCB functions in accordance with the SPMP. The CCB evaluates the problem report and then assigns a priority to the report of either *immediate*, *to be done*, or *optional*. The problem report is then assigned by the CCB either to the *Encounter* development team, QA, or CM for resolution. The CCB determines the schedule for problem report resolution based upon problem report priority and analysis report results. After the problem in the report is corrected, the QA team reviews the results and the QA manager reports on the review to the CCB. If necessary, the process is repeated.

9. TOOLS, TECHNIQUES, AND METHODOLOGIES

SQA (Software Quality Assurance) *techniques* include the auditing of standards, requirements tracing, design verification, software inspections, and the verification of formal methods. The SQA *tools* consist of software verification programs, checklists, media labels, and acceptance stamps. Checklists will be obtained from the company's software engineering laboratory, and tailored for *Encounter*. These are augmented by NASA checklists at [Na]. Checklists include the following:

• Review checklists are used at formal meetings, for document reviews, and for inspections.

1. Defect Number:	2. Proposer:

3. Documents/sections affected:

Source code affected*:   4. Package(s) _____
5. Class(es) _____   6. Method(s) _____
7. Severity: _____   8. Type: _____

9. Phase injected**:
Req ☐   Arch ☐   Dtld. Dsg ☐   Code ☐   Int ☐

10. Detailed description: _____
11. Resolution: 12. Status closed / open:

Sign-off: Description and plan inspected: _____
14. Resolution code and test plan inspected: _____
15. Change approved for incorporation: _____

*for source code defects   **earliest phase with the defect

Figure 2.55 Problem Reporting Form Example

- Checklists will be used for verifying the quality of the following activities and documents: Preliminary Design Review, Critical Design Review, Test Readiness Review, Functional Configuration Audit, Physical Configuration Audit, SRS, SDD, SPMP, and Software Development Folders.

- Separate checklists and forms are used for software audit purposes.

[Note to the student: This book contains several checklists in the form of "One way to ..." figures. These checklists involve meeting and inspection procedures, for example. Teams often begin with published checklists, and augment them according to additional specific needs of their projects.]

Additional SQA tools, techniques, and methodologies for configuration management are described in the SPMP.

10. CODE CONTROL

The methods and facilities used to maintain, store, secure, and document versions of completed code during all phases of the software life cycle are specified in the SCMP. The SQA team verifies that the code control procedures specified in the SCMP are followed.

The media labels for the baseline code have separate markings for verification, duplication, and validation. After the completion of a formal test that is witnessed or validated by SQA personnel, SQA stamps "Validated by SQA" on the media label for the baseline code, and the responsible QA member present signs the label. The SQA engineer conducting the test is required to sign. Baseline code is checked by SQA before being used to ensure that it is identical to the engineering master. The methods for integrity confirmation include physical possession by SQA personnel, stamped and signed media labels, checksum testing, bit-for-bit comparison, and visual comparison of output data for given certain input data.

11. MEDIA CONTROL

[Note to the student: Describe the means by which disks, tapes, etc. will be managed.]

The SQA team verifies that the software media are built and configured per the SCMP and that authorized changes have been installed and tested. In addition, the SQA team verifies that the software media are duplicated using only the procedures identified in the SCMP. SQA acceptance is indicated by an SQA stamp on the media label. The SQA audit reports for media control are intended as further evidence that QA procedures have been followed.

12. SUPPLIER CONTROL

[Note to the student: This section concerns relationships with suppliers of software and hardware. It describes how and by whom these relationships are to be handled. The SQA team verifies commercial off-the-shelf (COTS) products provided by the suppliers during incoming inspection by reviewing the packing slips that identify the product and its version number. The products are validated through installation and acceptance tests.]

13. RECORDS COLLECTION, MAINTENANCE, AND RETENTION

[Note to the student: This section describes how physical records will be handled, and who will be responsible for them. Include disk files that are not under configuration control.]

The SQA records collected and archived shall include

- Task reports
- Anomaly reports not handled by the regular problem reporting mechanism
- Memos, including recommendations to responsible parties

- Logbooks of SQA activities
- Audit reports
- Signed-off checklists from reviews and audits
- Minutes of inspections

Besides verifying the archive procedures specified in the SCMP, SQA shall separately archive its own records at least once a week. These records are retained throughout the operation and maintenance phase.

14. TRAINING

[Note to the student: SQA training specific to this project]

The SQA organization will conduct an initial four hour orientation on quality for the development team. This will include a presentation on the metrics to be used, and a workshop on how to use tools for recording metrics. SQA will also conduct monthly three hour classes for development team members to keep them informed of quality goals, tools, and techniques. Team members can waive attendance at these meetings by scoring perfectly on a multiple-choice quiz available at GCI/monthly/SQA/quiz.

15. RISK MANAGEMENT

SQA team members are encouraged to identify risks as early as possible. The procedures for risk management are specified in Section 3.3 of the SPMP.

REQUIREMENTS ANALYSIS I

Give every man thy ear ...
—Polonius to his son, from *Hamlet*

Obtaining the right requirements is a difficult process. It consists of careful interaction with those holding a stake in the application.

Figure 3.1 indicates the phase discussed in this chapter. Figure 3.2 lists the learning goals for this chapter.

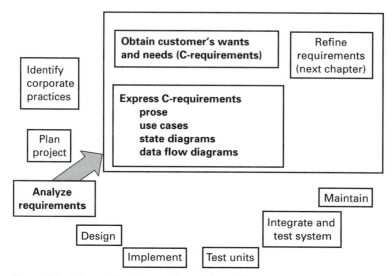

Figure 3.1 Software Engineering Road Map: Chapter 3 Focus

- Distinguish C- (Customer) requirements from D- (Detailed) requirements
- Be equipped with ways to express C- requirements
  - exploit use cases
  - exploit state diagrams
  - exploit data flow diagrams
  - sketch user interfaces
- Be able to write first parts of a Software Requirements Specification

Figure 3.2 Chapter Learning Goals

1. INTRODUCTION TO REQUIREMENTS ANALYSIS

This chapter discusses the overall analysis of the requirements for an application, which is a process of conceptualizing and then expressing concepts in concrete form. Most defects found in delivered software originate during requirements analysis. In general, such defects are also the most expensive to repair.

1.1 The Meaning of Requirements Analysis

To build something, we must first understand what that "something" is to be. The process of understanding and documenting this something is called "requirements analysis." Requirements generally express *what* an application is meant to do: Generally, they do not try to express *how* to accomplish these functions. For example, the following statement (Y) is a requirement for an accounting application.

The system shall allow the user to access his account balance.

Generally speaking, the following statement (N) is not a requirement for application.

> *Customers' account balances will be stored in a table called "balance" in an Access*[TM] *database.*

The latter statement concerns *how* the application is to be constructed, rather than *what* the application is meant to do.

A requirement at one level often translates into more specific requirement(s) at the next more detailed level. To understand this, imagine that your requirement for a house is that it has "a 180 degree view of the mountains." This could translate into the statement that it has "a deck at the right side with dimensions 20 feet by 50 feet." This is a more specific requirement at the more detailed level. Similarly, the statement (N) above could actually be a requirement at a subsequent level within the development process.

In addition, there are exceptions to the rule that requirements avoid specifying how something should be done. For example, the customer in the above example could, for some reason, specifically want account balances stored in an Access™ database of the name indicated. In that case, the statement (N) would indeed be a requirement.

The output of requirements analysis is a document generally referred to as a *requirements specification* or *software requirements specification* (SRS).

1.2 C-Requirements and D-Requirements

Debates have raged for some time on who "owns" requirements: the customer or the developers (see, for example, [Be1]). To deal with this issue, we divide "requirements analysis" into two levels (see [Ro1], [Br]). The first level documents the customer's wants and needs, and is expressed in language clear to him. The results are sometimes called "Customer requirements" or "C-requirements." The primary audience for C-requirements is the customer community, and the secondary audience is the developer community. The second level documents the requirements in a specific, structured form. These are called "developer requirements" or "D-requirements." The primary audience for D-requirements is the developer community, and the secondary audience is the customer community.

This book uses the IEEE standard for documenting requirements. The distinction between C- and D- requirement types within the major headings of the IEEE standard document template is illustrated in Figure 3.3. This chapter covers C-requirements; Chapter 4 covers D-requirements.

Although the primary audiences for C- and D-requirements are different, customers and developers work together closely to create successful products. One way to ensure good communication is to have representatives of the customer work alongside the developers. Some development organizations even refuse to take assignments without this provision. This is a tenet of the "extreme programming" method mentioned in Chapter 1. Seeding development staff with customer representatives, often technical, is a common U.S. Department of Defense practice. As a U.S. Navy employee, for example, the author once worked on a shipboard system alongside contractor engineers.

1.3 Why Requirements Must Be Written

Even to the novice, it may seem obvious that one should express in writing what a program is supposed to do when complete. Nevertheless, this writing process is often ignored or allowed to lapse. In such cases, it is sometimes believed that the source code expresses all the requirements: Since we cannot do without the source code, why not

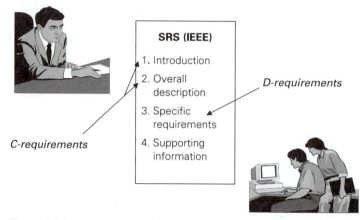

Figure 3.3 Customer Requirements Compared with Detailed Requirements (Graphics reproduced with permission from Corel)

reduce the whole process to this one essential document? The answer is that this does not work. The discipline of software engineering, the most authoritative of our engineers, and this book, all insist on carefully written requirements documents. Without such documents the team does not really know what goals it is trying to accomplish, cannot inspect its work properly, cannot test its work properly, cannot track its productivity, cannot get adequate data on its practices, cannot predict the size and effort of its next job, and cannot satisfy its customers. In short, there is no professional engineering without written requirements.

To illustrate these points, consider the following requirement for a scientific application.

The application shall display the length of the X12345 gene in the system window (requirement 7824)

Figure 3.4 shows a list of what must be done with this and all other requirements. In addition, the time taken to perform each of these steps must be recorded, so that the time

Each requirement must be

- expressed properly
- made easily accessible
- numbered
- accompanied by tests that verify it
- provided for in the design
- accounted for by code
- tested in isolation
- tested in concert with other requirements
- validated by testing after the application has been built

Figure 3.4 To Be Performed with Each Requirement

to implement similar requirements in similar contexts can be estimated in the future. Consider the chaos that would result if requirement 7824 were *not* written down. Few of the steps mentioned in Figure 3.4 could be carried out properly. Would it be any wonder if the application in question were unreliable?

When one contemplates carrying out the steps in Figure 3.4 for each and every requirement, one gets the idea of just why software engineering deals extensively in individual requirements. They are the currency—the basic "coinage"—of the profession.

1.4 A Typical Road Map of the Requirements Analysis Process

Figure 3.5 is a typical road map for the C-requirements analysis process described in this chapter. We revisit this road map on each iteration. The last step of the roadmap gathers the detailed D-requirements, a process explained in the next chapter. The team collects metrics on the stages of this process to enable the estimation of future iterations and future applications.

There are several ways in which a Software Requirements Specification can be organized. We will use—and modify—IEEE standard 830-1993, shown in Figure 3.6. The contents of IEEE 830-1993 will be explained throughout this chapter. IEEE 830-1993 is also an ANSI standard. Section 3 of the standard, the "specific requirements" (the D-requirements), is expanded and applied in the next chapter.

Software engineers debate the merits of various forms of requirements documentation. The disadvantage of the IEEE standard is that it is relatively old, and usually requires some modification and augmentation (e.g., to reflect advances in object-oriented analysis and design and emerging Internet issues). The advantage of the IEEE standard is that it encompasses most of the issues that must be expressed in one way or the other.

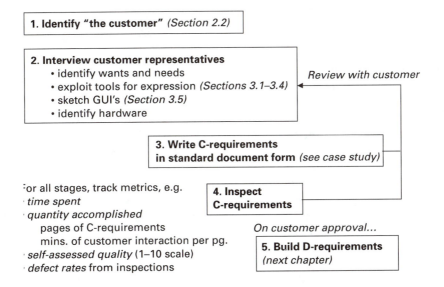

Figure 3.5 Typical Road Map for Customer (C-) Requirements

1. **Introduction**
   1.1. Purpose
   1.2. Scope
   1.3. Definitions, acronyms, and ab-
        breviations
   1.4. References
   1.5. Overview
2. **Overall description**
   2.1. Product perspective
       2.1.1. System interfaces
       2.1.2. User interfaces
       2.1.3. Hardware interfaces
       2.1.4. Software interfaces
       2.1.5. Communications
               interfaces
       2.1.6. Memory constraints
       2.1.7. Operations
       2.1.8. Site adaptation
               requirements
   2.2. Product functions
   2.3. User characteristics
   2.4. Constraints
   2.5. Assumptions and dependencies
   2.6. Apportioning of requirements
3. **Specific requirements**
   [see Chapter 4]
4. **Supporting information**
   [see Chapter 4]

*Figure 3.6 Contents of IEEE Standard 830–1993: Software Requirements Specification
Copyright © 1994 IEEE*

1.5 The Challenges and Benefits of Requirements Analysis

A defective requirement (i.e., one not repaired before the requirements document is final-ized) is very expensive. It is an estimated 20 to 50 times more expensive to repair if al-lowed to slip through the development process. In financial terms, if the cost of finding and repairing a defect at requirements time is $100, then the cost of finding and fixing that same defect at the end of the development process is $2000 to $5000. Who would refuse an investment of $100 that guarantees a payback of $2000 to $5000 within a year or two? Think of every early requirements defect search as just such an investment.

The damage that results from the customer's poor experience with the application is a factor entirely additional to the expense involved.

Given the tremendous benefit of detecting and repairing defects at requirements time, why are so many projects damaged by poor or nonexistent requirements analysis? A princi-pal reason is that customers usually do not know at the beginning of a project just what they want or need. The video game case study at the end of the chapter is an example of this un-certainty: It is a project with a purpose, but one whose outline is still in formation. This book emphasizes iterative development and the close alignment between the requirements, the de-sign, and the implementation. Engineers using a well-organized iterative process gather re-quirements, design for them, and implement them in coordinated iterations.

Requirements analysis is a necessity, not a luxury. Consider its effects on testing. Most development organizations consider testing an absolute necessity. But if someone were to give you just a black box with one purple, one pink, and one orange wire protrud-ing from it, and ask you to test it, you would probably refuse. Testing it would be impos-sible without knowing what the box is supposed to accomplish! In other words, without requirements, one cannot test properly.

Many organizations fail to write down requirements. This does not mean that they do not use requirements—it means only that the requirements exist in the minds of particular software engineers. When one considers the general ineffectiveness of unrecorded requirements, and the large number of requirements in any real application, and the realities of staff turnover, is it any wonder that a large fraction of software projects are never completed? A more subtle problem is created by organizations that write down requirements for the initial iteration, build against it, but do not keep the requirements document up to date on subsequent iterations. The reason for this is that it is often harder to update a requirements document than to write the first version. (This underscores the importance of good organization of the requirements document.) The fact that updating may be more difficult, however, does not alter the truism that failure to write down requirements will cause a great degree of difficulty.

An important payoff from requirements analysis is an understanding of and agreement about the application to be built (Brackett [Br]). This is the basis for contracts of all kinds.

Most of us have been told that "writing is thinking," and this is particularly true of writing requirements. Quite a few developers try to avoid writing requirements, eagerly jumping into code. One developer in the author's experience, impatient with the process, suddenly churned out prodigious quantities of code. He then announced to the team, "I've done my part—you guys are free to waste your time on boilerplate. I'm out of here." Coding prematurely like this is pouring quantities of concrete for a bridge without knowing what locations the bridge is supposed to span (let alone what the design is to be). The author feels that the reluctance to write requirements is not because writing them is too simple to bother with, as some claim, but that writing them properly is difficult. Concrete, realistic, and measurable procedures for writing requirements make the task much more of a professional challenge.

2. CUSTOMER INTERACTION

2.1 The Sources of Requirements

This section concentrates on interaction with people for requirements analysis. People are by no means the only source of requirements, however. As shown in Figure 3.7, Brackett [Br] has plotted several types of applications to illustrate the degree to which

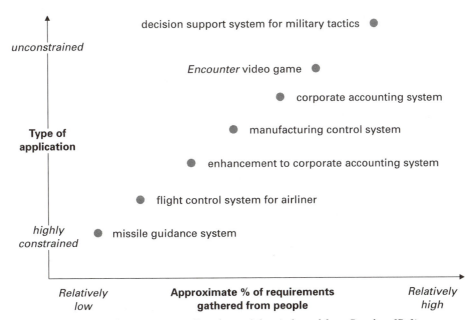

Figure 3.7 Sources of Requirements: People vs. Other (adapted from Brackett [Br])

requirements are gathered from people, rather than from other sources such as written material. The chart classifies applications in terms of the degree to which they are *constrained*. This refers to restrictions on the application that cannot be altered. For example, an application that describes the trajectory of a ball is constrained by gravity; chemical reactions are constrained by physical laws. The less constrained the problem, the more its requirements must be obtained from people. At one extreme, for example, our video game case study, being the product of pure imagination, relies on people for most of its requirements. Missile guidance systems, on the other hand, are constrained by the physics of motion rather than the desires of people, and so most of the requirements in this case arise from physics equations.

2.2 Stakeholder Identification

The people who have a stake in the outcome of the product are called its *stakeholders*. Collectively speaking, they are the application's "customer." As an example, consider the creation of an e-commerce website. One set of stakeholders consists of the site's visitors: Typically their primary requirement is the ease with which they can find and purchase needed items. The company's owners are stakeholders, too: Their primary requirement may be profit, short- or long-term. For this reason, they may want the site to emphasize high-margin items. Managers, another group of stakeholders, may require the application to track visitors. The application's developers are stakeholders too: They may want to use new development technology to keep up to date.

In the case of packaged ("shrink-wrapped") applications such as word processors, spreadsheets, and development environments, designers pay most attention to the acceptability of the application by as many users as possible. Although this can be a difficult marketing problem, it is clear that the users are the most significant stakeholders. For many large projects, however, identifying the most important stakeholders is complex. The "customer" is often the party paying to have the application developed, but even this is not clear-cut. For example, the Navy may be paying for an application, but the developers' day-to-day customer may be a civil servant rather than a naval officer: Then again, are not the taxpayers the "customers" since they are actually paying for the application? The customer of a subcontractor is the prime contractor. The customer for shrink-wrapped applications is a composite of potential customers established by the marketing department. When an application is intended for internal company use, such as claims processing within an insurance company, the customer is an internal organization.

Conflicting stakeholder interests can easily result in inconsistent requirements. An example of this is when two different groups within a company, with different motivations, want apparently the "same" application built. As a result, the requirements may not really be consistent. When requirements cannot be reconciled, projects tend to flounder, and are frequently canceled. Even when stakeholders' requirements are consistent, they can be too expensive to satisfy entirely.

Developers are subject to professional responsibilities, which can profoundly affect requirements. Suppose, for example, that developers are asked to build software for a medical device with a fixed budget, but they determine that the required features cannot all be adequately tested within that budget. Unless the budget is changed, they would have to eliminate requirements. Even when lives are not at stake, software engineers have a societal responsibility to produce products that thoroughly satisfy their requirements. A good deal of this involves managing the scope of the requirements so as to make them satisfiable within given budgetary and schedule constraints.

The good project leader surmounts these difficulties—a process which requires managerial, personal, business, and political skills.

2.3 Examples of Customer Wants

When the development community begins requirements analysis, the customer is typically still forming concepts of what he wants and needs. This is analogous to the requirements gathering phase between an architect and a client. For example, the client may want a ranch house with four bedrooms and a large living room. She relies on the architect, however, to help her clarify what she wants (e.g., a spacious living room with seating for 10).

The case study used in this book is a video game called *Encounter*. The following is a fragment of customer thinking obtained by a mythical marketing department.

> *Encounter is to be a role-playing game which simulates all or part of the player's lifetime. It should be of interest to both men and women.*

Figure 3.8 and Figure 3.9 summarize the C-requirements for the case study. The complete text statement is listed in the "Overall Description" section of the case study. Examples of unresolved issues are whether there is to be one or several characters under the control of the player; what exactly occurs when two characters interact; and whether the game can be played over the Internet. It is the task of the engineer to work with the customer to clarify these wants and needs.

Customer *needs* are a little more subtle to classify than their *wants*. For example, the customer may *want* a music application to allow computer novices to write music in a secure manner, but may also *need* a periodic autosave function to avoid losing work. Is the latter feature a requirement or is it part of the design? This depends on agreement between the developer and the customer. If the customer, having understood autosaving, becomes convinced that this is a feature he specifically wants, then it becomes a requirement. The customer may be content, however, to leave it to the designer as to how to accommodate

- This is a role-playing game that simulates all or part of the lifetime of the player's character.
- Game characters not under the player's control are called "foreign" characters.
- Game characters have a number of *qualities* such as *strength, speed, patience.*
- Each quality has a value.
- Characters "encounter" each other when in the same area, and may then "engage" each other.

Figure 3.8 Example Application "Encounter," 1 of 2

- The result of the engagement depends on the values of their qualities and on the area in which the engagement takes place.
- Player characters may reallocate their qualities, except while a foreign character is present.
- Reallocation takes effect after a delay, during which the player may be forced to engage.
- Success is measured by one of the following:
  - the "life points" maximum attained by the player
  - living as long as possible

Figure 3.9 Example Application "Encounter," 2 of 2

the secure computing of novice users. In this case autosaving is not a requirement, but a design element which contributes to satisfying the requirements.

2.4 The Interview and Documentation Process

Much of the analysis of requirements is a person-to-person activity, carefully organized to produce the best application. Figure 3.10 summarizes the process of preparing for and interviewing the customer.

Since there are typically several stakeholders who want to provide their input, the first issue is deciding whom to interview. Instead of trying to give everyone equal time, which can result in contradictory requirements and wasted effort, the author recommends selecting one or perhaps two primary individuals, interviewing them, and then soliciting comments from other key stakeholders. The process of interviewing a customer is typically expensive in that it consumes a significant amount of time of more than one person. For this reason, it is carefully scheduled. Two interviewers at each session are preferable to one, since a typical interviewer tends to miss points. Bringing a tape recorder can also help, but be sure to ask for permission in advance.

Although it is important to listen carefully to the customer at the interview, one usually cannot obtain requirements by listening alone. Typically, the customer formulates requirements as he goes along, and needs help. Although the vision formed is primarily the customer's, the interviewer and the customer develop a vision jointly to some degree. The customer usually requires some prompting to complete their vision, a little (but not too much) like a witness on the stand.

We emphasize use cases as an effective way to obtain and express requirements for a wide variety of applications. Some requirements need to be diagrammed, and ways to do this are described in Sections 3.3 and 3.4. To validate the requirements as written out, the

---

One Way To. . . Handle Interviews

Before interview:

1. List and prioritize "customer" interviewees
   - most likely to determine project's success
2. Schedule interview with fixed start and end times
   - at least two from development team should attend
   - prepare to tape?

At interview:

3. Concentrate on listening
   Don't be passive: probe and encourage
   - persist in understanding *wants* and exploring *needs*
   - walk through use cases, also data flow? state diagrams?
   Take thorough notes
4. Schedule follow-up meeting

After interview:

5. Draft SRS C-requirements using a standard
6. E-mail customer for comments

Figure 3.10 One Way to Handle Interviews with the Customer

interviewers follow up via e-mail, holding a subsequent meeting if necessary. Recall that the D-requirements have yet to be gathered and will require more meeting time.

After the meeting, the C-requirements are drafted in a format such as the IEEE standard. The draft is e-mailed to the customer community for comments, and successive interviews are conducted until there is satisfaction with the C-requirements.

3. DESCRIBING CUSTOMER (C-)REQUIREMENTS

The great challenge we face is expressing clearly what customers want and need. Words alone can be appropriate, but for many applications, narrative text needs to be supplemented by figures of various kinds. Section 3.6 summarizes procedures for expressing requirements.

3.1 Concept of Operations

Customers develop a vision—frequently unconscious and incomplete—of how their application will operate. This vision is sometimes referred to as the application's *model* or *concept of operations.* Different people generally hold differing concepts of what a software application entails. For example, the possible concept of operations for "a weather system" could be one of

- a facility for turning raw weather service information into graphical form
- a real-time system for forecasting the weather
- an application for alerting users to weather anomalies

These differing concepts of operations lead to very different applications.

The project manager or requirements engineer helps the customer to clarify his concept of operations. Since customers usually lack the techniques with which to express such concepts, engineers can propose appropriate techniques, such as *use cases, data flow,* or *state-transitions,* which are described below. Note that these techniques are also used for design, as shown in Chapters 5 and 6.

3.2 Use Cases

Requirements are often naturally expressed as an interaction between the application and an agency external to it, such as the user. The *use case,* a concept invented by Jacobson [Ja], is a very useful way to express customer requirements in the form of such interactions. A use case is identified first by its name, and by the type of user of the application, called the *actor.* It consists of a typical interaction between an actor and the application. For example, *Retrieve a file* would be a typical use case for a word processor, with the user as actor. It could consist of the following sequence of steps.

1. *User* clicks *File* menu
2. *System* displays options *new* and *open*
3. *User* clicks *open*
4. *System* displays file window

5. *User* enters directory and file name

6. *User* hits *open* button

7. *System* retrieves referenced file into word processor window

Since their "story" form is easy to understand, use cases are a particularly useful means of communication with customers. We will actually carry the use case idea well beyond C-requirements.

One person could use a system in several different ways, adopting the roles of different actors. Figure 3.11 and Figure 3.12 show examples of four use cases for the video game case study, two of which are shown in detail.

In the UML notation, an ellipse denotes a use case. For two of these use cases, the actor is the player of *Encounter.* Each use case is a sequence of actions taken by the player and the *Encounter* game, as shown for the *Initialize* use case. The *Engage Foreign Character* use case is a typical sequence of actions by *Encounter* and the player, whenever the player's main character and a foreign character are in the same area at the same time.

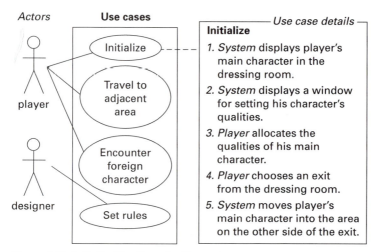

Figure 3.11 Initialize Use Case for Encounter

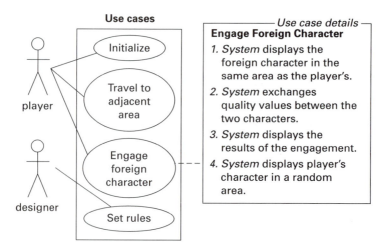

Figure 3.12 Engage Foreign Character Use Case for Encounter

The actor in the *Set rules* use case is a game designer: *The actor* describes the ability of *Encounter* to support the editing of rules for character interaction. Note that the *Travel to Adjacent Area* use case is explained in the case study at the end of the chapter, and that the *Set rules* use case is not included in the case study requirements.

The actor need not be a human role: It could be another system that uses the application. For example, if the application under development is a robot control system, then the actor could be a factory automation system that uses the robot control system.

Use cases can handle limited branching, but if there is more than one level of branching, the use case should probably be decomposed into other use cases. Even a single branch in a use case leads to an awkward description. For example, the following could be a use case for a personal budgeting application.

1. User selects "add checks" or "reconcile account"
2. If "add checks" selected:
3. One action happens
4. Another action happens
5. ....
6. If "reconcile account" selected:
7. One action happens
8. Another action happens
9. ....

This would be better decomposed into "select options," "add checks," and "reconcile account" use cases.

Since use cases are like stories, they are effective for eliciting information from customers, and they provide excellent insight into applications. Use cases can be expressed at differing levels of generality. The Unified Software Development Process, ([Ja1]) recommends using detailed use cases to specify a large fraction of the requirements.

It is evident that similar use cases do not yield much additional value. Relative to one another, use cases should either be *sequential*, or *orthogonal*. Two use cases are sequential if one can follow directly after the other. Orthogonal use cases take completely different views or options. For example, in a warehouse application, use cases based on a *foreman* actor and a *financial analyst* actor would typically be orthogonal. In the *Encounter* case study, *Set rules* is orthogonal to *Encounter foreign character*. Chapter 4 shows how use cases are combined to produce new use cases; it also introduces inheritance among use cases.

Jacobson [Ja] originated the idea of use cases by observing that, despite the huge number of potential executions, most applications are conceived of in terms of a relatively small number of typical interactions. He suggests starting application design by writing use cases, then using them to drive class selection. This technique is demonstrated in Chapter 4. Use cases can also be used to develop a prototype (see below). They are a basis for system-level test plans. We will demonstrate these strategies for the case study.

Most established documentation standards, including the IEEE's, predate use cases, and must be augmented to accommodate them. Use cases are useful for specifying requirements, design, and test cases. Since high level use cases can express the customer's vision of how the application is to work, the case study includes them under the "concept of operations" section of the Software Requirement Specification.

Although use cases are often identified with object-oriented methods, they can be used with any development methodology.

3.3 Data Flow Diagrams for Customer Communication

Some requirements are naturally described as the flow of data among processing elements. In a *data flow diagram*, the nodes—shown as circles or rectangles—represent processing units. The arrows among them denote the flow of data, and are annotated with the data's type. Data stores—places where data reside, such as databases—are denoted by a pair of horizontal lines enclosing the name of the data store. External agencies such as the user and printers are represented by rectangles.

Suppose, for example, that our customer is trying to explain the kind of banking application that she wants, starting with deposits into an account. The deposit functions might be *getting the deposit* from the user, and *checking the deposit transaction* to make sure that it is legitimate. These functions are represented by circles in Figure 3.13. Next, the type of data flowing between these functions is noted on the figure—the account number and the deposit amount. The user is involved, too, and so should be represented. A function to create a summary of accounts, to give another example, requires input from a store, as shown. A more complete data flow diagram for the banking requirements would be as shown in Figure 3.14.

The complete diagram includes thc "mcmber banks" data store, which is a list of banks allowing a deposit at this ATM. It also shows the data flow for the response to a query, in which details about an account are displayed.

Expressing these requirements in text form only would be more difficult than using a data flow diagram. Notice that data flow diagrams do not show control, however. For example, the ATM application does not indicate what function occurs first.

Standards used for the symbols differ among organizations: For example, rectangles are often used for the processing elements rather than circles.

Whether or not data flow diagrams are helpful for expressing requirements depends upon the application. For example, the banking data flow diagram in Figure 3.14 clarifies for many readers how the application is meant to behave, whereas video game requirements would probably not be readily described using a data flow diagram. Data flow dia-

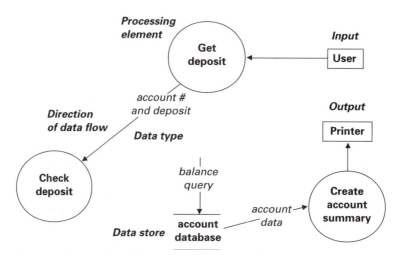

Figure 3.13 Data Flow Diagram: Explanation of Symbols

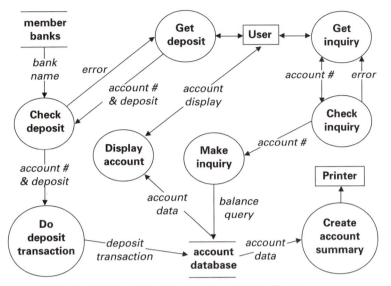

Figure 3.14 Partial Data Flow Diagram for ATM Application

grams are commonly used to describe designs, and we will revisit them in the design Chapters 5 and 6.

3.4 State-Transition Diagrams for Customer Communication

Sometimes, an application—or part thereof—is best thought of as being in one of several states. The *state* of an application is its situation or status. States are sometimes called "phases" or "stages." The idea is to divide the application into states so that the application is always in exactly one of these states. For example, it might be useful to think of an online shopper at a bookselling site as being either in *browsing* state (looking at book information) or in *purchasing* state (providing credit card information, etc.). The concept of state has a precise definition in the context of implementation, but in the present context the definition is still informal.

These are several possible *Encounter* states. They include the following.

- *Setting up:* the state during which the game is being set up
- *Preparing:* equipping the player's character with qualities such as "strength" and "intelligence" can be performed as long as no foreign character is present
- *Waiting:* when nothing is happening in the game that is experienced by the user
- *Engaging:* the state in which the player's character and the foreign character are exchanging quality values

These states are shown in the Figure 3.15. For event-driven applications, diagrams like this can sometimes be an effective way for the customer and developer to obtain a mutual concept of how the application is meant to work.

After identifying the states, the transitions between states are added. Transitions are denoted by arrows, each labeled with the name of the event which causes the application to change from one state to another. Sometimes, when an object is in a given state,

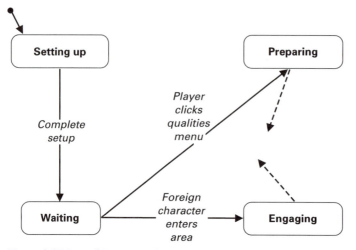

Figure 3.15 Partial Encounter State-Transition Diagram

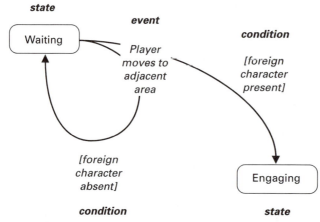

Figure 3.16 Using Conditions in State-Transition Diagrams

and an event occurs, the object can transition to one of several states, depending on a *condition*. For example, when the player decides to move her character to an adjacent area, the game transitions from the *Waiting* state into one of two states. One possibility is to transition back to the *Waiting* state again (if the foreign character is absent from the entered area); the other is to transition to the *Engaging* state (if the foreign character is present in the entered area). In the UML, conditions are denoted by square brackets, as shown in Figure 3.16.

The complete state-transition diagram for *Encounter* is shown in Figure 3.17. Once the player has finished setting up the *Encounter* game, the latter transitions from *Setting up* state into *Waiting* state. If *Encounter* is in *Waiting* state, and a foreign character enters, then *Encounter* transitions into *Engaging* state. Note that the process of setting quality values, and the process of reporting the results of an encounter can be interrupted by the arrival of the foreign character, which causes a new encounter to commence immediately.

The state-transition model is a good way to explain the concept of operations of *Encounter*. State-transition models are commonly used as design tools as well (see Chapters 5 and 6). Whether or not they should be used to express C-requirements, as we

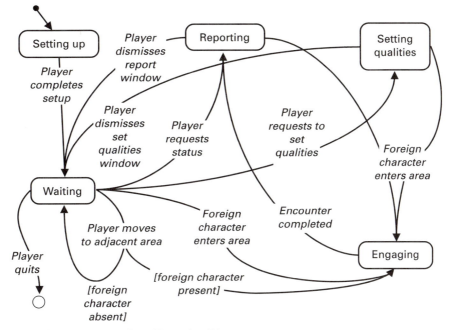

Figure 3.17 Encounter State-Transition Diagram

are doing here, depends on the application in question, and how helpful it is for the customer. This typically requires some education of the customer.

3.5 Drafting User Interfaces and Other Interfaces

User interface design is included with the "design" phase of software development, but could also be considered part of the requirements phase. This is a question of preference. This book takes the latter perspective, including only *software* design in the "design" phase.

Customers commonly conceive of an application by visualizing its graphical user interface (GUI), and so a good way to help them describe the application is to develop draft GUIs. Chapter 4, particularly the case study, concludes the specification of user interfaces in the context of detailed requirements. Our goal here is to provide some of the essentials of user interface design. This is quite different from the *technical* design of the application, which is covered in Chapters 5 and 6.

In developing user interfaces for our applications, the fortunate among us are able to either work with a professional designer, or to at least obtain help from one. For many projects, however, especially smaller ones, software engineers must design user interfaces on their own. Thus, we list some guidelines for user interface design.

3.5.1 Steps for Developing User Interfaces   In [Ga2], Galitz provides 11 steps for developing user interfaces. The author has adapted these, as shown in Figure 3.18. Each of these steps is applicable to the customer requirements process and/or the Detailed requirements processes.

Step 1 (know your user). This step recommends understanding the nature of the application's eventual users. Figure 3.19 and Figure 3.20 outline the factors involved. The checklist is a way of ensuring that we know the basic characteristics of the anticipated users, and that we

Step   *1:* Know your user (C) [a C-requirement process]

Step   *2:* Understand the business function in question (C)

Step   *3:* Apply principles of good screen design (C, D)

Step   *4:* Select the appropriate kind of windows (C, D)

Step   *5:* Develop system menus (C, D)

Step   *6:* Select the appropriate device-based controls (C)

Step   *7:* Choose the appropriate screen-based controls (C)

Step   *8:* Organize and lay out windows (C, D)

Step   *9:* Choose appropriate colors (D)

Step *10:* Create meaningful icons (C, D)

Step *11:* Provide effective message, feedback, and guidance (D)

Figure 3.18 Steps for Constructing User Interfaces (Adapted from Galitz [Ga2])

Level of knowledge and experience

• computer literacy	high / moderate / [low $\Rightarrow$ *explain every term**]
• system experience	high / moderate / [low $\Rightarrow$ *provide examples and animations*]
• experience with similar applications	high / moderate / [low $\Rightarrow$ *provide examples and animations*]
• education	advanced degree / college/ [high school $\Rightarrow$ *use 12th-grade terms*]
• reading level	>12 years' schooling / 5–12 / [< 5 $\Rightarrow$ *use very simple language*]
• typing skill	135 wpm / 55 wpm / [10 wpm $\Rightarrow$ *provide smaller text boxes; provide samples; emphasize fill-in-the-blank forms*]

Physical characteristics of the user

• age	young / middle aged / elderly
• gender	male / female
• handedness	left / right / ambidextrous
• physical handicaps	blind / defective vision / deaf / motor handicap

*Suggested actions for the latter, added by the author

Figure 3.19 Know Your Users, 1 of 2 (Adapted from Galitz [Ga2])

document our assumptions. These characteristics then determine the nature of the user interface. In general, users with less education, training, skill, and motivation require greater simplicity, more explanation, and more help. This may have to be traded off against efficiency and speed. It is often desirable to provide several levels of user interface, depending on the level of the user.

Step 2 (understand the business function). This step asks the designer to understand the purpose of the particular proposed user interface in terms of the application's overall pur-

Characteristics of the user's tasks and jobs

- type of use of this application
  discretionary / [mandatory ⇒ *make application fun to use*]

- frequency of use
  continual / frequent / occasional / [once-in-a-lifetime ⇒ *provide all procedures and help with every screen*]

- turnover rate for employees
  low / moderate / [high ⇒ *provide all procedures and help with every screen*]

- importance of task
  high / moderate / [low ⇒ *make fun to use*]

- repetitiveness of task
  low / moderate / high ⇒ [*automate as many steps as possible; provide variety in presenting data; provide opportunities to learn*]

- training anticipated
  none / self-training through manuals / extensive ⇒ [*provide graduated opportunities to learn on line*]

- job category
  executive / manager / professional / secretary / clerk etc. ⇒ [*use language, examples and descriptions familiar to typical clerk*]

Psychological characteristics of the user

- probable attitude toward job
  positive / neutral / negative

- probable motivation
  high / moderate / [low ⇒ *make especially attractive*]

- cognitive style
  verbal vs. [spatial ⇒ *emphasize geometrical views*]

  analytic vs. [intuitive ⇒ *emphasize symbols over text*]

  concrete vs. [abstract ⇒ *exploit generalizations*]

Figure 3.20 Know Your Users, 2 of 2

pose. For example, if the business purpose is the stocking of a warehouse, then we may want the user interface to reflect the layout of the warehouse floor. The sequence of screens that appear may reflect the manner in which users normally carry out their tasks for the business at hand.

Step 3 (understand the principles of good screen design). Figure 3.21 lists some major elements of good screen design. The figure includes several factors that often apply to making an interface "pleasing." Although these serve only to introduce the subject of visual effects, they are nevertheless quite useful even at this level. As an example, we apply some of these principles to an example of a screen used to input information about customers and their accounts. To improve the interface, we start at the top left, placing the most important elements first, and grouping like elements. Figure 3.22 and Figure 3.23 illustrate the improvement that the application of these principles can bring. Figure 3.24 shows where some of the principles of good screen design were applied.

Step 4 (select the appropriate kind of windows). Each user interface purpose can be served most effectively by one or two particular types of windows. Figure 3.25 and Figure 3.26 list five common GUI purposes and a window type which satisfies each of them. The window types employ Windows™ terminology, but are typical.

Step 5 (develop system menus). Some rules for the creation of main menus, provided by Galitz [Ga2], are shown in Figure 3.27. Users require a stable, comprehensible anchor for

Ensure consistency among the screens of designated applications, and among screens within each

● conventions; procedures; look-and-feel; locations

Anticipate where the user will usually start

● frequently upper left—place "first" element there

Make navigation as simple as possible

● align like elements
● group like elements
● consider borders around like elements

Apply a hierarchy to emphasize order of importance

Apply principles of pleasing visuals

● balance; symmetry; regularity; predictability
● simplicity; unity; proportion; economy

Provide captions

Figure 3.21 Principles of Good Screen Design (see Galitz [Ga2])

Type	checking ○	saving ○	mmf ○	CD ○

Branch   Main St. ○   Elm St. ○   High St. ○

Privileges   newsletter ☐   discounts ☐   quick loans ☐

First name   [   ]

Middle name   [   ]

Last name   [   ]

Street   [   ]

City   [   ]

State/county   [   ]

OK	Apply	Cancel	Help

*Figure 3.22 Applying Principles of Good Screen Design: "Before" (*see Galitz [Ga1])*

applications: Hence the need for a constant main menu. The number of items on this menu should usually be between five and nine, because most of us feel comfortable with choices of this size. For example, the word processor with which this book is being typed has nine main menu items: *File, Edit, View, Insert, Format, Tools, Table, Window*, and *Help*. The number of items could have been far higher, since there is plenty of space for more: However, we would probably have to continually search the list for the option we require, and this outweighs the benefit of increasing the choices. The main menu items are determined by the business at

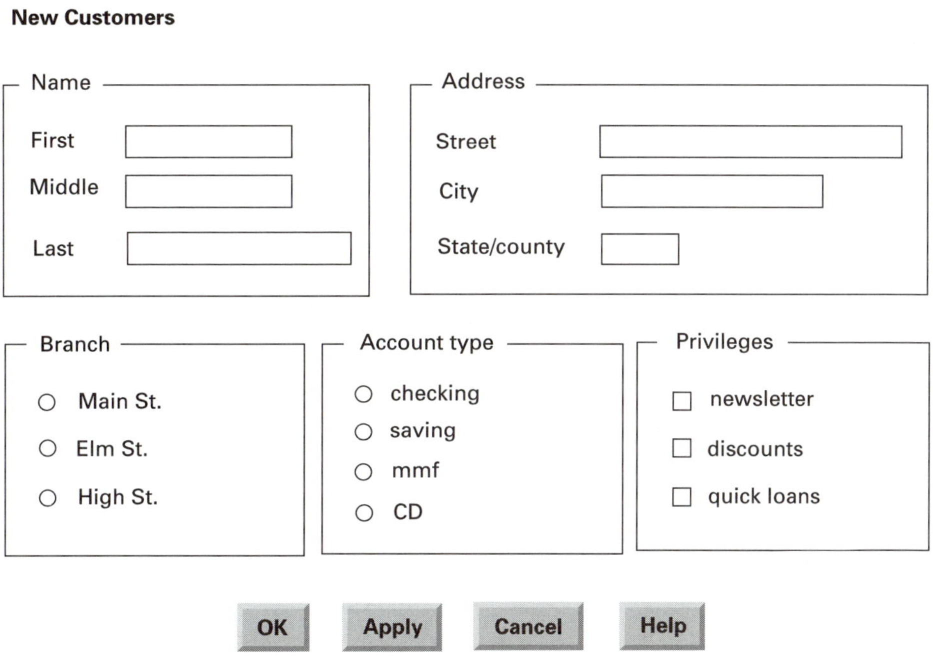

New Customers

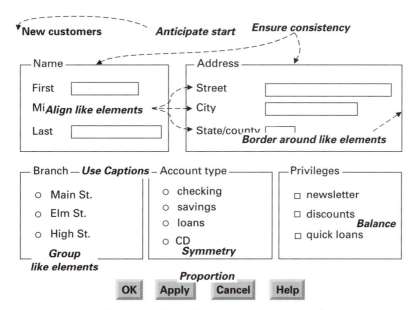

Figure 3.23 Applying Principles of Good Screen Design: "After"

Figure 3.24 How Principles of Good Screen Design Were Applied

hand—in this case the processing of text. Thus, for example, graphics commands are placed on a secondary menu.

Step 6 (select the appropriate device-based controls). "Device-based controls" are the physical means by which users communicate their desires to the application. They include joysticks, trackballs, graphics tablets, touch screens, mouses, microphones, and keyboards.

1. *Purpose:* display properties of an entity
   — *property window*

Properties of automobile 189	
Property	Value
Brand	Toyota
Model	Camry
ID	893-8913-789014

2. *Purpose:* obtain additional information so as to
   carry out a particular task or command
   — *dialog window*

Help	
Word:	
This screen ○ All screens ○	

Figure 3.25 Window Usage 1 of 2

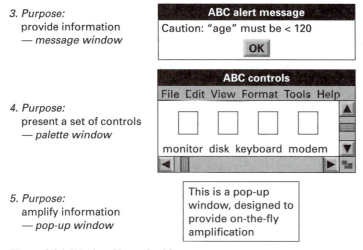

3. *Purpose:*
   provide information
   — *message window*

4. *Purpose:*
   present a set of controls
   — *palette window*

5. *Purpose:*
   amplify information
   — *pop-up window*

Figure 3.26 Window Usage 2 of 2

Step 7 (select the appropriate screen-based controls). "Screen-based controls" are symbols that appear on the monitor, by means of which the user notifies the application of his or her input and intentions. These include icons, buttons, text boxes, selections, and radio buttons, which are described in Figure 3.28. The rules for arranging screen-based controls in a window are virtually the same as those for screen design in general (see Figure 3.21 on page 154). Their number is, again, typically between five and nine. This number can be increased, however, if a hierarchy is used. For example, in Figure 3.23 on page 155, there are 20 options to select from, but the interface is manageable because these 20 items are organized into 6 groups.

Step 8 (organize and lay out windows). The rules for laying out multiple windows are similar to those for individual screen design (involving symmetry, proportion, etc., as in Figure 3.21 on page 154), but they involve arrangements such as tiling and cascading. The latter terms are illustrated in Figure 3.28.

Step 9 (choose appropriate colors). When used with skill and taste, color can enhance displays. Colors do not automatically make a user interface more useful or

- Provide a main menu
- Display all relevant alternatives (but only these)
- Match the menu structure to the structure of the application's task
- Minimize the number of menu levels

Figure 3.27 Develop System Menus

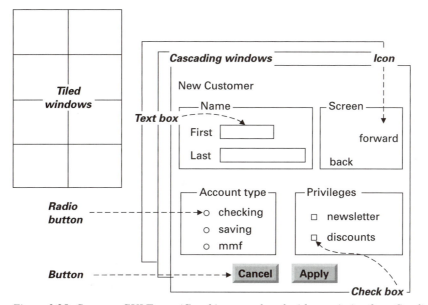

Figure 3.28 Common GUI Terms (Graphics reproduced with permission from Corel)

more attractive, however, and they can easily worsen it. According to renowned designer Paul Rand, "color is complexity personified" [Ra1]. Software engineers who do not have a professional designer with whom to work should be very sparing and conservative about the use of color. Try black and white first. If there is a clear purpose to it, introduce one color. Make sure that this helps the user. Think seriously before adding more colors. The observation of well-established applications, such as widely used word processors, can suggest how to use colors well. You can be assured that experienced professionals designed these interfaces, and the untrained software engineer can benefit from imitating them. The color blue is common in real-world screens of all kinds. Symmetry of colors is often recommended, and this symmetry can be of several varieties. For example, the author's word processor uses mainly three different shades of blue, which occur in a symmetrical pattern on the standard color palette. The other two colors used are yellow and, to a lesser extent, green. These are used in small quantities, accenting additional functionality only, and they do not compete with the major items, which are in black and gray.

3.5.2 Examples of Preliminary Requirements Sketches for the Case Study   Sometimes the execution of a program can be simulated by displaying a series of GUI images. For example, one could give someone a fair conception of *Encounter* by

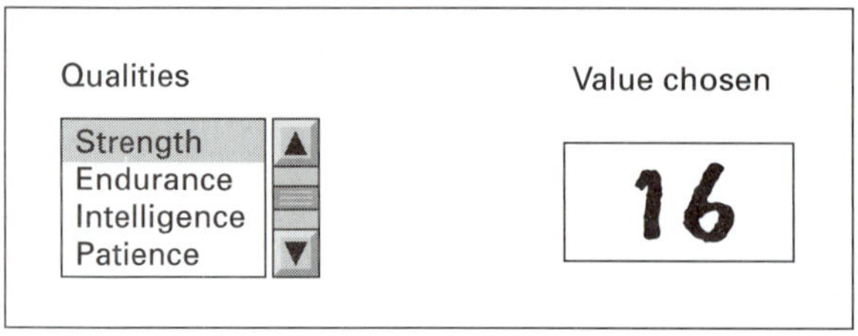

*Figure 3.29 Preliminary Sketch of User Interface for Setting
Game Character Qualities*

displaying a sequence of screen shots. In any case, the refinement of GUIs can involve a lengthy process of interaction with the customer.

Figure 3.29 shows a pencil-and-paper sketch of a GUI for setting the qualities of an *Encounter* character. Software such as Visual Basic™ and Java Beans™ support rapid GUI construction. It is natural to want this interface work to be an actual part of the final product, but this is practical only if

1. The GUI language is an acceptable source language for this part of the application.
2. The GUI-building tool generates maintainable code.

Otherwise, GUIs can be tentatively drafted using paint tools alone as shown in the preliminary screen shot in Figure 3.30. This GUI is specified in detail in Chapter 4.

Upon being shown GUIs, the customer typically realizes that he needs more or wants something different. In the example shown in Figure 3.29, it could well occur to the customer that the GUI for changing the value of qualities is awkward, because the total number of points may not change. The customer would also probably observe that the GUI is not particularly appealing. The process of finalizing the GUI is very interactive. The D-requirements provide precise GUI specification, as explained in Chapter 4.

3.5.3. Other Interfaces   Besides interfacing with users, applications must frequently interface with other systems, in which case the SRS specifies the interface. An example is a Web page application, which interfaces with server-resident CGI (Common Gateway Interface) programs. The format required by the CGI program must be specified: for example, the function form

> *<URL>/cgi-bin/query?pg=<value>&dk=<value>*
> (*pg* and *dk* are parameters of the server side function at .../*query*)

Interface specifications often consist of the names of the functions to be called, the type they return, and the types of arguments they require (their signature): for example, the function specification

> *float getValue(float principle, int numYears)*

This could specify a method that can be called by the application to be constructed, or a method that the latter must provide.

Interfaces may also consist of message formats or the specification of events generated and handled.

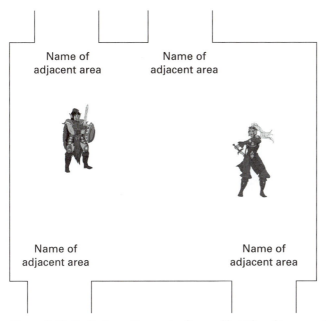

Figure 3.30 Preliminary Encounter Screen Shot (Graphics reproduced with permission from Corel)

3.6 Summary and Guide to Expressing C-Requirements

Figure 3.31 and Figure 3.32 summarize techniques for expressing the customer's requirements. The figures provide four alternative forms for expressing the customer's requirements. The form selected depends on the customer, as well as the requirement being described. Many requirements stand on their own, such as "the user shall be able to set the color of the type to blue, red, or black." Simple text is sufficient to express such requirements. Chapter 4 discusses their placement within the SRS.

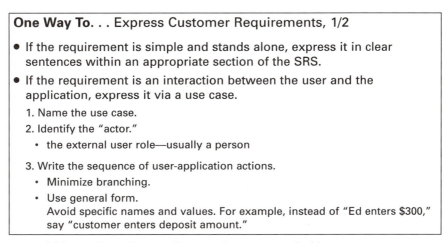

One Way To. . . Express Customer Requirements, 1/2

- If the requirement is simple and stands alone, express it in clear sentences within an appropriate section of the SRS.
- If the requirement is an interaction between the user and the application, express it via a use case.

    1. Name the use case.
    2. Identify the "actor."
       - the external user role—usually a person
    3. Write the sequence of user-application actions.
       - Minimize branching.
       - Use general form.
         Avoid specific names and values. For example, instead of "Ed enters $300," say "customer enters deposit amount."

Figure 3.31 One Way to Express Customer Requirements, 1 of 2

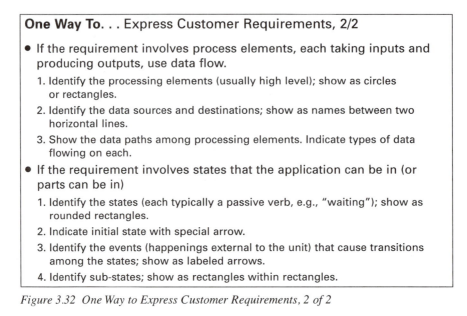

Figure 3.32 One Way to Express Customer Requirements, 2 of 2

Use cases are widely applicable for describing customer requirements because they capture user application interactions. If a state-transition diagram expresses what the customer wants and needs, and the customer understands the diagram, then its use is appropriate. The same holds for data flow diagrams. Data flow and state-transition techniques are commonly used for expressing *designs*. When using them for requirements specification, there is a significant danger of slipping into performing design instead of concentrating on requirements. For example, if an application is required to track the flow of orders within a company, then a data flow diagram (DFD) showing this process at a high level would be an appropriate form for C-requirements, because the DFD is needed to express what is to be done. On the other hand, consider an application that is required to produce the result of applying a complex formula. A DFD explaining the calculation process would be part of the design, but not the requirements.

4.   METHODOLOGIES, TOOLS, AND WEB USE FOR C-REQUIREMENTS

Numerous methodologies have been used to express requirements. Here is a summary of several methodologies.

Structured analysis formalizes data flow and functional decomposition. In particular, SADT (Structured Analysis and Design Technique) [Ro] is a systematic approach to handling system specifications. SADT describes the problem at the highest functional level as a rectangle with inputs, constraints, and outputs (the "context diagram"). This is decomposed into the next level of data flow diagram, which is then likewise decomposed. This produces a hierarchy of increasingly detailed data flow diagrams. Structured analysis views applications primarily from the functional perspective. This functional perspective is then realized by a hierarchy of functions.

Real-time systems can be effectively described by state-transition diagrams, used with or without object orientation (see, for example, Ward and Mellor [Wa]). In particular, *Statemate* is a graphical tool based on the state-transition work of David Harel [Ha3]. It provides a state-based method in which complex systems can be planned and analyzed. For example, modern ships have several redundant navigation systems. As a result of combinations of system disabilities, the navigation capability on some ships can get into a large number of possible states. These can be very difficult to understand without a graphical, state-oriented view (personal experience of the author). We have already seen that the *Encounter* case study can be usefully viewed as an event-driven state-transition system. Much of Statemate's notation has been adopted by the Unified Modeling Language.

PSL/PSA (Problem Statement Language / Problem Statement Analyzer) (for example, [Te]) was one of the earliest systems for expressing requirements. The original versions were text-based. Typical headings for components were PROCESS NAME, DESCRIPTION, GENERATES, RECEIVES, PART-OF, DERIVES/USING. Component descriptions are stored in a database, which can be accessed and summarized in a variety of ways.

5. RAPID PROTOTYPING, FEASIBILITY STUDIES, AND PROOFS OF CONCEPT

Failed software projects can waste millions of dollars. In Chapter 2, we discussed risk identification and retirement as an essential activity for anticipating project problems. This section discusses a way to begin obtaining risk feedback concurrently with the C-requirements process.

5.1 Rapid Prototyping

A "rapid prototype" is a partial implementation of the target application, usually involving a significant graphical user interface (GUI) component. Building a rapid prototype is a useful way to elicit the customer's requirements and also to identify and retire risky parts of a project. An increase in understanding can save expensive rework and remove future roadblocks in advance.

Large programs, such as billion dollar defense projects, utilize extensive prototyping because their requirements are so difficult to assemble. For small projects, simple graphics showing GUIs using paint-type tools may be sufficient, but this depends on the nature of the project. Student projects often benefit from a prototype, provided that the prototype is extremely modest. It enables the team to try out its development process before embarking on the real thing.

The more extensive the prototype, the more easily a customer's requirements can be understood. On the other hand, prototypes are themselves software applications, so the more extensive they are, the more expensive they become. A first cut at the decision of whether or not to build a prototype is shown in Figure 3.33. The table in Figure 3.33 shows, for example, that a relatively inexpensive prototype with high value should probably be built. "High value" means that building the prototype helps the customer understand better what kind of product is likely to emerge, helps the engineers understand better what kind of product should emerge, and / or retires a development risk.

Many cases fall into the "maybe" category of the table in Figure 3.33, and require the use of metrics. We are seeking an optimal level of effort to be spent on a prototype, as suggested by Figure 3.34. As the expenditure on a prototype increases, its usefulness increases, but so does its drain on the project's budget. As a result, there is probably a point at which the payoff is optimal (the maximum point for the curve), and some point beyond which funds are being squandered (where the curve intersects the horizontal axis).

As an example, consider an e-commerce application in which a clothing company wants to sell goods online, retain customer profiles, and allow customers to obtain pictures

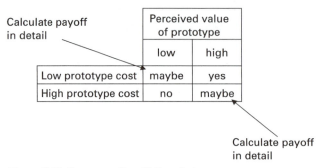

Calculate payoff in detail

Figure 3.33 Prototype Payoff: Rough Assessment

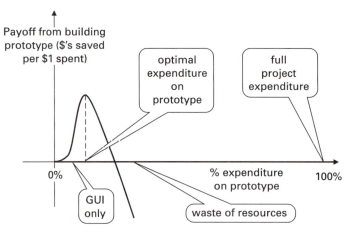

Figure 3.34 Prototype Payoff

of themselves wearing clothing from the catalog. Figure 3.35 below gives financial estimates for various levels of prototyping for the clothing vendor application. For each of the four features considered for the prototype, several estimates are made: the cost of building the feature, the percentage of the feature's implementation that will be reused in the application itself (i.e., not discarded), and the "gross benefit" from the effort. The gross benefit here is an estimate of what will be gained by implementing the feature in a prototype, excluding the reuse of the actual code, and excluding all expenses. For example, we have estimated that if the "trying on clothes" prototype were to be built, it would save a minimum $20,000 in development costs. This estimate is based on factors such as the following.

- Preventing time wasted on proposed requirements that the prototype shows are not really needed (e.g., minimum of three unneeded requirements out of 100; $300,000 budgeted for the requirements phase = $9000 saved)

- Implementing a software design for the "trying on clothes" feature, thereby retiring some development risks (e.g., estimate that this will save minimum of one person-week of design time = $2000)

- Rework that would have resulted from the customer changing requirements only after seeing the developed product (e.g., rework minimum of three requirements at $3000 each = $9000)

	Estimated Cost	Gross Benefit Excluding Code Reuse		Percentage of Prototype Code Reused in Application
		min	max	
Prototype feature				
1. GUI screenshots	$10,000	$10,000	$80,000	50%
2. Transaction security	$50,000	$10,000	$300,000	80%
3. Complete transaction	$80,000	$10,000	$400,000	50%
4. Customer tries on clothing	$120,000	$20,000	$140,000	30%

Figure 3.35 Estimates for E-Commerce Clothing Application

These minimum savings total to $9000 + $2000 + $9000 = $20,000.

Estimating the cost of building the prototype can use estimation techniques like those described in Chapter 2. The estimation of code reuse can be performed by identifying the classes of the prototype and determining which are likely to be usable in the actual application.

Estimation like this consists of adding up the estimation of smaller parts, which is still a difficult task. Bracketing each estimate between a minimum and a maximum can help to make this difficult process a little easier.

Once these estimates are made, the easy part is computing the best- and worst-case scenarios for each of these. This is shown in Figure 3.36. The minimum payoff value is obtained by taking the most pessimistic combination—the highest costs, the lowest gross benefits, and the lowest reuse percentages. The maximum payoff is calculated similarly. For example, the maximum payoff (the most optimistic alternative) for the "GUI screenshot" prototype feature is:

$$[\text{ maximum estimated benefit }] - [\text{ minimum estimated costs }]$$
$$= \$80,000 - [\text{ (minimum estimated cost)} \times \text{(percent not reusable)}]$$
$$= \$80,000 - [\$10,000 \times 50\%] = \$75,000$$

	Estimated Cost	Gross Benefit Excluding Code Reuse		Percentage of Prototype Code Reused in Application	Net Payoff		
		min	max		min	max	average
Prototype feature	B	D	E	C	D-(1-C)B	E-(1-C)B	
1. GUI screenshots	$10,000	$10,000	$80,000	50%	$5,000	$75,000	$40,000
2. Transaction security	$50,000	$10,000	$300,000	80%	$0	$290,000	$145,000
3. Complete transaction	$80,000	$10,000	$400,000	50%	−$30,000	$200,000	$85,000
4. Customer tries on clothing	$120,000	$20,000	$140,000	30%	−$64,000	$56,000	−$4,000

Figure 3.36 Prototype Payoff Calculations for E-commerce Clothing Application

Averaging is one way to deal with the spread between best and worst cases. The result suggests a positive payoff for all proposed prototype features except for the "trying on clothes" feature, which projects −$4000: an overall waste of $4000. The causes for the latter are the relatively low payoff, high development cost, and low reuse.

It may be advisable for the prototype to evolve into the application itself, but this should be planned for, not accidental. By their very nature, prototypes are rapidly constructed and rarely documented. They are frequently implemented with languages which get results quickly but which may be unsuitable for the application itself. It is quite common for developers to show the customer a prototype written in a language such as Visual Basic or PERL. Often the customer is then very impressed and assumes erroneously that the job is close to completion. An unfortunate consequence can be that the developer takes the apparently easy course of trying to evolve the prototype into the application. Unless the prototype was developed with this in mind, the project may take much longer to complete if this evolution is attempted, and an inferior product will be produced. An analogy to this is specifying a house for a customer by building a prototype house from bales of hay, giving the customer a good idea of what the eventual house will look like from a distance. Few would suggest, however, that the hay bales should form the basis for the actual construction.

"Rapid application development" (RAD) refers to prototyping. In the author's opinion, the name "rapid application development" is a misnomer. If RAD really was a way to develop *proper* applications rapidly then everyone would use it. This magic way would quickly become the norm, and would no longer be considered rapid.

5.2 Feasibility Studies

It is sometimes uncertain whether proposed requirements can be implemented at all. In other words, there is a risk to the entire project, rather than risks focused on specific requirements. In addition, the project would not be feasible—not worth building—if the risk were to be a reality. In such cases, *feasibility studies* may have to be performed. These studies are partial implementations or simulations of the application. For example, consider the feasibility of a Java Internet-based *Encounter*, and let's say we suspect performance will be so slow that the game would therefore be of negligible interest to anyone. A feasibility study could consist of setting up a message passing simulation at the anticipated rate from a number of players, but with dummy content. Delays could then be estimated by measuring the simulation.

Simulations are expensive since they are applications themselves, requiring the software engineering artifacts described in this book, such as their own SRS! The author was once involved with a simulation of a large system under development. The simulation grew into a large program in its own right, and was needed for several years, while the real system was being developed. No one took the requirements for the simulation seriously because it was not "the real thing." As a result, the cost of maintaining and using the simulation became astronomical. For example, to make changes required first tracking down an employee who "knew the system." Feasibility simulations are common in large defense programs which involve extensive software and hardware.

When we simply cannot tell whether an envisaged application concept would be worthwhile, a *proof-of-concept* may sometimes be constructed. This is a partial implementation of, or program similar to the envisaged application. Before the U.S. Navy built the Aegis generation of shipboard systems, for example, it built an entire scaled-back shipboard system, complete with software and hardware. This proof-of-concept served to satisfy the Navy that there was a good chance that the concepts envisioned for Aegis could be built within an acceptable time, for an acceptable cost.

6. UPDATING THE PROJECT TO REFLECT C-REQUIREMENTS ANALYSIS

The document set is a living entity: It has to be fed and cared for at regular intervals throughout the life of the project. Typically, when a phase is executed, several documents are affected. Managing this process, often beyond the capability of organizations, is key to the health of a project.

6.1 C-Requirements and Project Scales

For large projects, the process of analyzing the customer's requirements is relatively formal and organized. For example, the U.S. Department of Defense (DoD) often publishes a request for proposals (RFP) just to develop an SRS. Such an RFP contains only a very high-level description of the project. The RFP can be thought of as a C-requirement, and the contractor's product as the D-requirements. Several DoD personnel are assigned to deal with the SRS contractor, which may or may not be the contractor chosen to perform the design and development of the actual application. To ensure that the requirements are satisfactory, numerous meetings are held. These meetings involve contractor personnel, civil servant specialists and managers, and uniformed officers of the Navy or Air Force, etc. The SRS can easily add up to thousands of pages.

6.2 Effects of C-Requirements Analysis on the Project Plan

Once C-requirements have been gathered, the SPMP can be updated as shown in Table 3.1. Such updating occurs throughout the life cycle of an application.

The resulting schedule would typically be like that shown in Figure 3.37, with more detail than the schedule shown when the SPMP was originally drafted (Chapter 2), but still not very detailed.

Although the requirements analysis process can iterate throughout the life of the project, there are practical limits to such iteration. The customer typically needs to know the cost of the job early in the process, but developers will typically commit to a price only after the requirements are frozen. This limits the degree to which requirements are iterated.

TABLE 3.1 Updating Project Plan after Obtaining C-Requirements

	Status after Initial Draft	Result of Updating SPMP after Obtaining C-Requirements
Milestones	Initial	More milestones; more specific
Risks	Identify initial risks	Retire risks identified previously; identify more risks now that more is known about the project
Schedule	Very rough	Preliminary project schedule
Personnel	Designate C-Requirements engineers	Designated engineers for D-Requirements analysis
Cost estimation	Very rough	First estimates based on job content

Cost estimation can be improved once C-requirements have been analyzed. The main improvement stems from the increased understanding which the developers have for the scope and nature of the application. The function point estimates can be made more complete, and so can the estimates derived from them for schedule and labor. Direct bottom-up estimates can be improved as well.

The Software Requirements Specification and its sections are *software configuration items (CIs)*, as defined in Section 7.3.1 of Chapter 1 (page 51). Figure 3.38 shows a typical snapshot of the SRS configuration status. Notice that the revision number of a heading cannot be any less than that of its subsection CIs. For example, the *Introduction* revision number is at least 3 because its *scope* subsection went through 3 revisions, and each of these revisions would have caused a separate revision of the *Introduction*.

7. FUTURE DIRECTIONS AND SUMMARY OF C-REQUIREMENTS

7.1 Future Directions

Since requirements analysis is crucial to the software engineering enterprise, research has been performed on it for a number of years. One line of research, "executable specifications," involves specifying requirements in a way that can be automatically translated into executable code. Since the style of requirements is declarative (statements of fact), executable specifications require a process that converts declarative statements into the command statements of computers. The Prolog computer language is declarative and also executable, and has been used for many applications. It proves that a set of statements which resemble requirements ("what is" rather than "how to") can be made to execute.

For a number of years it was widely felt that CASE (Computer-aided Software Engineering) tools could greatly simplify the process of tracking requirements. The use of such tools has undergone cycles of optimism and pessimism. Another line of research (e.g., [Su]) goes further than the use case idea by providing a library of high-level object-oriented patterns against which the requirements engineer attempts to match the project at hand. Some feel that many requirements can be constituted from libraries of existing use cases. There have been several attempts to apply Artificial Intelligence to requirements analysis, often in the form of an intelligent assistant: None of these is in widespread use as the millennium turns, however. The growing extent of user-computer interaction is having a profound effect on requirements analysis, introducing many new issues (see, for example, [We]).

7.2 Summary

This chapter has described the process whereby the customer's requirements for the product are obtained and recorded in a manner clear to the customer. The customer's requirements are documented in a form such as Sections 1 and 2 of IEEE 830-1993 Software Requirements Specifications. Various techniques for eliciting and recording C-requirements are used, including use cases.

Requirements analysis is a challenging process because understanding what's wanted and needed requires considerable active elicitation from the customer. The points of this chapter are summarized in Figure 3.39.

	17- May	31-May	13-Jun	27-Jun	11-Jul	25-Jul	11-Aug	25-Aug	8-Sep
Milestones	Complete release 0.1 X								
								Complete release 0.2 X	
Develop release 0.1	██	██	██						
C-requirements	▓								
D-requirements	▓								
Architecture		▓							
Detailed design		▓							
Implementation			▓						
Test			▓						
Develop release 0.2			██	██	██	██	██	██	██
C-requirements			▓						
D-requirements			▓						
Architecture				▓					
Detailed design					▓				
Implementation						▓	▓		
Unit test						▓	▓		
Integration								▓	
System test								▓	

Figure 3.37 Typical Schedule After C-Requirements Analysis

SRS rev. 2.1   5/27/98

1. Introduction	rev 3
1.1. Purpose	rev 2
1.2. Scope	rev 3
1.3. Definitions, acronyms, and abbreviations	rev 2
1.4. References	rev 1
1.5. Overview	rev 3
2. Overall description	rev 4
2.1. Product perspective	rev 4
2.1.1. System interfaces	rev 2
2.1.2. User interfaces	rev 1
2.1.3. Hardware interfaces	rev 1
2.1.4. Software interfaces	rev 4
2.1.5. Communications interfaces	rev 1
2.1.6. Memory constraints	rev 4
2.1.7. Operations	rev 1
2.1.8. Site adaptation requirements	rev 4
2.2. Product functions	rev 3
2.3. User characteristics	rev 3
2.4. Constraints	rev 3
2.5. Assumptions and dependencies	rev 4
2.6. Apportioning of requirements	rev 1
3. Specific requirements	rev 6
(see next chapter)	
4. Supporting information	rev 3

Figure 3.38 Typical Snapshot of SRS Configuration Status   Copyright © 1994 IEEE

- C-requirements primarily for customer
  - include user interfaces
- D-requirements for developers
- Use standard SRS (e.g., IEEE)
- Use cases very effective
  - reuse as test cases
- State- and data flow-diagrams can be effective specifications as well

Figure 3.39 Summary of Chapter

This section explains how the principles covered in this chapter are translated into practice, by using the case study as the example. The student is also referred to the "One way to . . ." figures throughout this chapter, which act as a general guide to the process.

SPG1. PREPARING

Hal Furness, having been elected the requirements leader, was responsible for organizing the analysis of the requirements. As per the project organization, Hal was backed up by Karen Peters. They decided to gather requirements in two stages. The first would be primarily from the customer's perspective (C-requirements), and the second primarily for developers (D-requirements). [This guide describes the C-requirements process. The student guide in the next chapter describes the D-requirements.]

Hal and Karen prepared to gather metrics on the requirements process. They classified the stages of the process by *preparation, interview, write-up,* and *review.* The metrics they chose were dictated mostly by company policy, and were

- *Time taken*
- *Pages of C-requirements written*
- *Self-assessment* of the artifacts on a scale of 1-10 (not mandated by company policy)

- *Defects found* during inspections, as applicable

The reader is referred to Section 4 of this guide to see these metrics arranged in tabular form.

Karen made sure that the system for logging and tracking defects was in place and that Hal was equipped with the documentation of how to use it.

The company's investors considered video games a promising area, and were willing to provide seed money for requirements analysis and a prototype. It was now Hal and Karen's task to determine with whom to speak to get C-requirements. Hal understood that none of the team knew much about video games. He decided to interview people who frequently play games and are interested in giving their time for a modest fee. He made contact with Betty Sims, President of Amateur Gamers International, an enthusiastic game player who saw a bright future for video games as vehicles for fun, community involvement, and education. Betty also knew many gamers. Hal and Karen decided to write up requirements specifications based on Betty's input, and then show the specifications to others. The rest of the team was to investigate other avenues for input at the same time.

At a weekly meeting, Hal presented a plan for requirements analysis, as follows.

Week 1:

Hal and Karen: Interview Betty; Begin drafting C-requirements.

Fern and Al: Seek other candidates for requirements input.

Week 2:

Fern and Al: Report candidates to weekly meeting.

Team: Select one or two additional people to supply requirements.

Hal and Karen: Complete draft of C-requirements, e-mail to Betty for comments; arrange to interview the designated additional people; e-mail existing specification to them; create a complete requirements document for iteration 1; place under configuration control.

Week 3:

Team: Approve the SRS for iteration 1.

Hal and Karen: Interview designated people; edit and expand the specification; e-mail to all interviewees; collate responses; edit document, leaving selected issues for team resolution; plan D-requirements analysis [see next chapter].

Week 4:

Team: Provide input on the draft SRS; approve plan for D-requirements analysis [see next chapter].

Hal and Karen: Write up SRS and e-mail to all interviewees.

Week 5:

Hal and Karen: Resolve issues raised by interviewees; write up results; e-mail to team; begin implementing D-requirements process [see next chapter].

Team: Inspect C-requirements.

Despite the expense, Hal felt it important to have the entire team inspect the C-requirements because of the document's importance. In general, the team planned to use three-person inspection teams.

Hal scheduled the first interview with Betty in Room 1428 of the Stewart Building from 10:00 A.M. to 11:30 A.M. He e-mailed her a brief write-up of the project's history, and created the following very simple agenda.

10:00 A.M. – 10:15 A.M. Hal: motives for the project

10:15 A.M. – 11:30 A.M. Interview of Betty: customer requirements

Hal decided not to introduce more details because he wanted Betty's requirements to influence the rest of the meeting.

SPG2. INTERVIEWING THE CUSTOMER

Hal and Karen arrived at the interview with Betty, equipped with good sound recording equipment. Betty could not understand why anyone would want to build a video game unless it competed with the best available. Hal explained that this was just a first step, to provide the team with experience in this kind of programming, to get an idea of the scope of work required, and to show the investors what could be accomplished with a given amount of funding. Other motives were to determine whether there was any merit to the ideas that video games have potentially wide appeal, and are applicable to education. After this, the meeting became more focused. The tape recorder was turned on and Hal and Karen began to take detailed notes.

Betty's contention was that role-playing games (not action games) held the most promise for broadening the player community. She discussed the minimum capability that a prototype would need. This included areas where the game characters would engage, ways to get from one area to the other, ways to cause interactions among characters, and what would happen when the characters engaged. Hal and Karen tried to separate the issues and features as they arose, into "crucial for the first iteration," "can be postponed," and "other" (i.e., they used a triage method). The importance of the requirements listed in "other" would be determined later.

Given the script-like nature of the requirements Betty described, Hal focused on obtaining use cases from her. He asked her to describe typical scenarios for the game.

Betty described what happens when two characters interact. Karen took notes and expressed this as a use case—a sequence of actions taken by the player and/or the game—and then read it back to Betty.

Betty couldn't think of any other scenarios. Hal felt that there must be more, and asked how the game gets started. This resulted in a second use case. The third use case that they recognized explained how the player moves his character from one area to another. These three use cases seemed to be a satisfactory beginning. Hal and Karen felt that there might be additional essential use cases, but they would have to gather them later.

Betty, Karen, and Hal sketched a few screens together. One showed a typical encounter, and another showed a screen for entering the qualities of game characters. There was considerable discussion of the perspective that the player would have. Betty wanted a player perspective where the view shown on the monitor is the view seen by the player. Karen felt that the required complexity for that view would take the project well beyond their modest initial budget. It was agreed that a modified from-above view would be adequate for the prototype. The screen sketches reflected this. They agreed that considerable refinement of the user interface would be required.

As a result of the interfaces that they sketched, Karen felt that the game could really be understood only by means of states. Betty was not familiar with this term, but she was comfortable describing what she called the "modes" of a typical role-playing game, which turned out to be the same concept. Karen and Hal then sketched out the required states of the game, and reviewed with Karen how the game gets from one state to another.

Hal briefly considered clarifying the game further by analyzing the flow of data, but soon realized that the data flow perspective added little value.

Karen reviewed her notes with the others. A few points needed correcting but there was general agreement on the description.

SPG3.   WRITING UP THE SOFTWARE REQUIREMENTS SPECIFICATION

Hal and Karen divided the task of writing up the SRS by sections. They used the IEEE SRS standard, Sections 1 and 2 (Section 3 consists of the detailed requirements, the process for which is discussed in the Student Project Guide for Chapter 4). To avoid conflicting write-ups, they made sure that their sections were as independent as possible. Hal remembered his previous project, where the team spent so much time reconciling pieces written by different people, that it would have been quicker for one person to perform the entire task alone.

They discussed how to prioritize the requirements, because it was becoming clear that otherwise the list of requirements would become far larger than the team could handle. Hal wanted to rank them all, but Karen pointed out that the effort involved would be largely wasted: Most of the top-ranking requirements would get done anyway, so their exact order would not be important. Almost none of the bottom ones would get done, so the time spent ranking them would also be wasted. They decided to use a triage method to rank requirements into *essential* at one extreme, *optional* at the other, and *desirable* for the middle category (which simply means neither essential nor optional). They felt that it might be necessary to rank the desirable requirements later. This saved a great deal of useless debating time. They described their classification scheme in Section 2.6 of the SRS ("Apportioning of requirements").

Section 2.1.1 (concept of operations, containing the state diagram for the game) took Hal the longest time to write because he had to translate Betty's informal comments into a concrete form. They tried to cross-reference appropriate sections of the SRS with corresponding tests even though the tests were still sketchy. This helped to clarify the requirements themselves, however. When Betty looked at the test for Section 2.1.1, she recognized that Hal and

Karen did not understand some of the issues. In particular, when the game is in *Reporting* state and the foreign character enters the area containing the player's character, the test did not expect anything to happen. Betty saw this as detrimental and as a way for the player to effectively halt the game. The defect was added to the list of defects with a "major" categorization.

Karen sketched the user interfaces using Powerpoint™ as a drawing tool, rather than building them with Java, the target language. She considered PowerPoint™ adequate because the UIs in this part of the SRS are meant to be sketches—the detailed UIs are specified in Section 3—and, in any case, they were liable to be changed a great deal. This helped Hal and Karen to show the sketches to Betty and the others, obtain feedback, and then specify the UIs exactly for the D-requirements.

SPG4. FOLLOWING UP

The SRS Sections 1 and 2 were e-mailed to Betty. She realized that Hal and Karen had included only two of the three use cases, and the third use case describing movement of the player's character was absent. This defect was logged with a high priority.

Betty was surprised to see that the SRS did not reflect several issues that she thought she had made clear were important, and humbled to see that the SRS reflected "requirements" that she had offhandedly mentioned but now realized would be a waste of time. The latter included the ability of the player to change outfits while an engagement is progressing. She had numerous comments, most of which Hal and Karen responded to, and some of which were added to the list of defects.

Hal e-mailed the SRS Sections 1 and 2 to the team to enable them to prepare for an inspection.

Team leader Ed had learned about Arlan Howard, a marketing executive who was very familiar with the video game industry. The financial backers were willing to fund further requirements analysis at the customer level, and Hal and Karen prepared to meet with Howard. The latter was not able to grant them more than half an hour since he was very busy. Karen developed a prioritized list of questions and topics and mailed them and the existing draft of SRS Chapters 1 and 2 to Howard. They planned to wrap up the C-requirements with Howard.

The team also planned the process of developing the D-requirements. [See the student project guide for Chapter 4.]

SPG5. METRICS AND POSTMORTEM

The C-requirements were subjected to an inspection by the entire team and the defects were recorded.

For the next weekly meeting, Hal and Karen summarized the metrics as shown in Table 3.2. The team agreed on the postmortem observations shown.

EXERCISES

Solutions and hints are given at the end of this chapter to all exercises marked with "s" and "h" respectively.

REVIEW QUESTIONS

R3.1[s] What is the difference between a C-requirement and a D-requirement?

R3.2[s] What are the advantages and disadvantages of separating requirements into C- and D- categories?

TABLE 3.2 Postmortem Results

	Preparation	Interview	Write-up (results of inspection)	Review	Total
Time spent (minutes)	200 mins	170 mins	270 mins	250 mins	14.8 hours
% Time spent	200/890 = 22% // **20%***	170/890 = 19% // **23%***	270/890 = 30% // **27%***	250/890 = 28% // **29%***	
Quantity produced			15 pages		
Productivity (Time/quantity)			15/14.8 = 1.01 pages per hour // **0.95***		
Self-assessed quality (1-10)	9	5	9	2	
Defect rate			1.3 per page // **1.01 per page***		
Process improvement	Spend 20% less time preparing	Spread interview time more evenly among different people	Material well written initially, but should be checked more thoroughly prior to inspection	Spend ±30% more time reviewing	

*This project's organization norms.

R3.3[s] What is a use case?

R3.4[s] Is the following a use case?

"The system shall provide advice for the beginning Windows™ user on how to execute Windows™ operations."

R3.5[s] In which of the following applications does it make sense to build complete prototypes? (yes, no, or maybe)

a. A parcel tracking system for a major parcel delivery company

b. A simple system to store information about personal compact disc collections

c. A system to track retirement accounts in a small business

R3.6[s] Which of the following applications requires a feasibility study?

a. A database system for storing and accessing employee records

b. A system that automatically summarizes an input paragraph into a single sentence

GENERAL EXERCISES

G3.1[h] Brackett makes the point that the more constrained an application, the less reliance we have on people as the source of requirements. (Refer to his graph in Fig. 3.7 comparing "approximate percent of requirements gathered from people" with "type of application.") Can you think of any applications that do *not* fall on the graph's diagonal?

G3.2 Suppose that you are trying to describe an automobile application that reports the status of the starter system to the dashboard. How could you describe this in overall terms?

G3.3 In less than 3 pages, give requirements for an application that tracks bar-coded company invoices.

G3.4 Your customer needs to specify user interfaces. Discuss the pros and cons of the following means for doing this in the context of the application (large or small) and the nature of the GUI (complex or simple).

    a. Sketch using hand drawings—drawn by a graphic artist or yourself

    b. Sketch using graphics tools, such as Paint or PowerPoint

    c. Use the GUI-building features of the target language of the application

TEAM EXERCISES

T3.1 Write the C-requirements for an application decided upon by the team. Follow the form of IEEE 830-1993. Track the amount of time spent doing this exercise. Decide what fraction of the requirements are understood by the team. Estimate how long it would take to obtain 95% of the requirements. State how the process you used could have been improved. Be specific, and provide examples.

T3.2 a. Identify an individual outside the team who needs a modest application. You will be gathering C-requirements from this individual, then showing them to her.

b. With your "customer," identify metrics for how she will evaluate your C-requirements. Also determine the time limit for an interview (e.g., $1/2$ hour).

c. Interview the customer, and write the C-requirements.

d. Have the customer evaluate and comment on your C-requirements in accordance with the chosen metrics.

HINTS FOR QUESTIONS

G3.1 a. Find an application that is relatively constrained but whose requirements are to be gathered mostly from people.

b. Find an application that is relatively unconstrained but whose requirements are to be gathered mostly from sources other than people.

SOLUTIONS TO QUESTIONS

R3.1 C-requirements express the requirements in a form suitable for the customer, and consist mainly of a high-level description. The form of D-requirements is suitable for developers. D-requirements are a detailed form of the C-requirements.

R3.2 Customers and developers have different requirement needs. The advantages of separating C-requirements and D-requirements include the fact that they are likely to satisfy these different needs. The disadvantages include the possibility that the two forms of description are not consistent.

R3.3 A use case is a sequence of user/application interactions for a typical usage.

R3.4 This is not a use case because it is not a sequence of actions taken by the application and a user of the application.

R3.5   a. Parcel tracking: yes

   b. CD collections: probably too small to warrant a prototype

   c. Retirement accounts: maybe (no if the application is intended for one customer; perhaps, if it is intended for sale to many customers as a product)

R3.6   a. Database system: probably too standard to require a feasibility study

   b. Automatic summarizer: yes

CASE STUDY:

SOFTWARE REQUIREMENTS SPECIFICATION (SRS) FOR THE *ENCOUNTER* VIDEO GAME, PART 1 OF 2

[Note to the student: Using a standard to write the SRS helps one to cover all of the aspects of requirements that readers need to know about, and provides a recognized structure. Several standards are available but we will concentrate on the IEEE standard. The complete IEEE 830-1993 standard can be found in [IE]. Most organizations allow modification of the standard to tailor it for their own use. The template used below modifies the standard by omitting some less important sections and by adding sections on concept of operations and use cases. The student can compare the case study headings with the standards shown in Figure 3.6 on page 140.]

[Note to the student: The case study portion in this chapter, Sections 1 and 2, covers the customer (C-)requirements. The remainder of the document, Sections 3 and 4, containing the specific (D-)requirements, is provided in the case study at the end of Chapter 4. Recall that C-requirements are not intended to be detailed enough to develop the design and implementation: This is the purpose of the D-requirements.]

History of versions of this document.

x/yy/zzz Hal Furness: Initial draft

x/yy/zzz Karen Peters: Reviewed for technical accuracy; changes made throughout

x/yy/zzz Hal Furness: Entire document reviewed for small improvements

x/yy/zzz Karen Peters: Document reviewed and suggestions made

x/yy/zzz Karen Peters: Moved use cases to Section 2.2

x/yy/zzz Hal Furness: Improved wording throughout; sense not changed

1.   INTRODUCTION

1.1 Purpose

[Note to the student: The purpose of this entire document (not the purpose of the application)]

This document provides all of the requirements for the *Encounter* video game. Parts 1 and 2 are intended primarily for customers of the application, but will also be of interest to software engineers building or maintaining the software. Part 3 is intended primarily for software engineers, but will also be of interest to customers.

1.2 Scope

[Note to the student: What aspects of the application this document is intended to cover?]

This document covers the requirements for release 0.0.1 of *Encounter*. Mention

TABLE 3.3 Acronyms

Acronym or Term	Definition
Alive	A game character is said to be "alive" if it has at least one quality with nonzero value.
C-requirement	Statement of the requirements for the application, expressed in a form clear to the customer.
D-requirement	Statement of the requirements for the application, given in a form detailed enough to be used by the developers for design and implementation. If possible, D-requirements should also be understandable to the customer.
Encounter	Name of this application; also, a meeting between two game characters in an area (but not necessarily an "engagement"—see below).
Engagement	An interaction between characters of the game, which typically affects the characters.
RPG	"Role-playing game": a game typically played on a computer, in which the players adopt character roles.
Role-playing game	See RPG.
Video game	A game played on a computer.

will be made throughout this document of selected probable features of future releases. The purpose of this is to guide developers in selecting a design that will be able to accommodate the full-scale application.

1.3 Definitions, Acronyms, and Abbreviations

See Table 3.3.

1.4 References

Software Configuration Management Plan (SCMP) for *Encounter version 1.0*

Software Design Description (SDD) for *Encounter version 1.2*

Software Project Management Plan (SPMP) for *Encounter version 1.2*

Software Quality Assurance Plan (SQAP) for *Encounter version 1.0*

Software User Documentation Plan (SUDP) for *Encounter version 1.0*

Software Test Documentation (STD) for *Encounter version 1.0*

1.5 Overview

Intentionally omitted.

[Note to the student: The author of this document felt no need for this section, and intends to cover the overview in Section 2.]

2. OVERALL DESCRIPTION

[Note to the student: Make this general enough so that it is unlikely to change much in future versions. Avoid statements that are repeated in later sections.]

Encounter is to be a role-playing game which simulates all or part of the lifetime of the player's main character. It should be of interest to both men and women. The measure of "success" in playing *Encounter* is up to the player. Typically, success will be measured by the "life points" maximum attained by the player or by the ability of the player to live as long a life as possible.

Some game characters are to be under the control of the player. The rest, called "foreign" characters, are to be under the application's control. Game characters will have a fixed total number of points allocated among qualities such as *strength, stamina, patience,* etc. Characters encounter each other when they are in the same area at the same time, and may then engage each other. The result of the engagement depends on the values of their qualities and on the environment in which the engagement takes place. Engagements are not necessarily violent or adversarial. Players have restricted opportunities to reallocate their qualities. One of the player-controlled characters will be referred to as the "main" player character.

In early versions of this game, there will be only one player-controlled character and one foreign character.

The eventual nature of the characters is to be determined from insights gained from surveys and focus groups. It is expected that initial releases will not have animation.

Encounter should eventually be highly customizable, so that users can either start with predefined games, substitute predesigned characters and rules of engagement, or devise their own characters and rules of engagement.

The design should support expansion into a family of games, including Internet-based multiple player versions.

2.1 Product Perspective

[Note to the student: In this section, Encounter *is compared with other related or competing products. This is a useful way to provide perspective on the application. Subheading 2.1.1. of this section has been changed from the IEEE standard to accommodate "concept of operations."]*

Encounter is intended to fulfill the need for programmers to have a greater influence over the contents of video games with additional programming. It is also intended for a somewhat mature clientele. *Encounter* is intended to appeal to both genders. The design and documentation for *Encounter* will make it convenient to expand and modify the game. It

is anticipated that *Encounter* will be used as a legacy application for expansion into applications such as office interaction simulations.

2.1.1 Concept of Operations

[Note to the student: This section conveys the overall concept of the application by whatever means are most natural for doing so. In the case of Encounter, *the requirements developers decided that state/transitions best convey the concept.]*

Encounter can be in one of the following states (also shown in Figure 3.40).

- *Setting up:* the state in which the game is being set up by the player

- *Reporting:* The system is displaying a window showing the status of the player's character(s).

- *Setting qualities:* equipping the player's character with qualities. This process consumes arbitrary amounts of time, and can be performed as long as no foreign character is present.

- *Engaging:* the state which applies whenever a foreign character and the player's main character are present in an area at the same time.

- *Waiting:* The player and the foreign character(s) are not active.

This state/transition is tested by integration test <to be supplied>.

2.1.2 User Interface Concepts

[Note to the student: The following figures are preliminary sketches of key user interfaces only, used to provide perspective on the product. All the user interfaces are specified in detail in Section 3. We have modified the standard IEEE heading "user interfaces" to emphasize that these are not the detailed UIs.]

2.1.2.1 Area User Interface Concept.
The areas in which encounters take place shall have an appearance very roughly like that shown in Figure 3.41.

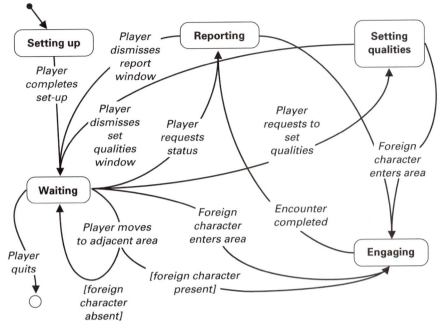

Figure 3.40 Encounter State-Transition Diagram

2.1.2.2 User Interface Concept for Setting Quality Values. When setting the values of game characters under his control, the player retrieves an interface of the form sketched approximately in Figure 3.42. The scroll box is used to identify the quality to be set, and the text box is used for setting the value.

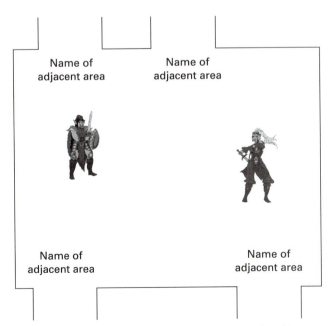

Figure 3.41 Preliminary Encounter Screen Shot (Graphics reproduced with permission from Corel)

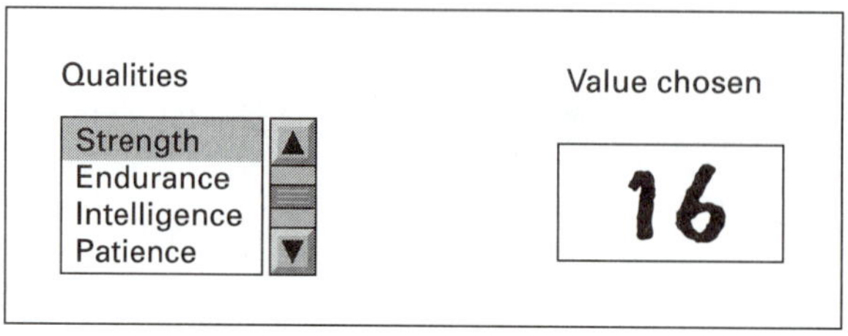

*Figure 3.42 Preliminary Sketch of User Interface for
Setting Game Character Qualities*

2.1.3 Hardware Interfaces
None. Future releases will utilize a joystick.

2.1.4 Software Interfaces
None.

2.1.5 Communications Interfaces
None. Future releases will interface with the Internet via a modem.

2.1.6 Memory Constraints
Encounter shall require no more than 16 MB of RAM and 20 MB of secondary storage (see test plan <test reference to be supplied>).

2.1.7 Operations
[Note to the student: Normal and special operations required by the user]

[Future release] It shall be possible to save and retrieve a game.

2.1.8 Site Adaptation Requirements
[Note to the student: Requirements for execution on a particular installation; versions in various languages (e.g., French, Japanese, Spanish)]

None.

2.2 Product Functions
[Note to the student: Summary of the major functions of the application. More detailed than Section 1.5; less detailed than Section 3. The writers of this SRS decided that use cases are an appropriate manner in which to specify the overall functionality of *Encounter.]*

This section specifies the required overall functionality of the application, but is not intended to provide the complete specifications. Section 3 provides the requirements in complete detail.

2.2.1 "Initialize" Use Case
Actor: player of *Encounter*

Use case: Figure 3.43 gives the text of the *Initialize* use case. The use case is shown in context with the *Encounter foreign character* use case and the *Set rules* use cases. *Initialize* is the typical sequence users execute at the beginning of a session.

This use case corresponds to test <test reference to be supplied> in the Software Test Documentation.

2.2.2 "Travel to Adjacent Area" Use Case
Actor: player of *Encounter*

Use case:

1. *Player* hits hyperlink connecting displayed area to adjacent area.

2. *System* displays the indicated adjacent area including player's character.

2.2.3 "Encounter Foreign Character" Use Case
Actor: player of *Encounter*

Use case:

1. *System* moves a foreign game character into the area occupied by the player,

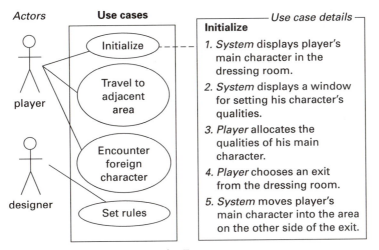

Figure 3.43 Initialize Use Case for Encounter

or *Player* moves into an area containing a foreign character.

2. *System* causes the two characters to engage.

3. *System* displays the result of the engagement.

4. If either the player's character or the foreign character has no points, the game terminates.

5. Otherwise, *System* moves the player's character to a random area different from that in which the encounter took place, and displays it there.

2.3 User Characteristics

[Note to the student: Indicate what kind of people the typical users are likely to be. Examples: novice, software professional, accountant with 5 years of computer usage, etc.]

The user is expected to be approximately 20–35 years of age.

2.4 Constraints

[Note to the student: all conditions that may limit the developer's options. These can originate from many sources.]

Encounter shall operate on PCs running Windows 95 or later at a minimum speed of 100 MHz. Java shall be the implementation language.

2.5 Assumptions and Dependencies

[Note to the student: any assumptions being made, e.g., future hardware]

None.

2.6 Apportioning of Requirements

[Note to the student: Order in which requirements are to be implemented.]

The requirements described in Sections 1 and 2 of this document are referred to as "C-requirements"; those in Section 3 are referred to as "D-requirements." The primary audience for C-requirements is the customer community, and the secondary audience is the developer community. The reverse is true for the D-requirements. These two levels of requirements are intended to be consistent. Inconsistencies are to be logged as defects. In the event that a requirement is stated within both the C-requirements and the D-requirements, the application shall be built from the D-requirement version since it is more detailed.

"Essential" requirements (referred to in Section 3) are to be implemented for this version of *Encounter*. "Desirable" requirements are to be implemented in this release if possible, but are not committed to by the developers. It is anticipated that they will be part of a future release. "Optional" requirements will be implemented at the discretion of the developers.

CHAPTER 4

REQUIREMENTS ANALYSIS II: COMPLETING THE SRS WITH SPECIFIC D-REQUIREMENTS

... rich, not gaudy

-Polonius, from *Hamlet*

Detailed requirements are the only place where the exact nature of the application is written down. The level of detail should be complete, but not redundant.

Figure 4.1 shows the content of this chapter in the context of the software engineering process. Figure 4.2 lists the learning goals for this chapter.

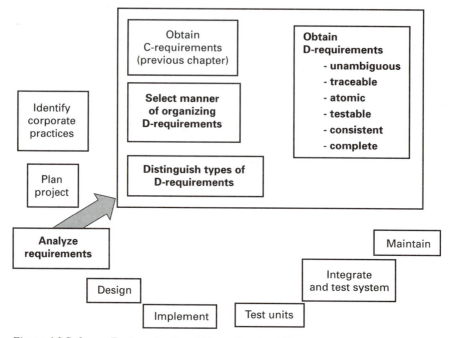

Figure 4.1 Software Engineering Road Map: Chapter 4 Focus

- Be equipped with options for organizing D-requirements
  - by class
  - by use case
  - by feature
  - by event

- Be able to complete requirements
  - be detailed enough to enable complete design and implementation
  - be able to express the nonfunctional requirements, e.g., performance

Figure 4.2 Chapter Learning Goals

► PART I : ESSENTIALS

1. INTRODUCTION TO SPECIFIC (OR D-) REQUIREMENTS

1.1 The Meaning of Specific or D-Requirements

Software engineers need a basis for design and implementation. This basis consists of the *detailed requirements*. These are also called "specific requirements," "functional specifications," "developer requirements," or "D-requirements." D-requirements consist of a complete list of specific properties and functionality that the application must possess, expressed in final detail. Each of these requirements is numbered, labeled, and tracked through implementation. They are consistent with, and elaborate upon, the C-requirements.

The D-requirements are intended to be read primarily by developers. Customers are interested in them as well and are typically able to understand and comment on many of them. Recall that the primary audience for the C-requirements consists of customers.

When it comes to software engineering, "the devil is in the details." For example, in 1999 NASA lost a weather satellite worth hundreds of millions of dollars, reportedly because control data they had assumed to be in metric form was not [Bo3]. The fascinating issue here is that this defect was identified within mere days of the disaster. What a pity it had not been identified at development time! The first line of defense against corruption or omission of details is the set of D-requirements. Far from being the mindless activity that it might first appear, getting *all* the requirements down in complete detail involves the difficult task of organizing people and documentation. To understand this challenge, imagine the task of organizing a 20-volume requirements document set so that a NASA engineer, for example, would know exactly where to look for a specific requirement.

1.2 A Typical Road Map of D-Requirements Analysis

Figure 4.3 shows a typical sequence of activities for gathering and documenting D-requirements. Section 5 describes ways in which specific requirements can be organized. D-requirements are written from the C-requirements as explained in Section 3. Ideally, we begin writing tests for each of the specific requirements simultaneously with writing the requirements themselves. Although D-requirements are written primarily for developers, the requirements and their tests are also reviewed with the customer. The D-requirements should then be inspected and released (see Section 6.3).

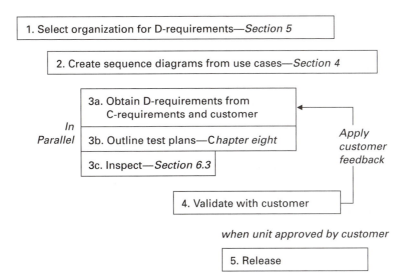

Figure 4.3 Road Map for Detailed (D-)Requirements

2.   TYPES OF D-REQUIREMENTS

There are several types of requirements, as summarized in Figure 4.4 and Figure 4.5. This classification applies to both C- and D-requirements. During the writing of C-requirements, these distinctions are often secondary to getting points across to the customer about the application in general. The classification becomes much more significant when writing the D-requirements, however, because it guides the development and testing process in different ways. The classification in Figures 4.4 and 4.5 is modified from Ross [Ro]. The various types of requirements are described next.

2.1 Functional Requirements

Functional requirements specify services that the application must provide (e.g., "The application shall compute the value of the user's stock portfolio."). On the other hand, a requirement such as "the application shall complete each portfolio value computation in less than one second" is not a functional requirement, because it does not specify a specific service. Instead, it qualifies a service or services (specifies something *about* them).

1. Functional requirements
   - the application's functionality
2. Nonfunctional requirements
   2.1 Performance
   - speed
   - capacity (traffic rates)
   - memory usage
     - RAM
     - disk
   2.2 Reliability and availability
   2.3 Error handling

Figure 4.4 Types of Requirements, 1 of 2

   2.4 Interface requirements
   how the application interacts with the
   user, and with other applications
   2.5 Constraints
   - accuracy
   - tool and language constraints
     - e.g. "FORTRAN 88 must be used"
   - design constraints
   - standards to be used
   - hardware platforms to be used
3. Inverse requirements
   what the application does not do

Figure 4.5 Types of Requirements, 2 of 2

2.2 Nonfunctional Requirements: Performance Requirements

Performance requirements specify timing constraints that the application must observe. Customers and developers negotiate constraints on elapsed time for computations, RAM usage, secondary storage usage, and so forth. For example:

> *For any beam, the Stress Analyzer shall produce a stress report of type five in less than a minute of elapsed time.*

Performance requirements are a critical part of real-time applications in which actions must complete within specified time limits. Examples of real-time applications include collision avoidance software, flight control applications, and antilock brake controls.

2.3 Nonfunctional Requirements: Reliability and Availability

Reliability requirements specify reliability in quantified terms. This kind of requirement recognizes that applications are unlikely to be perfect, and so circumscribes their extent of imperfection. For example:

> *The Airport Radar Application(ARA) shall experience no more than two level one faults per month.*

Availability, closely related to reliability, quantifies the degree to which the application is to be available to its users. For example:

> *ARA shall be available at level one or two on either the primary or backup computer at all times. ARA shall be unavailable on one of these computers at level one or two for no more than 2% of the time in any 30-day period.*

2.4 Nonfunctional Requirements: Error Handling

This category of requirements explains how the application must respond to errors in its environment. For example, what should the application do if it receives a message from another application which is not in an agreed-upon format? These are not errors generated by the application itself.

In some cases, "Error handling" refers to actions which the application should take if it finds *itself* having committed an error because of a defect in its construction. This kind of error requirement should be applied selectively, however, because our aim is to produce defect-free applications, rather than cover our mistakes with endless error handling code. In particular, when a function is called with improper parameters, we program a continuation of the application only if such an (erroneous) continuation is preferable to the cessation of the application.

For example, suppose that we have to specify the requirements for a device that automatically applies doses of intravenous drugs. We assume that the application will be thoroughly specified, designed, implemented, and inspected, so that the drug composition and dosage computations are supposed to be correct. Still, it would be wise in a case like this to specify an independent check of the composition and dosage of the drugs before administering them, and to specify error handling accordingly.

In summary, error checking on the application itself is appropriate for critical parts of the application at a minimum.

2.5 Nonfunctional Requirements: Interface Requirements

Interface requirements describe the format with which the application communicates with its environment. For example:

> *The cost of shipping the article from the source to the destination shall be displayed at all times in the "cost" text box.*
>
> *The format used to transmit "article expected" messages to cooperating shipping companies shall be a string of the form* exp<source>, *where* <source> *is a string from the* Standard City Table.

The first example specifies a requirement pertaining to users of the application. The second provides a message format for communication with other applications. Both are interface requirements.

2.6 Nonfunctional Requirements: Constraints

Design or implementation constraints describe limits or conditions on how the application is to be designed or implemented. These requirements are not intended to replace the design process—they merely specify conditions imposed upon the project by the customer, the environment, or other circumstances. They include accuracy, for example:

> *The damage computations of the Automobile Impact Facility(AEF) shall be accurate within one centimeter.*

Tool and language constraints are often imposed. These include historical practices within the organization, compatibility, and programmer experience. For example:

> *The AEF is to be implemented in FORTRAN 88.*

Design constraints are imposed on the project because stakeholders require them. Such constraints restrict the design freedom of the developers. For example:

> *The AEF shall utilize the Universal Crunch Facility to display impact results.*

The constraint of having to follow certain standards is often determined by company or customer policies. For example:

> *Documentation for* AEF *shall conform to Federal Guideline 1234.56.*
>
> *The* AEF *code is to be documented using company code documentation guidelines version 5.2.*

Projects are frequently constrained by the hardware platforms they must use. For example:

> AEF *shall run on Ajax 999 model 12345 computers with 128 megabytes of RAM and 12 Gigabytes of disk space.*

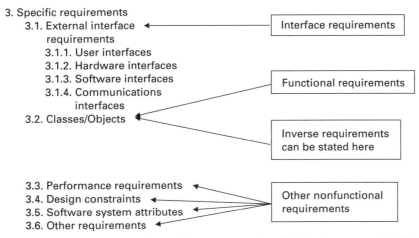

Figure 4.6 The IEEE 830-1994 SRS Organization: Specific Requirements with Object-Oriented Organization   Copyright © 1994 IEEE

2.7 Inverse Requirements

Inverse requirements state what the software will *not* do. Logically, there are an infinite number of inverse requirements: We select those which clarify the true requirements, and which clear up possible misunderstandings. For example:

> *AEF (see preceding section) is not required to analyze crash data.*

2.8 Mapping Requirement Types to IEEE SRS Standard IEEE 830-1993

Figure 4.6 lists the main topics in the IEEE SRS standard IEEE 830-1993, mapping them to the types outlined above.

3. DESIRED PROPERTIES OF D-REQUIREMENTS

We have pointed out the great impact on projects that missing details can have. To help ensure that the details are covered we identify the qualities that D-requirements should possess. In particular, the D-requirements should be complete and consistent. Each one should be capable of being traced through to the design and the implementation, tested for validity, and implemented according to a rational priority. We will review and inspect requirements for these properties when performing quality reviews, as explained in Section 6. At the end of the present section, a sequence of steps is provided that can be taken to express detailed requirements.

3.1 Traceability

3.1.1 Tracing Functional Requirements   Imagine an application with 1000 specific requirements. Without a clean trace from each requirement through the design of the application to the actual code that implements it, it is very difficult to ensure that such an ap-

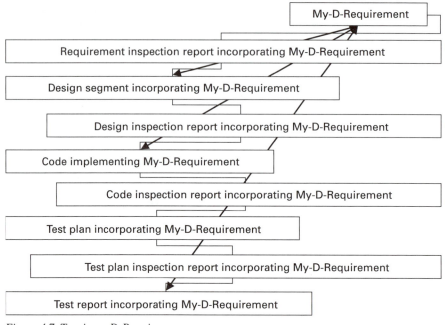

Figure 4.7 Tracing a D-Requirement
* Arrows represent key traces

plication remains in compliance with the requirements. When the requirements change, which is safe to assume, this becomes even more difficult. The capacity to map each requirement to its relevant part(s) of the design and implementation is called *traceability.* One way to help accomplish this is to map each functional D-requirement to a specific function of the target language. This technique is used in the case study. Figure 4.7 shows parts of the project that must be linked to have true traceability. Achieving and maintaining this degree of traceability during development is a major challenge.

As an example, consider the requirement for the *Encounter* video game case study:

> *When a foreign game character enters an area containing the player's main character, or vice versa, they engage each other.*

The meaning of this statement is clear: What remains to be seen, however, is what part of the design and code will be responsible for implementing this requirement. When using the OO paradigm we can link this requirement to a specific function of a specific class. The issue of what class is responsible for a function is not trivial, and it arises repeatedly when using the OO style. For the above example, *Area* objects would be able to recognize that an engagement is to take place since they would presumably be aware of their inhabitants. In particular, this requirement will be traceable to specific event-handling code for the *Area* class.

As the project proceeds, the requirements document should be kept consistent with the design and the implementation. When requirements are hard to trace through design and code, however, developers tend to avoid updating the requirements document when making changes to the source code because of the extensive effort required. Ultimately, such a deterioration of documents results in escalating development and maintenance expenses. This phenomenon is illustrated by the following example.

1. Developer Bill is asked to make changes to the implementation. Bill finds it difficult to connect the code he is modifying with the corresponding parts of the requirements document, and does not update it.

2. Developer Carmen is tasked to make new modifications. She implements and tests new code, and starts the process of updating the requirements document. But everyone tells her not to bother because they say the requirements document is out of date in several places and no one trusts it any more. They tell her it makes no sense to take the time to perfect her part when no one is going to read the document anyway. So Carmen moves on to do other programming. The discrepancies between the requirements document and the code become greater.

Even the most conscientious developer balks at properly updating his or her particular part of the requirements document when the document as a whole is untrustworthy. On the other hand, when the documents are tightly and simply referenced to each other, and management makes documentation a job performance requirement, engineers do keep them in very good professional shape. In other words, the system used to match D-requirements with the designs and code that implement them must be very clear and concrete.

When the code implementing a requirement exists in several parts of the implementation, tracing is achieved by means of a *requirements traceability matrix* of which Table 4.1 is an example.

As Table 4.1 shows, requirement 1783 is implemented by the action of functions *showName()* in module 1, *computeBal()* in module 2, and *getInterest()* in module 3. A change in this requirement necessitates a change in one or more of these functions. This must be carefully managed because these functions may participate in satisfying other requirements (e.g., *showName()* is used to implement requirement 1784 as well). As a result, changes made to satisfy one requirement may compromise another. Since many-to-many relationships are difficult to manage, we try to make the mapping between requirement and function one-to-one.

We want each D-requirement to be traceable *forward* and *backward.* The preceding discussion concerns forward traceability from D-requirement to implementation. Backward traceability of a D-requirement means that the requirement is a clear consequence of one or more C-requirements. For example, the D-requirement

Foreign characters should move from area to area at intervals averaging 5 seconds.

can be traced back to the following C-requirement, which was part of Section 2.0 in the SRS.

The rest [of the characters], called "foreign" characters, are to be under the application's control.

This backward traceability is a basis for the inspection of D-requirements.

TABLE 4.1 Requirements Traceability Matrix

Requirement	Module 1	Module 2	Module 3
1783	showName()	computeBal()	getInterest()
1784	showAccount()	showAddress()	showName()

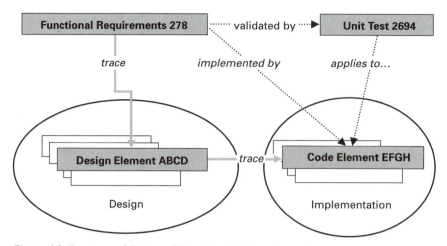

Figure 4.8 Tracing and Testing of Functional D-Requirements

Complete traceability means that each D-requirement is linked to a specific element of design, and also to a unit test, as suggested by Figure 4.8. The figure indicates the advantage of a tight trace (correspondence) between each individual functional requirement, the part of the design intended to handle the requirement, and the part of the code which implements it. These are coupled with the focused test for the requirement, called a unit test. Unit tests are the subject of Chapter 8.

3.1.2 Tracing Nonfunctional Requirements

The preceding discussion concerned functional requirements, but how do we trace *nonfunctional* requirements? This can be difficult because more than one part of the design and implementation may contribute to satisfying a nonfunctional requirement. For example, a requirement that every *Encounter* engagement complete in less than one second could involve code in an *Engagement* class, and/or a *GameCharacter* class, and/or an *Area* class. Our job at requirements time is to specify nonfunctional requirements as clearly as possible. In order to clarify nonfunctional requirements, we will also touch on design and implementation issues.

One goal of the design phase is to isolate each nonfunctional requirement in a separate design element. In the case of performance requirements, an attempt is made to isolate the slowest processing units. Appropriate, inspectable, nonfunctional comments accompany each function that is affected by performance requirements. Preferably, these are quantitative, as in "must complete in less than one millisecond in the worst case." Similarly, in cases where storage constraints are specified, we identify functions which generate the most storage.

Research shows that a relatively small percentage of functions in an application account for most of the processing, and so the search for a few principal time consumers can be fruitful. Let's return to the one-second performance requirement example for *Encounter* engagements, mentioned above. At design and implementation time, we seek typical time consuming components in the computation of engagements. These components include loops, graphics displays, and network communication. Loops and communication are not involved in computing engagements, and a test is implemented to ensure that the graphics and GUIs required for an engagement execute fast enough. The function that consumes most of the time is probably either the function to "engage a foreign character" of the *Engagement* class, or the function to display engagement results.

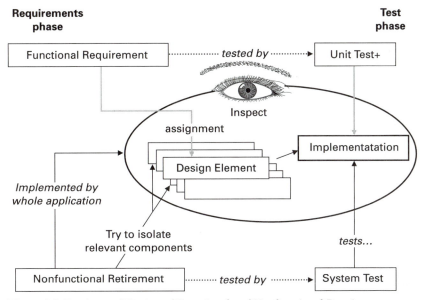

Figure 4.9 Tracing and Testing of Functional and Nonfunctional Requirements (Graphics reproduced with permission from Corel.)

To *validate* nonfunctional requirements we therefore tie each of them to a test plan—preferably at the time of writing the requirement. Figure 4.9 illustrates the typical relationship of functional and nonfunctional requirements to implementation and testing, discussed above. The figure illustrates the fact that several elements may contribute to nonfunctional requirements, and that system- or integration-testing is typically required to validate nonfunctional requirements because verifying them (i.e., prior to execution) can be difficult.

3.2 Testability and Nonambiguity

It must be possible to validate a requirement by testing that the requirement has been properly implemented. (Recall from Chapter 1 that "validation" refers to checking that an artifact functions the way it is supposed to.) Requirements that can be tested for are called *testable*. Untestable "requirements" have little practical value. Figure 4.10 provides an example of a nontestable requirement, and shows what it would take to make the requirement testable.

Unless a D-requirement is written clearly and unambiguously, we will not be able to determine whether or not it has been properly implemented. Figure 4.11 illustrates an example of an ambiguous requirement, followed by an improved version.

3.3 Priority

It is usually difficult to implement all of the planned functionality of an application on schedule and within budget. As mentioned in Section 1.3 of Chapter 2 (page 75), one can vary one or more of *capability, schedule, quality level,* and *cost.* Thus, if the schedule, budget, and quality level cannot be changed, the only alternative is to vary capability, i.e. to reduce the requirements that are implemented. This winnowing process is performed in a planned manner. One technique is to prioritize the specific requirements. Ranking

> *The system shall display the difference in salary between the client and the worldwide average for the same trade.*
>
> —can't be tested because the average mentioned cannot be determined (even though it exists)

> **Better version:**
>
> *The system shall display the difference in salary between the client and the estimated worldwide average for the same trade as published by the United Nations on its website . . . at the time of the display.*

Figure 4.10 Testability

> *The player can decide the qualities/values of* Encounter *characters*
>
> —At any time? Probably not. Would have to test under all circumstances, many not intended, incurring unnecessary expense, and producing a wrong result.

> **Better version:**
>
> *Whenever all foreign players are absent from the area containing the player's main charac- ter, the player may change the quality values of this character, keeping the sum total of the quality values unchanged. The Player Quality Window (as described in section 3.2.PQ) is used for this purpose. Changes take effect four seconds after the "OK" button is pressed.*

Figure 4.11 Ambiguity

all requirements is usually a waste of time: Instead, many organizations classify re-quirements into three (and sometimes four) categories. We will call them "essential," "desirable," and "optional." We make sure that the project implements the "essential" re-quirements. The use of three categories is an application of triage mentioned in Chapter 2. The prioritizing of requirements impacts the design, because the desirable and op-tional requirements often indicate the direction in which the application is headed. Figure 4.12 gives an example of requirements triage. It is a commonly held wisdom that as much as 80% of the business benefits of many applications accrues from as few as 20% of the requirements. Thus, if prioritization is performed well (e.g., calling roughly 20%, no more, "essential"), one can achieve most of an application's benefit with only a fraction of the work. This is a useful factor to keep in mind if the project begins to run out of time.

The "Preliminary Draft" below contains some prioritized D-requirements for the first release of *Encounter*. They are provided here, warts and all, to give the reader a feel for the issues that must be dealt with. Some of the "desirables" will become "essentials" in future releases. The requirements are in draft form and are clearly in need of reorgani-zation. They are improved upon later in this chapter and also in the case study.

[*essential*]   Every game character has the same set of qualities.

[*desirable*]   Each area has a set of *preferred* qualities.

[*optional*]   The player's character shall age with every encounter. The age rate can be provided at setup time. Its default is one year per encounter.

Figure 4.12 Prioritizing D-Requirements

PRELIMINARY DRAFT of *Encounter* D-requirements

(These are not yet organized: See the case study for the improved form.)

(un-inspected:) [essential] *Every game character in the* Encounter *video game shall have a name.*

(un-inspected:) [essential] *Every game character has the same set of qualities, each having a floating point value.*

(un-inspected:) [essential] Encounter *takes place in* areas, *each of which is connected to other areas by* exits.

(un-inspected:) [essential] *Whenever an* Encounter *game character enters an area containing another game character and one of them is player-controlled, the characters may either choose, or be obliged by the game, to engage each other.*

(un-inspected:) [essential] *Whenever a player-controlled game character is alone, the player can change the values of its qualities.*

(un-inspected:) [desirable] *The name of every character in* Encounter *shall have no more than 15 characters.*

(un-inspected:) [desirable] *At any given time every game character shall possess a number of* living *points. These are the sum of the values of its qualities.*

(un-inspected:) [desirable] *Each area has a set of* preferred *qualities.*

(un-inspected:) [desirable] *Combat areas require* strength *and* stamina; *living room areas require* listening ability *and* intellect.

(un-inspected:) [desirable] *The sum of the values of qualities of a game character relevant to the area in question shall be referred to as the character's area value. In an engagement, the system compares the area values of the characters and transfers to the stronger half the points of the weaker.* For example, suppose the player engages a foreign character in an area requiring stamina and attention to detail, and p_s is the value of the player's stamina. Assuming $p_s + p_a > f_s + f_a$, we would have $p_s' = p_s + f_s/2, p_a' = p_a + f_a/2, f_s' = f_s/2, f_a' = f_a/2$ where x' denotes the value of x after the transaction.

(un-inspected:) [optional] Encounter *shall take less than a second to compute the results of an engagement.*

(un-inspected:) [optional] *The player's character shall age with every engagement. The age rate can be set at setup time. Its default is one year per engagement.*

(un-inspected:) [optional] *Player-controlled characters lose or gain the values of their characters at the end of every engagement at the rate of +2% when under 30 and −2% when over 30.*

The prioritization of requirements relates to the iteration that will implement them. For example, if we do not manage to implement the "optional" requirement

"Encounter shall take less than a second to compute the results of an engagement"

on the second iteration, then it could appear with higher priority on the next iteration. The requirements for an iteration are maintained as a separate document. This helps in understanding subsequent requirements.

Begin Requirements

1. The application shall display a video in stock when a title is entered at the prompt, or "OUT" when not in stock.

2. The application shall display all of the store's videos by any director whose last name is entered at the prompt.

    2.1 Sequencing shall be controlled by the forward arrow key.

3. The application shall display all of the store's videos by any actor whose last name is entered at the prompt.

    3.1 Sequencing shall be controlled by the forward arrow key.

End Requirements

Omitted: Specify how to "display" a video!

Figure 4.13 Completeness in Detailed Requirements

3.4 Completeness

We strive to make each detailed requirement self-contained but this is rarely possible in practice, where requirements frequently refer to other requirements. The *completeness* of a set of requirements ensures that there are no omissions which compromise the stated requirements. Figure 4.13 illustrates an incomplete set of requirements. Without the specification of how a video is to be "displayed," this set of requirements is incomplete.

Considering the *Encounter* video game case study, let's take stock of whether we are heading toward a complete set of requirements. Perhaps a good way to take inventory of the requirements' current status is to review them via use cases.

- We set up the qualities of the player's character in the dressing room. We can check that all of the required functionality is present to specify this, and that all of the required data and images are present, too.

- We move to an adjacent area. We check that all of the required functionality is present to do this.

- We encounter a foreign character. We ensure that all of the details for this are provided.

3.5 Error Conditions

For each requirement, we ask what would happen if it were to take place under erroneous circumstances. As an example, let's take a requirement example put forward by Myers [My], as shown in Figure 4.14. This requirements specification is not complete because it does not account for error conditions. The version in Figure 4.15 would be more complete. A lack of error conditions in requirements specifications becomes especially glaring when the function is tested, since the tester forces error conditions and must know what the required output should be.

Sound requirements analysis deals with "illegal" input. It is tempting to assume that a GUI for the triangle requirement does not permit the input of negative numbers, and so the function does not have to deal with erroneous data. Generally speaking, such an assumption is unwise because it transfers the "legality" part of the triangle requirement to requirements on *users* of our triangle function. This increases the dependence among parts of the application. Although it *is* good practice to trap invalid user input at the GUI level and to oblige the user to enter only legal values, this does not substitute for tightening re-

> *A function that tells whether three numbers produce an equilateral triangle (whose sides are all equal), an isosceles triangle (containing exactly two equal sides), or a scalene triangle (a triangle which is neither equilateral nor isosceles).*

Figure 4.14 Requirement Lacking Necessary Error Conditions

> *A function that tells whether a triplet of numbers produces:*
>
> *(1) an equilateral triangle (whose sides are all greater than zero and equal), in which case it outputs 'E' at the prompt, or*
>
> *(2) an isosceles triangle (whose sides are greater than zero, exactly two of which are equal, and which form a triangle), in which case it outputs 'I' at the system, or*
>
> *(3) a scalene triangle (whose sides are all greater than zero and which form a triangle, and which is neither equilateral nor isosceles), in which case it outputs 'S' at the prompt, or*
>
> *(4) no triangle, in which case it outputs 'N' at the prompt.*

Figure 4.15 A More Complete Version of the Requirement

quirements elsewhere. The author recommends requiring the trapping of incorrect data at many, if not all, possible points. This is one equivalent to a long-established practice in engineering where redundancy is practiced in order to promote safety.

3.6 Consistency

A set of D-requirements is *consistent* if there are no contradictions among them. As the number of D-requirements grows, consistency can become difficult to accomplish, as illustrated by the three inconsistent requirements in Figure 4.16.

The object-oriented organization of requirements helps to avoid inconsistencies by classifying D-requirements by class, as in the case study, and by decomposing them into a very simple form. This is not a guarantee of consistency, however, and so requirements inspections check for consistency along with the other qualities mentioned.

Requirement 14. Only basic food staples will be carried by game characters.

...

Requirement 223. Every game character will carry water.

...

Requirement 497. Flour, butter, milk, and salt will be considered the only basic food staples.

Figure 4.16 Consistency in Detailed Requirements

3.7 Summary of the Process of Writing a Detailed Requirement

Figure 4.17 and Figure 4.18 summarize the process that can be followed in expressing a single requirement. Most of the steps outlined in the figures were described in this section as desirable qualities for requirements. Here are additional notes keyed to the numbering in the figures.

1. Section 5 in this chapter discusses ways in which detailed requirements can be organized, with an emphasis on the object-oriented style. The organization method has to be worked out before the D-requirements are written.

3. Assessing whether or not a requirement is traceable amounts to imagining a design for the application and imagining how the requirement would have to be satisfied by the design. This is easiest if the requirement corresponds directly to a method.

4. It helps to outline a test for a requirement at the same time the requirement is written. This not only clarifies the requirement but also establishes whether or not it is testable.

5. Many requirements depend on particular data and we need to indicate how the requirement is to operate in case the data is wrong or inconsistent. For critical requirements this should include errors due to bad design or programming (routine requirements may not account for defective design or defective programming of the application). For example:

    An OK requirement: When the *on* button is pressed, the high-intensity X-ray shall turn on if the parameters satisfy the following conditions.

    Not an OK requirement: The tic-tac-toe positions shall be displayed provided that no player has had two moves more than the other player.

4. SEQUENCE DIAGRAMS

Sequence diagrams are graphical representations of control flow and are particularly useful for visualizing the execution of use cases. Besides using them for requirements analysis, as shown in this chapter, we also use more detailed versions for design, as shown in Chapter 6.

Sequence diagrams require us to think in terms of objects. In a sequence diagram, the lifetime of each object involved is shown as a solid vertical line with the name of the object and its class at the top. Each interaction between objects is shown by means of a horizontal arrow from the object initiating the service to the object which supplies the service. The beginning of a sequence diagram for the *Encounter* use case is given in Figure 4.19. The following notes apply to Figure 4.19.

Note 1: First, we represent with a UML rectangle the object which initiates the use case. This is the object of the class *EncounterGame*. The fact that no object is mentioned, just the entire class, indicates that either no object is required (e.g., using static methods) or that an object without any particular name (an "anonymous" object) will suffice.

Note 2: The thin, elongated rectangle denotes the execution of a function of the object.

Note 3: Next we indicate the operation of the *Area* object initiated by *EncounterGame:* in this case, a creation operation, which is typically a constructor. The object constructed is the *dressing room Area* object. Incidentally, we are making the decision here that *Area* will be a class. (The name we have chosen for this class is actually a defect—*"Area"* is

---

One Way To. . . Write a Detailed Requirement 1

1. Classify requirement as functional or nonfunctional
    - IEEE SRS prompts for most nonfunctional requirements
    - select method for organizing functional requirements
2. Size carefully
    - a functional requirement corresponds ± to a method
    - too large: hard to manage
    - too small: not worth tracking separately
3. Make traceable if possible
    - ensure suitable for tracking through design and implementation
4. Make testable
    - sketch a specific test that establishes satisfaction

Figure 4.17 One Way to Write a Detailed Requirement, 1 of 2

One Way To. . . Write a Detailed Requirement 2

5. Make sure not ambiguous
    - ensure hard to misunderstand intention
6. Give the requirement a priority
    - e.g., highest ("essential"); lowest ("optional"); neither ("desirable")
7. Check that requirement set complete
    - for each requirement, ensure all other necessary accompanying requirements are also present
8. Include error conditions
    - state what's specifically required for non-nominal situations
    - include programmer errors for critical places
9. Check for consistency
    - ensure that each requirement does not contradict any aspect of any other requirement

---

Figure 4.18 One Way to Write a Detailed Requirement, 2 of 2

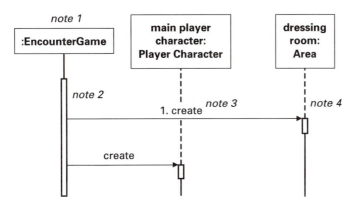

Figure 4.19 Beginning of Sequence Diagram for Initialize Use Case

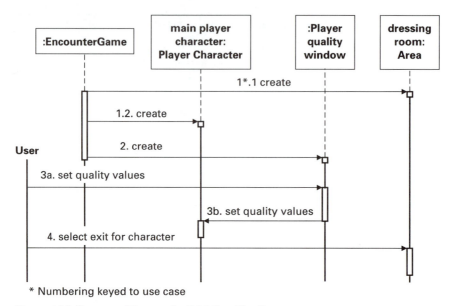

Figure 4.20 Sequence Diagram for Initialize *Use Case*

too general. We should have called it *EncounterArea;* we'll see the effect of this defect later.

Note 4: Notice that the solid line for the dressing room object begins only when the object begins its existence.

In the completed sequence diagram in Figure 4.20 operations are introduced. These operations indicate work that is initiated by the object at the head of the arrow, and carried out by the object at the arrow's end. Each operation usually translates into a specific function during the design phase.

The complete sequence diagram for the use case is given in Figure 4.20. The idea is that as one walks through a use case the necessity for particular objects becomes evident. These objects suggest classes to be introduced. In the *Initialize* use case the first action taken by the application is the displaying of the dressing room and the player's main game character. We need an object to perform this creation process. A reasonable choice for this purpose is the single object of a class *EncounterGame*. *EncounterGame* creates the *dressing room* object of an *Area* class, then tells *dressing room* to display itself. Each vertical bar denotes the execution of the function called. Some of the numbered steps in the use case result in more than one function request. We have introduced the class *PlayerCharacter* of which there is only one object, *mainPlayerCharacter*.

At this stage the sequence diagram serves to identify key domain classes. Typically, the sequence diagram has to be modified and made more precise at design time. One example of this is the identification of the class responsible for creating the dressing room object. The architecture (see next chapter) may actually call for *dressing room* to be created not by *EncounterGame* but by *Area* itself, or by a class yet to be named.

Sequence diagrams can be used to specify concurrent threads. For example, we might want the game characters of *Encounter* to move independently from area to area during the action. As shown in Figure 4.21, the UML notation for this is an arrow from one column to another with only the lower half of the arrowhead showing. This indicates the initiation of a thread at the arrowhead end.

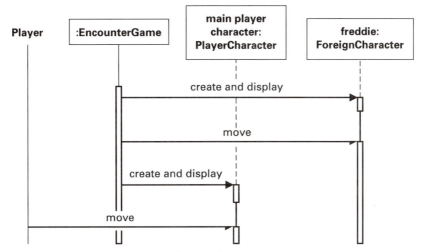

Figure 4.21 Sequence Diagram Showing Concurrency

The parallel vertical strips are well suited to visualizing concurrency. Sequence diagrams are unsuitable for describing synchronization, however. This can be done with UML *activity diagrams* (see [Ja1]). Unless they are required to express customer requirements, issues such as synchronization can be deferred to design time.

Figure 4.22 and Figure 4.23 summarize the steps needed to create a sequence diagram. When the first entity is the user a simple label at the top rather than a rectangle suffices. Note that the entity responsible for doing the work labeled on the arrow is the one at the *end* (not the head) of the arrow. The most significant part of the process is the selection of classes. We have to decide what general kind of thing (the objects of what class?) should handle the work we are asking the application to do.

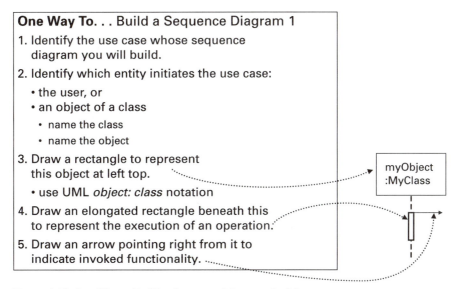

Figure 4.22 One Way to Build a Sequence Diagram, 1 of 2

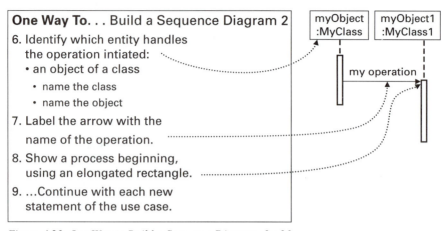

Figure 4.23 One Way to Build a Sequence Diagram, 2 of 2

5. ORGANIZING D-REQUIREMENTS

5.1 Why the Organization of Detailed Requirements Is Important

To appreciate the value of carefully organizing D-requirements consider the following rather random attempt at writing D-requirements for the *Encounter* game. Note that these requirements are still raw and uninspected.

> *Every character in the* Encounter *video game shall have a name.*
>
> *Every game character has the same set of qualities, each with a floating point value.*
>
> Encounter *shall take less than a second to compute the results of an engagement.*
>
> *Each area has a specific set of "qualities needed." For example, combat areas require* strength *and* stamina; *living rooms require* sensitivity *and* intellect.
>
> *When two* Encounter *game characters are in the same area at the same time they may either choose or be obliged by the game to engage each other.*
>
> *Every game character shall have an amount of* life *points.*
>
> *The sum of the values of qualities of a game character relevant to the area in question shall be referred to as the character's area value. In an engagement the system compares the area values of the characters and computes the result of the engagement.*
>
> *The name of any character in* Encounter *shall have no more than 15 letters.*

An unorganized list like the one above quickly becomes unmanageable as it grows.

- Its very size makes it hard to understand as a unit even before it grows into the hundreds, if not thousands.
- The requirements are of mixed types: *performance* requirements must be dealt differently from *behavioral* requirements, for example.
- Some requirements naturally belong with related ones.
- It is difficult to locate a specific requirement.

5.2 Methods of Organizing
Specific Requirements

D-requirements can be organized according to several schemes, principally:

- By *feature* (desired service perceived externally, usually defined by stimulus-response pairs)

  This is the organization often thought of as "requirements"—namely, the requirements are arranged by the observable features of the application. Note that this by itself does not really provide any systematic organization since it allows jumping from a feature in one part of the application to a feature in a completely different part.

- By *mode* (e.g., radar systems may have *training, normal,* and *emergency* modes)

- By *use case* (sometimes called "by *scenario*"). This organization, favored by the Unified Software Development Process, is elaborated on below. The idea is that most detailed requirements are part of a use case.

- By *class*. This is an object-oriented style which is explained extensively below. In this organization we classify requirements in classes. This way of organizing requirements is used in the case study.

- By *function hierarchy* (i.e., by decomposing the application into a set of high-level functions, and then these into sub-functions, etc.). For example, the requirements for a home budget program can be decomposed into (1) checking functions, (2) savings functions, and (3) investment functions. The checking functionality can be further decomposed into checkbooks functions, reconciliation, and reporting, etc. This is a traditional manner of imposing order on detailed requirements.

- By *state* (by indicating the specific requirements that apply to each state). For example, the requirements for an application that controls a chemical process might be best classified by the states in which the process can find itself (*starting up, reacting, cooling,* etc.). Within each state classification, the events that affect the application while in that state are listed.

Classification by state can be appropriate whenever the requirements for each state are very different. For example, an accounting system may behave differently depending on whether it is in the *configuring, executing,* or *backing up* state. Although the *Encounter* case study requirements could be organized by state we have decided that doing so would be less helpful than organizing them by class.

Methods for organizing D-requirements are summarized in Figure 4.24. Several of the ways of classifying the D-requirements are adapted from the IEEE standard 830-1993 which provides document templates for most of them. Figure 4.25 shows the conventional and the object-oriented classification templates of the IEEE 830-1993 standard. Users of outlines like this add sections as appropriate. For example, the OO organization lacks a section equivalent to 3.4 in the non-OO organization "logical database requirements." The case study at the end of this chapter uses a modified form of the IEEE OO style and includes a section for use cases.

It may be advisable to organize the specific requirements into a combination of classifications. Within the *configuring, executing,* and *backing up* states of an accounting application, for example, a feature-based organization could be used. The requirements for a factory automation system could be organized at the highest level by function (*intake, part manufacturing,* and *assembly*), then organized by class within each of these.

by . . .   Feature
         Use case
         Class
         Function hierarchy
         State

Figure 4.24 Ways of Organizing Detailed Requirements
(Graphics reproduced with permission from Corel.)

The method of organizing D-requirements is frequently related to the probable architecture of the application. For example, if the design is to be object-oriented, organization by *use case* or *class* should be considered because they facilitate traceability. These are explained in the next two sections. If the application lends itself to an obvious functional breakdown then organizing the requirements by *function hierarchy* may be appropriate. If there are actors who encompass all of the present and conceivable requirements quite separately, then organization by *actor* may be preferable.

3. **Specific requirements (non-OO)**	3. **Specific requirements (OO format)**
3.1 External interfaces	3.1 External interface requirements
3.2 Functions	3.1.1 User interfaces
3.3 Performance requirements	3.1.2 Hardware interfaces
3.4 Logical database requirements	3.1.3 Software interfaces
3.5 Design constraints	3.1.4 Communications interfaces
3.5.1 Standards compliance	3.2 Classes/Objects
3.6 Software system attributes	3.2.1 Class/Object 1
3.6.1 Reliability	3.2.1.1 Attributes (direct or inherited)
3.6.2 Availability	3.2.1.1.1 Attribute 1 . . .
3.6.3 Security	3.2.1.2 Functions (services, methods, direct or inherited)
3.6.4 Maintainability	3.2.1.2.1 Functional requirement . . .
3.6.5 Portability	. . .
3.7 Organizing the specific requirements	3.3 Performance requirements
3.7.1 System mode—*or*	3.4 Design constraints
3.7.2 User class—*or*	3.5 Software system attributes
3.7.3 Objects (see right)—*or*	3.6 Other requirements
3.7.4 Feature—*or*	
3.7.5 Stimulus—*or*	
3.7.6 Response—*or*	
3.7.7 Functional hierarchy—*or*	
3.7.8 Additional comments	

Figure 4.25 IEEE 830-99: Specific ("D-") Requirements OO and Other Styles
Copyright © 1994 IEEE

5.3 Organizing Detailed Requirements by Use Case

The Unified Software Development method exploits the observation that many requirements naturally occur in operational sequences. For example, the individual requirement that a video store application will allow entering the title of a new video, typically takes place as part of a sequence of transactions. These are the use cases, sometimes referred to as "scenarios" (in the UML a "scenario" is actually an instance of a use case). A collection of use cases for a video store application is illustrated in Figure 4.26.

The Unified Software Development Process favors organizing requirements by use cases. If one organizes D-requirements in this way it is useful to produce larger use cases from smaller ones. The Figure 4.27 shows one way of doing this with the UML, using "generalization." Use case *B* (for *Base*) generalizes use case *D* (for *Derived*) if *D* contains all of the steps in *B* (and, typically, additional steps).

For additional ways to obtain new use cases from existing ones, see Rumbaugh [Ru1].

5.4 Organizing Requirements by Classes

We will concentrate on an object-oriented style for organizing requirements, in which a categorization is first identified—the equivalent of selecting classes—then the individual requirements are placed into the resulting categories or classes. There are two approaches to this. One regards the classes as applicable for organizing the requirements but does not consider them necessarily usable for the actual design. Another approach, followed in the case study, does use the classes developed for the requirements in the actual object-oriented design (and implementation). The latter approach promotes one-to-one traceability from D-requirements to methods by making each functional D-requirement correspond to a function in the target language.

One downside of this approach is the risk that we later change the classes used, thereby breaking the correspondence between requirements and class selection. This is discussed by Jordan, Smilan, and Wilkinson in [Jo1]. Another disadvantage of this classification is that it requires us to select classes very early in the development cycle, and many

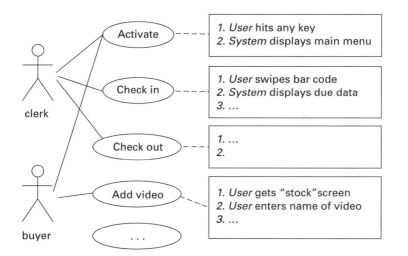

Figure 4.26 Organizing Requirements by Use Case: Video Store Example

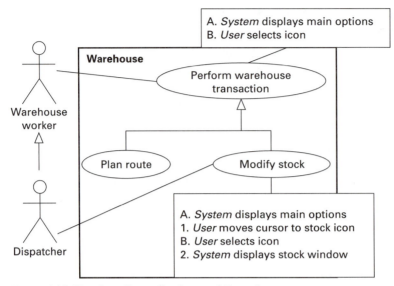

Figure 4.27 Use Case Generalizations and Extensions

argue that we are effectively performing design in doing so. Let's look at the *Encounter* game case study as an example. Picking classes such as *PlayerCharacter* and *Area* at requirements time is harmless since these are very likely to be consistent with any architecture chosen. In other words, the implementation is very likely to use these classes. On the other hand, having the *AreaConnection* objects reference the *Area* objects that they connect, can be regarded as a design decision.

The great advantage to organizing requirements by classes that will be used in the design is that it promotes tight correspondence between requirements, design, and implementation. This is a key benefit for using the OO paradigm. In addition, classes that correspond to real-world concepts are much more likely to be reused than those that do not. For many applications the benefits of using a class-oriented classification method outweigh its drawbacks.

A typical sequence for obtaining functional D-requirements using the OO style is as follows.

1. The process starts by listing the classes mentioned in the use cases.

2. The resulting collection of classes is typically incomplete and an effort should be made to uncover remaining "domain" classes. This process is explained below.

   The collection of classes is then inspected.

3. For each of the classes obtained, the requirements engineer writes down all of the required functionality of the application primarily pertaining to that class, as shown in the case study at the end of the chapter. This is done in the form of attributes and functions. For example "every customer shall have a name" (an attribute listed under class *Customer*) and "the application shall be able to compute the total assets of each customer" (a function listed under *Customer*).

   Each known required object of the class should be specifically listed as a requirement with that class. For example, "the *Rockefeller Family Trust* shall be a customer."

   The events that the objects of the class are required to handle should be specified.

The D-requirements are inspected as the process progresses.

Ideally, the test plans for each D-requirement should be devised at the same time, as explained below.

4. The D-requirements are then inspected against the C-requirements.

5. The D-requirements are verified with the customer and then released. Recall that the primary audience for D-requirements consists of developers: However, customers are vitally interested in the details, too.

Figure 4.28 summarizes these steps.

A common error made in classifying requirements by class is treating the process as if it were design. The language used should be plain English. For example, the following language is **acceptable:**

> *It shall be possible to obtain the number of days delinquent on any account.*

The following is **not acceptable:**

> *getDelinquentDays()* returns the number of days delinquent on the account.

In other words, object-orientation is used here only as an organizing principle for the requirements. The use of 00 for design and implementation is performed later.

5.5 Identifying Classes

The classes to be used as our organizing principle are carefully and conservatively identified. This is done by identifying the *domain* classes of the application—those pertaining specifically to the application. For example, the domain of an application simulating a

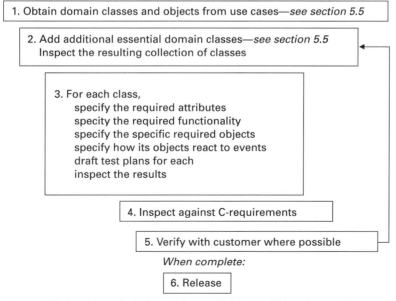

Figure 4.28 Road Map for D-Requirements Using the Object-Oriented Style

bank might contain classes *BankCustomer* and *Teller* but not *File* or *Database*—not even *Customer* or *Transaction*. The latter are not special to the application in question. The use of domain classes is a way to organize, think through, and track requirements. Our goal is to identify a minimum but sufficient set of domain classes that include all of the specific requirements.

As another example of domain class selection, consider an application that manages visits to a website. Some candidate domain classes are *SiteVisitor, SiteVisit,* and *SiteMission.* Requirements pertaining to the visitor (e.g., data about visitors, and functionality such as displaying visitor profiles) would be collected with the *SiteVisitor* classification. If the application requires us to track the reasons for each visit, then a domain class *SiteMission* would be appropriate. The corresponding requirements would be collected within *SiteMission.* For example, the requirement on the application would be that visitors submit a form stating their goals in visiting the site.

Use cases are a primary source for domain classes. Recall the sequence diagram for the *Encounter* "Initialize" use case in Figure 4.20 on page 198.

Unless the application is primarily a graphical user interface, the author recommends postponing the introduction of GUI classes until design time whenever possible. This is because these are not key domain classes and because designers tend to change them frequently. One can try to use only command-line interfaces for initial versions. On the other hand, GUI classes may be required early because the customer typically wants to see some GUIs early on. In the case study, for example, we have to include *PlayerQualityWindow* early in the process because it is called for in a C-requirement use case. Recall that the sequence diagram uses the classes in Figure 4.29. Classes *ConnectionHyperlink, AreaConnection, Area,* and *PlayerCharacter* are required by the "Travel to adjacent area" sequence diagram shown in Figure 4.30, which corresponds to the use case in the C-requirement of the same name. Classes *ForeignCharacter, Engagement,* and *EngagementDisplay* are called for by the "Engage foreign character" sequence diagram shown in Figure 4.31. The numbering in the sequence diagram is the same as that in the use case. Step 1 consists of showing the foreign character in the area. The sequence diagram shows the creation, and then execution of an *Engagement* event to handle the resulting engagement. This event changes the values of the participants (step 2.1) according to the rules of engagement. The engagement then calls an operation of its own to display the results (step 3.1), and so on.

After obtaining classes from the use cases an effective way to complete the identification of key domain classes is to use a "list and cut" process. This consists of (1) listing every reasonable candidate class you can think of, and then (2) aggressively paring down the list to a few essential classes.

EncounterGame
- a class with a single object

PlayerCharacter
- with object *mainPlayerCharacter*

Area
- with object *dressingRoom*

PlayerQualityWindow
- a GUI class included to complete the use case

Figure 4.29 Classes in Initialize *Sequence Diagram*

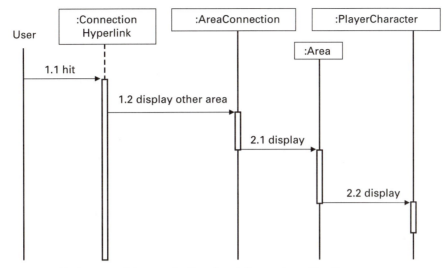

Figure 4.30 Sequence Diagram for Travel to Adjacent Area *Use Case*

1. Figure 4.32 shows candidate classes for the *Encounter* game selected from sequence diagrams, together with nouns from the preceding text in this chapter concerning the game. The Unified Modeling Language (UML) notation for a class is a rectangle containing the class name.

2. We now filter these. Note first that it is far easier to add a class later than to remove one that has become embedded in the design and implementation, so that if there is doubt about the usefulness of a candidate class we eliminate it. The rationale used for the final selection of domain classes for the case study is given next.

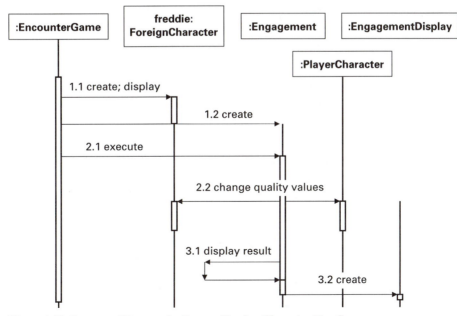

Figure 4.31 Sequence Diagram for Engage Foreign Character *Use Case*

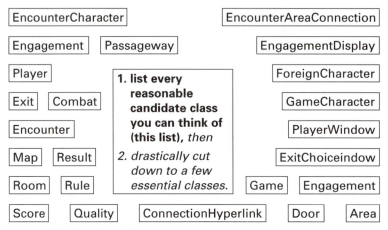

Figure 4.32 Candidate Classes for Encounter *Game*

- *Encounter:* Change to *EncounterGame* to make its purpose clearer (we may also need the plain "encounter" concept as well).
- *Game:* Not a domain class—too general (we may reintroduce this later when seeking useful generalizations)
- *GameCharacter:* too general to be in the domain (we may reintroduce this later when seeking useful generalizations)
- *Player: PlayerCharacter* is a preferable name (more specific to the domain).
- *ForeignCharacter:* OK (foreign characters act in ways that are different from player characters)
- *EncounterCharacter:* OK (generalization of *PlayerCharacter, ForeignCharacter,* etc.—still within the domain of the application)
- *Quality:* omit—try to handle as simple attribute of *EncounterCharacter*
- *Room:* omit—not sure if we need this; already have *Area*
- *Door:* omit—not sure we'll need it
- *Exit:* not sure if we need this: leads to neighboring area—try as simple attribute of *Area*—omit for now
- *Rule:* omit—not sure we'll need it
- *Area:* OK [The astute reader will note that this decision is defective.]
- *Engagement:* OK
- *Passageway:* We do need to connect areas but we do not yet know what form these connections will take. Use *EncounterAreaConnection* instead.
- *Result:* omit—vague
- *Combat:* omit—not sure we'll need it—already have *Engagement*
- *Score:* omit—Try as attribute of other classes.
- *PlayerQualityWindow:* This is needed to express the *Initialize* use case.
- *ExitChoiceWindow:* omit—not needed—click on exit hyperlinks.
- *Map:* omit—not required at this stage: maybe in a future version

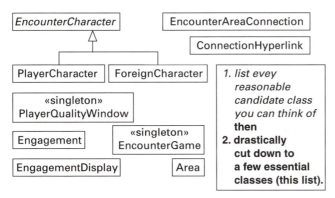

Figure 4.33 Classes for Encounter *Video Game Showing Only Inheritance*

- *EngagementDisplay:* OK—needed by use case though will try postpone by substituting a command line interface

The resulting classes are shown in Figure 4.33. The figure includes the inheritance relationships present among these classes denoted with a triangle. Some basics of the UML notation can be found inside the covers of this book.

There are other ways besides inheritance in which the classes in Figure 4.33 potentially relate. For example, *EncounterAreaConnection* will probably aggregate two *Area* objects. Our concern here is only with the core application classes, using them to organize the requirements. Relationships among classes are shown where necessary. The use of inheritance enables some degree of leverage. For example, after stating the requirements for *EncounterCharacter* we do not need to repeat these requirements in describing *PlayerCharacter* and *ForeignCharacter.* The *EncounterCharacter* class is shown in italics in Figure 4.33 because it is abstract: This declares that there will be no actual characters besides player-controlled and foreign characters.

The method outlined above to collect classes for categorizing detailed requirements is summarized in Figure 4.34.

One Way To. . . Select Domain Classes for Classifying Requirements

1. Develop a comprehensive, non-overlapping collection of use cases.
2. Create a sequence diagram for every use case.
    - take care in identifying the classes and objects
3. Gather the classes used in the sequence diagrams.
4. Determine essential additional domain classes.
5. Classify the detailed functional requirements by these classes.
    5.1 list each attribute as a requirement
    5.2 list each specific object of this class that must exist
    5.3 list each function required of objects in this classification
    5.4 list the events that all objects of the class must react to

---

Figure 4.34 One Way to Select Domain Classes for Classifying Requirements

The IEEE 830-1993 SRS standard designates a place where the purpose of each class is stated, together with its key attributes and functions. The standard calls for using the decimal numbering system from each class (e.g., 3.2.5) to each of its attribute requirements (e.g., 3.2.5.1) and each of its function requirements (e.g., 3.2.5.2). Instead we will arrange classes alphabetically to make it easier to add and remove classes. Such insertions are necessary as the application grows. It is important to number requirements, however, in order to be able to manage them, so we do this within each class as shown in the case study.

Sometimes, only "essential" requirements are numbered since only they must be traced for now. A good reference for this style of organizing specific requirements is Jordan, Smilan, and Wilkinson ([Jo1]). To assist in tracing D-requirements it can help to give a name to each one as in the case study. For example:

> 3.2.A.7 Preferred qualities
> [essential] Each area shall favor a set of qualities.

Including "desirable" and "optional" detailed requirements is beneficial for several reasons. First, the scope of the application can be controlled by implementing the requirements in a planned order. Second, stating future requirements provides direction to designers, helping them to create designs that can accommodate future features.

One technique for indicating which requirements have actually been designed for and implemented is to start by including a disclaimer with each, as in the following example.

> 3.2.A.7 Preferred qualities
> [desirable; not implemented yet] Each area shall be displayable in any one of three different styles.

When and if the requirement is accommodated by the design, "not implemented yet" can be removed.

5.6 Selecting the Right Class for a Given Requirement

Perhaps the most challenging issue when organizing D-requirements by class is to decide under what class to state the requirement. An easy example is the following.

> Requirement: *Every* Encounter *character shall have a name*

This requirement should be classified with "Encounter Characters." An example requiring more consideration is the following.

> Requirement: *Whenever the player's main character enters an area, that area and all the characters in it shall be displayed on the monitor.*

Obvious class candidates to classify this function are *PlayerCharacter* and *Area*. The requirement effectively calls for an event handler. According to the *courtyard* GUI shown in Chapter 3, the player's character enters an area after the player clicks on an area hyperlink. Thus, a natural triggering object for handling the entry event would be the area entered because it is aware of which characters inhabit it. The area entered could display itself and the characters it contains. Thus, the requirement stated above could reasonably be classified under *Area*.

5.7 Classifying *Entities* (Instances)

Applications require the existence of particular entities (or *instances* or *objects,* as opposed to particular classes). For example, our video game application requires that *Area* entities *courtyard* and *dressing room* exist. Where should we state these requirements? There are at least three options. The first option is to state them under the class that creates the objects. According to the sequence diagram, *EncounterGame* creates *dressing room.* This has the advantage of matching some code because the creating function of *EncounterGame* will refer to *dressing room.* A disadvantage of this approach is that the decision about which object creates the required object is liable to change, and so the requirements would have to be moved. It should also be noted that other objects, although not creating the required object, may refer to it more frequently than the creating object.

A second option is to introduce a special class that aggregates the required objects of each relevant class (e.g., a class *Areas* that aggregates the objects of *Area*). This can be awkward, and it may add unnecessary classes. We will exercise a third option: listing the requirement for objects with the class to which they belong. Thus, in the case study, the requirements for the existence of objects *dressing room* and *courtyard* are listed under the *Area* class as follows.

> *Area* **class**
> *All activities of the game (including engagements) take place in "Areas."*
>
> ...
>
> Area Requirement *("Dressing room ").* *There shall be an* Area *object with name "dressing room." Its image shall be . . . Its preferred qualities shall be* concentration *and* stamina.
> Area Requirement *("Courtyard").* *There shall be an* Area *object with name "courtyard." Its image shall be . . . . Its preferred quality shall be* strength.

5.8 Linking to Test Documentation

As each D-requirement is written, some work should be performed on the tests for that particular requirement. There are several advantages to writing tests simultaneously with the requirement. First, doing so helps to clarify the specific requirement. Second, it shifts some work from the testing phase of the project to the requirements phase. This relieves some of the pressure on the latter half of the project when there is less flexibility in the use of time.

For example, one of our requirements is as follows.

> *Requirement NNN. Every game character in the* Encounter *video game shall have a unique name containing between 1 and 15 characters.*

Requirements of the attribute type like this really specify *get-* and *set-* functions, so that the Table 4.2 constitutes the beginnings of a test plan for this requirement. Chapter 8 covers these tests in detail.

Recall from Chapter 1 that concurrent testing is an essential feature of incremental development, and also of "extreme programming." A methodology known as the "Y methodology" is actually built around the concept of concurrent testing. It carries this name because it is diagrammed with the waterfall descending from the left and a corresponding sequence of testing phases descending from the right, thereby forming the arms of a "Y." These two strands come together at integration time, after which system testing takes place (see Chapter 9).

TABLE 4.2 Test Input and Expected Output

Test input for Requirement NNN	Expected output
Harry	Harry
X	X
" " (blank)	" " (blank)
123456789012345	123456789012345
1234567890123456	123456789012345
. . .	. . .

▶ PART II: AT LENGTH

This part of the chapter can be covered after covering subsequent chapters. Understanding the material in this part, however, is required to produce a quality software product.

6. QUALITY OF SPECIFIC REQUIREMENTS

Keeping in mind the potentially disastrous consequences of failing to specify every last requirement detail (e.g., lost satellites), we try to rate the quality of our requirements as quantitatively as possible.

6.1 QA Involvement in the Analysis of D-Requirements

The quality assurance organization reviews the D-requirements. The IEEE Quality Assurance Planning standard (730.1-1995) states, for example, that the Software Quality Assurance Plan

> [should] identify or reference the standard practices, conventions and metrics to be used during the requirements phase. Cite standards . . . with which requirements baselining and traceability must comply. Uses formal requirements statement languages . . . wherever possible. Provision should be made for a scheme which uniquely identifies each requirement. . . .

The standard goes on to describe the form and nature of software requirements reviews (Section 3.6.2.1 of IEEE 730.1-1995).

In large projects, guidelines like these are sometimes followed. In many medium or small organizations, however, QA is brought into the process only after requirements have been determined. At times, QA is even asked after the fact to "check that this thing was built according to spec." QA typically complains that there are no adequate requirements to check the application *against*. Sometimes they have to try to construct requirements from the application as it has been built, a process known as *reverse engineering* (see Chapter 10). This situation is changing for the better, however, as development organizations become increasingly serious about process.

6.2 Metrics for D-Requirements Analysis

The selective use of metrics maximizes the investment in inspection by focusing the inspection process on useful, quantified results.

Each metric provides benefits, but costs money and time to collect, store, analyze, and report on. The art of metric application is to optimize the cost/benefit ratio. This depends on the organization's culture, the state of the project, the nature of the project, etc. Collecting metrics simply because they might be used in the future is a dubious practice. The author has seen roomfuls of metric data collecting dust because someone thought they might be useful but did not specify how. A triage process for selecting metrics is a useful practice that categorizes them as "must" metrics (one extreme), "nice to have" metrics (the other extreme), and "other" metrics (neither extreme). A few tryouts of the "other" metrics will clarify their costs and benefits.

The following list of quality assurance metrics includes requirements analysis metrics in IEEE Standard 982.2-1988 ("IEEE Guide for The Use of IEEE Standard Dictionary of Measures to Produce Reliable Software").

Quality assurance measures of specific requirements include:

- Measures of how well the requirements are written
  - Percentage of unambiguous specific requirements (IEEE metric 6)
  - Degree of completeness (IEEE metrics 23 and 35)
  - Percentage of misclassified D-requirements (in the object-oriented style this measures the percentage allocated to the wrong class)
  - Percentage of specific requirements that are not
    - testable
    - traceable (IEEE metric 7)
    - prioritized
    - atomic (indivisible into smaller parts)
    - consistent with the remaining requirements (IEEE metrics 12 and 23)

- Measures of the effectiveness of requirements inspection
  - Percentage of missing or defective requirements found per hour of inspection

- Measures of the effectiveness of the requirements analysis process
  - Cost per D-requirement
    - On a gross basis (total time spent / number of D-requirements)
    - On a marginal basis (cost to get one more)
    - Rate at which specific requirements are
      - modified
      - eliminated
      - added

- Measure of the degree of completeness of the requirements
  - This can be estimated from the rate, after the official end of D-requirements collection, at which specific requirements are
    - modified
    - added

The metrics are useful when their target values are specified in advance. For example, we could state that, based on past experience, requirements will be considered "complete" when the rate of modification and addition is less that 1% per week.

6.3 Inspection of D-Requirements Analysis

The reader is referred to Chapter 1 for a description of the inspection process in general.

Specific requirements (or D-requirements) are the first software process documents which can be inspected against prior documentation (the C-requirements). Inspectors prepare for the inspection by reading over the C-requirements (e.g., IEEE 830-1993 Sections 1 and 2), and comparing the specific requirements with them.

6.3.1 Example of Uninspected D-Requirements

Here is an uninspected version of D-requirements upon which we will perform an example inspection, entering the results in a table (see Table 4.3 on page 216). The final version of these requirements, resulting from the inspection, is shown in the case study.

Area Requirement 1 ("Area name"). [Not inspected yet] Every area shall have a name of up to 15 characters.

Area Requirement 2 ("Area image"). [Not inspected yet] There shall be an image in *gif* form to display each *Area* object.

Area Requirement 3 ("Display area method"). [Not inspected yet] Whenever a player character enters an area, that area and the characters in it shall be displayed.

Area Requirement 4 ("Courtyard object"). [Not inspected yet] There shall be an *Area* object with name "courtyard." Its image shall be that shown in Figure 4.59 on page 244.

Area Requirement 5 ("Dressing room object"). [Not inspected yet] There shall be an *Area* object with name "dressing room" and blank background image. The dressing room shall be adjacent to the courtyard area.

Encounter Requirement 1 ("Engaging a foreign character"). [Not inspected yet] When an engagement takes place, the following computation is performed: The sum of the values of qualities of a game character relevant to the area in question shall be referred to as the character's area value. [In this release, all qualities will count as equal.] In an engagement, the system compares the area values of the characters and transfers to the stronger, half of the points of the weaker. For example, suppose the player engages a foreign character in an area requiring stamina and attention span, and ps is the value of the player's stamina, etc. Assuming $ps + pa > fs + fa$, we would have $ps' = ps + fs/2, pa' = pa + fa/2, fs' = fs/2, fa' = fs/2$ where x' is the value of x after the transaction.

EncounterCharacter Requirement 1 ("Name of game character"). [Not inspected yet] Every game character in the *Encounter* video game shall have a unique name of up to 15 characters.

EncounterCharacter Requirement 2 ("Qualities of game characters"). [Not inspected yet] Every game character has the same set of qualities, each having a floating point value. These are initialized to *100/n,* where *n* is the number of qualities. The qualities are attention span, endurance, intelligence, patience, and strength.

EncounterCharacter Requirement 3 ("Image of game character"). [Not inspected yet] Every game character will be shown using an image that takes up no more than 1/8 of the monitor screen.

EncounterCharacter Requirement 4 ("Engagement with foreign character"). [Not inspected yet] Whenever an *Encounter* game character enters an area containing another game character, and one of them is player-controlled, the player character may either choose or be obliged by the game to engage the other character. Whether there is a choice or not is controlled by the game in a random way on a 50% basis.

Encounter Game Requirement 1 ("Encounter game object"). [Not inspected yet] There shall be a single *Encounter Game* object.

Foreign Character Requirement 1 ("Freddie foreign character object"). [Not inspected yet] There shall be a foreign character named "Freddie," all of whose qualities have equal values and whose image is shown in Figure 4.57 on page 242.

Player Character Requirement 1 ("Configurability"). [Not inspected yet] Whenever all foreign players are absent from an area, the player may set the values of his qualities using the *Player Quality Window,* as long as the sum of the quality values remains the same.

Player Character Requirement 2 ("main player character"). [Not inspected yet] The player shall have complete control over a particular game character called the main character.

Player Character Requirement 3 ("Living points") [Not inspected yet]. *Encounter* shall produce the sum of the values of the character's qualities, called its *living* points.

6.3.2 Example of Inspection Results on D-Requirements In this section, we will show typical results of an inspection of these requirements.

One comment about this set as a whole could be that the requirements do not support enough expansion of the game into a competitive product. A more particular defect is that the requirements do not properly specify the delay involved in setting a player's quality values; during the delay the player is subjected to an engagement in an unprepared state. (If the delay is too small, the player simply sets the qualities required for the area as high as possible and the game is not much of a challenge.) Let's inspect the list of proposed specific requirements one at a time.

Table 4.3 is an example of a form that can be used for the inspection of D-requirements, applied to the above list. The properties in Table 4.3 are defined above in Section 3 on page 187 (adapted from Ross [Ro]). Most of the metrics described in that section can be computed from this table. The table contains "Notes" and "No" notes. Here are the "No" notes:

1. Can a game character or area have a name with no characters?
2. The number 15 is rigid.
3. Only one?
4. If the player controls several characters, are all of their areas to be displayed or does this have to do only with the main player character?
5. Filling the entire monitor screen?
6. It should be easier to add new qualities or remove them.
7. When is there a Freddie? When does he appear?
8. In future releases characters may mutate.
9. Clarify what stays the same.
10. Can the value of a quality be negative?
11. Ambiguous because the player can't control everything that happens to the main character at all times.
12. Refine "complete control."

TABLE 4.3 Example of Inspection Results on D-Requirements

Requirement	Traceable backward	Complete	Consistent	Feasible	Non-ambiguous	Clear	Precise	Modifiable	Testable	Traceable forward (Note 14)
Area Requirement 1	Note 2	Note 1	Yes	Yes	No 1	Yes	No 1	No 2	No 1, 2	Yes
Area Requirement 2	Yes	Yes	Yes	Yes	No 3	Yes	No 3	Note 3	Yes	Yes
Area Requirement 6	Yes	Note 5	Note 5	Yes	No 3	No 3	No 5	Yes	Yes	Yes
Area Requirement 3	Yes	Yes	Yes	Yes	Yes	Yes	Note 6	Note 3	Yes	Yes
Area Requirement 4	Yes	Note 7	Yes	Yes	Yes	Yes	Yes	Yes	Yes	Yes
Engagement Requirement 1	Note 2	Yes	Yes	Yes	Yes	Yes	Yes	Note 3	Yes	Yes
EncounterCharacter Requirement 1	Yes	Note 1	Yes	Yes	No 1	Yes	No 1	No 2	No 1, 2	Note 9
EncounterCharacter Requirement 2	Yes	Yes	Yes	Yes	Yes	Note 8	Yes	No 6	Yes	Yes
EncounterCharacter Requirement 3	Yes	Yes	Yes	Yes	Yes	Yes	Yes	Note 3	Yes	Yes
EncounterCharacter Requirement 4	Note 11	Yes	Yes	Yes	Yes	Yes	Yes	No 7	Yes	Yes
EncounterGame Requirement 1	Yes	Yes	Yes	Yes	Yes	Yes	Yes	Note 12	Yes	Yes
ForeignCharacter Requirement 1	Note 14	Yes	Yes	Yes	Yes	No 10	No 8, 9	Yes	Yes	Yes
PlayerCharacter Requirement 1	Yes	Yes	Yes	Yes	Yes	No 12	Yes	Yes	Yes	Yes
PlayerCharacter Requirement 2	Yes	Yes	Yes	Yes	No 11	No 12	No 12	Note 3	No 12	Yes
PlayerCharacter Requirement 3	Yes	Yes	Yes	Yes	Note 10	Note 10	Yes	Yes	Yes	Yes

The "Notes" are as follows:

1. Is any keyboard character acceptable?
2. Check validity with customer.
3. It is unclear how modifiable this should be.
4. It is hard to answer "complete" because it is unclear. See the note referenced in the clear column for the issue.
5. We assume that the customer has some leeway in exactly what "courtyard" will look like.
6. Are there dressing room exits to any other area?
7. This is somewhat clumsily written: could lead to misunderstanding.
8. It is usually preferable to have a single requirement match each attribute. This does not appear necessary, as the qualities will be treated alike.
9. Produce at any time? On request? Show at all times?
10. These details are not mentioned in the C-requirements: check with customer.
11. Clarify "50% basis," if possible.
12. For Internet versions it may become necessary to have more than one instance of an *Encounter Game* object. We will not exclude this possibility in future iterations.
13. It is not clear in what directions this could be modified.
14. Is the requirement written in such a way that it will be possible to trace it through to the code that implements it?

In addition to these, the IEEE defines a measure of completeness. Described in 982.2-1988 A35.1, this is a formula involving 18 observed quantities (e.g., "number of condition options without processing") and 10 weights (e.g., the relative importance of "defined functions used"). Basically, it measures the degree to which there are loose ends within a set of D-requirements.

7. USING TOOLS AND THE WEB FOR REQUIREMENTS ANALYSIS

Tools can help the process of capturing and managing requirements; e.g., by sorting, prioritizing, assigning, and tracking them. One benefit of such tools is to know who is working on what requirement at what time. Tools can also help to control "feature creep"—the process by which features which are not really necessary are added to the application. With the appropriate tools, a project leader can more easily assess the status of requirements analysis. He or she can determine, for example, "what percentage of the essential D-requirements have been implemented and fully unit tested by QA"?

For simple projects, much of this can be performed using a simple Web-based spreadsheet, as illustrated in Figure 4.35. The "designed for" designation indicates that the requirement is accounted for in the design. "Unit tested" means that the code implementing the requirement has undergone testing in stand-alone fashion. "Integration testing" means that the application has been tested to verify that it implements the requirement.

A table such as that in Figure 4.35 is kept as part of a project status document which can be attached to the SPMP. The cells in this matrix could be hyperlinked to relevant parts of the project's documents.

Requirement number	Priority			Status						
	Essential	Optional	Not started	Fraction complete		Ready for Inspection	Designed for	Integration		
	Desirable			1/3	2/3	Inspected		Unit tested	tested	
Responsible engineer										

Figure 4.35 Example Spreadsheet for Tracking Requirements

Hyperlinks can be used to preserve single-source engineering for D-requirements (i.e., eliminating duplication). For example, hyperlinks from the source code to the corresponding D-requirement can be accomplished with tools such as *Javadoc*. Javadoc converts certain Java source code comments into an HTML document describing the classes and their methods (see for example [Su]). By inserting hyperlinks to the SRS within these comments, the HTML document produced by Javadoc hyperlinks to the SRS. This is illustrated in Figure 4.36 where the specific requirement corresponding to the method *engageForeignCharacter* is hyperlinked from the document that Javadoc produces from the source code.

The trend is for continual improvements in the process by which programmers will be able to more easily go back and forth between the SRS, the design, the graphical user interfaces, and the source code.

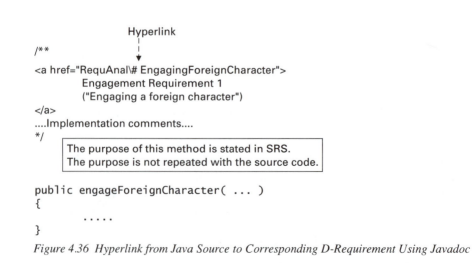

Figure 4.36 Hyperlink from Java Source to Corresponding D-Requirement Using Javadoc

8. FORMAL METHODS FOR REQUIREMENTS SPECIFICATION

8.1 Introduction to Formal Specifications

Mathematics is very good at expressing state: in other words "what is." This contrasts with the "how to" of procedures and algorithms. Since requirements specifications mostly describe the state of the application before and after actions, mathematical notation can be more appropriate than natural language for specifying detailed requirements. The use of mathematics in this context is part of what's called "formal methods." Formal methods are useful to mathematically trained engineers. This section is intended to give the reader an idea of formal methods for stating requirements. The reader is referred to Hayes [Ha] and also Gehani and Lally [Ge] for a full description of formal specification methods.

Many scientists believe that mathematics has a significant role to play in specifying all of the critical details that can so easily trip up the best-intentioned project. They believe that such a use of mathematics can thereby prevent wasting money, destroying property, and even losing lives (e.g., in critical care applications).

As an example, consider the following specification for a procedure:

Returns a sorted array consisting of the elements of the array A.

This simple-sounding requirement is surprisingly fraught with ambiguity. The elements of A could have several keys on which to sort. Even if A is a set of integers, "sort" needs to be defined: sorted into evens and odds? in decreasing order? Even if the order is supposed to be increasing, the requirement remains ambiguous.

For example, if $A = (4,6,3,4,6,8)$, then all three of the following arrays satisfy the above requirement:

$(3,4,6,8)$, $(3,4,4,6,8)$, and $(3,4,4,6,6,8)$.

Working on the natural language form of the requirements statement can improve it. For example:

Returns a sorted array of all of the individual elements of the array A.

Unfortunately, the word *individual* is ambiguous. One could go on rewording the specification, but this would simply be struggling to avoid mathematics. We return later in this section to this particular example.

A common notation for expressing requirements formally is known as "Z"-specifications (actually pronounced "Zed"). Z-specifications are a standard way to describe the required state before and after a procedure. Some selected (and slightly modified) Z notation is presented below.

8.1.1 Selected Mathematical Notation

$\Rightarrow$ means *implies* or *infers*; thus $P \Rightarrow Q$ means "if statement P is true, then statement Q is true."

$\forall$ means *for every;* for example: $\forall$ living person L, L has a head.

$\vee$ means "or"; $\wedge$ means "and".

N denotes the set of integers.

For a set A, $a \in A$ means *a is an element (a member) of A;* for example, $17 \in N$.

$A \subseteq B$ means *A is a subset of B;* that is, every element of A is an element of B. For example, $E \subseteq N$, where E is the set of even integers.

$A \times B$, where A and B are sets, denotes the product of these two sets; the product of A and B is the set of pairs (a, b) where $a \in A$ and $b \in B$.

Finite sets can be denoted by brackets and commas. For example, $\{4, 7, 2\}$ is the set consisting of the integer elements 4, 7, and 2. In this notation, elements are not repeated, and their order is not relevant.

$\{x: P\}$ means the *sets of elements x satisfying property P;* for example, $\{x: x^2 = x + 3\}$ is the set of numbers whose square equals the number plus 3.

If S is a finite set, card (S) is the number of elements in S. For example, card $(\{g, e, q\}) = 3$.

Functions

A *function f* from a set A to a set B is a subset of $A \times B$, in which no element of A occurs more than once as the first element of a pair. This is denoted $f: A \rightarrow B$. Put more symbolically, $f \subseteq A \times B$ and $[(a, b_1) \in f$ and $(a, b_2) \in f] \Rightarrow [b_1 = b_2]$.

The *domain* of a function is the set consisting of the first elements of the pairs constituting the function. For example, the domain of $g: N \rightarrow N$, where $g = \{(3, 5), (7, -1), (8, 2)\}$, is $\{3, 7, 8\}$.

The *range* of a function is the set consisting of the second elements of the pairs constituting the function. For example, the range of $h: N \rightarrow N$, where $h = \{(3, 5), (7, -1), (8, 5)\}$, is $\{5, -1\}$.

If f is a function and y is in the range of f, then $f^{-1}(y)$ is the set of domain elements of f that map onto y. Formally, $f^{-1}(y)$ is defined by $f^{-1}(y) = \{x: f(x) = y\}$. For example, $h^{-1}(5) = \{3, 8\}$ for the function h defined above.

The symbols $f: R \mapsto P$, expressed "f is a partial function from R to P," means that $f: Q \rightarrow P$, where $Q \subseteq R$ (Q is a subset of R). [For example, $R = \{4,7,2\}$, $P = \{8,1,5\}$, $Q = \{4,7\}$, $f(4)=5$, and $f(7)=8$.]

$a \mapsto b$ means that a maps to b in the context of the function being described [e.g., for the function f just defined, $4 \mapsto 5$ and $7 \mapsto 8$].

Suppose also that $f: A \mapsto B$ and $g: A \mapsto B$. Then $f \oplus g$, the extension (or "overriding") of g by f, is defined by
   • $f \oplus g(x) = g(x)$ if x is in the domain of g
   • $f \oplus g(x) = f(x)$ if x is not in the domain of g, but x is in the domain of f

[For example, taking the function f defined above, and g defined by $g(4)=11$ and $g(8) = 3$, we have $f \oplus g(4) = 11$, $f \oplus g(8) = 3$, and $f \oplus g(7) = 8$.]

8.2 Examples of Formal Specifications

A Z-specification consists of two connected rectangles with missing corners. The upper rectangle describes the types of the inputs, parameters, and outputs. The lower rectangle describes the state (situation) after the application of the procedure. The prime (') of a variable denotes its value at the conclusion of the procedure. For example, x' is the value of the variable x after applying the procedure being specified. Inputs are denoted with question marks. (Instead of saying "*z* is an input," we simply state *z*?) Once it becomes familiar, this notation is quite convenient.

This section shows how to use Z-specifications to (1) specify the requirements for augmenting a table and (2) perform a table lookup.

Example Augment 1: Augmenting a Table Suppose that we want to specify precisely a procedure which takes two integer inputs *l* and *r*, and updates a two-dimensional table t of integers by adding the pair *(l, r)* if *l* is not already present as a first element, overwriting with *r* if *l* is already present. The table *t* is assumed to have no repeating first elements: such tables are really functions from integers to integers.

We will build a Z-specification for the augmentation of a table of integers with no repeating first elements. It states that the table *t* is transformed by procedure *Augment* into a new function *t'*. The function *t'* behaves identically with *t* except that it maps *l* to *r*.

For example, if *t* is the table

5	7
2	11
1	2

then augmenting *t* with input (2, 4) yields the table

5	7
2	4
1	2

and augmenting *t* with input (3, 6) yields the following table.

5	7
2	11
1	2
3	6

The Z-specification is shown in Figure 4.37 and Figure 4.38. To a reader sufficiently versed in Z-notation, this specification is about as unambiguous as can be obtained.

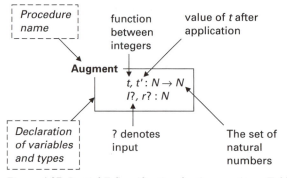

Figure 4.37 Partial Z-Specification for Augmenting a Table: Explanation of Symbols

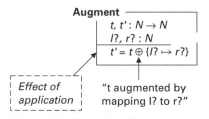

Figure 4.38 Full Z-Specification for Augmenting a Table

Example 2: Lookup   Figure 4.39 specifies a function *Lookup,* which looks up an entry in a table, returning the result (the corresponding integer) if the entry is present, and zero otherwise. The Z-specification states that *t* is a table, *l?* an input (that we are looking up) and *r!* the resulting integer when *l?* is in the left hand column of the table. For example, applying *Lookup* to the tables listed above, with *l?* having the value 5 would result in *r!* having the value 7. The specification gives the value of 0 to *r!* if *l?* is not in the left hand column of the table.

The way in which the result (lower box) can be read is:

either (1) the input *l?* is not in the domain of *t,* the output *r!* is zero, and *t* is unchanged

or (2) the input *l?* is in the domain of *t,* the output *r!* is the result of applying *t* to *l?,* and *t* is unchanged.

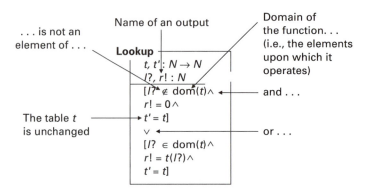

Figure 4.39 Z-Specification for Looking Up an Entry in a Table (see Hayes [Ha])

TABLE 4.4 The Array A

Domain element A	Range element A(x)
1	4
2	6
3	3
4	4
5	6
6	8

Why do we have to state specifically that t is unchanged? If we did not, we could not complain about an implementation that changes t (perhaps for programming convenience), because such an implementation would still satisfy the requirements.

Example 3: Sorting   For the next example, let's return to the sorting example at the beginning of this section. Recall that the (imperfect) natural language requirement was:

> *Returns a sorted array of all of the individual elements of the array.*

Mathematically, arrays are functions with a domain of the form $\{1, 2, 3, ..., n\}$ for some positive integer n. For example, the array $A = (4,6,3,4,6,8)$ is equivalent to the function shown in Table 4.4.

We want the Z-specification to state that t' has the same domain and range as t, that its range elements are in order (and could be equal). It is easy to express the fact that the range elements of A are in order, but we must also deal with repetitions. Recall that pure mathematical sets do not have repetition. For example, 6 appears twice in the range of A: We must ensure that it also appears twice in the range of A'. To do this, we can use the inverse function notation f^{-1}. The meaning of $f^{-1}(x)$ is "the set of domain elements that map to x." The set of elements that A maps to 6 consists of 1 and 5, so $A^{-1}(6) = \{1,5\}$. We need only ensure that $A'^{-1}(6)$ also contains exactly two elements, ensuring the same repetition in A' as in A. Thus, what we need is the equality in size of $A^{-1}(x)$ and $A'^{-1}(x)$ for all relevant values of x.

Using Z-notation, a specification would be as in Figure 4.40.

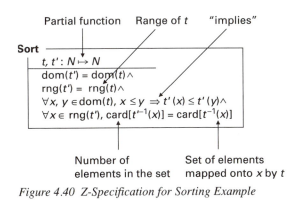

Figure 4.40 Z-Specification for Sorting Example

Maximum ─────────────────────────────

> $t : N \mapsto N \wedge card\ (\ dom(t)\ ) < 1000$
> $m!, n! : N$
> ──────────────────────────────
> $n! \in dom(t)\ \wedge$
> $m! = t(n!)\ \wedge$
> $\forall i \in dom(t),\ [t(n!) \geq t(i),$ and
> $\qquad\qquad$ if $t(n!) = t(i)$ then $n! \leq i]$

Figure 4.41 Z-Specification for Maximum

Example 4: Maximum   As a final example, let's take a common, simple requirement which is better expressed formally than informally. This time we express it formally
first, as shown in Figure 4.41. This specification is for the maximum of the integer array
t and the index of that maximum element. What makes the formal specification appealing is the ease with which it specifies that if there are several maximum entries, the one
with the lowest index is selected.

8.3 When Should One Use Formal Specifications?

Formal specifications have numerous supporters, as well as numerous detractors. Several
commercial systems, including parts of IBM's widely used CICS (Customer Information
Control System), have utilized formal methods in general and Z-specifications in particular.

Effectiveness in communicating requirements is the litmus test for when to use formal vs. informal requirements. Expressing requirements is sometimes best done using natural language and sometimes best done using a formal specification. For the latter to be
effective, implementers and users of the SRS must be sufficiently trained to understand
them. Z-specifications appear to be mostly applicable for processes which can be described in terms of their outcomes alone (i.e., an algorithm by which their outcomes are to
be attained does not need to be specified). Research on formal specifications continues, including studies on their use for specifying graphical user interfaces. The reach of mathematics can hardly be underestimated. Einstein once jokingly called the power of
mathematics "unreasonable." It is possible that new research will expand the practical applicability of formal methods.

In short, if the requirement is explainable in terms of concrete output, and the developers are educated in formal methods, then formal requirements can be a viable means
for expressing specific requirements. In any case, we can borrow specific parts of the formal specifications, such as the use of the "!" and "?" notations.

Formal specifications are required to implement "executable specifications" (see, for
example, Schwartz et al. [Sc]). These are specifications which can be automatically translated into object code, and must therefore be precise. Active research in this area has taken
place for many years, reporting qualified successes (e.g., Jones [Jo2]), and qualified failures (e.g., Ostrolenk et al. [Os]). A published example of formal requirements for a large
real-time application is the Operational Flight Program for the US Navy's A-7E (Alspaugh
[Al1]). It should be noted, however, that these particular requirements were written to the
as-built system as a demonstration.

We will return to the use of mathematics in Chapter 7 when we discuss the implementation of functions. The sites at [Z] provide additional contemporary information about
Z-specifications.

Maximum

$$t : N \mapsto N \wedge card \; (\; dom(t) \;) < 1000$$
$$m!, n! : N$$

$n! \in dom(t) \wedge$
$m! = t(n!) \wedge$
$\forall i \in dom(t), \; t(i) \geq t(n!)$
$\Rightarrow i \geq n!$

Precondition:

   t is an array of length *lg*
$$0 < lg < 1000$$

Postcondition:

   $0 \leq n < lg$ // *n* index of max
   $m = t[n]$ // *m* is max value
   $t[i] \leq m$ for $i = 0, \ldots, lg - 1$
   if $t[j] = m$ then $j \geq n$ // first

Figure 4.42 Z-Specifications vs. Preconditions and Postconditions for Maximum

8.4 Preconditions and Postconditions

A commonly used form of specifications which is less formal than Z-specifications consists of *preconditions* and *postconditions*. These are descriptions of the required state of the application before and after a computation. Preconditions and postconditions generally use pseudocode, as well as parts of the implementation language (Java, C++, etc.), rather than mathematics alone. For this reason, they are frequently applied for specifying designs. More precisely, they are usually used to specify function requirements for programmers based on designs. (Recall that, although we name only one waterfall phase "requirements," the products of any phase, design, for example, actually become the requirements for the next phase — in this case, implementation. "Requirements" is actually a term that applies to many phases.)

To give an example, the maximum example used above could be stated in a manner shown in Figure 4.42.

This requirement can be stated more succinctly: Refer to exercise G4.4.

9. THE EFFECTS ON PROJECTS OF THE D-REQUIREMENTS PROCESS

Once D-requirements have been collected, the project documents are updated to reflect the improved project knowledge. We will take as an example the required updates to the SPMP.

9.1 Effects on the SPMP

Once D-requirements have been gathered, the SPMP can be updated as shown in Table 4.5. D-requirements are placed under configuration control. One issue to be addressed is what level of detail should be counted as a software configuration item (CI). Certainly, Section 3 as a whole ("Specific requirements") of the SRS (using the IEEE standard) could be a CI. Each class could be a CI. Individual requirements are typically too fine-grained to be CIs.

9.2 The Effects of Large Scales on D-Requirements

When the list of requirements grows into the hundreds, inconsistencies of the kind mentioned in Section 3.6 on page 195 can easily arise. Classifying requirements by classes, classes by packages, and packages by sub-packages, and the like becomes a necessity. The packages typically correspond to subsystems in the overall organization of the application.

TABLE 4.5 Updating the Project on Completing D-Requirements

	Status after initial draft	Result of updating after C-requirements	Result of updating after D-requirements
Milestones	Initial	More detailed	More detailed
Risks	Identify	Retire risks identified previously; seek more risks	Retire risks identified; identify more risks
Schedule	Very high level	Preliminary project schedule	More detailed: shows class and method development tasking
Personnel	Designate C-requirements engineers	Engineers designated for D-requirements analysis	Designate software architects
Cost Estimation	Crude estimates	First estimates based on job content	Improved estimate based on more specific function points or past experience with similar individual requirements

Although *completeness* is a goal for which we strive in collecting requirements, it is an elusive goal. For substantial applications, there is seldom a natural "last" requirement — just the last one before requirements freeze.

As outlined in the corresponding section about scale in the previous chapter, large-scale projects require increasing organizational formality (not to be confused with formal methods). The SRS may have to be divided into separate volumes. A single section in our (tiny!) case study could expand into a 700-page volume. Extensive management work is required to schedule the development and inspection of D-requirements. Projects with hundreds of specific requirements need requirements management tools. The successful widespread usage of the Java packages has shown, however, that large collections of requirements are manageable when the functionality is organized by well-defined packages, sub-packages, and classes.

The rewards of good requirements analysis are substantial. Conversely, the penalties for poor requirements are substantial too. For example, Faulk (in [Th]), reports on a Government Accounting Office study of the Cheyenne Mountain Upgrade project on which "requirements-related problems" resulted in a $600 million cost overrun, an eight-year delay, and diminished capability. Debates rage about the percentage of large projects that turn out badly versus the percentage that turn out well. Suffice it to say that many large projects do a fine job of requirements analysis. The author can attest to this from personal experience.

10. SUMMARY OF THE D-REQUIREMENTS PROCESS

D-requirements ("developer" or "detailed" requirements) are written primarily for designers and developers. They are created from C-requirements, as well as from continued customer interaction. D-requirements must be testable, traceable, and consistent. Since they become numerous, they must be classified systematically. A useful way to organize D-requirements is by domain class and function. There are several metrics against which D-requirements can be inspected. Good requirements analysis yields extensive benefits. This summary is shown in Figure 4.43.

- D-requirements for developers
- Goals: clarity, traceability
- Good organization helps
  - e.g., OO style
- Use formal methods as appropriate
- Update SPMP as a result

Figure 4.43 Summary of Chapter 4

STUDENT PROJECT GUIDE:
D-REQUIREMENTS FOR THE *ENCOUNTER* CASE STUDY

This section explains how the principles for obtaining and representing D-requirements, explained in this chapter, are translated into practice. The case study is used as the example. The student is also referred to the "One way to ..." Figures throughout this chapter, which act as a guide to the process.

SPG1. PREPARING

Hal and Karen had completed their write-up of the C-requirements based on discussions and interviews with Betty Sims and Arlan Howard. They used the headings of the IEEE standard (refer to Figure 3.6) as prompts for the nonfunctional requirements such as GUIs, performance, and hardware platforms. Now they had to identify the manner in which they would organize the functional D-requirements. They anticipated having to revisit and update the SRS many times, coordinating the design and code with it: They wanted this process to be as simple as possible. As a result, their major criterion was the ability to easily maintain consistency between the SRS, the design, and the code.

They first discussed organizing the detailed requirements by states and actions, based on the state-transition diagram described in the C-requirements. This organization method would consist of a list of the actions that a player would take, such as clicking an exit hyperlink on an area, fol-

lowed by the effects of this action. They both agreed that this would be an understandable organization, but decided that it would not trace to the implementation as well as they wanted. They began searching for other ways in which to organize the D-requirements.

Hal was in favor of organizing the functional D-requirements by use case, especially since he wanted to follow the Unified Software Development Process. He pointed out that, at this stage, the video game could most easily be thought of in terms of the *setting up* use case, the *moving among the game areas* use case, and the *engaging the foreign character* use case. He pointed out how convenient it would be to use just these three use cases to describe all of the functional requirements. He was also excited about the prospect of perhaps being able to reuse these use cases for specifying future games.

Karen agreed that the requirements would be quite easy to understand if organized by use case, but she had several objections. The first was that some requirements would be part of more than one use case. An example is what happens when an exit from a room is clicked. This could be part of all three use cases they had identified, and so it would not be clear where to look for it. Karen's other objection was the fact the mapping from the use cases to the code would not be as clean as the organization she had in mind. Finally, she pointed out that the company was not yet equipped to properly archive use cases for future reuse.

Karen wanted to organize functional requirements by class, which, she said, facilitated traceability from requirements to implementation. She wanted to pick classes carefully enough to ensure that they would be used as part of the design (and implementation). Hal pointed out a disadvantage of this approach: the fact that it forced them to decide very early on some of the classes that they would use in implementing the application. He was worried about the possibility that they may later change their minds about the selection. After further discussion, they decided that organizing the detailed requirements by class had more benefits than drawbacks, and they committed to this method. They decided to be very conservative about class selection, however.

SPG2. CLASSIFYING THE D-REQUIREMENTS

Hal and Karen first took each use case and expressed it as a sequence diagram. Looking at each step, they identified what object of what class initiated the action, and what object had the responsibility for carrying out the action. This process prompted them to create and/or identify classes. They found it necessary to call Betty and Arlan several times to clarify use case steps that they thought they had understood but really didn't.

Hal listed the classes and objects mentioned in the use cases. They then brainstormed, scouring every aspect of *Encounter* they could reasonably imagine for additional possible classes. As a final step in the class selection process they drastically cut the list down to an essential few, still taking care to preserve all of the classes referred to in the use cases. The final list consisted of *Area, EncounterCharacter, EncounterGame, Engagement, EngagementDisplay, ConnectionHyperlink, ForeignCharacter, PlayerCharacter,* and *PlayerQualityWindow.*

They now finalized the headings of the SRS in Section 3.2 ("Specific requirements on Figure 3.6"). They collected the detailed requirements related to areas in subsection 3.2.A, corresponding to the *Area* class. They ordered these subsections alphabetically because they anticipated adding classes later. They surmised that if they were to have ordered topics by number (e.g., *PlayerCharacter* being 3.2.14), then locating an individual requirement would have been more difficult because the user of the SRS would have to search many of the 3.2.N subsections before finding the one applicable. The next class being *EncounterAreaConnection*, they numbered the next subsection 3.2.*EAC*, etc. Within each classification they created subsections for *attributes, entities, functionality,* and *events.*

SPG3. WRITING THE D-REQUIREMENTS

Karen and Hal wrote section 3.1 on user interfaces by supplying details on the sketches they had made for the C-requirements, then asking Betty, as well as the human factors department, to review them. Knowing that this would be the final document from which these were to be built, they had the customer agree on every detail.

They entered the sequence diagrams in Figures 4.55, 4.56, and 4.57.

They checked their interview notes with Betty and Arlan as to the properties ("attributes") of each classification (class). For example, they asked what properties were required for the connections between two *Encounter* areas. (One property of such connections was "the first area" connected, and another was "the second area".) For each class, they asked themselves what entities (instances of the class) were required for the game. For example, there would have to be a dressing room area, and a courtyard area. They then asked what functionality the class had to possess. For example, a functionality of each *Encounter* character is the ability to configure the values of its qualities (requirement 3.2.EC.3.2). Finally, they listed all of the events that instances of the class were required to respond to. (For example, clicking on an exit from an area.)

One aspect that disturbed them was the time required for new values to take effect. They realized that this was a key aspect to the game: If no time were to elapse, the player would simply set the qualities pertaining to the current area to a maximum, and little skill would be required to play the game. A delay made the game interesting but the problem was how much delay should there be? They considered stating "to be decided" for the duration, but finally decided to specify four seconds, feeling that changing this amount would be a straightforward process.

Karen was concerned about the imprecision of some of the requirements, especially those concerning the manner in which quality points should be exchanged when two characters engage each other. She felt that programmers could easily misunderstand the requirements. This would waste time on defects and produce a defective game. She suggested using Z-specifications. Hal made the point that no one except Karen would understand them well enough, since the rest of the team did not have the required education. They compromised by agreeing to use appropriate mathematics in specifying this require-

ment, but not the Z-specification format. Karen made a mental note that if she ever taught software engineering, she would insist that all students be completely comfortable with Z-specifications.

Prompted by the section headings in the IEEE SRS standard, Karen and Hal made sure to cover all of the performance requirements (mostly pertaining to the speed that the game would have to possess to be interesting) and check them with Betty and Arlan. They also thought through the memory requirements (RAM and disk). They then completed the document.

SG4. FOLLOWING UP: METRICS AND POSTMORTEM

The requirements analysis team asked Betty, Arlan, and the rest of the team to inspect the D-requirements. They performed this inspection primarily against the C-requirements by ensuring that every part of the C-requirements was elaborated upon by D-requirements. They also employed a checklist like that used in Table 4.3 on page 216. Several defects were found, which Hal and Karen recorded and repaired. The results of this process were similar to those described in the Student Project Guide for C-requirements (Chapter 4).

EXERCISES

Solutions and hints are given at the end of this chapter to all exercises marked with "s" and "h" respectively.

REVIEW QUESTIONS

R4.1[s] To whom are D-requirements primarily targeted?

R4.2[s] A typical application has many requirements. Name an important issue in creating and dealing with requirements.

R4.3[s] Name 3–5 categories of detailed requirements.

R4.4[s] Name 5–7 desirable properties for detailed requirements.

R4.5[s] Name 4–6 ways of organizing detailed requirements.

R4.6[s] a. Is there a sequence diagram corresponding to every use case?

b. Is there a use case corresponding to every sequence diagram?

GENERAL EXERCISES

G4.1[h] Write 10 D-requirements for a simulation application that simulates the movement of customers in a bank.

G4.2 What is wrong with the following D-requirements?

a. *HomeBudget* shall display a convenient interface for entering personal data.

b. *SatControl* shall compute the predicted time it takes to circle the Earth on the current orbit, and the actual time taken to circle the Earth on the previous orbit.

c. *InvestKing* shall determine the best investment strategy.

G4.3 Give precise measures of quality to the D-requirements in exercise G4.2.

G4.4 State the maximum requirement of example 4 on page 224 in a more succinct form. Use the precondition and postcondition form.

G4.5 Give a use case and the corresponding sequence diagram for a system with the following C-requirement.

"The system shall provide advice for the beginning Windows user on how to execute Windows operations."

TEAM EXERCISES

T4.1 ("SRS")

Write the SRS for your application. Use or modify the IEEE standard. If you are using an iterative approach, try to indicate what requirements are to be implemented in each iteration.

Track the time spent on this by individuals and by the group. Break this time into appropriate activities. Measure the effectiveness of your effort. (Feel free to develop your own metrics; see also team exercises in prior chapters.) Indicate how the process you used to develop the SRS could have been improved.

Evaluation criteria:
α. *Degree of clarity*—A = very clear writing
β. *Extent to which the plan includes all relevant details and excludes irrelevant material*—A = more than 95% of knowable details included and less than 5% of details irrelevant
γ. *Effectiveness of your self-measurement and process improvement description*—A = very effective metrics; very specific assertions on how the process would have been improved without spending more time

HINTS TO QUESTIONS

G4.1 Classifying by class, the following classes should be included. *BankCustomer, Bank, Teller*.

SOLUTIONS TO QUESTIONS

R4.1 Developers, primarily; customers, secondarily

R4.2 Classifying them so that they can be readily accessed and maintained

R4.3 Functional, nonfunctional, inverse, interface, design, and implementation constraints

R4.4 Traceability, testability, nonambiguity, priority, completeness, error conditions, and consistency

R4.5 By mode, use case actor, class (the OO style), feature, function hierarchy, or state

R4.6 a. Yes. Given a use case, it is always possible to identify the objects involved, then convert the sequence of user/system actions into a sequence of function calls among these objects.

b. No. A sequence diagram expresses a sequence of function calls among objects. Not every such sequence is a typical interaction between the user and the application.

SOFTWARE REQUIREMENTS SPECIFICATION (SRS) FOR THE *ENCOUNTER* VIDEO GAME, PART 2 OF 2

History of versions of this document.

x/yy/zzz Initial draft by Karen Peters

x/yy/zzz Reviewed for technical accuracy by Hal Furnass; requirements swapped between *Area* and *PlayerCharacter*

x/yy/zzz Release 0.1 approved by Karen Peters

3. SPECIFIC REQUIREMENTS

3.1 External Interface Requirements

3.1.1 User Interfaces

[Note to the student: Section 2.1.2 in the SRS for the Encounter video game showed only sketches of user interfaces in order to provide product perspective. It lacked details and should not be regarded as the last word.

If user interfaces are not completely specified later in this document, then all details should be given in this section. Since we are using the object style of specification in this case study, the details of each window are packaged with their classes in Section 3.2.2. in the SRS.

In any case, this section should explain the physical relationships among graphical elements (e.g., cascading, tiled, superimposed).]

Encounter takes place in areas. Figure 4.44 shows a typical screen shot of the

courtyard area, with a player-controlled character, a foreign character, and the results of an engagement. This interface takes up the entire monitor screen. Areas have connections to adjacent areas, labeled by hyperlinks. Clicking on one of these hyperlinks moves the player's character into the corresponding area.

The entire set of interfaces is as follows:

a. One user interface for each area, specified in Section 3.2AR below.

b. A user interface for setting the quality values of the player's character, specified in Section 3.2.PQ.

c. A user interface for displaying the results of an engagement, specified in Section 3.2.ED. The same user interface is used to show the status of the player's character.

An interface of type *a* above will always be present on the monitor. When called for by these requirements, interfaces of type *b* or *c* will be superimposed.

This requirement is tested in Software Test Documentation (STD). <test reference goes here>.

3.1.2 Hardware Interfaces

[Note to the student: The hardware that Encounter *(which is a software application) deals with]*

[Future release: *Encounter* will be controllable by a joystick.]

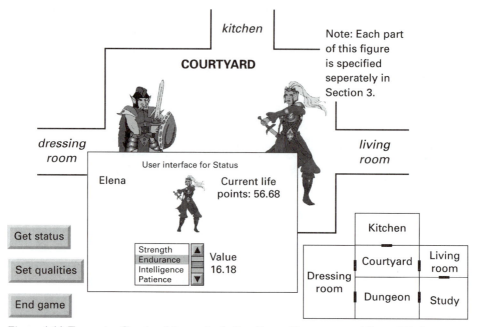

Figure 4.44 Encounter Courtyard *Image Including Game Characters and Status Window (Graphics reproduced with permission of Corel)*

3.1.3 Software Interfaces

[Note to the student: Other software with which Encounter must interface: an example would be a printer driver]

[Future release: *Encounter* will be playable from Intergalactic Internet Gaming Site.]

3.1.4 Communication Interfaces.

[Future release: *Encounter* shall interface with the Internet via a modem with at least 56 Kb/s.]

3.2 Specific Requirements

[Note to the student: This section takes some liberties with the IEEE standards in order to account for use cases. First it describes the sequence diagrams required to express the use cases of Section 2.2 of this SRS (Section 3.2.1). The classes required to express these use cases are then used to classify the detailed requirements (Sec-

tion 3.2.2). Sequence diagrams were explained in Section 4 of this chapter on Page 196.]

3.2.1 Sequence Diagrams

[Note to the student: Here we show a sequence diagram for each of the use cases identified in Section 2.1 of the SRS. The IEEE SRS standard does not have a section called "sequence diagrams"; it has been tailored to accommodate this concept.]

3.2.1.1 Initialize Use Case. The sequence diagram for the *Initialize* use case is shown in Figure 4.45. This use case requires classes *EncounterGame* (of which there is only one instance), *PlayerCharacter* (with instance main player character), *PlayerQualityWindow* (of which there is only one instance), and *Area* (with instance dressing room).

3.2.1.2 Travel to Adjacent Area Use Case. The sequence diagram for the *Travel to adjacent area* use case is shown in

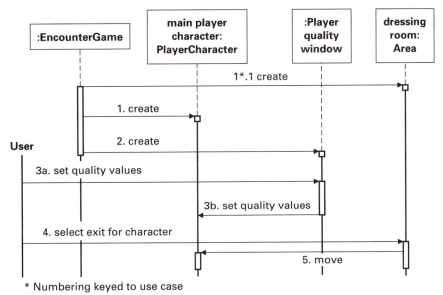

Figure 4.45 Sequence Diagram for Initialize *Use Case*

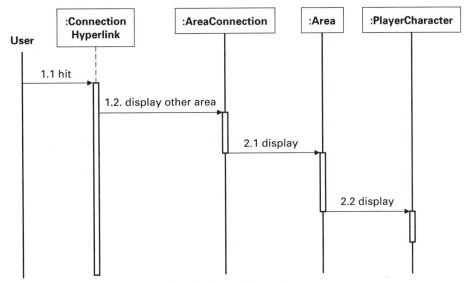

Figure 4.46 Sequence Diagram for Travel to Adjacent Area *Use Case*

Figure 4.46. This use case requires classes *ConnectionHyperlink, AreaConnection, Area,* and *PlayerCharacter.*

3.2.1.3 Engage Foreign Character Use Case.
The sequence diagram for the *Engage foreign character* use case is shown in Figure 4.47. This use case requires classes *EncounterGame* (of which there is only one instance), *ForeignCharacter* (with instance

freddie), *Engagement, PlayerCharacter, PlayerQualityWindow,* and *Engagement-Display.*

3.2.2 Classes for Classification of Specific Requirements

[Note to the student: Since we are classifying the detailed requirements by class, we first list the classes that we have (very

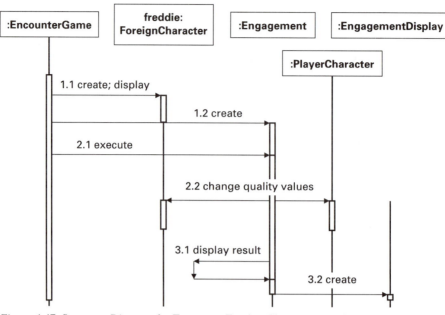

Figure 4.47 Sequence Diagram for Encounter Foreign Character *Use Case*

carefully!) chosen. These are not all of the classes that will be used by the application—merely the core classes pertaining to the domain of the application, which are adequate for organizing all of the requirements. In this case, for example, all of them are aspects of the Encounter video game.]

The classes for the *Encounter* video game sufficient for expressing the requirements are *Area, EncounterCharacter, EncounterGame, Engagement, Engage-* mentDisplay, ForeignCharacter, Player-Character, and PlayerQualityWindow. These are shown in the object model of Figure 4.48.

[Note to the student: The numbering "3.2.Area.N.N...," etc. used in Section 3.2 makes it easier for us to insert, remove, and locate requirements by organizing alphabetically the classes that contain them. Think in terms of hundreds of requirements. If we were to number the classes

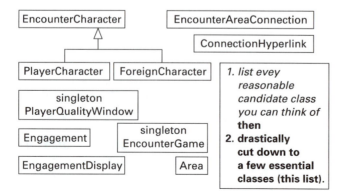

Figure 4.48 Classes for Encounter *Video Game Showing Only Inheritance Relationships*

using "3.2.1...", "3.2.2...," etc., then inserting new classes would have to be done at the end of the list, since existing numbering, already referred to elsewhere in the project, could not be disturbed. The requirements would not be alphabetically ordered. As a result, one would have to go through the requirements one by one to locate a particular one.]

3.2.AR Areas

[Note to the student: First, we describe what the class (i.e., this classification of requirements) refers to.]

An area is a place viewable on the monitor. All activities of *Encounter* (including engagements) take place in areas. Rooms, gardens, and courtyards are examples of areas.

3.2.AR.1 Attributes of Areas

[Note to the student: Here we tell what properties each object (specific entity) of the class must possess.]

3.2.AR.1.1 AREA NAME. [essential; not yet implemented]

[Notes to the student: The bracketed statement above indicates the priority and the status of the requirement. Once the requirement is coded and tested, the statement "not yet implemented" is either deleted or changed to "implemented."

"Essential" requirements are implemented first. Once a requirement has been designed for and implemented, "essential" can be removed. This is one technique for tracking the state of the application and its relationship with this SRS. Another technique is to specify the iteration to which the requirement applies.]

Every area will have a unique name consisting of 1 to 15 characters. Acceptable characters shall consist of blanks, 0 through 9, *a* through *z*, and *A* through *Z* only.

Test plan < reference to test goes here>.

[Notes to the student: Each attribute-type requirement maps to a pair of get-

and set- functions. This document suggests how each requirement can be hyperlinked to a unit test in the Software Test Documentation.]

3.2.AR.1.2 AREA IMAGE [essential; not yet implemented] There shall be an image to display each *Area* object on the entire monitor. The image shall fill the entire monitor.

3.2.AR.1.3 AREA-SPECIFIC QUALITIES [essential; not yet implemented] Only some game character qualities shall be applicable in each area. The specific qualities required for each area are specified in Section 3.2.AR.2.

3.2.AR.1.4 ACTION BUTTONS [essential; not yet implemented] Every area shall show a "Get status" button, a "Set qualities" button, and an "End game" button, in the lower left corner.

3.2.AR.2 Area Entities

[Note to the student: We designate specific area objects that must exist within the application.]

3.2.AR.2.1 COURTYARD AREA [essential; not yet implemented} There shall be an *Area* object with name "courtyard" requiring qualities *stamina,* and *strength.* The preliminary courtyard image shown in Figure 4.49 includes a map of nearby areas.

3.2.AR.2.2 DRESSING ROOM AREA [essential; not yet implemented] There shall be an area with name "dressing room" requiring no qualities. Its preliminary image, shown in Figure 4.50, includes a map of nearby areas.

3.2.AR.2.3 DUNGEON AREA [essential; not yet implemented] There shall be an area with name "dungeon" requiring qualities *stamina* and *patience.* Its preliminary image shown in Figure 4.51 includes a map of nearby areas.

3.2.AR.2.4 KITCHEN AREA [essential; not yet implemented] There shall be an area

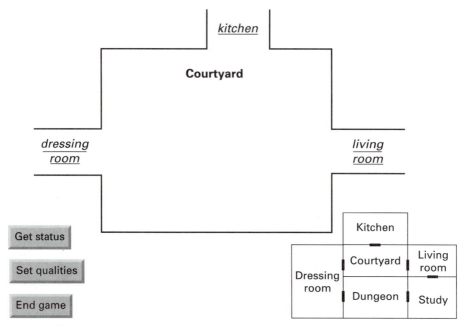

Figure 4.49 Encounter Courtyard *Image*

with name "kitchen" requiring the quality *concentration*. The preliminary kitchen image shown in Figure 4.52 includes a map of nearby areas.

3.2.AR.2.5 LIVING ROOM AREA [essential; not yet implemented] There shall be

an area with name "living room" requiring qualities *concentration* and *stamina*. Its preliminary image shown in Figure 4.53 includes a map of nearby areas.

3.2.AR.2.6 STUDY AREA [essential; not yet implemented] There shall be an area with

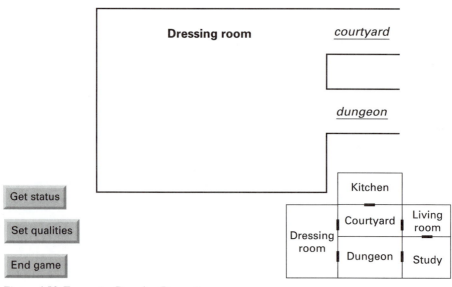

Figure 4.50 Encounter Dressing Room *Image*

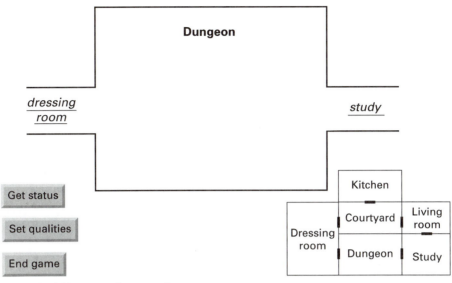

Figure 4.51 Encounter Dungeon *Image*

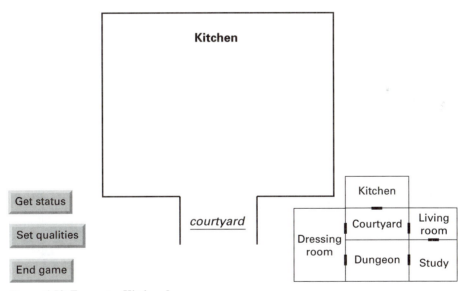

Figure 4.52 Encounter Kitchen *Image*

name "study" requiring quality *concentration*. Its preliminary image shown in Figure 4.54 includes a map of nearby areas.

3.2.AR.3 Area Functionality

[Note to the student: This is the required functionality that pertains specifically to areas. Every functional capability of the application should belong to one of these sections.]

3.2.AR.4 Events Pertaining to Areas

[Note to the student: We separate the events that pertain to areas from the at-

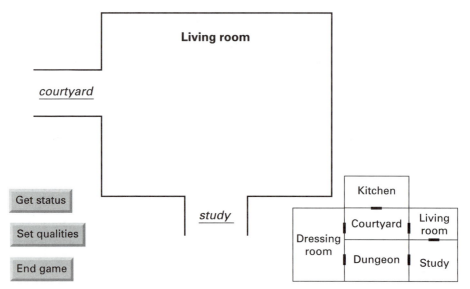

Figure 4.53 Encounter Living Room *Image*

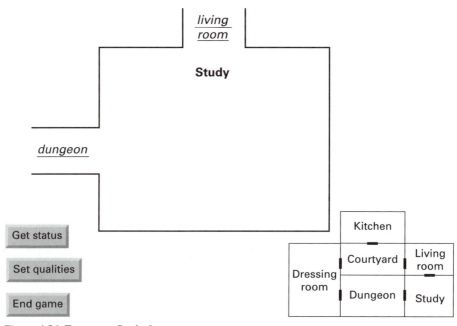

Figure 4.54 Encounter Study *Image*

tributes, objects, and methods. An event is an action that occurs to the application and is instigated from outside of the application.]

3.2.AR.4.1 DISPLAY ON ENTRY OF PLAYER CHARACTER [essential; not yet imple-

mented] Whenever the player's main character enters an area, that area and the characters in it shall be displayed on the monitor, filling the monitor.

3.2.AR.4.2 HANDLING ENGAGEMENTS [essential; not yet implemented] When a foreign game character enters an area containing the player's main character, or vice versa, they engage each other.

3.2.AR.4.3 INTERRUPTING ENGAGEMENTS [optional; not yet implemented] Players are able to interrupt engagements on a random basis. On average, the player can stop one of every ten engagements by executing the procedure to set qualities. The user tries to interrupt an engagement by attempting to set the player's qualities. If the game does not allow this, no indication is given: The game proceeds as if the attempt had not been made.

3.2.AR.4.4 PRESSING THE *SET QUALITIES* BUTTON [essential; not yet implemented] When the user presses the *set qualities* button, a window for setting the values of qualities appears superimposed on the area, provided that there is no foreign character in the area. See 3.2.PQ for the specifications of this window.

3.2.AR.4.5 PRESSING THE *END GAME* BUTTON [optional; not yet implemented] When the user presses the *end game* button, the game terminates. No additional screens appear.

[Note to the student: The previous sentence, an inverse requirement, was felt necessary because games often do display a summary of a session.]

3.2.AR.4.6 PRESSING THE *GET STATUS* BUTTON [optional; not yet implemented] When the user presses the *get status* button, an engagement display window appears showing the status of the player's character before and after the last engagement.

3.2.CH Connection Hyperlinks Between Areas Connection hyperlinks are hyperlinks placed at each area exit, showing the area to which it is connected.

3.2.CH.1 Attributes of Connections Hyperlinks

3.2.CH.1.1 CONNECTION [essential; not yet implemented] Each connection hyperlink corresponds to an area connection.

3.2.CH.2   Connection   Hyperlink Entities

[essential; not yet implemented] There are two connection hyperlinks corresponding to each area connection, one in each area of the connection.

3.2.CH.3 Functionality of Connection Hyperlinks
none

3.2.CH.4   Events   Pertaining   to Connection Hyperlinks

3.2.CH.4.1 USER CLICKS ON A CONNECTION HYPERLINK The effect of clicking a connection hyperlink is that the player's character is displayed in the area on the other side of the area connection.

3.2.CO Connections Between Areas
Characters travel from area to adjacent area by means of connections. Each of these connects two areas. Figure 4.55 shows the required connections among the areas.

3.2.CO.1 Attributes of Connections Between Areas

3.2.CO.1.1 FIRST AND SECOND AREAS [essential; not yet implemented] Each connection will connect a pair of areas which we will call the "first" and "second" areas.

3.2.CO.2 Connections Entities

3.2.CO.2.1 DRESSING ROOM–COURTYARD [essential; not yet implemented] There will be a connection between the dressing room and the courtyard.

3.2.CO.2.2 DUNGEON–STUDY [essential; not yet implemented] There will be a connection between the dungeon and the study.

3.2.CO.2.3 STUDY–LIVING ROOM [essential; not yet implemented] There will be a connection between the study and the living room.

3.2.CO.2.4 COURTYARD–LIVING ROOM [essential; not yet implemented] There will

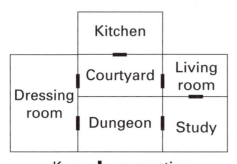

Key: ▌ = connection

Figure 4.55 Encounter *Area Configuration (Desirable Requirement)*

be a connection between the courtyard and the living room.

3.2.CO.2.5 DRESSING ROOM–DUNGEON [essential; not yet implemented] There will be a connection between the dressing room and the dungeon.

3.2.CO.2.6 COURTYARD–KITCHEN [essential; not yet implemented] There will be a connection between the courtyard and the kitchen.

3.2.CO.3 Functionality of Area Connections
none

3.2.CO.4 Events Pertaining to Area Connections

3.2.CO.4.1 MOVING A CHARACTER THROUGH A CONNECTION [essential; not yet implemented] Connections are displayed as hyperlinks at the borders of areas whenever the player's character is in the area. When the user clicks such a hyperlink, the linked area is displayed with the character in this area.

3.2.EC Encounter *Characters*

3.2.EC.1 Attributes of Encounter Characters

3.2.EC.1.1 NAMES OF *ENCOUNTER* CHARACTERS. [essential; not yet implemented]

Every game character in the *Encounter* video game shall have a unique name. The specifications for names shall be the same as those for Area names, specified in 3.2.AR.1.

3.2.EC.1.2 QUALITIES OF ENCOUNTER CHARACTERS. [essential; not yet implemented] Every game character has the same set of qualities. Each quality shall be a nonnegative floating point number with at least one decimal of precision. These are all initialized equally so that the sum of their values is 100. The value of a quality cannot be both greater than 0 and less than 0.5.

For the first release the qualities will be *concentration, intelligence, patience, stamina,* and *strength.*

3.2.EC.1.2 IMAGE OF *ENCOUNTER* CHARACTERS [essential; not yet implemented] Every game character will have an image.

3.2.EC.2 Encounter Character Entities
The characters of the game are described among the types of *Encounter* characters.

3.2.EC.3 Functionality of Encounter Characters

3.2.EC.3.1 LIVING POINTS [essential; not yet implemented] The *Encounter* game will be able to produce the sum of the values of

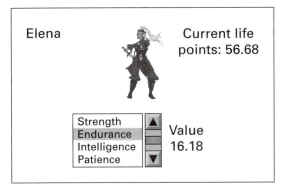

Figure 4.56 User Interface for Showing Status (Graphics reproduced with permission from Corel)

any character's qualities, called its *living points*.

3.2.EC.3.2 CONFIGURABILITY OF *ENCOUNTER* CHARACTER QUALITY VALUES [essential; not yet implemented] Whenever an *Encounter* character is alone in an area, the value of any of its qualities may be set. The value chosen must be less than or equal to the sum of the quality values. The values of the remaining qualities are automatically adjusted so as to maintain their mutual proportions, except for resulting quantities less than one, which are replaced by quality values of zero.

3.2.ED Engagement Displays [essential; not yet implemented] There will be a window displaying the result of engagements. The format is shown in Figure 4.56.

3.2.ED.4 Engagement Display Events

3.2.ED.4.1 DISMISSING THE DISPLAY [essential; not yet implemented] When the user hits OK, the display disappears.

3.2.EG The Encounter Game The requirements in this section pertain to the game as a whole.

3.2.EG.1 Attributes of the Encounter Game

3.2.EG.1.1 DURATION [optional; not yet implemented] A record will be kept of the

duration of each game, timed from when the player begins the game.

3.2.EG.2 Entities of the Encounter Game

3.2.EG.2.1 SINGLE GAME [essential; not yet implemented] There will be a single game.

[Note to the student: Future releases will allow several versions of the game to run at the same time.]

3.2.EN Engagements An *engagement* is the interaction between a game character controlled by the player and a foreign character.

3.2.EN.1 Attributes of Engagements none

3.2.EN.2 Engagement Entities There are no permanent engagement entities.

3.2.EN.3 Functionality of Engagements

3.2.EN.3.1 ENGAGING A FOREIGN CHARACTER

[Note to the student: This particular requirement is mathematical in nature and so there is no attempt to replace the mathematics with natural language, which would risk compromising its precision. The use of nat-

Figure 4.57 Image for Freddie Foreign Character (Graphics reproduced with permission from Corel)

ural language to explain the mathematics is a good practice, however.]

[essential; not yet implemented]

When an engagement takes place, the "stronger" of the two characters is the one whose values of area-specific qualities sum to the greater amount. The system transfers half the values of each area-specific quality of the weaker to the stronger. No transfer of points takes place if neither character is stronger.

If either character has no points after the value reallocations are made, the game ends. If the game does not end, the player's character is moved to a random area and the results of the engagement are displayed.

As an example of the value reallocations, suppose that the player engages a foreign character in an area preferring *stamina* and *concentration*. If p_s is the value of the player's stamina, and assuming $p_s + p_c > f_s + f_c$, we would have $p_s' = p_s + f_s/2$, $p_c' = p_c + f_c/2$, $f_s' = f_s/2$, and $f_c' = f_a/2$ where x' is the value of x after the transaction.

[The reader will recognize the defect in the last equation, which should be $f_c' = f_c/2$. We will leave the defect intact as an example.]

To take a numerical example of an engagement in this area: If the player's stamina value is 7, and concentration value is 19, and Freddie the foreigner's stamina is 11, and concentration 0.6, then the player is stronger. The result of the engagement would be:

Player: stamina $7 + 11/2 = 12.5$; concentration $19 + (0.6)/2 = 19.3$

Freddie: stamina $11/2 = 5.5$; concentration 0 because $(0.6)/2$ is less than 0.5

3.2.FC Foreign Characters

A foreign character is an *Encounter* character not under the player's control.

3.2.FC.1 Attributes of Foreign Characters

See *Encounter* character requirements. These are initialized to be equal.

[In future releases, foreign characters may mutate into new forms.]

3.2.FC.2 Foreign Character Entities

[Note to the student: This section tells that there is only one foreign character.]

3.2.FC.2.1 FREDDIE FOREIGN CHARACTER [essential; not yet implemented] There will be a foreign character named "Freddie," whose image is shown in Figure 4.57. This character will initially have a total of 100 points, that are distributed equally among its qualities.

3.2.FC.3 Functionality of Foreign Characters

3.2.FC.3.1 FOREIGN CHARACTER MOVEMENT [essential; not yet implemented] As long as it is alive, a foreign character should move from area to adjacent area at random intervals averaging two seconds. After being present in an area for a random amount of time averaging one second, all of the character's life points are divided among the qualities relevant to the area, such that the values of each quality are as close to equal as possible.

3.2.PC Player Characters

These are *Encounter* characters under the control of the player.

3.2.PC.1 Attributes of Player Characters

See *Encounter* character attributes. Player character images can be selected from one of the images in Figure 4.58.

3.2.PC.2 Player Character Entities

3.2.PC.2.1 PLAYER'S MAIN CHARACTER The player will have control over a particular game character called the "main" character. The nature of this control is subject to the restrictions specified in the remaining requirements. This character shall initially have a total of 100 points, that are distributed equally among its qualities.

3.2.PC.2.2 ADDITIONAL CHARACTERS UNDER THE CONTROL OF THE PLAYER [optional; not yet implemented] The player will be able to introduce characters other than the main player that he controls. Details are to be decided.

3.2.PC.3 Player Character Functionality

3.2.PC.3.1 CONFIGURABILITY OF THE PLAYER CHARACTER QUALITY VALUES [essential; not yet implemented] Whenever all foreign players are absent from the area

containing the player's main character, the player may set the value of any quality of the main character using the *Player-QualityWindow* shown in Figure 4.59. The value chosen must be less than or equal to the sum of the quality values. The values of the remaining qualities are automatically adjusted so as to maintain their mutual proportions, except for resulting quantities less than 0.5, which are replaced by quality values of zero.

3.2.PC.3.2 CONFIGURABILITY OF THE PLAYER CHARACTER IMAGES [desirable; not yet implemented] The player will have the option to choose the image representing his or her main character from at least two images. These options are shown in Figure 4.58.

3.2.PC.3.3 AGING OF THE PLAYER CHARACTER IMAGES [optional; not yet implemented] The main player character will automatically increase each quality by a percentage for the first half of his or her life, then decrease each quality by the same percentage for the second half. Details are to be decided.

3.2.PQ The Player Quality Window

This is a window from which the player may allocate the values of his or her characters.

3.2.PQ.1 Attributes of the Player Quality Window

The window for setting the qualities of a player character in *Encounter* is shown by

| Elena | Sean | Boris |

*Figure 4.58 Player Character Image Options
(Graphics reproduced with permission from Corel)*

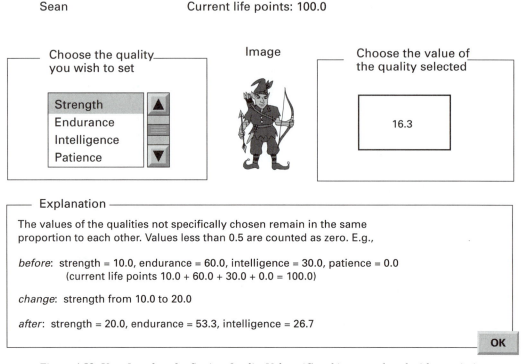

Figure 4.59 User Interface for Setting Quality Values (Graphics reproduced with permission from Corel)

means of a typical example in Figure 4.59. The game character icon appears in the center, and its name appears at the left top of the screen. The character's life points appear in the center. On the left center is a list box displaying four of the qualities at a time. Clicking on one of these qualities allows the player to select a value for it in the text box on the right. An explanation of how the arithmetic is performed is shown in a pale yellow box in the lower part of the screen. Color backgrounds for the name, life points, and value boxes are to be pale turquoise.

3.2.PQ.2 Player Quality Window Entity

3.2.PQ.2.1 WINDOW FOR ALLOCATING QUALITIES [essential; not yet implemented] A window shall be available under the conditions described above to allocate the values of the player character. The window shall have the appearance of

the GUI shown in Section 3.1.1.2 of this specification.

3.2.PQ.3 Player Quality Functionality

3.2.PQ.3.1 INITIATING THE DISPLAY [essential; not yet implemented] The player quality menu shall be able to display itself.

3.2.PQ.4 Player Quality Window Events

3.2.PQ.4.1 DISPLAYING THE VALUE OF A QUALITY [essential; not yet implemented] When the player clicks on a quality in the list box on the left, the value of that quality shall be displayed in the text box on the right.

3.2.PQ.4.2 SETTING THE VALUE OF A QUALITY [essential; not yet implemented] When the user enters a legitimate value for a quality and hits the "enter" button, the value of that quality is set to the amount entered. If the value is invalid, an error window shall appear stating "invalid value: try again."

3.2.PQ.4.3 DISMISSING THE WINDOW [essential; not yet implemented] When the user hits the OK button, a time of four seconds elapses, after which the window disappears. At the end of this time period (i.e., if there are no interruptions) the value allocations are made.

3.2.PQ.4.4 INTERRUPTION [essential; not yet implemented] Upon interruption of the display of the quality value window, the window vanishes.

Note that interruptions will be caused by a foreign character entering the area. Note also in this case that the quality values are not changed and that an engagement takes place.

3.3 Performance Requirements

[Note to the student: Performance requirements include required speeds and/or time to complete. Unless documented in a different section of the SRS, they may also include memory usage (RAM and/or disk), noted either statically or dynamically (i.e., memory required at runtime).]

The application will load and display the initial image in less than a minute.

Engagements should execute in less than one second.

These requirements are tested in STD < reference to test goes here>.

3.4 Design Constraints

[Note to the student: This section specifies restrictions on design. If there is no material in this section, designers are free to create any (good) design that satisfies the requirements. For example, we can add the design constraint "one-story" to the following: "A house with four bedrooms, all of which are less than a thirty-second walk from the family room."]

Encounter shall be designed using UML and object-oriented design. It shall be implemented in Java. The software will run as a Java application on Windows 95. It shall be

designed in a way that makes it relatively easy to change the rules under which the game operates so that others can customize the game.

3.5 Software System Attributes

3.5.1 Reliability *Encounter* shall fail not more than once in every 1000 encounters. Test documentation < reference to test goes here>.

3.5.2 Availability *Encounter* shall be available for play on any PC running Windows 95 only (i.e., no other applications simultaneously). Test documentation < reference to test goes here>.

3.5.3 Security [Future releases will allow access to saved games only with a password.]

3.5.4 Maintainability

3.5.4.1 Changing Characters and Areas [essential] It shall be straightforward to change characters and areas.

3.5.4.2 Globally Altering Styles [desirable] It shall be straightforward to globally alter the style of the areas and connections. (Style changes reflect different levels of game play in the same environment.)

3.5.4.3 Altering Rules of Engagement [optional] Rules of engagement should be relatively easy to change.

3.6 Other Requirements

4. SUPPORTING INFORMATION

4.1 Table of Contents and Index

To be supplied

4.2 Appendixes

To be supplied

[Note to the student: Appendices may include

a. Sample I/O formats, descriptions of cost analysis studies, or results of user surveys

b. Supporting or background information that can help the readers of the SRS

c. A description of the problem to be solved by the software

d. Special packaging instructions for the code and the media to meet security, export, initial loading, or other requirements

State explicitly whether or not each appendix is to be an official part of the SRS.]

CHAPTER 5

SOFTWARE
ARCHITECTURE

" ... in form and moving how express and admirable!"
— Hamlet

Software engineers seek clean, elegant architectures because these facilitate defect-free implementations and are more amenable to extension and reuse. The context of this chapter is shown in the Figure 5.1. The learning goals of this chapter are shown in Figure 5.2.

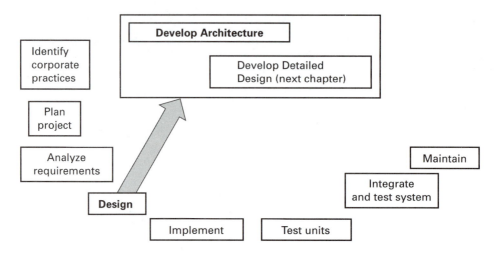

Figure 5.1 Software Engineering Road Map: Chapter 5 Focus

- Understand the term "Software Architecture"
- Utilize frameworks, design patterns, and models
- Develop architecture alternatives
- Relate architectures to detailed designs
- Apply the IEEE SDD standard

Figure 5.2 Chapter Learning Goals

▶ PART I : ESSENTIALS

1. INTRODUCTION TO SYSTEM ENGINEERING AND SOFTWARE ARCHITECTURE

After decades during which software engineers created their own designs from scratch, or reused designs that they had seen by chance, a discipline of software architecture and design is now emerging. To an increasing extent, we can express high-level and low-level designs using terms that are common to all professional software engineers. In the same way that we may admire great works of civil engineering like the "Chunnel" between Britain and France, or mechanical engineering works like the Space Station, we will soon admire great software architectures.

1.1 The Big Picture: System Engineering

Applications invariably require both hardware and software components. An example is an antilock braking system, which has mechanical, electronic, and software parts that work together to maximize braking without letting the vehicle skid. An interactive chat

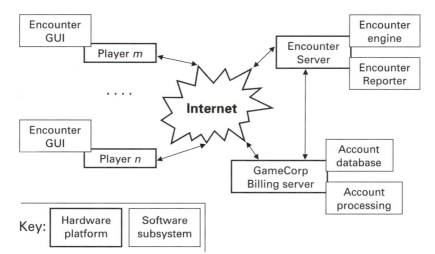

Figure 5.3 A Physical Configuration for Internet-based Encounter

facility on the Web is another example of a system with hardware and software components.

System Engineering is the design and analysis process which decomposes an application into software and hardware. Some aspects of this decomposition may be required by the customer, and some designed by engineers. For example, Figure 5.3 shows a possible configuration for an Internet-based version of the *Encounter* game run by the *GameCorp* gaming service.

The system engineering process starts with total system requirements, then makes hardware/software tradeoffs and determines a decomposition into hardware and software. After this, the software engineering process is applied to the software portions, starting with software requirements analysis, etc. It is beyond the scope of this book to do justice to the full process of system engineering. We will deal only with relatively straightforward hardware/software allocations such as the Internet *Encounter* game discussed above. As shown in Figure 5.3, the game system is decomposed physically into player computers, a game server, and a billing computer. The software components are decomposed into modules, each of which resides on a computer as shown in Figure 5.3.

Embedded software interacts at the microsecond timing level with hardware other than the computer on which it resides. Antilock brakes, for example, contain such software, as illustrated in Figure 5.4. The Internet version of *Encounter* described above would not qualify as embedded software.

Embedded applications pose the greatest challenge for system engineering because their response timing is generally critical. The U.S. Department of Defense is a long-time user of advanced systems engineering because of the extensive software/hardware integration required by defense systems. Defense contractors employ numerous system engineers. These engineers develop system requirements and perform studies to assess appropriate hardware/software configurations.

The IEEE and other standards bodies have published standards for system engineering such as IEEE P1233 "Guide to Developing System Requirements Specifications." This includes broad considerations such as dimensions and weight of mechanical components,

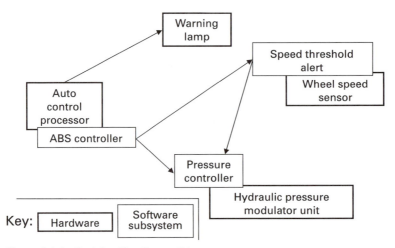

Figure 5.4 Antilock Braking System Diagram

resource limitations, environmental constraints, performance, functionality, compatibility, reliability, maintainability, and producibility.

1.2 The Meaning of "Software Architecture"

If we compare software engineering with the process of bridge building, the requirements analysis process is like deciding where the bridge must begin, where it must end, and what kind of loads the bridge must accommodate. Continuing the analogy, the bridge designer would have to decide whether a suspension bridge, a cantilever bridge, a cable-stayed bridge, or some other type should be chosen to satisfy the requirements. These are bridge *architectures*. Software engineers are faced with a similar decision process. This chapter describes the software engineer's choice of architectures.

"Architecture" is equivalent to "design at the highest level." We will refer to the remainder of the design process as "detailed design."

The clear specification of software architectures, important for all applications, is indispensable in the case of multiperson development jobs. This is because large applications must be designed and implemented in parts ("modularized") and then assembled. Architecture selection provides this modularization. The engineers charged with the task of developing the architecture, the "technical architects," are usually the team's most experienced engineers.

1.3 Goals of Architecture Selection

For a given software development project there may be several appropriate architectures to choose from, and deciding which is best depends upon the goals. It is typically difficult to satisfy all goals because a design that satisfies one may not satisfy another. For this reason, the goals are prioritized. Figure 5.5 lists some key design goals.

The "Extension" goal describes the degree to which we want to accommodate new features. Frequently, if the architecture is to easily allow for the addition of new features, then more design work is required and the resulting design is more complex. This usually involves introducing more abstraction into the process. For example, we might want the architecture for the *Encounter* video game to support not just this particular game (the lowest level of generality),

- Extension
  - facilitate adding features
- Change
  - facilitate changing requirements
- Simplicity
  - make easy to understand
  - make easy to implement
- Efficiency
  - attain high *speed*: execution and/or compilation
  - attain low *size*: run time and/or code base

Figure 5.5 Selected Design Goals

but any role-playing video game. There are many advantages to generality, but it does require an investment of time. One major task in establishing generality is to assess the kinds of extensions that will emerge. We can't design for all possible extensions. Here is where "optional" and "desirable" requirements are useful because they point to where the application is heading.

Designing for change is a different goal from designing for extension, although the design techniques are often similar. Here, we want our design to allow alterations in the requirements such as replacing "the player shall have control over his game character" to "at random times the player shall lose control of his game character."

Simplicity is a design goal under all circumstances. Architectures which are simple and accommodate extension and change are rare and much sought after. Other goals for architecture selection include promoting the efficient use of CPU cycles and/or space.

1.4 Decomposition

With enough practice it is not hard to write small programs: Large applications, however, present very different problems and have been found to be extremely difficult to create in practice. The principal problem of software systems is complexity—not the number of lines of code per se, but their interrelationships. A very good weapon against complexity is to decompose the problem so it has the characteristics of a small program. For this reason, decomposition (or "modularizing") the problem is of critical importance and is one of the most exciting design challenges. The designer should form a mental model of how the application will work at a high level, then develop a decomposition to match this mental model. For example, what four or five modules would neatly encompass the *Encounter* game case study? Or, what five or six modules should we use to decompose a personal finance application? The next problem becomes the decomposition of the resulting components, etc. This process is sometimes called "recursive design."

We start with the goals of software decomposition.

Cohesion within a module is the degree to which communication takes place among the module's elements. *Coupling* describes the degree to which modules communicate with other modules. Effective modularization is accomplished by maximizing cohesion and minimizing coupling. This makes it possible to decompose complex tasks into simpler ones. Figure 5.6 suggests coupling/cohesion goals by showing an idealized architecture for a bridge in which each of its six components has a great deal of cohesion, and the coupling between the components is low.

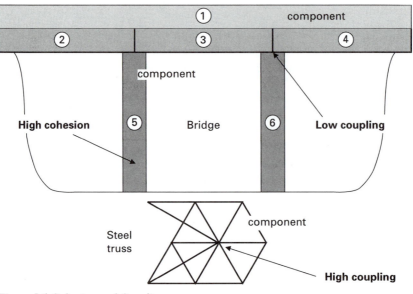

Figure 5.6 Cohesion and Coupling

The parts (e.g., the bricks) of each bridge component (e.g., the columns) are mutually dependent. This is high cohesion. On the other hand, each component depends on just a few other components. For example, each column is coupled to only two cross pieces. This is low coupling. On the other hand, the "steel truss" in the figure shows eight components depending on each other at one place, which is a relatively high degree of coupling.

Low coupling/high cohesion are particularly important for software design because of the necessity to continually modify applications. Compare the life cycle of a typical software application with that of a bridge. The need for modification is many times more likely for the software than for the bridge. Low coupled/high cohesion architectures are far easier to modify since changes tend to have comparatively local effects on them. These types of architectures are not easy to attain, however.

The number of top-level packages in an architecture should be small. A range of "7 ± 2" is a useful guideline, although specific projects can vary greatly from this range for special reasons. The difference between small- and large-scale projects is the amount of nesting of modules or packages. Large-scale projects organize each top-level package into sub-packages, these into sub-sub-packages, etc. The "7 ± 2" guideline applies to each of these decompositions.

As an example of decomposition consider the *Encounter* game. One way to decompose it is to separate all of its parts into the following four modules.

- Environment in which the game takes place (areas, connections, etc.)
- Mechanism controlling the game (encounters, reactions to events, etc.)
- Participants in the game (player and foreign characters, etc.)
- Artifacts involved in the game (swords, books, shields, etc. These will appear in future releases.)

Each of these modules is quite cohesive. For example, the game characters interact extensively with each other. The coupling between these modules, on the other hand, is stronger than we might want. For example, when characters encounter each other, the environment, the controlling mechanism, the participants and, ultimately, the artifacts are all involved.

One Way To. . . Begin Selecting a Basic Architecture

1. Develop a mental model of the application at a high level
   - as if it were a small application

     e.g., personal finance application

     works by receiving money or paying out money, in any order, controlled through a user interface

2. Decompose into the required components
   - look for high cohesion and low coupling

     e.g., personal finance application

     decomposes into Assets, Suppliers, *and* Interface

3. Repeat this process for the components

Note: For an account of *established* architectures, see the rest of this chapter.

Figure 5.7 One Way to Begin Selecting a Basic Architecture

As another example, consider how to decompose the design of a personal finance application. One decomposition possibility is as follows.

- Accounts (checking, savings, etc.)
- Bill paying (electronic, by check, etc.)
- Global reports (total assets, liabilities, etc.)
- Loans (car, education, house, etc.)
- Investments (stocks, bonds, commodities, etc.)

Although this decomposition is appealing from the user point of view, it has weaknesses as a design decomposition. For example, there is little cohesion in the *Accounts* module, since our different accounts may not interact much. There is a great deal of coupling. For example, making a loan payment involves accounts, bill paying, loans, and possibly reports.

An alternative architecture is as follows.

- Interface (user interface, communications interface, reporting, etc.)
- Suppliers (landlord, loans, utilities, etc.)
- Assets (checking accounts, stocks, bonds, etc.)

Perfect decomposition is a worthy goal, but difficult to accomplish. Software is not the only kind of engineering in which clean modularization is difficult to attain. In [Sh1] Shnayerson showed that despite General Motors' best attempts to modularize the design of their first production electric car EV1, form and fit factors (the requirement to fit the car's working parts into a confined space) forced uncomfortably high coupling among components.

This section is summarized in Figure 5.7.

▶ PART II: AT LENGTH

This part of the chapter *can* be covered after covering subsequent chapters. Understanding the ideas in this part, however, is required to produce a quality software product.

2.   MODELS, FRAMEWORKS, AND DESIGN PATTERNS

Decomposing a design into components is an essential step, but much more architecture work is generally required. First, we need to coordinate the use cases, the classes, the state transitions, and the decomposition. We call these perspectives *models,* as discussed in Section 2.1.

In devising the class model we often find it advisable to develop or use a preexisting collection of software which forms the basis for a *family* of similar applications. Such a family, called a *framework,* is described in Section 2.3.

The *detailed design* consists of all of the design work that excludes architecture on one hand and implementation on the other. It includes defining the classes which connect the domain classes with the architecture classes. This is the subject of Chapter 6.

Instead of "reinventing the wheel" we try to reuse designs which have proved effective in prior applications. *Design patterns* are patterns of interrelated classes and methods which have proven their value for many applications. An example is a collection of classes that implements a tree of objects. Design patterns apply at both the architectural level discussed below in Section 2.5 and at the detailed design levels discussed in Chapter 6.

Taking the role-playing game case study and its class model as an example, we will develop a framework for role-playing games (RPG) in general. Based on this framework, an architecture for *Encounter* will be provided in this chapter. To complete the design of *Encounter*, the domain classes developed during requirements analysis must be made to operate with the architecture classes. We do this by adding the detailed design classes (see Chapter 6).

2.1 Using "Models"

It is usually necessary to describe applications from several perspectives. This can be compared to the architecture of a house, which requires multiple perspectives such as a plot plan, a vertical view, a frontal view, a plumbing plan, etc. In the software world, the perspectives are called *models*. There has been much exciting development in this field during the last years of the twentieth century. Figure 5.8 and Figure 5.9 show various models of the target application, many taken from the Unified Software Development Method (see Jacobson et al [Ja1]; also Kruchten [Kr]).

The *use case model* is the collection of use cases. They tell much of what the application is intended to do. The initial use case versions are suitable for use as C-requirements (sometimes called "business use cases"). As the project progresses, they are expressed as sequence diagrams in increasingly specific form. They are realized as specific scenarios, which are used for testing. An example of a use case is the engagement with a foreign character in the *Encounter* case study.

The *class model*: We have seen a good deal of the class model (class diagrams) already. They explain the building blocks with which the application will be built. Class models are often called "object models." Within class models, methods and attributes can be shown.

The *component model* is the collection of data flow diagrams. These describe the way in which the application is to perform its work in terms of moving data. A component model in the *Encounter* case study would include a diagram of quality value data flowing from an engagement object to the player character object and the foreign character object when these encounter each other in an area.

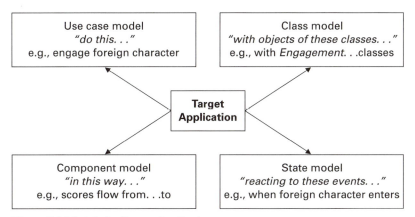

Figure 5.8 Models for Expressing Designs

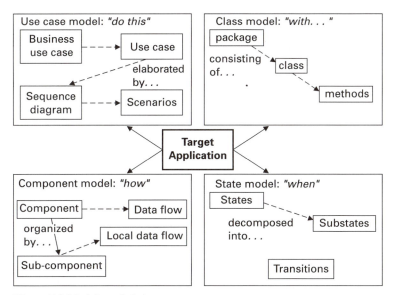

Figure 5.9 Models and their parts

The *state model* is the collection of state/transition diagrams. State models describe *when* the application does its work. In *Encounter* we developed such a model (the state diagram in Chapter 3), showing the game's responses to foreign character arrivals and to user requests to set values, dismiss windows, quit the game, etc.

Within each of these models we provide increasing levels of detail. Depending on the size of the job we may recursively apply one or more level of details within each model. The architecture of an application is often expressed mainly in terms of one of the models, and is supported by one or more of the remaining models. The Unified Software Development Process includes the "implementation" model, which has to do with the way in which code is organized. Every architecture has at least one class model capable of implementing it.

package of classes

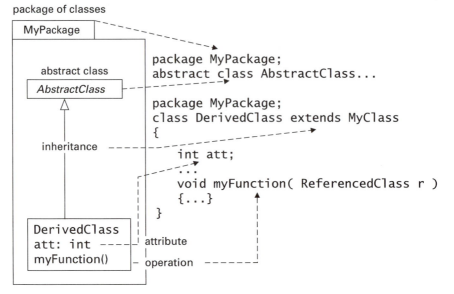

Figure 5.10 Packages, Abstraction, Inheritance, Attributes, and Operations in UML

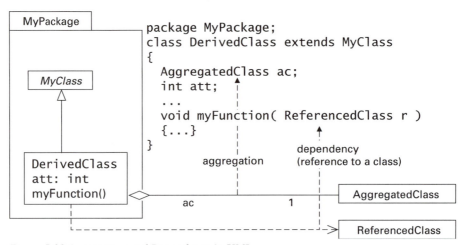

Figure 5.11 Aggregation and Dependency in UML

2.2 The Unified Modeling Language

We will use the Unified Modeling Language (UML) extensively in the class models that follow (see, for example, [Booch-UML] and [Ru1]). We have already been using UML notation for use cases and sequence diagrams. Figure 5.10 and Figure 5.11 illustrate key UML notation for class models as we will interpret them in this book.

At the highest level of a class model, the UML uses the term *package* for the components of an architecture. *Packages* are collections of classes. "Package" also happens to be the name of collections of Java classes, and so the names map well in this case. Java packages translate into file directories, their sub-packages decompose into subdirectories, etc. The UML actually allows "packages" to contain any materials associated with an application, including code, designs, documentation, etc.

Abstract classes, i.e., those that cannot be instantiated into objects, are denoted with italics. *Aggregation*, denoted with a diamond, indicates the inclusion of objects of one class by another, and is usually implemented by means of a class having an attribute whose type is the included class. The numeral at the end of an aggregation line denotes the number of objects aggregated. For example, the "1" at the end of the *DerivedClass/ AggregatedClass* relationship implies that each *DerivedClass* object aggregates exactly one *AggregatedClass* object. Instead of single numerals, a range can be given, such as 3..7; "*" denotes "some number" of objects aggregated. *Dependency*, denoted with a dotted line arrow, commonly means that a method of the dependent class refers to the second class.

2.3 Frameworks

A framework is a collection of classes that are usable by several different applications. Frequently classes of a framework are related. They may also be abstract and intended for use through inheritance.

The Java Application Programming Interface (API), an example of useful framework packages, has shown how eager the development community is for rich frameworks with which to do their work. The core Java API packages are intended to serve huge ranges of applications, whereas our intention in developing an application is usually to serve only applications somewhat like the one we are designing. We relate application packages to framework packages via aggregation and/or inheritance. For example, consider how we use the Java Abstract Windowing Toolkit (*awt*) package. We don't modify the *awt* but instead we create GUI classes for our application that inherit from *awt* classes, or aggregate *awt* objects as attributes.

Some believe that frameworks should be designed only if they will be used by a large number of applications, as is the Java API. There are often significant advantages, however, to developing a partial framework in parallel with an application, even when a large number of applications of the framework is not assured. This partial framework often serves as an invaluable abstract layer from which many of the application's classes inherit.

As an example, let's create a framework which the *Encounter* case study can use. We seek a decomposition for role-playing video games, as well as a decomposition of the *Encounter* application. Decompositions are suggested by looking for possible groupings among the domain classes we obtained from requirements analysis (*Area, Encounter-Character, EncounterGame, Engagement, EngagementDisplay, ForeignCharacter, Player-Character,* and *PlayerQualityWindow*).

Each of these classes must fit into an application package and each application package must use one or more framework packages. For example, following this principle, one framework package called *Characters* could describe the entities participating in role playing games. There could be an application package, *EncounterCharacters,* which uses *Characters* and contains the classes for *EncounterGame*'s characters. This is shown in Figure 5.12. Figure 5.13 shows a decomposition into role-playing game framework packages and *Encounter* application packages.

The *Characters* framework package involves both the characters controlled by the player and those controlled by the application. The *Artifacts* framework package involves items that do not belong with the other packages. The necessity for the *GameArtifacts* package is not yet clear at this stage. It is perhaps too early to tell whether furniture (for

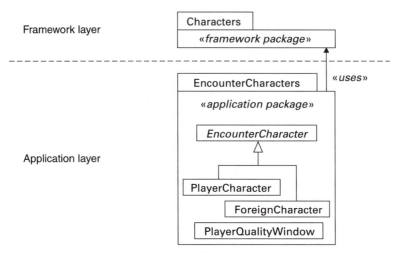

Figure 5.12 Layering for Role-Playing Video Games

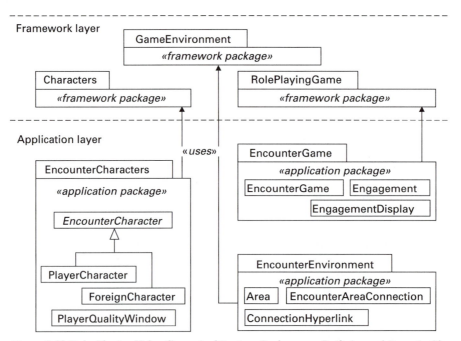

Figure 5.13 Role-Playing Video Game Architecture Packages — Built Around Domain Classes

example) should be considered part of the layout, whether "shields" are to be handled by the *Character* package, etc.

We have tried to attain high cohesion and low coupling in our *Encounter* application packages (Figure 5.12) by grouping logical entities (characters, game, control, and layout separated). If we had grouped classes as they appear on a monitor (characters with areas), the packages would have had unacceptably low cohesion since these are not tightly related classes. Coupling would have been unacceptably high because we would need to be able to access the areas as well as the characters (very different entities) from outside the package.

Figure 5.14 summarizes the way in which we are arriving at the class model. The domain classes are obtained by performing requirements analysis. The framework classes are obtained by developing an architecture for applications like the one under development. Its classes are either part of a preexisting package or are developed as part of the architectural analysis. Finally, the rest of the classes (the "design" classes) are added to complete the design. The complete design for the application consists of all the domain classes, all of the design classes, and some of the framework classes. (Typically, we do not use all framework classes.) This is shown in Figure 5.15. The framework classes used in the design are part of the application's architecture. The domain classes are all part of the detailed design since they are completely specific to the application, are conceived from requirements, and are not architectural. An example from the case study is the class *PlayerCharacter*. It

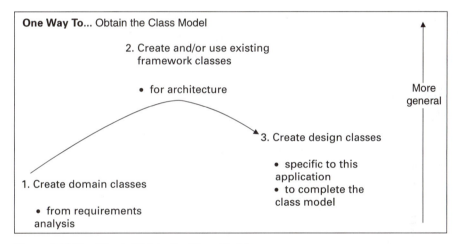

Figure 5.14 One Way to Obtain the Class Model

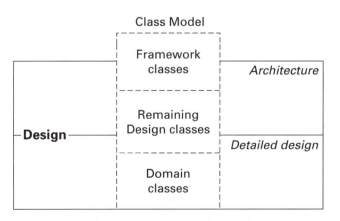

Figure 5.15 Class Model vs. Architectural and Detailed Design   Software Architecture: Perspectives on an Emerging Discipline, by Shaw, Mary and David Garlan. Copyright © 1996 Reprinted by permission of Prentice-Hall, Inc. Upper Saddle River, NJ.

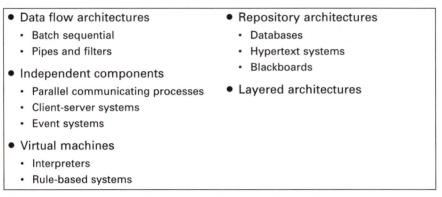

Figure 5.16 Categorization of Software Architectures (Shaw and Garlan)

stands virtually alone, expressing what this game character is meant to do. Some of the design classes are created as part of the architecture process and others as part of the detailed design process.

2.4 A Categorization of Architectures

Shaw and Garlan [Ga1] have classified software architectures in a useful manner. In other words, they have collected together software patterns for architectures. Their classification, somewhat adapted, is shown in Figure 5.16. Section 3 below elaborates upon most of these architectures. There is a very wide variety of problems requiring software solutions, and there is a wide variety of architectures needed to deal with them. Still, one of the architectures identified by Shaw and Garlan may match the problem or, at least, provide ideas for modularization.

2.5 Design Patterns I: Introduction

Design Patterns are combinations of components, typically classes and objects, which have been found by experience to solve certain common design problems. To make an analogy with house architecture, consider the problem of designing a house on ample land that allows for a great deal of privacy. The *Ranch* (one-story) architecture satisfies this requirement. Note that "Ranch" refers to a design idea that allows for many alternative realizations: It is not a single unalterable set of house plans.

Design Patterns were brought to the attention of the wider developer community by Gamma et al. in their now classic book [Ga]. Gamma et al. describe 23 common design patterns, dividing them into *structural*, *creational*, and *behavioral* categories. *Structural* design patterns deal with ways to represent ensembles of objects (e.g., trees and linked lists) gaining elegance in many cases by enabling the treatment of the ensemble as a single entity. *Creational* design patterns deal with ways of creating complex objects such as mazes and trees. *Behavioral* design patterns enable us to capture the behavior of objects, for example, by reporting on a collection of objects in a particular order. Although there are more design patterns than those mentioned in [Ga] we will concentrate only on applying the patterns described there.

Design patterns may be applicable at the architectural level and/or at the detailed design level. Figure 5.17 names selected design patterns that are particularly useful at the architectural level. They are described throughout this chapter.

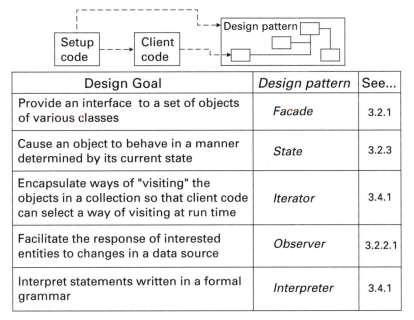

Design Goal	Design pattern	See...
Provide an interface to a set of objects of various classes	Facade	3.2.1
Cause an object to behave in a manner determined by its current state	State	3.2.3
Encapsulate ways of "visiting" the objects in a collection so that client code can select a way of visiting at run time	Iterator	3.4.1
Facilitate the response of interested entities to changes in a data source	Observer	3.2.2.1
Interpret statements written in a formal grammar	Interpreter	3.4.1

Figure 5.17 Summary of Architectural Design Patterns

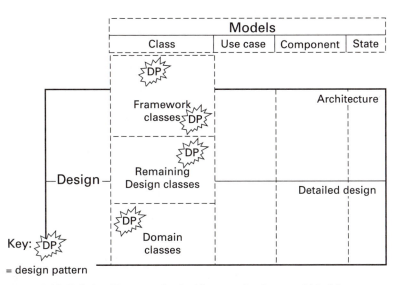

Figure 5.18. Relating Frameworks, Architecture, Designs, and Models

As Figure 5.17 indicates, each design pattern performs on behalf of clients—code which needs the services that the pattern provides. Clients reference an entry point to the design pattern, usually a method of a class within it. Generally speaking, a third type of code, which can be considered ad hoc "setup code," is also involved. It sets up the state of the design pattern. Setup code, which is not intended for reuse, makes it possible for clients to interface cleanly with the design pattern. In particular, clients should have to know as little as possible about the structure and inner workings of the design pattern.

2.6 Components

As of the latter half of the 1990s, there has been increased interest in the notion of "components." These are reusable entities that do not require knowledge of the software using them. COM objects and Javabeans are example component technologies. Components can be objects in the usual object-oriented sense except that they satisfy additional guidelines aimed at making them self-contained. They use other components by aggregation, and generally interact with other components through events.

Figure 5.18 summarizes the relationship between frameworks, architectures, detailed designs, models, and design patterns. The figure shows that design patterns may be applicable at the framework level, within the design classes at the architecture level, and also within detailed design. Typically, we do not try to apply design patterns within the domain classes since the latter are devised individually and closely match sets of requirements. As

TABLE 5.1 Architecture Alternatives (Garlan and Shaw)

Architecture (Garlan and Shaw)			
Category	Subcategory	*Frequently applicable design pattern(s)*	Comments
Data flow	Batch sequential		*Decorator* pattern may apply (see [Ga])
Independent components	Pipes and filters Parallel communicating processes	*Observer (Section 3.2.2.1)*	
	Client-server systems	*Facade (Section 3.2.1)*	
	Event systems	*State (Section 3.23) Observer*	
Virtual machines	Interpreters	*Interpreter (Section 3.3)*	
	Rule-based systems		See [Ha4] for explanation of rules
Repository architectures	Databases	*Observer, Iterator (Section 3.4.1)*	
	Hypertext systems		See *Decorator* in [Ga]
	Blackboards		See [En] for definition of blackboards
Layered architectures			Most design patterns consist of an abstract layer and a nonabstract layer

will be seen, design patterns usually require the introduction of nondomain classes such as abstract classes.

3. SOFTWARE ARCHITECTURE ALTERNATIVES AND THEIR CLASS MODELS

The software architect develops a mental model of how the application is meant to work, with five to seven components (very roughly). The result depends on the application, of course, but may benefit from architectures that others have developed in the past, just as a suspension bridge design benefits from the study of previously built suspension bridges. This section elaborates on the architectures classified by Shaw and Garlan [Ga1], and indicates design patterns which may help to implement them.

We first summarize these in Table 5.1 and then explain most of them in turn.

3.1 Data Flow Architectures

Some applications are best viewed as data flowing among processing units. Data flow diagrams (DFDs) illustrate such views. Each processing unit of the DFD is designed independently of the others. Data emanates from sources, such as the user, and eventually flows back to users, or into sinks such as *account databases*. The elements of the DFD notation were explained in Section 3.3 of Chapter 3 (page 148). A banking application is shown in Figure 5.19.

Data flow from the user to a *Get deposit* process, which sends the account number and the deposit amount to a process designed to check these data for consistency.

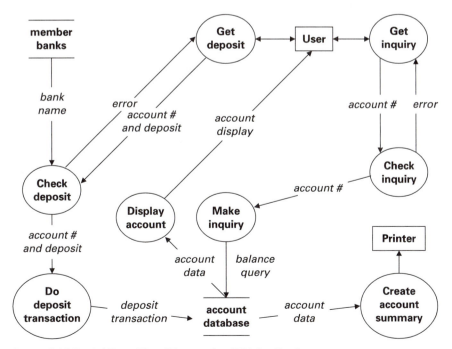

Figure 5.19 Partial Data Flow Diagram for ATM Application

If they are consistent, the data may be sent to a process that creates a transaction, and so on. DFDs can be nested. For example, the "Create inquiry transaction" can itself be decomposed into a more detailed data flow diagram, as explained in Chapter 6. One kind of data flow architecture, shown in Figure 5.20, is referred to as the "pipe and filter" architecture. These are data flow architectures in which the processing elements ("filters") accept *streams* as input (sequences of a uniform data element) at any time, and produce output streams. Each filter must be designed to be independent of the other filters. The architectural feature in Figure 5.20 is implemented by UNIX pipes, for example.

Pipe and filter architectures have the advantage of modularity. An example is shown in Figure 5.21. In this example the application maintains accounts as transactions arrive at random times from communication lines. The architecture includes a step for logging

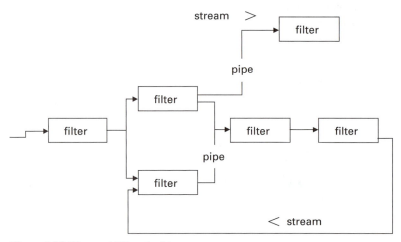

Figure 5.20 Pipe and Filter Architecture

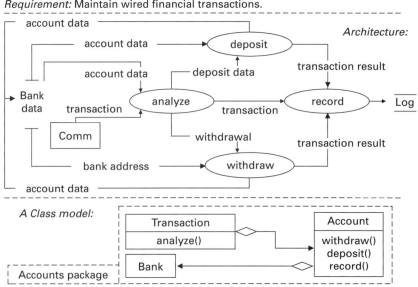

Figure 5.21 Example of Pipe and Filter Data Flow Architecture Choice

transactions in case of system failure. The *withdraw* function would have *withdrawal* input such as `JohnDoeAccountNum12345Amount$3500.00`, or just `JohnDoe12345$3500.00`—i.e., a character stream—and bank address input such as `BankNum9876`. The processing elements, shown in ellipses, wait until all of the required input has arrived before "firing"— performing their operation.

There is generally not a uniform way to map data flow diagrams (DFDs) onto class models; however, functional units of the DFD can sometimes map directly onto methods of classes, as shown in Figure 5.21.

The increasing use of distributed computing is accelerating the application of stream-oriented computing because remote function calling is often implemented by converting the call to a stream of characters. This is done in Java's Remote Method Invocation (RMI), for example. RMI uses serialization, which converts objects to character streams. In addition, I/O is often implemented using streams, and performing I/O in a language such as Java often amounts to a filtering process.

In the special case where the filters are only given batches of data, the result is a *batch sequential* form of data flow. As an example, consider a banking application that computes the amount of money available for mortgage loans (secured by properties) and the amount available for unsecured loans. A data flow diagram (DFD) is suggested by Figure 5.22. This DFD is batch sequential because the functions are executed using virtually all of the input data taken together. For example, we collect the funds available for mortgage loans by using all of the account data. This is in contrast with the transaction example in Figure 5.21, in which there are many—virtually continuous—transactions, each using selected data from their sources.

Figure 5.22 also shows one mapping into a class model in which the functions of the data flow are realized as methods of the *Bank* class. The "batches" of processing are executed by running the relevant methods of this class.

For decades, data flow has been the most common way of expressing architectures, and it is bound to be useful for some time to come. Engineers naturally think of data flowing from one processing "station" to the next and of processing taking place at each station. The disadvantages of data flow diagrams include the fact that they do not map very cleanly to code—whether object-oriented or not.

The data flow model will be used once again when we discuss detailed design in the next chapter.

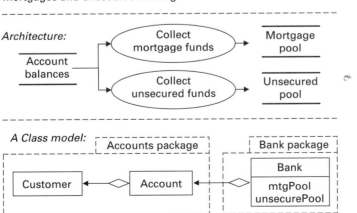

Figure 5.22 Example of Batch Sequential Data Flow *Architecture*

3.2 Independent Components

The "independent components" architecture consists of components operating in parallel (at least in principle) and communicating with each other from time to time. Probably the most obvious instance of this can be found on the World Wide Web where thousands of servers and millions of browsers operate in parallel all day and periodically communicate with each other.

3.2.1 *Client-server* Architectures and the *Facade* Design Pattern   In a client-server relationship, the server component serves the needs of the client upon request. Client-server relationships have the advantage of low coupling between the two participating components. These relationships apply to software engineering in general, when more than one person performs implementation. It is natural to parcel out a package of classes to each developer or group of developers, and developers typically require the services of classes for which others are responsible. In other words, developers' packages are often related as client and server. The problem is that these services are typically in varied states of readiness as the project progresses.

A component acts more effectively as a server when its interface is narrow. "Narrow" means that the interface (essentially a collection of functions) contains no unnecessary parts, is collected in one place, and is clearly defined. The *Facade* design pattern establishes just such an interface to a package of classes. *Facade* regulates communication with the objects in its package by exposing only one object of the package to code using the package, hiding all of the other classes. This exposed object is usually the one and only member of the *Facade* class. The *Facade* structure is illustrated in Figure 5.23.

A call that would otherwise refer to an object of a class within the package is replaced by a call to a method of the *Facade* object. This method can then reference the object in question.

The use of *Facade* for each of the *Encounter* packages is shown in Figure 5.24. Communication with game characters must occur via the single *EncounterCast* object. Reference to parts of *Encounter*'s environment must occur through the *EncounterEnvironment* object.

One difficulty in applying *Facade* is the prohibition against mentioning the member classes of the *Facade* object's package. For example, users of the *EncounterCharacters* package typically need to access individual game characters but are permitted to access only the class *EncounterCast*: In particular, users of the *EncounterCharacters* package can't even *mention* the class "*EncounterCharacter*" because that would contradict the principle of hiding this class! This is a severe restriction. If a (public) framework package exists containing the class *GameCharacter*, however, then users of *EncounterCharacters* may mention *GameCharacter*. This is usually sufficient to deal with the access issue.

In particular, the *EncounterCharacters Facade* class could have public methods such as

```
GameCharacter getMainCharacter();
```

Client code could contain statements such as

```
GameCharacter mainPlayerCharacter =
EncounterCharacters.getMainCharacter();
```

All permissible actions affecting the main player character are controlled by the *EncounterCharacters* Facade object.

One can think of this usage of the *Facade* design pattern with the following analogy. Suppose that you call *CampaLot Corp.* with the intention of buying a tent. To do this, you

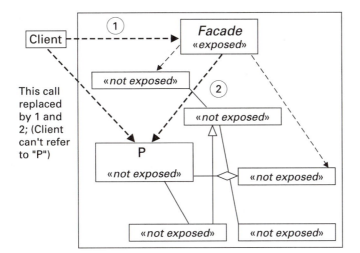

Figure 5.23 Facade Design Pattern Structure

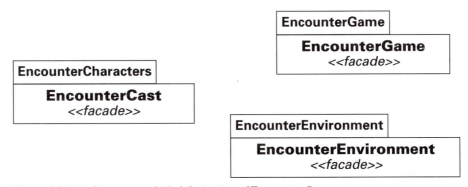

Figure 5.24 Architecture and Modularization of Encounter *Game*

need to know about tents in general (this is like being able to reference a *Tent* framework class), but you rely on *CampaLot*'s interface (the person at the other end of the telephone— the "Facade" object) to provide access to their particular line of tents.

An issue to keep in mind when considering the use of *Facade* is the additional effort required to make methods available to users of the package. For example, suppose that we have a package called *Chemistry* which contains a class called *Molecule*, which in turn contains a useful method called *atomicWeight()*. If we are using a *Facade* class *MoleculeFacade*, then *MoleculeFacade* would have to contain a public method such as *getAtomicWeight()* that passes control to *atomicWeight()*. This requires additional work and coordination within the development process. A price like this is usually worth paying when the reward is increased modularization.

Client-server architectures were a steady feature of the 1980s and 1990s. Many of them replaced mainframe/terminal architectures. Client/server architectures have subsequently become more sophisticated and more varied. Some are now designed as three-tier architectures instead of the original two tiers (client and server). The third tier lies between the client and the server, providing a useful level of indirection. A common allocation is to design the GUI for the client, the database management system, or procedure management for the middle layer, and assorted application programs and/or the database itself for the third layer. The middle layer can be a common data "bus" such as the Common Object Request Broker (CORBA). Alternatively, the middle layer can operate via a binary standard such as COM (Microsoft's Common Object Model). Finally, the World Wide Web can be considered a breed of client/server architecture in which "one server / tens of clients." is replaced by "one server / millions of clients."

3.2.2. The *Parallel Communicating Processors* Architecture

Another type of "independent component" architecture identified by Shaw and Garlan is named *parallel communicating processes*. This architecture is characterized by several processes executing at the same time (Threads, in Java terms). *Encounter* uses this architectural element by having the foreign character Freddie move independently from area to adjacent area while the game progresses. This thread "communicates" whenever Freddie finds himself in the same area as the player character.

A UML notation which expresses parallelism was discussed in Chapter 4. This notation used in Figure 5.25, shows an architecture for a banking application designed to handle multiple transactions occurring simultaneously on automated teller machines (ATMs).

When customer *n* uses an ATM, object *customer n* is created (1 in Figure 5.25). This object creates *session m*, a thread, or parallel process (2), denoted by a half arrow. *Session m* then retrieves an *Account* object such as *customer n checking* (3). The customer then performs a deposit transaction on the checking object (4). In parallel, other *Customer* objects such as *customer n+1* are creating and operating on other threads such as *session k*. The beginnings of an object model which handles this kind of architecture is shown in Figure. 5.24.

When an application demands parallel processing, the *parallel communicating processors* architecture is a common choice. This architecture can be used for schemes that coordinate conceptually independent tasks. In his classic book [Di], Dijkstra showed that conceiving a process such as the combination of parallel parts can often simplify designs. An example of this is a simulation of customers in a bank. Traditionally many such simulations were designed

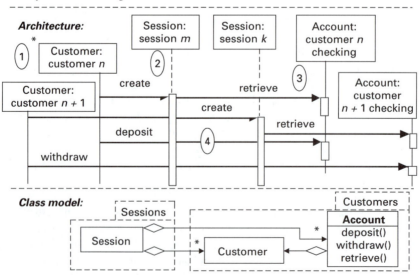

* numbering for explanation in text

Figure 5.25 Example of Parallel Communicating Processes *Architecture*

without parallelism by storing and handling the events involved. Such designs can sometimes be simplified, however, if the movement of each customer is a separate process (e.g., a *Thread* object in Java). Such a parallel communicating process design has the advantage that it matches more closely to the activities which it simulates.

A good reference to parallel communicating processes in the Java context is [Le].

3.2.2.1 The *Observer* Design Pattern An "independent elements" architecture frequently consists of a source of data, together with a number of clients that must be updated whenever the data changes. For example, suppose that the headquarters of the International Hamburger Corporation maintains data on its server about hamburger sales throughout its empire. Distributed clients for this data include Senior Management, Marketing, and Operations. The data change continually, and each of headquarters' clients needs to update its display according to its needs. For example, Senior Management's bar chart is updated after a 5% change has taken place, Marketing is shown a new pie chart when a change of at least 1% takes place, and Operations displays tables which are updated when any change takes place.

The *Observer* design pattern can be used as an architecture for dealing with these requirements. The parties requiring updating are known as observers and are subclasses of a single abstract class which we will call *Observer*. The *Observer* design pattern is shown in Figure 5.26. We will follow a sequence of steps to show how *Observer* operates.

(Step 1) The client references a fixed object, requesting that the observers be notified. For example, the client object could be a process programmed to notice that the data has changed, or it could be a clock-driven task. In the model, this is shown as a *Client* object telling the *Source* object to execute its *notify()* function.

(Step 2) The *notify()* method tells each of the *Observer* objects to execute its *update()* function.

(Step 3) The implementation of *update()* depends on the particular *ConcreteObserver* to which it belongs. The function *update()* compares the *ConcreteObserver* object's state (variable values) with that of the central data source on the server, then decides whether or not to change its variable values accordingly or possibly perform other actions such as creating a new display.

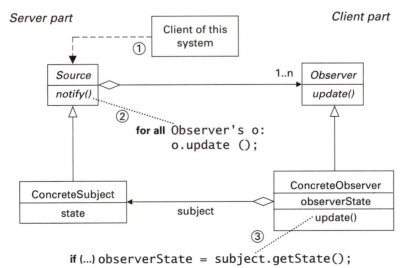

Figure 5.26 Observer *Design Pattern*

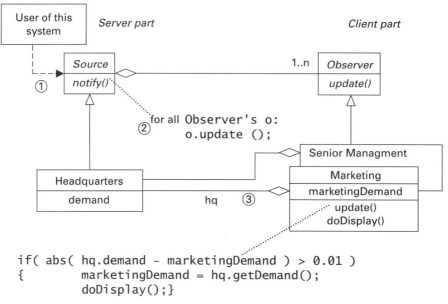

```
if( abs( hq.demand - marketingDemand ) > 0.01 )
{         marketingDemand = hq.getDemand();
          doDisplay();}
```

Figure 5.27 Observer *Applied to "International Hamburger Co."*

Applying *Observer* to our International Hamburger Corporation problem, we obtain the architecture shown in Figure 5.27. *Observer* has the advantage of being a recognized pattern (Java even contains *Observer* and *Observable* classes). Another advantage is that it allows the addition and removal of observers without disrupting the remaining observers. The pattern is disadvantageous if very few of the observers need to react to changes (in which case the numerous notifications waste resources). *Observer* is also disadvantageous when update policies are more naturally prompted by the observers, or where update policies among observers have very little in common.

3.2.3 *Event Systems* Architectures and the *State* Design Pattern

Let's turn to *Event Systems*, the third type of "independent component" architecture classified by Shaw and Garlan. This architecture views applications as a set of components, each of which waits until an event occurs that affects it. Many contemporary applications are Event Systems. A word processor, for example, waits for the user to click on an icon or menu item. It then reacts accordingly, by storing the file, enlarging fonts, etc. Event systems are often fulfilled as state transition systems, which were introduced in Chapter 3.

When a system behaves by essentially transitioning among a set of *states*, the *State* design pattern can be considered for the design. For example, we have described the overall requirement for *Encounter* in terms of the state diagram in Figure 3.17 of chapter 3 on page 151. *Encounter* transitions among the *Setting up, Waiting, Setting qualities, Reporting,* and *Engaging* states, among others. Our design should capture this behavior effectively. It should also be capable of gracefully absorbing new states and action handling as the game becomes more complete, without disrupting the existing design. For these reasons, we will apply the *State* design pattern.

The *State* design pattern solves the problem of how to use an object without having to know its state. In the context of *Encounter* we want to be able to write controlling code which handles mouse actions but which does not reference the possible states that the

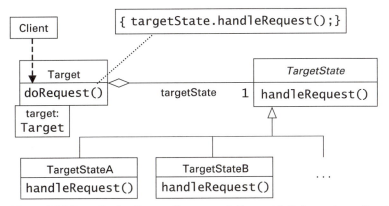

Figure 5.28 State *Design Pattern Structure:* doRequest() *Behaves According to State of* Target *Object*

game can be in, or the specific effects of the mouse actions. This makes it possible to add new game situations without disrupting this controlling code.

In general terms, suppose that we want to use a method *doRequest()* of an object *target* of class *Target*, where *doRequest()* behaves differently according to *target*'s state. This can be solved by introducing a class which we will call *TargetState*, and giving *Target* an attribute (we'll call it *targetState*) of type *TargetState. We make sure that at all times* targetState *properly represents* target's *current state in that it is an object of the appropriate* TargetState *subclass.* This is shown in Figure 5.28.

The method *doRequest()* simply calls *targetState.handleRequest()* in turn, so the call to *doRequest()* is translated by the virtual function property into the particular version of *handleRequest()* appropriate to the state of *target*. All of this is invisible to the client calling *doRequest()*. In other words, the client does not need to know the state of *target*.

Figure 5.29 shows how the *State* design pattern can be used to handle the states and actions of *Encounter*. The framework class *RPGame* ("Role-playing game") has an attribute called *state* of type *GameState*. The type of *state* (i.e., which subclass of *GameState* it belongs to) determines what happens when *handleEvent()* is called on an *RPGame* object. The code for *handleEvent()* in *RPGame* passes control to the *handleEvent()* function of *state*. Each subclass of *GameState* implements *handleEvent()* in its own manner. For example, if *Encounter* is in *Setting qualities* state, and the event is the arrival of a foreign character, then the window permitting the setting of character quality values disappears because this is what the method *handleEvent()* in *Preparing* is programmed to do. An additional consequence of this particular event/state combination is that *Encounter* transitions to *Engaging* state, as required by the state transition diagram. This is transition is implemented by code such as

```
EncounterGame.setState( new Engaging() );
```

The next time an event occurs in the game, the *handleEvent()* function of *Engaging* will execute, reflecting the fact that the game is now in *Engaging* state.

The *State* architecture and design pattern is particularly beneficial when new states are likely to be needed in the future. A shortcoming of the *State* design pattern is that it does not handle the issue of how to set up the successive state once *handleEvent()* has been performed. An alternative to the *State* design pattern is the use of a simple state/action table whose entries indicate what actions should be taken when the application is in a given state

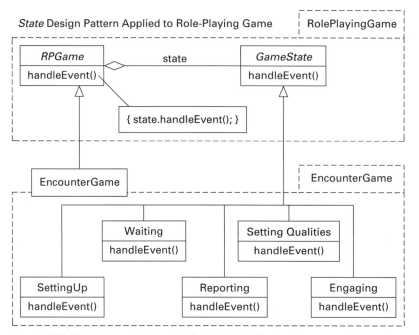

Figure 5.29 State *Design Pattern Applied to Role Playing Games and* Encounter

and a given event occurs. An example is provided in Section 5.2 on page 285, where pros and cons of using *State* are listed.

Whether or not the *State* design pattern is applied, state-oriented architectures have been used with success for many applications (see, especially, the work of Shlaer and Mellor [Sh2]). Real-time applications, such as a mobile telephone routing application, tend to benefit especially from the state architecture.

3.3 Virtual Machines

A virtual machine architecture treats an application as a program written in a special-purpose language. Because an interpreter of this language has to be built, this architecture pays off if several "programs" are to be written in this language, generating several applications.

As an example of a virtual machine architecture, consider an application that processes orders for certain networked computer systems. The processing of orders is expressed in a special-purpose language with the following grammar.

```
Program ::= 'assemble' Program | 'price' Program | System
System ::= Computer | '{' System 'and' System '}'
Computer ::= '{' CPU '&' RAM '}'
CPU ::= '260MHz' | '300MHz' | '400MHz'
RAM ::= '32MB' | '64MB' | '128MB'
```

For example, the order shown in Figure 5.30 consists of a 260MHz system with 64MB of RAM connected to a system which consists of the following two connected computers:

a 400MHz system with 128MB of RAM

a 260MHz system with 32MB of RAM

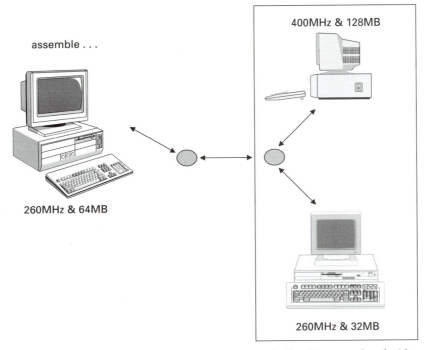

Figure 5.30 Example of a Virtual Machine "Program" (Graphics reproduced with permission from Corel.)

This order is expressed using the grammar as follows.

```
Assemble
{
        {
        { 260MHz & 64MB }
        }
        and
        {
                { 400MHz & 128MB }
                and
                { 260MHz & 32MB }
        }
}
```

This is a legal statement in the grammar, as explained by the following.

Program
assemble Program
assemble System
assemble { System and System }
assemble { Computer and { System and System } }
assemble { { CPU & RAM } and { Computer and Computer } }
assemble { { 260MHz & 64MB } } and { { CPU & RAM } and { CPU & RAM } } }

assemble { { 260MHz & 64MB } and { { 400MHz & 128MB } and { 260MHz & 32MB } } }

The output produced by the virtual machine would be something like the following.

```
Construct system 1 as follows:              – line 1
     Computer with 260Mhz CPU and 64MB RAM  – line 2
Construct system 2 as follows:              – line 3
Construct system 3 as follows:
     Computer with 400MHz CPU and 128MB RAM
Construct system 4 as follows:
     Computer with 260MHz CPU and 32MB RAM
Connect system 3 and system 4
Connect system 1 and system 2
```

We could make the output easier for the installer to use, but the output above simplifies the example.

The advantage of the *Virtual Machine* architecture is the freedom to generate applications simply by expressing them in the special-purpose language. For example, the following would be another "program," giving the price and the assembly instructions:

```
price assemble { . . . }
```

Our language can be made much more capable, of course. Also, its text-based style can be replaced by a graphical one. The same basic virtual machine architecture would apply.

The implementation of a complete virtual machine requires the building of an interpreter, which can be a significant task. In general, the interpretation requires us to execute an operation—let's call it *interpret()*—on a program written in our language. The interpretation of a *primitive* element alone (e.g., a CPU in the example) is generally simple (for the example, this could be simply to print "take CPU out of its box"). The problem is how to execute an *interpret()* function when applied to a more complex "program."

One way to do this is to use the *Interpreter* design pattern. Gamma et al. ([Ga]) point out that it is appropriate to use this design pattern when the grammar is small and speed is not a significant factor. This is the case in the example we have been using. The *Interpreter* design pattern is shown in Figure 5.31.

AbstractExpression objects are either *TerminalExpression* objects on which the interpretation function is simple, or *NonTerminalExpression* objects. The latter aggregate one or

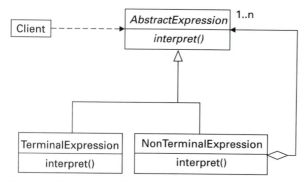

Figure 5.31 Interpreter *Design Pattern*

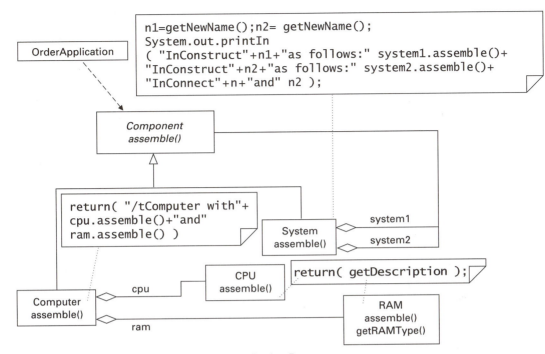

Figure 5.32 Application of Interpreter *Design Pattern*

more *AbstractExpression* objects. The *interpret( )* function on a *NonTerminalExpression* object operates by commanding each of its aggregated *AbstractExpression* objects to execute its version of *interpret( )*.

As an example, we will describe the architecture of an interpreter for the grammar of the example we have been using, omitting price for the sake of simplicity. Applying the *Interpreter* design pattern, we obtain the class diagram shown in Figure 5.32. We are confining ourselves to the assembly of just two components, so the class *System* aggregates two *Component* objects. This can be easily extended to more than two.

The customer assembly order in the program fragment given previously would be translated (using readily available tools) into

```
assemble( order )
```

with order being the following System object.

```
System order = new System (
// System1 set to first constructor parameter:
new Computer( 260, 64 ),
// System2 set to second constructor parameter:
new System( new Computer ( 400, 128 ), new Computer ( 260, 32 ) )
);
```

The command assemble(order) in *Component* reverts to the *assemble()* method of a *System* object. This produces line 1 of the output, and executes *assemble()* on each of its two attributes, as shown by the code fragment in Figure 5.32. On the first attribute, a *Computer* object, *assemble()* produces line 2 of the output. Line 3 is then produced. Executing *assemble()* on the second attribute causes *assemble()* to execute on a *System* object, which first delegates *assemble()* to two *Computer* objects, etc.

Virtual machine architectures are advantageous if the application consists of the processing of complex entities, and if these entities, such as the orders in the example, are readily describable by a grammar. An additional example is an application which provides simple user-level programming of a special purpose language. A nonprogrammer user, for example, is capable of writing a script such as

Balance checking / add excess to account + subtract deficit from saving;

Save report / c:Reports + standard headings + except replace "Ed" by "Al"

PrintReport / standard headings

e-mail report to Jayne@xyz.net.

A virtual machine architecture parses and interprets such scripts.

3.4 Repository Architectures

An architecture built primarily around data is called a *Repository* architecture. The most common of these are systems designed to perform transactions against a database. For example, an electric company maintains a database of customers that includes details about them, such as power usage each month, balance, payment history, repairs, etc. Typical operations against this database are adding a new customer, crediting a payment, requesting a payment history, requesting a list of all customers more than three months in arrears, etc. A typical design for this kind of repository architecture is shown in Figure 5.33.

Other examples of applications with repository architectures include interactive development environments (IDEs). IDEs apply various processes such as editing and compiling to a database of source and object files.

There is an extensive literature on database architectures, and this book does not attempt to cover this ground. Many applications, such as IDEs, while not pure database applications, do involve databases. Our *Encounter* example in its simplest form does not include a database. If, however, it were to grow into a game with tens of individual characters then we might require a database rather than a flat file for storing the characters. This would certainly be true if we wanted to allow the user to call up statistics such as "list the characters with strength under 10," etc. Structured Query Language (SQL) is a common way to express queries (see, for example, [Ka]).

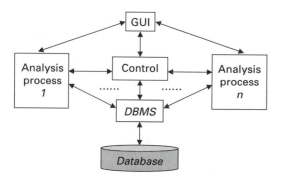

Figure 5.33 A Typical Repository *Architecture*

Blackboard architectures, developed for artificial intelligence applications, are repositories which behave in accordance with posting rules. The reader is referred to [Ja2] for a detailed treatment of blackboard architectures.

The final type of repository architectures we will mention is the *hypertext* architecture. The most common use of hypertext is on the Web. An application that manages the documentation of a software engineering application (see Figure 1.35 in Chapter 1, on page 50) is another example.

The word "repository" is often used in industry to denote an application that provides a unified view of a collection of databases. Repositories do not change the structure of these databases, but they allow uniform access to them. This is a special case of repository architectures as defined by Garlan and Shaw [Ga1].

Repository architectures occupy a large fraction of applications, since so many architectures make databases their core. When the processing is negligible compared to the formatting of data from the database, repository architectures are appropriate. On the other hand, the presence of a large database can sometimes mask the fact that a large amount of processing may drive the architecture. Ad hoc programming (e.g., "stored procedures") can easily mushroom into messy applications which should have been conceived differently from the repository model.

3.4.1 "Visiting" the Members of a Repository with the Iterator Design Pattern

Repository architectures are often appropriate for applications requiring aggregates (collections) of objects. Aggregates are maintained so that their parts can be "visited." If the aggregated objects must be visited in a *variety* of ways, the *Iterator* design pattern can be applied. An example is a personnel management system designed to list employees in various ways. Let's say that the employee objects are stored in a tree structure reflecting an organizational chart. Client software of the set of employees can be made to visit this structure in a manner indicated by an *Iterator* parameter, performing an operation on each individual object, such as printing the name or transferring the employee's image to a file. One way of visiting could be alphabetical; another could visit by seniority; a third could visit all clerks, etc.

Suppose that *agg* is an aggregate of objects of class *C*. Iterator objects visiting *agg* must have the four functions shown in Figure 5.34. Once iterators define these four functions we can write code which uses them, thereby performing operations on the aggregate at run time in the order determined by the iterators. This is illustrated in Figure 5.35. We would not use *Iterator* if the aggregate is to be traversed in just one way.

- Iterator "points" to first element:
  ```
  void setToFirst();
  ```
- true if iterator "points" to the last element:
  ```
  boolean isDone();
  ```
- Causes the iterator to point to its next element:
  ```
  void increment();
  ```
- Return the element pointed to by the iterator:
  ```
  C getcurrentElement();
  ```

Figure 5.34 Functions Required by Iterator

```
/*
To perform desiredOperation() on elements of the
aggregate according to the iteration (order) i:
*/
for(i.setToFirst(); i.isDone(); i.increment())
    desiredOperation(i.getcurrentElement());
```

Figure 5.35 Using Iterator *Functions*

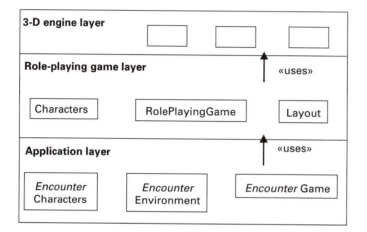

Figure 5.36 Layered Architectures

3.5 Layered Architectures

An architectural *layer* is a coherent collection of software artifacts, typically a package of classes. In its common form, a layer uses at most one other layer, and is used by at most one other layer. Building applications layer by layer can greatly simplify the process. Some layers, such as frameworks, can serve several applications.

We have already seen the layered approach applied to the *Encounter* application, where classes in the *Encounter* packages inherit from classes in the framework packages. This is shown in Figure 5.36. The figure shows how we might organize the use of a 3-D graphics engine as a layer accessible from the Role-playing game layer.

Figure 5.37 shows an example of a layered architecture for an Ajax bank printing application. There are four layers in this architecture, and Figure 5.38 shows dependency in the reverse direction compared to Figure 5.37. The application layer, *Ajax Bank Printing*, has to do with printing and formatting. It is built upon (i.e., uses) the *Accounts* and the *Ajax Bank Common Class* layers. The latter are built upon a vendor-supplied layer, not shown, which contains general utilities such as sorting and searching. Typically, a layer is realized as a package of classes. For example, the Ajax common library comprises classes used throughout Ajax applications, and addresses such issues as the bank's logo, and its regulations. The "using" relationship can be inheritance, aggregation, or object reference. In the example, only aggregation is applied between layers.

One common layered form is the client-server architecture. In this form, the client layer relies on the server layer to provide the services it requires. The client is typically

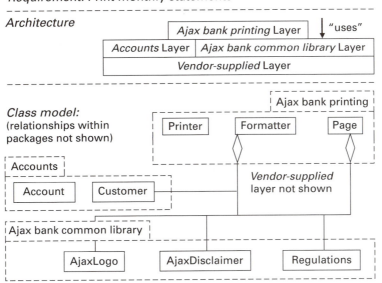

Requirement: Print monthly statements

Figure 5.37 Layered Architecture Example Using Aggregation

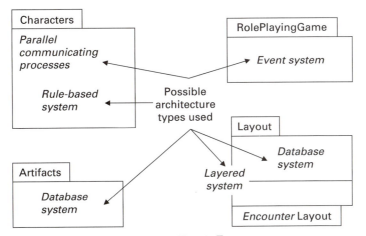

Figure 5.38 Possible Architecture Uses in Encounter

resident on the user's computer, and the server on a larger, more centralized computer. The server often references a database.

Classical client-server architectures suffer from a high degree of dependence in the sense that the clients and/or servers are hard-coded with knowledge about each other. This problem can be solved using the three-tier architecture. In this architecture, a middle layer is introduced which serves to insulate the client and server from each other. The middle layer can be used to increase the architecture's flexibility in a variety of ways. For example, if several servers can service a client request, the middle layer can be designed to find an appropriate server dynamically. The middle layer is often implemented by a type of

---

One Way To. . . Select an Architecture 1

1. Decompose into self-contained modules.
2. Compare with a standard architecture (e.g., Garlan and Shaw's classification). Improve decomposition.
   - Data flowing in batches between processing stations?
     - *batch sequential dataflow*
   - Processing stations waiting for data, then executing?
     - *pipe and filter dataflow*
   - Processes executing in parallel?
     - *parallel communicating processors*
   - A process supplying the needs of user processes?
     - *client-server*
   - A process reacting only to events occurring upon it?
     - *event systems*
   - Each execution the interpretation of a script?
     - *interpreters*
   - An application centered on a data store?
     - *repository*
   - Arranged in layers?
     - *layered*

Try to develop at least two alternative architectures.

Figure 5.39 One Way to Select an Architecture, 1 of 2

One Way To. . . Select an Architecture 2

3. Select among the alternatives identified.
4. Add classes to those from requirements analysis, to accommodate the architecture selected.
   - e.g., *data flow:* . . . to control flow among the elements
   - e.g., *event systems:* . . . to control transmission among states
5. Apply an existing framework and/or design pattern.
   - if a helpful one can be identified
6. Partition the collection of classes into packages.
   - ideally, 4–8 (nest packages for larger applications)
   - each package should make sense in the language of the application (e.g., "videos" OK; "big classes" not OK)
7. Verify high cohesion within parts; low coupling among parts— otherwise, adjust choice.
8. Consider introducing a *Facade* class/object to control the interface to each package.

Figure 5.40 One Way to Select an Architecture, 2 of 2

software known as *middleware*. CORBA, developed by the Object Management Group consortium, is a common middleware standard.

Layered architectures have extensive reuse benefits. The Java class library is effectively a very successful system of layers (e.g., the *applet* package (layer) relies on the *awt* package, which relies on the *lang* package, etc.).

3.6 Using Multiple Architectures Within an Application

Applications typically use several architectures. Figure 5.38 shows how the framework for role-playing video games could use several of the architecture types listed by Garlan and Shaw. It could make sense, for example, to organize the *Artifacts* package as a database. The game characters could be viewed as parallel communicating processes. We will design the overall control of the game as an event-driven system.

3.7 Summary and Procedures for Selecting Architectures

Figure 5.39 and Figure 5.40 summarize a way in which an architecture can be developed.

4. ARCHITECTURE NOTATION, STANDARDS, AND TOOLS

4.1 Notation

The Unified Modeling Language (UML) is a widely accepted graphical notation for describing object-oriented designs. Some aspects of the UML are briefly summarized inside the covers of this book. Other aspects are described and used throughout the book.

We described state/transition notations in Section 3.4 of Chapter 3 (page 149), and data flow diagrams in Section 3.1 of this chapter (page 263). These are applicable independently of object-orientation. The same is true for entity-relationship diagrams, which describe the relationships between the data in data stores.

4.2 Tools

Various computer-aided software engineering (CASE) tools are used to facilitate the software engineering process. Some tools represent classes and their relationships, such as *Rational Rose* by Rational Corporation, and *Together* by Object International. These tools facilitate the drafting of object models, linking them with the corresponding source code and sequence diagrams.

In selecting a modeling tool, a list of the requirements for the tool is drawn up using procedures similar to the requirements analysis process for software application development. Here is an example of some requirements for modeling tools.

- [essential] Facilitate drawing object models and sequence diagrams
  - Create classes quickly
  - Edit classes easily
  - Zoom into parts of the model
- [desirable] Possible to jump directly from the object model to the source code
- [essential] Should cost no more than X per user
- [optional] Reverse engineering available (i.e., create object models from source code)

4.2.1 Architecture-level Tools vs. Tools for Detailed Design and Implementation   Tool packages frequently try to span architecture, detailed design, and implementation. Various vendors are developing the capability to hyperlink from

source code to documentation and vice versa. Implementation-oriented tools such as *Javadoc* can sometimes be useful to supplement the design process. Client-server tools such as Powerbuilder can be applied to specifying architectures, even though they also specify implementations. *Javadoc* is useful for navigating packages because it provides an alphabetical listing of classes and the parent hierarchy of each class.

Interactive development environments (IDEs) are delivered with compilers and are widely used as partial modeling tools. OO IDEs generally show inheritance in graphical form, and developers are frequently attracted to these tools because of their closeness to the compilation and debugging process. As of October 1999, IDEs are typically not rich enough to facilitate true architecture and design work.

Component assembly tools create applications by dragging and dropping icons which represent processing elements. Java Bean environments are typical of these. Within such environments, beans (Java objects whose classes conform to the Java Beans standard) can be obtained from libraries, customized, and related to each other by means of events. The *Java Beans* standard was created with the express purpose of facilitating such simple assemblies by means of graphical tools.

A disadvantage of using modeling tools is the project's dependence on a third party vendor. In addition to the complications of the application and the project itself, engineers must be concerned with the viability of the tool's vendor. Suppose the vendor goes out of business or tool upgrades become too expensive: How will the project be affected?

Despite these issues, the use of design and development tools has increased steadily. The right tools leverage productivity, and economic factors are bound to continue favoring their usage in the long run.

4.3 IEEE/ANSI Standards for Expressing Designs

The IEEE Software Design Document (SDD) standard 1016-1987 (reaffirmed 1993) provides guidelines for the documentation of design. The table of contents is shown in Figure 5.41. The

Architecture*

*1. Introduction
  1.1. Purpose
  1.2. Scope
  1.3. Definitions, acronyms,
     and abbreviations
*2. References
*3. Decomposition description
  3.1. Module decomposition
    3.1.1 Module 1 description
    3.1.2 Module 2 description
  3.2. Concurrent process
    decomposition
    3.2.1 Process 1 description
    3.2.2 Process 2 description
  3.3 Data decomposition
    3.3.1 Data entry 1 description
    3.3.2 Data entry 2 description

*4. Dependency description
  4.1. Intermodule dependencies
  4.2. Interprocess dependencies
  4.3. Data dependencies
*5. Interface description
  5.1. Module interface
    5.1.1 Module 1 description
    5.1.2 Module 2 description
  5.2. Process interface
    5.2.1 Process 1 description
    5.2.2 Process 2 description
6. Detailed design
  6.1. Module detailed design
    6.1.1 Module 1 detail
    6.2.2 Module 2 detail
  6.2. Data detailed design
    6.2.1 Data entity 1 detail
    6.2.2 Data entity 2 detail

Figure 5.41 IEEE 1016-1987 Software Design Document Table of Contents (Reaffirmed 1993) Copyright © 1987 IEEE

IEEE guidelines accompanying the standard (1016.1-1993) explain how the SDD could be written for various architectural styles, most of which are described above. The case study uses the IEEE standard with a few modifications to account for an emphasis on the object-oriented perspective. As shown in the figure, Sections 1 through 5 can be considered software architecture, and Section 6 can be considered the detailed design, to be covered in the next chapter.

5. ARCHITECTURE SELECTION QA

Quality assurance personnel should participate in reviews of the architecture. In addition, QA develops test plans for each component of the architecture as soon as it is defined.

5.1 Quality in Architecture Selection

5.1.1 Metrics for Architecture Selection   Most applications can be implemented using one of several possible architectures, but some choices may be far superior to others. Important decisions like architecture selection are not made without first developing and comparing alternatives. Proposed architectures are thoroughly examined for defects because finding a defect at an early development stage has a huge payoff compared with allowing one to persist through the process and then trying to repair it.

In this section we will provide metrics for architecture selection; in the next section we will give examples of selection among architectural candidates.

As described in Table 5.2, one simple way to compare architectures is to weight the attributes required and then assign a fuzzy qualifier to each candidate. Table 5.2 can be used to compare alternatives in many areas, provided that criteria can be selected and weighted. The following metrics from [IEEE 982] apply to software designs in general.

13. *Number of entries and exits per module (package).* This can be counted by the number of public methods accessible from outside the module. The number of exit points can be counted by the number of public functions that return

TABLE 5.2 Fuzzy Method for Comparing Architectures

	Architecture 1	Architecture 2	Architecture 3
Quality (Quality weight:1-10)	9 =High; 5 = Medium; 2 = Low		
Extension(*e*)	*ea1*	*ea2*	*ea3*
Change(*c*)	*ca1*	*ca2*	*ca3*
Simplicity(*s*)	*sa1*	*sa2*	*sa3*
Efficiency: speed(*esp*)	*espa1*	*espa2*	*espa3*
Efficiency: storage(*est*)	*esta1*	*esta2*	*esta3*
Total	$e*ea1 + c*ca1+$ $s*sa1 +$ $esp*espa1 +$ $est*esta1$	$e*ea2 + c*ca2 +$ $s*sa2 +$ $esp*espa2 +$ $est*esta2$	$e*ea3 + c*ca3 +$ $s*sa3 +$ $esp*espa3 +$ $est*esta3$

values to the caller or make changes in the environment external to themselves. The goal is to keep this measure as low as possible to favor narrow interfaces.

15. *Graph-theoretic complexity for architecture.* The simpler ("static") version of this metric is

(Number of modules in the architecture) −

(Number of modules having at least one function call between them) + 1

We apply metric 15 to the architecture of a bank simulation shown in Figure 5.42. The architecture divides the simulation into the following packages.

SimConfiguration—which describes the way in which the stations are laid out within the bank

SimItems—which describes the entities that move about within the bank (primarily customers)

SimEvents—which handles the present and future simulated events that take place in the bank (e.g., a customer arriving at a teller window)

Simulation—the mechanism that drives the simulation (primarily by selecting the next event to execute, executing it, then orchestrating the consequences, including the generation of resulting events, and queuing them in the *ScheduledEvents* object)

Random—the package that handles the generation of random numbers according to various distributions (for example, producing the duration of service for the next transaction)

This architecture is designed using the *Facade* design pattern, and we will suppose that the only references between packages are those shown. There are five nodes (packages), and there are five pairs of modules between which there are function calls (either way). Thus, the static architecture complexity is 5 − 5 + 1 = 1. This number also measures the number of cycles within the architecture (which can be seen directly to be 1–*SimDriver/Events/Configuration*). This suggests an uncomplicated architecture, which is generally good.

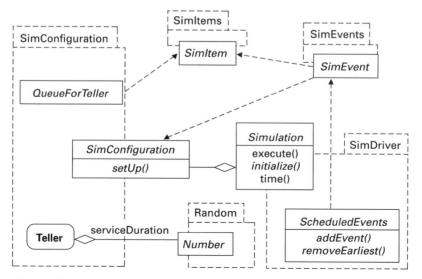

Figure 5.42 Architecture for a Simulation

25. *Data or information flow complexity.* This measures the information flow of large-scale structures, the procedure and module flow complexity, and the complexity of the interconnections between modules. The reader is referred to metric 4.25 of [IEEE 982] for the details.

Metrics like these provide quantification, but how do we use the resulting numbers? One answer lies in historical data. For example, we can easily tell that the *EncounterGame* package has four public functions at this point (see the case study at the end of the chapter). Perhaps we can forecast that this number will grow to between 10 and 15. These numbers are compared with the corresponding average numbers for past projects. If the average number is 10 and we have been satisfied with the modularization of past projects then this value causes no alarm. If the average number for past projects was 8 and we are headed towards 15, then a closer look at the architecture is in order, etc.

5.2 Choosing an Architecture Among Alternatives

We resist the urge to plunge immediately into one architecture by comparing alternatives. As an example, let's consider the architecture of the *Encounter* case study.

Alternative 1 for the *Encounter* case study: *state design pattern.* The *State* design pattern is a possible architecture for *Encounter* (discussed in Section 3.2.3 on page 270), and we will trade it off against other candidates. We will call the alternative discussed in Section 3.2.3 "alternative 1."

Alternative 2 for the *Encounter* case study: *ad hoc GUI-driven architecture.* A second architecture might dispense with the idea of state altogether and build separate event-handling code into each GUI object that is sensitive to mouse or keyboard actions. Such an architecture is shown in Figure 5.43, where selected methods are included to clarify it. In this architecture the exit hyperlinks are GUI representations of *AreaConnector* objects and each connector has event-handling code. For example, clicking on the *dungeon* exit

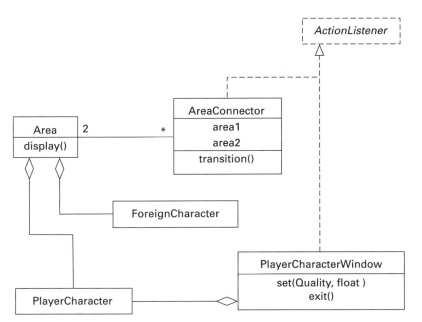

Figure 5.43 Ad hoc GUI-driven Architecture for Encounter

TABLE 5.3 Table-Driven State Transition Event Handling

Current state		Event			
	Click on exit	**Request quality change**	**Dismiss quality window**	**Foreign character enters**	**Foreign character leaves**
Waiting	Display player character in adjacent area	Show quality window		Show Both characters, and transition to *Engaging* state	
Engaging					Compute results of engagement and transition to *Waiting* state
Setting qualities			Remove quality widow and transition to *Waiting* state	Remove quality widow and transition to *Engaging* state	Transition to *Waiting* state

should cause the screen to display the dungeon area. The dungeon hyperlink's class must be associated with an appropriate event handler (e.g., a Java *Listener* object). The resulting design is more GUI-driven, more ad hoc, and more language-specific. There is little separation, however, between the code using this design and the state-specific parts. On the other hand, the class model contains fewer classes.

Alternative 3 for the *Encounter* case study: *state transition table*. A third architectural alternative is to retain the idea of states, but express the state transitions by means of a table. Table-driven state transitions are emphasized by Shlaer and Mellor [Sh2], for example. Table 5.3 is an example of such a table. This architecture uses the *State* concept, but it does not use the *State* design pattern.

We could now evaluate the values of the metrics mentioned above for this architecture. Here is a list of pros and cons contrasting the *State* design pattern with the table-driven approach. A fuller comparison of the three architectures follows, in Table 5.4.

Pros of using the *State* design pattern:

- Can easily add or modify states to accommodate change in game design
- Clarifies what actions can be done in various circumstances
- Classifies all mouse events that can affect *Encounter*

Cons of using the *State* design pattern:

- Class model is more involved and initially more difficult to understand.
- Duplicate data: The state of *Encounter* could be deduced from variables other than the *state* object, incurring the possibility of programmer error if these variables and the state object become inconsistent.

TABLE 5.4 Fuzzy Method for Comparing Architectures

		Architecture alternative		
		1. *State* design pattern	2. Ad hoc GUI-driven	3. State-transition table
Quality	Quality weight: 1–10	High = 9; Medium = 5; Low = 2		
Extension	9	High	Low	Medium
Change	7	High	Low	Medium
Simplicity	5	Low	High	Medium
Efficiency: speed	5	Medium	High	Medium
Efficiency: storage	2	Low	Low	Medium
Total: (higher = better)		183	126	140

Pros of using a table for describing state:

• The table is easy to understand and the contents are easy to change.
• This architecture can be implemented in a non–Object-Oriented language.
• Documentation on this approach is available using the Shlaer-Mellor method [Sh2].

Cons of using a table for describing state:

• Requires a data structure that is virtually global (the table)
• Augmenting the table with new states and actions may disrupt existing code and design.

Table 5.4 shows a comparison of the three architectures using the technique described in Table 5.2. Given the weighting chosen, which favors extensibility and change, the architecture based on the *State* design pattern comes out ahead. Regardless of the metrics used, wise teams try to apply common sense to look over each architecture in an independent manner.

5.3 Checking Architectures with Use Cases

Use cases are developed from customer requirements. Therefore, use cases cannot take into account the application's architecture since it will not yet have been determined. Once the architecture has been selected, however, it is useful to revisit the use cases to check that the architecture supports them adequately. For example, the *Engage Foreign Character* use case shown in Figure 3.12 of Chapter 3 (page 146) must execute upon the architecture we have developed in this chapter (as described in Figure 5.13). Since we retain the domain classes throughout the process, the classes originally referred to in the use case should be present among the classes in use. Typically, the sequence diagrams for the use cases now involve additional architectural classes.

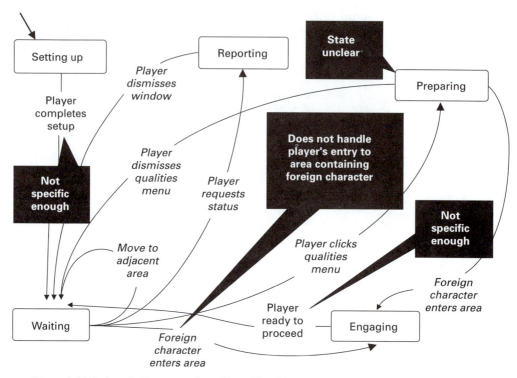

Figure 5.44 Defects in Encounter State-Transition Diagram

5.4 Inspection of Architecture Selection

Architectures are inspected against requirements. Recall that the payoff for defect detection is highest at the early project stages such as architecture selection. The metrics mentioned above provide one basis for the inspection.

Inspection of the architectural framework packages for *Encounter* could lead to the conclusion that there are no requirements yet for game artifacts and that the presence of the *Artifact* package is a defect.

We will take the *Encounter* state-transition diagram shown in Figure 5.44 as an additional example. A perusal of this state diagram could yield the defects shown in the figure. These defects can be removed by clarifying the names and/or descriptions of the events referenced.

5.5 Effects on the SPMP of Architecture Selection

Now that an architecture has been selected, the schedule can be made more specific and more detailed. In particular, the order in which parts are built can be determined. For example, in the case study it makes sense to first develop the *Characters* framework package, followed by the specific *EncounterCharacters* application package. Since these packages will not be completed in the first iteration of the spiral, we name the corresponding tasks "Characters I" and "EncounterCharacters I." Arrows indicate dependence of packages on

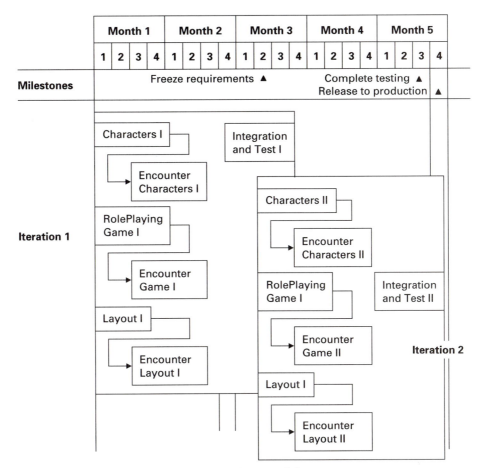

Figure 5.45 Updated Schedule Following Architecture Selection

others. For example, "EncounterCharacters I" cannot be completed without the completion of "Characters I," as shown in Figure 5.45. The schedule shows that "Integration and Test I" cannot begin until all of the other tasks in Iteration I have been completed.

6. SUMMARY

The term "software architecture" refers to the overall, high-level design of an application. Garlan and Shaw [Ga1] have classified software architectures in the categories shown in Figure 5.46. A *framework* is a collection of classes that applies to a family of applications. *Design patterns* are reusable combinations of classes that solve frequent design problems. Some apply to the development of architectures. The IEEE standard applicable to design is called the SDD ("software design document"). The choice of an architecture, a critical step, is made by selecting from among alternatives as summarized in Figure 5.47. The literature contains many definitions of "software architecture." Some of these are synopsized by the Software Engineering Institute in [Ar].

- "Software Architecture"=overall design
- Some architecture alternatives:
  - Dataflow architectures
    - Batch sequential
    - Pipes and filters
  - Independent components
    - Parallel communicating processes
    - Client-server systems
- Event systems
- Virtual machines
  - Interpreters
  - Rule-based systems
- Repository architectures
  - Databases
  - Hypertext systems
  - Blackboards
- Layered architectures

Figure 5.46 Summary of This Chapter, 1 of 2

- *"Frameworks"* = generic setting
- *"Design patterns"* = reusable combinations of classes solving frequent design problems
- *IEEE SDD* standard useful outline
- *Create and compare* architecture alternatives

Figure 5.47 Summary of This Chapter, 2 of 2

STUDENT PROJECT GUIDE:

ARCHITECTURE OF *ENCOUNTER* CASE STUDY

This section explains how the principles and methods for selecting and representing the architecture, explained earlier in this chapter, are translated into practice. The case study is used as the example. The student is also referred to the "One way to ..." figures in this chapter, which act as a guide to the process.

SPG1. PREPARING

In accordance with the SPMP, Karen Peters was the design leader, with Ed Braun backing her up and inspecting all of the design work. Karen aimed to develop two thoroughly prepared alternative architectures for the *Encounter* project and bring them to the team's preliminary design review. She was determined to avoid unpleasant haggling over architectures that were devised by different engineers. She felt that ego rather than technical issues predominated

in such cases. She had even worse memories of architecture "compromises" that were created to reconcile competing architectures. These frequently resulted in poor designs that everyone had to live and work with daily for months, if not years. On the other hand, Karen did not want to produce an architecture in isolation. She decided that she and Ed would select architecture candidates together, research them thoroughly, and present the choices to the team.

SPG2. SELECTING ARCHITECTURES

Al Pruitt had been thinking about the design of the game application, and he gave Karen a sketch of the ad hoc GUI-driven architecture described in Figure 5.43 above. He pointed out that it was simple and would be quick to implement.

Ed and Karen reviewed Garlan and Shaw's classification of architectures to determine if *Encounter* appeared to match any of the alternatives.

They first asked whether *Encounter* could be described as the flow of data from one processing element to another. The data would have to be the positions of the game characters and/or their quality values. This view did not seem to them to match their conception of the game.

Next, they turned to Garlan and Shaw's "independent components" architectures, the first of which was "parallel communicating processes." To Karen this seemed to be a possible match because each game character could be considered one of the processes. Each could be run on a separate parallel thread, and these threads would communicate whenever the characters encountered each other. They noted this as a candidate architecture.

They considered "client server" next, but it was unclear to them what the "client" and "server" roles would be, so they dismissed this alternative.

"Event systems," the next type listed, appeared to be a candidate architecture since the game responded to either user-initiated events, such as the pressing of an area hyperlink to enter an area, or to the arrival of the foreign character in the same area as the player character. They noted this as another candidate architecture.

Next, Ed and Karen considered "virtual machines," asking whether each game execution consisted essentially of the interpretation of a script. This did not appear to them to be the case.

They considered whether the game could be thought of as built around a repository of data (a "repository system"). The data could be the values of the characters and the status of the game. They decided that this might indeed be a possibility if there were many characters and many artifacts, because in that case, the manipulation of large amounts of data might predominate. Since *Encounter* was not to be data-centric, however, they rejected this candidate.

Finally, they considered a layered architecture. The question here was whether *Encounter* could be viewed as a series of class groupings with each grouping using one or two of the others. Karen felt that there would indeed be at least two useful layers: one for role-playing games in general, and one for *Encounter*. They made a note of this candidate architecture, and ended their consideration of Garlan and Shaw's options.

Now they listed the architecture candidates.

Al Pruitt's GUI-driven architecture

Parallel communicating processes

Event systems

Layered

They discussed which of these described the *overall* architecture and which were subsidiary to the overall architecture. Their conclusion was that the layering was the primary architectural principle since there was a generic role-playing game layer and the *Encounter* layer itself. They envisaged the "event systems" architecture as subsidiary to the layers. They postponed a detailed discussion of parallel communicating processes for the game characters. Conceptually, their main architecture selection is reflected in Figure 5.12 on page 258.

They decided to express the "event systems" architecture by means of states and transitions. They then debated whether to use the *State* design pattern or a state/action table to describe the event/transitions, and decided to apply metrics to assist in choosing from the architectures under consideration, including Al Pruitt's.

They used e-mail to try and get agreement on the weighting of criteria for architectures (*extension, change,* etc.,—see Table 5.4) in advance of the meeting, without mentioning the architecture candidates themselves. They then e-mailed Al a draft of the comparison table in advance of the meeting to make sure that they had not missed any aspects of his proposal. Al pointed out that the choice of architecture was heavily dependent on the weighting, but was willing to accept the team's weighting. Karen and Ed drew up the spreadsheet Table 5.4, comparing Al Pruitt's architecture (alternative 2) and two others they had developed, and mailed it to the team members so that they would be prepared for the meeting.

SPG3. TEAM MEETING ("PRELIMINARY DESIGN REVIEW")

At the meeting, Karen and Ed first confirmed agreement on the weighting of criteria. Because of their use of e-mail prior to the meeting, the team did not take long to iron out the few remaining inconsistencies. No mention was made yet of the architectures themselves.

They presented the architecture alternatives to the team, showing the spreadsheet results. After some discussion and modification of their assessments, the team confirmed their selection of the layered architecture and the use of the *State* design pattern. Karen and Ed's thought process and presentation had been thorough. The team's discussion focused on how to improve the architecture selected.

They solicited ideas for refining the architecture but Karen did not try to rank the ideas or create a single refined version of the architecture at the meeting. She wanted to think through the suggestions offline.

SPG4. REFINING THE ARCHITECTURE

Karen and Ed were now faced with the task of decomposing each layer. They performed this by placing the two additional architectural elements in separate packages. In the role-playing game layer they formed a package for the state machine called *RolePlaying-Game*. To handle the game characters, which move around in parallel, they created a

Characters package. They also created a *GameEnvironment* package to contain classes describing the places in which the characters would move. Finally, they envisaged an *Artifacts* package for the future to describe the miscellaneous items such as shields and swords that would be involved. This package, postponed for future releases, would have a repository architecture.

Their decomposition of the *Encounter* application layer was analogous since many of its classes had to inherit from the generic game level. They decided to create narrow access paths to the packages of this layer to prevent a situation where any class could reference any other class. They felt that such unrestricted references would soon become impossible to manage during development and maintenance. To accomplish this narrow access they used the *Facade* design pattern for each application package. Ed had some reservations about doing this because it increased the amount of code the team would have to create and manage. Methods would not be called directly, he pointed out, but only through special methods of the facade objects, thereby increasing the total number of methods. It also introduced complications in that internal classes could not even be mentioned by objects external to the package (although their generic base classes could be), but Karen convinced him that the price was worth the benefit of having a clear interface for each package.

They obtained approval for their architecture at a subsequent team meeting.

SPG5. DOCUMENTING THE ARCHITECTURE

Ed and Karen used Sections 1 through 5 of the IEEE standard 1016 to express the architecture in a Software Design Document (SDD). Since they had divided the application into two layers, one of which was slated for reuse, they decided to document the framework "role-playing game" layer in a separate SDD.

EXERCISES

Solutions and hints are given at the end of this chapter to all exercises marked with "s" and "h" respectively.

REVIEW QUESTIONS

R5.1[s] State in a sentence or two how "architecture" relates to "design."

R5.2[s] State in a sentence or two how "architecture" relates to "framework."

R5.3 Garlan and Shaw classify architectures into five categories. Name at least three of these categories. The answers are in Section 2.4 ("A categorization of architectures").

R5.4[s] Some design patterns are particularly relevant at the architectural level. Name three or four of these.

GENERAL EXERCISES

G5.1[h] Students are frequently confused about the difference between data flow diagrams and state transition diagrams. Suppose that your application is a batch simulation of customers in a bank. Being a batch simulation, the characteristics of the simulation are first set, then the simulation is executed without intervention. How could you describe this as a data flow application? Use a simple skeleton consisting of four parts to the diagram. (Identify your four parts, then look at how you could describe this application as a state-transition diagram. Which perspective offers more value in describing the architecture?)

G5.2 Which of the *State/Observer/Interpreter* design patterns are clearly candidate architectures for the following applications?

a. an application for informing clients of unusual changes in the stock market

b. an application that enables users to easily express types of standard letters to be created

c. a real-time application that shows the health of an automobile

TEAM EXERCISES

T5.1 ("Architecture")

Develop the architecture for your project. Describe your architecture using the IEEE standard, as in the case study accompanying this chapter. Make it clear what type of architecture and design patterns are being applied. Show at least one other architecture that you considered, and explain why you chose the alternative described. Include the use of metrics. It is not required that you automatically choose the architectures via metrics alone.

Track the time you spend doing this exercise in increments of five minutes, and include a time sheet showing the time spent by individuals and by the team. Use or improve upon the form in Table 5.5 that records the time spent per person on each module. Give your opinion on whether your tracking of time paid off, and whether your time could have been better managed.

TABLE 5.5   Form Showing Time Spent Per Module

		Module			
		1	2	3	4
Team member	Smith	10	4		
	Jones		5	12	
	Brown	2			14

Evaluation criteria:

α. Quality of the architecture — A = architecture intelligently chosen and very modular
β. Quality of self-improvement — A = self criticism very useful and very clearly written

SOLUTIONS TO QUESTIONS

R5.1 The architecture is part of the design; namely the high-level part.

R5.2 A framework is a reusable architecture that may also contain design and even implementation components.

R5.4 Facade, State, Observer, and Interpreter.

HINTS FOR QUESTIONS

G5.1 *hint*

The following are possible processing elements for a data flow diagram: *executeNextEvent*, *updatePositionOfCustomers*. Appropriate data stores are *PendingEvents*, which stores all events scheduled for future execution, and *StatusOfCustomers*, which stores the information about which customer is where. Complete the data flow diagram with these.

The following are possible states for the application: *beingConfigured*, *executingSimulation*, *reportingResults*.

CASE STUDY

We have two designs to describe. The first is that of the Role-Playing Video game framework; the second is that of the *Encounter* role-playing game.

The SDDs for both designs are split into two parts. The first parts, SDD Sections 1 through 5, shown below, consist of the architectural aspects of the designs. The second part, SDD section six, appearing at the end of Chapter 6, consists of the detailed designs.

The dependence of *Encounter* on the framework is specified in the *Encounter* case study.

I. ROLE-PLAYING GAME ARCHITECTURE FRAMEWORK

[Note to the student: see Figure 5.41 for table of contents]

History of versions of this document.
x/yy/zzz K. Peters: initial draft
x/yy/zzz K. Peters: refined; layout package modified extensively
x/yy/zzz E. Braun: reviewed
x/yy/zzz K. Peters: revised, incorporating comments by R. Bostwick
x/yy/zzz K. Peters: moved details of classes to Section 3

1. INTRODUCTION

1.1 Purpose

This document describes the packages and classes of a framework for role-playing video games.

1.2 Scope

This framework covers essentials of role-playing game classes. Its main intention is

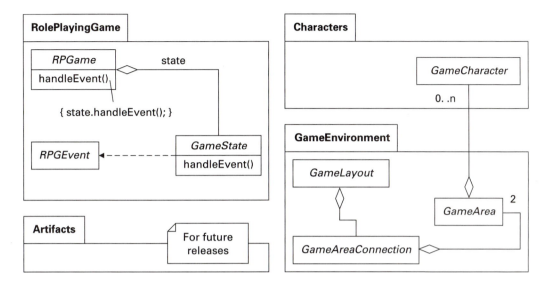

Figure 5.48 RPG Framework for Role-Playing Video Games

to provide an example of a framework for educational purposes. It is not intended as a framework for commercial games since its size is kept small to facilitate learning.

1.3 Definitions, Acronyms, and Abbreviations

Framework: a collection of interrelated classes used, via inheritance or aggregation, to produce families of applications

RPG: Role-playing game — a video game in which characters interact in a manner which depends on their characteristics and their environment

2. REFERENCES

Software Engineering: an Object-oriented perspective, by E. J. Braude, Wiley; 2001.

UML: The Unified Modeling Language User Guide, by G. Booch, J. Rumbaugh, and I. Jacobson, Addison-Wesley Pub Co; ISBN: 0-201-57168-4.

IEEE standard 1016-1987 (reaffirmed 1993) guidelines for generating a Software Design Document.

3. DECOMPOSITION DESCRIPTION

[Note to the student: specifies how the framework classes for role-playing video games are to be grouped. This reflects the top-level decomposition: the detailed decomposition into methods, for example, is left for the detailed design (see case study at the end of the next chapter).]

3.1 Module Decomposition

[Note to the student: This section shows the decomposition, then explains each part in a subsection.]

The framework consists of the *RolePlayingGame*, *Characters*, *Artifacts*, and *Layout* packages. These are decomposed into the classes shown in Figure 5.48. The classes in these packages are explained below. Unless otherwise stated, all classes in these packages are public. As indicated by the (UML) italics notation, all of the framework classes are abstract.

3.1.1 RolePlayingGame *Package*

This package is designed as a state-transition machine. The concept is that a role-playing game is always in one of several states. This package makes it possible to describe the possible states of the game and the actions that can take place in response to events. It implements the *State* design pattern (see [Ga]). The state of the game is encapsulated (represented) by the particular *GameState* object aggregated by the (single) *RPGame* object. This aggregated object is named *state*. In other words, *state* is an attribute of *RPGame* of type *GameState*.

The function *handleEvent( )* of *RPGame* is called to handle each event occurring on the monitor (mouse clicks, etc.). It executes by calling the *handleEvent( )* function of *state*. The applicable version of *handleEvent( )* depends on the particular subclass of *GameState* that *state* belongs to.

3.1.2 Characters *Package*

[Note to the student: It may seem strange to have a package containing just one class, but everything in software design has a tendency to grow. Even if the class does not grow, this does not disqualify its usefulness. For another example of a package with just one class, see java.applet, whose only class is Applet (but which also contains a few interfaces).]

This package contains the *GameCharacter* class, which describes the characters of the game.

3.1.3 GameEnvironment *Package*

This package describes the physical environment of the game. The class *GameLayout* aggregates connection objects. Each connection object aggregates the pair of *GameArea* objects which it connects. This architecture allows for multiple connections between two areas.

Each *GameArea* object aggregates the game characters that it contains (if any) and can detect encounters among characters.

3.1.4 Artifacts *Package*

[Not Implemented—for Future Releases] This package is intended to store elements to be located in areas, such as trees or tables, and entities possessed by characters, such as shields and briefcases.

3.2 Concurrent Process Decomposition

The framework does not involve concurrent processes.

4. DEPENDENCY DESCRIPTION

[Note to the student: This section describes all the ways in which the modules depend on each other.]

The only dependency among the framework modules is the aggregation by *GameArea* of *GameCharacter*.

5. INTERFACE DESCRIPTION

All classes in these packages are public, and thus the interfaces consist of all of the methods in their classes.

II. ARCHITECTURE OF *ENCOUNTER* ROLE-PLAYING GAME PART 1 OF 2 OF THE SOFTWARE DESIGN DOCUMENT, (SEE THE DETAILED DESIGN CASE STUDY FOR PART 2)

[Note to the student: See Figure 4.3 on page 183 for table of contents]

History of versions of this document.
x/yy/zzz K. Peters: initial draft
x/yy/zzz K. Peters: outline completed

x/yy/zzz E. Braun: detection of defects
x/yy/zzz K. Peters: incorporated comments by E. Braun
x/yy/zzz K. Peters: added decomposition by use case model and state model

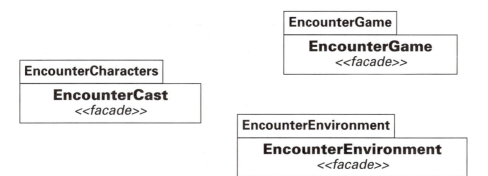

Figure 5.49 Architecture and Modularization of Encounter *Role-Playing Game*

1. INTRODUCTION

1.1 Purpose

This document describes the design of the *Encounter* role-playing game.

1.2 Scope

This design is for the prototype version of *Encounter*, which is a demonstration of architecture, detailed design, and documentation techniques. The architecture is intended as the basis for interesting versions in the future. This description excludes the framework classes, whose design is provided in the SDD entitled "Role-Playing Game Architecture Framework."

1.3 Definitions, Acronyms, and Abbreviations

2. REFERENCES

"Role-Playing Game Architecture Framework," section in *Software Engineering: an Object-oriented Perspective*, by Braude, E. J.; Wiley; 2001.

UML: The Unified Modeling Language User Guide, by G. Booch, J. Rumbaugh and I. Jacobson; Addison-Wesley Pub Co; ISBN: 0-201-57168-4.

IEEE standard 1016-1987 (reaffirmed 1993) guidelines for generating a Software Design Document.

3. DECOMPOSITION DESCRIPTION

The *Encounter* architecture is described using three models: use case, class (object) model, and state. In addition, the relationship between the domain packages of *Encounter* and the framework described in the SDD entitled "Role-Playing Game Architecture Framework" will be shown.

[Note to the student: The IEEE standard is extended using Sections 3.4 and 3.5 in order to describe these models. Recall that the other possible model is data flow, which we have not considered useful in this case. In the particular case of this video game, we chose to use the state description as part of the requirement as well as the design.]

3.1 Module Decomposition (Object Model)

[Note to the student: This section should not duplicate the "detailed design" section described in the next chapter. We do not go into detail here regarding the contents of the packages.]

The package architecture for *Encounter* is shown in Figure 5.49. The three packages are

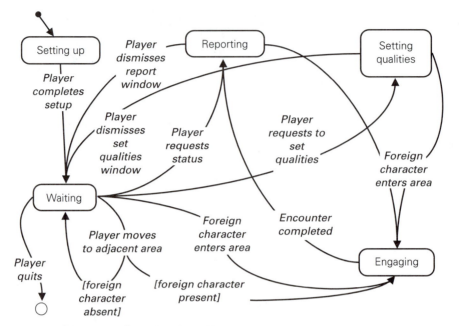

Figure 5.50 Encounter *State Transition Diagram*

EncounterGame, EncounterCharacters, and *EncounterEnvironment*. These have facade classes *EncounterGame, EncounterCast*, and *EncounterEnvironment* respectively. The facade class of each package has exactly one instantiation, and is an interface through which all dealings with the package take place. The remaining classes are not accessible from outside the package. (See Section 3.2.1 on page 266 and [Ga] for a complete description of the Facade design pattern.)

3.1.1 EncounterGame *Package*   The *EncounterGame* package consists of the classes controlling the progress of the game as a whole. The package is designed to react to user actions (events).

3.1.2 EncounterCharacters *Package*
The *EncounterCharacters* package encompasses the characters involved in the game. These include character(s) under the control of the player together with the foreign characters.

3.1.3 EncounterEnvironment *Package*
The *EncounterEnvironment* package describes the physical layout of Encounter in-

cluding the areas and the connections between them. It does not include moveable items, if any.

3.2 Concurrent Process Decomposition

There are two concurrent processes in *Encounter*. The first is the main visible action of the game, in which the player manually moves the main character from area to adjacent area. The second consists of the movement of the foreign character from area to adjacent areas.

3.3 Data Decomposition

[Note to the student: describes the structure of the data within the application]

The data structures flowing among the packages are defined by the *Area, EncounterCharacter*, and *EncounterAreaConnection* classes.

3.4 State Model Decomposition
Encounter consists of the states shown in Figure 5.50. *[Note to the student: This state*

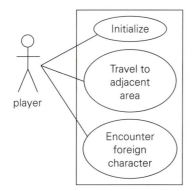

Figure 5.51 Encounter *use cases*

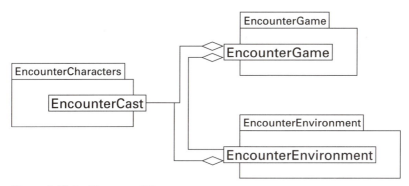

Figure 5.52 Architecture of Encounter

diagram was provided in the SRS, Section 3.40, where it was used to describe the requirements for Encounter. *The remaining states mentioned in the requirements will be implemented in subsequent releases.]*

3.5 Use Case Model Decomposition

[Note to the student: This section is added to the IEEE specification, which does not address the use case concept. It has been added at the end of this section so as not to disturb the standard order.]

Encounter consists of three use cases: *Initialize, Travel to adjacent area*, and *EncounterForeign Character*, as shown in Figure 5.51. These use cases are explained in detail in the SRS, Sections 2.2, and are detailed in sections later in this document.

[Note to the student: Details are given in the "detailed design" section.]

4. DEPENDENCY DESCRIPTION

This section describes the dependencies for the various decompositions described in Section 3.

[Note to the student: There are no significant dependencies among the use cases.]

4.1 Intermodule Dependencies (Object Model)

The dependencies among package interfaces are shown in Figure 5.52. The *EncounterGame* package depends on all of the other *Encounter* packages.

The *EncounterEnvironment* package is designed to depend on the *EncounterCharacters* package. This is because the game's character interaction takes place only in the context of the environment. In

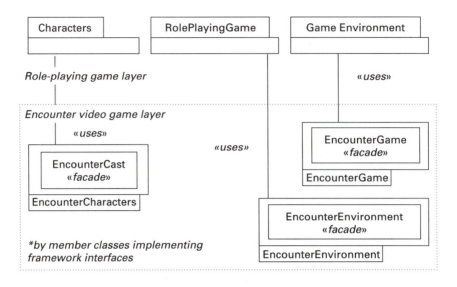

Figure 5.53 Framework / Application Dependency

particular, *Area* objects are responsible for determining the presence of the player's character together with the foreign character.

Dependencies among noninterface classes are explained later in this document.

[Note to the student: Such dependencies are detailed design specifications.]

4.2 Interprocess Dependencies

When an engagement takes place, the process of moving the main character about and the process controlling the movement of the foreign character interact.

4.3 Data Dependencies

The data structures flowing among the packages are defined by the classes, whose mutual dependencies are described in Section 6 of this document.

4.4 State Dependencies

Each state is related to the states into which the game can transition from it.

4.5 Layer Dependencies

The *Encounter* application depends on the Role-playing game framework as shown in Figure 5.53. Each application package uses exactly one framework package.

5. INTERFACE DESCRIPTION

This section describes the interfaces for the object model. Note that several of the classes described are defined in the design description of the Role-playing Game Framework.

5.1 Module Interfaces

[Note to the student: describes the interaction among the packages]

5.1.1 Interface to the EncounterGame *Package* The interface to the *EncounterGame* package is provided by the *theEncounterGame* object of the *Encoun-*

terGame facade class. It consists of the following.

1. `EncounterGame getTheEncounter-Game()` // gets the only instance

2. `GameState getState()` // current state of the EncounterGame instance

3. `void setState( GameState ) //` — of the EncounterGame instance

// Any event affecting the single `EncounterGame` instance:

4. `void handleEvent( AWTEvent )`

5.1.2 Interface to the Encounter-Characters *Package*

The interface to the *EncounterCharacters* package is provided by the *theEncounterCast* object of the *EncounterCast* facade class. It consists of the following.

1. `EncounterCast getTheEncounter-Cast()` // gets the single instance

2. `GameCharacter getThePlayer-Character()` // i.e., the unique character

3. `GameCharacter getTheForeign-Character()` // the unique character

// Exchange quality values specific to the game area

4. `void engagePlayerWithForeign-Character( GameArea )`

5.1.3 Interface to Encounter-Environment *Package*

The interface to the *EncounterEnvironment* package is provided by the *EncounterEnvironment* object of *EncounterEnvironment* Facade class. It consists of the following.

1. `EncounterEnvironment getTheEn-counterEnvironment()` // gets the Facade object

2. `GameArea getArea( String )`

3. `GameAreaConnection getArea-Connection( String )`

4. `void movePlayerTo( Area )`

5. `void moveForeignCharacterTo ( Area ) throws AreaNotAdjacent-Exception`

6. `Image getNeighborhoodAreas( Area )` // gets `Area` and areas one or two connections distant

5.2 Process Interface

[Note to the student: We stated in Section 3.2 that there are two processes involved in Encounter. *There is a significant design decision to be made in regard to the interface to the foreign character movement process, and we describe the result here. One option is to have the foreign character a thread, controlling itself. This has advantages, but requires this character either to know the environment — a disadvantage in terms of changing and expanding the game — or to be able to find out about the environment dynamically, which would be an elegant design but too ambitious for the scope of this case study. The architecture opts for another alternative, which is stated here.]*

5.2.1 Player Character Movement Process

The interfaces to the process which moves the player's character about the game consist of the graphical user interfaces specified in the SRS. The process reacts to events described in Section 3.4, which are handled by the *EncounterGame* package in accordance with its specifications, described later in this document.

5.2.2 Foreign Character Movement Process

The process of moving the foreign character is a separate process associated with and controlled by the *EncounterGame* singleton object. This process is controlled by the methods inherited from *java.lang.Thread.*

DETAILED DESIGN

"the mould of form . . ."
—Ophelia, describing Hamlet

Elegant application designs greatly enhance implementation and maintenance.

Figure 6.1 indicates the phase with which this chapter deals. Figure 6.2 lists the learning goals of this chapter.

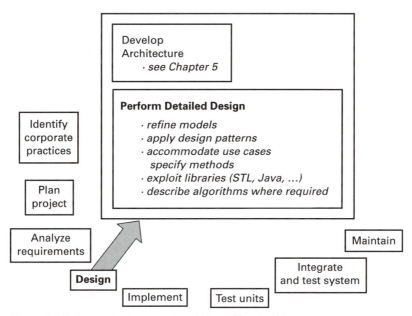

Figure 6.1 Software Engineering Road Map: Chapter 6 Focus

● Understand how design patterns describe some detailed designs

● Specify classes and functions completely

● Specify algorithms

   • use flowcharts

   • use pseudocode

Figure 6.2 Chapter Learning Goals

▶ PART I: ESSENTIALS

1. INTRODUCTION TO DETAILED DESIGN

1.1 The Meaning of "Detailed Design"

Detailed design is the technical activity that follows architecture selection. Its goal is to fully prepare the project for implementation. In other words, programmers should be able to implement a detailed design, concentrating on purely code issues.

1.2 Relating Use Cases, Architecture, and Detailed Design

The relationship between the use cases, the architecture, and the detailed design can be described by analogy with designing a bridge. Use cases would be part of the requirements

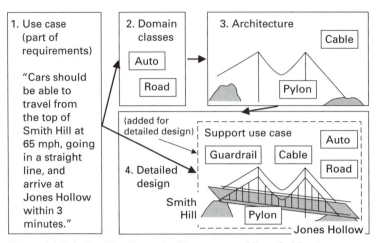

Figure 6.3 Relating Use Cases, Architectures, and Detailed Design

for the bridge. Based on the requirements, engineers select an architecture (e.g., a suspension bridge). After this, they develop the detailed design so as to enable the required use case with the architecture selected. This is suggested by Figure 6.3.

In the software analogy, each corresponding stage accumulates additional classes. In step 1, use cases are specified as part of the requirements. In step 2, these, together with other sources, are used to identify the domain classes. In step 3, we develop the software architecture, as described in Chapter 5. The last step is to verify that the architecture and detailed design support the required use cases. For the bridge analogy, we verify that cars can indeed use the bridge design to travel from Smith Hill to James Hollow as specified. For software design, we verify that the classes and methods specified by the detailed design are capable of executing the required use cases.

1.3 A Typical Road Map for the "Detailed Design" Process

Detailed design starts with the results of the architecture phase and ends with a complete blueprint for the programming phase. Figure 6.4 shows a typical sequence of steps taken to perform detailed design. In particular, step 2 creates the classes that associate the architecture on one hand with the domain classes on the other hand, as illustrated in the previous section. Design patterns may help in doing this. It is advisable to start the detailed design process with those aspects of the design that present the most risk. For example, in designing *Encounter* we might consider risky the way in which the classes were modularized (all characters in one package, etc.). This should be settled as soon as possible by specifying the details of the interface methods so that we can get an intimate idea of how this modularization works out. If the use of the *State* design pattern were perceived as a risk, we would specify its details first.

Step 3 includes checking that we have a complete design. It also includes ensuring that the object model supports the use cases, as discussed in Section 1.2.

Step 6 continues the practice of specifying a test as soon as each element is specified.

Figure 6.5 and Figure 6.6 show one way for a team to organize for the detailed design process.

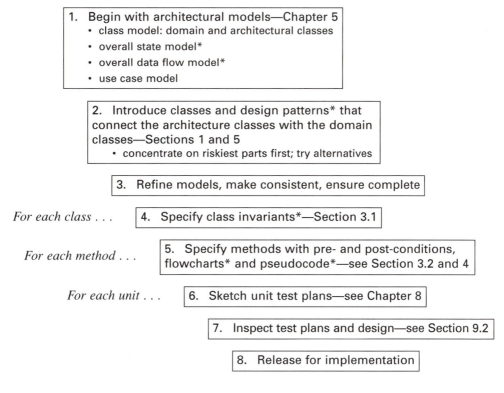

1. Begin with architectural models—Chapter 5
   • class model: domain and architectural classes
   • overall state model*
   • overall data flow model*
   • use case model

2. Introduce classes and design patterns* that connect the architecture classes with the domain classes—Sections 1 and 5
   • concentrate on riskiest parts first; try alternatives

3. Refine models, make consistent, ensure complete

For each class . . .   4. Specify class invariants*—Section 3.1

For each method . . .   5. Specify methods with pre- and post-conditions, flowcharts* and pseudocode*—see Section 3.2 and 4

For each unit . . .   6. Sketch unit test plans—see Chapter 8

7. Inspect test plans and design—see Section 9.2

8. Release for implementation

*if applicable

Figure 6.4 Typical Road Map for Detailed Design

One Way To. . . Organize the Team for Detailed Design, 1 of 2

1. Prepare for a detailed design kickoff meeting.
   • Ensure team members aware of the models (views) they are expected to produce
     • *typically object model, sequence diagrams, state, and data flow*
   • Ensure team members aware of the notation expected
     • *typically UML plus a pseudocode standard and/or example*
   • Design leader prepares list of modules
   • Design leader creates a meeting agenda
   • Project leader allocates time to agenda items
     (people can speak about detailed designs indefinitely if allowed to!)
     • *allocate the time among the agenda items*

Figure 6.5 One Way to Organize a Team for Detailed Design, 1 of 2

1.4 Design in the Unified Development Process

In the Unified development process of Jacobson et al., design takes place primarily during the "Elaboration" and "Construction" iterations, as emphasized in Figure 6.7. An "Analysis" phase is frequently identified as part of the waterfall process. Compared with the terminology of this book, the Analysis phase consists partly of requirements analysis and partly of architecture

---

One Way To. . . Organize the Team for Detailed Design, 2 of 2

2. Hold the kickoff meeting
    - Designate someone to monitor the agenda item time
    - Confirm that the architecture is ready for detailed design
        - Make sure that module interfaces are clear
            - *revise as a group if not*
        - Don't try to develop detailed designs as a group
            - *not necessary;* individuals *have the responsibility*
            - *groups are seldom good at designing details together*
    - Allocate modules to members
        - Request time estimates to design lead by a fixed date
    - Write out the conclusions and copy/e-mail every member
    - Decide how and when the results are to be reviewed

3. Update the documentation set
    - more detailed schedule with modules and inspections

4. Inspect the detailed designs
    - see Section 9.2

5. Rework as a result of inspections

6. Conduct post mortem and write out lessons learned

Figure 6.6 One Way to Organize a Team for Detailed Design, 2 of 2

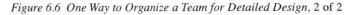

U.P. Term	Inception	Elaboration	Construction	Transition
1 Requirements				
2 Analysis				
3 **Design**				
Implementation				
Test				
	Preliminary iterations	Iter. #1 Iter. #n	Iter. #n + 1 ... Iter. #m	Iter. #m + 1 ... Iter. #k

Key: terminology used in this book   ☐1 = Requirements   ☐2 = Architecture   ☐3 = Detailed design

Figure 6.7 Design *in the Unified Software Development Process [Ja1]*

selection. Jacobson et al. make the comparison between the "Analysis" process and the "Design" process, shown in Figure 6.8 and Figure 6.9.

Item three in Figure 6.8 requires special explanation. The Unified process encourages three types ("stereotypes") of classes at the analysis level: *entity, boundary,* and *control* classes, whereas there is no such restriction on design classes. *Entity* classes express the essence of the concept, and are unlikely to require change over time or between applications. *Boundary* classes handle communication with entity objects, and *control* classes contain methods that pertain to the entity objects, but that are typically special to the application in which the entity class is being used. Boundary classes are typically like the *Mediator* object in the *Mediator* design pattern described in Section 5.3.3.

The creators of the Unified process feel that visual tools can be profitably used for design (see item 7). An example of this is the Rational Rose tool sold by their company, the Rational Corporation. Item 8 states that it is more important to maintain the detailed design throughout the development process than to maintain the results of the Analysis phase — assuming that a choice between the two must be made. Finally, item 10 expresses the point made above that we return to the use cases to ensure that their sequence diagrams are accommodated.

Analysis	Design
1. Conceptual and abstract	1. Concrete: implementation blueprint
2. *Applicable to several designs*	2. *Specific for an implementation*
3. <<control>>, <<entity>> and <<boundary>> stereotypes	3. No limit on class stereotypes
4. *Less formal*	4. *More formal*
5. Less expensive to develop	5. More expensive to develop (approximately 5 times as expensive)

Figure 6.8 Comparison of "Analysis" and "Design" [Ja1], 1 of 2

Analysis	Design
6. Outlines the design	6. Manifests the design (architecture one view)
7. *Emerges from conceptual thinking*	7. *May use tools (e.g., visual, round-trip engineering)*
8. Lower priority for in-process information	8. Higher priority for in-process information
9. *Relatively unconstrained*	9. *Constrained by the analysis and architecture*
10. Less focus on sequence diagrams	10. More focus on sequence
11. *Few layers*	11. *Many layers*

Figure 6.9 Comparison of "Analysis" and "Design" [Ja1], 2 of 2

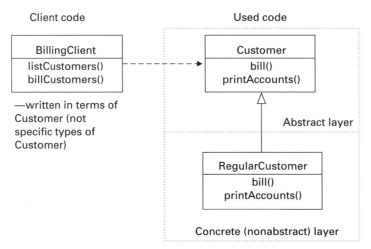

Figure 6.10 Designing against Interfaces

1.5 Designing Against Interfaces

In our discussion of architectures in Chapter 5 we exploited the *Facade* design pattern as a way of providing a clean interface to a package of classes. The idea of designing against interfaces is like employing a contract. The program element (e.g., the *Customer* class) supplying the functionality guarantees to provide functions with specified names, parameter types, and return types (e.g., `void bill( void )` and `boolean printAccounts( String accountType )`). The program elements using the supplier of functionality can then be designed without having to know how the functionality is implemented.

Designing against interfaces takes many forms. One is the use of abstraction. For example, if code is to be written about *Mammal* objects, then we try to write it so as to mention only *Animal* objects. In other words, we try to use only the *Animal interface*. This allows greater applicability and greater flexibility for our design.

As a further example, suppose that we are writing code about customers. This can be understood as writing against the *Customer* interface. We can actually consider using an abstract class *Customer*, with a nonabstract subclass such as *RegularCustomer*, as shown in Figure 6.10. This design is more flexible than writing against a concrete (nonabstract) class *Customer*, because we can easily add other types of customers, such as *SavingsCustomer* objects, with specialized versions of *bill()*, without having to change the code that uses *Customer* objects. The division into an abstract and a concrete layer is characteristic of many design patterns.

1.6 Reusing Components

Most engineering disciplines (electrical, mechanical, etc.) rely on the use of components that can be procured separately. Bridge designers, for example, do not generally design their own I-beams. For years, it has been observed that software engineers continually "reinvent the wheel" by implementing routines that already exist elsewhere. One reason for this lack of software reuse is the historically inadequate organization of existing architectures, designs, and code. The widespread adoption of object-oriented, object-like, and other component paradigms has helped to promote software reuse. Because of the large number of methods packaged with each class, functionality that we need is often included and is relatively convenient to locate.

The use of the Microsoft MFC library, Visual Basic controls, COM objects, Java Beans, and other Java Application Programming Interface (API) classes are examples of code reuse. The Object Management Group's Common Object Request Broker Architecture (CORBA) is a standard for distributed reuse.

We discussed frameworks in the previous chapter on architecture. These are packages of components designed for reuse. We developed frameworks to support application architectures, and so they are effectively reusable. The Java core API is another example of a widely used framework.

Java Beans provide reusable components for Java applications. They include graphics beans and "enterprise" beans, which encapsulate corporate tasks such as database access. In addition to the advantages afforded by being classes, beans obey standards that make them capable of manipulation within development environments.

Web-based programs (i.e., not components) such as JavaScript and CGI scripts are often reused.

At a different level, the Standard Template Library (STL) provides mix-and-match capability of standard algorithms such as sorting and searching. STL is applicable to a variety of data structures and to objects of virtually any class. STL is described below in Section 6.

In summary, a component marketplace has emerged and is growing continually.

Having found a component that could possibly be used in an application, *should* it be used? The following factors are typical in making this decision.

- Is the component documented as thoroughly as the rest of the application?
  —If not, can it be?
- How much customization of the component and/or the application is required?
- Has the component been tested to the same level as, or more extensively than, the rest of the application?
  —If not, *can* it be?

A table comparing the costs can be developed, similar to that in Section 5.2 of Chapter 2 (page 90) where a make-vs.-buy example was shown.

2. SEQUENCE AND DATA FLOW DIAGRAMS FOR DETAILED DESIGN

Recall that sequence diagrams (Chapter 4) and data flow diagrams (Chapter 3) can be useful for describing requirements. They are more commonly used as design tools. Figure 6.11 and Figure 6.12 provide guidance on what needs to be done to carry out detailed design, and the text following it provides details and examples.

2.1 Detailed Sequence Diagrams

Recall that use cases can be utilized to express requirements and that we also use them to determine the key domain classes for the application. We now take the sequence diagrams built from the use cases and provide the classes involved with the methods required to execute the sequences.

One Way To. . . Refine Models for Detailed Design 1 of 2:
Sequence Diagrams

1. Begin with the sequence diagrams constructed for detailed requirements or architecture (if any) corresponding to the use cases.

2. Introduce additional use cases, if necessary, to describe how parts of the design typically interact with the rest of the application

3. Provide sequence diagrams with complete details
    • be sure that the exact objects and their classes are specified
    • select specific function names in place of natural language
       (calls of one object to another to perform an operation)

Figure 6.11 One Way to Refine Models for Detailed Design: Sequence Diagrams, 1 of 2

One Way To. . . Refine Models for Detailed Design 2 of 2:
Data Flow Diagrams

1. Gather data flow diagrams (DFDs) constructed for detailed requirements and/or architecture (if any).

2. Introduce additional DFDs, if necessary, to explain data and processing flows.

3. Indicate what part(s) of the other models the DFDs correspond to.
    • e.g., "the following DFD is for each *Account* object in the class model"

4. Provide all details on the DFDs
    • indicate the nature of the processing at each node
    • indicate the kind of data transmitted
    • expand processing nodes into DFDs if the processing description requires more detail

---

Figure 6.12 One Way to Refine Models for Detailed Design: Data Flow Diagrams, 2 of 2

For example, the sequence diagram for the "Encounter Foreign Character" use case in the case study is shown in Figure 6.13, except that instead of the verbal descriptions of functionality called, which we used for requirements (see Section 4 of Chapter 4 on page 196), we designate specific functions. The other refinement is due to the fact that we introduced the *Facade* class *EncounterCast*, through which all external references to the game characters must pass. The reasoning behind the functions chosen is as follows.

1. *ForeignCharacter* is to have a display function. We will implement this with a method *display()*. (Since all characters will need to be displayed we can actually ensure this requirement by giving the base class *GameCharacter* a *display()* method.) The sequence diagram shows *EncounterGame* creating the foreign character (step 1.2) and also an *Engagement* object, and then calling *display()*.

2. This step in the use case indicates that we need an *execute()* method in *Engagement*.
    2.1 This step requires that *freddie* and the main player character be able to change their quality values. Since this capability is common to all *Encounter* characters we provide the base *EncounterCharacter* class with a *setQuality()* method.

3. This step requires that the result of the engagement be shown. The following two sub-steps constitute one way to do this.
    3.1 First *Engagement* creates an *EngagementDisplay* object.
    3.2 Now we show the engagement display by calling its *displayResult()* method.

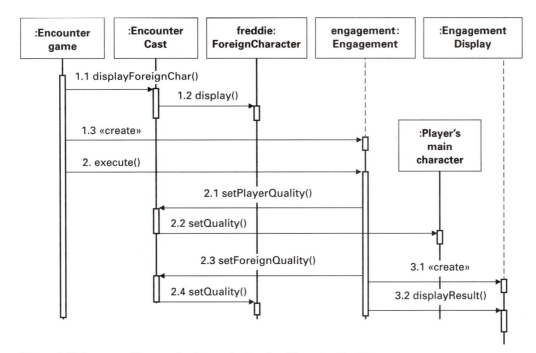

Figure 6.13 Sequence Diagram for Encounter Foreign Character *Use Case*

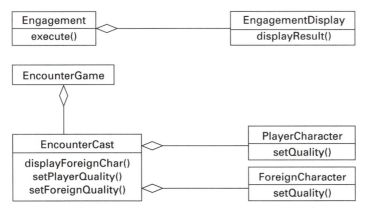

Figure 6.14 Classes of the Encounter Foreign Character *Use Case*

Since the methods required to execute this use case are now known, we can indicate them on the object model, as in Figure 6.14. Continuing this process, the class model and the use case model (in the form of sequence diagrams) are completed in detail, as shown in the case study. The state model (if applicable) must also be completed in detail. A data flow diagram is yet another model, and is discussed next.

2.2 Detailed Data Flow Diagrams

In Chapter 3 the data flow diagram (DFD) was discussed as a vehicle for expressing requirements. A banking example was described. For detailed design, data models have to be described in full detail and then mapped to functions or to classes and methods. Figure 6.15 illustrates what has to be done to describe all of the details for the banking DFD in Section 3.1 of Chapter 5 (page 263).

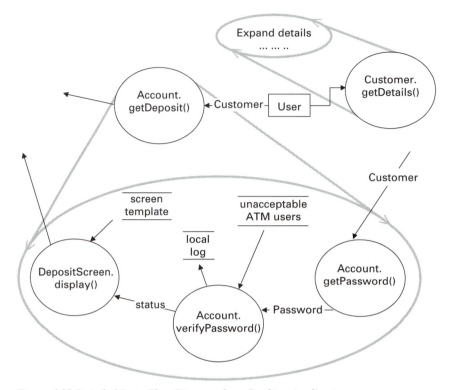

Figure 6.15 Detailed Data Flow Diagram for a Banking Application

Each processing element is expanded into a more detailed DFD, and this expansion process is continued until the lowest level processing elements are reached. The latter are typically individual functions, possibly of different classes. For example, the *getDeposit( )* function is expanded into three functions (getting the password, verifying it, and making a display). Two of these interact with data stores (a local log of transactions, a list of problem users, and a template for screen displays) that were not shown in the high-level DFD. Note that the data entrances and exits from the detailed expansions match those in the versions from which they are expanded.

DFDs are not helpful for all applications. For example, they do not appear to add much to the *Encounter* case study.

3. SPECIFYING CLASSES AND FUNCTIONS

The goal of detailed design is to provide a complete blueprint from which a program can be constructed. A good house blueprint leaves the builder with as few doubts as possible about the intentions of the designer, and the same is true for detailed software design. Figure 6.16 and Figure 6.17 provide typical steps in carrying out detailed design for each class function, and the succeeding text explains the steps in detail.

The detailed class diagrams should include all attribute and operation names, signatures, visibility, return types, etc. Accessor methods are commonly omitted. Figure 6.18 shows a class from the detailed design of an application that controls the flow in a chip

---

One Way To. . . Specify a Class

1. Gather the attributes listed in the SRS.
   - easy if the SRS is organized by class
2. Add additional attributes required for the design.
3. Name a method corresponding to each of the requirements for this class.
   - easy if the SRS is organized by class
4. Name additional methods required for the design.
5. Show the attributes and methods on the object model
6. State class invariants (see section 3.1)

Figure 6.16 One Way to Specify a Class, 1 of 2

One Way To. . . Specify a Function

1. Note the section(s) of the SRS or SDD that this function (method) satisfies.
2. State what expressions the function must leave invariant.
3. State the method's preconditions (what it assumes).
4. State the method's postconditions (its effects).
5. Provide pseudocode or a flow chart to specify the algorithm to be used.
   - unless straightforward

Figure 6.17 One Way to Specify a Class, 2 of 2

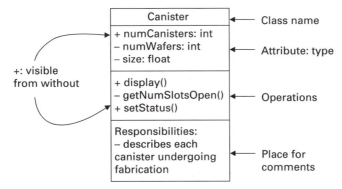

Figure 6.18 Detailed UML Notation for Classes

manufacturing plant of canisters holding wafers. The notation is part of the Unified Modeling Language (see also the inside front cover).

Notice that not all of the attributes are specified. Some required attributes may be left to the discretion of the implementers. It is also customary to omit accessor functions (e.g., *getSize*() and *setSize*()), since these can be inferred from the presence of the corresponding attributes (*size*).

Tools have the benefit of allowing designers to suppress (i.e., to not show) certain elements of the figure — e.g., the "responsibilities" section, or the variable types. Many tools allow designers to view only the classes and their relationships, in order to get the big picture.

One useful manner in which to specify classes is through the CORBA Interface Definition Language (IDL). This is a standard, textual format for specifying the interfaces provided by collections of classes, their attributes, and their functions. For the specification of IDL, see [Om2].

3.1 Class Invariants

An invariant is an assertion that remains true throughout a designated computation. Well thought out classes often have invariants. For example, our *Encounter* game characters have the property that the values of their qualities always sum to a positive nonzero amount. In an *Account* class, an appropriate invariant might be the following:

$$liquidAssetsI \leq checkBalanceI + savingBalanceI$$

This states that any change to these *Account* attributes does not allow the *Account* object to go into the red—savings included.

Class invariants are effectively requirements on the objects of the class, and they are expressed in terms of the attributes of the class. These requirements may map directly onto requirements of the application, and are thus found in the SRS. Alternatively, they may be mandated by the design. Class invariants take the form of constraints on the values. As C-requirements, they are often termed *business rules*. An example is "all Web auction participants must provide a credit card number," which could translate into a specific class invariant on the class *Participant* such as

isResistered == true AND 4 00000001 $\leq$ creditCardNum $\leq$ 699999999

OR

isResistered == false AND creditCardNum == 0

3.2 Function Invariants, Preconditions, and Postconditions

One way to control the behavior of functions is to use *function invariants*. These are assertions about relationships among variables that functions are guaranteed to obey. An example from *Encounter* is the following possible invariant for the *adjustQuality*() method.

Invariant: *the sum of the values of the qualities.*

In other words, when the value of one quality is changed with *adjustQuality( )* the values of the remaining qualities change in a way that leaves their sum unchanged.

An effective way to specify functions is by means of preconditions and postconditions. These were covered in Section 8.4 of Chapter 4 on page 225. Preconditions specify the relationships among variables and constants that are assumed to exist prior to the function's execution; postconditions specify these relationships after the function's execution. For example, the function *doWithdrawal(int withdrawalAmountP)* of an *Account* class could be specified as shown in Figure 6.19. Note that the bank's definition of "available funds" does not include the customer's overdraft privilege. Every invariant can be replaced by repeating the invariant assertion among both the preconditions and the postconditions.

Invariant of *withdraw(withdrawalAmountP)*:

   availableFundsI = max (0, *balanceI*)

Precondition:*

   withdrawalAmountP ≥ 0 AND

   balance – withdrawalAmountP ≥ *–OVERDRAFT_MAX*

Postcondition:*

   balanceI' = balanceI – withdrawalAmountP

xI denotes an attribute; *xP* denotes a function parameter; *x'* is the value of *x* after execution; *X* denotes a class constant
*The function invariant is effectively an additional pre- and post-condition

Figure 6.19 Specifying Functions: withdraw() *in Class* Account

4. SPECIFYING ALGORITHMS

Having identified the functions to be implemented, it may be desirable to describe the algorithm to be used in a way that stops short of source code. The advantage of doing this is that engineers can inspect the algorithm separately without the intrusion of programming complexities, thereby trapping defects before they magnify into code defects. The more critical the method, the more important this activity. Methods with complicated branching are prime candidates for flowcharting.

4.1 Flowcharts

Flowcharts are among the oldest of the graphical methods for depicting algorithms. Figure 6.20 contains a flowchart for the *setName()* method of *GameCharacter* showing two of the most commonly used flowchart constructs, namely decision (diamonds) and process (rectangles). An inspection of the flowchart in Figure 6.20 would make it apparent that the logic for checking the legitimacy of a parameter name is unclear.

Tools are available that create flowcharts from source code — a kind of reverse engineering that creates inspectable artifacts, but which compromises inspection *prior* to programming, one of the main purposes of flowcharts.

The use of flowcharting diminished during the 1980s and 1990s. This is partly because object orientation, which rose in popularity during that time, tends to reduce the amount of branching by splitting functionality into separate classes and by exploiting virtual functions.

4.1.1 A Flowchart Example The following example, the "backward chaining" algorithm for expert systems, illustrates how flowcharting can be helpful in explaining algorithms.

Expert systems are usually based on knowledge in the form of rules, which take the form

   antecedent AND *antecedent* AND ... AND *antecedent* => *consequent,*

where *antecedent*'s and *consequent*'s are facts. For example,

   animal is mammal AND *animal is striped* => *animal is zebra.*

Our facts will simply be strings.

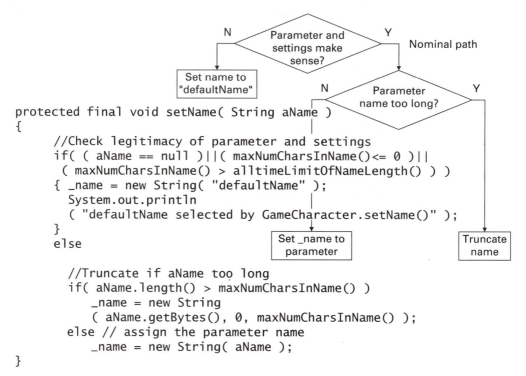

```
protected final void setName( String aName )
{
      //Check legitimacy of parameter and settings
      if( ( aName == null )||( maxNumCharsInName()<= 0 )||
       ( maxNumCharsInName() > alltimeLimitOfNameLength() ) )
      { _name = new String( "defaultName" );
        System.out.println
        ( "defaultName selected by GameCharacter.setName()" );
      }
      else

         //Truncate if aName too long
         if( aName.length() > maxNumCharsInName() )
            _name = new String
            ( aName.getBytes(), 0, maxNumCharsInName() );
         else // assign the parameter name
            _name = new String( aName );
}
```

Figure 6.20 Flowchart Example

The problem is to build a program that, given the following, determines whether or not a given fact, such as *L*, can be deduced. (The answer is "yes" for the example given.)

1. A list of facts, such as *A, B, Q*

2. A list of rules, such as *A&R => L, A&B => C,* and *B&C => F*

One possible object model is shown in Figure 6.21. The model stores the current list of known facts as a static structure of *Fact* called *factList*. It stores the list of known rules as a static structure in *Rule* called *ruleBase*. We will simplify the setup of these lists by hard coding the example given above in the *Fact* and *Rule* classes. Our emphasis is on the

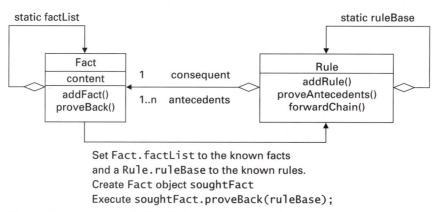

Figure 6.21 An Architecture for Chaining

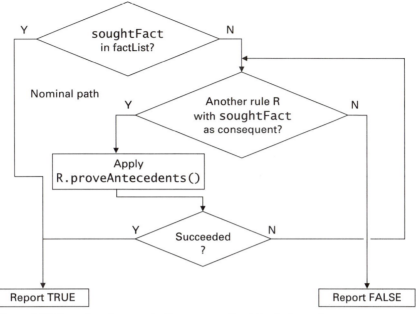

Figure 6.22 Flowchart for `soughtFact.proveBack(ruleBase )`

harder part: the "backchaining" algorithm *proveBack()* for establishing whether or not a given fact, called *soughtFact*, can be deduced from the given facts and rules. A flowchart for this algorithm is shown in Figure 6.22. A good inspection of this flowchart would uncover the fact that it fails to terminate if the rule base contains circularity, such as a pair of rules of the form $X => Y$, and $Y => X$.

4.2 Pseudocode

Pseudocode is a means of expressing an algorithm textually without having to specify programming languages details. As an example, pseudocode for a hypothetical automated X-ray controller is shown in Figure 6.23. An advantage of pseudocode is that it is easy to

FOR number of microseconds supplied by operator
    IF number of microseconds exceeds critical value
        Try to get supervisor's approval
        IF no supervisor's approval
            abort with "no supervisor approval for unusual duration"
            message ENDIF ENDIF
    IF power level exceeds critical value
        abort with "power level exceeded" message ENDIF
    IF (patient properly aligned and shield properly placed and
    machine self-test passed)
        Apply X-ray at power level p ENDIF . . . ENDFOR

See Section 9.22 for inspection of pseudocode.

Figure 6.23 Pseudocode Example for "X-ray controller"

```
//p FOR number of microseconds supplied by operator
for( int i=0; i<numMicrosecs; ++I ){
    //p IF number of microseconds exceeds critical value
    if( numMicrosecs >
        XRayPolicies.CRITICAL_NUM_MICROSECS)
            //p Try to get supervisor's approval
            int supervisorMicrosecsApproval=
                getApprovalOfSuperForLongExposure();
            //p IF no supervisor approval
            if( supervisorMicrosecsApproval <= 0 )
                throw( new SupervisorMicrosecsApprovalException() );
. . .
```

Figure 6.24 Pseudocode Extraction

understand but can also be made precise enough to express algorithms. Another advantage is that algorithms can be inspected for correctness independently of the clutter of language. A third advantage is that defect rates in pseudocode can be collected and used as a predictor for defect rates in the product, using historical defect data.

Many organizations use inspected pseudocode as annotated comments in the source code listing. Tools are then able to extract the pseudocode from the source. For example, using "//p" to preface pseudocode, the code in Figure 6.24 could implement the pseudocode cited above.

4.3 When to Use Flowcharts and Pseudocode

Pseudocode and flowcharts each have the advantages listed in Figure 6.25 and Figure 6.26. The decision whether or not to use pseudocode and/or flowcharts depends on factors particular to the application. Some developers shun flowcharts as old-fashioned, but flowcharts and pseudocode can be worth the trouble for selected parts of applications, where they help to produce better quality products.

- Clarify algorithms in many cases
- Impose increased discipline on the process of documenting detailed design
- Provide additional level at which inspection can be performed
  - Help to trap defects before they become code
  - Increase product reliability
- Often decrease overall costs

Figure 6.25 Advantages of Pseudocode and Flowcharts

- Create an additional level of documentation to maintain
- Introduce error possibilities in translating to code
- May require tool to extract pseudocode and facilitate drawing flowcharts

Figure 6.26 Disadvantages of Pseudocode and Flowcharts

▶ PART II OF DETAILED REQUIREMENTS: AT LENGTH

This **part** of the chapter *can* be covered after covering subsequent chapters. Understanding the ideas in it, however, is required to produce a quality software product.

5. DESIGN PATTERNS II: TECHNIQUES OF DETAILED DESIGN

In Section 2.5 of Chapter 5 (page 260), we discussed the application of design patterns to architecture. In this chapter, we apply them to detailed design. As the name "pattern" suggests, it is the overall combination rather than the specific parts that can sometimes help us to deal with design problems. Patterns should be applied only when the fit feels entirely comfortable; otherwise they can easily complicate a simple design. Despite these caveats, the author believes that the discipline of design patterns is an essential tool for the software engineer.

This section catalogs design patterns in accordance with the classification used by Gamma et al. ([Ga]). For the sake of reference, we include the design patterns already mentioned in the preceding *Architecture* chapter, but without repeating a detailed explanation. Web resources, such as Huang ([Hu5]), show how the design patterns in [Ga] can be implemented in Java and C++.

There are usually two aspects to each design pattern. The first is its typical class model, which shows the classes and their relationships; the second aspect is how the pattern operates. A use case model can be used to describe the latter.

Gamma et al. divide design patterns into three categories. The first, "creational" patterns, concerns the process by which objects are constructed; the second, "structural," deals with representing combinations of objects; the third, "behavioral," captures selected behavior among objects. Figure 6.27 provides guidance on how to go about applying design patterns, and refers to the text following it.

One Way To. . . Apply Design Patterns in *Detailed Design*

1. Become familiar with the design problems solved by design patterns
    - at a minimum, understand the distinction among (C) *creational* vs. (S) *structural* vs. (B) *behavioral* patterns

Consider each part of the detailed design in turn:

2. Determine whether the problem has to do with (C) creating something complex, (S) representing a complex structure, or (B) capturing behavior

3. Determine whether there is a design pattern that addresses the problem
    - try looking in the category identified (C, S, or B)
      - use this book and/or Gamma et al [Ga]

4. Decide if benefits outweigh drawbacks
    - benefits usually include increased flexibility
    - drawbacks often include increased complexity, and reduced efficiency

---

Figure 6.27 One Way to Apply Design Patterns in Detailed Design

5.1 Creational Patterns for Detailed Design

Creational patterns are used to vary and control the creation of objects, including coordinated families of objects, selected at run time. Without creational patterns, we have to write separate code for each kind of object or family of objects that could be required at run time. *Creational patterns typically create objects by means of a separate object or method, rather than by using constructors directly.* The following creational patterns appear in Gamma et al. [Ga].

5.1.1 Singleton The problem: Suppose that there is to be only a single object s of a class C. For example, in the case study, there is to be only one video game and so there is to be just one instance of the *EncounterGame* class. As described in the case study, several objects need to reference this object.

The *Singleton* pattern: The *Singleton* idea is implemented by making the constructor of the class private (or, possibly, protected). This prevents the creation of C objects except by methods of C itself. C is given a static data member of type C which will be the singleton. Let us name this *theCObject*. A public method of C, *getTheCObjec*t() is defined, which returns *theCObject* if it already exists, and constructs it otherwise. Thus, to get this one and only element of C, we merely invoke C.*getTheCObject*().

The static C object *theCObject* can be declared *null* initially, and set to *new C*() the first time *getTheCObject*() is called. Whether or not the value of *theCObject* is *null* can be used as the test for its "existence" mentioned above.

In the case study, the class *EncounterGame*, among others, applies the *Singleton* design pattern.

5.1.2 Factory The problem: Be able to write client code that creates objects of a *Base* class at run time without having to reference (mention) any subclasses of *Base*.

The *Factory* pattern: Equip *Base* with a method that creates a *Base* object. Let's call this method getNewBaseObject(). In the client code we use getNewBaseObject() instead of new-Base(). This exploits the virtual function property. At run time b.getNewBaseObject() creates an object of the subclass of *Base* to which b belongs. Figure 6.28 shows the *Factory* idea applied to client code referencing only the base class *BiologicalCell*. At run time either an *AnimalCell* or a *PlantCell* object is created, depending on the type of the *BiologicalCell* class that Client refers to.

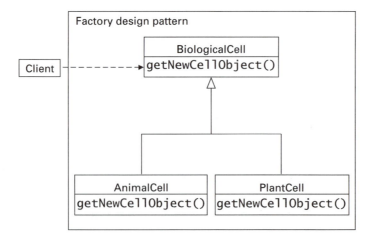

Figure 6.28 Factory *Example*

We have given a simple application of *Factory*. The *Factory* method can create the object with many different motives, however. For example, the *Factory* method *getGraphics()* in the Java *Component* API class obtains a *Graphics* object that draws on the specific *Component* object to which *getGraphics()* belongs.

5.1.3 Prototype   The problem: Suppose that we are designing an office application that deals with *Document* objects and *Customer* objects. For example

```
title = d.getTitle();      // d is a Document object
d.printSummary(c);         // c is a Customer object
d.addToDatabase();
c.addToDatabase();         // etc.
```

Suppose that each time the office application executes, it does so with just one subtype of *Document* throughout (e.g., only *InvoiceDocument* objects) and just one subtype of *Customer* throughout. The application identifies these subtypes at run time. Thus, one of four possible combinations of *Document* and *Customer* objects can apply at run time. Using statements of the form

```
Document d = new Document(); and Customer c = new Customer();
```

— creates base objects, but not objects of the specific type required at run time. This severely hampers the ability of the code to execute with all kinds of *Document* objects.

The *Prototype* pattern: A good way to handle this problem is to write the application using a particular static *Document* object (called a "prototype," which we will name *documentPrototypeS*) and a prototype *Customer* object (which we will name *customerPrototypeS*). In addition, each subclass of *Document* must have a *clone()* method: one which makes an entirely separate copy of a *Document* object: similarly for *Customer*. This is shown in the object model in Figure 6.29, where *Client* is a user class of *MyOfficeApplication*. The code in *MyOfficeApplication* does not need to know which type of *Document* object it is dealing with. Whenever method code in *MyOfficeApplication* needs a new *Document* object, it executes

```
Document d = documentPrototypeS.clone()
```
— instead of
```
Document d = new Document().
```

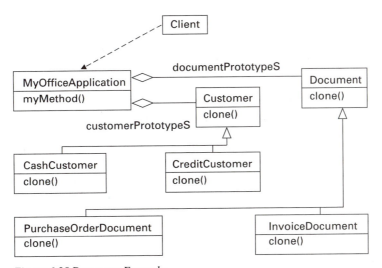

Figure 6.29 Prototype *Example*

```
public class MyOfficeApplication
{   private static Document documentPrototypeS;
    private static Customer customerPrototypeS;
    public MyOfficeApplication
      (Document dPrototypeP, Customer cPrototypeP)
    {   documentPrototypeS = dPrototypeP;
        customerPrototypeS = cPrototypeP;}
      public myMethod
        .... // Need a new Document object:
        Document d = documentPrototypeS.clone();
        .... // Need a new Customer object:
        Customer c = customerPrototypeS.clone(); . . .
```

This class is unaware of which type (subclass) of *Document* or *Customer* it is being executed with

Figure 6.30 Prototype *Design Pattern*, 1 of 2

```
abstract class Document
{   protected Document clone();
}
```

```
public class InvoiceDocument extends Document
{   . . . .
    protected Document clone()
    {. . . return new InvoiceDocument();
    }
```

Customer has an equivalent hierarchy of classes implementing clone()

```
public class PurchaseOrderDocument extends Document
{   . . . .
    protected Document clone()
    {. . . . return new PurchaseOrderDocument();
    }
```

Figure 6.31 Prototype *Design Pattern*, 2 of 2

This ensures that a consistent type of *Document* object is produced throughout the application. Code for this would look like that shown in Figure 6.30 and Figure 6.31.

We mentioned in Section 2.5 of Chapter 5 that the use of a design pattern by client code generally requires additional setup code. Setup code would supply *MyOfficeApplication* with a *Document* prototype (subtype) and a *Customer* prototype at run time with a statement in a manner such as

```
m = new MyOfficeApplication // supply the prototypes
( new PurchaseOrderDocument(), new CashCustomer() );
```

5.1.4 Abstract Factory *and* Builder

The problem: A family of related objects must be created at run time from several possible families. For example, consider an architecture package that generates house plans. At run time we would like to be able to see what one particular house plan looks like in Tudor style (where the walls, doors, roof, etc., are all in Tudor style), or in Modern style, etc. simply by selecting the style rather than drawing the house each time with separate code.

The *Abstract Factory* pattern: *Abstract Factory* consists of using the method

```
anAbstractFactoryObject.getThing()
```

in client code, instead of new Thing(). At run time, *anAbstractFactoryObject* is set to an object of the desired subclass of *AbstractFactory,* so that the objects it creates are coordinated.

Turning to the case study, suppose that we want to reward *Encounter* players when they reach higher levels by showing the areas and connections in new, coordinated styles. The areas with various styles are naturally subclasses of the *Area* class, and the connection classes are subclasses of *AreaConnection*. The challenge for our design of *Encounter* is to enable client code that does not mention the various levels. "Client" code here refers to the code that uses *Area* objects. This design would make upgrading and maintenance much easier.

It would be clumsy and inflexible to write the following statements in the client code or in *EncounterEnvironment*

```
area[5] = new Area(); // to be replaced!
connection[5] = new AreaConnection(); // to be replaced!
```

For example, it would be awkward to vary the area levels and connection levels at run time (e.g., change them from level 3 to level 4 style). In particular we would have to replace these lines with switch statements and pairs of statements such as

```
area[5] = new Lev8Area(); // clumsy
connection[5] = new Lev8AreaConnection(); // clumsy
```

Besides cluttering the client code, this also increases the dependence ("coupling") among parts of the design.

We can solve this problem by using an *Abstract Factory* class. This is a class — *Environment Factory* in this case — with abstract methods that promise to create the desired components. Subclasses — *Level1Factory, Level2Factory,* and *Level3Factory,* etc., in this case — each have coordinated working versions of these methods. Figure 6.32 shows the relationship among the classes in the case of *Level2Factory*.

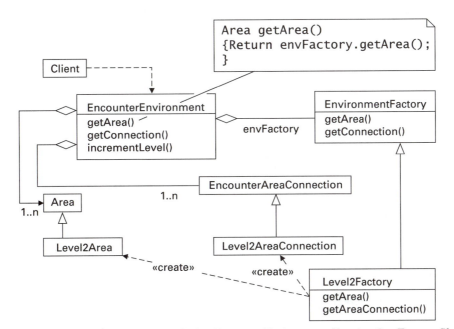

Figure 6.32 Abstract Factory *Applied to* EncounterEnvironment *Showing One* Factory *Class*

EncounterEnvironment aggregates an *EnvironmentFactory* object which we have named *envFactory*. When the client calls *getArea()* on the *EncounterEnvironment* object, this call is converted into the call *getArea()* on *envFactory*. If the game is at level 2, this results in the creation of a level 2 area. Similarly, calls to *getConnection()* will result in the creation of level 2 connections.

When the player reaches the next level, the client could call *incrementLevel()* on *EncounterEnvironment*. This has the effect of setting *envFactory* to a *Level3Builder* object. Alternatively, external controlling code could be asked to do this (see Section 2.5 of Chapter 5). The same client code will now create level 3 areas and connections. The client code does mention the levels themselves.

Figure 6.33 shows the object model with three levels. With this object model, instead of using lines in *EncounterEnvironment* of the form

```
area[5] = new Area(); // replace!
```

we use

```
area[5] = envFactory.getArea();
```

and instead of

```
connection[5] = new AreaConnection(); // replace!
```

we use

```
connection[5] = envFactory.getAreaConnection()
```

When the program is executed, *envFactory* is instantiated as an instance of a *subclass* of *EnvironmentFactory* (for example, a *Level9Factory* object). In this case, *EnvironmentFactory*'s version of *getArea()* produces only *Level9Area* objects, as illustrated by the dotted lines in the figure. Its version of *getAreaConnection()* produces only *Level9AreaConnection* objects, so that a consistent style is produced by the *EncounterEnvironment* code at run time.

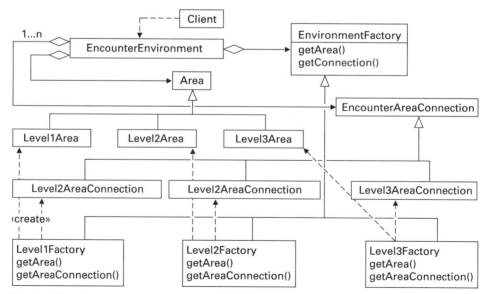

Figure 6.33 Abstract Factory *Applied to* EncounterEnvironment *Showing Several* Factory *Classes*

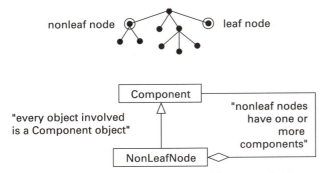

Figure 6.34 The Basis for Composite *and* Decorator *Structures*

5.2 Structural Patterns for Detailed Design

Structural patterns represent complex objects such as lists, collections, and trees as objects with convenient interfaces.

5.2.1 Composite *and* Decorator

The problem: Suppose that we want to represent a tree of objects (e.g., a company organization chart) or a linked list of objects.

The *Composite* and *Decorator* design patterns: The heart of a solution is to use the inherit/aggregate relationship illustrated in Figure 6.34. The idea is to show that some components aggregate other components. This is fleshed out in Figure 6.35. The class model includes components, *Leaf* objects, that do not aggregate other components. The pattern operates in the following manner. A *Composite* object executes *doIt()* in a manner that depends on a *Leaf* object, which is a simple execution, or a *NonLeafNode* object. A *NonLeafNode* object calls on each of its aggregated "descendents" to execute *doIt()*. These *Component* objects continue the process down the tree structure.

Suppose, for example, that the tree is actually a management organizational chart and "*doIt()*" is "*displayEmployee()*." In this case *Component* would be better called *Employee* and *NonLeafNode* would be better called *Supervisor*. *Leaf* would be termed something like *IndividualContributor*. Calling *displayEmployee()* on the *Component* object, which represents the whole organization, causes each of the objects to execute its *displayEmployee()* method and then call *displayEmployee()* on all of its subordinates. For vice presidents (e.g., *TypeANonLeafNode* being *SeniorVP*) the method *displayEmployee()*

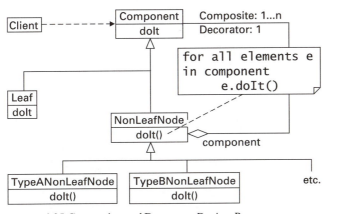

Figure 6.35 Composite *and* Decorator *Design Patterns*

could have a different effect, such as the inclusion of a biographical press release, compared with *displayEmployee()* for first-line supervisors (*TypeBNonLeafNode* being *FirstLineSupervisor*), etc.

Decorator has a simpler delegation property. *Decorator* creates a linked list, and the aggregation in Figure 6.34 involves only a single *Component* object. For example, if *textWindow* is a *Decorator* object that links several embellishments surrounding a block of text (e.g., scroll bars), then calling a method *display()* on *textWindow* has the effect of displaying each of the embellishments in sequence followed by the text itself. The text would be encapsulated as an object of the *Leaf* class.

5.2.2 Facade

The problem: Applications can consist of hundreds of classes, whereas humans are able to comfortably comprehend only five to nine entities at once. How can classes be organized into a comfortable number of collections, each with a clearly understandable interface?

The *Facade* design pattern: We have already used the *Facade* structural design pattern in Chapter 5 on Architectures (see Section 3.2.1 on page 266). When *Facade* is used, the resulting number of packages is manageable, as illustrated in Figure 6.36. The *Facade* objects are provided with enough (public) methods to enable users of the packages to access all of the objects and functionality that they require. Discussions in Chapter 5 emphasize the utility of framework classes in conjunction with *Facade*.

5.2.3 Adapter

The problem: Suppose that an existing application, or even just an existing object, provides functionality that our own application requires. For example, suppose that an existing application computes the principal obtained from investing a given quantity at a given interest rate for a given number of years in a special type of investment. We want to modify our own application as little as possible, but we want it to take advantage of the existing computation, and we also want to be prepared to later utilize alternative existing computations.

The *Adapter* design pattern: We first write our application by giving our own appropriate names to the function of interest, and the class/object that owns the function. For example, the method

```
amount( float originalAmount, float numYears, float intRate )
```

in the class *Financial*. This class is made abstract.

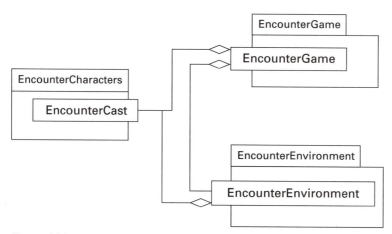

Figure 6.36 Architecture of Encounter: *Class Model*

Suppose that the functionality in the *existing* application is expressed as a method of a class, for example

```
computeValue( float years, float interest, float amount )
```

in the class *Principal*. This is illustrated in Figure 6.37

The *Adapter* design pattern consists of a class that we will name *FinancialAdapter* for illustration, that inherits from the application's class (*Financial* in our case), and that aggregates the legacy class (in this case *Principal*).

This could be implemented in Java, for example, as follows.

```
class FinancialAdapter extends Financial {
    Principal legacyAdaptee = null;
    // Constructors go here . . .
    /** This method uses the legacy computeValue() method */
    float amount( float originalAmount, float numYears, float intRate ) {
        return legacyAdaptee.computeValue
            ( originalAmount, numYears, intRate );
    } // end of method amount()
} // end of class FinancialAdapter
```

The new application is *written* against the class *Financial* and executed at run time against a *FinancialAdapter* object. (As the object model shows, *FinancialAdapter* objects are *Financial* objects, so this is permissible.) For example, the application could be *written* with a method parameterizing *Financial,* such as

```
void executeFinanceApplication( Financial aFinancial );
```

It could then be *executed* with the statement

```
executeFinanceApplication( new FinancialAdapter() );
```

All calls to the *amount()* method of *Financial* are passed to the legacy method *computeValue()*.

It is simple to adapt the application to a new implementation of *amount()* in a new class. We would only have to change the code in *FinancialAdapter:* The rest of the application would not be affected.

To preserve the option to retarget at run time we could retain *FinancialAdapter* but introduce a new *Adapter* class *FinancialAdapter2,* inheriting from *Financial.* Whenever

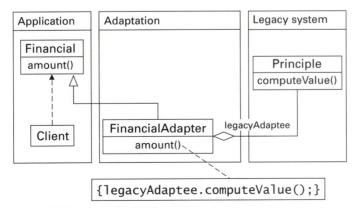

Figure 6.37 Adapter *Design Pattern*

we want to target the application to the second legacy system we would execute the application with

```
executeFinanceApplication( new FinancialAdapter2() );
```

Being able to retarget code by making localized changes like this (as opposed to changes in several locations) is valuable for development and maintenance.

The same effect can be obtained by *inheriting* `FinancialAdapter` from `Financial` and `Principle` instead of using aggregation.

5.2.4 Flyweight   The problem: Suppose that an application needs to deal with a large number of almost indistinguishable "small" objects. For example, suppose that our video game uses artifacts like *energy packets* and *swords*. A hundred energy packets (small indistinguishable objects) could be active at the same time.

Another example is an application that reformats text for various formats (print format, browser format, hand held device format, etc.). In principle, it might be useful to define each "c" in the text as a different object. On the other hand, the proliferation of large numbers of separate objects can be hard to manage and wasteful of storage space.

The *Flyweight* design pattern: *Flyweight* avoids making a separate object for every fine-grained entity by using a single object for the entities and by parameterizing the methods. In the above example, we would use only one object for all the "c" characters. The alternative to multiple video game *EnergyPacket* objects is a single *EnergyPacket* object with methods parameterized by the context in which this *EnergyPacket* object is being used. The game characters would need only to retain the number of energy packets that they possess. Thus, instead of

```
energyPacket[23].expend() ...... energyPacket[74].expend (),
```

we would use

```
theEnergyPacket.expend( mainCharacter, courtyard ) ......

theEnergyPacket.expend( freddie, dungeon )
```

Flyweight is typically used in conjunction with a *Factory* object that checks whether or not an appropriate object has already been created. If so, the object is returned; if not, it is created and made available for future reuse.

5.2.5 Proxy   The problem: Suppose that a method is expensive to execute because it requires a time-consuming process like downloading an image from the network or drawing graphics. We may not be able to prevent the method from being called, but we do want to prevent the method from performing its expensive portions unnecessarily.

The *Proxy* design pattern: Suppose that *RealActiveClass* is a class containing a method *expensiveMethod()*, which we want to avoid executing unnecessarily. We introduce an abstract class *BaseActiveClass* from which *RealActiveClass* inherits. The *Proxy* design pattern involves introducing a class that we will call *Proxy* that also inherits from *BaseActiveClass*. *Proxy* also contains a method called *expensiveMethod()*, which references *RealActiveClass*, as shown in Figure 6.38.

The idea is that *Proxy*'s *expensiveMethod()* is a "fake" expensive method. The client application is written in terms of *BaseActiveClass*. At run time the application executes with a *Proxy* object. This object effectively intercepts references that would otherwise refer directly to *RealActiveClass*. *Proxy* does not allow *RealActiveClass* objects to be created except where necessary. In addition, *Proxy*'s version of *expensiveMethod()*, which the ap-

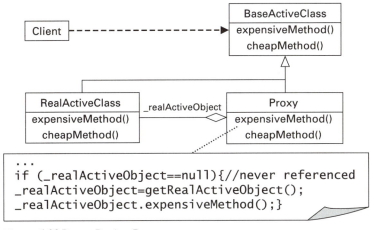

Figure 6.38 Proxy *Design Pattern*

plication calls, does not perform expensive parts more than is necessary. When such a call is necessary the *Proxy* object transfers the call on its *expensiveMethod()* to a call on *expensiveMethod()* of the *RealActiveClass* object.

For example, *RealActiveClass* could have a large disk-resident bit map attribute. *Proxy*'s *draw()* method would retrieve the bit map only if it had not already been loaded. If *draw()* is never called, the bit map is never retrieved from disk. Where possible, the bit map would already be resident in memory when *draw()* is called again.

5.3 Behavioral Patterns for Detailed Design

Behavioral patterns encapsulate application behavior options, allowing the behavior to vary at run time. Without these patterns, we would have to design and implement each behavior entirely separately.

5.3.1 Interpreter, Observer, and State
The *Interpreter* design pattern is described in Section 3.3 of Chapter 5 (page 272). The *Observer* pattern is described in Section 3.2.2.1 of Chapter 5 (page 269). The *State* design patterns is described in Section 3.2.3 of Chapter 5 (page 270).

5.3.2 Iterator
The problem: Many applications require code that "visits" a set of objects in different ways. One example of such a set is an organization chart. An example of visiting behavior on this set is the process of printing the names in alphabetical order; another is printing them by organizational responsibility (senior managers first, etc.). Another example of "visiting," this time on a database, is a search, as in "give me all customers who owe more than $500 and who are late on their accounts." We want to write the visiting code generically, concentrating on the actions that must be performed when the objects are visited. We want to be able to specify the required visiting sequence at run time.

The *Iterator* design pattern: The *Iterator* design patterns centers on *Iterator* classes, sometimes called "smart pointers." Every *Iterator* class has *state*—effectively a reference to an element of the set of objects that it is designed to visit. A simple example is an *Iterator* that applies to an array. In this case, the iterator's state could consist simply of an integer—an index in the array. Figure 6.39 illustrates how *Iterator* works.

Iterators are equipped to visit a set of *Item* objects if they have the following methods.

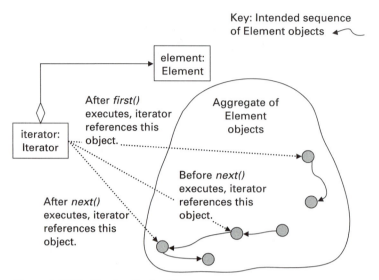

Figure 6.39 The Iterator *Design Pattern*

1. *first()*—sets the *Iterator* object to reference what it considers the "first" element of the set
2. *getItem()*—returns a reference to the current item
3. *next()*—bumps the *Iterator* ("pointer") object to reference what it considers the "next" element
4. *last()*—returns TRUE if *Iterator* object is "pointing" past the end of its sequential "route" through the set

Sometimes, *getItem()* and *next()* are combined.

The code for a complete visit sequence of a particular *Iterator* i to its set of objects is shown next. The elements involved, and also the order, are effectively specified by i. When each item is identified, *doWhatever()* performs its function on the item.

```
for( i.first(); i.last(); i.next() )
        i.getItem().doWhatever();
```

5.3.3 Mediator   The problem: Objects of classes frequently interact with each other in complex ways. We want to capture behavioral relationships between objects without building knowledge about each other into those objects. For example, when a GUI display is called for to set the qualities of a game character in the *Encounter* case study, a list box of qualities appears (a Java *Component* object). Also appearing is a text box for setting the value of a particular game character quality (another *Component* object). Actions performed on the list box affect the text box.

We don't want to build into the "game character quality list box display," knowledge about text boxes displaying or setting the values of these qualities. The latter would compromise the portability of the list box, would inhibit modifications to the design, and would make it hard for us to use the same list box in another display interacting with other components.

Another example of the interaction among objects is the "graying out" of word processor menu items when they do not apply to the text displayed. The menu and the current display interact.

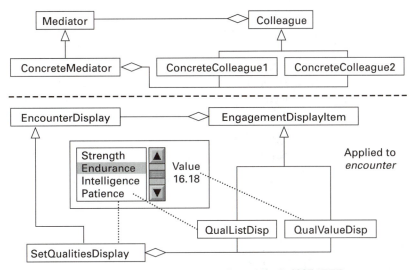

Figure 6.40 The Mediator *Design Pattern   Copyright © 1987 IEEE*

The *Mediator* design pattern: *Mediator* solves this problem by building into every mediated component a reference to a generic mediating object (but not a reference to any particular mediated object). This mediating object assumes the burden of maintaining the relationship between the objects. This is shown in Figure 6.40.

The design pattern in Figure 6.40 consists of a base class *Mediator,* each subclass of which encapsulates desired interaction among objects of *ConcreteColleague1, ConcreteColleague2,* and so on. All interacting objects belong to subclasses of a base class *Colleague,* which references *Mediator.* This ensures that the interacting objects need not know about each other. The lower part of Figure 6.40 applies *Mediator* to the *Encounter* example. When a quality on the list box is clicked (in the left part of the figure), the *QualListDisp* object tells us it aggregated *EncounterDisplay* mediator object to handle the event. This mediator object, set at run time to an object of *SetQualitiesDisplay,* tells the *QualValueDisp* object to display the value of the quality in question. It's a roundabout route but it accomplishes the goal of having *QualListDisp* and *QualValueDisp* not refer to each other. They can thus be used as part of other behavior, as is done in the case study.

6. THE STANDARD TEMPLATE LIBRARY

Invented by Stepanov, the Standard Template Library (STL) is a template-based library of standard, reusable data structures and algorithms. STL is a part of the ANSI C++ standard. A good reference is Musser, Saini, and Stepanov [Mu]. STL consists mainly of

- **Containers.** These contain collections of objects. They include vectors, lists, stacks, and queues. For example, for classes *X, list<X>* is a container which provides access to variable length sequences of objects in the form of a doubly linked list. *list<X>* has methods such as *push_back(X)* to push objects onto the end of the list.

- **Generic algorithms.** Generic algorithms manipulate STL containers and include insertion, deletion, searching, and sorting. For example, *find(*X begin, *X end, X objectWanted)*, where *X* is a class, is a generic function.

- **Iterators.** Iterators perform an operation on the elements of a container, as discussed in Section 5.3.2 above.

- **Function objects.** Each function object takes an argument and returns a result, but is an entire object in itself. Function objects include *divide, logical_and, not_equal_to,* and the like. One example is a general function for accumulating selected elements in a sequence:

```
accumulate( InputIterator first, InputIterator last, X initialValue,
BinaryOperation binaryOp )
```

where the base classes referenced in the parameter list are defined in STL.

- **Adapters.** Adapters were discussed in Section 5.2.3 above.

7. STANDARDS, NOTATION AND TOOLS FOR DETAILED DESIGN

7.1 IEEE Standard 890 for Detailed Design

Recall IEEE standard 890 for Software Design Documents shown in Chapter 5 on software architecture, as shown in Figure 6.41. This format for the detailed design section of this document consists simply of a description of each module (package) in turn, with a detailed description of each data part. For OO designs, the latter can be replaced with a detailed description of each class.

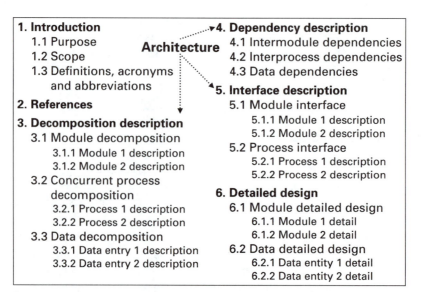

```
1. Introduction                    ▸4. Dependency description
   1.1 Purpose      Architecture     4.1 Intermodule dependencies
   1.2 Scope                         4.2 Interprocess dependencies
   1.3 Definitions, acronyms         4.3 Data dependencies
       and abbreviations           5. Interface description
2. References                        5.1 Module interface
                                          5.1.1 Module 1 description
3. Decomposition description              5.1.2 Module 2 description
   3.1 Module decomposition          5.2 Process interface
       3.1.1 Module 1 description         5.2.1 Process 1 description
       3.1.2 Module 2 description         5.2.2 Process 2 description
   3.2 Concurrent process
       decomposition              6. Detailed design
       3.2.1 Process 1 description    6.1 Module detailed design
       3.2.2 Process 2 description        6.1.1 Module 1 detail
   3.3 Data decomposition               6.1.2 Module 2 detail
       3.3.1 Data entry 1 description 6.2 Data detailed design
       3.3.2 Data entry 2 description     6.2.1 Data entity 1 detail
                                          6.2.2 Data entity 2 detail
```

Figure 6.41 IEEE 1016-1989 (Reaffirmed 1993) Software Design Document

7.2 The Unified Modeling Language (UML) for Detailed Object Models

We have already used the UML to describe the use cases and the classes involved in an architecture (see Section 3 on page 312, and Section 2.2 in Chapter 5, on page 256). The UML allows for the display of all of the methods in a detailed design, as illustrated on the inside cover. Since classes generally contain many methods, it is often desirable to display them selectively. Tools such as Rational Rose™ and Together/J™ allow selective displays. They also facilitate zooming onto portions of the object model.

7.3 Source-Based Tools: Javadoc

Hyperlinked class hierarchy diagrams can be generated from source code. For example, *Javadoc* produces lists of the classes belonging to packages, and of the methods belonging to classes. From source comments obeying a specific format, Javadoc also generates descriptions of these components. Source with Javadoc comments is illustrated in Figure 6.42 and Figure 6.43. Extensive use of Javadoc is made in the case studies at the ends of Chapters 7 and 8. The meaning of the "/**.....*/," "@author," "@version," and "@param" keywords are evident from the output shown below.

```
/**
Character of role-playing games.
@author Eric Braude
@version 0.1, 7/14/98
*/
public abstract class GameCharacter
{
    /**
    Name of the game character;
    initially null
    */
    private String _name;
    /**
    No character name will
    ever exceed this length
    */
    public final int
    alltimeLimitOfNameLength()

    . . .

    /** For logging*/
    protected void display()

    . . .
    /**
    Accessor of_name.
    "defaultName" assigned
    if this is first-time
    access
    */
    public String getName()

    . . .
```

Figure 6.42 Java Source with Javadoc, 1 of 2

```
/**
Subclasses must declare limit on size of character names
*/
protected abstract int maxNumCharsInName();

/**
Sets _name to aName if length is within aMaxNumChars
in length; otherwise truncates
Inheritors should use this for setName(String), but not override
@param aName: proposed name for _name
@param aMaxNumChars — at which to truncate aName
*/
protected final void setName( String aName ) . . .
. . . . . . . .
```

Figure 6.43 Java Source with Javadoc, 2 of 2

The code in the figures generates the following *Javadoc* documentation, which is shown in an edited form. The *Javadoc* output can be made more appealing by inserting HTML tags in the source.

Class Characters.GameCharacter

```
java.lang.Object
   |
   + − − − Characters.GameCharacter
```

---

public abstract class **GameCharacter**
extends Object
Character of role-playing games.

Variable Index
_name
  Name of the game character; initially null

Constructor Index
__GameCharacter__( )

Method Index
__alltimeLimitOfNameLength__( )
  No character name will ever exceed this length
__display__( )
  For logging
__getName__( )
  Accessor of _name
__main__(String[])
  Runs test of this class
__maxNumCharsInName__( )
  Name of the game character; initially null
__setName__(String, int)
  Sets _name to aName if length is within aMaxNumChars in length; otherwise truncates Inheritors should use this for setName, never override
__testForGameCharacterClass__(String)
  Tests all the methods of this class

Variables
_name
```
private String _name
```
Name of the game character; initially null

Constructors
GameCharacter
```
public GameCharacter()
```

Methods
alltimeLimitOfNameLength
```
private int alltimeLimitOfNameLength()
```
  No character name will ever exceed this length
display
```
protected void display()
```
  For logging
getName
```
protected String getName()
```
  Accessor of _name
maxNumCharsInName
```
protected static int maxNumCharsInName()
```
  Name of the game character; initially null
setName
```
protected final void setName(String aName,
                             int aMaxNumChars)
```
  Sets _name to aName if length is within aMaxNumChars in length; otherwise
    truncates Inheritors should use this for setName, never override
Parameters:
  aName: - proposed name for _name
  aMaxNumChars - --at which to truncate aName
main
```
public static void main(String args[])
```
  Runs test of this class
testForGameCharacterClass
```
public static void testForGameCharacterClass(String
                          aDestination) throws IOException
```
  Tests all the methods of this class

Tools such as *Javadoc* implement a kind of *reverse engineering*. This means that the documentation for a product (including the design) is produced after, rather than before, the product has been built. Some degree of reverse engineering invariably takes place even in well-engineered projects. In particular, programmers find it necessary to add methods which are not specified by the detailed design. Reverse engineering is counterproductive, however, if it *replaces* architecture selection and detailed design.

The case study uses *Javadoc*. A full reference to *Javadoc* can be found in [Ja4].

8. EFFECTS OF DETAILED DESIGNS ON PROJECTS

With a detailed design in hand, the project plan can be made more specific in several respects. In particular, cost estimation can be made much more precise, schedules can be

---

One Way To. . . Bring the Project Up-to-Date After Completing Detailed Design

1. Make sure the SDD reflects the latest version of detailed design, as settled on after inspections.

2. Give complete detail to the schedule (SPMP).

3. Allocate precise tasks to team members (SPMP).

4. Improve project cost and time estimates (see below).

5. Update the SCMP to reflect the new parts.

6. Review process by which the detailed design was created, and determine improvements. Include
   • time taken; broken down to include
     • *preparation of the designs*
     • *inspection*
     • *change*
   • defect summary
     • *number remaining open, found at detailed stage, closed at detailed design*
     • *where injected; include previous phases and detailed design stages*

Figure 6.44 One Way to Bring the Project Up to Date after Completing Detailed Design

broken down into tasks, and tasks can be allocated to individuals. Figure 6.44 includes most of the important updates to be performed once detailed design is complete.

8.1 Estimating Size from Detailed Designs

Since we can estimate the number and size of the methods involved in the application using detailed designs, a more precise estimation of the job size is possible. As described in Chapter 2, job costs can then be inferred from the size. Figure 6.45 shows steps for carrying this out.

The COCOMO model can now be used again to refine the estimate of job duration. It is best to use personal data to estimate the LOC for *very small, small*, etc. jobs.

One Way To. . . Estimate Size and Time from Detailed Designs

1. Start with the list of methods
   • ensures completeness, otherwise underestimate will result

2. Estimate the lines of code (LOC) for each
   • classify as *very small, small, medium, large, very large*
     • *normally in ± 7%/24%/38%/24%/7% proportions*
   • use personal data to convert to LOC
     • *otherwise use Humphrey's table below*

3. Sum the LOC

4. Convert LOC to person-hours
   • use personal conversion factor if possible
     • *otherwise use published factor*

5. Ensure that your estimates of method sizes and time will be compared and saved at project end.

Figure 6.45 One Way to Estimate Size and Time from Detailed Designs

TABLE 6.1 Lines of code (Humphrey)

Method type	Category				
	Very small	Small	Medium	Large	Very large
Calculation	2.34	5.13	11.25	24.66	54.04
Data	2.60	4.79	8.84	16.31	30.09
I/O	9.01	12.06	16.15	21.62	28.93
Logic	7.55	10.98	15.98	23.25	33.83
Set-up	3.88	5.04	6.56	8.53	11.09
Text	3.75	8.00	17.07	36.41	77.67

In the absence of such data, department, division, or corporate data can be used. Otherwise, Humphrey's table (Table 6.1) [Hu] can be used. Table 6.1 applies to C++ LOC per method.

Calculation methods perform numerical computation; *data* methods manipulate data (e.g., reformatting); *logic* methods consist mainly of branching; *setup* methods initialize situations; *text* methods manipulate text. Estimates for methods which combine several of these can be computed by averaging. For example, an unexceptional ("medium") method that performs calculations but also has a substantial logic component can be estimated as having $(11.25 + 15.98) / 2 = 13.62$ lines of code.

Capers Jones [Jo3] estimates that, on the average, Java and C++ require the same number of LOC to accomplish given functionality.

Descriptors such as *Very Small*, and *Small* are "fuzzy" in that they describe ranges rather than precise amounts. These ranges can overlap, in which case an average of the corresponding table values can be used. (This is actually a simplification of fuzziness, but adequate for our purpose.) Fuzzy descriptors are practical because they are easy to understand. They can be made more precise by categorization with the normal distribution, as shown in Figure 6.46.

On the average, about 38% of the methods should be classified as "medium," 24% "small," and 7% "very small," as illustrated in Figure 6.45. These numbers are obtained from the fact that about 38% of the values in a normal distribution are within a half of a

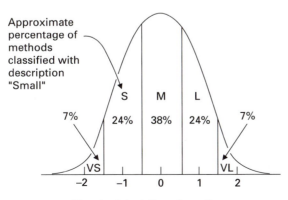

Standard deviations from the mean

Figure 6.46 Normal distribution of "Medium," "Small," etc.

standard deviation of the mean. In practical terms, if the fraction of methods you estimate as "very large" differs much from 7%, for example, then you should be satisfied that your application really does have an unusual number of very large methods. Otherwise, you should revise your estimates.

As an example, let's estimate the size of the *execute()* method of the *Engagement* class. This method involves the recalculation of quality values, which is the essential mechanism of executing the engagement process. For this reason, we could classify the *execute()* method as a "calculation." The size of the *execute()* method is not particularly remarkable, since it consists of a fairly straightforward computation of values, so we'll classify it as "medium." Thus, the estimated contribution of *execute()* is 11.25 LOC.

A level 5 organization (see Section 8.3, page 57 of Chapter 1 on the Capability Maturity Model) would typically plot method size estimates against actual sizes in order to improve this estimation process.

In the case study, these estimates are applied to the *Encounter* video game.

9.   QUALITY IN DETAILED DESIGNS

In order to obtain a good detailed design we should be able to recognize one when we see it. Some of this is aesthetic in nature, and a clean design has appeal in its own right. Nevertheless, there are useful quantitative measures of design quality. In this section we review quantitative measures of effectiveness in detailed design. Figure 6.47 and Figure 6.48 provide steps for ensuring the quality of detailed designs.

Some metrics for detailed design are provided in this section, satisfying step 1 in Figure 6.47. Steps 2, 3, and 4 are checks that the detailed design expands on all of the architecture, and nothing more.

Step 5 ensures that the design is complete. It is easy enough to check, as we do in step 7, that every method of every class is properly specified, but how do we know that we have included all of the classes and methods that are necessary? To do this, we return to the requirements and ensure that the detailed design we have developed accommodates all of the requirements. If we use the requirements organization as in the case study, then we know that every functional requirement corresponds to a specific method. Thus, the func-

---

One Way To. . . Inspect Detailed Designs, 1 of 2

1. Prepare to record metrics during the design process.
    - Include (1.1) time taken; (1.2) type of defect; (1.3) severity
2. Ensure each architecture module is expanded.
3. Ensure each detail is part of the architecture.
    - if a detail does not belong to any such module, the architecture may have to be revised
4. Ensure the design fulfills its required functions.
5. Ensure that design is complete (classes and methods).
6. Ensure that design is testable.

See Chapter 1 for inspection procedures.

Figure 6.47 One Way to Inspect Detailed Designs, 1 of 2

One Way To. . . Inspect Detailed Designs, 2 of 2

7. Check detailed design for
   - simplicity

     a design that few can understand (after a legitimate effort!) is expensive to maintain and can result in defects
   - generality

     enables design of similar applications?
   - expandability

     enables enhancements?
   - efficiency

     speed, storage
   - portability
8. Ensure all details are provided
   - only code itself is excluded as a "detail"
   - the detail work must be done eventually, and this is the best time to do it: don't postpone

---

Figure 6.48 One Way to Inspect Detailed Designs, 2 of 2

tional completeness task is reduced to ensuring that each of these methods can be called at an appropriate point in the execution. Consider, for example, the requirement

> ***3.2.EC.3.2*** *Configurability of* **Encounter** *character quality values*
> *Whenever an* Encounter *character is alone in an area, the value of any of its qualities may be set. The value chosen must be less than or equal to the sum of the quality values.*

We have already ensured that a function to perform this requirement exists, but to verify that our design supports the execution of this function, we have to effectively walk through a fully representative set of function calling sequences, each of which exercises the function. This amounts to developing a set of mental test cases, and the results should be saved for the testing phase. Here is such a set.

> *Begin game; call up window to set qualities; set quality; set quality again; dismiss window.*
> *Move to area with no foreign character; call up window to set qualities; set quality; dismiss window.*
> *Complete engagement; wait until foreign character departs; call up window to set qualities; set quality; dismiss window.*

For each of these scenarios, we verify that the classes and methods do indeed exist to accommodate it. Once we have done this for every functional requirement, we will have verified our design from the functional point of view. We can do the same thing with our detailed design for every nonfunctional requirement: We can verify mentally, and via calculation (e.g., in the case of timing) that the design supports each of them. Once again, the work we do to create each of these sequences can be used to develop tests which we apply once the implementation has been performed. We continue the steps in Figures 6.47 and 6.48.

Step 6 calls for testability. In other words, is it convenient to test the elements of the design? A design that can't be readily separated into parts tends to be untestable. An effective way to ensure this property is to write tests for each design element as soon as it is specified.

Step 7 has to do with the properties that we desire from our detailed designs. Ideally, we want all of these properties, but this is usually not possible. In particular, simplicity may be in conflict with generality and expandability. For example, to obtain generality in the design of Figure 1.5 on page 20, we used three classes instead of two, thereby compromising its simplicity. Design patterns often introduce additional classes, too. Thus, it is best to specify in advance which of these properties we care most about, then evaluate the design against them. If portability is required, we can establish scenarios for implementation on each desired platform.

Step 8 checks that every detail is given, short of code. It is common for designers to postpone many details until implementation time because it is time consuming. This is usually a mistake, however. The fact is that we have many issues to consider at implementation time, and so thinking through details beforehand, and inspecting them separately, can pay off handsomely.

9.1 Qualities and Metrics for Detailed Design

Detailed design metrics typically include counting the number of modules, functions, entry points, and exit points. For object-oriented implementations, this translates into counting the number of packages, the number of classes, the number of methods, the number of parameters, the number of attributes, etc.

A somewhat more comprehensive, though more complicated metric is IEEE metric 19 "design structure" (see [IEEE 982]), which determines "the simplicity of the detailed design" of a program.

9.2 Inspection of Detailed Designs

The principles and practice of inspections were expressed in Section 6.4 of Chapter 1 (page 41). The inspection of detailed designs consists of inspecting classes, their method prototypes (name, return type, and parameter types), the flowcharts and pseudocode, and the relationships among classes and methods within various models. These models can include the use case models and their associated sequence diagrams, the class model, the state models, and the data flow model.

9.2.1 Classifying Defects   As with all inspections, data about each defect are noted, including its severity, its type, and also the probable source of the defect in the project life cycle. In particular, the IEEE standard 1044.1 classifies severity as shown in Table 6.2.

A less expensive (i.e., less time-consuming to collect), but also less useful classification can be obtained using triage (see Table 6.3).

Defect *types* can include those listed below, which have been taken from IEEE standard 1044.1-1995. The types that apply to detailed designs for *Javadoc*-level inspections are marked "XDOC," and for pseudocode-level inspections are marked "PS".

Logic problem (forgotten cases or steps; duplicate logic; extreme conditions neglected; unnecessary functions; misinterpretation; missing condition test; checking wrong variable; iterating loop incorrectly, etc.) [PS]

Computational problem (equation insufficient or incorrect; precision loss; sign convention fault) [PS]

Interface/Timing problem (interrupts handled incorrectly; I/O timing incorrect; subroutine/module mismatch) [PS]

TABLE 6.2 IEEE 1044.1 Severity Classification

Severity	Description
Urgent	Failure causes system crash, unrecoverable data loss; or jeopardizes personnel
High	Causes impairment of critical system functions, and no workaround solution exists
Medium	Causes impairment of critical system functions, although a workaround solution does exist
Low	Causes inconvenience or annoyance
None	None of the above

Copyright © 1996 IEEE

TABLE 6.3 Defect Severity Classification Using Triage

Severity	Description
Major	Requirement(s) not satisfied
Medium	Neither major nor trivial
Trivial	A defect which will not affect operation or maintenance

Data handling problem (initialized data incorrectly; accessed or stored data incorrectly; scaling or units of data incorrect; dimension of data incorrect) [XDOC, PS]

Scope of data incorrect [XDOC, PS]

Data problem (sensor data incorrect or missing; operator data incorrect or missing; embedded data in tables incorrect or missing; external data incorrect or missing; output data incorrect or missing; input data incorrect or missing) [XDOC, PS]

Documentation problem (ambiguous description, etc.) [XDOC, PS]

Document quality problem (applicable standards not met, etc.) [XDOC, PS]

Enhancement (change in program requirements, etc.) [XDOC, PS]

Failure caused by a previous fix [XDOC, PS]

Performance problem (associated with test phase)

Interoperability problem (not compatible with other software or components) [XDOC, PS]

Standards conformance problem [XDOC, PS]

Other (none of the above) [XDOC, PS]

9.2.2 Examples of Detailed Requirement Inspection

In this section we will inspect pseudocode examples. The inspection focuses on defects in *commission* (whether the methods chosen are appropriate) and *omission* (whether there are other methods that should be included).

The pseudocode for a method should be checked against the corresponding requirement in the SRS or in the SDD. For example, the following is an early draft of a D-requirements of *Encounter* from the SRS:

> *"[essential] Every game character has the same set of qualities. Each quality shall be a non-negative floating point number with at least one decimal of precision. These are all initialized equally so that the sum of their values is 100. For the first release the qualities shall be* concentration, stamina, intelligence, patience, *and* strength. *The value of a quality cannot be both greater than zero and less than 0.5."*

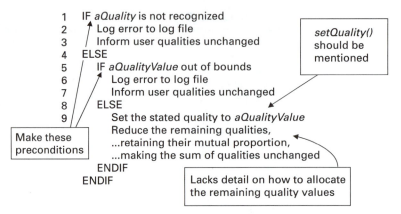

Figure 6.49 Inspecting Pseudocode

This requirement is implemented by the function *adjustQuality(String aQuality, float aQualityValue)* with the pseudocode to be inspected as shown in Figure 6.49.

An inspection of this pseudocode should expose the following defects.

1. Line 9: method *setQuality()* should be mentioned
2. Line 10: lacks detail on how to allocate the remaining quality values; also, why always "reduce" (why not sometimes "increase")?

Recall that the inspection process should merely establish that there *is* a defect here, but no time should be spent by the inspection team trying to repair this defect during the inspection meeting. The triage severity classification of defect 2 (relating to line 10) is *major* because its interpretation can lead to significant differences in the product. Using the IEEE 1044.1 standard, its classification is *computational*.

10. SUMMARY

Figure 6.50 summarizes this chapter.

- Make sufficient to code from
- Try standard design patterns
- Define selected algorithms
  - flowcharts
  - pseudocode
- Apply select tools
  - e.g., *Javadoc*

Figure 6.50 Summary of Detailed Design

EXERCISES

Solutions and hints are given at the end of this chapter to all exercises marked with "s" and "h" respectively.

REVIEW QUESTIONS

R6.1[s] State in three sentences each, or less, circumstances under which you would use the following in detailed design.

　　a. flowcharts

　　b. pseudocode

R6.2[s] Name three creational design patterns, stating their purpose in at most two sentences.

R6.3[s] Name three structural design patterns, stating their purpose in at most two sentences.

R6.4[s] Name three behavioral design patterns, stating their purpose in at most two sentences.

GENERAL EXERCISES

G6.1 Estimate the number of lines of Java code for the following set of methods. They are roughly ordered from smallest to largest. Assume that nothing else is known about the job.

> *Method 1 — I/O; Method 2 — Text; Method 3 — Calculation ; Method 4 — Logic;*
> *Method 5 — Data; Method 6 — Calculation; Method 7 — Text; Method 8 — Data;*
> *Method 9 — Set-up; Method 10—Calculation; Method 11 — Text; Method 12 — Data*

G6.2 Perform a design (both architectural and detailed) for a check balancing application with the following requirements. Fix defects in the requirements if you find them. You can play the role of customer if and when the customer's input is required. Report the time you spend on significant activities to the nearest five minutes.

1. The system shall display the current balance in the system window.

2. The system permits the user to record deposits of up to $10,000.

3. The system permits the user to withdraw any amount from the current balance. An error message "This withdrawal amount exceeds your balance" is displayed when the user attempts to withdraw an amount exceeding the balance.

TEAM EXERCISES

T6.1 ("SDD")

Provide an SDD for your project. Use, or improve upon the IEEE standard. Please enclose the latest version of your SRS.

Report the time spent by the individuals and the group on the parts of this assignment. Break this down into activities, including architecture, inspection, review, and detailed design. Comment on how the time spent could have been better allocated.

Evaluation Criteria:
α. *Clarity (A = straightforward to understand your architecture and detailed design)*
β. *Completeness (A = sufficient to cover your requirements)*
γ. *Elegance (A = expandable; maintainable)*
δ. *Meaningfulness of process improvement (A = showed specific, quantifiable improvement)*

SOLUTIONS TO QUESTIONS

R6.1 (a) Use flowcharts when the logic consists of multiple branching.

(b) Use pseudocode when the procedure needs to be described in detail and you do not want those details left up to the programmer.

R6.2 Singleton, Abstract Factory, and Prototype

Singleton: guarantees that a class has just one object

Abstract Factory: enables run time selection among families of objects

Prototype: enables run time selection among subclasses

R6.3 Composite, Proxy, and Flyweight

Composite: represents trees, so that clients can treat whole trees in the same way as subtrees

Proxy: stands in for an object to save time on unnecessary method invocations

Flyweight: avoids the proliferation of small objects with extensive commonality

R6.4 Iterator, Mediator, and Strategy

Iterator: encapsulates means of visiting a set of objects

Mediator: encapsulates the interaction among a set of objects

Strategy: allows the version of a method to vary at run time

CASE STUDY

We have to describe two detailed designs. The first is the detailed design of the Role-playing video game framework, and the second, that of the *Encounter* application. By separating them, we are making it easier to reuse and maintain the framework.

I. DETAILED DESIGN OF ROLE-PLAYING GAME FRAMEWORK, *CONTINUED* (REMAINING PARTS OF THE SOFTWARE DESIGN DOCUMENT)

[Note to the student: This is a continuation of the SDD whose table of contents is summarized in Chapter 5.]

6. DETAILED DESIGN OF ROLE-PLAYING GAME FRAMEWORK

The overall architecture of the packages described in this section can be found in Figure 5.52 of Chapter 5, on page 299.

6.1 Module Detailed Design

[Note to the student: These sections give all of the non trivial required details on each of the modules described in Section 3.1 in this SDD for the game framework.]

6.1.1 Role-playing Game Package

All mouse events are listened for by objects of the class *RPGMouseEventListener*, which inherits from *MouseListener* as shown in Figure 6.51. Each object which is sensitive to

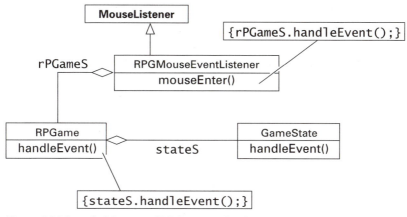

Figure 6.51 Detailed Design of RPGame *(Role-playing Game)Package*

mouse events asks an *RPGame* object to handle the event. *RPGame* passes control to the *handleEvent()* method of its aggregated *GameState* object. The sequence diagram for this is shown in Figure 6.52. For the current release, the methods are either trivial or are shown in Figure 6.52.

[Note to the student: Pseudocode for selected methods within selected classes may be included here. In addition, detailed use cases can be included. Since the methods and their details are still one or two lines in this case, it is sufficient to elaborate on the (barely) nontrivial methods with the notation shown in Figure 6.52.]

6.1.2 The Characters Package This

section elaborates on Section 3.1.2 of this SDD.

There is one class in the *Character* package: *GameCharacter*.

6.1.2.1 GameCharacter Class
Methods of GameCharacter
setName().

> Preconditions: none; postconditions: none; invariants: none Its pseudocode is as follows.

```
IF aName parameter OR maxNumChars-
InName() make no sense
```

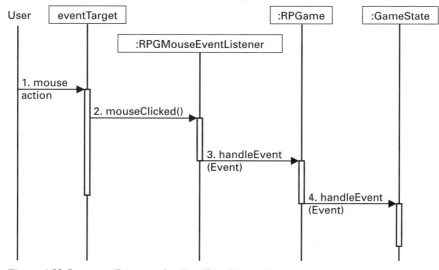

Figure 6.52 Sequence Diagram for Handling Mouse Events

```
Set name to default value and show
   this in system window
ELSE
   IF parameter string too long
      truncate at maxNumCharsInName()
   ELSE assign the parameter name
```

6.1.3 The GameEnvironment Package
This package is described completely by Figure 5.48 in Section 3.1 of this SDD (Chapter 5, page 295).

6.1.4 The Artifacts Package   [Not applicable in this iteration.]
[End of Detailed Design for the Framework packages]

II. DETAILED DESIGN OF ENCOUNTER, *CONTINUED* (REMAINING PARTS OF THE SOFTWARE DESIGN DOCUMENT)

[This is a continuation of the SDD, the table of contents of which are in Figure 6.41 on page 332.]

6. DETAILED DESIGN FOR *ENCOUNTER*

The overall architecture, showing the relationships among the packages and the domain classes described in this section, is shown in Figure 6.53.

6.1 Module Detailed Design for *Encounter*

[Note to the student: These sections give all of the required details on each of the modules described in Section 3.1 in this SDD (i.e., for Encounter).]

6.1.1 The EncounterGame *Package*

[Note to the student: This section gives all of the required details on Section 3.1.1 in this SDD. It describes completely the classes of the EncounterGame *package, and all of their nontrivial behavior. Most of this is described by the state transition diagram. In the interests of keeping the class model free of clutter, we do not show all object references.]*

The state diagram for *Encounter* is shown in Figure 3.17 of Chapter 3 on page 151. To realize these states and transitions, the *EncounterGame* package object model is designed as in Figure 6.54. There is exactly one instance of the *EncounterGame* class. The states of this object reflect the states and substates shown in the above state-transition diagram. The *Encountering* state aggregates an *Engagement* object that encapsulates the engagement of the game characters. The *Engagement* class aggregates a display called *EngagementDisplay*. The latter is mouse-sensitive, registering with an *RPGMouseEventListener* object. When the *Encounter* game is executed, this listener object references the *EncounterGame* object (an *RPGame* object). This enables *EncounterGame* to handle all events according to the game's state, using the *State* design pattern. The *EncounterGame* package has the responsibility of directing the movement of the foreign character over time. This is performed by methods of the class *CharacterMovement*, which is a thread class.

State classes need to reference other packages in order to implement *handleEvent( )*, and this is done through the Facade objects *EncounterCast* and *EncounterEnvironment*.

6.1.1.1 The EncounterGameDisplays *sub-package of the* EncounterGame *package*
Displays corresponding to some of the states are handled by a separate sub-package, *EncounterGameDisplays*, which is shown in Figure 6.55. *QualListDispl* is a list box consisting of the qualities of *Encounter* charac-

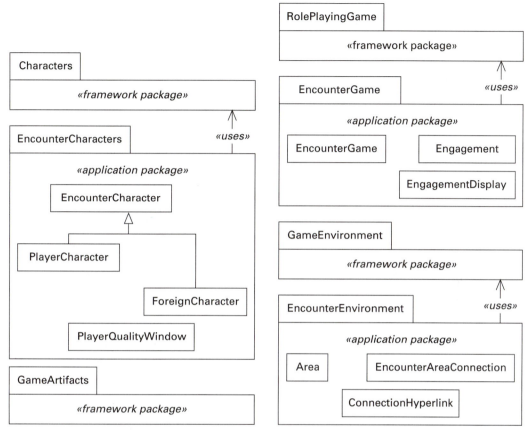

Figure 6.53 Video Game Architecture Packages, Showing Domain Classes

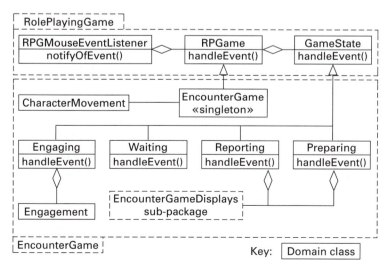

Figure 6.54 Detailed Design of EncounterGame *Package*

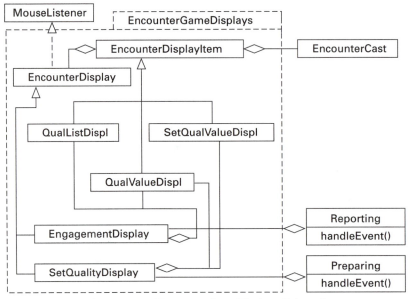

Figure 6.55 Detailed Design of EncounterGameDisplays *Sub-package*

ters. *QualValueDispl* is a read-only text box for displaying the value of a quality. *SetQualValueDispl* is an editable text box for setting the value of a quality. *EncounterDisplayItem* abstracts the properties and methods of displayable *Encounter* items such as these.

EngagementDisplay is designed to display the current value of any selected quality.

SetQualityDisplay is designed to enable the player to set the value of any quality.

EncounterDisplay abstracts the properties of these displays, and is a mediator base class.

This document does not provide further details of the design of these classes.

6.1.1.2 Sequence Diagrams for Event Handling

6.1.1.2.1 PLAYER DISMISSES REPORT WINDOW EVENT
Figure 6.56 shows the sequence involved in dismissing the engagement display. (This dismissal event is shown on the state transition diagram.)

6.1.1.2.2 PLAYER COMPLETES SETUP EVENT
Figure 6.57 shows the sequence in-

volved when the player completes the setup. (This dismissal event is shown on the state transition diagram.)

6.1.1.2.3 PLAYER MOVES TO ADJACENT AREA EVENT
Figure 6.58 shows the sequence when the player moves to an adjacent area by clicking on a connection hyperlink. (This dismissal event is shown on the state transition diagram.)

6.1.1.2.4 SEQUENCE DIAGRAMS FOR REMAINING EVENTS
The remaining events are handled very similarly to those described in Sections 6.1.1.1 through 6.1.1.3.

6.1.1.CM The CharacterMovement Class

[Note to the student: As in the SRS, we are using an alphabetical "numbering" scheme to make it easier to find and insert classes. There is also a benefit in being able to trace the requirements to the SRS.]

This class controls the movement of the foreign character.

Inheritance

This class inherits from *java.lang. Thread.*

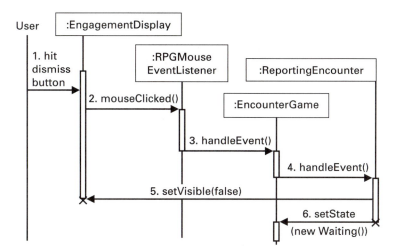

Figure 6.56 Sequence Diagram for Dismiss Engagement Display

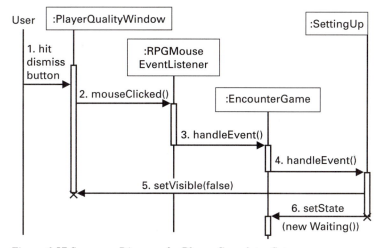

Figure 6.57 Sequence Diagram for Player Completes Setup

Methods of CharacterMovement

`public static EncounterGame run();`

Starts the foreign character in the dungeon. Moves the foreign character from area to area via area connections, changing areas to a randomly selected neighbor, at random times averaging every two seconds.

6.1.1.EG The EncounterGame *Class*
This is the facade singleton for the *EncounterGame* package.

Inheritance

This class inherits from *RPGame* in the framework.

Attributes of *EncounterGame*

`EncounterGame encounterGameS`: This is the singleton *EncounterGame* object.

Constructors of EncounterGame

`private EncounterGame():`

Preconditions: none
Postconditions: creates   an *EncounterGame* instance

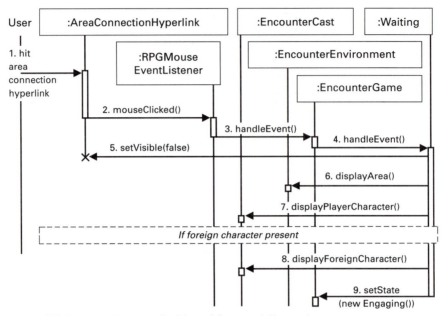

Figure 6.58 Sequence Diagram for Player Moves to Adjacent Area

Methods of EncounterGame

```
public static EncounterGame get-
TheEncounterGame();
```

    Preconditions: none

    Postconditions: `encounterGameS` not null

    Returns: `encounterGameS`

6.1.1.EN The* Engagement *Class This class encapsulates engagements between the player's character and the foreign character, and corresponds to requirement 3.2.EN.

Methods

```
public void engage(); // corre-
```
sponds to requirement 3.2.EN.3.1

    Preconditions: The player's character and the foreign character are in the same area.

    Postconditions: The values of the characters' qualities are as required by SRS requirement 3.2.EN.3.1; the player's character and the foreign character are in random, but different areas.

6.1.1.ZZ The* Engaging, Waiting, Preparing, *and* Reporting *Classes

[The "ZZ" numbering is used to collect classes that are not specified individually.]

Inheritance

    These classes inherit from *GameState* in the framework package.

    Each of these classes implements its *handleEvent()* method in accordance with the sequence diagrams of section 6.1.1.1.

6.1.2 The* EncounterCharacters *package

[This section elaborates on section 3.1.2 in this SDD.]

The design of the *EncounterCharacters* package is shown in Figure 6.59. It is implemented by the *Facade* design pattern, with *EncounterCast* as the facade object.

6.1.2.EC The* EncounterCharacter *Class This class encapsulates the re-

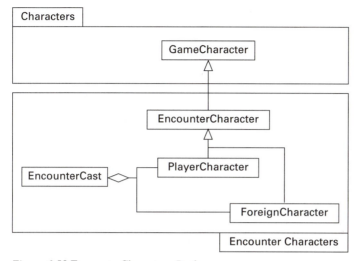

Figure 6.59 EncounterCharacters *Package*

quirements for *Encounter* characters that are not covered by *RPGameCharacters*. It satisfies requirements SRS 3.2.EC.

Class invariant: The values of qualValueI are non-negative (see "attributes" below for the definitions of qualValueI).

Inheritance

This class inherits from *Game-Character* in the framework package.

Attributes of *EncounterCharacter*

These satisfy requirement SRS 3.2.EC.1

```
private static final String[]
qualityTypeS
```

This represents the qualities that *Encounter* characters possess. These are concentration, stamina, intelligence, patience, and strength.

```
private float[] qualValueI
```

This is an array containing the values of the qualities.

Constructor of *EncounterCharacter*

These satisfy requirements 3.2.EC.3 of the SRS

Null constructor

Postcondition: The qualities are all equal fractions of 100.

```
protected   EncounterCharacter(
String nameP )
```

Postconditions:

(1) the qualities are all equal fractions of 100.

(2) the character's name is *NameP*

Methods of *EncounterCharacter*

```
public synchronized void
adjustQuality( String qualityP,
float qualityValueP )
```

This method satisfies requirement 3.2.EC.3.2.

Invariants: none
Preconditions:

qualityP is in *qualityTypesS[]*
AND *qualityValueP* >=0
AND *qualityValueP* <= the sum of the quality values
Postconditions:

qualityP has the value *quality-ValueP*

AND

the remaining quality values are in the same proportion as

prior to invocation, except that values less than 0.5 are zero.

The following is the pseudocode for the method *adjustQuality()*.

Set the stated quality to the desired amount

IF the caller adjusts the only non-zero quality value,

    divide the adjustment amount equally among all other qualities.

    ELSE change the remaining qualities, retaining their mutual proportion,

    Set each quality whose value is now less than 0.5 to zero

```
public float getQualityValue( String
qualityP )
```

Preconditions: *qualityP* is a valid quality string

Returns: the value of *qualityP*

```
public float getTolerance( )
```

Returns: the value below which quality values cannot go

```
protected int maxNumCharsInName()
```

Returns: the maximum number of characters in the names of *Encounter* characters

```
public float sumOfQualities()
```

Returns: the sum of the values of the qualities

This method satisfies requirement 3.2.EC.3.2.

```
public void showCharacter( Com-
ponent componentP, Graphics drawP,
Point posP, int heightPixP, boolean
faceLeftP )
```

    Displays the character in *componentP*, with center at *posP*, with height *heightPixP*, facing left if *faceLeftP* true

    This method satisfies requirements 3.2.PC.1 and 3.2.PQ.1.

```
private void setQuality( String
qualityP, float valueP )
```

    Preconditions: *qualityP* is a valid quality string.

    Sets the quality indicated by the parameter to *valueP* if the latter is >= 0.5, otherwise sets *valueP* to zero

    This method satisfies requirement 3.2.EC.2 (lower limit on nonzero quality values).

6.1.2.ES The EncounterCast *Class*

The method specifications for this singleton, interface class are given in Section 5 of this document.

6.1.2.FC The ForeignCharacter *class*

This class is analogous to *PlayerCharacter*, described next, and is designed to satisfy the SRS 3.2.FC.

6.1.2.PC The PlayerCharacter *Class*

This class is designed to satisfy the requirements 3.2.PC.

Inheritance

    This class inherits from *EncounterCharacter*.

Attributes:

```
private static final Player-
Character playerCharacterS;
```

    This is the singleton object representing the player's character.

Methods:

```
public static final PlayerChar-
acter getPlayerCharacter();
```

    This method returns playerCharacterS.

6.1.3 The EncounterEnvironment *Package*

The classes of this package describe the environment in which the game takes place. It is shown in Figure 6.60.

6.1.3.AR Area Class

This class encapsulates the places in which the characters exist, and corresponds to requirement 3.2.AR.

Inheritance

    This class inherits from *GameArea*.

Attributes:

```
private String nameI; // corre-
```
sponding to requirement 3.2.AR.1.1

```
private Image imageI; // corre-
```
sponding to requirement 3.2.AR.1.2

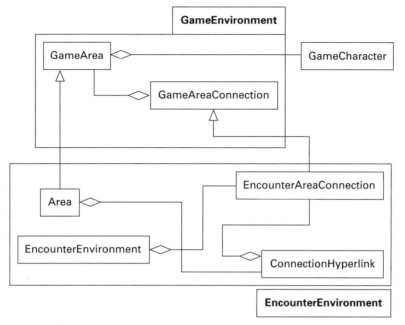

Figure 6.60 EncounterEnvironment *Package*

```
private String[] qualitiesI; //
```
corresponding to requirement 3.2.AR.
1.3
```
private Vector connectionHyper-
linksI;
```

Methods

`public void display()` shows the area object's image on the monitor.

`public static Area getArea( String areaNameP )` returns the area corresponding to `areaNameP` according to requirement 3.2.AR.2.2.

`public static AreaConnection get-AreaConnection( String area ConnectionNameP )` returns the area Connection object corresponding to `areaConnectionNameP` according to requirement 3.2.AR.2.2.

6.1.3.CO EncounterAreaConnection Class

This class encapsulates the ways to get from areas to adjacent areas. It inherits from *AreaConnection* and corresponds to requirement 3.2.CO.

Inheritance

This class inherits from *GameAreaConnection* in the framework package.

Attributes:

```
private Area firstAreaI; // cor-
```
responding to requirement 3.2.CO.1.1
```
private Area secondAreaI; // cor-
```
responding to requirement 3.2.CO.1.1

Methods: These are accessors for the attributes above.

6.1.3.EE EncounterEnvironment Class

This is the facade class for the *EncounterEnvironment* package.

Attributes:

```
private EncounterEnvironment
encounterEnvironmentS; // the singleton
```
Facade object
```
// [Area name][Area connection
```
name]["North" | "South" | "East" | "West"]:
```
private String[3] layoutS;
```

Methods:

```
public static EncounterEnvironment
getEncounterEnvironment ()
  Returns: encounterEnvironmentS
public static String[3] getLayout()
  Returns: layoutS
```

The remaining methods are specified in Section 5 of this document.

6.1.3.CH ConnectionHyperlink Class

This class encapsulates the ways to get from areas to adjacent areas. It corresponds to requirement 3.2.CH. This class implements the *MouseListener* interface.

Attributes:

```
private Connection connectionI; //
the corresponding connection
```

Methods:

The only meaningful method is `mouseClick()`.

6.2 Data Detailed Design

There are no data structures besides those mentioned as part of the classes in Section 6.1.

CHAPTER **7**

UNIT IMPLEMENTATION

This sweaty haste
Doth make the night joint-labourer with the day.

Hamlet

Writing programs in haste produces immediate, but dubious results; a disciplined approach, on the other hand, produces superior quality in less time.

This chapter will not attempt to cover the ground of a complete programming book such as Hoare and Jones [Ho]. Instead, we will discuss programming principles and guidelines that relate most directly to the software engineering enterprise. The context is shown in Figure 7.1, and the goals of this chapter are stated in Figure 7.2.

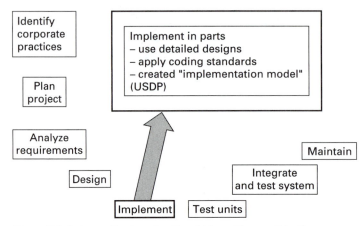

Figure 7.1 Software Engineering Road Map: Chapter 7 in Context

Be able to

- specify standards
- select coding style
- code with correctness justification
- identify quality goals

Figure 7.2 Learning Goals for This Chapter (Graphics reproduced with permission from Corel.)

1. INTRODUCTION TO IMPLEMENTATION

1.1 The Definition of "Unit Implementation"

"Implementation" refers to programming. "Unit" refers to the smallest part of the implementation that will be separately maintained. This could be an individual method or a class. In the examples, we will take methods as the lowest level unit.

1.2 Goals of Implementation

Implementation is intended to satisfy the requirements in the manner specified by the detailed design. Although the detailed design should suffice as the document against which programming is performed, the programmer typically examines all of the predecessor documents at the same time (the architecture, the D-requirements, and the C-requirements), which helps to smooth out inconsistencies among the documents.

1.3 A Typical Road Map of the Unit Implementation Process

Figure 7.3 shows a typical process by which code is produced.

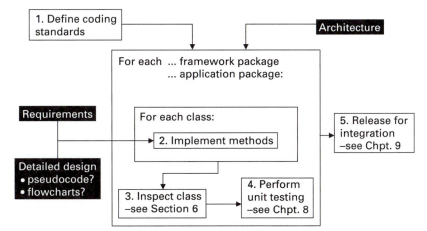

Figure 7.3 Road Map for Unit Implementation

1. In Figure 7.3, coding standards are identified, so that the source code has a common appearance (see Section 3).

2. The architecture determines what the framework and application packages are. Each class of each package is then implemented by coding the methods determined by the requirements, and by the detailed design. The framework packages are required before the application packages can be built.

3. Each class is inspected as soon as it is ready.

4. Each class is then tested, as described in Chapter 8.

5. Package or classes are then released for integration into the evolving application.

Figure 7.4 lists a sequence of actions that prepare the programmer for implementation. Some of the more complex methods will have been given pseudocode or flowcharts. The

---

One Way To. . . Prepare for Implementation

1. Confirm the detailed designs you must implement
   • code only from a written design (part of the SDD)

2. Prepare to measure time spent, classified by:
   • residual detailed design; detailed design review; coding; coding review; compiling and repairing syntax defects; unit testing (see Chapter 8) and repairing defects found in testing

3. Prepare to record defects using a form
   • severity: *major* (requirement unsatisfied), *trivial,* or *neither*
   • type: *error, naming, environment, system, data, other*

4. Understand required standards
   • for coding
   • for the personal documentation you must keep
      • *see the case study for an example*

5. Estimate size and time based on your past data

6. Plan the work in segments of ±100 LOC

Figure 7.4 One Way to Prepare for Implementation

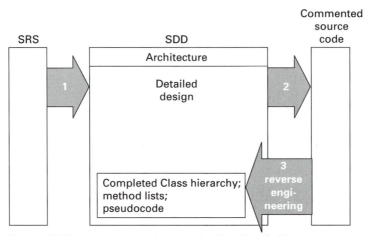

Figure 7.5 Using Reverse Engineering for Very Detailed Design

pseudocode from the detailed design document can become code comments. A test plan is developed for each unit, as described in the next chapter. Each of the units shown in the diagram is inspected. Once a class has been implemented, a reverse engineering tool (e.g., *Javadoc*) can be used to regenerate aspects of the detailed design, as illustrated in Figure 7.5.

Reverse engineering may be advisable after the initial implementation because the source code tends to become more up-to-date than the lowest level of detailed design. It can also be very useful for legacy code whose design is poorly documented. Generally speaking, reverse engineering should be resorted to only if truly necessary. The author has observed many situations in which reverse engineering is used to cover up for a lack of design. In other words, engineers dive into coding prematurely, then justify it with a "design" reverse engineered from the code. Readers of such "designs" are rarely fooled.

Reverse engineering is also discussed in Chapters 6 and 10.

1.4 Implementation in the Unified Software Development Process

Recall that the Unified Software Development Process (USDP) gives names to groups of iterations. Most iterations involve some implementation, and the "construction" iterations, their third quarter, involve the highest proportion of implementation. This is illustrated in Figure 7.6.

The USDP considers implementation to be yet another "model" (along with the use case model, the test model, etc.). Although the constituents of the design should map as faithfully as possible to those of the physical file system, a simple mapping may not be practical. For example, several classes could map onto a single file, and the implementation artifacts could include README files, source files, object files, and compressed versions such as JAR files. The *implementation model* shows how the physical artifacts of the implementation are organized, and how the design elements map to them. This is illustrated in Figure 7.7.

The model shows that the classes *Area* and *AnotherClass* are implemented on the same file — *Area.java* (*AnotherClass* could be an inner class of *Area*).

The implementation model consists of nested subsystems. These consist of components such as files and implementation interfaces, as illustrated by Figure 7.8. The figure says that the source code for classes *Area* and *AnotherClass* are in the file *Area.java*. The

	Inception	Elaboration		Construction			Transition		
	Prelim. iterations	Iter. #1	Iter. #n	Iter. #n + 1	...	Iter. #m	Iter. #m + 1	...	Iter. #k
Requirements									
Analysis									
Design									
Implemen-tation									
Test									

Figure 7.6 Implementation *in the Unified Process ([Ja1])*

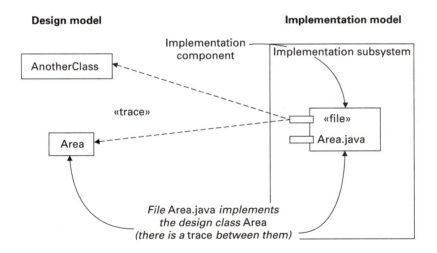

Design model

Implementation model

AnotherClass

Implementation component

Implementation subsystem

«trace»

«file»

Area

Area.java

File Area.java *implements the design class* Area *(there is a* trace *between them)*

Figure 7.7 Constituents of the Unified Process Implementation Model, 1 of 2

interface of *Area* (a collection of public functions) in the design corresponds to actual functionality provided by *Area.java* in the implementation. The implementation model also provides a notation for showing the relationships between files, such as "compiles into," "describes," and "compresses," using the "« »" notation. (An organization is free to define these.) The figure indicates that a README file, the source code of *Area,* and its object code, are in one physical collection, and that the file *impl.jar* is a jar'd (compressed "Java Archive") version of these.

The implementation model describes the classes and language-level interfaces responsible for implementing the system's interface. This is illustrated in Figure 7.9 for the *Encounter* case study, using a single interface class. This notation can show several classes

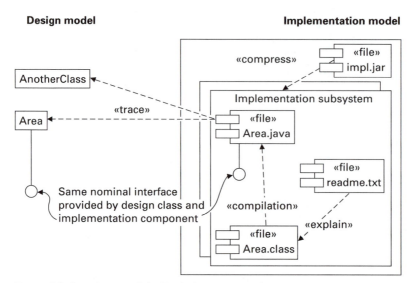

Figure 7.8 Constituents of the Unified Process Implementation Model, 2 of 2

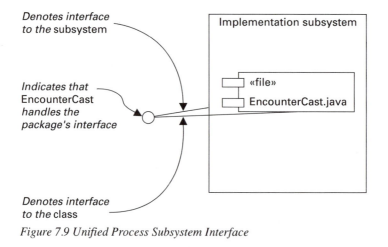

Figure 7.9 Unified Process Subsystem Interface

being responsible for parts of the subsystem's interface. These can be combined into an interface package that is responsible for an interface, and so on.

1.5 Programming Languages

There is a plethora of programming languages, ranging from specialized ones (e.g., hardware test languages) to general higher order languages such as C++, Java, and COBOL. Internet development alone involves a wide array of languages. The principles of this book can be applied to any of these languages, although OO languages stand to leverage its principles most directly. The application's anticipated target language does influence its design. For example, it may be preferable to design in more of a top-down, functional manner when using a language such as C, even though object-oriented designs can be applied in C to a degree. Some languages, such as Javascript and earlier Visual Basic, are *object-based,* giving programmers the ability to utilize encapsulation and aggregation, but not inheritance.

2. PROGRAMMING AND STYLE

The popular image of programming as the act of submitting typed material to a compiler is only a small part of the picture. The software engineer's real goal is to create *correct* code (i.e., entirely appropriate for its requirements), but compilers can only check syntax and generate object code. Correctness is a human responsibility. It is therefore essential that the professional be thoroughly convinced of code's correctness *before* submitting it to a compiler. Although it is possible in principle to compile first and verify correctness afterwards, this is as ineffective as correcting a letter's syntax before checking that it expresses its intended thoughts. Moreover, programmers tend to omit checking program code thoroughly once it has compiled without (syntax) error.

Figure 7.10 and Figure 7.11 indicate the steps that programmers can take to program: The steps are elaborated upon in the remainder of this chapter. This section outlines

---

One Way To. . . Implement Code, 1/2

1. Plan the structure and residual design for your code
   (complete missing detailed design, if any)
   - note preconditions and post conditions
   - note the time spent
2. Self-inspect your design and/or structure
   - note time spent, defect type, source (phase), severity
3. Type your code
   - do not compile yet
   - try methods listed below
   - apply required standards
   - code in a manner that is easiest to verify
     - *use formal methods if appropriate*

Figure 7.10 One Way to Implement Code, 1 of 2

One Way To. . . Implement Code, 2/2

4. Self-inspect your code—do not compile yet
   - convince yourself that your code does the required job
     - *the compiler will never do this for you: it merely checks syntax!*
   - note time spent, defects found, type, source, severity
   - See the code inspection checklist (Figs. 7.26–7.30 in Section pages 376 and 377) for details commonly required for method and class construction.
5. Compile your code
   - repair syntax defects
   - note time spent, defect type, source, severity, and lines of code
6. Test your code
   - apply unit test methods in Chapter 7

Figure 7.11 One Way to Implement Code, 2 of 2

1. TRY TO REUSE FIRST
2. ENFORCE INTENTIONS

   If your code is intended to be used in
   particular ways only, write it so that the code
   cannot be used in any other way.

   Figure 7.12 General Principles in Programming Practice

typical advice on programming style. There are many fine books offering advice on programming substance, which this chapter does not attempt to duplicate.

2.1 General Principles of Sound Implementation

Figure 7.12 recommends two general principles for programming.

1. We have stressed the need to design our own applications in such a way as to permit the reuse of components that we build: In the same spirit, we strongly consider reusing trusted existing code before writing our own. For example, consider using a Java Swing GUI component or an existing Java Bean before developing your own GUI component. A quick Web search for components to reuse is usually a worthwhile investment.

2. If you intend something about how the code you are constructing is to be used by other parts of the application, then try to enforce this intention. The author calls this the *"Enforce Intentions"* principle. It is often evident in user interfaces, where the user is prohibited from entering illegal data. We are stressing it for internal processing, however.

The *"Enforce Intentions"* principle is analogous to constructing curbs and islands on roadways to direct traffic along just those paths intended by traffic engineers, and no others. Such enforcement of intentions makes roads safer, and is widespread in every branch of engineering. The following includes examples of the *"Enforce Intentions"* principle in software engineering.

- Use qualifiers such as `final`, `const` in C++, and `abstract` to enforce the corresponding intentions. `final` classes can't be inherited from; `final` methods can't be overridden in inherited classes; the value of `final` variables can't be changed. If this causes compile-time errors, it means that you do not fully understand your own program yet, and no harm has been done. What we especially seek to avoid are run time errors.

- Make constants, variables, and classes as local as reasonably possible. For example, define loop counters within the loop: Don't give them wider scope.

- Use the *Singleton* design pattern if there is to be only one instance of a class (see Chapter 6).

- Generally speaking, make members inaccessible if they are not specifically intended to be accessed directly.
  - Make attributes `private`. Access them through more public accessor functions if required. (In Java, making attributes `protected` gives objects of subclasses access to members of their base classes, which is often undesirable.)
  - Make methods `private` if they are for use only by methods of the same class.

- Include examples in documentation. Programmers usually hesitate to do this, but examples can help the reader a great deal. The case study provides an example in the comments to the method `adjustQuality()` of the class `EncounterGame`.

- List methods alphabetically rather than trying to find a calling order among them. Some programmers like to group private, protected, and public methods, and then subgroup static and nonstatic methods. (The case study does not follow this practice.)

2.2 Pointers and References

The following hints are from Horstmann [Ho3].

- Avoid using pointer parameters in C++; use references instead.

- Never return a pointer to a new heap reference in C++. This has the effect of referring to memory that will become unusable later, and places the burden on the programmer to reclaim the space.

- Collect your garbage (C++); use `delete()` on unneeded objects. Failure to reclaim space ("memory leaks") is a leading cause of failures in C++ programs, and policies are developed to avoid this problem. Some C++ organizations allow programmers to allocate memory only through specified utility functions, in order to improve control over the allocation process. In other words, `new C()` is avoided: Programmers have to use factory-type utilities such as `F::getNewCObject()` for some class `F`.

  Commercial tools are also available that attempt to indicate potential memory leaks. Garbage collection in Java is automatic, so that memory leaks are not possible in the same serious manner as C++. Java programs can, however, accumulate resources such as files and sockets, and the programmer should be aware of the resources that his or her program is using at run time.

2.3 Functions

- Avoid type inquiry (e.g., `if( myObject instanceOf MyClass )` unless it is obviously beneficial. Use virtual functions instead. (See the *State* design pattern in Chapter 5, for example.)

- Avoid C++ *friend* functions except when the benefits obviously outweigh their drawbacks.

- Take special care in overloading operators, because others reading your program may misunderstand the meaning of your operations. Java does not allow overloading because of this.

2.4 Exceptions

Catch only those exceptions that you know how to handle. A method handling an exception looks like

```
ReturnType myMethod( ... ) {...
      try{...// call method throwing ExceptionX }
      catch( ExceptionX e ) {...// handle it }
  ...}
```

A method not handling an exception looks like the following.

```
ReturnType myMethod(...) throws ExceptionX{...}
```

- If the present method cannot handle the exception, there has to be a handler in an outer scope that can do so.
- If you can handle part of the exception, then handle that part and then rethrow the exception for handling within an outer scope.
- Make reasonable expectations about the ability of callers to handle the exception you are throwing; otherwise, find an alternative design since unhandled exceptions crash applications.
- Be careful not to use exceptions in situations that should be the subject of testing. For example, if it is specified as a precondition that a method should never be called with a parameter whose value is null, then *testing* should verify this. Throwing an exception when the parameter is not null should not be a routine way to handle such a problem.
- "If you must choose between throwing an exception and continuing the computation, continue if you can" (Horstmann [Ho.3]). His point here is that the continuation of an application can be preferable to shutting it down in cases when the consequences have been thought through.

    As an example, the case study continues to perform with a default name when given a faulty parameter string (e.g., *null*), since this is preferable to shutting down the game just because a name is illegal. On the other hand, a banking transaction with an illegal amount would not be allowed to continue.

Horstmann points out several reasons why constructors may fail.

- The first reason for constructor failure is a bad argument; he recommends setting the object to a default state and then passing control to an error handler.
- The second reason is that required resources are unavailable, a situation best handled by throwing an exception, since we may not be able to do anything about this.
- C++ programmers especially have to be concerned with memory that will be abandoned when an exception is thrown in response to a constructor failure.

2.5 Handling Errors

Developers are constantly faced with the issue of what to do with potentially illegal data. An example of illegal data is an account number which does not correspond to an actual bank account. Although we try to make implementations as simple as possible, the real world is not simple. A large fraction of programming goes towards the handling of errors. A disciplined approach is essential: Pick an approach, state it, and be sure everyone on the team understands and abides by it. One way to handle errors, shown in Figure 7.13, is explained in the succeeding paragraphs.

Our real goal is error *prevention* rather than correction. Using a well-defined process, inspecting the phases, and so on are the essential first line of defense. Certain design patterns can also help to prevent errors. For example, if a method *evaluate( )* accepts only "car," "truck," or "bus" as parameters, then it might be worthwhile not to use *String* as a parameter because it introduces the possibility of illegal parameters. It would be better to define a class such as *SpecializedVehicle* with a private constructor and factory functions:

One Way To. . . Implement Error Handling

1. Follow agreed-upon development process; inspect.
2. Consider introducing classes to encapsulate legal parameter values.
   - private constructor; factory functions to create instances
   - catches many errors at compile time
3. Where error handling is specified by requirements, implement as required.
   - use exceptions if passing on error-handling responsibility
4. For applications that must *never* crash, anticipate all possible implementation defects (e.g., use defaults).
   - only if unknown performance better than none (unusual!)
5. Otherwise, follow a consistent policy for checking parameters.
   - rely mostly on good design and development process

Figure 7.13 One Way to Implement Error Handling

```
SpecializedVehicle createACar()
SpecializedVehicle createATruck()
SpecializedVehicle createABus()
```

The method in question can then take only a parameter of this type. In other words, instead of

```
evaluate( String vehicleP ) ... // problem with illegal strings
```

use

```
evaluate( SpecializedVehicle vehicleP ) ... // parameter value cannot be illegal
```

When the possible parameter values are restricted but infinite, a separate class can still be valuable. For example, a person's age is an integer between 0 and 105, let's say, and so a method

```
getYearOfBirth( int ageP )
```

may have to deal with errors. In fact the same error processing would have to be repeated for all methods taking age as a parameter. On the other hand, a class *Age* with a private constructor and a public factory method

```
Age getAge( int ageP )
```

would handle erroneous input in a consistent manner, located in the same place as all the other aspects of age. Some options for dealing with this error are described below. The disadvantage of this method is the proliferation of additional classes, and the slight awkwardness of calls such as

```
... getYearOfBirth( getAge( n ) ) ...
```

in place of such simpler calls as

```
... getYearOfBirth( n ) ...
```

A second line of defense in dealing with potentially illegal data is to interact with the data source until the input is changed to a legal one before the processing continues.

This is possible for much of user interface programming, where we can often ensure that only legal inputs are permitted. If the only allowable strings that can be entered in a text field are "car," "truck," or "bus," it is easy to prevent the user from continuing until a legal entry is made. A list box is a common way to do this. Even here, however, subtle errors may creep in. For example, the user may enter date-of-birth as 1/1/80 and age (in 2000) of 30. It is possible to check consistencies, but the onus is on the designer to think of all possible consistency and boundary checks (sometimes called "business rules"). This checking can be very hard to perfect, however, when many fields are involved. When the external agency supplying the data is a separate application, there is even more possibility of error.

Given that the possibility of errors must be dealt with, how does one program a method to handle illegal input? (For example, a method that gives the balance on an account number when the method's preconditions clearly require that the account parameter be legal.) If all of the aspects of the development process have been properly practiced, then the method's parameters will always be legal whenever the method is called: But should we program a check of the parameter value in case our design or implementation is flawed? This depends on the requirements and is discussed in the rest of this section.

For example, suppose that there is a system requirement that the continued execution of the application is paramount, even if the execution is degraded or flawed. In this case, the programmer must deal with all inputs, even those that make no sense. As an example, consider an application that monitors heart functions and controls an oxygen supply to a patient. Let's suppose that we are coding a method *process(int measurementType, ...)* where *measurementType* must be positive. Let us assume that this application cannot afford to crash even when an internal method has been given an illegal integer due to a development defect. Thus, the code would check the input, and (1) set default values that are safe, if possible, or (2) place the entire application in a default mode of operation, or (3) throw an exception, passing the responsibility to the caller. The application would typically also report an alert.

Sometimes the reception of illegal inputs can be handled in a way that is consistent with explicit requirements. This occurs, for example, when data are transmitted over a faulty communication line. The receiving method may be designed to expect certain data, but the application is often explicitly required to continue execution, even when the data are not legal. Here, the data must be checked and errors processed in accordance with the requirements (e.g., "If the signal is not between 3.6 and 10.9, discard the signal and listen for the next signal . . . ").

What about methods whose exceptional behavior is not determined by the requirements? First, their preconditions must be thoroughly specified, so that the conditions under which they are called are clear. But even so, should their parameter values be checked to ensure that the preconditions are met? We distinguish between execution during development, and execution during deployment.

Executing during development allows test and verification code in many parts of an application, and we might well want to insert code that checks preconditions, as in the following.

```
/** precondition: parameters are positive */
int sum( int int1P, int int2P ) {
// verification code for use in development: check parameters positive
. . .
// now do the work
. . . }
```

Executing the *delivered product* requires a different perspective. If the method is called with negative parameters, this indicates a defect in the application itself. We would like to protect ourselves against our own mistakes, but the cure must be preferable to the illness.

```
/** precondition: parameters are positive */
int sum( int int1P, int int2P ) {
        // verification code for deployed application: check parameters positive
        // only if we have a clear philosophy of what to do if not
        ...
        // now do the work
        ... }
```

The "illness" in this example is that a parameter that should not be negative, is negative. A "cure" would return an answer inconsistent with the state of the application.

Without clear policies, checking like this for delivered products is a slippery slope: It is not feasible to check every part of an application (e.g., should the checking code also be checked?). Given a fixed amount of time, there is a significant potential to waste it on inserting self-protection code at the expense of inspecting the material itself for correctness.

Developers lose control of their application when using an arbitrary default whose consequences are not known. There are several reasons for this. It is unethical to distribute, without warning, an application that handles defective development with a deliberately incorrect continuation (i.e., a continuation not stated in the requirements). A defect is a mistake, but an arbitrary default not explicitly specified in the requirements is a cover-up. In practical terms, it is often preferable to reboot an aborted application rather than have it execute incorrectly (think of an application plotting airplane courses). Second, undisciplined error processing hides the defect, and it becomes expensive to find the defect compared with allowing the application to crash (hopefully at test time). Third, we must be consistent in design expectations. Code that effectively says, "I think we designed this correctly, but here is how we hope to keep the application executing if we did not," does not solve the design problem and is poor engineering.

2.6 Other Points of Practice

- Before committing to changing a variable, make sure that there has been no failure in reading the value. In Java, programmers are encouraged to abide by this because an exception is raised in the event of a faulty read: The exception should not be ignored, however, and the value read should be considered worthless.
- Use special caution when applying multiple inheritance in C++. (Java avoids these problems by prohibiting multiple inheritance.) For example, when both parent classes have a variable of the same name, the common descendent has two versions of the variable—a messy situation.

3. PROGRAMMING STANDARDS

The use of standards improves discipline, readability, and portability in programming. We will present a set of standards that can be used for example and reflection. Some of the following standards are adapted from Scott Ambler [Am]. Others can be found at Sun Corporation's Java site.

3.1 Naming Conventions—Java Examples

Use a naming convention for variables. Engineers tend to become emotional about their favorite conventions, and consensus is often impossible. Still, conventions are necessary. A limited time should be set aside for deciding on conventions and a method for finalizing them. For example, a team member can be designated to draft conventions, e-mail them to the other members for comments, then have the choices finalized by the designated person with the approval of the team leader. There should be guidelines as to when exceptions to conventions are to be allowed.

The following is an example of naming conventions.

- Name entities with concatenated words as in `lengthCylinder`. These are easy to understand and they conserve space. Blanket exceptions may be permitted at the discretion of the programmer. For example, `aAAAAAAAuto` would be better expressed `a_AAA_AA_A_Auto` instead of slavishly following the convention.

- Begin class names with capitals. This distinguishes them from variables. Some tools precede the name of entities with standard letters or combinations of letters, such as `C...` for classes as in `CCustomer`. This is useful when the importance of knowing the types of names exceeds the resulting awkwardness.

- Name variables beginning with lowercase letters. Constants may be excepted.

- Name constants with capitals as in `I_AM_A_CONSTANT` (use `static final`). `IAMA-CONSTANT` is hard to read; `IamAConstant` could be confused with a class; `iAmAName` gives no indication that it is a constant.

- Begin (or end) the name of instance variables of classes with an underscore as in `_timeOfDay` to distinguish them from other variables, since they are global to their object. This convention is used (e.g., [Ga]) and also derided (e.g., [Am]).

  A convention used in the case study is to append the suffix *I* to indicate instance variables, as in `timeOfDayI`. Each instance variable is global to each class instance, and when one is encountered in a block of code, it is useful to know this.

- Consider using a notation to distinguish the static variables of a class. The case study uses the suffix S, as in `numCarsEverBuiltS`. Recall that a static variable is global to a class, and it is helpful to know that a variable encountered in a block of code is one of these.

- Use `get...`, `set...`, and `is...` for accessor methods as in `getName()`, `setName()`, `isBox()` (where the latter returns a boolean value).

  Alternatively use `name()` and `name( String )`, for attribute `name` (e.g., in CORBA—see [OM]).

- Augment these with standardized additional "getters" and "setters" of collections, for example `insertIntoName()`, `removeFromName()`, `newName()`.

- Consider a convention for parameters. One convention is to use the prefix *a*, as in `sum( int aNum1P, int aNum2P )`. The case study uses the suffix *P*, as in `sum( int num1P, int num2P )`.

Document methods with a description of the following.

- Preconditions and postconditions (see the discussion on program correctness below)
- What the method does

- Why it does what it does
- What parameters it must be passed (for Javadoc, use @param tag)
- Exceptions it throws (for Javadoc, use @exception tag)
- Reason for choice of visibility (`private`, etc.)
- Ways in which instance variables (i.e., attributes) are changed
- Known bugs
- Test description, stating whether the method has been tested, and the location of its test script
- History of changes if you are not using a configuration management system
- Example of how the method works
- Special documentation for threaded and synchronized methods

Use a consistent standard for separation. Since single blank lines are useful for separating code sections within methods, a consistent standard is to use double blank lines between methods.

Within methods, consider standards such as the following.

- Perform only one operation per line.
- Try to keep methods to a single screen.
- Use parentheses within expressions to clarify their meaning, even if the syntax of the language makes them unnecessary. This is an application of "if you know it, show it."

In naming classes, use singular names such as `Customer`, unless the express purpose is to collect objects (in which case `Customers` might be appropriate). To prevent the proliferation of classes, it is sometimes desirable to have a class collect its own instances. This would be done with a static data member of the class.

3.2 Documenting Attributes (adapted from [Am])

- Provide all applicable invariants (quantitative facts about the attributes, such as " 36 < _length *_width < 193".)

For each attribute,

- State its purpose.
- Provide all applicable invariants (quantitative facts about the attribute, such as "1 < _age < 130" or " 36 < _length *_width < 193".)

See Section 4 of this chapter for a full description of *invariants*.

3.3 Constants

Before designating a variable as final (constant), be sure that it is indeed final. Ambler [Am] suggests using a method to represent a constant instead of using a constant, as shown in Figure 7.14. This technique retains the benefit of expressing the quantity in words (`getMaxCharsInName()`) instead of unexplained numerals ("20"), but allows flexibility at the same time.

instead of . . .

```
protected static final MAX_CHARS_IN_NAME = 20;
```

consider using . . .

```
protected final static int getMaxCharsInName()
{   return 20;
}
```

Figure 7.14 Constants

3.4 Initializing Attributes

Attributes should always be initialized so that the programmer has control of his or her program. We usually think of initialization to be in the form

```
private float balanceI = 0;  // convention: xxxI instance variable
```

The attribute requiring initialization may be an object of another class, however, as in

```
private Customer customerI;
```

This initialization is often done using a constructor, as in

```
private Customer customerI = new Customer( "Edward", "Jones" );
```

The problem with this technique, as Ambler points out, is its maintainability. When new attributes are added to `Customer`, all of these initializations may have to be updated. In other words, it violates the object-oriented goal of encapsulating all `Customer`-oriented issues with the class `Customer`. The other issue is that such construction may require unnecessary persistent storage.

A consistent solution is to use initialization only when the value is first accessed (a kind of "lazy initialization"). In general, we supply `MyClass` with a static function, which we will name `getDefaultMyClass()`. Attributes in other classes of type `MyClass` can now be declared without initialization, and assigned values only when they are accessed for the first time. An example is shown in Figure 7.15, Figure 7.16, and Figure 7.17, where `MyClass` is the class `Customer`.

4. PROVABLY CORRECT PROGRAMS

To say that a program is "provably correct" means that *a mathematical proof is provided* to show that the program satisfies its requirements. The proof is based on the requirements for the code and the text of the code. The proof is independent of compilation by a compiler and is independent of testing. This is an ideal capability.

A good mathematical proof is a well-constructed argument that convinces the author and others that a statement is true. The language of mathematics is the key to proofs, but mathematics can be applied to prove only statements that are expressed mathematically in the first place.

First, the requirement itself must be stated precisely. In Chapter 4 we described Z-specifications for stating requirements formally. Here, we will use a simpler form of requirements introduced in Chapter 4, *preconditions* and *postconditions*. The precondi-

Use initialization when the value is first accessed.
Supply `MyClass` with static `getDefaultMyClass()`.
Attributes are declared without initialization, and
assigned values the first time they are accessed.

In class Customer: `Account` ◁▷━━━▶ `Customer`

```
...
public static Customer getDefaultCustomer()
// ... reasons values below are chosen for the default
{        return new Customer
            ( "John", "Doe", 0, 1000, -2000 );
}
```

Figure 7.15 One Solution to Object Initialization, 1 of 3

```
private float balanceI = -10;
private Customer customerI;

public Account ( . . . ) . . .

public float getBalance()
{   return balanceI;
}
```

Figure 7.16 One Solution to Object Initialization, 2 of 3

```
public Customer getCustomer()    // access customerI
{
    if( customerI == null )      // never accessed
        customerI =              //initial value
           Customer.getDefaultCustomer();
    return customerI;            //current value
}

public getDefaultAccount()       // for users of Account
{   return new Account( -10, 3, "regular" );
}
```

Figure 7.17 One Solution to Object Initialization, 3 of 3

tions specify all assumptions made when the function is invoked. The postconditions
specify the required state at the conclusion of the function's execution.

As an example, consider the following requirement for a function $f()$.

Precondition: g is an array of integers of length n (g is "given").

Postcondition: $r = \max\{\ g[0],\ g[1],\ \ldots,\ g[n-1]\ \}$ (r is the "result").

Informally, this requirement calls for $f()$ to determine the maximum value of the array g. This
is easy to program, of course, but we will do so in a form that is much easier to prove correct.

```
while (the variables don't have the values required)
          perform appropriate actions
```

/* Need only *prove that this loop terminates* to
ensure that the variables have the values required*/

Figure 7.18 A Simple Correctness Framework

One way to become familiar with programming provably correct code fragments is to apply the (pseudocode) form shown in Figure 7.18. To prove that the variables end up with their required values, the programmer has only to verify that the loop terminates. If the programmer can prove this, then the statement *the variables don't have the values required* is no longer true when the loop terminates (a double negative), and so the desired state has been reached.

At first glance, provably correct programs appear to be a very different way of going about programming. This is not actually so. The intuitive process one normally uses is not different: Formality merely helps to control the process with much more precision. For example, most of us would program a *max()* function by setting up a loop and accumulating the maximum "so far." In other words, we would keep the following statement true during the computation:

$$[j <= n{-}1] \text{ AND } [r = \text{maximum}\{ g[0], g[1], \ldots, g[j] \}] \text{ // statement I}$$

As mentioned in previous chapters, a statement that is to be kept true like this is known as an *invariant*. We also say that the statement is "kept invariant" (unchanged). Although the values of the individual variables within it (j and r) do change, *the statement as a whole remains true*. One can think of an invariant as a kind of seesaw in which the variables are continually coordinated to keep it level. As the *max()* computation progresses and j increases, the values of r and j are coordinated to keep statement I true. Note that *max()* is the name of the function we are developing, whereas the word "maximum," used in the statement of the invariant, is intended for human consumption and refers to a mathematical concept that readers are supposed to be familiar with.

An invariant is used in a program as a kind of scaffold on which the rest of the program is built. It is analogous to an infrastructure in structural engineering: a "given" on which we can build, in order to satisfy requirements. This is suggested by Figure 7.19, in which an infrastructure has been developed that provides an "invariant" upon which an elevated highway can be built.

A provably correct program for *max()* is shown in Figure 7.20. Notice that we are using a *while()* loop instead of a *for* loop because *while* loops are easier to use with correctness proofs. A limit is placed on n because real computers cannot guarantee the program's effectiveness for any n without limit. A proof that this program is correct is stated in Figure 7.21.

This simple example illustrates the argument of scientists and engineers who feel that software engineering will increasingly use formal methods over time. They point out that formal methods merely make more professional and precise the way we already implement applications. In "A Discipline of Programming," Dijkstra [Di] shows how even the simplest programs can possess a wealth of potential variations, some efficient and some not, some satisfying their requirement and some not. Thus, it is not at all surprising that

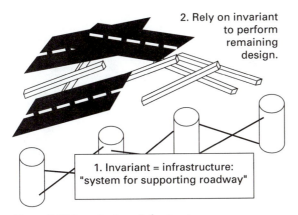

2. Rely on invariant to perform remaining design.

1. Invariant = infrastructure: "system for supporting roadway"

Figure 7.19 Invariants as Infrastructures

```
//Define I: 0 ≤ j ≤ n−1 < 100 & r = max{g[0], g[1], . . . , g[j]}
//After the following two commands, I is true:
int r=g[0];
int j=0;

//This block keeps I true
while( j < n-1 )
{    if( g[ j+1 ]>r )
             r=g[ j+1 ];
     ++j;
}
```

Figure 7.20 Provably Correct Program to Sum an Array of Length n, 1 of 2

```
/* Assuming that the loop terminates (proved below), we know at
this point that j < n–1 is no longer true. We have also kept I invari-
ant (true). Putting these together,
    • j < n–1 is false, AND
    • j <= n–1 (from statement I), AND
    • r = max {g[0], g[1], . . . , g[j]} (from statement I)

so that j = n–1 AND r = max {g[0], g[1], . . . , g[n–1]}

—which was our goal.

It remains only to prove that the while loop terminates. Because I
is kept invariant, the quantity n–j is always positive: in addition,
n–j diminishes by 1 on each iteration. The only way this can occur
is if the loop terminates. */
```

Figure 7.21 Provably Correct Program to Sum an Array of Length n, 2 of 2

bugs lurk in the code of even the best programmers. Consequently, we need all the available tools and techniques to produce reliable applications.

The following example is adapted from "A Discipline of Programming" [Di]. A similar, but easier to read, reference is Gries ([Gr]). The problem is to find the greatest common divisor (GCD) of two positive integers: the greatest natural number (1, 2, . . .) that divides both. For example, the GCD of 18 and 12 is 6.

Preconditions:
   xP and *yP* are both natural numbers
Postconditions: (restates definition of GCD)
   1. *gcd*(*xP*, *yP*) is a positive integer
   2. *gcd*(*xP*, *yP*) divides *xP* and *yP*
   3. if *z* is any natural number dividing
       both *xP* and *yP*, then *z* <= *gcd*(*xP*, *yP*)

*Figure 7.22 Requirements for gcd (xP, yP) as
            Preconditions and Postconditions*

```
// Let I be the assertion "GCD(xP, yP) = GCD (x, y)"
```

```
// Initialize the variables to make I true:
```

```
int x = xP;
int y = yP;
```

```
/* The loop below preserves I and results in x == y.
When it terminates (termination proof later):
      GCD(xP, yP) = GCD(x, y)    from the invariant
      = GCD(x, x)                because x == y
      = x
Report x as the result and our work will be done. */
```

Figure 7.23 Provably Correct Code for Greatest Common Divisor, 1 of 2

```
while( !( x==y ) )
{     if( x>y )
            x = x - y;    //preserves I (property of GCD)
      else                // !(x == y) and !(x > y), thus x < y
            y = y - x;    //preserves I (same property of GCD)
}
/* The quantity  x + y  diminishes by at least 1 on every iteration, but re-
mains positive. Thus, the number of iterations must be finite. */
System.out.println("Greatest common divisor of" +
xP + "and" + yP + "is" + x);
```

Figure 7.24 Provably Correct Code for Greatest Common Divisor, 2 of 2

We will distinguish between "GCD," the concept as we humans understand it (ex-plained in the preceding paragraph), and "gcd()," the code we are constructing to implement GCD. The program in Figures 7.22, 7.23, and 7.24 uses the mathematical fact that the GCD of two positive integers *a* and *b* is the same as the GCD of the pair *a* − *b* and *b*, provided the quantity *a* − *b* is positive. For example, the GCD of 30 and 18 (which is 6) is the same as the GCD of 30 − 18 and 18. The latter pair, 12 and 18, also has a GCD of 6.

The requirements for the method—*gcd(int xP, int yP)*—can be stated as in Figure 7.22. Code for the function *gcd(int anX, int aY)*, including a proof, is shown in Figure 7.23

1. Devise a relationship *I* among the variables which is easy to establish, and a relationship *r* so that *I AND r* together yield the postcondition.

2. Write code that makes *I* true.

3. Follow by code in the form
   `while(!r)`
   > {   *Perform operations that*
   > * *keep I invariant and*
   > * *cause the loop to terminate eventually*
   > }

4. Prove that the `while` loop terminates.

Figure 7.25 A Common Way to Write Provably Correct Loops

and Figure 7.24. The termination proof is just one of several possible explanations of why the loop must have a finite number of iterations.

We can summarize many applications of provably correct code as in Figure 7.25.

5. TOOLS AND ENVIRONMENTS FOR PROGRAMMING

It has often been said that man is a toolmaker, and this is no less true of software developers. There are an increasing number of tools that help with programming.

Interactive development environments (IDEs) are widely used to enable programmers to produce more code in less time. They include drag-and-drop facilities for forming GUI components, graphical representation of directories, debuggers, "wizards," and so forth. The approach taken in JavaBeans is to standardize the source so that any JavaBean development environment can handle the source. This approach has the advantage of not tying developers to a single IDE. The ease with which COM objects can be generated has greatly improved.

Profilers such as *JProbe* can be used to accumulate statistics such as

* Cumulative CPU and elapsed time
* Time spent by each method
* Cumulative count of objects generated
* Number of calls
* Average method time

Applications must have some form of source code in order to be deliverable. Many organizations at CMM level 1 take this to extremes by producing nothing but source code. The realization by tool vendors that their customers can be counted on to produce source code, hopefully documented, has motivated them to produce reverse engineering tools that take source code as input, and which develop limited documentation. An example of a reverse engineering source code tool is *Javadoc*, which was discussed in Section 7.3 of Chapter 6 (page 333). Reverse engineering is discussed more fully in Chapter 9.

Several object-oriented tools (such as Rational Rose, Together/J/C++) generate source code from object models. These forward engineering tools cannot be expected to generate more than code skeletons within which the programmer must work to produce the eventual implementation. The same tools also perform reverse engineering by mechanically producing object models from source code (hence the term "round trip engineering").

The history of tools in other branches of engineering (e.g., CAD/CAM) suggests that programming tools will continue to improve significantly, that they will continue to leverage programming skills, and that they will reduce drudgery and mechanical tasks.

6. QUALITY IN IMPLEMENTATION

This section discusses metrics and methods for attaining quality implementations. Figures 7.26, 7.27, 7.28, 7.29, and 7.30 provide a code inspection checklist.

One Way To. . . Inspect Code I: *Classes Overall*

C1. Is its (the class') name appropriate?
  • consistent with the requirements or the design?
  • sufficiently specialized/general?

C2. Could it be abstract (to be used only as a base)?

C3. Does its header describe its purpose?

C4. Does its header reference the requirements or design element to which it corresponds?

C5. Does it state the package to which it belongs?

C6. Is it as private as it can be?

C7. Should it be *final* (Java)?

C8. Have the documentation standards been applied?
  • e.g., Javadoc

Figure 7.26 One Way to Inspect Code I: Classes Overall

One Way To. . . Inspect Code II: *Attributes*

A1. Is it (the attribute) necessary?

A2. Could it be *static*?
  • Does every instance really need its own variable?

A3. Should it be *final*?
  • Does its value really change?
    • Would a "getter" method alone be preferable?

A4. Are the naming conventions properly applied?

A5. Is it as private as possible?

A6. Are the attributes as independent as possible?

A7. Is there a comprehensive initialization strategy?
  • at declaration time?
  • with constructor(s)?
  • using *static*{}?
  • Mix the above? How?

Figure 7.27 One Way to Inspect Code II: Attributes

```
One Way To. . . Inspect Code III: Constructors

CO1.   Is it (the constructor) necessary?
         • Would a factory method be preferable?
             • More flexible
             • Extra function call per construction
CO2.   Does it leverage existing constructors?
         •   (a Java-only capability)
CO3.   Does it initialize all the attributes?
CO4.   Is it as private as possible?
CO5.   Does it execute the inherited constructor(s) where necessary?
```

Figure 7.28 One Way to Inspect Code III: Constructors

```
One Way To. . . Inspect Code IV: Method Headers

MH1.   Is the method appropriately named?
         • method name consistent with requirements or design?
MH2.   Is it as private as possible?
MH3.   Could it be static?
MH4.   Should it be final?
MH5.   Does the header describe the method's purpose?
MH6.   Does the method header reference the requirements and/or design
       section that it satisfies?
MH7.   Does it state all necessary variants? (see Section 4)
MH8.   Does it state all preconditions?
MH9.   Does it state all postconditions?
MH10.  Does it apply documentation standards?
MH11.  Are the parameter types restricted? (see Section 2.5)
```

Figure 7.29 One Way to Inspect Code IV: Method Headers

```
One Way To. . . Inspect Code V: Method Bodies

MB1.   Is the algorithm consistent with the detailed design pseudocode or
       flowchart?
MB2.   Does the code assume no more than the stated preconditions?
MB3.   Does the code produce every one of the postconditions?
MB4.   Does the code respect the required invariant?
MB5.   Does every loop terminate?
MB6.   Are required notational standards observed?
MB7.   Has every line been thoroughly checked?
MB8.   Are all braces balanced?
MB9.   Are illegal parameters considered? (see Section 2.5)
MB10.  Does the code return the correct type?
MB11.  Is the code thoroughly commented?
```

Figure 7.30 One Way to Inspect Code V: Method Bodies

6.1 Standard Metrics for Source Code

6.1.1 Counting Lines "Lines of code," however imperfect, constitutes a useful programming metric. A standard way of counting has to be established. For example:

Decide how to count statements that occupy several lines (1 or "n"?).

Decide how to count comments (0?).

Decide how to count lines consisting of *while, for, do*, etc. (1?).

The choice depends on precedent, the standard used for historical data, and on automatic counting tools that are adopted. Keeping lines-of-code data consistent with the definition chosen is much more important than the exact choice of definition.

6.1.2 IEEE Metrics The following is a small sample of metrics from [IEEE 982] showing ways of quantifying the quality of source code. These do not depend on testing, which is covered in the next chapter.

IEEE Metric 14. Software Science Measures

Measured quantities used:

Let n_1 = number of distinct operators (+, * etc.) in the program. For example, in the program { $x=x+y; z=x*w;$ }, $n_1 = 2$.

Let n_2 = number of distinct operands in the program. For example, in { $x=x+y; z=x*w;$ }, $n_2 = 4$, since the + and the * each involve two operands.

Let N_1 = total number of occurrences of the operators in the program.

Let N_2 = total number of occurrences of the operands in the program.

Sample of Halstead estimates:

Estimated program length: $n_1(log\ n_1) + n_2(log\ n_2)$

Program difficulty: $(n_1N_2)/(2n_2)$

For more on Software Science measures, see [Ha5].

IEEE Metric 16. Cyclomatic Complexity.
This metric determines the structural complexity of a block of code by essentially counting loops, which are important factors for complexity. It can be used to identify modules whose complexity should be targeted for reduction.

An example of a policy based on this metric is to require all modules with cyclomatic complexity exceeding the mean by 20% to undergo special review.

Measured quantities used:

N: number of nodes (program statements)

E: number of edges (an "edge" joins node m to node n if statement n can immediately follow statement m)

One method for computing the cyclomatic complexity is to compute $E - N + 1$. Another way to obtain this number is to count the number of closed regions formed by edges which cannot be split into smaller closed regions. This is evident in Figure 7.31.

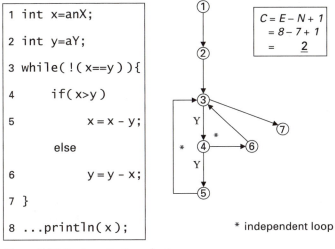

```
1 int x=anX;

2 int y=aY;

3 while(!(x==y)){

4      if(x>y)

5           x = x - y;

    else

6           y = y - x;

7 }

8 ...println(x);
```

$$C = E - N + 1$$
$$= 8 - 7 + 1$$
$$= \underline{2}$$

* independent loop

Figure 7.31 Cyclomatic Complexity

6.2 Custom Metrics for Source Code

Cyclomatic complexity expresses the number of loops in a program, but does not distinguish between nested and non-nested looping. In general, loops within loops are more error-prone than sequences of independent loops.

It is not hard to create metrics that measure significant identified issues. For example, to measure loop complexity, one could estimate that each nesting of a loop increases complexity by an order of magnitude (roughly, a factor of 10). The following nesting example could be given a nesting complexity factor as described.

Loop 1—counts as 1

Loop 2—counts as 1

        Loop 2.1—counts as 10 (a loop within loop 2)

        Loop 2.2—counts as 10

                Loop 2.2.1—counts as 100

Loop 3—counts as 1

Loop 4—counts as 1

Loop 5—counts as 1

        Loop 5.1—counts as 10

Using this metric, the complexity value of the result is 135. This metric can be normalized by dividing by lines-of-code, then compared with a company or division average.

6.3 Code Inspection

Recall that *severity* is an essential piece of inspection data since it allows the prioritization of defects, allowing a rational scheduling of the work. (See Table 7.1, reproduced from Chapter 6.) Trivial defects are not worth the time of an inspection meeting. A good way to handle trivial defects is for inspectors to give a marked up source listing directly to the author.

The other descriptors of defects are their *type*, one classification of which is repeated below from Chapter 6.

TABLE 7.1 Defect Severity Classification Using Triage

Severity	Description
Major	Requirement(s) not satisfied
Medium	Neither major nor trivial
Trivial	A defect that will not affect operation or maintenance

Logic problem (forgotten cases or steps; duplicate logic; extreme conditions neglected; unnecessary functions; misinterpretation; missing condition test; checking wrong variables; iterating loops incorrectly, etc.)

Computational (equation insufficient or incorrect; precision loss; sign convention fault)

Interface/timing (interrupts handled incorrectly; I/O timing incorrect; subroutine/module mismatch)

Data handling (initialized data incorrectly; accessed or stored data incorrectly; scaling or units of data incorrect; dimension of data incorrect)

Scope of data

Data (sensor data incorrect or missing; operator data incorrect or missing; embedded data in tables incorrect or missing; external data incorrect or missing; output data incorrect or missing; input data incorrect or missing)

Documentation (ambiguous description, etc.)

Document quality (applicable standards not met, etc.)

Enhancement (change in program requirements, etc.)

Failure caused by a previous fix

Interoperability (not compatible with other software or component)

Standards conformance

Other (none of the above)

```
/**
* Requirement 3.2.P.3.1 Configurability of the player character quality values
*/
public synchronized void adjustQuality
   (String qualityP, float qualityValueP)
     {
       float originalSumM = sumOfQualities(); // must remain invariant


       try
       {//pc IF qualityP is not recognized,
       //pc  Log error to log file and inform user qualities unchanged
       //Will need current value of qualityP
       float originalValueOfaQualityPM = qualValueP[indexOf( qualityP )];

       //pc IF qualityValueP out of bounds
       //pc   Log error to log file and inform user qualities unchanged........
       //pc ELSE
       //pc   Set the stated quality to qualityValueP
       setQuality( qualityP,qualityValueP );
```

> Pseudocode not followed; severity *medium*; type *data*

> Defect as above

Figure 7.32 Original adjustChar() *Source Code,* 1 of 2

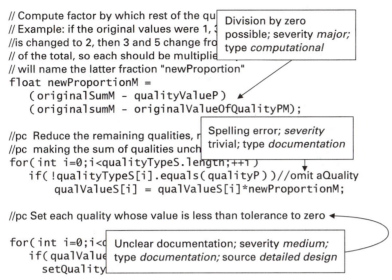

```
// Compute factor by which rest of the qu
// Example: if the original values were 1, 3
//is changed to 2, then 3 and 5 change fro
// of the total, so each should be multiplie
// will name the latter fraction "newProportion"
float newProportionM =
    ( originalSumM - qualityValueP )
    ( originalsumM - originalValueOfQualityPM);
```

Division by zero possible; severity *major;* type *computational*

```
//pc  Reduce the remaining qualities, r
//pc  making the sum of qualities unch
for( int i=0;i<qualityTypeS.length;++i )
    if( !qualityTypeS[i].equals( qualityP ) )//omit aQuality
        qualValueS[i] = qualValueS[i]*newProportionM;
```

Spelling error; *severity trivial;* type *documentation*

```
//pc Set each quality whose value is less than tolerance to zero
```

```
for( int i=0;i<
    if( qualValue
        setQuality
```

Unclear documentation; severity *medium;* type *documentation;* source *detailed design*

Figure 7.33 Original adjustChar() *Source Code,* 2 of 2

As an example of code inspection, we inspect the code for the method *adjustQuality( )* in the case study class *EncounterCharacter* as shown in Figure 7.32 and Figure 7.33.

6.4 Personal Software Documentation

Each engineer is required to maintain documentation of his current work. This documentation has a name such as the Software Development Folder, Personal Software Documentation (PSD). This enables the engineer to report status at all times, and some of it becomes part of the project's archive. The PSD can include the items in Figure 7.34.

- Source code
- Personal defect log
  - defects type
  - personal phase during which injected
  - personal phase during which removed
  The personal phases are
    1. *Additional detailed design (if applicable)*
    2. *Code (record defects injected or detected—and repaired——in source code before submission to the compiler)*
    3. *Compile record (record defects detected and repaired after attempted compilation)*
    4. *Unit test*
       - *Unit testing performed by QA, is not part of this documentation.*
  - Time log
    - *time spent on additional detailed design, coding, compiling, and testing*
  - Engineering notebook
    - *includes status of additional detailed design (if applicable) and code*
    - *incidents, noteworthy development issues*

Figure 7.34 Personal Software Documentation

The Software Engineering Institute's Personal Software Process mandates the time log and defect information. The team or project leader determines how to use and archive the PSD of the team members. The word "personal" should not be taken to mean that the PSD is the property of the engineer: Work for which an organization pays is ordinarily the property of that organization. Engineers are primarily evaluated on the end products of their personal process and on whether their process is properly documented. Generally speaking, they are not evaluated on all of the steps in that process.

7. SUMMARY OF THE IMPLEMENTATION PROCESS

The goals of implementation are to correctly program the detailed design in a manner that promotes maintainability. Programming standards help in this process. An organized way of specifying the purpose of each method is essential, and this can be accomplished by stating preconditions and postconditions. Code, especially potentially difficult code, can be proven to satisfy its requirements (i.e., independent of testing) by writing the program text in a disciplined, preferably provable, manner. These points are shown in Figure 7.35.

EXERCISES

Solutions and hints are given at the end of this chapter to all exercises marked with "s" and "h" respectively.

REVIEW QUESTIONS

R7.1[s] You are about to code a method. What are the two major sources telling you what this method is to do?

R7.2[s] State 3–5 steps that typically should happen once you have coded a method.

For answers to review questions 7.3 through 7.6, see text Sections 2.1–2.4 on pages 362–364.

R7.3 Give 3–4 general principles of sound implementation.

- Keep coding goals in mind
  - correctness
  - clarity
- Apply programming standards
- Specify preconditions and postconditions
- Prove selected segments correct—compiler-free
- Implement with measured time
- Maintain quality and professionalism

Figure 7.35 "Implementation" Chapter Summary

R7.4 Give 2–3 general principles of dealing with pointers.

R7.5 Give 2–3 general principles of dealing with functions.

R7.6 Give 4–6 general principles of dealing with exceptions.

R7.7[s] Suppose that you want a program fragment to accomplish a state S involving float variables x, y, and z. (For example, $x = \max(y, z)$.)

    a. Give a general, provably correct *while* structure for doing this.

    b. What is required to complete the proof?

    c. In what way does this *while* structure provide a possible handle on the efficiency of the procedure?

    d. Code fragments do not usually exist in a vacuum. The *while* loop is usually embedded in surrounding code. Generically, describe a way in which the loop relates to its environment that is often used to establish correctness.

R 7.8[s] Summarize a rigorous general way to specify what a method is intended to do.

R 7.9 Give 5 source code metrics. (For answers, see the "metrics" Section 6.1 on page 378.)

GENERAL EXERCISES

G7.1 Give 2–4 pros and 1–2 cons for enforcing coding standards.

TEAM EXERCISES

T7.1 ("Implementation")

Implement key parts of your application to form a prototype.

SOLUTIONS TO QUESTIONS

R7.1 The method either corresponds directly to a detailed (D-)requirement in the SRS, or it is required by the design.

R7.2 You should measure the time it took for you to do the work, as in the PSP. You should self-inspect and self-test it thoroughly. The method, either alone or together with other methods, is then subjected to regular code inspection. After completing this process, it is subjected to unit testing, and, when accepted, it is integrated into the application.

R 7.7 (a)

    while(not S)

        perform computation

R 7.7 (b) Prove that the loop terminates.

R 7.7 (c) It may be possible to compare the efficiency of algorithms of this form by comparing the number of iterations and the extent of the computations performed within the *while* block before it terminates.

R 7.7 (d) Often, there is an assertion (a relationship among the variables) that is left unchanged ("invariant").

R 7.8 Specify preconditions and postconditions.

CASE STUDY

I. UPDATES TO THE SQAP

(add to: 5. Standards, Practices, Conventions, and Metrics, [5.2 Content])

5.2.1 Programming Conventions (this section is added)

The following conventions will be used.

Parts of nonconstant names are delineated by capitalization: for example, *thisIsAName*.

Class and interface names begin with a capital: for example, *Account*.

Instance variables in classes begin with a lowercase character and end with "I": for example, *balanceI*.

Static (class) variables begin with a lowercase character, and end with "S": for example, *interestRateS*.

Variables defined in, and global to, a method begin with a lowercase character and end with "M": for example, *interestM*.

Parameters begin with a lowercase character and end with "P": for example, *principalP*.

Final variables shall be written in capitals and shall use underscores: for example, *BANK_NAME*.

5.2.2 Notation for Showing the Location of Files

We will use UML to describe the implementation (Booch et al. [Booch-UML]).

5.2.3 Personal Software Documentation

Each engineer will maintain documentation of his current work, which is referred to as his Personal Software Documentation (PSD). This enables the engineer to report status at all times and it becomes part of the project's archive. The team or project leader will determine how to organize the PSD of the team. Typically, a personal software document set corresponds to a task that has been allocated to the engineer, and consists of a set of classes.

[Note to the student: An example of PSD is provided in Section III below.]

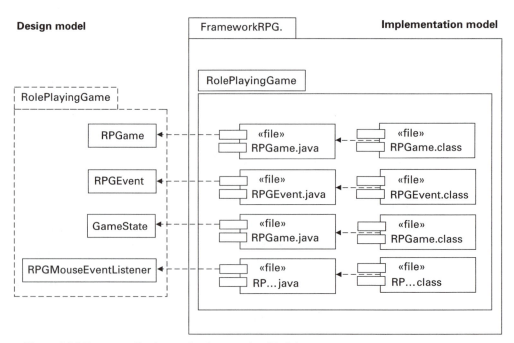

Figure 7.36 Encounter Design vs. Implementation Models

II. UPDATES TO THE SCMP APPENDIX: IMPLEMENTATION MODEL

Sample

A part of the *Encounter* implementation model is shown in Figure 7.36.

III. PERSONAL SOFTWARE DOCUMENTATION, PART 1 OF 2

[Note to the student: This document is maintained by individual engineers to describe the current state of their work. It should be complete enough to allow the engineer to report his or her status at meetings, or to allow another engineer to take over the work in a reasonable amount of time if necessary.

If the engineer is following the PSP or the TSP, then the format and content of this document is specified by those processes. The format below uses ideas from the PSP, but is not the full PSP form. See Chapter 8 for Part 2.]

1. INTRODUCTION

This document describes the work of John Jones on the class *EncounterCharacter*. It is under configuration control with the file name *PSD_EncounterCharacter*. The files referenced here are stored in the directory *Encounter\PSD\JJones* on the Galaxy system.

2. DEFECT RECORDING LOG

The log in Table 7.2 is maintained in file *defectLog*.

3. TIME RECORDING LOG

[Note to the student: Engineers maintain records of how long it takes them to perform the various activities required by software engineering (refer to Table 7.3). These data are essential for the project, and they also provide the engineer with a professional "toolkit." Timing data can be collected via written forms or via software tools residing on desktop computers, hand-helds and so on. Engineers have to develop a common understanding of the degree of precision required by the organization. Note that approximate time measurements can easily become too inconsistent for practical use.] These data are stored in *Time_Recording_Log*.

TABLE 7.2 Defect Recording Log (HUMPHREY)

Date	Number	Type	Phase Injected	Phase Removed	Repair Time (minutes)
6/14/99	142	Interface	Personal detailed design	Personal code review	10
Description: omitted checks on name length in EncounterCharacter					
6/16/99	143	Documentation	Code	Personal code review	4
Description: incorrect Javadoc description of EncounterCharacter					
. . . . . .	. . . . . .	. . . . . .	. . . . . .	. . . . . .	. . . . . .
. . . . . .					

This table concludes with defects found during unit test (see Chapter 8).

TABLE 7.3 Time Recording Log (Humphrey)

Date	Start	Stop	Interruptions	Time taken	Phase	Comments
6/99	10:04 am	10:25 am	4 + 6	11	Detailed Design	Consulted with V.N.
6/99	1:20 pm	4:34 pm	15 + 20	159	Personal Code review	Defect 14
7/99	. . . .					

(5. UNIT TEST PSD FOR ENCOUNTERCHARACTER)

—See Case Study: Chapter 8.

IV. SOURCE CODE (WITHOUT TEST CODE): *ENCOUNTERCHARACTER*

Source code for the *EncounterCharacter* class is shown in Figure 7.37, Figure 7.38, Figure 7.39, Figure 7.40, Figure 7.41, Figure 7.42, Figure 7.43, Figure 7.44, Figure 7.45, Figure 7.46, Figure 7.47, Figure 7.48, and Figure 7.49.

```
package Encounter.EncounterCharacters;
/* Class Name        : EncounterCharacter
* Date               : 01/13/2000
* Copyright Notice   : copyright © 1999-2000 by Eric J. Braude
*/
import java.awt.*;
import java.io.*;
import FrameworkRPG.Characters.*;
import TestUtilities.*;

/**Base class for the characters of the Encounter game. SDD reference: 6.2.1
* <p> Invariants:   The values of qualValueI[] are >= 0
* @author Eric Braude, Tom VanCourt
* @version 0.2
*/
public class EncounterCharacter extends GameCharacter
{
/** Total quality points at initialization. */
private static final float QUAL_TOTAL_INIT = 100.0f;
```

Figure 7.37 Listing—page 1

// Symbols used when other classes refer to specific qualities.

```
/** Symbol for one of a character's qualities */
public static final String QUAL_CONCENTRATION = "concentration";

/** Symbol for one of a character's qualities */
public static final String QUAL_INTELLIGENCE = "intelligence";

/** Symbol for one of a character's qualities */
public static final String QUAL_PATIENCE = "patience";

/** Symbol for one of a character's qualities */
public static final String QUAL_STAMINA = "stamina";

/** Symbol for one of a character's qualities */
public static final String QUAL_STRENGTH = "strength";

/** Qualities that each Encounter character possesses <p>Req:3.2.EC.1.2 */
private static final String[] qualityTypeS=
{   QUAL-CONCENTRATION, QUAL_STAMINA,
    QUAL_INTELLIGENCE,  QUAL_PATIENCE,
    QUAL_STRENGTH
};
```

Figure 7.38 Listing—page 2

```
/* INSTANCE VARIABLES */
/** Values of the qualities <p> Requirement 3.2.EC.1.2*/
private float[] qualValueI = new float[qualityTypeS.length];
/** Name of the GIF file containing the character's image
* The character in this image is assumed to be facing left
* Select this character's height, relative to heights of other characters, by padding the top
* and bottom with transparent pixels. No padding gives the tallest possible character.
*/
private String imageFileNameI = null;

/* CONSTRUCTORS */

/** Allocate initial total quality points equally among the qualities.
* <p> Requirement: 3.2.EC.1.2 (quality value initialization)
*/
protected EncounterCharacter()
{   super();
    for( int i = 0; i < qualityTypeS.length; ++i )
        qualValueI[i] = QUAL_TOTAL_INIT / qualityTypeS.length;
}
```

Figure 7.39 Listing—page 3

```
/** Construct a new character using the given name and image file.
 * <p> Requirement:    3.2.EC.1.1 (character naming)
 * @param     nameP    Printable name for the character
 * @param     imageFileP   Filename, relative to document base, for character image
 */
protected EncounterCharacter( String nameP, String imageFileP )
{   this();
    setName( nameP );
    imageFileNameI = imageFileP;
}
```

```
/** Construct a new character using the given name.
 * <p> Requirement:   3.2.EC.1.1 (character naming)
 * @param    nameP   Printable name for the character
 */
protected EncounterCharacter( String nameP )
{   this( nameP, null );
}
```

Figure 7.40 Listing—page 4

```
/* METHODS */
```

```
/** Requirements 3.2.EC.3.2: "Configurability of Encounter character quality values."
 * Synchronizatoin holds qualityValueI constant even with other threads running.
 * <p> SDD reference: 6.1.2.1.1
 * <p> Invariants: see the class invariants
 * <p> Preconditions: qualityP is in qualityTypeS[]
 *     AND qualityValueP >= 0
 *     AND qualityValueP <= the sum of the quality values
 * <p> Postconditions: qualityP has the value qualityValueP
 *     AND the remaining quality values are in the same proportion as prior to invocation,
 *         except that values less than some tolerance are zero.
 * @param     qualityP          Quality whose value is to be adjusted
 * @param     qualityValueP     The value to set this quality to
 */
public synchronized void adjustQuality( String qualityP, float qualityValueP )
{   // Value of the quality to be changed
    float qualityValueM = qualValueI[indexOf( qualityP )];

    // Save the sum of the values
    float originalSumM = sumOfQualities();

    // pc Set the stated quality to the desired amount, adjusted to the threshold value.
    setQuality( qualityP, qualityValueP );
```

> "//pc" references the pseudocode

Figure 7.41 Listing—page 5

```
// pc If the caller adjusts only the nonzero quality value,
// divide the adjustment amount equally among all other qualities.
if(originalSumM==qualityValueM)
{   float qualityDiffEach=(originalSumM-qualityValueP)/(qualityTypeS.length-1);
    for(int i=0; i<qualityTypeS.length; ++i)
        if(!qualityTypeS[i].equalsIgnoreCase(qualityP))
            setQuality(qualityTypeS[i], qualityDiffEach);
}
else {
    /* Compute factor ("proportionM") by which all other qualities must change.
     * Example: if the values were 1, 3, 5 (i.e. sum 9), and the first quality is changed
     * from 1 to 2, then "3" and "5" change from 8/9 of the total to 7/9
     * of the total, so each should be manipulated by 7/8, i.e., by (9 – 2)/(9 – 1).
     */
    float proportionM=(originalSumM-qualityValueP)/(originalSumM-qualityValueM);

    //pc Adjust the remaining qualities, retaining their mutual proportion
    for (int i=0; i<qualityTypeS.length; ++i)
        if(!qualityTypeS[i].equalsIgnoreCase(qualityP))
            setQuality(qualityTypeS[i], qualValueI[i]* proportionM);
    }
}
```

Figure 7.42 Listing—page 6

```
/** Get a copy of the list of names of quality values.
 * @return      working copies of name strings representing qualities
 */
public static String[] getQualityTypes()
{
    String[] returnListM=newString[qualityTypeS.length];        // Copy the string array.

    for(int i=0; i<qualityTypeS.length; i++)                    // Copy each string.
        returnListM[i]=newString(qualityTypeS[i]);

    return returnListM;                                          // Return the copy.
}

/** Returns the value of the specified quality
 * <p>Precondition:     qualityP is a valid member of qualityTypeS[].
 * @param      qualityP  The quality we want the value for
 * @return               The value of the specified quality
 */
public float getQualityValue(String qualityP)
{
    return qualValueI[indexOf(qualityP)];
}
```

Figure 7.43 Listing—page 7

```
/** Quality values below this threshold are set to zero to avoid having the game
* go on for an indeterminate amount of time.
* <p>Requirement: e.g.3.2.EC.1.2 (lower limit on non-zero quality values
* @return        Tolerance value
*/
static final float getTolerance()
{   return 0.5f;
}
```

Figure 7.44 Listing—page 8

```
/** Returns the index of the specified quality
* <p> Precondition          qualityP is in qualityTypeS[], give or take capitalization
* @param      qualityP       The quality we are searching for
* @return                    The quality index
*/
private static int indexOf (String qualityP)
{   int returnIndexM = -1   // Default to "missing" value.

    for(int i = 0; i < qualityTypeS.length; ++i)        // Search quality name table.
        if(qualityTypeS[i].equalsIgnoreCase(qualityP)) // Quality name match?
        {   returnIndexM = i;                           // Note the index value
            break;
        }

    return returnIndexM;
}

/** Set default maximum allowable number of characters in names of characters.
* <p>Requirement: //3.2.EC.1.1 (limit on character name length)
* @return          Maximum number of characters allowed in a character name
*/
protected int maxNumCharsInName()
{   return 15;
}
```

Figure 7.45 Listing—page 9

/** Set a quality value without regard to the values of other qualities.
* Truncate any value below the threshold value down to zero.
* Synchronization prevents changes to qualityValueI while other threads are using it.
* <p>Requirements: 3.2.EC.2 (lower limit on nonzero quality values)
* <p>Precondition: *qualityP* is a valid member of *qualityTypeS[]*
* <p>Postcondition: Quality values are greater than tolerance or are 0.
*
* @param   qualityP The quality to set the value of
* @param   valueP   The value to set the quality to
*/

```
public synchronized void setQuality( String qualityP, float valueP )
{
    if( valueP<getTolerance() )
        qualValueI[indexOf(qualityP)]=0.0f;
    else
        qualValueI[indexOf(qualityP)]=valueP;
}
```

Figure 7.46 Listing—page 10

/** Display the character
* <p>Requirements: 2.1.2.1 (character displayed in game Area),
*   3.2.PC.1 (character image selection),
*   3.2.PQ.1 (character image in quality update window)
* @param   compP   UI component in which to draw the character
* @param   drawP   Graphics context for doing the drawing
* @param   posP   Pixel coordinate within compP for the center of the image
* @param   heightPixP Desired image height, in pixels
* @param   faceLeftP   <tt>true</tt> if character faces left, <tt>false if faces right
*/

```
public void showCharacter( Component compP, Graphics drawP, Point posP,
    int heightPixP, Boolean faceLeftP )
{
    if( imageFileNameI==null )
    {   // No image file name. Print the character name instead.
        drawP.setColor( Color.magenta );              // Normally a visible color
        FontMetrics fm=drawP.getFontMetrics();
        drawP.drawString( getName(),                  // Print the name, centered
            posP.x-fm.stringWidth(getname())/2,       // at the character location.
            posP.y-fm.getHeight()/2 );
    }
```

Figure 7.47 Listing—page 11

```
else {       // File name was provided. Draw the image file.
    Image chImage = compP.getToolkit().getImage( imageFileNameI );
    int imageWidth = chImage.getWidth( compP );        // Raw size of the image
    int imageHeight = chImage.getHeight( compP );
    int scaledWidth = imageWidth*heightPixP/imageHeight;   // Scale width same as height


             // Assume that the normal image faces left. Decide whether to reverse the image.
    if( faceLeftP )
        drawP.drawImage( chImage,                              // Draw the image as given,
            posP.x - scaledWidth/2, posP.y - heightPixP/2,    // scaled and centered.
            posP.x + scaledWidth/2, posP.y + heightPixP/2,
            0,0,imageWidth-1, imageHeight-1, compP );
    else
        drawP.drawImage( chImage,                              // Draw the image reversed,
            posP.x + scaledWidth/2, posP.y - heightPixP/2,    // scaled, and centered.
            posP.x - scaledWidth/2, posP.y + heightPixP/2,
            0,0,imageWidth-1, imageHeight-1, compP);
    }

}            // End of showCharacter.
```

Figure 7.48 Listing—page 12

```
/** Computes the sum of the quality values.
* Synchronization makes sure that another thread won't change qualityValueI
* while this thread is part-way through computing the total.
* <p> Requirements:    3.2.EC.3.2 (proportions among quality values)
* @return             The sum of the player's qualities, a value 0 or greater.
*/
public synchronized float sumOfQualities()
{
    float sumM = 0.0f;

    for( int i = 0; i<qualityTypeS.length; ++i )
        sumM += qualValueI[i];

    return sumM;
}

} // end of EncounterCharacter
```

Figure 7.49 Listing—page 13

CHAPTER 8

UNIT TESTING

Carrying, I say, the stamp of one defect,

. . .

Shall in the general censure take corruption
From that particular fault.

Hamlet

The **potential** for harm in every application defect, and the increasing difficulty of detecting and repairing the defect as the application grows, makes it worthwhile to test early and often.

Upon implementing parts of the application, we immediately begin to test, as suggested by Figure 8.1. The learning goals of this chapter are shown in the Figure 8.2.

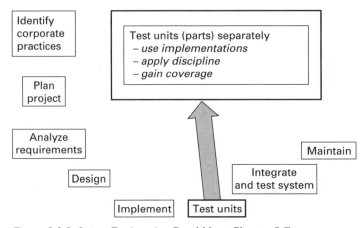

Figure 8.1 Software Engineering Road Map: Chapter 8 Focus

- Understand meaning of unit testing
- Distinguish black box vs. white box testing
- Attain proper test coverage
- Learn a testing standard
- Inspect a unit test plan

Figure 8.2 Learning Goals for This Chapter

1. INTRODUCTION TO UNIT TESTING

1.1 The Goals of Testing

We cannot test an application for every possibility, because the number of ways that a non-trivial computer program may execute is limitless. Thus, testing cannot prove that an application is free of defects, as proofs of correctness can. Testing can only show the *presence* of defects.

Testing is often misunderstood as being primarily a reassurance process, as in "test it to make sure it is right." Sometimes, this is indeed the goal of testing, especially shortly before delivery, or in regression testing (explained in the next chapter). A major purpose of testing is quite the opposite from reassurance, however. The purpose is not to show that the application is satisfactory, but to vigorously determine where the application is *not* satisfactory!

The time spent testing entails considerable expense, and we try to obtain the maximum benefit from this expense. For a given application under test, the more defects found per dollar of labor, the higher the payoff from the investment in testing. Thus, the purpose of testing is to find as many defects, with as high a level of severity, as possible. This is summarized in Figure 8.3.

Testing accounts for more than half of the time spent on projects. The reward for finding a defect early in the process is at least a tenfold saving compared with finding it at integration time or — worse — after delivery. Consequently, we test *early* and *often*.

As with ideal quality assurance in general, the testing of code should be performed by people other than those who developed it. When an engineer develops code, he forms a

Goal of testing: Maximiza the number and severity of defects found per dollar spent.

- thus: test early

Limits of testing: Testing can only determine the presence of defects, never their absence.

- use proofs of correctness to establish "absence"

Figure 8.3 Golden Rules of Testing

vision of what the code is meant to do, and, at the same time, he develops typical circumstances in which the code must execute. It is safe to assume that the code shows few problems in those particular circumstances. Consciously or not, these circumstances form the developer's test cases. Thus, when an individual tests his own code he tends to hide the very defects that need uncovering.

"Unit testing" is the earliest type of testing. The next level consists of integration testing. This validates the overall functionality of each stage of the partial application. Finally, the system and acceptance tests validate the final product, as described in the next chapter. The use cases already developed are used as a basis for some of these tests. Figure 8.4 illustrates types of testing and their relationship.

This chapter covers unit testing; all other tests are explained in Chapter 9.

1.2 The Meaning of "Unit Testing"

The goal of unit testing is structural, whereas the goal of other kinds of testing is typically functional. As an analogy, testing each bridge cable at the factory is a kind of unit testing since it involves structural units. A test which consists of driving a car across the partially constructed bridge, on the other hand, is not unit testing. As shown in Figure 8.4, functions are generally the smallest parts to which unit testing is applied. The next larger unit is the module (the class, in the case of object-orientation). Sometimes, combinations of modules are still considered "units" for the purposes of testing.

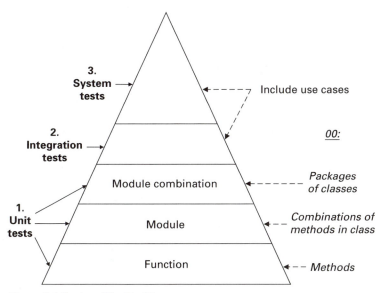

Figure 8.4 Testing: The Big Picture

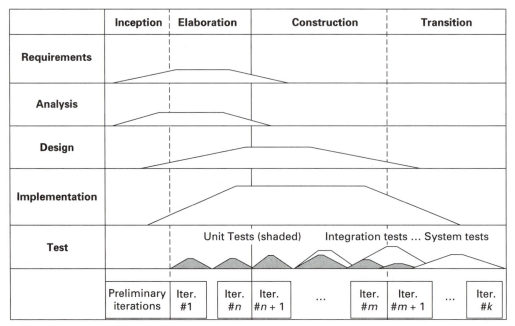

Figure 8.5 Unit Testing in the Unified Process [Ja1]

The units to which "unit testing" is applied are the building blocks of the application, rather like the individual bricks upon which a house rests. Whereas a house is not seriously affected by a few defective bricks, however, a software application can be very sensitive to defects in individual building blocks. Once defective parts become embedded in the application, enormous amounts of time can be taken to identify and repair them. Thus, software building blocks have to be completely reliable, and that is the goal of unit testing.

Unit testing is complementary to inspection and the use of formal correctness.

In terms of the Unified Software Development Process, unit testing takes place mainly during the *Elaboration* iterations and also the early *Construction* iterations, as suggested by Figure 8.5.

1.3 A Typical Unit Testing Road Map

Figure 8.6, which is based on IEEE standard 1008-1987, shows a typical road map for unit testing. The following explains the steps involved in the unit testing process.

1. The inputs to the test planning process consist of the requirements and the detailed design. Recall that each requirement corresponds to well-defined code (a function, where possible). The detailed design typically consists of additional classes and methods. These are also important to the quality of the application, and they must be tested to the same degree as the individual requirements. The output of the test planning process is a unit test plan (e.g., *"(1) test method 84; (2) test method 14;...; (m) test class 26, ..."*).

2. The next step is the acquisition of the input and output data associated with each test. Some of these data may have already been acquired for prior testing (e.g., previous iterations, previous versions of the product, or prior releases). The product of this step is called the test set.

3. Finally, the tests are executed.

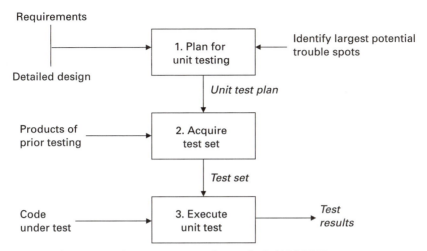

Figure 8.6 Road Map for Unit Testing   Copyright © 1986 IEEE

Here are the steps called for in the IEEE standard for unit testing (1008-1987). They expand the road map just described.

1. Plan the general approach, resources, and schedule.
2. Determine requirements-based characteristics to be tested.
3. Refine the general plan.
4. Design the set of tests.
5. Implement the refined plan and design.
6. Execute the test procedures.
7. Check for termination.
8. Evaluate the test effort and unit.

2. TEST TYPES

Although Glen Myers wrote "The Art of Software Testing" ([My]) back in 1978, this little book remains a classic and has inspired many of the notes in this chapter.

2.1 Black Box, White Box, and Gray Box Testing

This section defines black, white, and gray box testing. The rest of the chapter explains how to plan for, design, and execute such tests.

When we are interested exclusively in whether an application or part thereof provides the appropriate output, we test it for each requirement using appropriate input. This is called *black box testing* because we pay no attention to the insides of the "box" (the application): The box might just as well be "black." Black box tests might be sufficient if we could ensure that they exhaust all combinations of input. This would prove to the customer that all of the requirements are satisfied. No testing covers all possibilities, however.

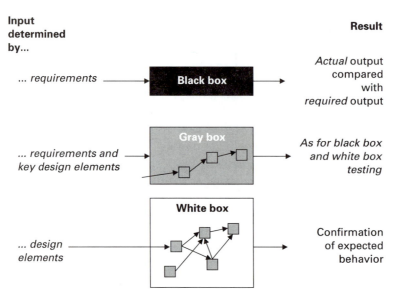

Figure 8.7 Black Box, Gray Box, and White Box Testing

Black box testing is like testing a bridge by driving several combinations of vehicles over it. This is not sufficient because we need to also check the constituents of the bridge and the manner in which it was assembled. The latter is the idea behind *white box testing*. Figure 8.7 illustrates black box and white box testing.

The goal of white box testing is to test along the most likely fault lines of the application. To perform white box testing, we first dissect the design of the application, looking for paths and other partitioning of control and data. Then we design tests which traverse all or some of these paths, and exercise all of the constituent parts. A more descriptive name for this activity is "glass box testing."

"Gray box" testing considers the inside workings of the application or the unit under test, but only to a limited extent. It can include aspects of black box testing as well.

2.2 Equivalence Partitioning for Black Box Testing

Since we cannot test all input combinations, we seek representative test cases. Figure 8.8 illustrates the set of possible test cases for three variables in a financial application: principal, interest rate, and inflation estimate. The problem is to best represent the infinite set of possibilities with as representative a finite set as possible. *Equivalence partitioning* is the division of the test input data into subsets such that if any single input from the partition succeeds, then all others are likely to succeed. For example, in testing the function *setName(String)* in *GameCharacter*, the passing of the test *setName-("Harry")* means that we probably will not find defects by testing *setName()* on every string of five alphabetical characters. Indeed, we can probably extend this equivalence set to "all names with more than zero characters and less than *maxNumCharsInName()* characters."

Figure 8.9 illustrates equivalence partitioning for a method that computes a quantity based on a given principle, a given interest rate, and a given inflation estimate. The shaded equivalence partition described by Figure 8.9, for example, is

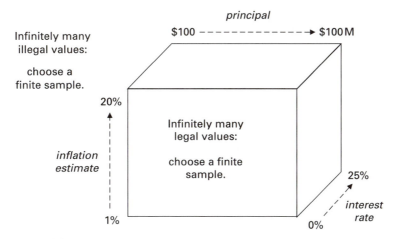

Figure 8.8 Test Input Ranges

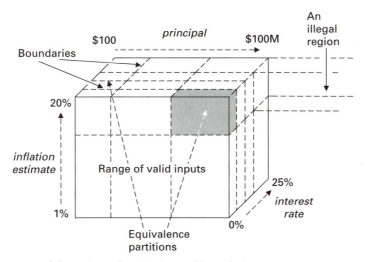

Figure 8.9 Test Input Partitioning and Boundaries

"inflation estimate between 15% and 20%" and "principle between $65M and $100M," and "interest rate between 0% and 5%."

The maximum payoff from testing is usually obtained from values at the boundaries, as explained next.

2.3 Boundary Value Analysis for Black Box Testing

Equivalence partitions are typically arrived at by investigating limiting values for the variables within the application. For example, if the inflation estimate has to be between 1% and 20%, this provides two boundaries. Suppose that the application treats estimates over 15% differently from those under 15%. This would introduce an additional boundary, as shown in Figure 8.9.

In the *setName(String)* function mentioned above, boundaries occur for strings of length zero and strings of length *maxNumCharsInName( )*.

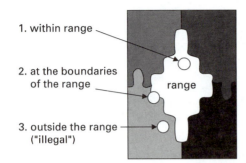

Figure 8.10 Testing Ranges: Elementary Cases

Boundaries can also take a form such as $x + y = 7$. This would result from a condition such as *while*($x + y \geq 7$).

In designing tests, values outside these boundaries (i.e., invalid inputs) are also used as test data. Once the boundaries of equivalence classes are established, test data is generated in a manner suggested by Figure 8.10.

2.4 Statement Coverage for White Box Testing

Every statement in a program should be executed by at least one test. Such statement coverage is *necessary*. As the example in Figure 8.11 shows, however, statement coverage is by no means *sufficient* to ensure that a program is correct (see Myers [My]). The requirements for the program in Figure 8.11 are specified by the flowchart. The test case "$u ==$ 2, $v == 0$, and $x == 3$" executes every command in the implementation and also generates the correct output ($x == 2.5$). The program is defective, however, since it does not implement the flowchart. For example, it generates $x == 1$ from the test case "$u == 3$, $v == 0$, and $x == 3$," whereas it should generate $x == 2$ as specified by the flowchart.

2.5 Decision Coverage for White Box Testing

Decision coverage ensures that the program takes every branch of every decision. For example, considering the flowchart in Figure 8.12, we verify that each "yes" and each "no" has been followed at least once by tests in the test set.

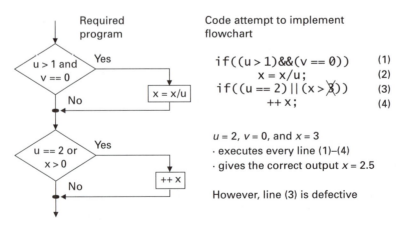

Figure 8.11 Covering Every Statement Is Not Sufficient ([My])

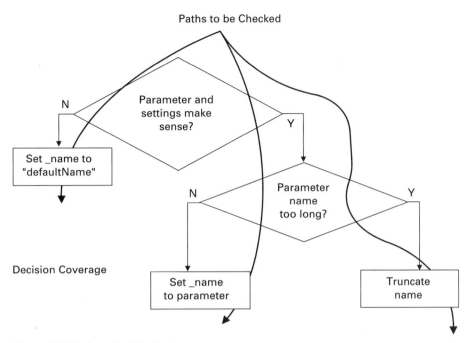

Figure 8.12 Paths to be Checked

Effectively, loops implement a sequence of condition statements. For example, the loop

```
for( i = 0; i < 3; ++i )
   v[i] = w[i+1] + w[i];
```

can be "unrolled" into the following sequence of conditional statements:

```
// For i == 0:
i = 0;
v[i] = w[i+1] + w[i];
++i;
// For i == 1:
if( i < 3 ) {
      v[i] = w[i+1] + w[i];
      ++i;
}
// For i == 2:
if( i < 3 ) {
      v[i] = w[i+1] + w[i];
      ++i;
}
```

Decision coverage ensures that every iteration of every loop is executed. This can be done by identifying each loop and setting the input values so that every iteration of every loop is executed at least once. This approach is not so difficult for *for* loops, but it introduces complications for *while* loops. For example, how would we test every iteration of

```
while( u < v ) { .... } // ?
```

Sometimes, the possibilities can be enumerated completely; Sometimes they can be partitioned into typical groups. Sometimes, however, complete decision coverage is practically impossible for *while* loops. Recall that *while* loops are often amenable to formal methods and inspections. This illustrates the complementary nature of formal methods, inspections, and testing.

Decision coverage usually includes statement coverage, since following all branch points in all combinations usually encounters every statement in the code. Exceptions to this are programs with multiple entry points. Decision coverage can be deficient because some decisions can mask others. For example, in the statement

```
if( A && B ) ...,
```

the condition B is never tested if the condition A is false. Similarly, in the statement

```
if( A || B ) ...,
```

the condition B is never tested if the condition A is true.

To deal with this problem, *multiple condition testing* can be applied. This is a thorough form of condition testing which tests every combination of every condition at least once. Devising test cases for these can be a tedious task because it is necessary to track backwards through the program from each condition to determine appropriate input. Automated test generation software is essential for devising these test sets.

So far, we have concentrated on ensuring that all statements are executed and that the outcomes are the ones we expected. This constitutes a gray box technique in that we are testing for input/output (black box) but also for all statements (white box). We also need to be sure that, as it executes, the program transitions through the states as we intend. Assertion-based testing accomplishes this.

2.6 Assertion-Based Testing

Recall that assertions are statements which relate variables. Assertions express state. For example, to express the state of an automated teller machine application after the user has inserted a card and entered a correct personal identification number, the following typical assertion applies.

```
( cardInserted == true ) && ( pin == VALID )
```

As described in Chapter 7, we use assertions to maintain intellectual control of computations and to prove the correctness of code. In many cases, assertions are invariant (unchanging) throughout strategic blocks of code. It is often useful to insert commands into the source code that report whether or not an assertion that we expect to be true is indeed true. This white box technique is called assertion-based testing. For example, if the sum of variables x and y is supposed to be 10 throughout a computation, then "assert(x + y == 10);" can be checked at run time. The function assert(<argument>) can report the truth or falsity of its argument. If desired, the computation can be suspended if the assertion is false, etc. Sometimes assert() functions are left in the source for run time execution, as in

```
assert( potentiallyFatalXRayDose < 137 );
```

although they are normally used for validation testing only.

Suppose that we want to use assertion-based testing for the *max*() program in the provable correctness Section 7.4 on page 370. The assertion that needs satisfying could be expressed by the method shown in Figure 8.13.

```
public static boolean checkAssertion
    ( int loopSoFarP, int indexOfMaxP, double[] arrayP )
{
```
    // Defining the assertion checker
    // First establish the following booleans:

```
    boolean b1M = true;    /* means values of arrayP[] are lower than
        arrayP [indexOfMaxP] for all indices <indexOfMaxP */
    if( indexOfMaxP != 0 ) // b1M true if max so far is first element
        for( int u = 0; u < indexOfMaxP; ++u )
            b1M &= ( arrayP[u] < arrayP[indexOfMaxP] );
    boolean b2M = true; /* means values of arrayP[] no higher than
        arrayP[indexOfMaxP] for indices indexOfMaxP ... loopSoFarP */
    for( int v = indexOfMaxP; v <= loopSoFarP; ++v )
        b2M &= ( arrayP[v] <= arrayP[indexOfMaxP] );

    if
    (         // Loop has progressed up to index loopSoFarP
            ( 0 <= loopSoFarP ) && ( loopSoFarP < arrayP.length )
            && // indexOfMaxP is the index <= loopSoFarP ...
            ( 0 <= indexOfMaxP ) && ( indexOfMaxP <= loopSoFarP )
                && b1M && b2M // ... where the first max occurs

    )
    {           System.out.printIn( "Assertion valid" );
                return true;
    }
    else
    {           System.out.printIn( "Assertion invalid" );
                return false;
    }
}
```

Figure 8.13 Assertion-based Testing for max()

The assertion test can now be applied whenever the assertion is supposed to be true within the program, as shown in Figure 8.14. This *max*() example is a very simple one, of course, and the amount of trouble required to test it via assertion testing is out of proportion to the code under test. For more complex code under test, however, the set- up time can sometimes be reasonable, and the payoff (defects found per hour spent) much higher.

Modern languages either build assertion capabilities into the language (C++ and Eiffel) or else allow the building of assertion functions by the software engineer or by third parties.

2.6.1 Limits of Automated Assertion Checking

Assertion checking has limits. For example, the assertion used for the simple *gcd()* example in Section 4 of Chapter 7 on page 370 cannot be checked in its current form with an assertion checker. Recall that invariant assertion used for the proof was

$$GCD(anX, aY) = GCD(x, y)$$

```
/** Finds index and value of first of the largest array elements ... */
public static void main( String [] mainArg )
{
double  a[] = getArray();
```

Applying Assertion-based
testing to *max*()

```
// Let I be the assertion ... (see Section 4 of Chapter 7) ... Establish I
int i=0;
int k=0;
boolean validityM = checkAssertion( i,k,a );                    // assertion test

// Following preserves I ... terminates ... (Section 4 of Chapter 7)
while( i!=a.length – 1 )
{    ++i;
        if( a[i] > a[k] )
                k = i;
validityM = validityM && checkAssertion( i, k, a );             // assertion test
}

System.out.printIn( "First max value is" + a[k] + "at index" + k );
System.out.printIn( "Validity:" + validityM );                  // assertion report
}
```

Figure 8.14 Applying Assertion-based Testing to max()

From the perspective of an actual execution, this involves the very computation (greatest common divisor) that we are trying to implement! Humans, on the other hand, *can* use their understanding of GCD to convince each other (and themselves) of the code's correctness.

2.7 Randomness in Testing

Generally speaking, we use random test input in order to avoid biased test samples. For example, if we want to assess the population's opinion of a politician we pick a sample from the population at random. This applies randomness in a focused manner: The type of test is identified first, then randomness is applied to obtain unbiased sample data for this test. The same is true for software testing. Once the type of test has been chosen (e.g., decision coverage) and the limits of the data are defined, substantial leeway remains for the possible input. Ideally, this input should be chosen at random.

As an example, consider performing decision coverage on the flowchart example in Section 2.4 above. Suppose that we want the answer to "name too long?" to be "yes." There is a large data set which makes the name too long, and it is in choosing from this data set that the use of randomness is ideal. One way to do this is to choose each name as follows

Choose an integer *i* greater than *maxNumCharsInName()* at random.

For *j=0 ... i*, choose a character at random and set *name[j]* to this character.

As a second example, consider performing boundary testing for an application that checks whether or not a sequence of four real numbers *x1, x2, x3,* and *x4* is valid data for a sample in an experiment. Suppose that "valid data" means that

$$-5 < x1 \leq 10$$

$$x1 + x2 \leq x3$$

$$x3 \geq x4$$

Boundary testing requires us to select testing data with the following constraints.

$$x1 = -5 \text{ (illegal)}; \ x1 = 10$$
$$x1 + x2 = x3$$
$$x3 = x4$$

Note that $x1$ is to have one of only two values, $x3$ is determined once $x1$ and $x2$ have been chosen, and $x4$ is determined by $x3$. Thus, we must choose from infinitely many values of $x2$, and so we choose these at random to avoid bias.

3. PLANNING UNIT TESTS

A systematic approach to testing is required because the number of potential units to be tested is usually very large. It is easy enough to state that "every part of the job must be tested": However, this has little meaning because the testing phase is allocated only a finite amount of resources (duration and person-hours). Thus, the goal is to detect as many errors as possible at as serious a level as possible, with the resources available. Steps to plan for unit testing are listed in Figure 8.15.

1. Decide on the philosophy of unit testing   The first issue is to identify what the "units" are to be and who is to test them.

For object-oriented development projects, a common organization of unit tests is to test the methods of each class, then the classes of each package, and then the package as a whole. In the case study, we would test the classes in each framework package first and then move on to the application packages, because the latter depend on the former.

Testing a unit is ideally planned and performed by someone other than the developer, and unit testing is, in fact, sometimes planned and performed by the QA organization.

One Way To. . . Plan for Unit Testing

1. Decide on the philosophy for unit testing.
   - individual engineer responsible (common)?
   - reviewed by others?
   - designed and performed by others?
2. Decide what / where / how to document.
   - individual's personal document set (common)?
   - how / when to incorporate into other types of testing?
   - incorporate in formal documents?
   - use tools / test utilities?
3. Determine extent of unit testing (i.e., in advance).
   - do not just "test until time expires"
   - prioritize, so that important tests definitely performed
4. Decide how and where to get the test input.
5. Estimate the resources required.
   - use historical data if available
6. Arrange to track time, defect count, type, and source.

Figure 8.15 One Way to Plan for Unit Testing

Although this has the benefit of independence, it requires QA engineers to understand the design in great detail. Some organizations do not support this capability, and so they assign QA to higher-level testing only. Unit testing is often left to the development group and is performed in a manner of their own choosing. In any case, tests are made available for inspection and for possible incorporation into higher level tests. Some of the independence of QA can be captured by having development engineers unit-test each other's code.

2. Decide how unit tests will be documented   Unit test documentation consists of test procedures, input data, the code that executes the test, and output data. Unit tests can be packaged with the code itself or in separate documents. The advantage of packaging them with the code that they test, is convenience. This technique is illustrated in Section 4.2.1. The disadvantage is the resulting bloat in the size of source code. Precompilers can be used to strip test code before compiling deliverables.

Test drivers and utilities are used to execute unit tests, and these are documented for future use. For example, the case study uses the following test utility function:

```
public static void reportToFile
    (
    FileWriter FileWriterP,
    String TestDescriptionP,
    String CorrectOutputStringP,
    String ActualOutputStringP
    )
```

3. Determine the extent of unit testing   Since it is impossible to test "everything," the extent of testing has to be defined in a conscious manner. For example, if a banking application consists of *withdrawals, deposits,* and *queries,* unit testing could specify that every method should be tested with an equal amount of legal, boundary, and illegal data; or perhaps *withdrawal* and *deposit* methods are tested three times as extensively as query methods, etc. In general, methods that change state (variable values) are usually tested more extensively than those that do not. The limits of what constitutes "unit" testing have to be defined. For example, do they include the testing of packages, or is this to be considered another type of testing (see Chapter 9)?

Engineers also specify the extent of testing in advance, i.e., when the testing process should end. For example, should each unit be tested for a fixed amount of online time? Until the first three failures are obtained? Stopping criteria are discussed further in Section 5.2 on page 416.

Recall that our theme for testing is to perform tests which are most likely to expose errors. By prioritizing tests in accordance with their likelihood to produce defects, we tend to optimize the time spent testing. The prioritization approach depends on the unit under test. Loops are a major source of errors, and so are boundaries and interfaces. In the latter category, tests involving sub-units such as functions are rife with potential defects, since each subunit expects the others to be of a certain kind, and these expectations are often wrong.

4. Decide how and where to get the test input   We have discussed legal, boundary, and illegal inputs for test data. Some random generation is also required. Where possible, tools are used that generate test input by parsing the source code and detecting data boundaries and branches. In addition, a good deal of test data may be available from previous versions of the application, from standard sources, industry benchmarks, etc. All of this is documented for future reference and reuse.

5. Estimate the resources required   As with all planning, we identify the person-months and the duration required to perform unit testing. The prime source for this estimation consists of historical data. Although unit testing is often bundled with the development process, executing it separately provides invaluable data.

6. Arrange to track time, defect count, type, and source   Participating engineers determine the exact form in which they will record the time spent on unit testing, the defect count, and the defect types. The resulting data are used to assess the state of the application and to forecast the job's eventual quality and completion date. The data also become part of the organization's historical record.

The next two sections provide examples of unit test planning at the method and the class levels. The case study at the end of the chapter shows the resulting code.

4.   CHECKLISTS AND EXAMPLES FOR METHOD TESTING

4.1 Unit Testing of Methods

Humphrey [Hu] recommends the checklists for performing method tests in Figures 8.16 and 8.17.

Methods are in one of two categories. The first category corresponds to the requirements placed upon the application. The second category has to do with the classes and methods added to form the design. These categories of test data are illustrated by Figure 8.18.

Unit testing includes the stand-alone testing, where possible, of each method corresponding directly to a requirement stated in the SRS. In other words, we verify that the method satisfies its requirement. Within its limited scope, this is a black box test. White box tests of each method are applied as well (e.g., to obtain statement and decision coverage).

For those methods arising from design, we often do not possess explicitly stated requirements against which to perform tests. An example of a test emanating from the design is

---

One Way To. . . Perform Method Testing, 1 of 2

1.   Verify operation at normal parameter values.
     (a black box test based on the unit's requirements)

2.   Verify operation at limit parameter values.
     (black box)

3.   Verify operation outside parameter values.
     (black box)

4.   Ensure that all instructions execute.
     (statement coverage)

5.   Check all paths, including both sides of all branches.
     (decision coverage)

6.   Check the use of all called objects.

7.   Verify the handling of all data structures.

8.   Verify the handling of all files.

Figure 8.16 One Way to Perform Method Testing (Humphrey), 1 of 2

One Way To. . . Perform Method Testing, 2 of 2

9. Check normal termination of all loops.
   (part of a correctness proof)

10. Check abnormal termination of all loops.

11. Check normal termination of all recursions.

12. Check abnormal termination of all recursions.

13. Verify the handling of all error conditions.

14. Check timing and synchronization.

15. Verify all hardware dependencies.

Figure 8.17 One Way to Perform Method Testing (Humphrey), 2 of 2

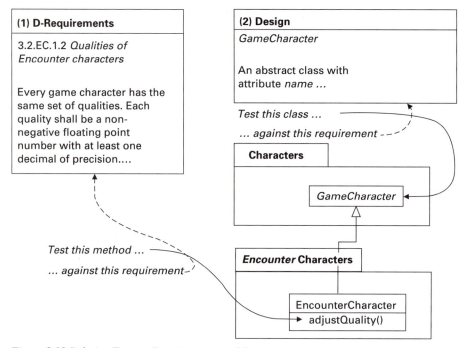

Figure 8.18 Relating Tests to Requirements and Design

one for the class *GameState*, a class that was introduced for the design of our video game: None of the original requirements specifically involve *GameState*. Ideally, separate requirements should be written for all design classes once the design is created. When such separate requirements are not written, as is often the case, test cases have to be devised against the functionality that the class is supposed (by the tester) to possess—a less than ideal situation.

4.2 Method Test Example

A plan to perform method unit testing on the *Encounter* case study methods could be as follows.

> *For each class a method-testing method is developed that executes each of the methods with various parameter values. The method-testing methods make use of the util-*

ity method `reportToFile()` *in the test utility class* `TestExecution`.
`reportToFile()` *has parameters*
> *< destination file > < output comment string > < actual value > < expected value>.*
> *To obtain the test data for each method, we manually identify the parameter bound-
aries, then manually pick at least one value inside, on, and outside these boundaries.*

The example below shows how the values for one method are picked. The code at the
end of the chapter shows this test plan in action for the *EncounterCharacter* class. As will
be seen below, developing systematic test cases even for these simple extremes is usually
not trivial.

We will test for the following D-requirement for the *Encounter* case study.

> ***3.2.EC.1.2 Qualities of Encounter characters.*** *Every game character has the same set
of qualities. Each quality shall be a non-negative floating point number with at least
one decimal of precision. These are all initialized equally so that the sum of their values is 100. The value of a quality cannot be both greater than zero and less than 0.5.*
>
> *For the first release the qualities shall be* concentration, stamina, intelligence, pa-
tience, *and* strength.

An appropriate test set for a method *adjustQuality(String qualityP, float valueP)* is
given next. This method sets the quality named by *qualityP* to *valueP* and adjusts the remaining qualities so that the proportion of the remaining available points remains the
same. A purely random combination of valid and invalid values of *qualityP* and *valueP* is
not the way to begin the development of a test set: First, thought is given to the ranges of
the parameters. Within each of the "on range boundaries," "outside range," and "within
range" categories, we try to obtain systematic coverage, which usually means seeking representatives of equivalence partitions. Table 8.1 is typical of a systematic decomposition
of the input space into equivalence partitions.

TABLE 8.1 Partitioning of Range for Unit Testing

Unit test		Results in a zero value?	Applied to ...	
			Concentration	Stamina
1. Within range		No: Test 1.1	Test 1.1.1	
			⋮	⋮
		Yes: Test 1.2	Test 1.2.1	
				⋮
2. Boundary	2.1 Called with one value zero	No: Test 2.1.1	Test 2.1.1.1	
				⋮
		Yes: Test 2.1.2	⋮	
	2.2 Called with one value 100	⋮		
	⋮			
3. Illegal	3.1 Called with a parameter < 0	⋮		
	etc.:			

The second level of partitioning could be determined by whether or not a zero value results in a quality when *adjustQuality*() is applied. A third level of partitioning is shown in Table 8.1, and the results are listed below.

1. Test cases with parameters within range:
    1.1 *adjustQuality*() does not result in a zero value:
        1.1.1 quality parameter = "concentration"
        Input: (Ideally, choose these at random between 0 and 100 to sum to an amount less than 100.)
            Concentration value 20;
            Stamina value 20; [Note: 1/4 of the non-"concentration" points]
            Intelligence value 20;
            Patience value 20;
            Strength value 20;
        Execute: `adjustQuality( "concentration," 10 )` (Ideally, this value is chosen at random within bounds guaranteed not to result in a zero "concentration" value.)
        Expected output:
            Concentration value 20 + 10 = 30;
            Stamina value 70/4 = 17.5; [Note: remains 1/4 of the non-"concentration" points]
            Intelligence value 70/4 = 17.5;
            Patience value 70/4 = 17.5;
            Strength value 70/4 = 17.5;
        Tests 1.1.2, 1.1.3, ... are similar, using the other qualities instead of concentration.
    1.2 *adjustQuality*() does result in a zero value:
    (Ideally, apply randomness within bounds in a similar manner to that described above.)
        1.2.1 quality parameter = "concentration"
        Input:
            Concentration value 20;
            Stamina value 20;
            Intelligence value 20;
            Patience value 20;
            Strength value 20;
        Execute: `adjustQuality( "concentration", 99 )`
        Expected output:
            Concentration value 99;
            Stamina value 0 (1/4 result replaced by zero);
            Intelligence value 0 (1/4 result replaced by zero);
            Patience value 0 (1/4 result replaced by zero);
            Strength value 0 (1/4 result replaced by zero);
        Tests 1.2.2, 1.2.3, ... are similar, using the other qualities instead of concentration.
2. Test cases with parameters at the range boundaries:
    2.1 *adjustQuality*() called with one parameter value zero:
        2.1.1 Results in no zero value
            2.1.1.1 quality parameter = "concentration"
        Input:
            Concentration value 0;
            Stamina value 25;
            Intelligence value 25;
            Patience value 25;

Strength value 25;
Execute: `adjustQuality( "stamina", 74 )`
Expected output:
Concentration value 0;
Stamina value 99;
Intelligence value 0 (result of 1/3 is set to zero)
Patience value 0 (result of 1/3 is set to zero)
Strength value 0 (result of 1/3 is set to zero)
Tests 2.1..1.2, 2.1.1.3, ... are similar

Tests 2.2, 2.3, ... pertain to other extremes. For example:

2.N *adjustQuality*() called with parameter equaling a current value

Input:
Concentration value 0;
Stamina value 25;
Intelligence value 25;
Patience value 25;
Strength value 25;
Execute: `adjustQuality( "stamina", -25 )`
Expected output:
Concentration value 0;
Stamina value 0;
Intelligence value 33;
Patience value 33;
Strength value 33;

3. Test cases with parameters outside the range:

3.1 Above upper limit of parameter values

3.1.1 parameter value = "concentration"

Input:
Concentration value 20;
Stamina value 20;
Intelligence value 20;
Patience value 20;
Strength value 20;
Execute: `adjustQuality( "concentration", 81 )`
Expected output:
Message to error log stating that adjustQuality() was called with out-of-range input
Concentration value 100; (20+81 set to 100)
Stamina value 0; (after concentration is set, there are no remaining quality points to distribute)
Intelligence value 0;
Patience value 0;
Strength value 0;

Tests 3.1.2, 3.1.3, ... are similar

Tests 3.2, 3.3, ... are similar to test 3.1

3.N Below lower limit of parameter values

3.N.1 parameter value = "concentration"

Input:
Concentration value 20;
Stamina value 20;

> *Intelligence value 20;*
> *Patience value 20;*
> *Strength value 20;*
> *Execute:* `adjustQuality( "concentration", -21 )`
> *Expected output:*
> *Message to error log stating that adjustQuality() was called with out-of-range input*
>> *Concentration value 0; (20–21 set to zero)*
>> *Stamina value 25; (100/4)*
>> *Intelligence value 25; (100/4)*
>> *Patience value 25; (100/4)*
>> *Strength value 25; (100/4)*

The remaining test set is generated in a similar manner.

4.2.1 Testing the Complete Methods of a Class

As an example, let us concentrate on the *GameCharacter* class in the *Characters* framework package. It is currently the only class in that package, and it was introduced during the architecture phase.

We will show code within *GameCharacter* that tests the member method *setName()*. This could be organized as shown below. (The notation "//ps" indicates pseudocode for an automated pseudocode extractor.) The case study at the end of this chapter provides the complete method test.

```
/*
* GameCharacter.java
*/
package FrameworkRPG.Characters;
import TestUtilities.*; //in-house test package
import java.util.*;
import java.io.*;


/**
* Character of role-playing games.
* @author Eric Braude
* @version          0.1,7/14/98
*/

public abstract class GameCharacter
{
// ATTRIBUTES ──────────────────────────────────────
/** Name of the game character; initially null */
private String nameI;

// METHODS ──────────────────────────────────────────

/** No character name will ever exceed this length */
public final static int limitOfNameLength()
{
return 100;
}
```

```
/** For logging */
protected void display()
{
System.out.println( "Game character " + nameI + " displayed" );
}


/** Accessor of nameI. "defaultName" assigned if this is first-time access. */
public String getName()
{
if( nameI == null ) // never before accessed
        setName( "defaultName" );
return nameI;
}


/** Subclasses must declare limit on size of character names */
protected abstract int maxNumCharsInName();


/**
* Sets nameI to nameP if length is within maxNumCharsInName() in length;
* otherwise truncates.
* Inheritors should use this for setName( String ), but not override
* @param nameP: proposed name for nameI
*/
protected final void setName( String nameP )
{
//ps IF string parameter OR maxNumCharsInName() make no sense
if( ( nameP == null ) || ( maxNumCharsInName() <= 0 ) ||
( maxNumCharsInName() > limitOfNameLength() ) )
{ // Set name to default value and show this in system window
        nameI = new String( "defaultName" );
        System.out.println
        ( "defaultName selected by GameCharacter.setName()");
}
//ps ELSE
else
        //ps IF parameter string too long
        if( nameP.length() > maxNumCharsInName() )
                //ps truncate at maxNumCharsInName()
                nameI = new String
                ( nameP.getBytes(), 0, maxNumCharsInName() );
        else
        //ps ELSE assign the parameter name
                nameI = new String( nameP );
}


/** Tests this class */
public static void main( String[] args )
{
        // Get file name for test results and run test
        String outputFileNameM;
```

```
            if( args == null || args.length == 0 )
            {
                    System.out.println( "Using output.txt as default for rest
                    results." );
                    outputFileNameM = "output.txt";
            }
            else
                    outputFileNameM = args[0];
            try
            {
                    testGameCharacterMethods( outputFileNameM );
            }
            catch( IOException e ) { System.out.println( e ); }
    }
```

/** **Tests all the methods of this class** */
```
public static void testGameCharacterMethods( String destinationP )
throws IOException
{
        // Prepare for the test:
        FileWriter outM = new FileWriter( new File( destinationP ) );

        // Because this is an abstract class, need a concrete one for testing
        class TempGameCharacter extends GameCharacter
        {
                public int maxNumCharsInName() { return 20; }
        }
        TempGameCharacter c = new TempGameCharacter();

        System.out.println
        ( "Test for GameCharacter class with maxNumCharsInName() ="
        + c.maxNumCharsInName() );

        System.out.println( "GameCharacter test results on" +
        destinationP + "\n" );
}
```

// **Tests for SetName()** —————————————————
/* SetName() 1. Equivalence partitioning (one partition): nominal, legal name. */
```
c.setName( "Harry" );
TestExecution.reportToFile
( outM, "SetName Test 1.1: Non-null string", c.nameI, "Harry" );
```

// SetName() 2. Boundary value analysis
```
c.setName( "X" ); // minimum legal length
TestExecution.reportToFile
( outM, "SetName Test 2.1: Min non-null string", c.nameI, "X" );
```

The unit test plans for the *getName(), display(),* and *getCharacter()* are performed similarly. The case study at the end of this chapter shows a test for the methods of *Encounter-GameCharacter.*

One Way To. . . Perform Class Unit Tests

1. Exercise methods in combination
   - 2–5, usually
   - choose most common sequences first
   - include sequences likely to cause defects
   - requires hand-computing the resulting attribute values

2. Focus unit tests on each attribute
   - initialize, then execute method sequences that affect it

3. Verify that each class invariant is unchanged
   - verify that the invariant is true with initial values
   - execute a sequence (e.g., the same as in Step 1).
   - verify that the invariant is still true

4. Verify that objects transition among expected states
   - plan the state / transition event sequence
   - set up the object in the initial state by setting variables
   - provide first event and check that transition occurred, etc.

Figure 8.19 One Way to Perform Class Unit Tests

5. CHECKLISTS AND EXAMPLES FOR CLASS TESTING

Having tested the individual methods of a class, we can move on to testing the class as a whole. This amounts to executing its methods in combination or subjecting objects of the class to events such as mouse action. Once again, a purely random set of method combinations is likely to waste time and still leave gaps in coverage. There are several complementary ways of testing classes, as shown in Figure 8.19.

A plan to perform class-level unit testing on the *Encounter* case study methods could be as follows.

> *For each class X, a self-testing method* testXClass() *is developed that executes the methods in various sequences.* testXClass() *can be executed from* main() *or from outside the class* X. *The method sequences are developed by means of the techniques listed in Figure 1234.*

5.1 Method Combination Test Example

Each method combination test consists of a sequence of function calls. For the class *Encounter-Character,* for example, the following methods would be tested in sequences.

Abbreviation	Method prototype
aq	`adjustQuality( String qualityP, float qualityValueP )`
d	`deleteFromEncounterCharacters(EncounterCharacter encounterCharacterP)`
ge	`EncounterCharacter getEncounterCharacter( String nameP )`
gq	`float getQualityValue( String qualityP )`
gs	`float getSumOfQualities()`

gt	`float getTolerance()`
io	`int indexOf( String qualityP ) throws Exception`
ii	`insertIntoEncounterCharacters( EncounterCharacter` `encounterCharacterP )`
m	`int maxNumCharsInName()`
sq	`setQuality( String qualityP, float valueP )`

We concentrate our testing resources in two ways. We identify

1. . . . sequences likely to be commonly used.
2. . . . sequences which appear most likely to harbor defects. This carries out the precept of seeking the highest number of defects per dollar spent.

The following sequences are common:

ge-aq-gs // get the character—adjust the qualities—get the sum of qualities

ge-sq-aq-gq // get the character—set a quality—adjust the qualities—get the quality

One is struck by the infinite number of possible tests that can be run, even for simple applications. (In view of this, inspections and correctness proofs are not as expensive, comparatively, as they might first appear.). A limit has to be placed on the length of method sequences: Since there are ten methods, we will limit the maximum length to ten. A triage approach can be useful in identifying common sequences. A given sequence of methods can be categorized as either most likely to or least likely to expose a defect. Otherwise, the sequence is consigned to the "neither" category. All of the "most likely" tests are executed, together with as many of the "neither" category as possible. The "least likely" are executed if there is time.

Since the process of adjusting quality values is relatively complicated, the following is an example of a sequence most likely to harbor defects.

ge-sq-aq-sq-aq-gq /* get the character—set a quality—adjust the qualities—set a quality— adjust the qualities—get the quality */

5.2 Attribute-Oriented Tests

Attribute-oriented tests are designed by focusing on a single attribute and predicting the effects of executing various methods in sequence (e.g., *setBalance(100); addToBalance(70); getBalance()*). We execute the sequence and verify that the resulting value of the attribute turns out as predicted. In effect, attribute-oriented tests are focused method sequence tests.

5.3 Testing Class Invariants

As described in Chapter 7, class invariants are constraints among the attributes of the class that must remain true at indicated places in the execution. Class invariant tests consist of noting the truth of each invariant, executing sequences of methods, then verifying that the invariant remains true. For example, one invariant for the class *EncounterCharacter* is that the sum of the quality values is less than 100. The following code fragment tests this invariant. It is taken from the method *testEncounterCharacterClass* in *EncounterCharacter*.

```
/*  .  .  .  .  .  .
Check for the invariant
"sum of the quality values of Character object characterP is ≦ 100"
*/
boolean truthM = true;
float sumM = 0.0;
for( int i = 0; i < qualityTypeS.length; ++i )
{
        sumM += characterP.qualValueI[i]; // accumulate sum of quality values
        truthM = truthM && ( sumM <= 100.0 ); // set false if sumM > 100
}
TestExecution.printReportToFile // utility comparing expected and actual values
(
        outM, // test log file
        "Class test for invariant sum of the quality values of Character object
        characterP is <= 100' ", // text description
        truthM, // value obtained
        true // desired value
);
```

Some languages (e.g., Eiffel) and some APIs (e.g., SunTest) are equipped with functions which test the validity of assertions, usually called *assert(...)*. An assertion is a statement that can be true or false: for example, "x == y." Assertions are often invariants.

5.4 State-Based Tests

As we have seen, the objects of classes can often be thought of as transitioning among states in response to events. We should therefore test such classes in terms of their state. For example, let us test the class *EncounterGame*. Figure 8.20 shows the first steps in the testing of the application's state-transitions. The complete state-transition test is shown in Figure 8.21. The numbers denote a typical event sequence for causing a meaningful sequence of events. One test would thus consist of stimulating the system so that it transitions through this sequence. One would also introduce events that do *not* apply for particular states, so as to ensure that they do not affect the application.

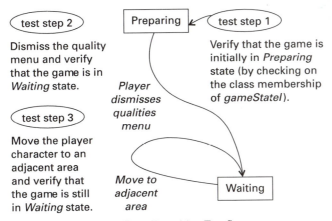

Figure 8.20 Encounter *State-Transition Test Sequence*

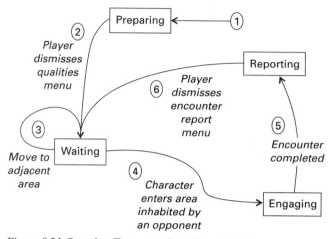

Figure 8.21 Complete Encounter State-Transition Test

To design and execute state-oriented testing requires considerable time, especially because extensive user inputs are required. Tools are available which record user interactions with the system, and which can reproduce these actions. In addition, assertion checkers can be embedded in the code to verify that the system is in the state it is supposed to be in.

6.   SUMMARY

In summary, unit testing consists of testing the structural parts of an application under development. This contrasts with integration testing, which tests functional parts of the application as it is constructed.

Black box testing is concerned that the code under test provides the correct output for each input. White box testing is concerned with verifying the process by which outputs are generated. There are several aspects to white box testing. One should test "early and often." In addition, test plans developed early help to clarify requirements. These points are shown in Figure 8.22.

- Unit testing = "pieces"
- Integration testing = "whole thing"
- Black box: input /output
- White box: verifies processing
  - many ways
  - ensure completeness

- Test planning earlier/better
  - helps clarify requirements

Figure 8.22 Unit Testing Summary

EXERCISES

A hint is provided for every exercise marked with the superscript "h." Solutions are provided for every problem marked with the superscript "s."

REVIEW QUESTIONS

R8.1[s] Describe 3-4 levels of testing.

R8.2[s] Describe the difference between black, white, and gray box testing. *Section 2 above on page 397 ("types of tests") is a solution to this question.*

R8.3[s] It is not possible to test for every combination of inputs. Name a black box technique that attempts to reduce the number of test cases.

R8.4[s] We test selectively.

a. State a practical criterion for selecting test input.

b. Generally speaking, what kinds of input values usually cause the most common errors?

R8.5[s] Give an example of a program with the following properties. The program is intended to implement a simple flowchart, but does not do so correctly. There is an input to the program that executes every line of the program and gives the correct answer. *Section 2.4 on page 400 ("statement coverage for white box testing") is a solution to this question.*

R8.6[s] Give an example of a program in the form of a flowchart with a single branch point. Construct a defective program with the following property. There is an input causing every branch of the program to be executed. *Section 2.5 on page 400 ("decision coverage for white box testing") is a solution to this question.*

R8.7[s] What assertion would you check for in a computation which finds the first minimum in the array *a* of size 100?

R8.8[s] Name four to six steps in planning for unit testing. *Section 3 on page 405 ("planning unit tests") is a solution to this question.*

R8.9[s] Name three black box tests for functions (methods).

R8.10[s] Name 6–12 white box tests for functions (methods).

R8.11[s] Give code that tests whether the class invariant I is satisfied in the class *EncounterCharacter.* I = "all quality values are non-negative." Refer to the variables in the code fragment from *EncounterCharacter* in Section 5.3 on page 416 ("testing class invariants").

R8.12[s] Describe state-oriented testing. *Section 5.4 on page 417 ("state-based tests") is a solution to this question.*

TEAM EXERCISES

T8.1 ("Unit test") Perform full unit tests on two significant methods of your application.

State how long individuals and the whole team spent on developing each part of these tests, and how the process used could have been improved.

> *Evaluation Criteria:*
> α. *Degree of clarity of the plan — A = very clear plan*
> β. *Extent to which the plan and test include all relevant aspects of the unit tests — A = all of the relevant coverage mentioned in this chapter*
> γ. *Realism of the self-evaluation data and improvement plan — A = very specific data on results, and specific changes to improve the process*

GENERAL EXERCISES

G8.1 Write the code for a class *Account* with attribute *_balance*, accessor methods, and method *add()*. Assume that *Account* has states *Sound*, *Empty*, and *Arrears*, and that these are implemented using the *State* design pattern. Write a complete set of unit tests for *Account*, including state-oriented tests.

SOLUTIONS FOR REVIEW QUESTIONS

R8.1 Function tests test each individual function or method. Class tests test each class. Package tests come next. (The latter two are sometimes called *module* tests.) Integration tests check partial builds of the application. Finally, system tests verify the application as a whole.

R8.3 Equivalence partitioning reduces the number of test cases by dividing the set of possible inputs into separate subsets. These subsets are chosen so that if a test with one input from a subset succeeds, then all possible inputs from that subset are likely to succeed as well.

R8.4 a. Select inputs that are most likely to expose defects.

b. Defects usually occur most often at boundaries (limits of permissible values).

R8.7 The assertion that needs satisfying is the following conjunction of four statements.

$0 \leq i < a.length - 1$ // progress of loop up to index i
AND
$0 \leq k \leq i$ // minimum up to now is at index k
AND // first minimum is at k
[EITHER k=0
OR [$a[u] > a[k]$ for $u = 0, 1, ..., k-1$] // values higher for all indices less than k
AND
[$a[u] \leq a[k]$ for $u = k, ..., i$] // no value lower for indices between k and i

R8.9 Black box function tests can be accomplished by the following kinds of test data:

1. within range

2. at the boundaries of the range

3. outside the range

R8.10 1. Check all paths, including both sides of all branches

2. Ensure that all instructions execute

3. Check the use of all called objects

4. Verify the handling of all data structures

5. Verify the handling of all files

6. Check normal termination of all loops

7. Check abnormal termination of all loops

8. Check normal termination of all recursions

9. Check abnormal termination of all recursions

10. Verify the handling of all error conditions

11. Check timing and synchronization

12. Verify all hardware dependencies

R8.11 The following code tests for the class invariant requiring all quality values to be non-negative.

```
// . . .
// Check for the invariant e.qualValueI[i] >=0
boolean truthM = true;
for( int i = 0; i < qualityTypeS.length; ++i )
        // Set truthM false if any entry in e.qualValueI not >= 0
        truthM = truthM && ( e.qualValueI[i] >= 0 );
TestExecution.printReportToFile // utility comparing expected and actual values
(
        out,  // test log file
        "Class test for the invariant 'qualValueI[i] >= 0'",// description
        truthM, // value obtained
        true // desired value
);
```

CASE STUDY:

ENCOUNTERCHARACTER. JAVA PERSONAL SOFTWARE DOCUMENTATION (PSD), PART 2 OF 2

[Note to the student: The following is Part 2 of the document that describes and points to the PSD for EncounterCharacter. *The format of this document is derived from the IEEE Standard for Software Test Documentation.*

The manner in which unit testing is carried out in this case study is one of many possibilities. An alternative strategy, for example, is to execute tests through static self-test methods from an external object. This object can be made to perform several unit tests, sending the results to specified output files by following the instruction on a test script file.]

5. UNIT TEST FOR ENCOUNTERCHARACTER

5.1 Test Design Specification

The unit test for *EncounterCharacter* consists of two public methods as follows.

testEncounterCharacterMethods() tests each of the methods in turn

testEncounterCharacterClass() tests sequences of methods

These methods can be executed by *EncounterCharacter's main()* method or by an external object.

5.2 Test Case Specification

The test cases for *EncounterCharacter* are built into *testEncounterCharacterMethods()* and *testEncounterCharacterClass().*

[Note to the student: For simplicity, this unit test includes test data with the method. Normally, however, the input data and the expected output are retrieved from a file.]

5.3 Test Procedure Specification

The unit tests for *EncounterCharacter* are initiated by executing the *main()* method of *EncounterCharacter.* The parameter supplied to *main()* specifies the file to which the results are written.

[Note to the student: This is a simple procedure: However, the procedure becomes considerably more complex when source files and user interaction are involved. For example, this will be the case in unit testing the class EncounterGame.*]*

5.4 Test Results Documentation

The test results documentation consists of the test log, test incident report, and test summary report.

5.4.1 Test Log

[Note to the student: an account of the test's results. See the example below.]

This is contained in file:
EncounterCharacter_Test_Log_day_ month_year.doc

5.4.2 Test Incident Report

[Note to the student: any occurrences or noteworthy events that occur during testing. See the example below.]

This is contained in file:
EncounterCharacter_Test_Incident_day _month_year.doc

5.4.3 Test Summary Report

This is contained in file
EncounterCharacter_Test_Summary_ Report_day_month_year.doc

Example of a Test Log (Section 5.4.1 of the Personal Software Documentation): *EncounterCharacter_Test_Log_ 26_Jul_1999*

Method tests:
>>>>>GetCharacter Test 1: nominal value<<<<<
querty<——Obtained
querty<—— Required
>>>>>GetCharacter Test 2: Outside parameter values <<<<<
defaultName<——Obtained
defaultName<—— Required
>>>>>EncounterCharacter Test 3: Limit parameter values<<<<<

123456789012345<——Obtained
123456789012345<—— Required
Expect one name for each character
querty
defaultName
123456789012345
>>>>>indexOf() Test 1: valid quality name<<<<<
Actual integer = expected integer.
>>>>>indexOf() Test 2: valid quality name<<<<<
Actual integer = expected integer.
>>>>>setQuality() Test 1: nominal value<<<<<
Actual float = expected float.
>>>>>setQuality() Test 2: nominal value<<<<<
Actual float = expected float.
>>>>>adjustQuality() test 0: verify that values add to 100<<<<<
Actual float = expected float.
>>>>>adjustQuality() test 1: verify values sum to 100 after adjusting<<<<<
Actual float = expected float.
>>>>>adjustQuality() test 2: verify values adjusted as commanded<<<<<
Actual float = expected float.
>>>>>adjustQuality() test 3: verify low value reverts to zero<<<<<
Actual float = expected float.
>>>>>adjustQuality() test 4: verify values sum to 100 after adjusting<<<<<
Actual float = expected float.

Class test:
>>>>>Class test ge-aq-so<<<<<
100.0<——Obtained
100.0<—— Required
>>>>>Class test ge-aq-aq-gq-so: part 1<<<<<
20.9876<——Obtained
20.9876<—— Required
>>>>>Class test ge-aq-aq-gq-so: part 2<<<<<
100.0<——Obtained
100.0<—— Required
>>>>>Class test for the invariant '_qualValue[i] >=0'<<<<<
true<——Obtained
true<—— Required

[Note to the student: The test log example does not show failed tests. These can be detailed in the log, transmitted to a separate file, and they can generate monitor text.]

Example of a Test Incident Report (Section 5.4.2 of the Personal Software Documention):
EncounterCharacter_Test_ Incident_26_Jul_1999.doc

The test was attempted with version 7.2.1 of EncounterCharacter using version 2.3 of the TestUtilities package. On the first try, the test failed to run. We think that this was due to the fact that we did not really have version 2.3 of TestUtilities. When we reloaded this package, the test ran without incident.

[Note to the student: This is a good place to mention mistakes made during testing. These are particularly prevalent when user actions are required, and it is impractical to rerun the entire test.]

Example of a Test Summary report(Section 5.4.3 of the Personal Software Documention):
EncounterCharacter_Test_Summary_ 26_Jul_1999.doc

This test was executed by John Jones at 2:00 P.M. using release 1.1.6 of Sun's virtual machine. Subject to the anomalies in the test incident report, the results were 100% pass on the built-in unit test methods. These methods were inserted by E. Braude in version 6.5.2 They are due to be expanded in later versions of EncounterCharacter.

Example of unit test source code

The following code, for the *EncounterCharacter* class, includes self-test methods.

The class *TestExecution* is used to execute the unit test. It contains a static method *printReportToFile()* whose parameters, in Javadoc notation, are as follows.

```
* @param-FileWriter-Destination
of report output.
* @param-String-A description of
the test.
* @param-int-The expected correct
result.
* @param-int-The actual result.
* @return-void
* @exception-None
```

There are no preconditions. The postconditions are that a file has been written to the destination indicated by the *FileWriter* input parameter, that contains the test description input, the expected result, and the actual result — each clearly indicated. The code is shown in Figures 8.23 through 8.34.

```java
/** To test this class.
* @param      argsP      destination of method test log, class test log respectively
*/
public static void main(String[] argsP)
{
    // Default files on which to write test output and run tests
    String methodOutputFileNameM= "methodOutput.txt";
    String class OutputFileNameM= "classOutput.txt";

    if( argsP!= null && argsP.length == 2 )// use defaults if input improper
    {   methodOutputFileNameM = argsP[0];
        class OutputFileNameM = argsP[1];
    }


    // 1. EXECUTE TESTS WHICH DO NOT REQUIRE HUMAN INTERVENTION


    // Test methods individually, then test class
    try
    {   testEncounterCharacterMethods( methodOutputFileNameM );
        testEncounterCharacterClass( classOutputFileNameM );
    } catch( IOException eP )
    {   System.out.println( eP );
    }
```

Figure 8.23 Listing—page 1

```java
    // 2. EXECUTE TESTS WHICH DO NOT REQUIRE HUMAN INTERVENTION

    Frame[] imageTests = {                              // Display test cases.
        new testCharacterImage(                         // Missing image.
            new EncounterCharacter( "GuyWithNoImage", null ) ),
        new testCharacterImage(                         // Image is present.
            new EncounterCharacter( "Elena", "elena.gif" ) )
    };

    for( int i = 0; i<imageTests.length; i++ ) {// Display each test window.
        imageTests[i].setSize( 400, 250 );              // Adequate size for character.
        imageTests[i].setVisible( true );
        imageTests[i].show();
    }

    try{                                                // Let user examine windows.
        Thread.currentThread().sleep( 30*1000 );
    } catch( Exception exc ){
    }

    for( int i = 0; i<imageTests.length; i++ ) // Shut the windows.
        imageTests[i].dispose();

    System.exit(0);
}
```

Figure 8.24 Listing—page 2

/** Tests this class by executing its methods in combination.
* @param   destinationP   Location to write results.
* @exception IOException   If there's a problem opening or accessing destinationP
*/
```
public static void testEncounterCharacterClass( String destinationP )
    throws IOException
{        /* Prepare for the test */
        PrintWriter outM = new PrintWriter( new FileOutputStream(destinationP ) );
        System.out.println(
            "InEncounterCharacter class test results on "+destinationP + "In" );

        /*
         * The following methods will be tested in sequences:
         *
         * a.     adjustQuality( String qualityP, float qualityValueP )
         * d.     deleteFromEncounterCharacters( EncounterCharacter encounterCharacterP )
         * ge.    EncounterCharacter getEncounterCharacter( String nameP )
         * gq.    float getQualityValue( String qualityP )
         * gt.    float getTolerance()
         * io.    int indexOf( String qualityP )
         * ii.    insertIntoEncounterCharacters( EncounterCharacter encounterCharacterP )
         * m.     int maxNumCharsInName()
         * sq.    setQuality( String qualityP, float qualityValueP )
         * so.    float sumOfQualities()
```

Figure 8.25 Listing—page 3

```
         *
         *     The following sequences occur commonly:
         *     ge-aq-so
         *     ge-sq-a-gq
         *     . . . . .
         *     The following sequences have a high potential for defects:
         *     ge-aq-aq-gq-so
         *     . . . . .
         */

/* Test C1: ge-aq-so */
EncounterCharacter eC1M = new EncounterCharacter( "CharForTestC1" ); // method "ge"
eC1M.adjustQuality( QUAL_STRENGTH, 40.0f );                          // aq
TestExecution.printReportToFile( outM,
    "Class test ge-aq-so", eC1M.sumOfQualities(), 100.0f );          // so

/* Test C2: ge-aq-aq-gq-so */
EncounterCharacter eC2M = new EncounterCharacter("CharForTestC2"); // ge
eC2M.adjustQuality( QUAL_STRENGTH, 40.0f );                         // aq
eC2M.adjustQuality( QUAL_STAMINA, 20.9876f );                       // aq
```

Figure 8.26 Listing—page 4

```
TestExecution.printReportToFile( outM, "Class test ge-aq-aq-gq-so: part 1",
    eC2M.getQualityValue( QUAL_STAMINA ), 20.9876f ); // gq

TestExecution.printReportToFile( outM, "Class test ge-aq-aq-gq-so: part 2",
    eC2M.sumOfQualities(), 100.0f );                        //so
```

```
/* INVARIANT-ORDERED TESTS
* Check for the invariant "qualValue[i] >=0"
* —after executing the sequences of methods executed above
*/
boolean truthM = true;
for( int i = 0; i < qualityTypeS.length; ++i )
{   /* Set truthM false if any entry in eC1M.qualValueI not >= 0 */
    truthM = truthM && ( eC1M.qualValue[i] >= 0.0f );
}
TestExecution.printReportToFile( outM,
    "Class test for the invariant 'qualValue[i] >= 0'", truthM, true );
```

```
/* Conclude */
outM.close();
System.out.printIn( "InClass tests of EncounterChar class concluded." );
}    // end of testEncounterCharacterClass
```

Figure 8.27 Listing—page 5

```
/** Tests all the methods of this class one at a time
 * @param    destinationP   Location to write results.
 * @param    IOException    If there's a problem opening or accessing destinationP
 */
public static void testEncountCharacterMethods ( String destinationP ) throws IOException
{  /* Prepare for the test */
   FileWriter outM = new FileWriter( new File(destinationP ) );
   System.out.println( "EncounterCharacter method test results on" + destinationP + "In" );

   /* Tests for getEncounterCharacter()*/

   EncounterCharacter eCNorM = new EncounterCharacter( "qwerty" );   //normal
   TestExecution.reportToFile( outM,
      "GetCharacter Test 1: nominal value", eCNorM.getName(), "qwerty" );

   EncounterCharacter eCNullM = new EncounterCharacter ( null );  //null
   TestExecution.reportToFile( outM, "GetCharacter Test2: null parameter",
      eCNullM.getName(), GameCharacter.DEFAULT_NAME );
```

Figure 8.28 Listing—page 6

```
StringtooLongM = "12345678901234567890123456789012345678901234567890";
EncounterCharacter eCTooLongM = new EncounterCharacter( tooLongM );   // too long
TestExecution.reportToFile( outM, "GetCharacter Test 3: Limit parameter values,"
    + "max name len = "+eCTooLongM.maxNumCharsInName(),
    eCTooLongM.getName(),
    tooLongM.substring( 0, eCTooLongM.maxNumCharsInName() ) );

EncounterCharacter eCZeroM = new EncounterCharacter( "" );              // zero-length
TestExecution.reportToFile( outM, "GetCharacter Test 4: zero-length",
    eCZeroM.getName(), GameCharacter.DEFAULT_NAME );

EncounterCharacter eCPuncM = new EncounterCharacter( "a+b" );          //bad chars
TestExecution.reportToFile( outM, "GetCharacter Test 5: bad char '+'",
    eCPuncM.getName(), GameCharacter.DEFAULT_NAME );
```

Figure 8.29 Listing—page 7

```
/* Tests for indexOf() for every valid quality name. */
for( int i = 0; i < qualityTypeS.length; ++i )
    try {TestExecution.reportToFile( outM,
        "indexOf()Test1." + i + ":valid name:" + qualityTypeS[i],
        indexOf( qualityTypeS[i] ), i );
    } catch( Exception eP )
    { TestExecution.reportToFile( outM, "indexOf() Test1:valid name: compare",
        "indexOf( '"+qualityTypeS[i] + "' )","with expected" + i );
    }

/* Tests for indexOf() for an invalid quality name. */
try {TestExecution.reportToFile( outM,
    "indexOf()Test2: invalid name: zorch", indexOf( "zorch" ), -1;
} catch( Exception eP )
{ TestExecution.reportToFile( outM,
    "indexOf() Test2: valid name: compare", "indexOf( \"zorch\" )", "with expected-1" );
}
```

Figure 8.30 Listing—page 8

/* Tests for setQuality() */

// Set up for test
```
EncounterCharacter hank = new EncounterCharacter( "Hank" );
```

// Nominal value
```
hank.setQuality( QUAL_STRENGTH, 10.3f );
TestExecution.reportToFile( outM, "setQuality() Test1:nominal value",
    hank.getQualityValue( QUAL_STRENGTH ), 10.3f );
```

// Out of range value
```
hank.setQuality( QUAL_PATIENCE, -6.2f );
TestExecution.reportToFile( outM, "setQuality() Test 2:nominal value",
    hank.getQualityValue( QUAL_PATIENCE ), 0.0f );
```

// Value below close-to-zero threshold
```
hank.setQuality( QUAL_STAMINA, getTolerance()* 0.9f );
TestExecution.reportToFile( outM, "setQuality() Test 3:value close to zero",
    hank.getQualityValue( QUAL_STAMINA ), 0.0f );
```

Figure 8.31 —page 9

```
// Tests for adjustQuality().

// Set up for test and verify: Values should be 20 each.
EncounterCharacter harvey = new EncounterCharacter( "Harvey" );
TestExecution.reportToFile( outM, "adjustQuality() test 0: verify that values add to 100",
    harvey.sumOfQualities(), 100.0f );

// Nominal adjustment
harvey.adjustQuality( QUAL_STRENGTH, 30.0f );  // strength 30 rest 70/4 each
TestExecution.reportToFile ( outM, "adjustQuality() test 1: values sum to 100 after adjusting",
    harvey.sumOfQualities(), 100.0f );
TestExecution.reportToFile ( outM, "adjustQuality() test 2: values adjusted as commanded",
    harvey.getQualityValue( QUAL_STRENGTH ), 30.0f );

// Adjustment resulting in a zero value
harvey.adjustQuality( QUAL_STAMINA, 99.0f );
TestExecution.reportToFile ( outM, "adjustQuality() test 3: verify low value reverts to zero",
    harvey.getQualityValue( QUAL_STRENGTH ), 0.0f );

// Conclude
outM.close();
System.out.printIn( "\nMethod tests of EncounterCharacter class concluded." );
}
```

Figure 8.32 —page 10

```
/** Class to test repainting of characters. Creates a window, which will contain
 * several copies of the character image.
 */
private static class testCharacterImage extends Frame
{

    /** Instance attribute that remembers which character image to display. */
    private EncounterCharacter characterI;

    /** Basic constructor—create a window for testing some character's image.
     * @param      characterP      Character whose image is to be tested.
     */
    testCharacterImage( EncounterCharacter characterP )
    {
        super( characterP.getName() );  // Do all normal Frame initialization.
        characterI = characterP;        // Remember which character we're testing.
    }
```

Figure 8.33 —page 11

```
/** Repaint the display area of the frame.
 * @param      drawP      Graphics context for drawing the character.
 */
public void paint( Graphics drawP )
{   Dimension frameSizeM = getSize();            // Size of the window area.
    int widthUnitM = frameSizeM.width /5;        // Convenient divisions of window.
    int heightUnitM = frameSizeM.height /5;

    characterI.showCharacter( this, drawP,       // Drawn small, facing right.
        new Point( widthUnitM, heightUnitM ), heightUnitM, false );

    characterI.showCharacter( this, drawP,       // Drawn large, facing left.
        new Point( widthUnitM*4, heightUnitM*3 ), heightUnitM*2, true );

    characterI.showCharacter( this, drawP,       // Drawn large, facing right.
        new Point( widthUnitM*2, heightUnitM*2 ), heightUnitM*2, false );

    characterI.showCharacter( this, drawP,       // Drawn small, facing left.
        new Point( widthUnitM*3, heightUnitM*4 ), heightUnitM, true );
}

}          // End of testCharacterImage inner class
```

Figure 8.34 —page 12

SYSTEM INTEGRATION, VERIFICATION, AND VALIDATION

Figure 9.1 shows the contents of this chapter in the context of the software engineering process. Figure 9.2 states the learning goals of this chapter.

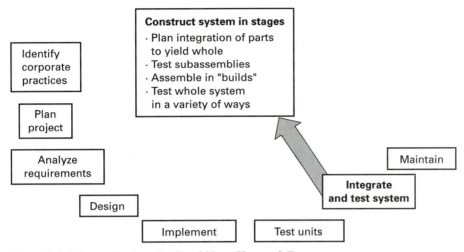

Figure 9.1 Software Engineering Road Map: Chapter 9 Focus

- Be able to plan the integration of modules
- Understand types of testing required
- Be able to plan and execute testing
  - beyond the unit level

Figure 9.2 Learning Goals for This Chapter

1. INTRODUCTION

1.1 The Meaning of "Integration"

Because applications are complex, they must be built of parts which are first developed separately and then assembled. "Integration" refers to this assembly process. Various kinds of testing are performed on the partially assembled application, and also on the entire application.

The integration phase of the Waterfall process is apt to produce nasty surprises due to incompatibility of the parts being integrated. For this reason, the Unified Software Development Process, in particular, tries to avoid "big bang" integration by means of continual integration using multiple iterations. The shaded parts of Figure 9.3 show that integration really takes place during the Construction and Transition iterations.

Losses of information are likely to occur in transitioning from one stage of the development process to the next. As pointed out by Myers [My], Figure 9.4 illustrates places within the waterfall process at which a loss of understanding can typically occur.

Because of these potential losses of information, continual testing and integration are used. While there is certainly great value in testing units within their final environment as part of the application, described in this chapter, this does not substitute for thorough unit testing prior to including each part (see Chapter 8).

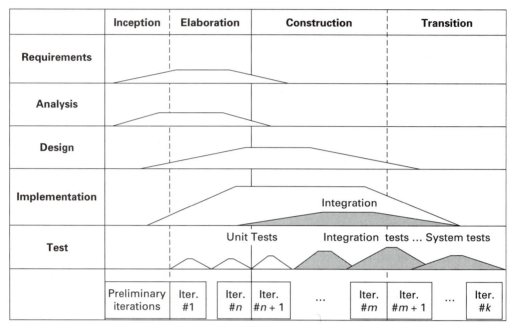

Figure 9.3 Unified Process for Integration and Test [Ja1]

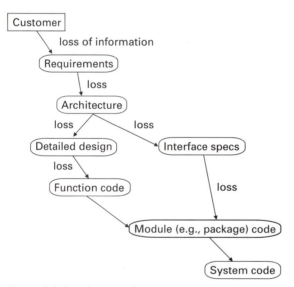

Figure 9.4 Development Overview

1.2 Verification, Validation, and System Testing

Recall that "verification" asks whether we are "building it right." In other words, are we building precisely those artifacts in the present phase which were specified in the previous phase? When applied to integration, verification amounts to confirming that we are putting together precisely the components we planned to assemble, in precisely the way we planned to assemble them. Such verification can be performed by inspecting the products of integration.

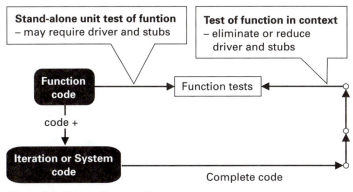

Figure 9.5 Testing Units in Context

"Validation" asks whether we are "building the right thing." In other words, are we satisfying the requirements as stated in the SRS? At the integration phase, this is performed by means of system testing.

Upon completing a build, an iteration, or the entire application, thorough testing requires that we first revisit the unit tests of functions (methods) and modules (classes or packages). This time, however, they are tested in context rather than in isolation. Fewer drivers and stubs are required, leading to fewer complications and resulting defects. If this is the final build, no drivers or stubs are required at all. The difference between stand-alone unit tests and unit tests performed in context is illustrated in Figure 9.5, where the units are functions.

For example, unit testing of the method `adjustQuality()` in the class `EncounterCharacter` was performed using a test method `testEncounterCharacterMethods()`, inserted into the `EncounterCharacter` class (see the case study in Chapter 8). On the other hand, testing `adjustQuality()` in the context of the completed application is performed by running the application in a way which ensures that this method is repeatedly executed. This can be done by periodically pulling up the window during the game and changing quality values.

Figure 9.6 shows the flow of artifacts (mainly documents and code) among the project phases, and among the various types of tests. Module and function tests are executed in two different modes. The first time, they are executed in isolation as unit tests. The second time, they are executed in the context of the entire application. They are numbered twice for this reason.

Figure 9.7 shows which document(s) the various tests are tested against. Recall that *validation* is the process of making sure that the right thing is being built, and is thus effected by testing against the original requirements. The other tests ensure that the application is being built in the manner that we intend, the process of *verification*. For example, interface tests verify that the implementation faithfully reflects the intended interfaces.

The tests mentioned in Figure 9.7 are described briefly below, then elaborated upon in the rest of this chapter.

Once the code for the system has been integrated or partially integrated (bottom of Figure 9.6), it becomes possible to test parts in the context of the entire system instead of in stand-alone fashion. To focus testing on designated parts of the application, we have to devise appropriate input.

1. We had to create stubs and drivers in order to perform unit testing on *functions and classes,* introducing the possibility of unnecessary errors and incomplete coverage. If it

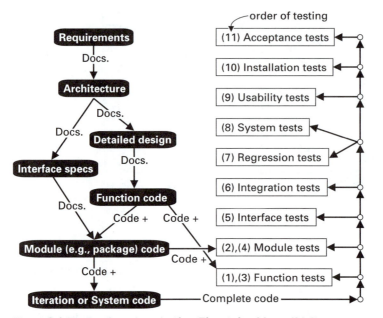

Figure 9.6 Testing Overview: Artifact Flow (after Myers [My])

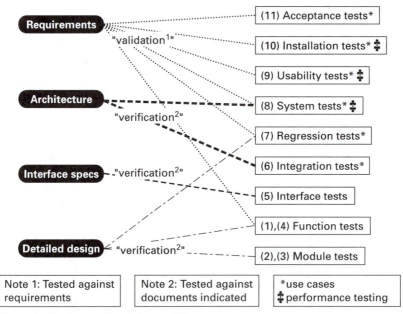

Figure 9.7 Testing for Validation and Verification

can't be left in the code, for space or organizational reasons, this software can be set aside in a retrievable way for future use. Another alternative is to include or exclude it by means of a precompiler which has switching *(include unit testing code / exclude unit testing code)*.

2. Similarly, it becomes possible to retest other *modules* (e.g., packages) in the system context.

3. *Interface* testing retests the validity of the interfaces among modules.

4. The purpose of *regression testing* is to verify that additions made to the system have not degraded its preexisting capabilities. In other words, regression testing is performed against requirements that were already satisfied, prior to the addition of new capabilities. Only when an artifact has passed regression testing are we ready to test the operation of the added code.

5. *Integration testing* is performed on the partially constructed system, to verify that the result of integrating additional software (e.g., classes) operates as planned. For example, we might implement the *EncounterEnvironment* package first, testing it thoroughly. After that, we might implement the *EncounterCast* package. After the latter is integrated with the *EncounterEnvironment* package, the process of verifying that the characters behave as required in the areas, is an example of an integration test.

6. *System testing* is performed on the application as a whole or on designated releases.

   System and integration tests take place against the architecture. In other words, they verify that the architecture has been followed, and that the architecture functions as intended. For example, the architecture of the *Encounter* case study is designed so that when a foreign character enters an area containing the player's character, an event is generated in the *EncounterLayout* package. The event is handled by the *EncounterGame* package. In some cases the foreign character may disappear, which would be evidenced in the *EncounterCast* package. *System* tests verify this kind of behavior.

   System testing also validates requirements, both functional and nonfunctional. The nonfunctional requirements include performance requirements such as execution speed and storage use.

7. *Usability testing* validates the acceptability of the application to its end users.

8. *Installation testing* is performed with the application installed on its target platforms.

9. *Acceptance testing* is performed by the customer in order to validate the acceptability of the application.

The testing types summarized above are discussed next in more detail.

2. THE INTEGRATION PROCESS

2.1 A Description of "Integration"

Figure 9.8 illustrates a possible integration process for the first "iteration" of a suspension bridge construction (the single-level version) as well as one for the second "iteration" (the double-level version). Each iteration is a coherent stage of construction. A careful sequence of activities called "builds," which completes the iteration, is planned.

The simplest kind of integration consists of adding new elements to the baseline (the existing code) on each iteration around the spiral. This is illustrated in Figure 9.9. The "implementation" phase consists of the coding of the new parts, followed by its integration into the baseline.

The integration process for software is no less of an art and science than the integration process for physical projects, and it can be very complex. As with the bridge example, each software iteration is constructed in stages. This is illustrated for the Unified Software Development Process in Figure 9.10.

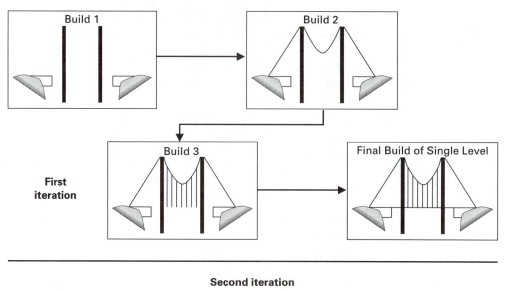

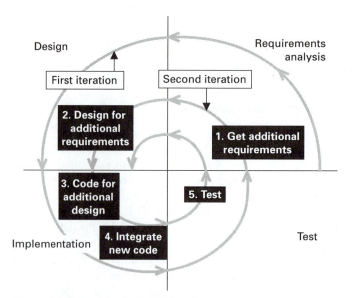

Figure 9.8 The Build *Process within Iterations*

Figure 9.9 Integration in Spiral Development

	Inception	Elaboration	Construction	Transition
Requirements				
Analysis				
Design		**First build for iteration** *i*		**Last build for iteration** *i*
Implementation				
Test				
	Preliminary iterations	Iter. #1	Iter. #n	Iter. #n + 1	Iter. #i	Iter. #m	Iter. #m + 1	Iter. #k

Figure 9.10 Relating Builds and Iterations in the Unified Process [Ja1]

Figure 9.10 shows groupings of iterations (the Construction iterations, for example) with each iteration (e.g., iteration *i*) divided into several builds. This extensive organization is relevant for large projects.

When the architecture is developed, an important consideration is the ease with which the parts can be integrated. Unlike some physical applications, however, it is seldom feasible to complete individual software modules prior to integration. One reason for this is that typical software modules serve several clients, whereas physical modules serve a very limited number of "clients," often just one. For example each bridge column supports just one or two road sections. On the other hand, as software requirements become better understood, new clients become apparent for each module. Thus, as illustrated in Figure 9.11, software builds must frequently integrate partially constructed units, as in the "typical" sequence rather than the "unit-oriented" sequence.

Although the typical build process has the disadvantage of working with incomplete units, it does have the advantage of exercising integration earlier in the development process. This helps to retire risks by avoiding "big bang" integration.

The difficulties of integrating applications underscore the importance of designing the units (e.g., classes and packages) to be as focused in purpose as possible, and their mutual interfaces as narrow as possible. These goals, "high cohesion" and "low coupling" respectively, were discussed in Section 1.4 of Chapter 5 on page 251.

Figure 9.12 gives one way in which to establish an integration and build plan, and the points mentioned there are explained further in this chapter.

Testing is simplified by incorporating whole use case implementations into each build rather than just use cases parts. Devising relatively small use cases in the first place makes it easier to fit them into builds. Since user interfaces will have to be built and tested eventually, it is preferable if they—or key parts of them—can be built early on so that testing of the evolving application can be conducted through them. The alternative is to build temporary interfaces for use during integration testing.

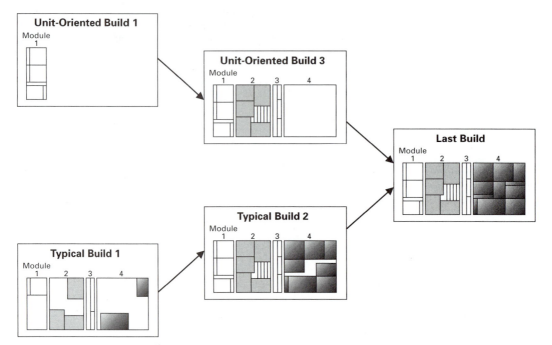

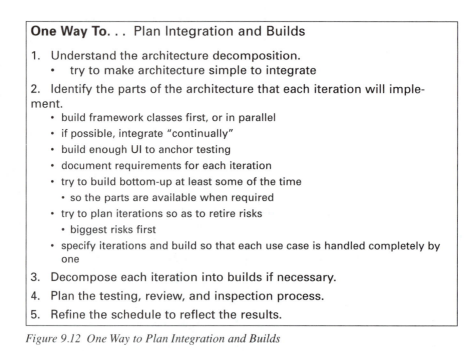

Figure 9.11 Build Sequences: "Unit-oriented" vs. Typical

One Way To. . . Plan Integration and Builds

1. Understand the architecture decomposition.
   - try to make architecture simple to integrate

2. Identify the parts of the architecture that each iteration will implement.
   - build framework classes first, or in parallel
   - if possible, integrate "continually"
   - build enough UI to anchor testing
   - document requirements for each iteration
   - try to build bottom-up at least some of the time
     - so the parts are available when required
   - try to plan iterations so as to retire risks
     - biggest risks first
   - specify iterations and build so that each use case is handled completely by one

3. Decompose each iteration into builds if necessary.

4. Plan the testing, review, and inspection process.

5. Refine the schedule to reflect the results.

Figure 9.12 One Way to Plan Integration and Builds

Jacobson et al. point out that bottom-up build development is generally easier to use as a guide to planning builds. This approach creates parts before they are used to construct larger units. The bottom-up process can usefully be combined with the implementation of frameworks classes, however, which is a top-down process.

2.2 A Typical Road Map of the Integration and System Testing Process

Figure 9.13 shows a typical sequence of actions for integrating a software system.

Recall that the packages chosen for the *Encounter* case study are those shown in Figure 9.14 (which also shows the domain classes selected). The integration of these packages consists of putting them together in stages, ending with the completed application. This is done according to the integration plan, which can be documented in the Software Configuration Management Plan. This is an example of the necessity for continually revising documents. Recall that the SCMP was one of the first project documents created. We revisit it once the architecture has been specified (in the SDD), in order to specify the integration sequence.

Figure 9.15 lists significant factors in determining the order of integration. The order depends on the demands of the project. For risky projects, we would concentrate on integrating the risky parts as soon as possible to gauge the effectiveness of our design. Showing particular parts of the application to the customer also dictates an order of integration. Otherwise, we would integrate used modules before the modules that use them, thereby minimizing the use of temporary driver code.

Since the *EncounterGame* package in the *Encounter* case study uses (refers to) the *EncounterEnvironment* package and the *EncounterCharacters* package, we first integrate the latter two packages. After this, the game engine can be integrated, allowing the game to be exercised. The resulting integration schedule is shown in Figure 9.16.

1. Decide extent of all tests.

2. For each iteration . . .
   2.1 For each build . . .
   2.1.1 Perform regression testing from prior build
   2.1.2 Retest functions if required
   2.1.3 Retest modules if required
   2.1.4 Test interfaces if required
   2.1.5 Perform build integration tests—*Section 3.1*

   Development of iteration complete

   2.2 Perform iteration system and usability tests—*Sections 3.4, 3.5*

System implemented

3. Perform installation tests—*Section 3.8*

System installed

4. Perform acceptance tests—*Section 3.7*

Job complete

Figure 9.13 Road Map for Integration and System Test

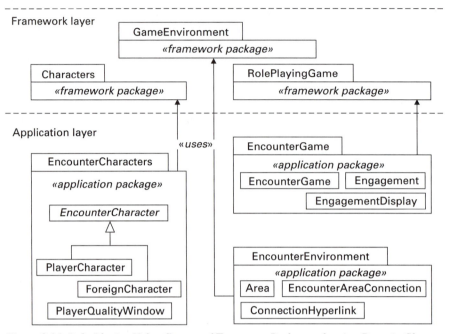

Figure 9.14 Role-Playing Video Game and Encounter *Packages showing Domain Classes*

technical factors	• *Usage of modules* by other modules • build and integrate modules *used* before modules that *use* them • Defining and using *framework* classes
risk reduction	• *Exercising integration* early • Exercising key *risky parts* of the application as early as possible
requirements	• *Showing parts* or *prototypes* to customers

Figure 9.15 Factors Determining the Sequence of Integration

Since we have only three application packages to integrate for the case study, and since the application is a prototype only, our plan is simple. It consists of two iterations broken into three builds. Since the case study is just the beginning of a real video game, we might want to describe the integration plan in terms of the Unified Software Development Process. Thus, the schedule in Figure 9.16 shows one *Inception* iteration, constructed in two builds. It then calls for the first *Elaboration* iteration, to be built in a single build. No further iterations are shown so far.

Instead of the integration plan in Figure 9.16, Figure 9.17 shows an alternative integration plan for the *Encounter* case study. This plan phases in classes from various packages. It does not try to complete a package and then integrate it with those already implemented. Instead, for each build, it adds classes to several packages. Its advantage is that it integrates as it goes along, trying to avoid catastrophic failures often encountered with "big bang" integration.

	Month 1				Month 2				Month 3				Month 4				Month 5			
	1	2	3	4	1	2	3	4	1	2	3	4	1	2	3	4	1	2	3	4
Milestones	Prototype requirements △									Complete prototype △										
Iterations	Inception iteration												Elaboration iterations ⟶							
Iterations (detail)	Iteration 1 "view characters in areas"												Iteration 2 "elementary interaction"							
Builds	build 1					build 2							build 3							
Modules	GameEnvironment package △ Encounter-Environment package △ Integrate and test					Characters package △ Encounter Characters package △ Integrate and test							RolePlaying Game package △ EncounterGame package △ △ :package integration Integrate and test							

Figure 9.16 Integration Schedule for Encounter *Case Study*

3. THE TESTING PROCESS

3.1 Integration Testing

Integration testing verifies each of the integration builds and iterations. Figure 9.18 shows a way in which integration testing can be planned and carried out in conjunction with unit and regression testing. The concepts referred to are explained in the rest of this chapter.

Use cases are an ideal source of test cases for integration tests. As mentioned above, Jacobson ([Ja]) et al. advise accommodating each use case within a build. The idea is for use cases to build upon ones already integrated, thus forming tests that are increasingly representative of the application's usage. This is illustrated in Figure 9.19.

A large number of tests are required to adequately validate an application, and they require methodical organization. One style of organizing test cases is to package them in classes specially created for testing. For example, a test of a package could be designed as a class belonging to the package. A class, or perhaps an entire test package, could be dedicated to testing the whole application. These can be shown as test artifact icons on the implementation model discussed in Section 1.4 of Chapter 7 (page 358).

Typically, builds consist of the code of several developers, and many problems are usually encountered when the code is integrated to create the build. For this reason, we try to begin integration and integration testing early in the process, thereby exercising the code in its ultimate context.

Integration testing is performed while builds are in progress. Such tests usually consist of regression tests, with additional testing added to validate the new additions. It is impractical to continually run complete, formal integration tests. Consequently, scaled-down, informal integration tests are frequently applied on a regular basis: They validate only that

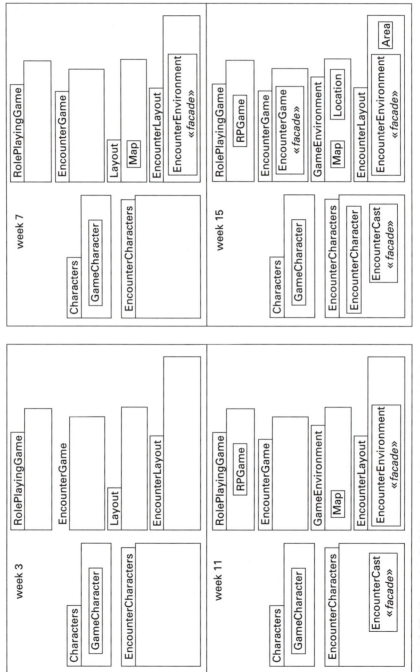

Figure 9.17 Alternative Build Process for Encounter Case Study

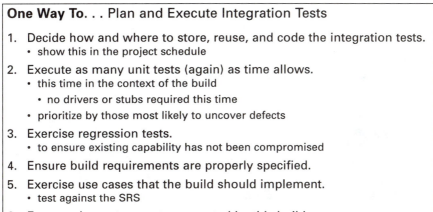

One Way To. . . Plan and Execute Integration Tests

1. Decide how and where to store, reuse, and code the integration tests.
   • show this in the project schedule
2. Execute as many unit tests (again) as time allows.
   • this time in the context of the build
      • no drivers or stubs required this time
   • prioritize by those most likely to uncover defects
3. Exercise regression tests.
   • to ensure existing capability has not been compromised
4. Ensure build requirements are properly specified.
5. Exercise use cases that the build should implement.
   • test against the SRS
6. Execute the system tests supported by this build.

Figure 9.18 One Way to Plan and Execute Integration Tests

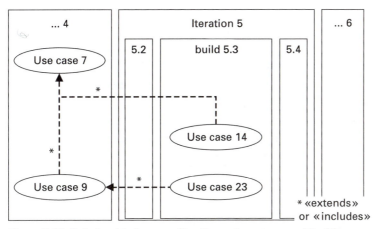

Figure 9.19 Relationship between Use Cases, Iterations, and Builds

the system appears to operate as it should. These are sometimes called "smoke tests." Smoke tests either reassure programmers that they can keep working in the same way (if no problems appear), or else indicate problems that could otherwise cause great delays at integration.

An integration schedule often takes the form shown in Figure 9.20, which takes a banking application as an example. As the task of building the modules comes to an end, they are integrated into the baseline (i.e., merged into the official emerging product) one at a time. In this case, the integration process takes place between weeks 23 and 41.

The process of compiling and testing partial builds is often performed overnight, development being frozen while compilation and testing is in progress. This is shown in the box within Figure 9.21.

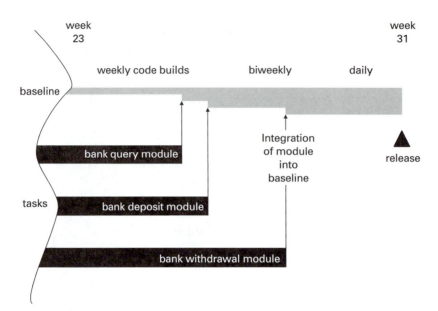

Figure 9.20 Final Code Build and Integration Schedule: Banking Example

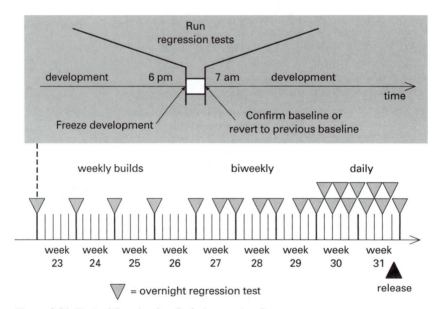

Figure 9.21 Typical Day-by-day Code Integration Process

As the release date for the build or the application approaches, the frequency of regression tests increases until they are performed daily—typically overnight, as shown in Figure 9.21. If regression testing shows that existing functionality is still present, then the integrated code becomes part of the baseline. On the other hand, if the regression tests show that the added code creates defects in the preexisting functionality, the decision can be made to revert to the code base that existed before the new material was integrated—effectively "dis"-integrating. This kind of daily integration and regression test schedule was reported by Cucumano and Selby [Cu] to be utilized by Microsoft, for example.

3.2 Testing Workers and Artifacts

In this section we will review the artifacts involved in the integration testing process, as suggested in the Unified Software Development Process (USDP). They are as follows.

- *The use case model:* the set of use cases describing the typical usage of the application, and the sequence diagrams which describe them in detail
- *The test cases:* the inputs for each of the tests
- *The test procedures:* the manner in which the tests are to be set up, executed, and the results evaluated. These could be a manual procedures, or ones using test automation tools.
- *The test evaluation:* the summary, details, and effects of the defects found
- *The test plan:* the overall plan for conducting the tests, including their order
- *The test components:* the source code for the tests themselves, and for the application code to be tested
- *The defects:* reports on the defects discovered as a result of this process, classified by severity and type

The USPD integration testing process involves the roles of test engineer, component engineer, integration tester, and system tester. Their responsibilities are shown in Figure 9.22. Most of the artifacts shown in Figure 9.22 are accounted for in the IEEE test documentation discussed below.

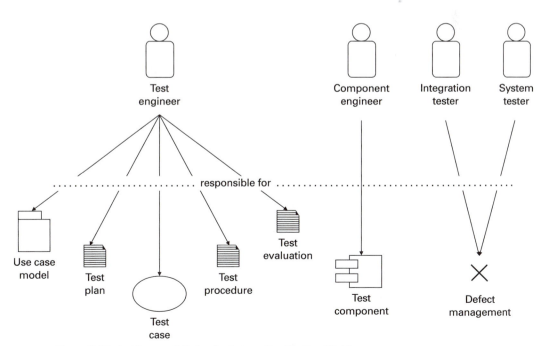

Figure 9.22 Artifacts and Roles for Integration Testing [Ja1]

3.3 Interface Testing

Many application failures are due to problems with the interfaces between components. In the chaos of project execution, groups find it much easier to communicate among themselves rather than with other groups, so that design and programming interfaces can easily be misunderstood. The Software Design Document's "Interface Specification" section is the "bible" for the application's internal interfaces. Once modules have been developed, the interfaces can be tested. This is done by generating traffic across each interface, typically in the form of function calls.

As an example, consider the interfaces of *Encounter* as shown in Figure 9.23. To test that the interfaces work as required, we can call interface methods sequentially in various combinations. The sequences we choose should exercise many interface method combinations, but should make sense in the context of the game. Otherwise, the outcome could be difficult to predict. Figure 9.24 shows an example of a comprehensible sequence from the case study whose effects can be readily observed on the monitor.

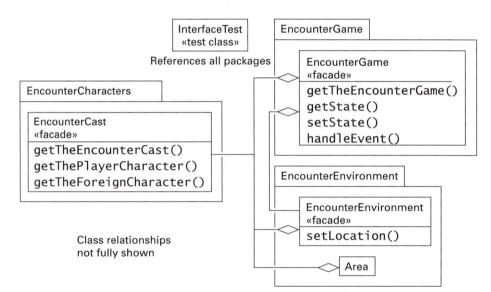

Figure 9.23 Interface Testing for Encounter

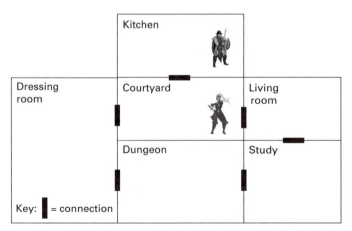

Figure 9.24 Interface Test Scenario for Encounter *(Graphics reproduced with permission from Corel)*

Sequence of methods called from `main()` in an `InterfaceTest` object:

1. // place the player character in the courtyard with default values ....
    // Get the EncounterCast (interface) object
    ```
    playerChar = EncounterCast.getThePlayerCharacter();
    ```
    // Set up the test to occur in the dungeon
    ```
    EncounterLayout.setLocation( playerChar, "courtyard" );
    ```
2. // Set the state of the game to *Waiting*
    ```
    EncounterGame.setState( "waiting" );
    ```
3. // Now verify the state of the game
    ```
    state = EncounterGame.getState();
    ```
4. // Print the name of `state`
    ```
    state.printStateName();
    ```
5. // Cause the foreign character Freddie to be in the Kitchen
    ```
    foreignChar = EncounterCast.getTheForeignCharacter();
    EncounterLayout.setLocation( foreignChar, "kitchen" );
    ```
6. // Cause the foreign character Freddie to enter the courtyard
    ```
    EncounterLayout.setLocation( foreignChar, "courtyard" );
    ```
7. // Verify that the state is now *Encountering*
    ```
    state = EncounterGame.getState();
    state.printStateName();
    ```
    // Cause the player's character to jump to the dungeon
    ```
    EncounterLayout.setLocation( foreignChar, "dungeon" );
    ```
8. // Verify that the player's qualities have changed as anticipated.

    . . . .

3.4 System Testing

System testing is the culmination of integration testing. It consists of black box tests which validate the entire application against its requirements. Whenever possible, system tests are performed with the application running in its required environment. Sometimes, however, we have to be content to run system tests in an environment or configuration that is not equivalent to the customer's. For example, we would not normally consider it necessary to test applets on every type of PC. On the other hand, applets should be tested on all major versions of all major browsers.

Since system tests ensure that the requirements have been met, they must systematically validate each requirement. It requires considerable test scripting to force the demonstration of each requirement in turn. At this time, we also validate the use cases.

The Unified Software Development Process tries to organize most requirements by use case, in which case testing is simpler in comparison with the testing of individual atomic requirements.

Figure 9.25 and Figure 9.26 list the major types of system tests.

Reliability/availability is measured by metrics such as the mean time between failure (MTBF). To obtain MTBF, a definition of "failure" is first stated—for example, a total disabling

- *Volume*

  Subject product to large amounts of input.

- *Usability*

  Measure user reaction (e.g., score 1–10).

- *Performance*

  Measure speed under various circumstances.

- *Configuration*

  Configure to various hardware / software
  - e.g., measure setup time

- *Compatibility*
  - with other designated applications

    e.g., measure adaptation time

- *Reliability / Availability*

  Measure uptime over extended period.

Figure 9.25 Types of System Tests, 1 of 2 (see Kit [Ki])

- *Security*

  Subject to compromise attempts
  - e.g., measure average time to break in

- *Resource usage*

  Measure usage of RAM and disk space, etc.

- *Installability*

  Install under various circumstances.
  - Measure time to install.

- *Recoverability*

  Force activities that take the application down.
  - Measure time to recover.

- *Serviceability*

  Service application under various situations.
  - Measure time to service.

- *Load / Stress*

  Subject to extreme data and event traffic.

Figure 9.26 Types of System Tests, 2 of 2 (see Kit [Ki])

of the application. Actually, several different levels of failure can be defined. To compute the MTBF, a tester starts the application, notes the time, then executes the application using (ideally) a random scenario, until the system fails. The time is noted, and the elapsed time computed. This process is performed repeatedly. The MTBF is the average of the times obtained.

The term *Serviceability,* mentioned in Figure 9.26, refers to the ease or difficulty with which the application can be kept operational. For example, an expert system application relies on its knowledge base, which must be capable of being easily modified.

Usability is explained next.

TABLE 9.1 Example of Usability Metric Values

	Average measure (out of 10)
Ease of viewing	8.5
Ease of use	9.5

3.5 Usability Testing

A good interface can greatly enhance the value of an application. *Usability testing* validates the application's acceptability to its users.

3.5.1 Testing for User Interface Requirements
The primary usability testing task is to ensure that the application satisfies its stated requirements. Recall from Section 3.5 of Chapter 3 (page 151) that there are numerous window types and that these can appear in several possible positions. In addition, specific timing may be required. For example, in the *Encounter* case study, there is a specified delay between the time when a character's quality values are set and when they take effect. Usability testing includes the validation of these requirements.

One way to do this is to quantify the level of satisfaction that users report in using the application.

3.5.2 Usability Metrics
Usability criteria are specified in advance. For example, we might require that a random sample of 30 users of our home finance application rate the application as shown in Table 9.1. The appropriate sample size is statistically determined, and it depends on the size of the anticipated customer base and the desired probability of erroneous conclusion.

In practice, usability data would be more detailed than that shown in Table 9.1. For example, Kit [Ki] lists the criteria in Figure 9.27 as essential for usability testing. The example metrics are the author's.

- *Accessibility*
  How easily can users enter, navigate, and exit?
  - e.g., measure by average time taken to . . .

- *Responsiveness*
  How quickly does the application allow the user to accomplish specified goals?
  - e.g., measure average time taken

- *Efficiency*
  How minimal are the required steps for selected functionality?
  - "minimal" deduced in theory
  - e.g., also measure by minimal time from user sample

- *Comprehensibility*
  How easy is the product to understand and use with documentation and *help*?
  - e.g., measure time taken for standard queries

Figure 9.27 Key Attributes for Usability Testing (adapted from Kit [Ki])

In addition to these qualities, we would need application-specific metrics such as the following.

> *How easy would you say it is to enter a standard accident report form (on a scale of 1–10)?*

In designing usability questionnaires, the challenge is to obtain data that enables engineers to focus development on remedying the most serious shortcomings, without exceeding the limits of users' time and patience. Usability data can be expensive to collect because users often expect compensation for the time and trouble of providing feedback. For example, a client company of the author's develops software for a device used by physicians. The company provides doctors with a free dinner and hundreds of dollars in return for viewing and commenting on screen shots and demonstrations. The developer considers the benefits well worth the cost.

3.6 Regression Testing

When an application becomes large, the system tests assume a special significance. This becomes especially noticeable when a change is made to a large application, and developers need to validate the fact that the change has not disturbed the existing functionality. The first question to ask after integrating the change is typically the following. "Is this product the same one that I had before, with the functionality added?" Reinspection is generally impractical, and so an important practical way to help answer this question is to verify that the system continues to pass the same designated set of system tests that it passed before the changes were made. This verification process is called *regression testing*.

Regression testing takes place frequently. If time does not allow for complete regression testing, then selections are made of those tests most likely to fail due to changes.

3.7 Acceptance Testing

The developer organization and the customer organization are parties to a contract. When the job is completed, a wise developer obtains a definitive statement from the customer stating that the application has indeed been delivered. The *acceptance tests* are designed to assure the customer that the stipulated application has indeed been built. Acceptance tests may be indistinguishable from the system tests devised by the developer, but this time they are witnessed officially by the customer organization and are executed on the target platform(s).

Customers are frequently required to make progress payments based on intermediate deliveries. These are partial implementations and designs, and they too require acceptance testing.

3.8 Installation Testing

The fact that we have tested an application in our own environment does not ensure that it will work properly in the customer's environment because there is plenty of room for new errors when changing environments. *Installation testing* consists of testing the application in its ultimate hardware configuration. This entails installing the application in its target environment, then executing the system test suite. For shrink-wrapped applications, installation testing consists of executing the application on platforms which typify customer environments.

4. DOCUMENTING INTEGRATION AND TESTS

4.1 Standards for Test Documentation

The ANSI/IEEE standard for test documentation is shown in Figure 9.28.

1. The *introduction* section explains the context of the tests and their overall philosophy. For example, if the application controls emergency room equipment then this is where we would generally explain our overall approach to testing the models, leading to testing under emergency room conditions.

2. The *test plan* explains how the necessary people, software, and equipment are to be organized to get the testing job done. For example, "The timing module will be tested by Joe between weeks 30 and 33; the heart monitor module will be tested by Sue between weeks 26 and 30; the integration of these will be tested by Ed between weeks 31 and 33, . . ."

3. The *test design* supplies the next level of detail beyond the test plan. It breaks out the software items involved, describes the order in which they are to be tested, and names the test cases to be applied. For example, "Joe will test the timing module in isolation between weeks 30 and 33 using test procedure 892 and driver 8910; Sue will test the heart monitor module in isolation between weeks 26 and 30, using test procedure 555 and driver 3024; Ed will test the build which integrates these two modules (build 7) using . . ."

4. The *test cases* consist of the input sets and the precise stimuli to be applied in order to carry out the test design. For example, the heart monitor module is to operate on test file 892, which provides specific patient data at specific times. We have to describe exactly where this test file is located.

5. The *test procedures* are the complete, detailed steps for carrying out the test plan. They include all setup procedures, the names of required source and object code files, output files, log files, tests case files, and reports. For example, test procedure 892 could be as follows

   a. Compile the Timing module together with driver 8910

   b. Set the directory path to . . .

---

1. **Introduction**

2. **Test plan**
   items under test, scope, approach, resources, schedule, personnel

3. **Test design**
   items to be tested, the approach, the plan in detail

4. **Test cases**
   sets of inputs and events

5. **Test procedures**
   steps for setting up and executing the test cases

6. **Test item transmittal report**
   item under test, physical location of results, person responsible for transmitting

7. **Test log**
   chronological record, physical location of test, tester name

8. **Test incident report**
   documentation of any event occurring during testing which requires further investigation

9. **Test summary report**
   summarizes the above

Figure 9.28 ANSI/IEEE 829-1983 Software Test Documentation (Reaffirmed 1991) Copyright © 1983 IEEE

c. Load the contents of file 672 onto a file with the name input in the same directory as the object code

d. Execute the code with the following options . . .

e. On the window that appears, enter "Jones" in the name text box . . .

. . . .

The reason for this level of detail is the fact that if and when a test indicates a defect, it is important to know the exact circumstances under which the defect occurred. Without detailed test step documentation, tests can't be reliably reproduced, and the defect may not be reproducible. In that case, it is hard or impossible to repair.

6. The *test item transmittal report* summarizes what tests were run, who performed them, what versions they were performed on, etc.

7. The *test log* is a detailed running account of what transpired during the test. This can be important in trying to reconstruct situations when tests fail.

8. The *test incident report* elaborates on noteworthy occurrences that took place during testing. Examples are deviations from the normal manner of operating the application, and mistakes made in the testing process.

The IEEE format in Figure 9.28 can be used for most of the test types mentioned in this chapter. It is used in the case study at the end of this chapter for the build integration tests.

4.2 Organizing Integration and Test Documentation

A good document in which to describe how the parts of an application are to be assembled is the configuration management document (the SCMP in IEEE parlance). This is illustrated in Figure 9.29. This document organization indicates that the SPMP describes

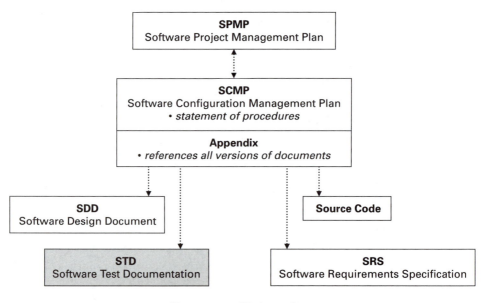

Key: ┈┈► "Refers to"

Figure 9.29 System Test Documentation in Context

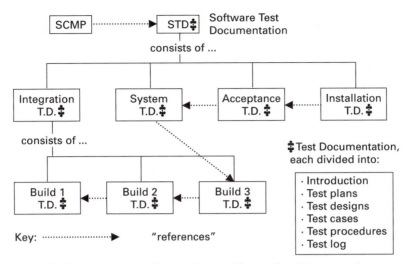

Figure 9.30 Organization of Integration- and System Test Documentation (with R. Bostwick)

the SCMP, and who is responsible for it. The SCMP itself describes the specific procedures for maintaining (storing, labeling, coordinating, etc.) the various versions of the various documents, including the SPMP. It also specifies exactly where these documents are located. The latter specification grows, and can be better described in an appendix for the SCMP. In particular, the SCMP and its appendix need to reference the test documentation (the STD—Software Test Documentation—in IEEE parlance), to keep careful track of the tests that are run, the corresponding test cases, procedures, plans, etc., and the actual versions of the code that these test.

Figure 9.30 illustrates the relationships among the various test documents and their relationship with existing documentation. The test documentation for the application, the STD, includes all of the various types of testing described in this chapter. It could also include unit testing, depending on the degree to which unit testing is documented. Figure 9.28 shows the IEEE standard for test documentation, and this organization is applied to each build and to each of the various test types, as shown in Figure 9.30.

Artifacts of various tests are reused, as indicated by the dotted lines in Figure 9.30. For example, *build* testing typically uses test plans, designs, cases, and procedures which were developed to test previous builds. *System* testing uses artifacts (test cases, etc.) which were developed to test the final build, *Acceptance* testing uses artifacts from *System* testing, and *Installation* testing uses artifacts from *Acceptance* testing.

5.   THE TRANSITION ITERATIONS

After the application has been integrated, several activities are required before it can be released. The steps are summarized by Jacobson et al. in the *Transition* iterations of their Unified Software Development Process. The goals of these iterations are described in Figure 9.31. Figure 9.31 also summarizes the relative amounts of requirements, analysis, etc. required for these iterations during the transition phase.

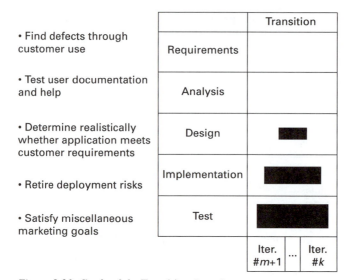

		Transition	
• Find defects through customer use	Requirements		
• Test user documentation and help	Analysis		
• Determine realistically whether application meets customer requirements	Design	▬	
• Retire deployment risks	Implementation	██	
• Satisfy miscellaneous marketing goals	Test	███	
		Iter. #*m*+1	...	Iter. #*k*

Figure 9.31 Goals of the Transition *Iterations*

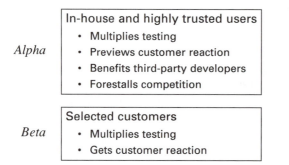

Alpha

In-house and highly trusted users
- Multiplies testing
- Previews customer reaction
- Benefits third-party developers
- Forestalls competition

Beta

Selected customers
- Multiplies testing
- Gets customer reaction

Figure 9.32 Alpha Releases and Beta Releases

5.1 Alpha and Beta Releases

In many cases, internal prospective users, as well as customers, are willing to participate in the system testing process. This process is controlled by alpha releases and beta releases, as illustrated by the Figure 9.32.

Alpha releases are given to in-house users or to a highly selective and trusted group of external users for early prerelease use. The purpose of alpha releases is to provide the development organization with feedback and defect information from a group larger than the testers, without affecting the reputation of the unreleased product. Following the dissemination of alpha releases, beta releases are given out.

Beta releases are given to part of the customer community with the understanding that they report defects found. In addition, alpha and beta releases are used to convince potential customers that there really is a product behind the vendor's promises. Sometimes, distributing prereleases is a strategic business technique used to discourage customers from purchasing competing products, inducing them to wait for the release of the application which is being beta tested. The ethical issues that this sometimes raises are beyond the scope of this book.

A principal motivation to be alpha testers and beta testers is to gain advanced knowledge of the product. Developers can gain information about the application (typically its APIs) so that they can begin to develop applications which use it. Users can begin to form decisions about purchasing the application.

5.2 Road Map for the Transition Iterations

Figure 9.33 shows common steps followed in carrying out the Transition (final) iterations. The "stopping criteria" are the conditions under which the product is to be released for acceptance testing. If these conditions are not determined in advance, testing typically proceeds until time runs out: This is usually not an effective use of testing time. An example of a stopping criterion is "a maximum of two medium-level or lower defects found per week of beta testing." Kit [Ki] has categorized stopping criteria as suggested by Figure 9.34.

Figure 9.34 mentions "remaining defects": But how can we estimate the number of defects remaining? One method is by "seeding." This consists of inserting a variety of defects into the application, then determining the percentage of these which are detected by independent testers within a given time period. This percentage is then used to estimate the number of defects remaining.

For example, if 3 of 50 seeded faults are found during a given test, we can estimate $47/3 = 15.67$ undetected faults for every fault that we actually detect. Thus, if a total of 100 unseeded faults are found during the same kind of test, then there are roughly $100 \times 15.67 = 1567$ remaining undetected faults in the system.

By applying some of these criteria, projects can use graphs such as those shown in Figure 9.35 in order to determine when to release the product. In this example, three stopping criteria are applied. The stopping criterion for the error detection rate is "at most seven defects found per thousand hours of testing per week for at least four consecutive weeks."

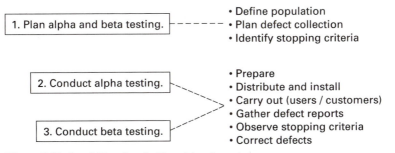

Figure 9.33 Road Map for the Transition *Iterations*

- Completing a particular test methodology
  - Complete the procedures of a method or tool

- Estimated percent coverage for each category
  - predetermine percent of each and show how to calculate
  - e.g., "95% statement coverage"

- Error detection rate
  - predetermine rate with given severity level
  - e.g., "2 medium severity defects or less per 100 hours of operation"

- Total number of errors found
  - (if possible) computed from a percentage of remaining defects
  - predetermine percent
  - e.g., "95% of estimated existing defects found"

Figure 9.34 Stopping Criteria (Kit [Ki])

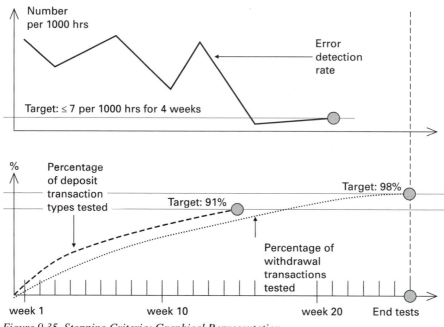

Figure 9.35 Stopping Criteria: Graphical Representation

(To squeeze a thousand hours of testing into a week, testing is executed on different copies of the application in parallel.) This is a banking application, and tests of "deposit" and "withdrawal" transactions are tallied separately. In the case illustrated by the figure, the last criterion to be satisfied is the "percentage of withdrawal transactions tested," and so the product is not released before this (week 26).

6.   QUALITY IN INTEGRATION, VERIFICATION, AND VALIDATION

6.1 Qualities to Aim For

Good integration plans are well thought out, and effective system and integration tests are thorough and comprehensive. Metrics such as the following promote these qualities.

6.2 Metrics for Integration and System Testing

The following metrics are taken from IEEE 982.1-1988, the standard dictionary of measures [IEEE 982].

IEEE 1. Fault density = [Number of unique faults found by testing] / [Number of lines of code]

IEEE 2. Defect density = [Number of unique faults found by inspection] / [Number of lines of code]

IEEE 5. Functional test coverage = [Number of functional requirements tested] / [Total number of requirements]

IEEE 10. Software maturity index = $[M - F_a - F_c - F_d] / M$, where

M = number of parts in the current baseline
F_a = number of parts in the current baseline added since the previous baseline
F_c = number of parts in the current baseline changed since the previous baseline
F_d = number of parts deleted from the previous baseline

"Parts" can be functions, classes, packages, modules, and the like chosen consistently throughout. Mature applications yield a maturity index close to 1, meaning that the number of affected parts is small compared with the total.

IEEE 18. Run reliability is the probability that k random runs of the system will produce correct results. This is estimated by executing a number, N, of runs, and counting the number, S, of successes. The probability of success is thus S/N, and the probability of being able to execute k successful runs is the product of the probability of each success: $[S/N][S/N] \ldots [S/N]$, or $[S/N]^k$. The inputs for each run are chosen randomly and independently of the choice for the previous run.

IEEE 20. The mean time to discover the next k faults. This quantity is estimated in a manner analogous to run reliability (18 above).

IEEE 21. Software purity level. This metric is an estimate of a program's freedom from faults during the operational phase (see [IEEE 982]).

IEEE 22. Estimates of the number of faults remaining (by seeding). This estimate is obtained by "seeding" the application with faults as randomly as possible—N of them, let us say. If s is the number of seeded faults subsequently found, and f the number of unseeded faults found in the same time period, then the estimate is $f \times N/s$.

IEEE 24. Test coverage. This measures the completeness of the testing performed (i.e., the fraction of the job implemented times the fraction of tests implemented). The formula is

TC (as a percentage) = [[No. Implemented requirements] / [No. Requirements]]
  × [[No. Program primitives tested] / [Total no. program primitives]]

  × 100 (converts to percentage)

Program primitives are the testable units of the program. These include the methods, the classes, and the packages.

IEEE 30. Mean-Time-to-Failure (MTTF). This is measured by recording the times between all pairs of observed successive failures, and averaging these times. "Time" is frequently elapsed time, not CPU time.

IEEE 36. Test accuracy. This test estimates the reliability of the testing process, and is a by-product of test 22 described above.

Test accuracy = N_f / N, where N is the number of seeded faults, and N_f is the number of seeded faults found during the designated testing period.

6.3 Inspection of Integration and System Testing

Several aspects of integration are amenable to the inspection process. They include the SCMP portions relating to the integration sequence, and the various test plans (e.g. Integration Plan and System Test Plan). An example of a defect in the integration plan is the absence of a necessary element (module, class, method, etc.) from a particular stage of integration, i.e., an element that must be present to form a testable build or a use case. An example of a defect in an integration test is the absence of a test step that is part of the corresponding use case.

The sequence of builds and their tests can be very complex: hence the benefit of inspections, in which several minds are brought to bear on the plans.

6.4 QA Involvement in Integration and System Test

Quality Assurance personnel are typically more active during build testing and system testing than during any other phase of the process. Nowhere is the principle that the testers differ from the authors of a product more relevant than during integration testing.

To understand the importance and difficulty of the QA process, take as an example a vendor of applications for TV weather casters. One major function of this application is to convert large amounts of data into images. Not only does the data change continually, but there are also many ways in which the data can be displayed. Competitive forces, and frequent demands from weather casters for improved features, result in continual changes and improvements to the application. In addition, the vendor has strong incentives to release upgrades in order to maintain revenue. This kind of development organization typically employs QA personnel to test new features and to run regression tests. Imagine the effects on the vendor's business prospects if the display system crashes in full view of millions of people.

One major issue for QA in a case like this is reproducibility. QA has to reproduce a session in which the weather caster clicked on particular spots at particular instants while displaying a moving thunderstorm. Tools which record and reproduce user actions, described below in Section 7, can help, but they do not cover every type of application. There is considerable additional work to be done to measure and maintain quality.

When defects at the system level are found, appropriate people have to be notified. This can be a significant diplomatic, management, and technical task. Diplomatic, because developers do not like to hear about their fallibility; management, because consistent defects have to be traced and responsibility determined among many contributors; technical because the act of isolating the causes of a defect can be complex.

6.5 System Integration and the Capability Maturity Model

The end of a project is a good time to assess the process used and to arrange for process improvement. A typical organization aspires to graduate to the next CMM level. Figure 9.36 recalls the five CMM levels.

As an example, suppose that our organization is at level 3 and is trying to attain level 4. Thus, the team will have tried to make detailed measurements and to control the project (rather than have the project control the team). A postmortem could take the form shown in Table 9.2.

1. *Initial*   undefined, ad hoc
2. *Repeatable* tracks cost, schedule, functionality after fact
3. *Defined*   documented, standardized, tailorable
4. *Managed*   detailed measurement; control
5. *Optimized*   continual quantified process improvement

Figure 9.36 Capability Maturity Models

**TABLE 9.2 Postmortem Example: Requirements
Analysis Through System Integration**

	Metric collection	Controllability	Action items
Requirements	Only 2 of 4 requirements metrics maintained	Good—problem was neglect, not lack of time	Designate QA engineer to maintain SRS and all four metrics. LD by 3/1.
Design	Failed to define metrics	Poor—completed in 140% of scheduled duration	H.R. to select best three metrics for this type of application; estimate cost and schedule consequences; by 3/5. LD to describe how we should prioritize design activities; by 4/1.
			ST to decide whether insufficient time was allocated to design, or whether the process was inefficient, and identify reasons why; by 3/15.
Implementation	Good	Completed in 130% of scheduled duration	Revise line-of-code estimation methods; identify top three reasons for overrun; J.A. by 3/5.
Integration and release	Applied too many useless metrics	Adequate	Eliminate "rate of beta site signup" metric. Reassess effectiveness of the other metrics used; BV by 3/10.

7. TOOLS FOR INTEGRATION AND SYSTEM TESTING

The sheer volume of testing usually requires the use of automated test tools. Jacobson et al. [Ja1] suggest that at least 75% of tests are best automated, the remainder manual. Selected testing tool capabilities are listed in Figure 9.37 and explained below.

Capabilities of Automated System Test Tools

1. Record mouse and keyboard actions to enable repeated playback
2. Run test scripts repeatedly
3. Enable recording of test results
4. Record execution timing
5. Record run time errors
6. Create and manage regression tests
7. Generate test reports
8. Generate test data
9. Record memory usage
10. Manage test cases
11. Analyze coverage

Figure 9.37 Capabilities of Automated System Test Tools

1. Record and Play Back. Without the ability to record and play back mouse and keyboard actions, testers are reduced to performing these tests repeatedly by hand. This is tedious and expensive. In addition, the results may not be directly comparable because humans cannot duplicate their actions precisely. Kit [Ki] has categorized capture/playback tools as shown in Figure 9.38.

The most common capture/playback tools are native/software intrusive tests. An example of nonintrusive system tests is the testing of a real-time military command-and-control application in which user interaction is simulate using separate hardware connected to the application under test. The external hardware is programmed to provide stimuli to the command-and-control in such a way that the application cannot distinguish these stimuli from actual user input.

Record/playback tools can be very useful, but they are sensitive to changes in the user interface. A small change in the UI can invalidate a whole set of mechanically executed tests.

2. Run Test Scripts Repeatedly. The ability to execute application tests automatically saves testers from having to repeat them manually with varying parameters.

3. Record Test Results. This spares testers from having to implement this function.

4. Record Time Usage. Automated test tools are capable of measuring and recording elapsed time and CPU usage.

5. Record Run Time Errors. Some automated testing tools can record errors encountered while the application executes.

6. Manage Regression Testing. Recall that regression testing is required to validate the fact that modifications to the previous version have not introduced new errors. Regression tests change over time, as more and more capabilities are implemented. Some automated test tools can keep track of these tests and apply them on demand.

7. Generate Test Reports. Automated test tools include test report generators which eliminate the need to write numerous test reports manually or to write one's own report generation tools. The latter was partially done for the case study.

- *Native / software intrusive*
  test software intermingled with software under test
  - could compromise software under test
  - least expensive
- *Native / hardware intrusive*
  test hardware intermingled with software under test
  - could compromise software under test
- *Nonintrusive*
  uses separate test hardware
  - does not compromise software under test
  - most expensive

Figure 9.38 Types of Capture/Playback Tests (adapted from [Ki]).

8. Generate Test Data. Among the most useful test tools are those for test data generation. These tools generate input data to satisfy many of the white box and black box test disciplines discussed in this chapter and Chapter 8. One example is the generation of random combinations of input. Some test tools also facilitate gray box integration and system tests that exercise module interaction. It should be noted that these tools cannot be expected to generate the correct output for each test case, however, since this capability is the reason we are building the application in the first place!

9. Memory Usage Test Tools. These tools are very useful in testing the run time performance of applications. Figure 9.39 summarizes their potential capabilities. As Figure 9.39 shows, some of these tests simply report statistics in tabular or graphical form while others are capable of detecting some errors.

10. Test Case Management Tools. Test management tools typically possess the capabilities described in Figure 9.40.

- *Memory leaks*
  - detect growing amounts of unusable memory inadvertently caused by the implementation
- *Memory usage behavior*
  - confirm expectations
  - identify bottlenecks
- *Data bounds behavior*
  - e.g., confirm integrity of arrays
  - e.g., detect attainment of limiting values
- *Variable initialization*
  - indicate uninitialized variables
- *Overwriting of active memory*

Figure 9.39 Memory Usage Test Tools

- *Provide user interface*
  - to manage tests
- *Organize tests*
  - for ease of use
  - for maintenance
- *Manage test execution sessions*
  - to run tests selected by user
- *Integrate with other test tools*
  - to capture and play back
  - to analyze coverage
- *Provide reporting*
- *Provide documentation*

Figure 9.40 Test Case Management (adapted from Kit [Ki])

11. Coverage analysis. Coverage analyzers take as input the product, together with the test suite. They provide an analysis of the coverage of the suite. These analyzers can verify various types of test coverage, including statement coverage.

Testing requires the repeated use of forms. Document templates are the most elementary but most widely used testing "tools." Templates can be based on testing documentation standards such as ANSI/IEEE 829-1983 (reaffirmed 1991) "Software Test Documentation," for example.

Although automated test programs replace many test-programming tasks, their use often requires significant programming skills. For example, recorders of mouse and keyboard actions must trap such events, and this requires programmers with a good knowledge of how events are generated, so that the test tools can intercept the application appropriately.

8. SUMMARY

This chapter has described the integration phase of software development, which consists of planning, executing, and verifying builds. Figure 9.41 summarizes the various forms of testing covered in this chapter.

EXERCISES

A hint is provided for every exercise marked with the superscript "h." Solutions are provided for every problem marked with the superscript "s."

REVIEW QUESTIONS

R9.1[s] In transitioning from one phase to the next, information is typically lost. Name three to five transitions during which such loss often occurs.

R9.2[s] What is the difference between verification and validation?

R9.3[s] Name four to eight different kinds of tests and state what they are for.

R9.4[s] What are *builds* and how do they relate to iterations?

R9.5[s] Name three to five artifacts for which test engineers may be responsible.

R9.6[s] What is regression testing and why is it necessary?

R9.7[s] What is the difference between alpha testing and beta testing?

R9.8[s] What is acceptance testing?

R9.9[s] Name four to eleven metrics for integration and system testing.

- *Integration process*: executed in carefully planned builds
- *Integration testing*: each build
- *System testing*: whole application
- *Regression testing*: verify that changes do not compromise preexisting capabilities

Figure 9.41 Summary of System Integration and Verification

TEAM EXERCISES

T9.1 ("Integration") Obtain project specifications from two other teams in the class. Specify informally a new application that contains significant elements of these applications. Specify an integration plan to build this new application.

Evaluation criteria:

α. *Degree of clarity of the plan—A = very clear plan*
β. *Degree to which the plan contains an appropriate order—A = feasible and appropriate order of operations*

GENERAL EXERCISES

G9.1 Figure 9.42 shows the architecture outline of an application that simulates the movement of customers in a bank. Provide a build plan for this application.

Evaluation criteria:

α. *Degree of clarity of the plan—A = very clear plan*
β. *Degree to which the plan contains an appropriate order—A = feasible and appropriate order of operations*

G9.2 Describe the various levels of testing to which you would subject the application in exercise G9.1, and indicate which of the classes and packages shown in Figure 9.42 would be involved in each. (Many more classes will be involved in building the complete application, but you are not required to show these.)

SOLUTIONS FOR REVIEW QUESTIONS

R9.1 Loss of information typically takes place in translating

requirements into architecture

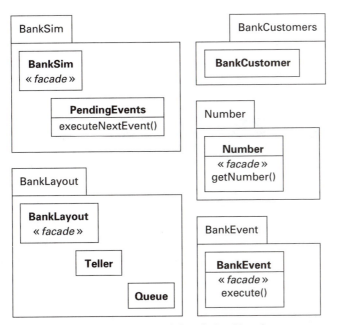

Figure 9.42 Architecture of Bank Simulation Exercise

architecture into detailed designs

architecture into interface specifications

detailed designs into the code for individual functions

interface specifications into module code

R9.2 "Verification" asks whether we are "building it right." "Validation" asks whether we are "building the right thing."

R9.3 *Function, class, and module* tests are unit tests that test these physical units.

Interface tests validate the way in which modules communicate with each other.

Integration tests validate the builds of the partial application.

System tests validate the operation of the application as a whole.

Acceptance tests provide the sign-off that the application does what the developers promised it would.

Installation tests validate that the application operates according to specification in its intended physical environment.

R9.4 Each iteration is constructed by means of a sequence of builds. Each build is an integration of part of the application and is designed to make the assembly process convenient. Each build takes the result of the previous build as its baseline.

R9.5 Test cases, test procedures, test plans, test evaluations, and possibly use case models.

R9.6 Regression tests are designed to validate the fact that a modification or addition to the code has not compromised its preexisting capabilities. They are required precisely because changes to code may change existing behavior. Changes in existing behavior may be the result of defective changes, or of defective existing design/code.

R9.7 Alpha releases are given to in-house users or highly selected customers. Beta releases are provided to a cross section of the user community.

R9.8 Acceptance testing is the official testing process whereby a customer can agree that the product meets the requirements of the contract, and can take delivery.

R9.9 The solution to this question can be found in Section 6.2 on page 458 "Metrics for integration and system testing."

CASE STUDY:

I. SCMP: APPENDIX A. PLAN FOR INTEGRATION BASELINES

[Note to the student: We need to describe the order in which the application will be integrated. The SCMP is an appropriate location for this description, since it describes configurations of the iterations and builds.]

History of versions of this document:

11/1/98 E. Braude: Initial Draft

4/4/99 E. Braude: Revised

8/23/99 R. Bostwick: Documents reviewed and recommendations made

8/24/1999 E. Braude: Recommendations integrated

8/26/1999 E. Braude: Reviewed, comments expanded

1. INTRODUCTION

During the integration process, the software for *Encounter* is constructed in stages or builds. This appendix describes the configuration of the first three builds. Integration testing is based on these builds. The last build is the basis for system testing.

2. CONSTRUCTION OF INTEGRATION BASELINES

The three successive builds for release 1 of Encounter are shown in Figure 9.43. The first build consists of the *GameCharacters* framework package and the *Encounter-Characters* package. The second build uses the first build. It consists of the *EncounterEnvironment* package, its corresponding framework, and the first build. The third build refers to builds 1, and 2. It consists of the *EncounterGame* package, its corresponding framework, build 1, and build 2.

2.1 Integration Build 1

Build 1 is illustrated in Figure 9.44. Build 1 implements the *GameCharacters* framework package and the *EncounterCharacters* package.

2.2 Integration Build 2

Build 2 is shown in Figure 9.45. Build 2 consists of the *EncounterEnvironment* package and the *GameEnvironment* framework package, together with the first build. The *GameEnvironment* and the *Encounter-Environment* packages use the build 1 *GameCharacter* and *EncounterCast* classes respectively. Courtyard, dungeon, and living room are examples of areas. Some of these areas are connected. For example, there is a connection between the dressing room and the courtyard.

At the conclusion of build 2, the framework/application decomposition is shown in Figure 9.46. The *EncounterGame* package and its *RolePlayingGame* framework package are not present because they are part of build 3.

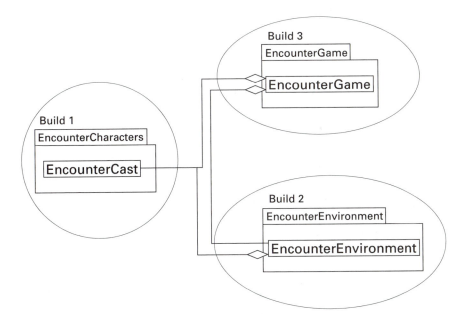

Figure 9.43 Integration Plan for Encounter

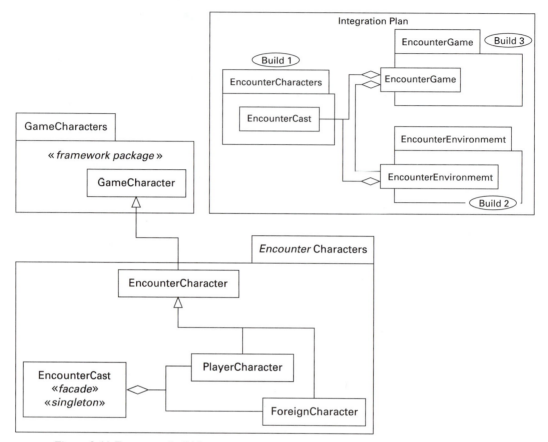

Figure 9.44 Encounter *Build 1*

2.3 Integration Build 3

The final build, build 3, is illustrated in Figure 9.47. Build 3 consists of the *EncounterGame* package, its *RolePlayingGame* framework package, build 1, and build 2.

II. SOFTWARE TEST DOCUMENTATION FOR *ENCOUNTER*

History of versions of this document:

 11/1/98 E. Braude: Initial Draft

 4/4/99 E. Braude: Revised

 8/23/99 R. Bostwick: Documents reviewed and recommendations made

 8/24/1999 E. Braude: Recommendations integrated

 Status: to be completed

 [Note: This document describes the overall testing of *Encounter*. The document uses the IEEE STD headings *(introduction, plan,* *design, test cases, procedures, test item transmittal report, log, incident report, summary)* and refers to the various particular tests (integration tests, system tests, acceptance tests, etc.). These, in turn, are described using the same IEEE STD headings.]

1. INTRODUCTION

This document contains the STD for *Encounter* and its Role-playing Game [RPG]

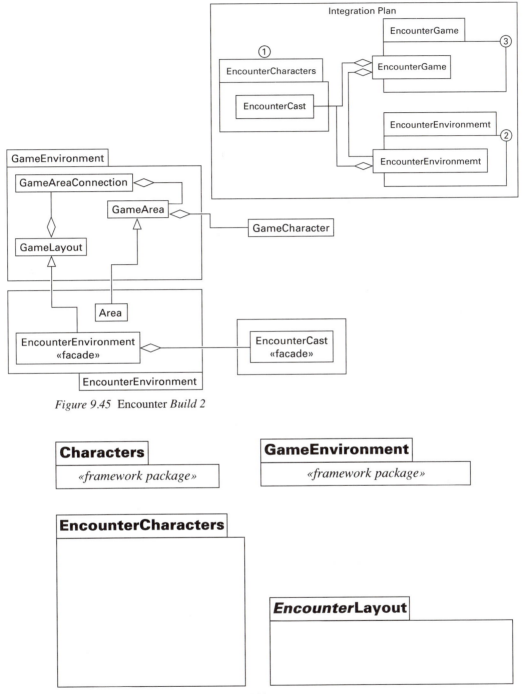

Figure 9.45 Encounter *Build 2*

Figure 9.46 Encounter *Status After Build 2*

framework. The categories of testing addressed in this document include unit, integration, system, acceptance, and installation testing. This document describes the testing required to validate the first three builds of the *Encounter* video game. IEEE standard 829-1983 for Software Testing Documentation is used at every level of testing.

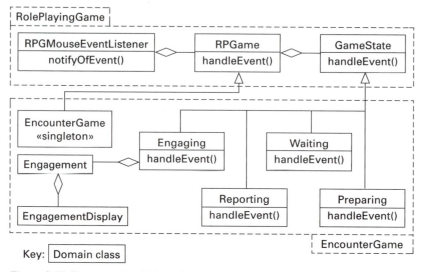

Figure 9.47 Encounter *Build 3 (includes builds 1 and 2—not shown)*

The test philosophy for the *Encounter* Video Game is summarized in Table 9.3.

[Notes to the student: This is the application to Encounter *of Figure 9.6 in Section 1.2. Although the SDD is not explicitly a requirements document, it effectively imposes requirements on the implementation. Sometimes these requirements are spelled out in a separate document. The case study in this book does not contain such a separate document.]*

2. *ENCOUNTER* VIDEO GAME TEST DOCUMENTATION

The STD for *Encounter* and the RPG framework covers test planning, specification, and reporting. There are separate test plans for unit, integration, system, acceptance, and installation testing. Each test plan references its test design, test case, and test procedure specifications. The test reporting documentation consists of the test log, incident report, and summary report.

2.1 Unit Test STD

Refer to the separate unit test document.

[Note to the student: See case study in the Unit Testing chapter.]

2.2 Integration Test STD

The STD for integration testing consists of the separate STDs for build 1, build 2, and build 3, as described next. Refer to Appendix A in the SCMP for an explanation of the construction of the build integration baselines.

2.2.1 Build 1 STD

2.2.1.1 Build 1 Test Plan

2.2.1.1.1 TEST PLAN IDENTIFIER *Build1_TP*

2.2.1.1.2 INTRODUCTION This test plan covers the integration test for the *GameCharacters* framework package and the *EncounterCharacters* package. It describes how to verify that the Player and Foreign characters can be retrieved, modified, and displayed through the singleton *EncounterCast* object.

2.2.1.1.3 TEST ITEMS The classes and methods in the *GameCharacters* and *EncounterCharacters* packages are tested through the *EncounterCast* singleton.

2.2.1.1.4 FEATURES TO BE TESTED The features tested by the test design specifica-

TABLE 9.3   Approaches and Documentation for Test Types

Test Type	Approach	Corresponding Document Sections
Unit	White box and black box; method and class tests; test against D-requirements and design.	SRS Section: 3.2 *Classes/Objects* SDD Section: 6. *Detailed design*
Integration	Gray box; mostly package-level; oriented to builds 1, 2, and 3; test against architecture and C-requirements.	SRS Sections: 2. *Overall description*, 3.1 *External interfaces*, validate representative requirements in 3.2 *Classes/Objects* SDD Sections: 3. *Decomposition description*, 4. *Dependency description*, 5. *Interface description*
System	Black box; all packages; whole system (build 3); test against nonfunctional requirements, architecture, and C-requirements.	SRS Sections: 2. *Overall description*, 3.1 *External interfaces*, validate representative requirements in 3.2 *Classes/Objects*, 3.3 *Performance requirements*, 3.4 *Design constraints*, 3.5 *Software system attributes*, 3.6 *Other requirements* SDD Sections: 3. *Decomposition description*, 4. *Dependency description*, 5. *Interface description;* validate representative requirements in 6. *Detailed design.*
Acceptance	Black box; all packages; whole system (build 3); test against C-requirements and D-requirements.	SRS Sections: 2. *Overall description*, 3.2 *Classes/Objects*
Installation	Black box; all packages; whole system (builds for customer specific configurations); test against C-requirements and D-requirements.	SRS Sections: 2. *Overall description*, 3.2 *Classes/Objects*

tion *Build1_TD* are based on the requirements within the SRS and SDD, as listed in Table 9.4.

2.2.1.1.5 FEATURES NOT TO BE TESTED

[Note to the student: There are infinitely many issues that are not tested, but identifying particular issues that will not be tested for sometimes helps to clarify the testing process.]

The testing of the features associated with the *EncounterEnvironment* and *EncounterGame* packages and their frameworks is deferred until the build 1 and build 2 integration testing.

2.2.1.1.6 APPROACH   The approach to the verification of build 1 consists of verifying that the characters of the game can be re-

trieved and displayed through the singleton *EncounterCast* object. The method and interface tests verify that the required (public) interface methods of the *Encounter Characters* package are available from the *EncounterCast* singleton.

2.2.1.1.7 ITEM PASS/FAIL CRITERIA
Pass/fail criteria are based upon satisfying the corresponding requirements in the SRS and SDD.

2.2.1.1.8 SUSPENSION CRITERIA AND RESUMPTION REQUIREMENTS (N/A)

2.2.1.1.9 TEST DELIVERABLES   The documents listed in Table 9.5 are to be delivered to the configuration management group at the completion of the build 1 integration test.

TABLE 9.4 Features to be Tested in Build 1

Document	Section	Requirement Title
SRS	2.1.2.2	User interface concept for setting quality values
	3.2.EC	Encounter characters
	3.2.FC	Foreign characters
	3.2.P	Player characters
	3.2.PQ	The player quality window
SDD for RPG framework	3.1.2	Characters package
	5.0	Interface description
SDD for Encounter	3.1.2	EncounterCharacters package
	4.2	Interprocess dependencies
	5.1.2	Interface to the EncounterCharacters package

TABLE 9.5 Test Document Identifiers

Test Document	Document Identifier
Build 1 Test Plan	Build1_TP
Build 1 Test Design Specification	Build1_TD
Build 1 Test Case Specifications	Build1_TC1 to Build1_TC...
Build 1 Test Procedure Specifications	Build1_TP1 to Build1_TP...
Build 1 Test Logs	Build1_LOG1 to Build1_LOG...
Build 1 Test Incident Report	Build1_InRep1 to Build1_InRep...
Build 1 Test Summary Report	Build1_SumRep1 to Build1SumRep

2.2.1.1.10 TESTING TASKS The testing tasks consist of the following steps:

(1) Load build 1 and the package *Build_1*. (2) Execute build 1 test procedures from the *main()* method of *Build_1Test* in package *Build_1*. (3) Write test report documentation in accordance with Section 2.2.1.1.9. (4) Store all test documentation and data in accordance with Section 2.2.1.1.9 under configuration management.

2.2.1.1.11 ENVIRONMENT NEEDS Depending upon equipment availability, either an IBM PC, Sun SPARC workstation, or an Apple IMAC hardware configuration can be used. The IBM Visual Age™ Integrated Development Environment (IDE) should be used for the build 1 testing.

2.2.1.1.12 RESPONSIBILITIES Sally Silver and Jose Hernandes from the SQA group are responsible for managing, preparing, and executing the build 1 integration test. In addition, the *Encounter* development group addresses technical questions and responds to test incident reports. Configuration control stores all test documentation and data.

2.2.1.1.13 STAFFING AND TRAINING NEEDS The SPMP specifies the overall staffing and training needs for integration testing.

2.2.1.1.14 SCHEDULE The schedule for integration testing is included in the SPMP section 5.5 version 5 and higher. (Section 5.5 of Chapter 5 on page 288 discusses the updating of the SPMP to reflect the architecture selected.)

[Note: The case studies in this book do not include the updated SPMP.]

2.2.1.1.15 RISKS AND CONTINGENCIES If the SQA team is unable to execute tests, or the number of defects causes an unacceptable number of system failures, then Alfred Murray of the *Encounter* development team will be assigned to the build 1 integration test.

TABLE 9.6   Integration Test Inputs, Outputs, and Actions

	Quality	Player input value	Foreign input value	Other	Action
B1.1	N/A	N/A	N/A	Get player character	Verify by name
B1.2	N/A	N/A	N/A	Get foreign character	Verify by name
B1.3	Concentration	30	40	N/A	Verify output values == input values
B1.4	Stamina	30	40	N/A	Verify output values== input values
B1.5	. . .	. . .	. . .	. . .	. . .

2.2.1.1.16 APPROVALS   The completion of this test requires the approval of the SQA Manager, the *Encounter* Development Manager, and the CCB Representative.

2.2.1.2 Build 1 Test Design

2.2.1.2.1 TEST DESIGN SPECIFICATION IDENTIFIER   To be decided.

2.2.1.2.2 FEATURES TO BE TESTED   The test for build 1 will get the *EncounterCast* object and the *Player* and *Foreign* characters, change the values of various qualities, get these values, then verify their correctness.

2.2.1.2.3 APPROACH REFINEMENTS   To be decided.

2.2.1.2.4 TEST IDENTIFICATION   To be decided.

2.2.1.2.5 FEATURE PASS/FAIL CRITERIA   To be decided.

2.2.1.3 Build 1 Test Cases

2.2.1.3.1 TEST CASE SPECIFICATION IDENTIFIER   To be decided.

2.2.1.3.2 TEST ITEMS   The functionality to be tested is contained in the specifications for the following public methods of *EncounterCast*.

```
EncounterCast getTheEncounterCast()
GameCharacter   getThePlayerChar-
acter()
GameCharacter   getTheForeignChar-
acter()
void    setPlayerCharacterQuality(
String quality, float value )
void    setForeignCharacterQuality(
String quality, float value )
float getPlayerCharacterQuality()
float getForeignCharacterQuality()
```

These are tested in accordance with the Table 9.6.

2.2.1.3.3 INPUT SPECIFICATIONS—SEE TABLE 9.6

2.2.1.3.4 OUTPUT SPECIFICATIONS—SEE TABLE 9.6

2.2.1.3.5 ENVIRONMENTAL NEEDS   This testing is performed with the *GameCharacters* and *EncounterCharacters* packages alone.

2.2.1.3.6 SPECIAL PROCEDURAL REQUIREMENTS—NONE

2.2.1.3.7 INTERFACE DEPENDENCIES   none

[Note to the student: This section describes the relationships among the various interfaces. This becomes significant for future builds, but is not an issue for build 1.]

TABLE 9.7   Build 1 Test Log

Test #	Result	Defect reference
1	Passed	N/A
2	Failed	1823
3	Data lost — to be repeated	N/A
4	Loss of precision in returned value	2872
5	. . .	. . .

2.2.1.4 Build 1 Test Procedures

2.2.1.4.1 TEST PROCEDURE SPECIFICATION IDENTIFIER

[Note to the student: identifies the class/method from which the test is executed]

Integration_Tests/Build1_Test in package *Tests*

2.2.1.4.2 PURPOSE   To set up a test of build 1 with a minimum of other parts of the application.

2.2.1.4.3 SPECIAL REQUIREMENTS   The test harness in *Integration Tests/Build1_Test,* consisting of a class with a single method, *main(),* is to be constructed, and tests 1, 2, 3, . . . are to be executed and the results compared.

2.2.1.4.4 PROCEDURE STEPS   Populate the file *Build1_test_data* with input data and expected output values for the qualities in the following format.

> *<quality name> <input><expected output>*
> *<quality name> <input><expected output>*
> *. . . .*

There is no additional beginning or ending text.

2.2.1.5 Build 1 Test Item Transmittal Report

2.2.1.5.1 TRANSMITTAL REPORT IDENTIFIER *Build1_SumRep1*

2.2.1.5.2 TRANSMITTED ITEMS   Test summary report; test log; test incident report

2.2.1.5.3 LOCATION   The documentation for build test 1 is located in . . .

2.2.1.5.4 STATUS   not yet executed

2.2.1.5.5 APPROVALS   Build 1 testing is to be approved by the QA manager.

2.2.1.6 Build 1 Test Log

2.2.1.6.1 TEST LOG IDENTIFIER   *Build1 test_log*

2.2.1.6.2 DESCRIPTION   This document describes the results of build 1 testing (see example in Table 9.7).

2.2.1.6.3 ACTIVITY AND EVENT ENTRIES

[Note to the student: The "defect reference" is the number used by the defect tracking system for this defect.]

2.2.1.7 Build 1 Test Incident Report

2.2.1.7.1 TEST INCIDENT REPORT IDENTIFIER   *Build1 test3*

2.2.1.7.2 SUMMARY—SEE TABLE 9.7.

2.2.1.7.3 INCIDENT DESCRIPTION   Ed Blake was distracted during the execution of test 3 by an alarm in the building, and could not record the results. It was decided not to interrupt or repeat the test sequence, and to conduct test 3 as part of the testing for build 2.

2.2.1.7.4 IMPACT   It was decided that the incident(s) reported above were not serious enough to require a repetition of this test.

2.2.1.8 Build 1 Test Summary Report

2.2.1.8.1 TEST SUMMARY REPORT IDENTIFIER   To be decided.

2.2.1.8.2 SUMMARY   The build 1 test passed with the exception of the defects noted. This will be handled by the regular defect repair process.

2.2.1.8.3 VARIANCES   See build 1 test incident report.

2.2.1.8.4 COMPREHENSIVE ASSESSMENT   To be supplied.

[Note to the student: additional remarks supplying details]

None

2.2.1.8.5 SUMMARY OF RESULTS   To be supplied.

2.2.1.8.6 EVALUATION   To be supplied.

2.2.1.8.7 SUMMARY OF ACTIVITIES   To be supplied.

2.2.1.8.8 APPROVALS

_____ Approved Disapproved
Manager of QA

2.2.2 Build 2 STD   [Similar format to build 1 STD]

2.2.2.1 Build 2 Test Plan
These tests will verify that the areas of the game can be retrieved and displayed through the *EncounterEnvironment* object, and that the connections among them are consistent with the SRS.

2.2.2.2 Build 2 Test Design
These tests will first verify that the correct *EncounterEnvironment* object can be obtained, and then show that the *Area* objects and *AreaConnection* objects can be retrieved as required.

2.2.2.3 Build 2 Test Case
The functionality to be tested is contained in the following public functions of *EncounterEnvironment*.

```
GameArea getTheDressingRoom()
GameArea getTheDungeon()
```

```
....
EncounterEnvironment    getTheEn-
counterEnvironment()
```

2.2.2.4 Build 2 Test Procedures—to be supplied

2.2.2.5 Build 2 Test Item Transmittal Report—to be supplied

2.2.2.6 Build 2 Test Log—to be supplied

2.2.2.7 Build 2 test incident report—to be supplied

2.2.2.8 Build 2 test summary report—to be supplied

2.2.3 Build 3 STD—to be supplied

2.3   System Test STD

[Note to the student: Recall from Figure 9.7 in Section 1.2 (page 436) that the system tests verify the fact that the architecture has been correctly implemented.]

2.3.1 System Test Plan   These tests are performed against the architecture, as described in Figure 9.48.

The tests verify that the effects of game actions in *EncounterGame* correctly manifest themselves as movements of *Encounter* characters within the environment.

2.3.2 System Test Design

[Note to the student: The system tests are designed to verify the architecture by executing and verifying sequences of interface methods.]

2.3.3 System Test Cases   System Test 1

1. Move player character into dungeon.
2. Move foreign character into courtyard.
3. Move foreign character into dungeon.
4. Execute an encounter in the dungeon.

System Test 2

1. ...

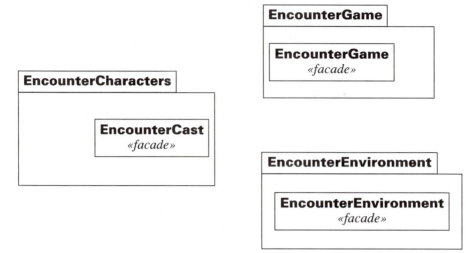

Figure 9.48 Architecture and Modularization of Encounter

2.3.4 System Test Procedures

The system tests are executed from the *SystemTest* package. System test *N* is executed by means of the *main()* method of class *SystemTestN*.

2.4 Acceptance Test STD

2.4.1 Acceptance test plan

[Note to the student: The integration tests verify that the requirements of Encounter, *as stated in the SRS, have been satisfied.]*

The acceptance tests are stored in the *AcceptanceTest* package, and include the use cases.

The *Initialize* use case is shown in Figure 9.49 and is executed by the *main()* method of the class *Initialize* in the *AcceptanceTest* package.

The *SimpleEncounter* use case is shown in Figure 9.50 and is executed by the *main()* method of the class *AcceptanceTest.Initialize.*

2.4.2 Acceptance Test Design

The use cases indicated in Section 2.4.1 are to be executed in sequence several times, in accordance with the test cases in Section 2.4.3.

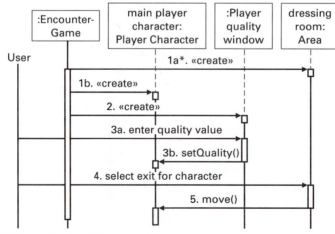

* Numbering keyed to use case

Figure 9.49 Sequence Diagram for Initialize Use Case

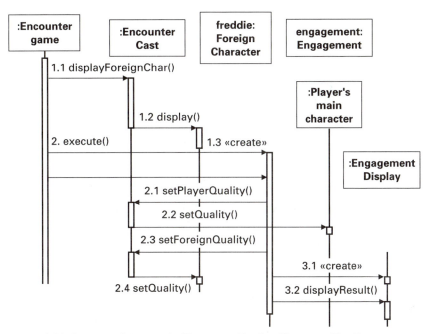

Figure 9.50 Sequence Diagram for Encounter *Foreign Character Use Case*

2.4.3 Acceptance Test Cases

2.4.3.1 Test Cases for Initialize Use Case

[Note to the student: The tests are instances of the Initialize *use case, also known as "scenarios."]*

2.4.3.1.1 INITIALIZE ACCEPTANCE TEST 1

Start up game.

Supply main character with the following quality values, in the order shown:

> Strength: 30
> Concentration: 20

Move the main character to the courtyard.

2.4.3.1.2 INITIALIZE ACCEPTANCE TEST 2

Start up game.

Supply main character with the following quality values, in the order shown:

> Strength: 30
> Concentration: 20
> Patience: 30

Move the main character to the courtyard.

2.4.3.1.3 INITIALIZE ACCEPTANCE TEST 3

Start up game.

Supply main character with the following quality values, in the order shown:

> Strength: 30
> Concentration: 20

Move the main character to the dungeon.

2.4.3.1.4 INITIALIZE ACCEPTANCE TEST 4 . . .

2.4.3.2 Test Cases for Encounter Foreign Character Use Case

2.4.3.2.1 ENCOUNTER FOREIGN CHARACTER ACCEPTANCE TEST 1

Set the main character's "patience" value to 30.

Set the foreign character's "patience" value to 20.

Move the main character to the drawing room.

Cause the foreign character to enter the drawing room.

Verify that an engagement has taken place.

Observe the engagement window showing the results.

(The player's patience value should be 40, and the foreign character's 10.)

2.4.3.2.2 ENCOUNTER FOREIGN CHARACTER ACCEPTANCE TEST 2

Set the main character's "strength" value to 30.

Set the foreign character's "strength" value to 20.

Move the main character to the dungeon.

Cause the foreign character to enter the dungeon.

Verify that an engagement has taken place.

Observe the engagement window showing the results.

(The player's strength value should be 40, and the foreign character's 10.)

2.4.3.2.3 ENCOUNTER FOREIGN CHARACTER ACCEPTANCE TEST 3

. . .

2.4.4 Acceptance Test Procedures

Acceptance tests shall be carried out with two designated representatives of the customer present. These representatives shall carry out all testing with the assistance of the vendor. Whenever possible, events should occur as a result of the random processes of the game instead of being stimulated. An example of this is the arrival of the foreign character in an area. A log of all tests shall be maintained by the customer representatives and signed by all parties: Any signatory can enter dissenting statements in the log.

2.5   Installation Test STD

[Note to the student: These are tests which verify that the application executes correctly in their required hardware and operating system environments.]

The installation tests for *Encounter* consist of executing the system tests on the following hardware configurations.

1. IBM-compatible PC with at least 32 megabytes of RAM and 100 megabytes of disk space.
2. SUN SPARC model mmm with at least 32 megabytes of RAM and 100 megabytes of disk space.
3. Apple IMAC model 1234 or later with 32 megabytes of RAM and 100 megabytes of disk space.

The installation tests shall consist of the acceptance tests conducted on all of the above platforms.

CHAPTER **10**

MAINTENANCE

Figure 10.1 places this chapter in the context of software engineering. Figure 10.2 lists this chapter's learning goals.

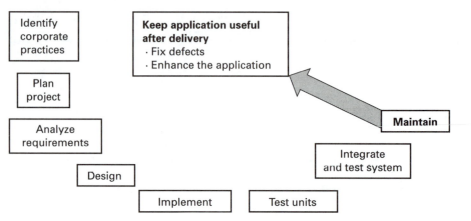

Figure 10.1 Software Engineering Road Map: Chapter 10 Focus

- Understand how "Software Maintenance" is defined
- Appreciate the cost of maintenance
- Understand software maintenance issues
- Organize for maintenance
- Use IEEE maintenance standard
- Apply maintenance metrics

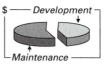

Figure 10.2 Learning Goals of This Chapter

1. INTRODUCTION

Figure 10.3 and Figure 10.4 show a typical sequence of actions required to service a maintenance request (MR): The rest of this chapter elaborates upon the steps mentioned and provides background.

One Way To. . . Service a Maintenance Request 1

1. Be prepared to keep required metrics. Include
   —lines of code added
   —lines of code changed
   —time taken: 1. preparation   2. design   3. code   4. test
2. Ensure that the request has been approved
3. Understand the problem thoroughly
   —reproduce the problem
   • otherwise get clarification
4. Classify the MR as *repair* or *enhancement*
5. Decide whether the implementation requires a redesign at a higher level
   —if so, consider batching with other MRs
6. Design the required modification
   (i.e., incorporate the change)

Figure 10.3 One Way to Service a Maintenance Request, 1 of 2

> **One Way To. . .** Service a Maintenance Request 2
>
> 7. Plan transition from current design
> 8. Assess change's impact throughout the application
>   —small changes can have major impact!
> 9. Implement the changes
> 10. Perform unit testing on the changed parts
> 11. Perform regression testing
>   —ensure changes haven't compromised existing capabilities
> 12. Perform system testing with new capabilities
> 13. Update the configuration, requirement, design, and test documentation

Figure 10.4 One Way to Service a Maintenance Request, 2 of 2

1.1 The Meaning of "Software Maintenance"

The *software maintenance* of a product consists of those activities performed upon the application after the product has been delivered. The IEEE glossary [IEEE 610] describes software maintenance as

> *The process of modifying a software system or component after delivery to correct faults, improve performance or other attributes, or adapt to a changed environment.*

It has been estimated that maintenance consumes 40% to 90% of the total life cycle costs of applications (e.g., [Fo], [Pi]). Some may quarrel that the definition of maintenance quoted above includes enhancements, which really should be considered additional development. In any case, maintenance is an activity of significant proportions. Perhaps the most famous maintenance effort involved the year 2000 (Y2K) problem, for which massive work was done to modify applications so that they could handle the years of the new millennium. This was a maintenance activity because it ensured that applications already delivered continued to provide their intended functionality.

Lehman ([Le1] and [Le2]) claims a "law" that if a program is not continually adapted to ongoing needs, it becomes less and less useful with time. In other words, if an application remains unchanged, its usefulness usually declines.

1.2 The Issues of Software Maintenance

To understand the problems of maintenance, imagine an application so large that no single person can be familiar with all of its details. The author has worked on large shipboard defense systems, for example, where this is the case. In maintaining such a subsystem, a major problem is the ripple effect of making a change. There are many, many instances of seemingly harmless changes made in "remote corners" of large applications that actually cripple them.

Bennett [Be2] has categorized problems of software maintenance as shown in Figure 10.5. Management tends to be fatigued by the effort required to deliver applications. In addition, funds spent on maintenance are usually not simple to justify as a return on investment.

To illustrate this point, let's imagine that the Navy has informed us (a military contractor) that the algorithm for reconciling three independent sources of shipboard navigation data is flawed. We need an estimate of the cost of making this repair. Our calculations

- *Management*
  - —Return on investment hard to define
- *Process*
  - —Extensive coordination required to handle stream of Maintenance Requests
- *Technical*
  - —Covering full impact of changes
  - —Testing very expensive compared with the utility of each change
    - focused tests ideal but expensive
    - regression testing still required

Figure 10.5 Software Maintenance Issues

could be as shown in Table 10.1. The cost of making this change at $50–$100 per hour of loaded labor (i.e., including benefits, etc.) is $5600–$28,000. This is a very wide variation.

If a single, focused change were the only one we had to handle, then our process problems would be minor. Typically, however, numerous maintenance requests stream continually through the organization. Some economy of scale can be obtained, reducing the cost of each change, but a stream of maintenance changes places a significant burden on the process. Programmers, testers, and writers have to be coordinated. To give an example, should the SRS be updated as soon as the customer indicates a requirement flaw, as soon as a patch succeeds, only after thorough testing, or only when grouped with other maintenance actions? Each of these options leaves the documentation and source code set in an inconsistent state for periods of time. Without careful management, these supposedly short-lived inconsistencies multiply and the documentation gets out of control, with the result that no one knows exactly what the application does.

The technical challenge is to make changes in an understandable, even elegant, manner. The absence or presence of elegance in maintenance is like the difference between adding a storage shed to a house to add space, versus adding space in a way that preserves the house's integrity. Adding a storage shed can compromise the appearance and structure

TABLE 10.1 Estimating the Cost of Servicing a Maintenance Request

Activity	Estimate (person-days)	Activity	Estimate (person-days)
1. Understand the problem and identify the functions that must be modified or added	2–5	6. Compile and integrate into baseline	2–3
2. Design the changes	1–4	7. Test functionality of changes	2–4
3. Perform impact analysis	1–4	8. Perform regression testing	2–4
4. Implement changes in source code	1–4	9. Release new baseline and report results	1
5. Change SRS, SDD, STP, configuration status	2–6	**Total**	**14–35**

of a house, whereas preserving a house's integrity using the skill of a good architect makes no such compromise.

Testing is the second significant technical issue. Simply focusing tests on the changed or added parts takes time enough, because special test plans must often be devised for this purpose. But focused testing is not enough. The possibility of ripple effects requires that we execute extensive regression testing to ensure that changes have not compromised the application's preexisting functionality. This is a major factor in the high cost of maintenance.

1.3 A Typical Road Map to Establish a Maintenance Process

Figure 10.6 shows a typical road map for establishing a maintenance operation. Steps 1a through 1d are actually carried out during development. "Designing for maintenance" includes trying to anticipate directions in which the requirements are likely to grow and accommodating these directions in the design. Design patterns, for example, often help to accomplish this. "Supportability" in step 1b means "capable of being maintained effectively." This includes, for example, the presence of liberal comments within the code. Maintainers are generally not as specialized in their knowledge of an application as developers since they have to deal with a much larger code base: Nevertheless, maintainers are required to fully understand each instruction under scrutiny before they make changes. Ensuring supportability is a continual quality issue.

Step 2 is to decide on the limits of the maintenance effort — mainly whether or not to include improvements. The options are described in Section 2.

Step 3 is to decide whether to perform maintenance in-house or not. Contracted maintenance has the advantages of competitive pricing and allowing the application's owner to concentrate on other business. A disadvantage is diminished familiarity with the code by employees.

The planning of the maintenance process itself is discussed in Section 5.

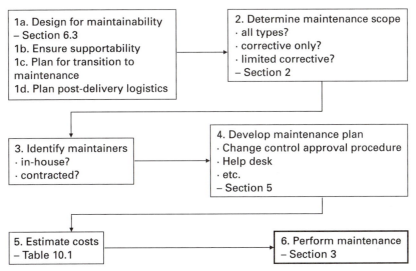

Figure 10.6 Road Map to Establish Maintenance (after Pigoski [Pi])

2.   TYPES OF SOFTWARE MAINTENANCE

We distinguish between those maintenance actions that *fix* defects and those that *enhance* the application. Various studies have shown that 60–80% of maintenance actions are enhancements rather than repairs (see, for example, [Pi] p. 34, and Glass [Gl]). As shown in Figure 10.7, Lientz, Swanson, et al. [Li] refine each of these two types of maintenance into two subcategories.

Adaptive maintenance is classified as "fixing" because the resulting application executes without any additional functionality, and its capability is not actually enhanced.

The need for *preventive* maintenance can be deduced from an observation of Lehman ([Le1] and [Le2]): *Without corrective action, the structure of a program being maintained tends to become increasingly complex, and eventually becomes too complex to change at reasonable cost.*

As an example of a type of maintenance, consider the *Encounter* video game case study. A *corrective* maintenance example is shown in Figure 10.8. MR #78, described there, requires the maintainer to decide whether the method *adjustQuality( )* is the culprit or whether the requirements for *Encounter* characters are defective. Actually, the latter is the case because the requirements mandate that

- The user be permitted to set any quality to any value less than or equal to the current sum of the qualities
- The remaining qualities retain their mutual proportions
- No quality shall have a value both greater than zero and less than 0.5
- The sum of the qualities remains invariant

Fixing
- Corrective
  - defect identification and removal
- Adaptive
  - changes resulting from operating system, hardware, or DBMS changes

Enhancing
- Perfective
  - changes resulting from user requests
- Preventive
  - changes made to the software to make it more maintainable

Figure 10.7 Types of Maintenance (Lientz, Swanson, et al. [Li])

Maintenance Request 78

The computations that ensue when the player changes the value of a quality are supposed to keep the total invariant but they do not. For example, if the qualities are *strength* = 10, *patience* = 0.8, and *endurance* = 0.8 (sum = 11.6), and the player adjusts *strength* to 11, then the result is *strength* = 11, *patience* = 0, and *endurance* = 0, which do not sum to 11.6.

Figure 10.8 Example of Corrective Maintenance Request

Maintenance Request 162

Modify *Encounter* so that the game begins with areas and connections in a coordinated style. When the player achieves level 2 status, all areas and connections are displayed in an enhanced coordinated style which is special to level 2, etc. The art department will provide the required images.

Figure 10.9 Example of Perfective Maintenance Request

As can be seen in the MR #78 example, these four conditions cannot all be satisfied at once. Since the defect is in the requirements, it is the customer's prerogative to make or permit the change. One way to do this is to relax the last (invariant) requirement to

$$0 \le (\text{sum of qualities})' \le \text{abs}(\text{sum of qualities} - N)$$

where N is the number of qualities, abs means "absolute value," and x' is the value of x after the adjustment process. This modification keeps the effect of discouraging the player from changing quality values too much and too many times, because points may be lost whenever this is done.

Now let us turn to a *perfective* maintenance request. We will suppose that the marketing department has decided to make the game more attractive because players require more tangible rewards for their skill. They want the entire look of the game to be enhanced whenever the player achieves a new level. The art department will supply the corresponding graphics and the maintenance organization is tasked with a modification to accommodate this additional requirement, as stated in Figure 10.9. A solution to MR 162 in Figure 10.9 is discussed later in this chapter.

3. MAINTENANCE TECHNIQUES

3.1 Impact Analysis

The analysis, design, and implementation sequence of maintenance requests is similar to that for ordinary development with the important exception of impact analysis. This is an assessment of the impact of the changes upon the product's artifacts. In a study by Weiss [We1], it was found that 19% of the defects emanated from the requirements phase, 52% from design, and 7% from programming. Many claim higher percentages for requirements defects. Figure 10.10 illustrates the artifacts potentially impacted by the repair of a defect.

In the minimal case, only a single artifact is affected. This occurs, for example, when the programmer has failed to follow a standard in naming a local variable or when an unused variable is removed. In the worst case, however, every part of the process is affected. Even for a code-level defect (i.e., a defect in the code only), the impact can range from minor to major. A seemingly simple change such as an increase in the size of a compile-time C++ array could have major ripple effects throughout the application.

Maintenance Request 162, described in Figure 10.9, affects every aspect of the process, as shown in Figure 10.11. When an application is designed with traceability in mind, the documentation of maintenance actions can be manageable. Otherwise, the consequences can be extremely expensive to manage. For more on impact analysis techniques for code-level maintenance actions, see Wilde [Wi].

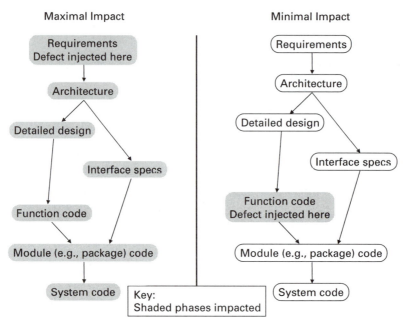

Figure 10.10 Impact of a Defect on Maintenance

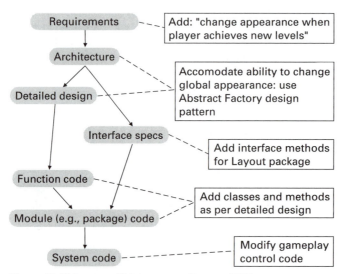

Figure 10.11 Impact of Maintenance Request #162

3.2 Reverse Engineering

Software products under maintenance have a wide variety of possible histories: Many existing applications are poorly or inconsistently documented. The first step in organizing a rational maintenance effort for such an application is to bring it to a consistent, documented state. This often includes trying to infer the design from the source code, a process called *reverse engineering*. Several tools are available to assist in this purpose. For example, *Rational Rose* (Rational Corporation) and *Together* (Object International) can generate object models from C++ or Java source code. The maintainer can then peruse these diagrams in order to surmise the purpose of the designer. Due to ambiguities in the meaning of UML diagrams, however, and the mechanical nature of the reverse process, reverse engineering cannot fully determine the designer's intentions. When a designer draws UML boxes and relationships, the geometrical placement conveys information (groupings, for example) that is appreciated by humans but not by mechanical processes.

Reverse engineering is actually more general than code-to-design transformation: It is the process of deducing the contents of a phase from the artifacts of a subsequent phase. Inferring purpose from structure is not always possible. The reader is referred to the example of undocumented code in Section 5.1 of Chapter 1 (page 34). Due to the absence of comments, the purpose of that undocumented code is impossible to deduce.

3.3 Reengineering

With their book on business process reengineering (BPR), Hammer and Champy [Ha1] suggested in the 1980s that companies examine anew the entire process by which they produce value for their clients, and then redesign it from scratch. Hammer and Champy's emphasis was on the process as a whole rather than on the parts. The process starts with input such as orders, ends with final delivery of the goods or services, and includes all contributory elements such as supporting software and employee contributions. Reengineering spurred efforts to look at the requirements for software applications within the requirements for the enterprise as a whole (the company, the branch, the organization, etc.). The resulting applications are sometimes called *enterprise applications,* although this concept is also used without the context of BPR. Typically, reengineering includes asking how legacy applications *should* fit, not how they *do* fit. In effect, business process reengineering applies the system engineering concepts described in Chapter 3 to business processes.

Reengineering is related to maintenance because it results in the redesign of applications. Figure 10.12 illustrates this point by comparing a hypothetical bridge that is not reengineered to accommodate increased traffic, with one that is reengineered.

As an example, suppose that a company reengineers its management training process. The reengineering approach consists of examining the process from beginning to end. Typically, it is impractical to build all of the software from scratch, so that existing applications have to be redesigned to fit within the reengineered design. Figure 10.13 suggests at a high level how *Encounter* could be reengineered to fit with such a management simulation. The workflow would supply *Encounter* with its new and changed requirements. The result of reengineering in this case is to adapt *Encounter* so as to yield a management simulation application, and also an application that evaluates the results.

3.3.1 Refactoring In many cases, programs need to be improved to a greater degree than just enhancing some lines of code, but to a lesser degree than complete reengineering. This process is sometimes called "refactoring." Fowler [Fo2] describes an example of a design for a video store that is not particularly good but is adequate for a simple application, then shows how the design can be refactored to handle additional requirements such as the generation of new kinds of reports. This process includes "extracting a method," (i.e., creating a method to replace an existing piece of code). Other examples of refactoring include the introduction of ideas from the *Implementation* chapter of this book into existing code, such as the replacement of a literal constant

```
final int MAX_NUM_VIDEOS = 18;
```

by a method

```
static final int getMaxNumVideos() . . .
```

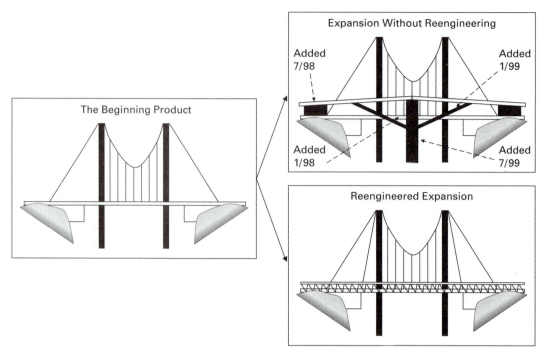

Figure 10.12 Maintenance with and without Reengineering

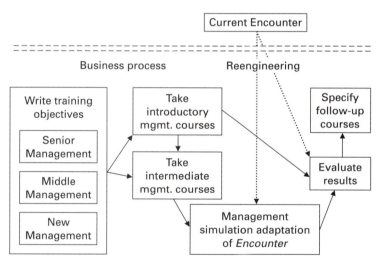

Figure 10.13 Reengineering Encounter *to Conform to Management Training*

3.4 Legacy Applications

Legacy systems are existing applications that serve a continuing useful purpose. The term is sometimes used more specifically for existing applications that are not worth modifying.

Bennett [Be2] has classified options which are included in Figure 10.14, for dealing with legacy systems. The incorporation and encapsulation options are illustrated in Figure 10.15.

Figure *i* in the diagram ("Incorporation") shows how the new application can be obtained from the original by extending or modifying it. In the *Encounter* case study, for example, this might apply if we were to make the game real-time with first-person perspective. We could do this by adding to *Encounter* (the legacy application in this case) a graphics engine

- Continue to maintain
- Discontinue maintenance and
  1. *Replace*
     - buy replacement
     - OR build replacement
       —reverse engineer legacy system
       —or develop new architecture
       —possibly replace in phases

OR 2. *Incorporate* as integral part of new application
   - freeze maintenance

OR 3. *Encapsulate* and use as server
   - consider using *Adapter* design pattern

Figure 10.14 Options for Dealing with Legacy Systems

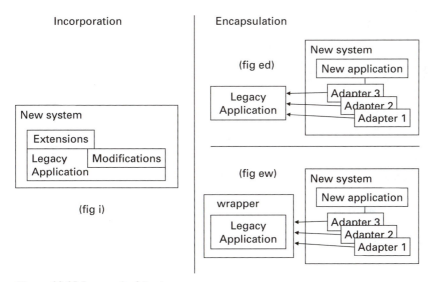

Figure 10.15 Legacy Architectures

(the "extension") that displays at all times what the player character sees, and by modifying the original code so that the displays are from the player's perspective, rather than from above.

When using a legacy application by *encapsulation,* the original application remains basically unchanged. The new application is built separately, and in the course of executing it, functionality of the legacy system is called as needed. This can be done directly, as in figure *ed*, or through a "wrapper," as in figure *ew*. Figure *ed* fits the *Adapter* design pattern (see Chapter 6) if the legacy application is object-oriented. A *wrapper* is software that provides an interface for the legacy application that clients can handle. In particular, a wrapper can make the application appear to be object-oriented. Once this is done, the *Adapter* design pattern can be applied.

3.5 Updating Documentation

Maintenance actions consist of far more than technical changes and additions. The entire documentation chain has to be updated to reflect each maintenance action. For example, a repair caused by a defect in the requirements results in updates to the requirements document, possibly the design document, certainly the implementation, and certainly the test documentation. In addition, the configuration management system has to reflect the new version of the product. For large programs in which the author has participated, the work required to repair a defect has been often been smaller than that required to update the documentation. The effect of ignoring the update process, however, is to leave the product and its documentation inconsistent, making continued maintenance increasingly expensive, and ultimately prohibitive.

4.   IEEE STANDARD 1219-1992

The table of contents for IEEE 1219-1992 for software maintenance [IEEE 1219] is shown in Figure 10.16. The seven steps listed in this standard are roughly the same as for the development process. Each of these steps has six attributes, as shown in Figure 10.17.

For each maintenance request, Tables 10.2 and 10.3 elaborate on the six attributes for each of the seven steps of the maintenance process.

1. *Problem identification* 　1.1 Input 　1.2 Process 　1.3 Control 　1.4 Output 　1.5 Quality factors 　1.6 Metrics	4. *Implementation* 　4.1 Input 　4.2 Process 　　　*4.2.1 Coding and testing* 　　　*4.2.3 Risk analysis and review* 　　　*4.2.4 Test readiness review* 　4.3–4.6 Control, Output, Quality 　　　factors, Metrics
2. *Analysis* 　2.1 Input 　2.2 Process 　　　*2.2.1 Feasibility analysis* 　　　*2.2.2 Detailed analysis* 　2.3–2.6 Control, Output, Quality 　　　factors, Metrics	5. *System test* 　5.1–5.6 Input, Process, Control, 　　　Output, Quality factors, Metrics
	6. *Acceptance test* 　6.1–6.6 Input, Process, Control, 　　　Output, Quality factors, Metrics
3. *Design* 　3.1–3.6 Input, Process, Control, 　　　Output, Quality factors, Metrics	7. *Delivery* 　7.1–7.6 Input, Process, Control, 　　　Output, Quality factors, Metrics

Figure 10.16 IEEE 1219-1992 "Software Maintenance" Standard Table of Contents Copyright © 1993 IEEE

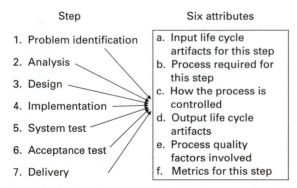

Step　　　　　　　　　　　Six attributes

1. Problem identification
2. Analysis
3. Design
4. Implementation
5. System test
6. Acceptance test
7. Delivery

a. Input life cycle artifacts for this step
b. Process required for this step
c. How the process is controlled
d. Output life cycle artifacts
e. Process quality factors involved
f. Metrics for this step

Figure 10.17 Six Attributes of Each Maintenance Step (IEEE)   Copyright © 1993 IEEE

4.1 Maintenance Problem Identification

Table 10.2 describes the process used in the identification phase for maintenance requests. "Problem Identification" in the case study at the end of this chapter, for example, was performed by the marketing department. They solicited and examined user complaints about the complicated way in which *Encounter* game characters exchange quality values as a result of engagements.

4.2 Maintenance Problem Analysis

Table 10.3 describes the analysis phase for maintenance requests.

4.2.1 Examples of Maintenance Problem Analysis
Maintenance problems range from the simple to the deeply challenging. For example, suppose that we want to provide the *Encounter* game player with additional image options for the main player. This appears to be a straightforward request: However, the extent of maintenance requests like this is often underestimated. The *analysis* process is designed to uncover the real work in carrying out modifications and additions. For example, we might determine that the increased number of image options requires a complete reworking of the way in which images are displayed and chosen.

Maintenance Request #162 for the case study (see Figure 10.9 above) will be analyzed to estimate the resources required to design and implement it. We will use the *Abstract Factory* design pattern for the design, as described in Chapter 6. Modifications to the object model to accommodate these and the new required classes are required. Once these modifications are made, we will need to replace all *Area* and *AreaConnection* references in the client code (the code using the new configuration) such as

```
... new Area() and
... new Connection()
```

with calls of the form

TABLE 10.2 Identifying a Maintenance Request

	IEEE 1219-1992 Maintenance Phase 1: Problem Identification
a. Input	The Maintenance Request (MR)
b. Process	Assign change number Classify by type and severity, etc. Accept or reject change Make preliminary cost estimate Prioritize
c. Control	Identify MR uniquely Enter MR into repository
d. Output	Validated MR
e. Selected quality factors	Clarity of the MR Correctness of the MR (e.g., type)
f. Selected metrics	Number of omissions in the MR Number of MR submissions to date Number of duplicate MRs Time expected to confirm the problem

TABLE 10.3 Analyzing a Maintenance Request

	IEEE 1219-1992 Maintenance Phase 2: Problem Analysis
a. Input	Original project documentation Validated MR from the identification phase
b. Process	Study feasibility of the MR Investigate impact of the MR Perform detailed analysis of the work required Refine the MR description

c. Control	Conduct technical review
	Verify
	   test strategy appropriate
	   documentation updated
	Identify safety and security issues

d. Output	Feasibility report Detailed analysis report, including impact Updated requirements Preliminary modification list Implementation plan Test strategy
e. Selected quality factors	Comprehensibility of the analysis
f. Selected metrics	Number of requirements that must be changed Effort (required to analyze the MR) Elapsed time

```
...  LevelNBuilder.getArea()  and
...  LevelNBuilder.getConnection()  etc.
```

The IEEE metrics quantifying these modifications are as follows.

- Number of requirements changes for MR #162: between 140 and 450. Since we have organized the requirements by class, we count
  - the number of new classes that must be described: 60 to 90 (there are 20 to 30 levels, let's say, and for each of these, *Abstract Factory* requires a factory class, a subclass of *Area*, and a subclass of *AreaConnection*)

  plus
  - the number of new methods: (2 to 5) per class × (60 to 90) classes = 120 to 450.
- Estimate of effort for MR #162: 2.4 to 9 person months: The effort can be estimated in terms of the number of person-days per requirement, based on these data for the project so far. For example, if the original project had 300 requirements and was completed with 6 person-months, we can use 0.02 person-months per requirement, so that MR #162 should be taken care of with [(120 × 0.02) to (450 × 0.02)] = 2.4 to 9 person-months. The repetitive nature of the classes suggests a lower number in this range, perhaps three person-months.
- Elapsed time estimate for MR #162: The elapsed time estimate can be computed from historical data in a similar manner to the *Effort* computation.

A better method for estimation is the use of linear regression, in which a set of past data is used to derive a straight line approximation, and this straight line is used to approximate the result.

TABLE 10.4 Designing for a Maintenance Request

	IEEE 1219-1992 Maintenance Phase 3: Design
a. Input	Original project documentation Analysis from the previous phase

b. Process	Create test cases
	Revise
	  requirements
	    implementation plan

c. Control	Verify design Inspect design and test cases

d. Output	Revised
	  modifications list
	  detailed analysis
	  implementation plan
	Updated
	  design baseline
	  test plans

e. Selected quality factors	Flexibility (of the design) Traceability Reusability Comprehensibilty
f. Selected metrics	Effort in person-hours Elapsed time Number of applications of the change

4.3 Designing for a Maintenance Request

Table 10.4 describes the design phase for MRs. The design to handle MR #162, for example, follows the Abstract Factory design pattern, which consists of modifying the original *EncounterEnvironment* package. The original documentation for this package is shown in Figure 10.18.

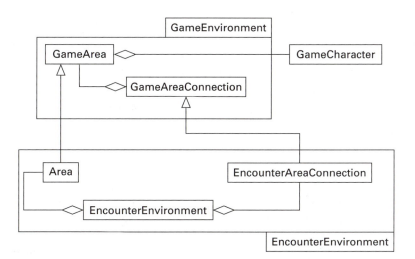

Figure 10.18 EncounterEnvironment *Package (Before Modification)*

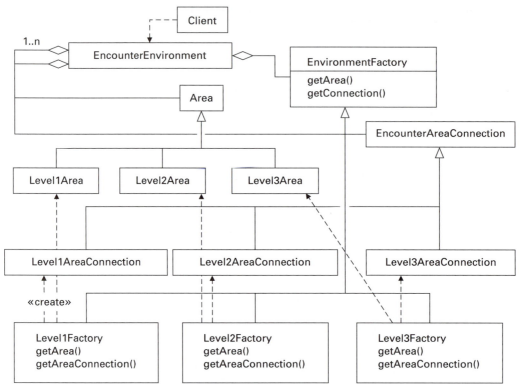

Figure 10.19 Abstract Factory Applied to Encounter

Instead of creating *Area* and *EncounterAreaConnection* objects directly, the modified application will do so through methods *getArea()* and *getAreaConnection()*. These are methods of a new class, *EnvironmentFactory*. Client code of the *EncounterEnvironment* package need have no knowledge of the type of *Area* and *AreaConnection* objects being built because all creation requests are channeled through the particular *EnvironmentFactory* object aggregated by *EncounterEnvironment*. At run time, the client code selects an object of the appropriate *EnvironmentFactory* subclass. For illustration purposes, the object model in Figure 10.19 shows *Area* and *AreaConnection* classes for three game-playing levels only, rather than for the much larger number planned.

A plan is required for getting from the old design to the new one. Figure 10.20 shows such a plan. This particular plan begins with the existing design, then adds and tests parts that do not disrupt the existing implementation, such as types of areas and connections. Before the last step, the redesign is ready to execute the abstract factory implementation, each of the parts having been thoroughly tested. In the final step, the new creation process is finally implemented and tested.

4.4 Implementing a Maintenance Request

Table 10.5 shows steps and documentation for the implementation of maintenance requests.

The response to maintenance requests can involve a significant amount of development, and this can introduce new defects. The *error rate* is the number of defects created by this maintenance effort per unit of effort (e.g., person-month). The measurement methodology for these new defects has to be precisely defined: for example, "the number

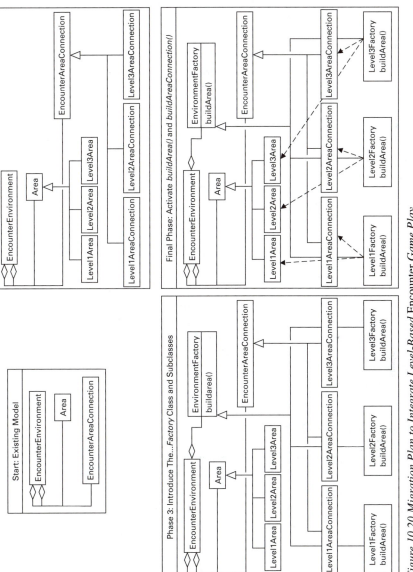

Figure 10.20 Migration Plan to Integrate Level-Based Encounter Game Play

TABLE 10.5 Implementing a Maintenance Request

	IEEE 1219-1992 Maintenance Phase 4: Implementation
a. Input	Original source code Original project documentation Detailed design from previous phase
b. Process	Make code changes and additions Perform unit tests Review readiness for system testing

c. Control	Inspect code
	Verify
	   CM control of new code
	   Traceability of new code

d. Output	Updated
	   software
	   unit test reports
	   user documents

e. Selected quality factors	Flexibility Traceability Comprehensibility Maintainability Reliability
f. Selected metrics	Lines of code Error rate

Copyright © 1993 IEEE

of defects found within three months of deployment." Let's suppose that the handling of MR #162 described above consumes 20 person-days and produces 10 new defects. The error rate for this MR would then be $10/20 = 0.5$ defects per person-day.

The remaining maintenance steps are system testing, acceptance testing, and updating the project documentation. The procedures followed for these are very similar to those for regular development.

5. THE MANAGEMENT OF MAINTENANCE

A *maintenance plan* describes the flow of Maintenance Requests (MRs) through the organization. Figure 10.21 shows a typical maintenance plan, where the thicker line indicates the nominal path of MRs. In the plan shown, customers provide comments on enhancements and defects through the help desk. These are written up as Maintenance Requests. An official unit, which may be a single person or a committee, decides which MRs will be implemented and prioritizes them. Such a committee is sometimes called the "change control board." MRs are then retired by technical maintenance staff. The thinner lines show other ways in which MRs can be generated and retired. The appropriate organization of maintenance activities depends on the scale of the application: The process for implementing MRs can be lengthy.

There are two timing problems associated with the implementation of MRs. The first is getting the prepared code to users. The second concerns the handling of defects in general. The defect may hamper the continuation of testing, and the route to repairing it may

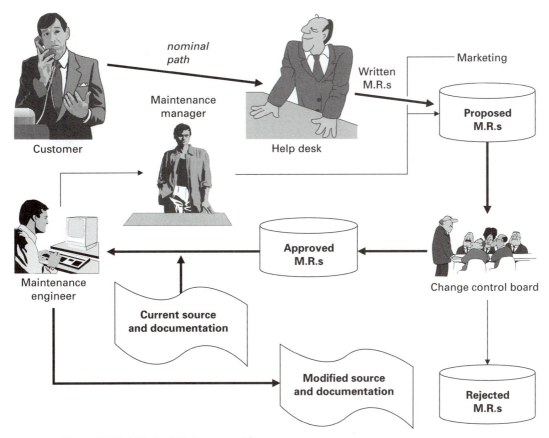

Figure 10.21 A Typical Maintenance Flow

be unacceptably long. To take an extreme example, in a military application with which the author was once involved, nine months could elapse between the identification of an MR and its complete implementation and documentation! In either case, a *patch* was often implemented. Patches are modifications or additions to the object code which either fix or work around the defect. Patches are supposed to be temporary. They often take the form of a set of files which replace object code already written. Figure 10.22 shows a way in which patches can be organizcd within the development organization. The advantages and disadvantages of patches include those listed in Figure 10.23.

The comment in Figure 10.23 about "masking" refers to the fact that allowing defects to remain can make it difficult to detect other defects whose effects are hidden by the effects of the nonrepaired defect.

After surveying maintenance organizations, Dekleva [De] found that maintenance organizations ranked problem-causing issues as shown in Figure 10.24. In particular, the frequency with which maintenance priorities are changed causes the most difficulty. To take an example in our video game case study, the changing priorities shown in Figure 10.25 are typical in a vendor organization.

The second and third largest sources of maintenance problems concern ways in which the application is tested, and its performance measured, respectively. As we have seen, possible tests are numerous and time-consuming. In addition, there are numerous ways to measure the effectiveness of the maintenance enterprise. Maintenance turns out to be a substantial, but often underestimated expense. Other sources of problems include handling

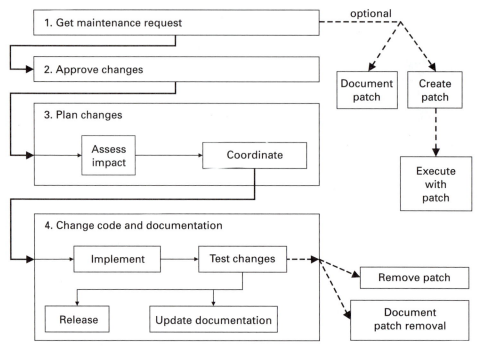

Figure 10.22 Maintenance and Patching

Advantages	**Disadvantages**
• Keeps customers satisfied in the short run	• Duplicates work
	• patch *and* final fix both implemented
• Enables continued operation and testing without repeated prevalence of the defect	• Sometimes never replaced
	• proper fix deferred forever!
• Avoids masking other defects	• Complicates final fix
• Enables test of fix	• must remove
	• Complicates documentation process

Figure 10.23 Advantages and Disadvantages of Using Maintenance Patches

1. Changing priorities	7. Measurement of contributions
2. Testing methods	8. Low morale due to lack of recognition or respect
3. Performance measurement	
3. Incomplete or nonexistent system documentation	9. Lack of personnel, especially experienced
5. Adapting to changing business requirements	10. Lack of maintenance methodology, standards, procedures, and tools . . .
6. Backlog size	

Figure 10.24 Ranked Problems in Maintenance (Deklava [De])

Top priority . . .

. . . at release:

- Make this the most bug-free game on the market
  - action: eliminate as many defects as possible

. . . two months after release:

- Add more features than our leading competitor
  - action: add enhancements rapidly

. . . six months after release:

- Reduce rising costs of maintenance
  - action: eliminate most severe defects only

Figure 10.25 Examples of Changing Priorities for Encounter

the backlog of MRs, which sometimes grows alarmingly. In addition, maintenance and testing have often been regarded as less prestigious and less glamorous than design.

6. QUALITIES IN MAINTENANCE

Although maintenance is often considered a burden, it can also be viewed as an opportunity to demonstrate good customer service. Bennett [Be3] reports that this latter view has been widespread in Japan. Quality maintenance can thus be tied directly to continuing customer satisfaction and future orders. Some enterprising companies have successfully adopted maintenance as a contracting business in its own right, because it generates reliable long-term revenue.

6.1 Maintenance Metrics

Since maintenance consumes a large fraction of life cycle costs, which is sometimes a surprise to management, it is particularly important that maintenance costs and benefits be quantified. Basic maintenance metrics are shown in Figure 10.26.

We first determine the maintenance goals for the application, and then select additional metrics that measure our degree of success in attaining those goals. Table 10.6, based on a table by Stark and Kern [St], illustrates this by showing how three different goals motivate the use of different metrics.

Here are more complete descriptions of the IEEE metrics mentioned in the table.

(1) Fault density: "Faults" are defects found during testing or operation.

[Number of faults found in the application] / KSLoC

- Number of lines of code under maintenance
- Person-months to perform various maintenance tasks
- Defect count

Figure 10.26 Metrics for Maintenance

TABLE 10.6 Maintenance Metrics Classified by Goal

Goal	Question	Selected Corresponding Metrics*
Maximize customer satisfaction	How many problems are affecting the customer?	* (1) Fault density * (30) Mean time to failure * Break / fix ratio [Number of defects introduced by maintenance actions] / [Number of defects repaired]
	How long does it take to fix a problem?	* Fault closure Average time required to correct a defect, from start of correction work * Fault open duration Average time from defect detection to validated correction
	Where are the bottlenecks?	* Staff utilization per task type Average person-months to (a) detect each defect and (b) repair each defect. * Computer utilization Average time / CPU time per defect
Optimize effort and schedule	Where are resources being used?	Effort and time spent, per defect and per severity category * planning * reproducing customer finding * reporting error * repairing * enhancing
Minimize defects (continue focused development-type testing)	Where are defects most likely to be found?	* (13) Number of entries and exits per module * (16) Cyclotomic complexity (see Section 6.1.2 of Chapter 7 on page 378)

*The numbered metrics are from the IEEE.

KSLoC = thousands of lines of noncommented source statements

(30) Mean time to failure: The average time it takes to obtain a failure of the application measured from startup.

This measure requires the definition of "failure" for the application under test. The definition depends on what the customer perceives as failure, and ranges from application crashes to specific types of problems. For a financial application, for example, any calculation resulting in a discrepancy of one dollar or more could be defined as a "failure."

6.2 Application of Maintenance Metrics

In this section, we discuss how metrics can be used to manage the maintenance activity. The *fraction of comment lines in the source code* helps to predict the relative magnitude of a maintenance effort, as illustrated in Figure 10.27. Compared with the other three modules, the *Sick Day Recorder* module is liable to produce the biggest maintenance challenge because it has a large proportion of uncommented lines-of-code, and is larger than average. The *Benefits Reporter* module is likely to be the least expensive to maintain because

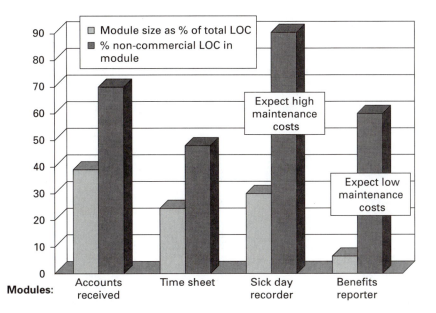

Figure 10.27 Predicting Relative Maintenance Effort

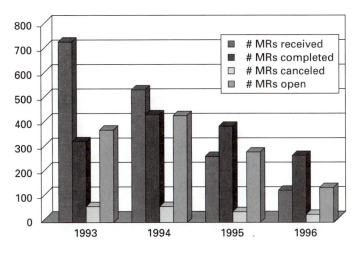

Figure 10.28 Example Profile of "Fixing" Type Maintenance Requests

it is the smallest and has a higher than average proportion of comments. The proportion of comment lines can be obtained using a utility program or by counting from a random sample of pages of code.

To manage a maintenance effort, graphs like that in Figure 10.28 are useful. According to the graph, a large number of requests for repair and enhancement arrived in the first two years, resulting in a peak backlog during the second year. This backlog was eventually worked off. The profile that appears in the figure is a typical one, whether the time scale is years, months, or weeks.

We emphasized earlier in this chapter the significant difference between *faults* and *enhancements*. Typically the maintenance manager tries to account for these separately so

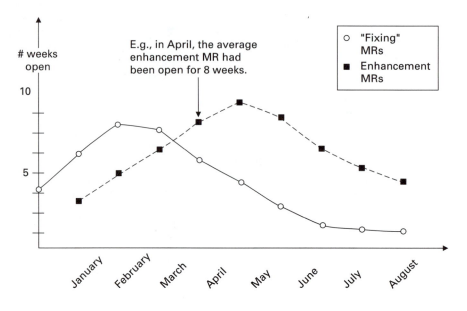

Figure 10.29 Example Profiles of Open Management Requests

that the customer pays for enhancements. To manage an organization's effectiveness in handling the maintenance workload, a graph such as that in Figure 10.29 can be used. The graph shows the average number of weeks that a maintenance request (whether a repair or an enhancement) has been waiting for resolution, measured from the time it was first reported. This chart shows a convergence to an average delay of about one week for repairs, and roughly four weeks for enhancements.

6.3 Maintainability

Oman [Om1] has identified factors in source code that make an application more maintainable. Figure 10.30 shows how he decomposed code into various types and focused on each type. The author has modified Oman's presentation of his results in an effort to make them easier to comprehend. A more complete version of Oman's results is shown in Figure 10.31.

For example, the more modular a system, the easier it is to maintain (see under *source code / control structure / system*). The more data is initialized, the easier it is to maintain (see under *source code / information structure / component*). The reader will recognize that many of these same qualities have been emphasized in this book for good design and implementation.

Recall that a major motivation for the use of design patterns is to make applications more maintainable. For example, the *State* design pattern makes it relatively easy to add new states without altering the functionality of the existing states. Ironically, improved methods of system development are reported to result in more, rather than less maintenance (see Dekleva [De1]). This is apparently because better-designed applications are easier to change, and consequently we are more likely to consider changing them to adapt to new circumstances.

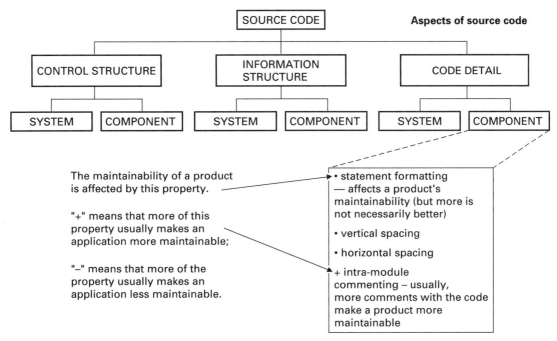

Figure 10.30 Effects on Maintainability of Source Code Properties, 1 of 2 *(from Oman [Om1])*

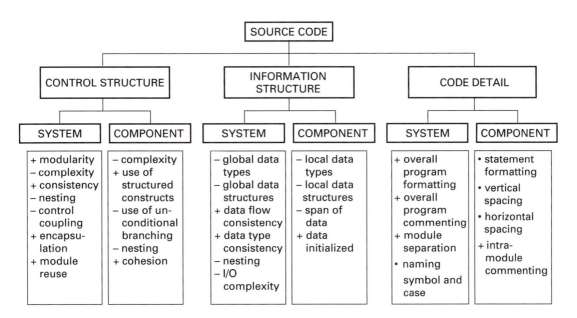

Examples:

"+ modularity" means greater modularity usually makes an application more maintainable;

"– span of data" means that the greater the scope of data structures, the less it is maintainable.

Figure 10.31 Effects on Maintainability of Source Code Properties, 2 of 2

- "Software Maintenance" = post delivery
- Impact analysis is key
- IEEE standard covers process
  - identification, input, process, control, output, process quality, process metrics
  - order similar to development process
- Presents several management challenges
  - manage flow of MRs
  - motivate personnel
  - ensure all documentation kept up-to-date
- Metrics: plot repairs and enhancements

Figure 10.32 Summary of Chapter

7. SUMMARY

Maintenance consumes a large fraction of the typical software development budget. The largest fraction of maintenance typically consists of enhancements rather than repairs. These points are included in Figure 10.32, which summarizes the main points of this chapter.

The author is indebted to Bennett [Be2] and Pigoski [Pi] for many of the ideas and references in this chapter. The reader is also referred to the valuable work of Oman [Om].

EXERCISES

A hint is provided for every exercise marked with the superscript "h." Solutions are provided for every problem marked with the superscript "s."

REVIEW QUESTIONS

R10.1[s] Define in one sentence the term "software maintenance."

R10.2[s] There are four types of maintenance, which fit into two general categories. Name these.

R10.3[s] Show a typical flow of maintenance requests. A solution can be found in Figure 10.8 on page 484 and Figure 10.9 on page 485.

R10.4[s] Suppose that a proposal is made to change the length of an array in an application to accommodate requirements that were not previously satisfied. What activity is required before actual changes in the code can be made?

R10.5[s] In a paragraph, define "reverse engineering." The solution to this is found in Section 3.2 on page 486.

R10.6[s] Give two or three ways in which legacy systems can be utilized by new applications.

R10.7[s] What does it mean to "reengineer" an application? Why would one do this?

R10.8[s] Give five to ten potential maintenance management problems. These can be found in Figure 10.24 on page 498.

GENERAL EXERCISES

G10.1 It is proposed to implement the following requirement, which was initially designated optional, for the *Encounter* case study.

> *PlayerCharacter Requirement [desirable] ("Player character image") The player shall have the option to choose the image representing her main character from at least four GIF files.*

   a. What type of Maintenance Request (MR) is this?

   b. Provide an impact assessment for this MR.

G10.2 Give examples of possible corrective, adaptive, and preventive changes for the *Encounter* case study.

G10.3 Which of the following would require reengineering. Explain.

   a. Convert a simulation of the operations of a bank into an automated bank security system.

   b. Add to a simulation of the operations of a bank so that it handles the movements of security personnel.

   c. Modify an online tutoring system so that it can provide multiple-choice quizzes at any time to permit students to assess their understanding of what they are currently reading.

TEAM EXERCISES

T10.1 ("Maintenance")

   (a) Obtain specifications from two other teams in the class. Propose at least one of each of the following types of modifications: corrective, adaptive, perfective, and preventive.

   (b) Another team will have proposed four such modifications to your project. Develop an impact assessment of your project for each of these modifications.

   (c) Negotiate with the team proposing modifications to your project to make the modifications reasonable in terms of the resources required; then implement these modifications.

   (d) Implement, test, and measure your modifications.

> *Evaluation criteria:*
>
> *α. Degree to which the proposed modifications are of the types specified — A = accurately belong to the modification category*
> *β. Completeness of your impact assessments — A = all dimensions of the impact covered*
> *γ. Degree to which the modifications have been tested — A = all changes thoroughly tested*

SOLUTIONS FOR REVIEW QUESTIONS

R10.1 *Software maintenance* refers to those activities performed on the application, that begin after the product has been delivered.

R10.2 *Repairing* (corrective and adaptive) and *Enhancing* (perfective and preventive)

R10.4 *Impact Analysis*, an activity that identifies those artifacts that will be impacted by the proposed change

R10.6 One option is to modify the legacy application and also add new application code. A second option is to use the legacy application by calling it directly from the new application. A third option is to provide a wrapper for the legacy application (code that provides it with an appropriate API) and then make use of it from the new application through this API.

R10.7 Reengineering an existing application is a process of redesign which is part way between piecemeal modifications on one hand and complete redesign and reimplementation on the other. Reengineering is advisable when anticipated continued modification would lead to a poorly designed whole, which would become very expensive to maintain.

CASE STUDY

MAINTENANCE OF *ENCOUNTER*

This case study examines Maintenance Requests to the *Encounter* video game application.

MAINTENANCE REQUEST 4593

[The reader is referred to the tables in Section 4 of this chapter, which describe the parts of this document.]

1. PROBLEM IDENTIFICATION

1.1 Problem Identification *Input*

Marketing director Mary Kraus has determined that the mechanism for exchanging quality values between two encountering game characters is too complicated for the average gamer.

1.2 Problem Identification *Process*

Work on this MR is to be part of change release 4. This MR was accepted for action by the project leader on January 12, 2000. Engineer Alan Owens estimates the repair cost at 12 person-hours (including all required tests) provided that regression testing for this MR is batted with the biweekly regression test. Its priority is 4 [out of 5, where 5 is the lowest priority].

1.3 Problem Identification *Control*

This MR was entered into the MR repository by engineer A. Jones on 1/13/00.

1.4 Problem Identification *Output*

This MR is to be number 4593, designated by engineer A. Jones on 1/13/00.

The statement of this MR is as follows.

Simplify the formula by which an engagement between a player character and a foreign character changes the values of their qualities as follows. Halve the values of the area-specific qualities possessed by the weaker game character. (The "area-specific qualities" are those relevant to the area in which the engagement takes place.) Do not change the qualities of the stronger game character.

1.5 Problem Identification *Quality Factors*

The quality factors are the completeness and clarity of the MR.

1.6 Problem Identification *Metrics*

MR 2984 was evaluated at the maintenance inspection of 1/22/00 with the following results.

Number of omissions in the MR: 1

Clarity of the MR: 8 (scale: 0 = incomprehensible; 10 = apparently cannot be made clearer)

Overlap of the MR: 0 (scale: 0 = no overlap with any other MR; 10 = capability included in one or more open MRs)

Estimated delay of the MR: 12 days

[Note to the student: The following summary information would not be repeated for every MR.]

As a result, the metrics applicable to the complete set of open MRs are as follows

Average omission per MR: 0.9 (group standard = 0.5)

Average MR clarity: 7.2 (group standard = 7)

Average MR overlap: 1.6 (group standard = 2.0)

Average delay: 18 days (target: 14)

2. PROBLEM ANALYSIS

2.1 Problem Analysis *Input*

1. MR 2984

2. SRS version 4.6.5, containing the following:

3.2.EN.3.1 Engaging a foreign character [essential] When an engagement takes place, the "stronger" of the two characters is the one whose values of area-specific qualities sum to the greater amount. The system transfers half the values of each area-specific quality of the weaker to qualities of the stronger.

For example, suppose that the player engages a foreign character in an area preferring *stamina* and *concentration*. If p_s is the value of the player's stamina, etc., and assuming $p_s + p_c > f_s + f_c$, we would have $p_s' = p_s + f_s/2$, $p_c' = p_c + f_c/2, f_s' = f_s/2, f_c' = f_a/2$ where x' is the value of x after the transaction.

To take a numerical example, if the player's stamina value is 7 and concentration value is 19, and Freddie the foreigner's stamina is 11 and concentration 0.1, then the player is stronger. The result of the engagement would be:

Player: stamina 7 + 11/2 = 12.5; concentration 19 + (0.1)/2 = 19.05 (displayed as 19.1)
Freddie: stamina 11/2 = 5.5; concentration 0 because (0.1)/2 is less than 0.1

2.2 Problem Analysis *Process*

Feasibility: This MR is considered feasible to implement because its impact is limited to engagement results and the resulting life of game characters.

Detailed analysis: The only class affected by this MR is *Engagement*. An *Engagement* object computes the resulting quality values of the characters involved in the engagement. The run time attribute values of the game character objects will be different, but their code does not require modification.

The MR description mentions the transformation $f_c' = f_a/2$, which should be $f_c' = f_c/2$, stating that the value is halved (not replaced by half of another value).

Documentation refinement: One requirement in the SRS will need to be changed. No others will be affected. The user's manual will need to be changed.

2.3 Problem Analysis *Control*

This MR was discussed at the maintenance meeting of 4/3/99, and determined to be of level 1 (technically straightforward).

Test documentation 7829 and 8924, determined to be the appropriate regression test segments, did not require change except that the table of expected results required modification.

[Note to the student: These test "documents" are not provided in the case study.]

2.4 Problem Analysis *Output*

One requirement in the SRS is changed, as shown below.

[Convention: Erased words are shown with a strike-through; added words are underlined.]

3.2.EN.3.1 Engaging a Foreign Character [essential] When an engagement takes place, the "stronger" of the two characters is the one whose values of area-specific qualities sum to the greater amount. ~~*The system transfers to qualities of the stronger, half the values of each area-specific quality of the weaker.*~~ *Each area-specific quality of the weaker of the two characters is halved.*

For example, suppose that the player engages a foreign character in an area preferring stamina *and* concentration. *If* p_s *is the value of the player's stamina, etc., and assuming* $p_s + p_c > f_s + f_c$, *we would have* ~~$p_s' = p_s + f_s / 2, p_c' = p_c + f_c / 2, f_s' = f_s / 2, f_c' = f_c / 2$~~

$$f_s' = \lfloor f_s / 2 \rfloor, \text{ and } f_c' = \lfloor f_c / 2 \rfloor$$

where *x'* is the value of *x* after the transaction.

The expression $\lfloor z \rfloor$ *("floor" operation) denotes the largest integer less than or equal to* z.

To take a numerical example, if the player's stamina value is 7 and its concentration value is 19, and Freddie the foreigner's stamina is 11 and concentration 0.1, then the player is stronger in this particular area. *The result of the engagement would be:*

Player: ~~*stamina 7 + 11/2 = 12.5; concentration 19 + 0.1/2 = 19.05 (displayed as 19.1)*~~ unchanged

Freddie: ~~*stamina 11/2 = 5.5; concentration 0 because 0.1/2 is less than 0.1*~~
$$\text{stamina} = \lfloor 11/2 \rfloor = 5$$
$$\text{concentration} = \lfloor 1/2 \rfloor = 0$$

The user manual will require change as follows... . [not supplied].

Implementation plan: Engineer T. Fine will implement this MR. Since the MR will cause significant change in how the game responds, it will be implemented and tested separately from all other MRs.

Since there is uncertainty that this change will meet with player approval, extensive usability testing will be carried out.

2.5 Problem Analysis *Quality Factors*

The principal quality factor is the soundness of the impact analysis.

2.6 Problem Analysis *Metrics*

Hours of impact analysis per method changed or added: 0.5.

Degree of separateness from other MRs: 6.5 (scale: not separate at all = 0; completely separate = 10). Remark: this MR also corrected the defect "$f_c' = f_a / 2$" in *Engagement requirement 1*, thus introducing effective overlap with another maintenance action.

Time expected for problem validation: 12 days of elapsed time

Number of requirements changes: 1

Documentation error rates: (not yet inspected)

Effort: two person-hours

Elapsed time: two days

Error rates: (not yet inspected)

As a result, the metrics applicable to the complete set of open MR's are as follows:

Average hours of impact analysis per method changed or added: 0.9 (group average = 0.6)

Average degree of separateness from other MRs: 5.1 (group standard: 4.0)

3. DESIGN

3.1 Design *Input*

MR 2984

3.2 Design *Process*

The SDD required modification. The pseudocode for the *execute()* function of the *Engagement* class had to be changed to the form shown below.

3.3 Design *Control*

The new pseudocode is to be inspected. The date of inspection is April 8, 1999.

3.4 Design *Output*

The earliest revision containing this MR is SDD version 5.4.3.

The following pseudocode will apply to the revised method *execute()* of the class *Engagement*.

Let `asq[]` be the area-specific qualities for the area in which the engagement takes place.
`SET p` to the sum of the player's `asq` values.
`SET f` to the sum of freddie's `asq` values.
`IF p == f`, the engagement has no effect
`IF p > f`
    Halve the values of freddie's `asq` qualities and apply "floor" operation.
`ELSE IF f > p`
    Halve the values of the player's `asq` qualities and apply "floor".

Test plans are to be modified as follows... .

Due to the importance of this MR, usability test #8902 has been devised by the marketing department to assess player reaction to the new formulas.

3.5 Design *Quality*

Our main concern is with the acceptability of this change to game players. Equally important are regression tests to ensure that the computation is not defective, and that it does not compromise any existing game capability.

3.6 Design *Metrics*

Number of pseudocode replacements: 1

Documentation error rates: to be inspected

Effort: one person-hour

Elapsed time: one day

Error rates: to be inspected

4. IMPLEMENTATION

4.1 Implementation *Input*

SDD version 5.4.2

Source code version 11.3.7

4.2 Implementation *Process*

The MR was coded by B. Marks. Nonsystem testing was performed by A. Antonini.

4.3 Implementation *Control*

The implementation and unit test plans were inspected by team 5 on January 30, 2000.

4.4 Implementation *Output*

The earliest source code containing the change is version 11.3.8.

The inspection report is found in the inspection archives, dated January 30, 2000.

Test reports can be found in Test Documentation packages 7820, 7621, and 8902.

4.5 Implementation *Quality Factors*

The project quality factors of the *Encounter* SQAP were applied.

4.6 Implementation *Metrics*

. . .

5. SYSTEM TEST

5.1 System Test *Input*

SDD version 5.4.2

SRS version 4.6.5

Source code version 11.3.8.

5.2 System Test *Process*

Regression tests 7893.4, 23689.14, 21376.0, and 1237.46 passed. The new regression tests, resulting from the new engagement computations, are 7893.5, 23689.15, 21376.1, and 1237.47, respectively.

The following tests will be executed on version 11.3.2: ....

The *usability* of the result is to be measured by running the following procedure three separate times. The complete test documentation is found as Test Documentation 89041.0.

> *A sample of 100 customers shall be selected at random from the player population. They rate the current version of the game on a scale of 1–10 in the following categories:*
>
> interest, challenge, realism, and overall fun
>
> *They are given the modified version, together with a user manual. They play the modified game for 10 to 15 hours over a period of a week, then provide responses to the same questionnaire as that described above.*
>
> *The above procedure is to be repeated with a different sample, and with the order reversed (new version first, old version next).*

The usability result is to be reported in the form of the percentage change in the score between the two computation methods.

5.3 System Test *Control*

See SCMP.

5.4 System Test *Output*

The results of these tests are found in the System Test Documentation 890451.

5.5 System Test *Quality Factors*

See System Test Documentation.

5.6 System Test *Metrics*

See System Test Documentation.

6. ACCEPTANCE TEST

The MR shall be considered a success if the following results are obtained for the total of 400 customers:

(1) All regression tests described above pass.

(2) Improvement occurs in every category.

(3) At least two categories of the usability test obtain a score of a 25% or greater, and no category has a score more than 3% lower than without the change.

ACRONYMS

ACRONYM	DEFINITION
ABS	Antilock braking system
ACM	Association for Computing Machinery
AIF	Automobile Impact Facility — a name created for a fictitious application
ANSI	American National Standards Institute
API	Application programming interface
ARA	Air Radar Application — a name created for a fictitious application
ATM	Asynchronous Transfer Mode
AWT or awt	Abstract Windowing Toolkit — a Java package
BPR	Business process Reengineering
CACM	Communications of the ACM
CAD/CAM	Computer aided design / Computer aided manufacturing
CASE	Computer-aided software engineering
CCB	Change Control Board
CDR	Critical design review
CGI	Common Gateway Interface
CI	Configuration item
CICS	Customer Information Control System — an IBM product
CM	Configuration management
CMM™	Capability Maturity Model
COCOMO	Constructive Cost Model (Barry Boehm)
COM	Common Object Model (Microsoft)
CORBA	Common object request broker architecture
COTS	Commercial off-the-shelf software
CPU	Computer processing unit
C-requirements	Customer-oriented requirements; a form of the requirements suitable for customers to work from, but also forming part of requirements for developers
DBMS	Database management system
DFD	Data flow diagram
DOD or DoD	U.S. Department of Defense
D-requirements	Detailed requirements; developer-oriented requirements; a form of the requirements suitable for developers to work from
EI	External inputs — for use in function point analysis
EIN	External inquires — for use in function point analysis
ELF	External logical files — for use in function point analysis
EO	External outputs — for use in function point analysis
FCA	Functional configuration audit
GCI	Gaming Consolidated Industries — a name created for a fictitious company
GUI	Graphical user interface

511

ACRONYM	DEFINITION
HTML	Hypertext markup language
IBM	International Business Machines
IDE	Interactive development environment
IDL	Interface definition language — mostly associated with CORBA
IEEE	Institute of Electrical and Electronics Engineers
IFPUG	International Function Point Users' Group
ILF	Internal logical files — for use in function point analysis
ISO	International Standards Organization
IV&V	Independent verification and validation
JAR files	Java ARchive
KLOC or KLoC	Thousand of lines of code (normally, excluding comment lines, but this should be specified)
LOC or LoC	Lines of code (normally, excluding comment lines, but this should be specified)
MR	Maintenance request
MTBF	Mean time between failures
NASA	National Aeronautics and Space Administration
NCSLOC	Non-comment source lines of code
OMG	Object Management Group
OO	Object-oriented
PCA	Physical configuration audit
PDR	Preliminary design review
PS	Pseudocode (acronym not in common use)
PSD	Personal software documentation
PSL/PSA	Problem statement language / Problem statement analyzer
PSP	Personal Software Process. PSP0, PSP1, PSP2, and PSP3 are defined levels of capability within the PSP
QA	Quality assurance (often refers to the quality assurance organization)
QC	Quality control
RAD	Rapid application development
RAM	Random access memory
RFP	Request for proposals
RPG	Role playing game
SADT	Structured analysis and design technique
SCM	Software configuration management
SCMP	Software configuration management plan
SDD	Software design document
SDF	Software development folder
SEI	Software Engineering Institute
SIP	Software integration plan
SPMP	Software project management plan
SQA	Software quality assurance
SQAP	Software quality assurance plan
SQL	Structured query language
SRS	Software requirements specification
STD	Software test document
STL	Standard Template Library
STP	Software test plan
SUDP	Software user documentation plan

SV&VP or SVVP	Software verification and validation plan
TBD or tbd	"To be decided"
TBS or tbs	To be supplied
TRR	Test readiness review
TSP^{SM}	Team Software Process
UML	Unified Modeling Language
USDP	Unified Software Development Process
V&V	Verification and validation
Y2K	Year 2000; maintenance activities that allow applications to operate on and after the year 2000

GLOSSARY

Actor A particular role adopted by the user of an application while participating in a use case.

Alpha release A preliminary version of an application given to highly trusted customers and/or internal users to obtain feedback.

Application Programming Interface (API) A list of classes and member function prototypes provided for the benefit of programmers. The function information consists of its name, the parameter types, the return types, and the exceptions thrown.

Architecture, Software An overall design of an application, including its decomposition into parts.

Artifact Any kind of data, source code, or information produced or used by a worker during the development process; used in particular in describing the Unified Software Development Process.

Association for Computing Machinery (ACM) An organization of professionals involved in the computing enterprise, emphasizing software.

Attribute A variable of a class as a whole (not a variable local to a method).

Beta release A preliminary version of an application, given to selected customers to help detect defects, and to obtain feedback.

Black box method A method, typically a testing method, applied to implemented code, which takes into account input and output only (i.e., not the internal manner in which the code operates).

Build A partial implementation of an application.

Business process reengineering (BPR) A systematic design of a business process, such as purchase order handling, from beginning to end, including human and non-human aspects, typically performed from scratch.

C-requirements Requirements stated in a form most convenient for an application's customer, but also forming part of the requirements for developers.

Capability assessment A process by which the capability of an organization, group, or person to produce software, is measured in a quantitative and objective manner.

Capability Maturity Model (CMM) A systematic manner of assessing the overall capability of an organization to develop software; developed by the Software Engineering Institute in Pittsburgh, PA.

Computer aided design / Computer aided manufacturing (CAD/CAM) Graphic-intensive software which assists in the design and manufacturing of electronic, construction, or mechanical products.

Computer-aided software engineering (CASE) The software engineering process, assisted by a coordinated set of software tools. These tools are tailored to the various phases of software development.

Change control board (CCB) A committee that decides whether or not a proposed enhancement or repair to an application should be implemented.

Commercial off-the-shelf (COTS) Commercially available software product. In this context, such software is used to work with code built from scratch to create an application.

Common object request broker architecture (CORBA) A standard under which applications can invoke functions residing on remote platforms, regardless of the language in which they are written.

Configuration item (CI) An artifact whose versions are specifically tracked from the beginning to the end of a project.

Configuration management (CM) The process of maintaining and managing the various versions of various artifacts of a software project.

Constraint A specified limitation.

Constructive Cost Model (COCOMO) Barry Boehm's formulas for computing the probable labor requirements, in person-months, to build an application, and the probably elapsed time, based on the estimated lines of code.

Critical design review (CDR) A process of deciding once and for all whether or not to proceed with a proposed design. The process includes, or may consist entirely of, a meeting.

D-requirements Developer requirements; a form of the requirements primarily suitable for developers to work from, but also forming part of the requirements for customers.

Data base management system (DBMS) A system for organizing and accessing data.

Data flow diagram (DFD) A diagram showing how data flows into, within, and out of an application. The data flows among the application's user, the data stores, and internal processing elements of the application.

Design pattern A pattern of commonly occurring classes, relationships among them, and accompanying algorithms.

Encounter The video game case study used in this book.

Event An occurrence affecting an object, initiated externally to the object.

Formal methods Rigorous methods for specifying requirements, design, or implementation; mathematical and logical in nature.

Framework A collection of general classes that forms the basis for several applications. The classes of each application aggregate or inherit from the framework's classes.

Function point (FP) A measure of an application's complexity.

Functional requirement A requirement expressing a function which an application must perform.

Graphical user interface (GUI) A graphic display, often interactive, by means of which a user interacts with an application.

Help desk A facility for providing help to users of an application.

Independent verification and validation (IV&V) The process of performing verification and validation by a third party (i.e., not by the organization performing the development).

Institute of Electrical, and Electronics Engineers (IEEE) An organization of professionals, dedicated to engineering involving electronics, electricity, and software.

Integration The fusing of application modules to form an application.

Integration testing The process of testing for the successful fusing of modules.

Interactive development environment (IDE) A software application that helps developers to create, edit, compile, and execute code.

Interface An interface for a system is a specification of a set of functions which the system provides; the specification includes the names of the functions, their parameter types, return types, and exceptions.

Invariant A relationship among variables which, within a specified context, does not change (the values of the individual variables may change, however).

Inverse requirement A specification which is specifically *not* a requirement of an application.

Iteration The process of repeatedly adding requirements, design, implementation, and testing to a partially built application.

Legacy application An application that has been delivered and used.

Maintenance The process of repairing and enhancing an application that has been delivered.

Maintenance request (MR) A request to modify or add to an existing application.

Mean time between failures (MTBF) (Time an application is in use) / (number of occasions the application failed during that time); the definition of "failure" has to be supplied.

Metric A specification for how to measure a software engineering artifact. For example, *lines of code* is a metric for source code.

Model A model of an application is a view of its design from a particular perspective, such as the combination of its classes, or its event-driven behavior.

Non-comment lines of source code (NCSLOC) A line of source code which is not a comment.

Non-functional requirement A requirement placed upon an application that does not involve any specific functionality. A constraint on memory is an example.

Object-oriented (OO) An organization of designs and code into classes and instances ("objects"). Every object in a given class is provided with a set of functions specified for the class; each object has its copy of a set of variables specified for the class.

Object Management Group (OMG) A non-profit organization of companies, which establishes standards for distributed object computing.

Paradigm A way of thinking, such as the object-oriented paradigm.

Personal software documentation (PSD) Documentation that an individual maintains about the current status of his or her code.

Personal Software Process^{SM} **(PSP)** A process, developed by Watts Humphrey at the Software Engineering Institute, for improving and measuring the software engineering capability of individual software engineers.

Physical configuration audit (PCA) A systematic review of a project's physical artifacts on hand, including the documents, source code, files, tapes, and disks.

Preliminary design review (PDR) A meeting at which an early draft of a design, of all or part of the project, is presented and critiqued by engineers and managers.

Process A "software process" is an order in which development activities are performed.

Project management The process of fulfilling the responsibility for the successful completion of a project.

Prototype An application that illustrates or demonstrates some aspect(s) of an application that is under construction.

Provably correct program A program written in such a manner that a mathematical and logical proof can be produced which proves that the program satisfies its requirements.

Pseudocode An English-like language which is formal enough to describe an algorithm.

Quality assurance (QA) The process of ensuring that a specified level of quality is being attained in the execution of a project; may also be used to refer to the organization performing this function, rather than the function itself.

Rapid application development (RAD) The process of quickly developing an application, or part thereof, typically sacrificing proper documentation, design, or extensibility.

Regression testing The process of validating the fact that the addition of code to an application under development does not diminish the capability the application possessed before the addition was made.

Requirements analysis The process of obtaining a complete, written statement of what functionality, appearance, performance, and behavior are required of an application.

Reverse engineering The process of deducing the contents of a software development phase from the artifacts of a subsequent phase (for example, deducing the design from the code).

Risk retirement The process of dealing with a perceived threat to the successful execution of a project (a risk), either by finding a way to avoid the risk, or by taking action to eliminate its impact.

Roadmap A list of activities which result in attaining a specified goal.

Role-playing game (RPG) A game, often a video game, in which the players assume roles, and interact with each other in those roles.

Sequence diagram A diagram involving objects of an application, which shows a sequence of function calls between the objects; sequence diagrams usually elaborate upon use cases.

Software configuration management plan (SCMP) A document that specifies how the code and documents of a project, and all of their versions, are to be managed.

Software development folder (SDF) A document specifying the current status of the code on which an individual software engineer is working. This includes all details about the unit testing which the engineer has performed to date.

Software Engineering Institute (SEI) An institute initially founded to improve the quality of U.S. defense software. Its work is used by many non-defense organizations as well.

Software project management plan (SPMP) A plan stating who will develop what parts of an application, and in what order they will do so.

Software requirements specification (SRS) A document stating what an application must accomplish.

Software test documentation (STD) A document that specifies all aspects of the testing process for an application.

Software test plan (STP) Documentation stating what parts of an application will be tested, and the schedule of when testing is to be performed.

Stakeholder A person, group, or organization with a stake in the outcome of an application that is being developed.

State An object's status; formally defined as set of values of the object's variables (for example, an Automobile object can be defined as in "classic" state if its manufacture year has a value less than 1955 and its condition variable is "fair" or better.)

System engineering The process of analyzing and designing an entire system, including the hardware and software.

System testing The process of testing an entire application (as opposed to testing its parts).

Team Software Process[SM] **(TSP)** A process, developed by Watts Humphrey at the Software Engineering Institute, for assessing and improving the performance of teams developing software.

Testable An artifact (e.g., a requirement) for which it is possible to write a specific test validating that the product is consistent with the artifact.

Traceable A requirement is traceable if the design and code fragments that implement it can be readily identified; a requirement is not traceable if it is unclear which parts of the design accommodate it, and which parts of the code implement it.

Transition (in a state diagram) The process under which an object changes from being in one state to being in another.

Unified modeling language (UML) A graphical notation for expressing object-oriented designs.

Unified Software Development Process (USDP) A development process created by Booch, Jacobson, and Rumbaugh, emphasizing use cases.

Unit testing The process of testing a part of an application in isolation from the rest of the application.

Use case A sequence of actions, some taken by an application and some by the user, which are common in using an application; the user assumes a particular role in this interaction, and is called an "actor" relative to the use case.

Validation The process of ensuring that a software application performs its intended functions in the manner specified.

Verification The process of ensuring that a software application is being built in the manner planned.

Waterfall A software development process in which requirements are first collected, a design is developed, the design implemented in code, and then tested. This is performed in sequence, with a small amount of overlap between the successive phases.

White box process A method, typically testing, applied to implemented code, which takes into account the manner in which the code is intended to operate.

REFERENCES

[Ab] Accreditation Board for Engineering and Technology (ABET), 1996.

[Al] Albrecht, A. J., "Measuring Application Development Productivity," Proceedings of the Joint SHARE/GUIDE/IBM Application Development Symposium, October 1979, pp. 83–92.

[All] Alspaugh, Thomas A.; Faulk, Stuart R.; Heninger Britton, Kathryn; Parker, R. Alan; Parnas, David L., and Shore, John E., "Software Requirements for the A-7E Aircraft," NRL Memorandum Report No. 3876, August 31, 1992.

[Am] Ambler, Scott, www.ambysoft.com (1999).

[An] Anderson, A. et al., "At Chrysler, Objects Pay," Distributed Computing, October 1998, pp. 25–28.

[Ar] "How Do You Define Software Architecture?" http://www.sei.cmu.edu/architecture/definitions.html (12/99).

[Be] Beck, Kent, "Extreme Programming: A Humanistic Discipline of Software Development," FASE, Lisbon, Portugal, part of ETAPS 1998, 1998.

[Be2] Bennett, K. "Software Maintenance: A Tutorial," Software Engineering, IEEE Computer Society, November, 1999, as noted in [Do].

[Be3] Bennett, K.H., "Software Maintenance in Japan" keynote paper, in Proc. 8th European Workshop on Software Maintenance, Durham, North Carolina, 1994.

[Be1] Berry, Daniel M., and Lawrence, Brian, "Requirements Engineering," IEEE Software, vol. 15, no. 2, March/April 1998.

[Bo] Boehm, Barry, Software Engineering Economics, Englewood Cliffs, NJ: Prentice Hall, 1981.

[Bo2] Bohm, C., and Jacopini, G., "Flow Diagrams, Turing Machines and Languages With Only Two Formation Rules," Communications of the ACM, May 1966, pp. 366-371.

[Bo1] Booch, G., Object Solutions: Managing the Object-Oriented Project, New York: Addison-Wesley, 1995.

[Bo3] Booch, G., Object-Oriented Analysis and Design with Applications, Reading, MA: Addison-Wesley, 1994.

[Booch-UML] Booch, G.; Jacobson, I.; and Rumbaugh, J., The Unified Modeling Language User Guide, Reading, MA: Addison-Wesley, 1998.

[Bo4] Boston Globe, October 1, 1999.

[Br] Brackett, J., ftp://ftp.sei.cmu.edu/pub/education/cm19.ps, (January 1990).

[Br1] Brooks, Frederick P., Jr., The Mythical Man-Month: Essays on Software Engineering, Anniversary Edition, Addison-Wesley, July 1995.

[Bu] "The Mother of All Software Projects," Business Week, February 22, 1999.

[Ch] http://www.egroups.com (4/2000).

[Cu] Cucumano, A. and Selby, R. W., "How Microsoft Builds Software," Communications of the ACM, vol. 40, no. 6, June 1997, pp. 53–61.

[De] Dekleva, S., "Delphi Study of Software Maintenance Problems," Proceedings of the IEEE Conference on Software Maintenance, Orlando, FL, November 1992, pp. 10–17.

[De1] Dekleva, Sasa M., "The Influence of the Information Systems Development Approach on Maintenance," MIS Quarterly, vol. 16, no. 3, pp. 355–372.

[De2] DeMarco, Tom, and Lister, Timothy, Peopleware: Productive Projects and Teams, 2nd edition, New York, NY: Dorset House,1999.

[Di] Dijkstra, E., A Discipline of Programming, Englewood Cliffs, NJ: Prentice Hall, 1976.

[Di1] Dijkstra, E.W., "GOTO statement considered harmful," letter in Communications of the ACM, March 1968.

[Do] Dorfman, M. (ed.) and Thayer, Richard H. (contributor), Software Engineering, IEEE Computer Society, November 1999.

[Dr] Dreger, J., Function Point Analysis, Englewood Cliffs, NJ: Prentice Hall, 1989.

[En] Engelmore, Robert, and Morgan, Tony (ed.), Blackboard Systems (The Insight Series in Artificial Intelligence), ASIN: 0201174316.

[Fa] Fagin, M., "Design and Code Inspections to Reduce Errors in Program Development," IBM Systems Journal, vol. 15, no. 3, pp.182–211.

[Fo] Foster, J. "Cost Factors in Software Maintenance," Ph. D. Thesis, University of Durham, NC, Computer Science Department, 1994, as noted in [Be2].

[Fo2] Fowler, Martin, Refactoring: Improving the Design of Existing Code, Reading, MA: Addison-Wesley, 1999.

[Ga] Gamma, Erich; Helm, Richard; Johnson, Ralph; and Vlissides, John, Design Patterns: Elements of Reusable Object-Oriented Software (Addison-Wesley Professional Computing), Addison-Wesley, August 1999.

[Ga1] Garlan, David, and Shaw, Mary, Software Architecture: Perspectives on an Emerging Discipline, Englewood Cliffs, NJ: Prentice Hall, 1996.

[Ga2] Galitz, W., The Essential Guide to User Interface Design: An Introduction to GUI Principles and Techniques, New York: John Wiley & Sons, 1996.

[Ge] Gehani, Narain, and Lally, S., Software Specification Techniques (International Computer Science), Reading, MA: Addison-Wesley, 1985.

[Gi] Gilb, T., and Graham, D., Software Inspection, Reading, MA: Addison-Wesley, 1993.

[Gl] Glass, R., "Maintenance: Less is Not More," IEEE Software, July/August 1998.

[Gr] Gres, David, "The Science of Programming," New York: Springer-Verlag, 1987.

[Ha1] Hammer, Michael, and Champy, James, Reengineering the Corporation : A Manifesto for Business Revolution, Reprint edition, Harperbusiness, May 1994.

[Ha3] Harel, D., "On Visual Formalisms," Communications of the ACM, May 1988, pp. 514-530.

[Ha] Hayes, I., Specification Case Studies, Englewood Cliffs, NJ: Prentice Hall, 1986.

[Ha4] Hayes-Roth, Frederick, Building Expert Systems, ASIN: 0201106868.

[Ho] Hoare, C. A. R., and Jones, C.B., Essays in Computing Science (Prentice Hall International Series in Computer Science), Englewood Cliffs, NJ: Prentice Hall, 1989, ASIN: 0132840278.

[Ho1] Horstmann, Cay S., and Cornell, Gary, Core Java 2 , Volume 1: Fundamentals, Upper Saddle River, NJ: Prentice Hall, 1998.

[Ho2] Horstmann, Cay S., and Cornell, Gary, Core Java 1.1, Volume II: Advanced Features, Upper Saddle River, NJ: Prentice Hall, 1998.

[Ho3] Horstmann, Cay S., Practical Object-Oriented Development in C++ and Java, New York: John Wiley & Sons, 1997.

[Hu] Humphrey, Watts S., A Discipline for Software Engineering (SEI Series in Software Engineering), Reading, MA: Addison-Wesley, 1995.

[Hu1] Humphrey, Watts S., Managing the Software Process (SEI Series in Software Engineering), Reading, MA: Addison-Wesley, 1989.

[Hu2] http://www.sei.cmu.edu/publications/articles/ sources/practice.preach/ index.html (12/99).

[Hu3] http://www.stsc.hill.af.mil/crosstalk/1998/apr/ dimensions.html (12/99).

[Hu4] Humphrey, Watts S., Introduction to the Personal Software Process (SEI Series in Software Engineering), Reading, MA: Addison-Wesley, December 1996.

[Hu5] http://csg.uwaterloo.ca/~huang/dptool/ interfac.htm (12/99).

[Hu6] Humphrey, Watts S., Managing Technical People: Innovation, Teamwork, and the Software Process (Sei Series in Software Engineering), Reading, MA: Addison-Wesley, 1996.

[Hu7] Humphrey, Watts S., Introduction to the Team Software Process (The SEI Series in Software Engineering), Addison-Wesley, August 1999.

[IE] IEEE Software Engineering Standards Collection, 1997 Edition, Piscataway, NJ: IEEE, 1997.

[IEEE 610] IEEE Standard Glossary of Software Engineering Terminology, IEEE 610.12-1990.

[IEEE 829] Software Test Documentation, ANSI/ IEEE 829We -1983 (reaffirmed 1991).

[IEEE 982] Guide to the Use of IEEE Standard Dictionary of Measures to Produce Reliable Software, ANSI/IEEE 982.2-1988.

[IEEE 1219] IEEE Std 1219-1998 (Revision of IEEE Std 1219-1992) IEEE Std 1219-1998 IEEE Standard for Software Maintenance, IEEE Computer Society.

[IF] International Function Point Users' Group, http://www.ifpug.org/ (12/99).

[IF1] International Function Point Users' Group reference to function point spreadsheets, http://www.ifpug.org/home/docs/freebies.html (as of 12/99).

[Ja] Jacobson, Ivar, Object-Oriented Software Engineering: A Use Case Driven Approach (Addison-Wesley Object Technology Series), Reading, MA: Addison-Wesley, 1994.

[Ja1] Jacobson, Ivar; Rumbaugh, James; and Booch, Grady, The Unified Software Development Process (Addison-Wesley Object Technology Series), Reading, MA: Addison-Wesley, 1999.

[Ja3] Jacobson, Ivar; Griss, Martin; and Jonsson, Patrik, Software Reuse: Architecture Process and Organization for Business Success, Reading, MA: Addison-Wesley, 1997.

[Ja2] Jagannathan, V.; Dodhiawala, Rajendra; and Baum, Lawrence S. (ed.), Blackboard Architectures and Applications (Perspectives in Artificial Intelligence, Vol. 3), ASIN: 0123799406.

[Ja4] http://www.java.sun.com/products/jdk/javadoc/index.html (12/99).

[Jo] Jones, Capers, and Jones, Capers T., Applied Software Measurement: Assuring Productivity and Quality, 2nd edition, New York: McGraw-Hill, 1996.

[Jo1] Jordan, Richard; Smilan, Ruth; and Wilkinson, Alex, "Streamlining the Project Cycle with Object-Oriented Requirements," OOPSLA Conference Proceedings, 1994, pp. 287–300.

[Jo2] Jones, C., Software Development: A Rigorous Approach, Englewood Cliffs, NJ: Prentice Hall, 1980.

[Jo3] http://www.spr.com/library/0langtbl.htm (12/99).

[Ka] Kaluzniacky, Eugene; Kanabar, Vijay; and Irwin, Richard D., Xbase Programming for the True Beginner: An Introduction to the Xbase Language in the Context of dBASE Iii+, Iv, 5, Foxpro, and Clipper, Burr Ridge, IL: Irwin, 1995.

[Ke] Keil, M.; Cule, P.; Lyytinen, K.; and Schmidt, R., "A Framework for Identifying Software Project Risks," Communications of the ACM, vol. 41, no. 11, November 1998.

[Ki] Kit, Edward, Software Testing in the Real World: Improving the Process, Reading, MA: Addison-Wesley, 1995.

[Kr] Kruchten, P., The Rational Unified Process, Reading, MA: Addison-Wesley, 1998.

[Le] Lea, Doug, Concurrent Programming in Java: Design Principles and Patterns (Java Series), Reading, MA: Addison-Wesley, 1996.

[Le1] Lehman, M., "Programs, Life Cycles, and the Laws of Software Evolution," Proc. IEEE, vol. 19, 1980, pp. 1060–1076.

[Le2] Lehman, M., "Program Evolution Information Processing Management," Proc. IEEE, vol. 20, 1984, pp. 19–36.

[Li] Lientz, Bennet P.; Swanson, E. Burton; and Tompkins, G. E., "Characteristics of Applications Software Maintenance," Communications of the ACM (CACM), vol. 21, 1978, pp. 466–471.

[Me] Meyer, Bertrand, "On to Components," Computer IEEE, January 1999.

[Mu] Musser, David R.; Saini, Atul (Contributor); Stepanov, Alexander; STL Tutorial & Reference Guide : C++ Programming With the Standard Template Library, (Addison-Wesley Professional Computing Series), Reading, MA: Addison-Wesley, 1996.

[My] Myers, Glenford J., The Art of Software Testing, New York, John Wiley & Sons, 1979.

[Na] http://www-isds.jpl.nasa.gov/cwo/cwo_23/handbook/Dsnswdhb.htm (12/99).

[Om] Oman, P.; Hagemeister, J.; and Ash, D., "A Definition and Taxonomy for Software Maintainability," University of Idaho, Moscow, Software Engineering Test Laboratory Report #91-08-TR, ID 83843, 1992.

[Om1] Oman, P., "HP_MAS: A Tool for Software Maintainability Assessment," University of Idaho, Moscow, Software Engineering Test Laboratory Technical Report #92-07-TR.

[Om2] The Object Management Group, http://www.omg.org (12/99).

[Os] Ostrolenk, Gary; Tobin, Mary; and Southworth, Mark; "Lessons from Using Z to Specify a Software Tool," IEEE Transactions on Software Engineering, vol. 24, no. 1, January 1998.

[Pa] Parnas, D. L., and Madey, J., "Functional Documentation for Computer Systems Engineering (Version 2)," McMaster University, Hamilton ONT, Canada, Technical Report CRL Report No. 237, September 1991.

[Pi] Pigoski, Thomas M., Practical Software Maintenance: Best Practices for Managing Your Software Investment, New York: John Wiley & Sons, 1996.

[Ra] http://www.rational.com (12/99).

[Ra1] Rand, Paul, A Designer's Art, New Haven, CT: Yale University Press, 1985.

[Ro] Ross, Douglas T., "Structured Analysis (SA): A Language for Communicating Ideas," IEEE Transactions on Software Engineering, vol. 3, no. 1, January 1977, pp. 16–33.

[Ro1] Software Specification: A Framework, http://www.sei.cmu.edu/topics/publications/documents/cms/cm.011.html (12/99).

[Ru] Rugaber, Spencer, and White, Jim, "Restoring a Legacy: Lessons Learned," IEEE Software, vol. 15, no. 4, July/August 1998.

[Ru1] Rumbaugh, James; Jacobson, Ivar; and Booch, Grady, The Unified Modeling Language Reference Manual, Reading, MA: Addison-Wesley, December 1998.

[Ru2] Rumbaugh, J.; Blaha, M; Premerlani, W.; Eddy, F.; and Lorenson, W., Object-Oriented Modeling and Design, Englewood Cliffs, NJ: Prentice Hall, 1990.

[Sc] Schwartz, J. T.; Dewar, R. B. K.; Dubinsky, E.; and Schonberg, E., Programming with Sets: An Introduction to SETL, New York: Springer-Verlag, 1986.

[Sh] Sheldon, F. et al., "Reliability Measurement from Theory to Practice," IEEE Software, vol. 9, no. 4, July 1992.

[Sh2] Shlaer, Sally, and Mellor, Stephen J., Object Lifecycles: Modeling the World in States, Englewood Cliffs, NJ: Yourdon, 1991.

[Sh1] Shnayerson, Michael, The Car That Could; The Inside Story of General Motors' Revolutionary Electric Vehicle, ASIN: 067942105X.

[St] Stark, George E., and Kern, Louise C., "A Software Metric Set for Program Maintenance Management," Journal of Systems and Software, vol. 24, 1994, pp. 239-249. http://www.members.aol.com/GEShome/met_prog/sustaining/estSus.html (12/99).

[Su] JavaTM Platform 1.1 Core API Specification http://www.java.sun.com/products/jdk/1.1/docs/api/packages.html (12/99).

[SPR] http://www.spr.com/library/0langtbl.htm (12/99).

[ST] http://www.suntest.com/ (8/99).

[Sz] Szyperski, Clemens, Component Software: Beyond Object-Oriented Programming, Reading, MA: Addison-Wesley, 1998.

[Te] Teichroew, Daniel, and Hershey, Ernest A. III, "PSL/PSA: A Computer Aided Technique for Structured Documentation and Analysis of Information Processing Systems," IEEE Transactions on Software Engineering (TSE), vol. 3, no. 1, January 1977, pp. 41–48.

[Th] Thayer, Richard H., Software Engineering Project Management, Second Edition, Piscataway, NJ: IEEE, 1997.

[Wa] Ward, Paul T., and Mellor, Stephen J., Structured Development for Real-Time Systems: Essential Modeling Techniques, Englewood Cliffs, NJ: Yourdon, 1986.

[We] Wegner, Peter, "Why Interaction Is More Powerful Than Algorithms," Communications of the ACM, May 1997, pp. 80–91.

[We1] Weiss, D. M., "Evaluating Software Development by Analysis of Change Data," SEL-81-011, NASA Software Engineering Laboratory, November 1981.

[Wi] Wilde, Norman, "Software Impact Analysis: Process and Issues," SERC-TR-70-F, March 1994. Software Engineering Research Center, National Science Foundation, http://www.hesperus.oboe.com/serc/ (12/99) and Durham University Technical Report, July 7, 1993.

[Yo] Yourdon, E., Decline and Fall of the American Programmer, Englewood Cliffs, NJ: Prentice Hall, 1992.

[Z] http://www.comlab.ox.ac.uk/archive/z.html (12/99).

[Zo] Zobel, Justin, Writing for Computer Science: The Art of Effective Communication, New York: Springer-Verlag, 1997.

CREDITS

Preface P.6, P. 4 Jacobson/Booch/Rumbaugh, THE UNIFIED SOFTWARE DEVELOPMENT PROCESS. Æ 1999 Addison Wesley Longman, Inc. Reprinted by permission of Addison Wesley Longman.

Chapter 1 1.9, 1.15, 1.17 Jacobson/Booch/Rumbaugh, THE UNIFIED SOFTWARE DEVELOPMENT PROCESS. Æ 1999 Addison Wesley Longman, Inc. Reprinted by permission of Addison Wesley Longman. 1.31 From IEEE Standard 730-1989. "IEEE Standard for Software Quality Assurance Plans" Copyright © 1989 IEEE. All rights reserved. 1.33 From IEEE Standard 1012-1986. "ANSI/IEEE Standard for Software Verification and Validation Plans." Copyright © 1986 IEEE. All rights reserved. 1.38 From IEEE Standard 828-1990. "IEEE Standard for Software Configuration Management Plans." Copyright © 1990 IEEE. All rights reserved. 1.40 Humphrey, A DISCIPLINE FOR SOFTWARE ENGINEERING pages 11, 117, 300 and 659 © 1995 Addison-Wesley Publishing Company. Reprinted by permission of Addison Wesley Longman. 1.43, 1.44, 1.45, 1.46, 1.47 Humphrey, MANAGING THE SOFTWARE PROCESS, page 5. © 1989 Addison-Wesley Publishing Company. Reprinted by permission of Addison Wesley Longman. 1.48 "Three Dimensions of Process Improvement; Part III: The Team Process; Crosstalk, April 1998," Humphrey. Copyright © 1998 Watts S. Humphrey. Reprinted with Permission.

Chapter 2 2.29, 2.30 From "IEEE Transactions on Software Engineering," Vol. SE-9, No. 6, November 1983, page 639. Copyright © 1983 IEEE. All rights reserved. 2.34, 2.35. 2.36 SOFTWARE ENGINEERING ECONOMICS by Boehm, B. W., © 1982 Reprinted by permission of Prentice-Hall, Inc., Upper Saddle River, NJ 2.40 Humphrey, INTRODUCTION TO THE TEAM SOFTWARE PROCESS, © 2000 Addison-Wesley Inc.. Reprinted by permission of Addison Wesley Longman. 2.41 From IEEE Standard 1058.1-1987. "ANSI/IEEE Standard for Software Project Management Plans." Copyright © 1988 IEEE. All rights reserved. 2.43 From IEEE Standard 730-1989. "IEEE Standard for Software Quality Assurance Plans." Copyright © 1989 IEEE. All rights reserved.

Chapter 3 3.6 From IEEE Standard 830-1993. "IEEE Recommended Practice for Software Requirements Specifications." Copyright © 1994 IEEE. All rights reserved. 3.7 Special permission to use Software Requirements, SEI Curriculum module SEI-CM-19-1,2, © 1990 by Carnegie Mellon University, is granted by the Software Engineering Institute 3.18, 3.19, 3.20 The Essential Guide to User Interface Design: An Introduction to GUI Design Principles and Techniques, Galitz. Copyright © 1997John Wiley & Sons, Inc. Reprinted by permission of John Wiley & Sons, Inc. 3.38 From IEEE Standard 830-1993. "IEEE Recommended Practice for Software Requirements Specifications." Copyright © 1994 IEEE. All rights reserved.

Chapter 4 4.6, 4.25 From IEEE Standard 830-1993. "IEEE Recommended Practice for Software Requirements Specifications." Copyright © 1994 IEEE. All rights reserved. 4.49 Ian Hayes, Specification Case Studies, Copyright © 1987 by Prentice-Hall International (UK) Ltd., p. 41. Reprinted by permission.

Chapter 5 5.15, Table 5.1 Software Architecture: Perspectives on an Emerging Discipline, by Shaw, Mary and David Garlan. Copyright © 1996, Reprinted by permission of Prentice-Hall, Inc., Upper Saddle River, NJ. 5.25, 5.31 Gamma/Helm/Johnson/Vlissides, DESIGNPATTERNS:

INDEX

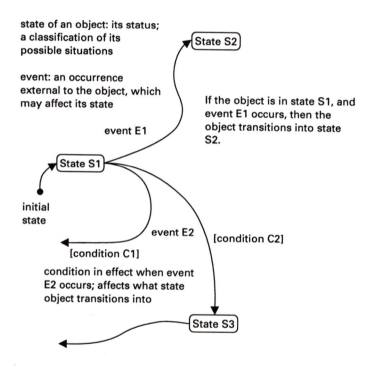

state of an object: its status;
a classification of its
possible situations

event: an occurrence
external to the object, which
may affect its state

State S2

event E1

If the object is in state S1, and
event E1 occurs, then the
object transitions into state
S2.

State S1

initial
state

event E2

[condition C2]

[condition C1]

condition in effect when event
E2 occurs; affects what state
object transitions into

State S3